政治學的理性與感性——

林繼文 精選集

冷則剛、吳文欽、吳玉山、吳親恩、謝復生 導讀

SENSE AND SENSITIVITY OF POLITICAL SCIENCE: SELECTED WORKS OF JIH-WEN LIN

中央研究院
政治學研究所
Institute of Political Science,
Academia Sinica (IPSAS)

編者序 Preface

　　中央研究院政治所第二任的所長林繼文教授是我國研究理性選擇理論首屈一指的學者。他將此一途徑運用到選舉制度、憲政體制、兩岸關係等各個領域，建立了國際性的聲望。繼文在學界擔任各種領導性的角色，嚴己寬人，以身作則，啓迪後進。雖然英年早逝，但是對於我國政治學發展的影響極爲深遠。

　　繼文的才華是跨越學科界線的。他早期最大的興趣是歷史和語文。當年台大徐州路法學院舊圖書館地下室藏有日本時代的大批文件，對他產生了極大的影響。繼文在台大政研所就讀碩士班時接受了國內輩份極高的日本專家許介鱗教授指導，於1991年撰成了碩士論文「日本據台末期（1930 — 1945）戰爭動員體系之研究」。像這樣一位對文史有興趣的學生，到了美國之後，又拜在 UCLA 政治系的賽局理論大師 George Tsebelis 教授門下，在 1996 年寫就了博士論文 "Consequences of the Single Non-Transferable Voting Rule: Comparing the Japan and Taiwan Experiences"，集中討論「複數選區單記非讓渡投票制」（SNTV），並在學成歸國後成爲在台灣推廣理性選擇途徑的一位領導學者。由於兼有文史與數理的專長和偏好，因此繼文一方面對於形式理論與量化的研究途徑推展不遺餘力，一方面又堅實地將之與案例研究相結合，把比較政治的理論和區域研究（特別是台灣與日本研究）連接得非常好，並且始終努力揉合量化與質化的研究途徑。這樣的功力和用心，在國內外的政治學者當中是極爲罕見的。

　　繼文於 1996 年回國，首先進入中研院中山人文社會科學研究所服務。由於台灣在 1990 年代初正在進行民主化，因此像所有的新興民主國家一樣，必需要進行政治制度的抉擇，這裡就包括選舉制度和憲政體制。選制（特別是 SNTV）一直是繼文研究政治制度的主軸，也成爲他建立學術聲望的基礎。另一方面，在他回國與進入中研院一年後，我國就進行了最重要的第四次修憲，建立了總統直選、而行政院長同時要率領內閣對立法院負責的半總統制。究竟這種介於總統制和內閣制之間

的憲政體制會怎樣地運作，對於我國是不是合適，這些都是研究政治制度的人所必
然關切的重大議題。由於繼文是採用理性選擇的方法論，又以 SNTV 選制作爲博士
論文的主題，因此他對於半總統制的研究就展現了兩個必然的特點：第一是沿用理
性選擇的分析途徑，第二是探討憲政體制如何和選舉制度配套，又會產生怎樣的結
果。在這兩方面，繼文都著述甚豐，爲國內的研究樹立了標竿。此外，兩岸關係對
台灣政治的影響不斷擴大，又和政治制度產生互動，並且帶入了國際環境的變數，
而成爲繼文適用理性選擇途徑的又一個新興領域。

　　在社科所的六年期間，不論在形式理論的倡導研究、憲制與選制的理性分析，
或是兩岸關係的模型建構，繼文都做出了可觀的貢獻，而成爲這幾個領域的年輕翹
楚，並於四年內完成了副研究員的升等。這樣的突出表現，立刻爲眾所矚目。在
2002 年中研院政治學研究所籌備處成立，負責規劃全局的是學術諮詢委員會的召
集人胡佛院士，吳玉山教授爲籌備處主任，決定從院內外徵聘核心的研究人員，最
初僅有三位，分別是來自台大政治系的朱雲漢與吳玉山教授，和來自中研院社科所
的繼文。在吳玉山教授的力邀下，繼文進入了新成立的政治所，一方面主持和發展
方法群組，一方面全力衝刺研究。在 2003 到 2018 年之間，繼文在形式理論、選舉
制度、半總統制，還有兩岸關係的各個領域持續進展，在過去的基礎上，精益求精
地提出新方法和新論點，建立了研究的領先地位。

　　繼文對於研究是竭盡心力的，他研究表現中最爲豐碩的部分是在 2003 年之後
完成，而這是在他發現腦瘤開刀之後。那次的手術雖然順利，也在一段時間內成功
地遏制了病情的擴散，但是繼文的視力是受到若干損傷的，他也因此要仰賴能將論
文讀出的軟體。對於一位研究者而言，視力受損是何等重大的打擊，但這並不影響
繼文在學術上的發展。相反地，他在各個研究面向上都能全方位地展開，並且做
出讓學界欽重的研究成果，可以想見這其中的艱辛與毅力，困難與克服。在 2007
年，繼文在政治所升等爲正研究員，當時是政治所辦理的第一個副研究員升等案，
審查的過程非常嚴謹。政治所以此向外傳遞了一個清楚的訊息：這就是政治所期盼
的研究員的典型。在學術社群貢獻方面，繼文是政治學計量方法營的創辦人之一，
並在 2003 到 2011 年之間長期擔任計量營計畫主持人，在這段期間計量營得以成長
與茁壯。其次，2012 年政治所在磨劍十年後正式脫離籌備處的地位而正式成所，
繼文後來擔任副所長，並在 2015 年繼任爲政治所的第二任所長，獲得了同仁的全
力支持。繼文全心領導所務，推動方法論的研究，加強國際聯繫，勞心勞力，把政
治所帶到一個新的發展層次。最後，他是在所長任內發病倒下，可謂對政治所鞠躬

盡瘁，而形塑了一代典型。

　　繼文於 2018 年 1 月 2 日不幸辭世，為了紀念他對中研院政治所以及我國政治學界的貢獻，政治所於 2 月 3 日舉辦「林繼文前所長學術紀念會」，邀請了王業立、謝復生、黃紀、吳玉山教授等重量級學者，回顧繼文為我國政治學不同領域所做的貢獻，另外也邀請吳介民、黃長玲、徐斯儉教授等和繼文自大學時代就相熟的好友，分享繼文的學術志業與成長歷程。紀念會當天座無虛席，參加者包括中研院廖俊智院長與人文社會科學組各所所長及中心主任、國內各大學政治相關科系主管與同行、繼文在學術界與學運界的朋友、以及繼文過去在中正大學、東吳大學、政治大學、台灣大學等校授課時的修課學生，足見繼文交遊之廣、育才之深。

　　由於繼文大部分的學術著作散見於國內外知名期刊，亦有部分收錄於專書合輯。為了更完整彰顯繼文的學術貢獻，中研院政治所於 2018 年 6 月，決議在繼文 50 餘篇的中、英文學術作品中，挑選代表著作集結成冊。經過編委會數次討論之後，我們精選出繼文 17 篇代表性研究成果，命名為《政治學的理性與感性——林繼文精選集》，作為「中研政治系列叢書」的第五卷。全書分成四大主題，包括「理性選擇與制度分析」、「憲政制度與半總統制」、「選舉體制」、「兩岸關係」，並由國內外各領域的權威學者撰寫主題導讀。本書同時也收錄繼文擔任科技部（原國科會）政治學門召集人時，一篇寫給年輕學術工作者的建議。整體來說，本書闡釋了繼文如何運用理性選擇途徑，從事關於政治制度和兩岸關係的研究，又反映了繼文感性的一面。我們希望這本書的問世，除了更完整呈現繼文學術成果之外，也能讓後人更瞭解繼文運用理性選擇理論分析台灣政治與兩岸關係的先驅者角色。

　　本書能夠順利出版，要感謝賴芊卉小姐居中聯繫與鉅細靡遺的校正，讓本書維持了「中研政治系列叢書」一貫的高編排水準，林文正、楊君婕、呂英鈿、謝孟君同學的細心校對，吳玉涵小姐協調封面的修改，五南圖書出版公司的劉靜芬、林佳瑩小姐在出版過程的全力支持，恣遊公司陳思辰（Paul）先生專業的封面設計，以及中央研究院法律學研究所與社會學研究所的出版事務諮詢。我們也要感謝中央研究院人文社會科學研究中心《人文及社會科學集刊》、五南圖書出版公司、東吳大學《東吳政治學報》、政治大學國際關係研究中心 Issues & Studies 以及《問題與研究》、政治大學選舉研究中心《選舉研究》、科技部《人文與社會科學簡訊》、台灣大學政治學系《政治科學論叢》、台灣民主基金會 Taiwan Journal of Democracy、台灣政治學會《台灣政治學刊》、Cambridge University Press 之 China

Quarterly 與 *Journal of East Asian Studies*、Elsevier 之 *Electoral Studies*、SAGE 之 *International Political Science Review* 及 *Party Politics*、University of Michigan Press 等學術及出版單位慨然同意我們轉載繼文的作品，讓他的這些代表著作，能以精選集的方式問世。

　　能夠作為繼文的同事與朋友，我們深感榮幸，謹透過這本論文精選集，向他精彩的一生致敬。

冷則剛、吳玉山、吳文欽、吳親恩
識於南港中央研究院
2019 年 8 月 1 日

【編者按：我們也在此向本書讀者介紹其它關於繼文的紀錄。繼文 39 歲第一次腦瘤開刀後，隔年春天蔡篤堅教授委請研究生來與繼文進行三次訪談。繼文的夫人劉怡昕教授根據訪談內容，為繼文編輯了電子書《繼文 40 自述》。在自述中，繼文詳細回顧自己從學齡前至取得博士學位、以及至中研院服務的生涯歷程，還有他對於基督信仰的認識。此外，繼文辭世之後，他的學生傅鈺如同學，為他架設一個紀念網站，收錄許多繼文的學界友人與學生對於繼文的追憶文字、前述「林繼文前所長學術紀念會」的錄影檔、以及《繼文 40 自述》電子書。對於想多瞭解繼文的讀者，可至以下網址進一步參考這些資料：https://jihwenlin.weebly.com/blog。】

目次　　　　　Table of Contents

編者序

理性選擇與制度分析

憲政制度與半總統制

圖表目次　　　Tables and Figures

圖目次

表目次

理性選擇與制度分析

主題導讀

林繼文與制度分析

謝復生

　　林繼文博士英年早逝，令人惋惜，是學界的一大損失。他在台灣的政治學者中，是非常勇於創新的一位，相當程度上體現了胡適先生所倡導的「大膽假設，小心求證」的治學方法。他的研究課題，涵蓋面相當廣，包含憲政體制、選舉制度、投票行爲、兩岸關係等；在研究方法上，則質化、量化並具。在台灣的政治學者中，尤其特出的，是他運用社會選擇理論（social choice theory）、空間模型（spatial model）、賽局理論（game theory）等數理模型，對相關現象，提出許多非常有趣的觀察與論證。

　　本文擬檢視林博士所撰寫的五篇有關制度設計與制度變革的論文，來探討他對政治學的貢獻，並提出我個人的一些看法。[1] 這五篇論文有兩篇論及半總統制的運作，一篇討論憲政體制、選舉制度與內閣組成，另有兩篇則探究選舉制度改革。下面的討論基本上依據這個順序來進行。

壹、研究途徑

　　林繼文博士的研究，主要植基於理性抉擇理論（rational choice theory），尤其是社會選擇理論、空間模型與賽局理論。爲使不熟悉相關理論的讀者，有一概括的理解，以下先簡要說明這類研究途徑的基本架構。

　　理性抉擇理論，簡而言之，就是以個人理性這樣一個假定出發，透過邏輯演繹，來推出各種各樣的行爲法則。經濟學，大體而言，就是依據這樣一個研究途徑來建構的。政治學中，在過去這五、六十年裡，也在一定程度上蔚爲風潮。[2]

---

[1] 這五篇論文都是林博士個人單獨撰述、發表的，分別是林繼文（1997）、林繼文（2000）、Lin（2011a）、Lin（2011b）與 Lin（2016a）。

[2] 林博士和筆者曾合撰一文，介紹理性抉擇理論在台灣政治學的發展，請參閱謝復生、林繼文（2013）。關於理性抉擇理論更進一步的說明，請參閱謝復生（2011、2013）。

　　所謂個人理性，指的是人有偏好，其偏好可排出順序，同時，他也會計算達成這些偏好的可能性，然後在這樣的考量下，決定其行動。所謂排出順序，意味對任兩個可加以比較之選項（如 a 和 b），他或喜歡 a 多於 b，或 b 多於 a，或覺得兩者無差別。並且，在有三個選項（如 a、b、c）的情況下，他若喜歡 a 多於（或至少一樣喜歡）b，而喜歡 b 又多於（或至少一樣喜歡）c，那麼他應該喜歡 a 多於（或至少一樣喜歡）c。假若他喜歡 a 多於 b，喜歡 b 多於 c，卻又喜歡 c 多於 a，那麼，他的偏好就無法排出順序來，就不符合我們對理性的定義。

　　這個理性的假定是針對個人的，但在政治學（或其他社會科學）的研究裡，我們無法總是環繞在無以計數的個人身上，而常常必須簡化為數量較少的群體（如國家、政黨、利益團體等），使我們的研究工作，成為可行—更勿論群體本身也是有趣的研究對象。但是，群體是否可以像個人一樣有偏好，而其偏好又可排出順序來呢？

　　我們可以「投票矛盾」（paradox of voting）的現象，來說明群體理性的問題。首先，假定某群體有甲、乙、丙三個人。這三個人對 a、b、c 三個選項的偏好順序排列如下：

　　甲：$aPbPc$；

　　乙：$bPcPa$；

　　丙：$cPaPb$。

　　其中，P 代表喜歡前者多於後者。在這樣偏好順序的組合下，若依兩兩相較、多數決之法，我們可以看出，就 a、b 而言，由於甲、丙兩人均喜歡 a 多於 b，只有乙喜 b 多於 a，因此這群體應喜 a 多於 b。同理，就 b、c 而言，由於甲、乙兩人均喜歡 b 多於 c，只有丙喜 c 多於 b，故此群體應喜 b 多於 c。如果這個群體是理性的，則既然他們喜歡 a 多於 b，而 b 又多於 c，對 a、c 而言，他們應喜 a 多於 c。但當我們將 a、c 直接相比，則可見乙、丙皆喜歡 c 多於 a，只有甲喜 a 多於 c，因而，他們整體而言，其實是喜歡 c 多於 a。這也就是說，這個群體不合乎我們對理性的要求，從而我們無法瞭解他們究竟會選擇 a 或 b 或 c，我們就無法預期他們的行為。

　　經濟學者 Kenneth J. Arrow（1953）將「投票矛盾」的現象，擴及到各種各樣的偏好加總工具（如市場、投票等），證明不論何種加總工具，「投票矛盾」的現象總是可能的。這也就是說，儘管我們可以假定個人是理性的，但無法假定群體是理性的。當然，如果群體中有一個獨裁者，或群體有共識，「投票矛盾」不會出現，我們就可以假定群體是理性的，這也可從 Arrow 定理的前提條件推出（Arrow, 1953）。

　　Arrow 定理是社會選擇理論的濫觴。由此所衍生出來的在單一面向或多面向議題

空間（unidimensional or multidimensional issue space）的均衡的問題，成為大家探討的重要課題。與此相關的是選舉的空間理論，同樣在探尋不同面向議題空間裡中間選民（median voter）或所謂均衡存在與否的問題。

　　林繼文博士在他的研究裡，經常引用社會選擇理論和空間理論的概念。例如，在探討日本選舉制度改革時，他就用了勝集（win-set）的概念，來說明政黨在多面向議題空間的合縱連橫（林繼文，1997：71-72）。當然，政黨是個群體，有 Arrow 矛盾的問題，但在政黨有強力的領導人或內部有相當共識的前提下，以政黨作為理性的參與者，倒無太大問題。

　　另外，林繼文博士也經常運用賽局理論在他的研究中。賽局理論基本上也是本於理性抉擇的研究途徑，強調參與者彼此之間的策略互動。簡而言之，基於各參與者的策略、報酬，我們可以推論各個參與者在考量對方的策略選擇的情形下，作出對自己最有利的選擇決定。例如，在探討半總統制的運作時，他就設定了一個包含總統、總理、國會的三人賽局，由此推論出各種半總統制的運作形態（林繼文，2000）。

貳、半總統制的運作

　　林繼文博士在 2000 年曾編著了一本題為《政治制度》的專書。在書中，他也納入了一篇他自己所寫的「半總統制下的三角政治均衡」的論文。這是一篇非常扎實的文章，理論鋪陳及經驗驗證兼具。

　　首先，半總統制不是一個非常清晰的概念。就 Maurice Duverger（1980）的定義而言，在這個制度下，總理對國會負責，但又有個民選總統，有一定實權。這個定義，在相當程度上，是替《法國第五共和憲法》所量身定做的。一個難以釐清的問題是總統的權力的大小：在人事上？在政策上？與總理或國會的權力對比？這些都是難以說清楚、講明白的。然而，如果總統（相對於總理或國會）的權力不明確，我們就很難對半總統制的運作，理出一個頭緒。這也是為什麼很多學者試圖對半總統制，作進一步分類的原因。Matthew Soberg Shugart 和 John M. Carey（1992）的總理總統制（premier-presidential system）（如第五共和法國）和總統議會制（president-parliamentary system）（如威瑪德國）的分類，就是著例。

　　林繼文博士在「半總統制下的三角政治均衡」的論文中，也在試圖對半總統制作更細緻的分類，並從分類中，得出一些推論。在文章中，他設定了一個半總統制下包

括總統、總理及國會的三人賽局：由總統先做選擇（主動介入或不介入決策），再由總理（接受或不接受總統立場）、國會（接受或不接受總理做法）依序做出選擇；在總統或總理遭受杯葛時，總統可選擇再次介入或不再介入。由於根據作者的設定，這是一個訊息完備（perfect information）的賽局，因此，我們可以用反向歸納（backward induction）的方法求解，得出所謂子局完備均衡（subgame perfect equilibrium）。基於各種可能報酬，作者得出總統干政、總統主導、總理主導與無政府等幾種可能結果，並由此推出幾個命題：

1. 當國會對總理的信任度低，而總統所面臨的問題具有緊迫性時，結果為總統干政。總統社會支持度越低，此種傾向越強。但是總統若是主動權過小，則可能陷入無政府狀態（頁 149）。

2. 當國會對總理信任度高時，總統主動權低或支持度低都可以導致總理主導（頁 150）。

3. 當國會對總理信任度高時，總統主動權高及支持度高同時為總統主導的必要條件（頁 150）。

這些命題都有一定的說明力，也與常識的理解，若合符節。作者並檢視了十個案例（其中法國、葡萄牙、波蘭等因憲政改革，各有兩個案例）。除了少數狀況（如 1993 至 1995 年的波蘭），大體都印證了這些推演的結果。

這篇文章體現了林繼文博士的一貫風格，透過嚴謹的推論，得到一些命題，然後蒐集相關案例，進行驗證。這是一篇難得的真正用比較的方法，所寫出來的比較政治的論文。

這篇論文出版於 2000 年，彼時台灣方才經歷憲政改革，因此，對於半總統制在台灣的運作狀況，還不是非常清晰。所以，在這篇論文中，對台灣的個案，著墨不多。但林繼文博士在結論中仍對台灣未來的可能發展，作了一些說明。雖然部分論述與未來的發展有些出入（如「未來立法院極可能沒有任何政黨掌握過半的席次」），但整體來看，其推論仍與近二十年來的進展，有相當程度的契合。

在發表於 *Journal of East Asian Studies* 的文章中，他則進一步闡述了半總統制在台灣運作的情形（Lin, 2011b）。這篇文章主要在解一個令人困惑的課題，即馬英九就任總統之後，他的政黨控制了立法院多數，因而在正常狀況下，政府運作應該非常順暢才是，然實際上，他的許多政策依然經常在國會碰壁。

作者在這篇文章，同樣建構了一個訊息完備的賽局，並借助否決者理論（veto player theory）來推斷在台灣的半總統制下，可能出現的運作狀況（所謂否決者，指的

是其同意是改變現狀所不可或缺的）。由此，作者推演出兩個主要的假說。其一、當同黨立法委員可以修改政府法案時，立法院有後發優勢（last-mover advantage），可以將法案修改至趨近立委們的理想點（ideal point）。其二、當法案同時涉及總統及行政院長時，如果立法院可加以修改，這會增加總統及行政院長意見相左的機會。作者另外檢視了一些實際案例，這兩個假說大體得到證實。

這個研究試圖解答在非分立政府的情況下，居然會有政治僵局的問題，是個很有趣的題目。不過，這其中有多少是源自憲政體制，當然值得斟酌。作者所提及的政黨內部分歧問題，顯然是個非常重要的憲政體制外的因素。但另外，立法院的政黨協商制度應也是造成僵局非常關鍵的原因。作者在附註裡提及政黨協商，但在本文中並未多所著墨。

這篇文章是在 2011 年出版的。2016 年又經歷了政黨輪替，顯然馬英九及蔡英文兩位總統治下的行政、立法關係大有不同，很值得做個比較。可惜林繼文博士已辭世，否則必可針對兩個政府的歧異，作更進一步的分析。

參、憲政體制、選舉制度與內閣組成

接下來我想談的是林繼文博士在 2016 年所出版的有關憲政體制與選舉制度的文章。這篇文章收錄於 Nathan F. Batto、Chi Huang、Alexander C. Tan 和 Gary W. Cox 所合編的 *Mixed-Member Majoritarian Electoral Systems in Constitutional Context* 一書。文章題目是憲政體制對政黨制度的影響，但從內文來看，實際上比較偏重憲政體制、選舉制度對第三黨或無黨籍人士參與內閣的分析。從某個意義來說，這些制度安排當然會影響到成立第三黨的誘因，但從這篇文章整體來看，還是比較側重第三黨或無黨籍人士是否會被引進至內閣的問題。然而，儘管標題與內文略有出入，這並不影響本文的價值。

首先，這篇論文不像前一節的兩篇文章使用了那麼多的符號邏輯，但依然是在理性抉擇的範疇之內。而且，最值得稱許的，是這篇文章的原創性。作者主要著眼點在不同制度安排下，內閣組成—特別是第三黨或無黨籍人士被引進內閣的問題上—的差異。

依作者所言，台灣實施半總統制，總統掌握了內閣組成的大權，總統可能引進無黨籍人士進入內閣，以彰顯內閣的代表性並掃除影響立法的障礙，特別是當總統的黨無法控制國會多數時。另外，當混合多數制（mixed-member majoritarian system 或所謂單一選區兩票制）取代單記非讓渡投票制（single nontransferable vote）後，也會增加無黨籍人士入閣的機會。

至於日本的狀況，則大有不同。日本是個內閣制國家，有參、眾兩院，儘管眾議院居主導地位，但參議院也有相當的決策權。而兩院的選舉制度不同，小黨較易進入參議院，因此，執政黨儘管控制眾議院，卻未必能在參議院取得優勢，以致執政黨常需籠絡小黨，以便順利執政。尤其，當眾議院的選舉制度從單記非讓渡投票制轉換爲混合多數制後，這種現象更加可能。

作者檢視了台灣及日本歷年的組閣狀況，基本上驗證了作者的推論。不過，有關小黨能否存活的問題，除了制度因素外，社會的分歧（cleavages）也是不可忽視的原因。台灣有明確的統獨分歧，而日本卻欠缺長期、穩定的分歧，這多少是造成兩者政黨制度歧異的重要原因之一（Hsieh, 2013）。不過，林繼文博士這篇論文，專注於制度成因，因此，這並不算是什麼缺失。

肆、選舉制度改革

我另外所選的兩篇文章，均涉及選舉制度改革。一般而言，選舉制度有一定的穩定性，這是因爲選舉制度造就了一批既得利益者，而這些人因現行制度得利，我們因此很難期望他們會改變現制而使自己的利益受損。故而，選舉制度改革，在成熟的民主國家，不常發生。不過，在過去這些年，我們依然看到一些改革之例。林繼文博士的兩篇文章，就在探討選制改革的成因。

第一篇文章是用中文寫就的，登載於 1997 年 12 月所出版的《台灣政治學刊》，討論日本在 1994 年如何將眾議院的選舉制度從單記非讓渡投票制轉換爲混合多數制。在這篇文章中，作者從空間理論的勝集的概念出發，鋪陳日本選制改革的歷程。在空間理論裡，我們假定每個參與者都有一個理想點，距離理想點愈遠，參與者偏好的程度愈低。在多面向的議題空間裡，我們可以想像理想點被許多無異曲線（如同心圓）所包圍。在無異曲線的任兩個點，參與者的偏好程度是一樣的，但愈遠的無異曲線，則偏好的程度愈低。假定有三個參與者（稱甲、乙、丙），並有一個點叫現狀，我們可以想像有三條代表三個參與者的無異曲線通過現狀。假若這三個參與者是三個政黨，在一場賽局裡都無法單獨獲勝（如無一黨取得過半議席），但任兩個參與者（如甲和乙）均可形成獲勝聯合，則在兩個參與者通過現狀的兩條無異曲線間的交集，即是所謂勝集。如果這兩個參與者組成獲勝聯合，我們可以預期他們會選擇勝集中的點，來取代現狀。不過，除非有康多塞贏家（Condorcet winner），否則這個獲勝聯合是不穩定的；另一個

獲勝聯合（如甲和丙）可以找到另外的點，來取代甲、乙所選擇的點。[3] 林繼文博士就是用這樣的論述，來說明自民黨、革新政黨與其他小黨間的合縱連橫，最終達到選制改革的結果。當然，這個結果不是康多塞贏家，但一旦通過，就變成新現狀，要再改易，有其難度。

　　這篇文章最有趣的，就是改革不易，往往要搭配其他議題，並且在無一黨獲得過半議席的情況下，才有可能成功。日本 1994 年的選制改革，就是在自民黨失掉政權，並搭配其他政治改革方案的情況下，才終於實現。諷刺的是，改革的結果竟是偏向被改革的自民黨的方案。作者臚列了各參與者在相關議題上的立場，並詳述了改革的軌跡，是一篇上乘之作。

　　另外一篇於 2010 年刊登於 *Party Politics* 的文章，則比較了日本及台灣在選舉制度改革的經驗。在這篇文章裡，作者強調日本及台灣在改革前所採用的單記非讓渡投票制，在特定時空背景下有利於最大黨，使得制度得以延續，但也往往埋下自我毀滅的種子，而導致最終的改革。

　　在單記非讓渡投票制下，一個政黨—尤其是大黨—常會在一個選區裡，提名數名候選人。而為了席次極大化，政黨會提名適量的候選人—不少，但也不多，以免選票分散—並力求各候選人獲得等量的選票，避免選票過度集中，這就是所謂配票。同時，同黨候選人之間也往往競爭慘烈。由於這些候選人均屬同黨，黨的標籤相同，政策也大同小異，因此，候選人個人的特質，變得至關重要。這使得選舉非常個人化，選區服務常成為獲勝的關鍵。依據 J. Mark Ramseyer 和 Frances M. Rosenbluth（1993）的論述，至少在日本，由於自民黨掌握政權，可以提供其候選人各式各樣的資源，使其成為選戰中的常勝軍，而長期掌控執政權力。林繼文博士這篇論文大體依循這樣一種說法，來檢視日本與台灣的狀況。不過，他更進一步論證這樣的優勢有其窮之時，最後可能導致制度本身的崩解。

　　按照林繼文博士的推論，當經濟狀況好的時候，執政黨可以提供更多的資源給它的候選人，來爭取選民的支持，但這種做法的效用會遞減。最終，經濟發展會導致選民往都市移動，傳統用資源換選票的做法，會愈來愈難以施展。同時，由於單記非讓渡投票制帶有一定的比例代表性，提供小黨某種程度的生存空間，使對施政不滿的選民可能轉而支持小黨。大黨為了生存，可能主張將選制改為比例代表性較低的制度，以壯大自己，削弱小黨。

---

[3]　相關論述，請參閱 Plott（1967）與謝復生（2011、2013）。

　　作者檢視了日本及台灣的案例，發現在單記非讓渡投票制下，經濟成長確實有利執政黨，但都市化則反之。這造成了執政黨的兩難：一方面，經濟成長是維繫其政權的必要手段，但另一方面，經濟成長也埋下了其選票流失的種子。在日本和台灣這兩個例子裡，選舉制度改革的來到，都是在長期的執政黨失掉其國會多數之時，實非偶然。

　　那麼，改革來臨，什麼樣的制度會是新的選擇呢？依作者所言，大黨（或自認有機會成為大黨的黨）會傾向採用比例代表性較低的選制，而小黨則反之。在日本，在自民黨、革新政黨和其他在野黨的合縱連橫下，選擇了有利大黨的混合多數制。而在台灣，由於修憲程序的困難，小黨對於選制改革沒有太多置喙的餘地，最後也選擇了對國民黨、民進黨兩大黨有利的混合多數制。無論日本或台灣，大黨都成了改革的贏家。

　　這篇論文延續了前一篇論文的主軸，但更進一步釐清了改革的前因後果，論證更明確，對相關現象的研究，作出了相當的貢獻。

伍、結論

　　林繼文博士是個治學非常嚴謹的學者。我有幸和他有過一些合作的機會，除了一篇以中文寫就有關理性抉擇理論的文章外（謝復生、林繼文，2013），還合寫過一篇有關東亞國家不同世代民眾對民主的支持度的專書論文（Hsieh and Lin, 2016）。在寫作過程中，看到他兢兢業業的工作態度，還歷歷在目。我們本來還商討過其他可能的研究計劃，不過，俱往矣。謹以本文，紀念這位傑出的學者。

第一章

制度選擇如何可能：論日本之選舉制度改革[*]

壹、導言

「新制度論」（new institutionalism）是近年來頗受政治學界注意的一個研究取向。[1]簡要地說，此一理論認為我們可以從個別行動者在特定制度條件下的策略互動，來解釋重要的政治現象。這種觀點同時和幾個重要學派連結。首先，在精神上，新制度論和經濟學中的制度學派具有共通性，認為資訊不充分及交易成本的存在使制度成為政治經濟生活的核心。其次，在分析單位上，該學派承續了行為論對個體的重視，以個別行動者的偏好（preference）作為分析的起點。儘管如此，新制度論的目的，仍是解釋集體選擇（collective choice）的結果。同時，相較於一般的「理性選擇論」（rational choice theory），新制度論更繼承了古典政治學對制度的重視，認為政治生活無法脫離制度的脈絡而存在。這樣的視野，不僅能使理論反映現實，更蘊含了以制度設計來達成政治實踐的意圖。

然而，從理論的周延性來看，新制度論蘊含了一項根本的難題。如果所有的政治現象都可以還原為個體的選擇，那麼制度本身也可以被選擇的。[2]如此一來，所謂制度只是一項中介性的變數。如果我們堅持制度擁有自主性，則新制度論將有變成「新結構論」的危險；這違反了該理論的基本假設及精神。新制度論者當然可以宣稱，他們還是遵循方法上的個體主義；制度之所以被當成分析要件，乃因其具有一定的持久性。制度之所以持久，是因為透過特定制度所選拔的政治菁英，往往具有維護現行體制的傾向；而菁英較非菁英更有可能進行制度選擇。如果一定要追究制度選擇從何而來，答案也很直接：因為菁英的偏好結構（preference structure）產生改變。簡言之，根據這種觀點，一項制度之所以被改變，只是因為大多數有權者的想法或利益改變了。

---

[*] 本文曾刊登於《台灣政治學刊》，第 2 期（1997 年 12 月），頁 63-106。感謝台灣政治學會《台灣政治學刊》同意轉載。

[1] 關於新制度論的興起，請參見 Ordeshook（1990）。關於新制度論在整個政治學界的最新發展，可參閱 Goodin 與 Klingemann（1996: 3-49, 133-222）。

[2] 必須強調的是，「可選擇」並不等同「可改變」。同樣的道理，大多數制度雖具有一定的穩定性，卻並不表示其不可改變。本文的主旨，就在於認定制度是可選擇的，並探討其在何種條件下是可變的。

選舉是民主政體的核心機制，選舉制度也構成新制度論最引以爲傲的研究領域。我們發現，從制度論的角度探討選舉制度的論著，大多亦具有前述特色。其一，既有研究多以選舉制度爲自變項，解釋政黨數目（Rae, 1967; Taagepera and Shugart, 1989; Lijphart, 1990; Ordeshook and Shvetsova, 1994; Amorim Neto and Cox, 1997）、政治行爲（Katz, 1980）或政治後果（McCubbins and Rosenbluth, 1995; 王業立，1995）。這些研究雖然獲致豐富的成果，但相形之下對於制度形成與變遷的討論就少得多。其次，在不得不論及選舉制度變革時，既有研究多將其歸因於選民對於政治現狀的不滿，進而迫使政治菁英以制度變革應對之。

本論文試圖修正這種觀點，並以日本選舉制度改革的具體個案支持所論。主要的論點可以歸結如下：

1. 偏好結構的改變不一定是選舉制度改革的充分條件。
2. 選舉制度改革的必要條件之一，在於制度選擇的議題面向和其他議題面向同時進入決策議程。
3. 我們可以根據議程的設定及參與制度改革者的立場，來預測改革的軌跡。

質言之，影響選舉制度改革的因素，不但在於個別行動者的利益計算與策略互動，更在於既有制度所提供的空間。如果這項理論成立，則前述「新制度論」的遞歸性（recursiveness）將可以被打破：只要特定條件存在，一項制度可以孕育出其自身的終結者。

論述的結構如下。次節回顧關於日本選舉制度之研究，探討其對於制度改革的思考。第參節建構關於選舉制度改革的一般模型，闡述改革的條件及類型。第肆節檢視日本個案是否符合模型適用的先決條件，並界定行動者及其立場。第伍、陸節透過模型及先行條件，推演出關於日本選舉制度改革的假設，並以實際的改革過程來驗證假設。結論則簡要地介紹其他選舉制度的改革經驗，說明模型的普遍適用性。

貳、制度選擇：選舉制度研究的盲點

本文的分析對象，是選舉制度中相當獨特的「多人區單記非讓渡投票制」（single nontransferable voting under multi-member district, SNTV-MMD），爲便於行文，文中將

其簡稱爲一般所熟知的「中選舉區制」。[3] 此一制度的定義非常簡單：每位選民投一票給特定的候選人；候選人所得的選票不得轉移給他人。每一選區應選名額通常大於一；當選與否完全取決於候選人的得票排名。這種制度看來無甚奇特，舉世各國中卻只有日本和台灣長期採用。[4] 中選舉區制在日本已有將近百年的歷史。事實上，日本自 1889 年通過《眾議院議員選舉法》迄今（1997），有 85% 的時間實施中選舉區制，或是在基本定義上相同的大選舉區制。至於在台灣，中選舉區制更是 1935 年實行地方選舉以來的主要制度（台灣總督府，1945）；目前上至國會議員，下至縣市議會議員，都採取此制進行選舉。

因此，中選舉區制雖然稀有，在所施行的國家卻稱得上是根深蒂固。一些學者乃以其爲解釋日本政治獨特性的關鍵。其中最具代表性的，就是 Ramseyer 與 Rosenbluth（1993）的著作。[5] 根據其分析，中選舉區制造成執政黨候選人同黨相爭的局面。執政黨因而必須協助其參選者提供選民特殊利益，以解決所謂的「票源區隔」（vote division）問題。因此，中選舉區制不但是金權政治的溫床，更是大黨能長期壟斷政權的原因（因爲少數黨無法透過利益分配來解決同樣的問題）。這樣的研究，從制度論的角度解釋了許多向來被視爲文化產物的政治現象。

然而，正如我們在導論中所指出的，以選舉制度作爲解釋政治後果的自變項，必然遭逢兩項難題：第一，我們無法從其理論中推導出制度改革的動因。正如許多學者所言，日本的中選舉區制可歸類爲「準比例代表制」（Bogdanor and Bulter, 1983; Lijphart, 1984）。也就是說，中選舉區制對於大黨的有利程度不及小選舉區制（Rae, 1971; Lijphart, 1990）。若然，長期壟斷政權的自民黨，爲何不乾脆將選舉制度改成小選舉區制？當然，也有學者從其他的角度來解釋中選舉區制如何有利自民黨一黨獨大（Pempel, 1990）。[6] 然而，如果中選舉區制的確造成了自民黨的長期執政，自民黨爲何又成爲制度改革的發動者？我們又如何解釋，在實際的改革過程中，自民黨所持的立場其實是小選舉區制（詳後）？

---

[3]　英文的文獻習慣將此一制度簡稱爲 SNTV。事實上，SNTV 的定義亦適用於英美等國的小選區制。即使在日本與台灣，也有部分的選區應選名額爲一。我們所稱的中選舉區，應選名額大於一。

[4]　1881 年的巴西憲法曾規定實行「大選區單一不可讓渡投票制」。南韓亦曾於 1980 至 1988 年間採用「兩人區單一不可讓渡投票制」與比例代表制的並用制（Brady and Mo, 1992）。此外，美國的一些地方議會也採用「多人區單一不可讓渡投票制」。

[5]　此外，McCubbins 與 Rosenbluth（1995）則爲相同的論點提供了細緻的量化證明。

[6]　Pempel 的說法是，中選舉區使執政黨可同時推出多人競選，而以個別候選人的落選替代了整個政黨的被淘汰。這種理論並不能解釋自民黨在選舉制度改革中的立場與行動。

　　第二，我們更難從既有理論解釋改革的過程與結果。現有理論在解釋日本何以能完成選舉制度改革時，大多尋求外生性或突發性的因素，例如金權政治導致的民意不滿（Shiratori, 1995; 張世賢，1995），或是因應新的經濟情勢（Rosenbluth, 1996）。這種看法，的確能解釋日本的選舉改革為何發生在一連串貪污醜聞爆發之後。然而，其所未及關照的，在於為何各政黨所提出的解決方案迥然不同。這種差異性，對於改革的具體內容有著決定性的影響。而更另人困惑的是，反對現行制度最力的正是金權政治的支持者自民黨，而向以改革著稱的左翼政黨對於新選舉制度卻抱持抵制的態度。

　　由上可知，要研究選舉制度的改革，必須考慮政治行動者本身對於制度的偏好，以及這種偏好如何轉化成集體的制度選擇。由於研究課題是特定制度條件下的策略行動，我們可以採用理性選擇理論的一些基本觀念，形構制度選擇的政治力學。這就是次節的主題。

參、選舉制度改革的理論模型

　　政治的本質在於權力分配。選舉制度之所以受到注意，正因為其決定了議席的歸屬，進而影響國會內權力分配的公平性。因此，我們要回答的問題是：在追求權力的前提下，政治菁英會在何種條件下，以何種方式更動選舉制度？[7]

　　以下我們先建構關於權力分配的一般模型，再考慮權力分配如何和選舉制度產生關聯。假設所有的黨派都是以極大化自身的權力為目標，而政治行動的單位是由立場相近的黨派所組成的權力集團（power group）。[8]換言之，每個權力集團都是「議題空間」（issue space）中的一點。若將每一行動者的權力量化，N 個權力集團即構成一 N 維（N-dimensional）的空間。再假設權力是常和的（constant sum；亦即一集團權力的增加意味著其他集團權力的減少），則任一時間點的權力分配狀態必落於一 N-1 維單體（N-simplex）上的某一點。我們稱此單體的每一個頂端（vertex）為某一權力集團的「理想點」（ideal point）。在此點上，該集團的權力等於常和之值，而他者權力為 0。

---

[7]　我們假設選舉制度的改變必須獲得國會多數派的認可。然而，某些國家透過公民投票來決定選舉制度的變革，使選民偏好成為制度選擇的主要基準。在此情況下，政治菁英的態度不一定與民意相符，也不能主導制度選擇的走向。

[8]　我們也可用個別議員為分析單位。但一個合理的假設是，議員為了降低風險，會尋找利益相近的議員而結成黨派，某些黨派也結成集團以增加影響力。權力集團成員間的契約是固定而長期的，而聯盟（coalition）成員的合作關係卻是暫時而隨議題轉變的。

圖 1.1 所描繪的是最單純的一種狀況，即兩黨政治。若不考慮其他的因素，則位於兩黨理想點間的線段就是議題空間：權力的分配狀態可以用此線段上的任一點來表示；此點越靠近某黨，該黨的權力就越大。我們把特定時間點上的權力分配狀態稱作「現狀」（status quo；簡稱 SQ）。權力的重分配，即是對現狀的改變。

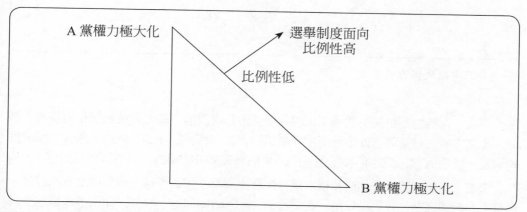

圖1.1　兩黨制下的選舉制度改革與權力重分配

　　決定權力分配的因素有許多。本文考慮以下兩種最常見的狀況：

　　首先，若無其他因素的介入，國會內的權力分配取決於黨派間的結盟。我們以圖1.2 作一說明。假設國會中有 A、B、C 三黨各自代表一權力集團，任兩黨皆構成多數。圖中由任兩黨的無異曲線交集所構成的區域，就是所謂的「勝集」（win set）。勝集中的任一點都比 SQ 對特定的多數更有利，因而可以取代 SQ。再設 A 黨為執政黨（但席次不過半），故 SQ 接近 A 點。從圖中可以看出，由 B、C 兩黨所占之勝集空間最大，顯示其對於打破現狀具有相當的共識。例如，B、C 兩黨可以聯手通過法案 SQ' 來增加自身的權力。[9]

---

[9]　雖然勝集中的任何一點都可以取代現狀，我們認為最合理的替代方案應位於 SQ 在聯盟成員的「帕雷圖集」（Pareto set）的垂直投射上。此點比集合外的方案更有利於聯盟成員，採垂直投射則是因為符合公平原則。所謂「帕雷圖集」是「帕雷圖最適點」（Pareto optimal）的集合。方案 X 是「帕雷圖最適點」的充要條件是：不存在一方案 Y，且所有聯盟成員對 Y 的喜好不下於 X，且至少有一成員喜 Y 勝於 X。以圖 1.2 來看，B、C 兩黨的帕雷圖集就是線段 BC。

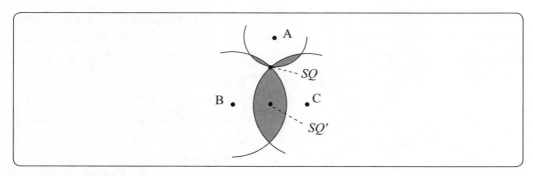

圖1.2　三黨間的權力重分配

　　其次，在結盟不更動的狀態下，現狀可能因為資源消長或外在情勢變化而移動。例如，A 黨可能因為某些意外事件而突然喪失影響力，使現狀往 *SQ'* 移動。還有一種常見的狀況，就是 A 黨因為不能滿足選民的要求而喪失部分的權力，自然圖利反對黨。

　　那麼，選舉制度改革如何和權力重分配產生關聯？如前所述，選舉制度本身就是一種權力分配的機制。我們可以用「比例性」（proportionality）這樣一個指標來描述不同的選舉制度對政權參與的滿足程度。一種選舉制度的比例性越高，即表示其越有利於小黨派的當選。依照通說，比例性最低的是小選舉區制。在此制下，政權往往為最大的兩個黨派所壟斷。相對地，在純粹的比例代表制之下，當選機率全然取決於自身的實力；制度本身不偏袒任一方。[10] 因此，選舉制度本身即構成一議題空間，各黨派可依各種制度對其之利弊決定立場。這個空間，對於黨派間的權力分配有著重大的影響。

　　然而，選舉制度並非影響權力分配的唯一因素。各黨派在進行權力競逐時，往往需要同時考慮包括選舉制度在內的多種機制。若然，則決策者面臨的是一個「多面向」（multi-dimensional）的議題空間。如果選舉制度和其他影響權力分配的機制（或議題）同時成為選擇的對象，我們即說「選舉制度改革和其他議題同時進入議程（agenda）」。更具體言之，這是指下列情形：所有參與決策的黨派，不但必須表明其所選擇的選舉制度，也須同時在其他議題上表明立場。此外，行動者可以在不同議題間進行交換。舉例而言，A 黨為可以支持 B 黨所喜歡的選舉制度，以交換 B 黨對於 X 法案的支持。另一個常見的例子是，執政黨支持某反對黨（或其中某派）的選舉制度改革案，以化解倒閣的危機。再以圖 1.1 為例，選舉制度改革一旦和原有的權力分配面向共

---

[10] 當然，這樣的制度只能在理想上存在。此外，比例代表制不必然導致多黨制（謝復生，1986）。

存，議題空間即成為二維。

　　根據同理，我們也可得知何謂「選舉制度改革不和其他議題同時出現在議程中」。這可能在兩種情形下發生。第一，由於受到議程設定的影響，各黨派僅能就單一事項進行抉擇。[11] 第二，各黨派對於選舉制度的立場完全一致，而現狀也符合這個立場。若然，則選舉制度改革的面向等於不存在，自然不會出現在議程中。[12]

　　由此可知，影響選舉制度改革的主要因素有二：整個議題空間的維度（dimensionality），以及各黨派在這個空間中的位置。我們所要探討的課題就是：在何種議題結構及偏好分布下，現有選舉制度能被新制度取代？何種新制度最可能產生？要回答這些問題，我們援引「空間模型」（spatial model）裡一項著名的定理：現狀 SQ 不可取代若且唯若 SQ 是一全方中位點（median in all directions）。[13] 用比較通常的語言來說，只有從各種角度來看都不偏不倚，現狀才不能被改變。為了能運用這項定理，我們採取兩項假設（assumptions）。

假設一：中選區制是選舉制度面向上的中位選擇（median voter）。

　　如前所言，許多學者將中選區制視為一種「準比例代表制」。這裡所謂的中選區制，是指選區規模約在四到十席的制度。[14] 對中、小黨（派）而言，這種制度比單一選區制更有利。對大黨而言，中選區制也比純粹的比例代表制為佳。換言之，中選區制可以說是選舉制度選擇面向上的「康氏贏家」（Condorcet winner）。[15] 當然，這個假設是純就制度的比例性來看，政黨也可能因為其他的考慮而更改其立場。但這已經是其他面向的問題。

---

[11] 兩項議案如果未同時進入議程，並不代表其間在本質上是不相關的。因此，即使選舉制度和其他權力面向相關，決策的方式和結果還是可以完全不同。換言之，我們談的是「議程設定」（agenda-setting）的問題。

[12] 如果各黨派對於選舉制度的偏好一致，但現狀卻不符這個偏好，則既有制度應會被改變。然而，在此過程中，選舉制度應該不會成為利益交換的對象。

[13] 「全方中位點」X 必須滿足如右的條件：X 本身為一理想點，且所有通過 X 的線皆將理想點分隔成兩邊，而每一邊理想點的數目都不超過半數。這個定理由 Davis、DeGroot 與 Hinich 在 1972 年所提出，適用於歐式議題空間（Euclidean issue space）。在這之前，C. Plott 在 1967 年針對一般化的效用函數，證明均衡存在的充分條件。

[14] 根據 Taagepera 與 Shugart（1989: 114）的看法，選區規模在四席以下仍有利於大黨獨占席次，而在十席以上則接近純粹的比例代表制。

[15] 若 X 是「康氏贏家」，則對所有的 Y ≠ X 而言，喜歡 X 勝於 Y（strictly prefer X to Y）的人多於喜歡 Y 勝於 X 的人。在簡單多數決的賽局（strong simple majority-rule voting game）中，「康氏贏家」的集合和「局心」（core）是相等的（Ordeshook, 1986: 347）。所謂局心，是所有不可被替代的方案所構成的集合。換言之，若現狀在局心中，則勝集為空集合。

假設二：如果某一權力集團經由既有的選舉制度取得優勢（dominant）地位，則在其他條件不變的情況下，此一制度是該集團最喜好的制度。

所謂優勢地位，是指不需其他黨派的合作即可掌控決策權。如果選舉制度是某一優勢政黨壟斷政權的要因，這個政黨自然會護衛這個制度。舉例而言，英美的兩大政黨都明顯地偏好單一選區制，而不願意改變現狀。不過，我們在採用這個假設時必須作兩點說明。第一，一個政黨並不一定要因為既有制度無法使其取得優勢地位而排斥這個制度。政黨的實力也是影響其國會席次的要因。因此，即使國會中沒有優勢政黨，我們還是可找出各黨派的理想點。第二，優勢政黨的支持率可能在其執政期間有所變化，而改變其對於不同選舉制度的期待。[16] 假設二只適用於政黨支持度沒有明顯變動的情況下。

根據以上的定理與假設，我們可以推演出關於中選區制改革的第一個命題：

命題一：如果中選區制度具有可變性，則以下兩種情況必須同時發生：1. 沒有權力集團掌握絕對多數；2. 選舉制度改革和其他影響權力分配的議題面向同時進入議程。

我們可以用反證法論之。如果某一權力集團掌握絕對多數的國會席次，則其理想點就是一全方中位點。[17] 根據假設二，其所支持的選舉制度和現狀也應相同。根據全方中位定理，這種現狀是不會被改變的。以常理言之：如果現有制度造就了一個壟斷決策權的既得利益黨派，這個黨派自然沒有動機改變現制。其次，根據假設一，中選區制是選舉制度面向上的中位選擇。因此，如果選舉制度被當作單一議案處理，作為現狀的中選區制即成為一個全方中位點。根據定理，這樣的現狀是不會被改變的。

命題一所揭示的是選舉制度改革的必要條件。個別言之，這兩個條件都不是充分條件。首先，由於兩者都是必要條件，只要這兩個條件中任何一者不被滿足，另一條件本身都不足以導致制度變遷。例如，即使沒有黨派壟斷決策權，中選區制還是可以因為議題的單一化而被維持。反之，即使是在多議題的空間，全方中位點仍然可以存在。

那麼，這兩個條件若是同時發生，選舉制度的變遷是否可能？這要看「其他」議題的性質。我們認為，其他議題一旦涉及權力的重分配，則命題一所敘述的兩個條件將可導致選舉制度的改革。其原因在於理性選擇論中的另一個著名定理：當權力（資源）之

---

[16] 舉例而言，南韓的執政黨曾藉由「兩人區單一不可讓渡投票制」而在 1980 至 1988 年間控制國會的多數席次。但經過 1987 年的總統大選，該黨認為其支持度上升，因而開始考慮單一選區制的好處（Brady and Mo, 1992）。

[17] 中位點（median）是指排列順序上的中間點。因此，只要任何一集團的人數超過半數，中位點必與此集團的理想點重合。

和爲常數，而又沒有黨派掌握多數時，沒有任何狀態是穩定的。[18] 換言之，只要選舉制度和權力分配產生關聯，而且沒有權力集團壟斷決策權，那麼即使現有制度是制度選擇面向上的中位方案，還是可以被改變。舉例而言，某些黨派可以爲了擴大權力（例如進入內閣），而適度地在制度選擇的議題上讓步。只要這些黨派構成多數，現在制度就可被改變。

以上的命題所指陳的，是常被論及的一個政治現象：制度一旦成爲權力交換的籌碼，就有被改變的可能。然而，制度的可變性只是我們要探討的第一個問題。我們還有興趣知道，現有制度一旦可以改變，新方案是什麼？新制度本身是不是穩定的？這是下一個命題的要旨。

命題二：現有選舉制度若具可變性，則替代方案通常不只一項。替代方案如果不是「康氏贏家」，則其本身是可被取代的。如果「康氏贏家」根本不存在，則任何新方案都是可以被更動的。

勝集是由聯盟成員的無異曲線所組成，具有無限多個構成元素。[19] 一般而言，勝集反映了不同聯盟的立場，而呈現不規則狀。以圖 1.2 爲例，組成勝集的三個「葉片」，分別由 {A, B}、{B, C} 與 {A, C} 等三聯盟的「利益交集」所構成。在這種多案競爭的狀態下，勝負往往取決於對議程的掌握。假設執政的 A 黨掌握了提案權，即可以提出勝集中最靠近其立場的方案爭取 B 黨的合作。由於該方案優於現狀（SQ），後者應當不會拒絕。這就是所謂議程設定者的權力（power of the agenda-setter）：即使 A 黨不能掌握多數席次，還是可以藉由此權維護其執政的地位。當然，議程不一定完全掌控在執政黨的手裡。如果 C 黨有相當的機會操控議事程序，就可拉攏 B 黨組成抗 A 聯盟。同理，A 黨也可聯合 C 黨防止 B 黨的挑戰。總之，命題二的要義在於說明，改革的可能性和改革成果的穩定性，應被當作兩回事看待。X 制度可以取代現狀，不代表 X 制度就不可被 Y 制度取代。最好的結果是，新制度 X 不但可以贏得多數支持，同時也是「康氏贏家」。然而，這樣的結果並不必然發生。我們甚且可以說，只要制度改革和資源或權力的重分配牽扯在一起，則新制度本身也是不穩定的（因爲「康氏贏家」不存在）。

---

[18] 這項陳述得自以下定理：特徵函數形態的實質超可加常和賽局（essential super-additive constant-sum games in characteristic function form）之局心爲空集合（Ordeshook, 1986: 350）。

[19] 隱藏在此的假設是，效用函數是連續（continuous）而準凹（quasi-concave）的。關於如何導出勝集的詳細說明，請參見 Laing、Nakabayashi 與 Slotznick（1983）。即使我們不採用這種效用函數假設，勝集的元素通常也不只一個。

同理，如果要維持新制度的穩定性，就要避免其再度成為權力交換的籌碼。[20]

我們可以藉由日本的選舉制度改革來驗證以上的分析。要將前述命題應用在日本個案上，我們須先瞭解日本的國會議員對於選舉制度的偏好，以及制度改革所處的議題空間。我們將於次節檢視這些問題，並概述日本各政黨的社會基礎如何影響其對選舉制度之偏好。在此前提下，第伍、陸節將上列命題加以操作化，形成關於日本選舉制度改革之假說，並以實際經驗檢證之。

肆、中選舉區制與選舉精英之制度偏好

對於選舉制度之偏好，主要取決於制度本身的比例性。既有研究在探討這個問題時，大多是以政黨為分析單位，而主張比例性越高的制度越能獲得小黨的支持（Rae, 1971; Lijphart, 1990）。要將這樣的結論應用在中選舉區制上，必須先克服一些難題。其一，在中選舉區制的競選過程中，候選人個人通常扮演主導性角色，而同黨相爭的傾向在大黨尤為明顯。因此，以政黨為單位分析比例性，不能完全看出選舉制度所蘊含的利益分歧。舉例而言，某大黨可能在選舉中取得超過得票率的席次率，但同黨當選人卻彼此敵對。黨內的不同派系，對於制度的喜好也可能有所不同，其次，只研究選舉制度的比例性，並不能告訴我們候選人所賴以當選的社會基礎為何。這種基礎，很可能影響當選者對於選舉制度改革的偏好，以及其在其他議題面向上的立場。

因此，我們必須瞭解在中選舉區制之下，各類型候選人當選機率的大小，而其勝選的基礎又是什麼。關於後一個問題，學者間有各種看法。某些新制度論者，認為日本（尤其是自民黨）的國會議員乃是以經濟性的分歧為票源區隔的基礎，彼此以經濟部門劃分勢力範圍（Ramseyer and Rosenbluth, 1993）。水崎節文及森裕城（1995）的實證研究則發現日本眾議院議員候選人的得票有明顯的地域性區隔。此外，意識形態或議題立場也可能在特定選區成為集票的依據。不論基礎為何，我們可以約略將候選人的支持基礎依勝選策略分為兩種理想類型：集中型與分散型。前者是指其得票明顯集中於特定的經濟性、地域性、或意識形態性團體。後者則是指因為候選人某些不可替代的特質（例如形象或知名度），使其贏得跨團體或地域的支持。除了支持基礎外，候選人個人實力也是一重要變數。譬如說，票源廣闊固然可能使人高票當選，對實力不足者而言過

---

[20] 當然，這也是必要條件而非充分條件。如要新制度本身不是中位方案，則即使沒有權力因素的干預，也可能是不穩定的。

度分散卻可能是致命傷。同樣的道理，狹隘的訴求固然有鞏固票源的作用，卻也可能導致得票不足。

選舉精英對於制度的偏好將受到其支持基礎及本身實力的影響。一般而言，實力越強的選舉精英，越容易在小選舉區制中得利。對集中型的候選人而言，只要選區劃分得當，也較易在小選舉區中壟斷席次。分散型的候選人，如果實力較弱，則較易在多席次的競爭中取得一定的游離票而當選。如果一名候選人實力雄厚但卻票源分散，則小選舉區制有利於其排除實力較差者的競爭，而中選舉區制卻可能使其不敵集中型（且實力相當）的候選人。[21]

選舉精英的選票基礎，也決定了他們在其他議題面向上的位置。試以對於金權政治的態度論之。一般而言，一個國會議員的支持基礎越特定化，就越可能運用政治權力圖利特殊利益。在中選舉區制下，由於只要得到特定少數團體的支持即可當選，這種傾向將更為明顯。同樣的道理，對於利益政治最不滿的，可能就是不具有明顯屬性而集體行動能力又較薄弱的選民。分散型的候選人應當就是受到此類選民的支持。

選票基礎的差異因此左右了當選者對於金權政治的立場，形成另一議題空間。各類型當選人所占的比重，也因而影響了制度改革議題空間的結構。一個合理的推斷是：由於中選舉區制是多席次當選，其所產生的當選人通常具有不同的實力和支持基礎；這種異質性亦導致對於選舉制度的不同評價。表 1.1 顯示日本各政黨當選人在 1990 及 1993 年眾議院選舉的排名分布狀況。從表中可以看出，自民黨當選人的排名在兩次選舉中都略呈常態分布。[22] 因此，我們可以推論自民黨議員對於選舉制度的偏好並非同質的。在其他政黨中，值得注意的是以改革為號召的政黨往往都有較大的機率拔得頭籌。這包括 1990 年的社會黨及 1993 年選舉中的新政黨。這些革新政黨的特徵，正在於候選人乃以批判傳統的「利益誘導政治」為訴求。換言之，其支持基礎屬於分散型，其票源則為對現狀不滿的游離票。改革派的候選人紛紛以高票當選，說明其實力的堅強。

由以上的資料可知，中選舉區制的特性再加上社會情勢的變化，使 1990 年前後的日本出現了各種形態的選舉菁英，各自抱持對選舉制度以及其他議題的不同立場。這種異質性，正是制度改革的前提。以下，我們將根據此前提，檢視關於選舉制度改革的諸項命題。

---

21 除此之外，選區劃分也影響當選機率。集中型的候選人，可能因選區劃分不當導致票源被切割，進而落選。相對而言，分散型候選人則較不受此因素影響。

22 關於日本各政黨在中選區制下得票率的長期分析，請見川人貞史（1987）。

表 1.1　1990 及 1993 年日本眾議院選舉各黨當選人排名分布表

A. 1990 年

排名	公明黨	民社黨	共產黨	社會黨	自民黨	其他	全部
1	1 (2.2%)		1 (20.0%)	74 (53.2%)	51 (17.7%)	3 (37.5%)	130 (25.4%)
2	4 (8.7%)	2 (14.3%)	1 (20.0%)	34 (24.5%)	87 (30.2%)	1 (12.5%)	129 (24.5%)
3	11 (23.9%)	4 (28.6%)	2 (40.0%)	15 (10.8%)	88 (30.6%)	3 (37.5%)	125 (24.5%)
4	17 (37.0%)	6 (42.9%)	1 (20.0%)	9 (6.5%)	44 (15.3%)	1 (12.5%)	83 (16.2%)
5	12 (26.1%)	2 (14.3%)		7 (5.0%)	18 (6.3%)		43 (8.4%)
6	1 (2.2%)						1 (0.2%)
總計	46	14	16	139	288	8	511

B. 1993 年

排名	公明黨	民社黨	共產黨	社會黨	自民黨	日本新黨	新生黨	全部
1	7 (13.5%)	5 (27.8%)	2 (14.3%)	3 (4.2%)	62 (27.1%)	21 (42.9%)	24 (44.4%)	129 (25.3%)
2	12 (23.1%)	3 (16.7%)	3 (21.4%)	1 (16.7%)	6 (27.9%)	1 (26.5%)	17 (31.5%)	129 (25.3%)
3	17 (32.7%)	5 (27.8%)	2 (14.3%)	27 (37.5%)	50 (21.8%)	7 (14.3%)	5 (9.3%)	121 (23.8%)
4	13 (25.0%)	1 (5.6%)	4 (28.6%)	20 (27.8%)	32 (14.0%)	3 (6.1%)	6 (11.1%)	81 (15.9%)
5	3 (5.8%)	4 (22.2%)	3 (21.4%)	9 (12.5%)	20 (8.7%)	5 (10.2%)	2 (3.7%)	47 (9.2%)
6				1 (1.4%)	1 (0.4%)			2 (0.4%)
總計	52	18	14	72	229	49	54	509

資料來源：根據宮川隆義（1991、1994）算出。

說明：僅列出政黨提名當選人。

伍、選舉制度改革與日本的政黨重組

前面提到，在中選舉區制下所產生的選舉精英，對此一制度將抱持不同的偏好。若然，中選舉區制爲何還能長期存在？我們又如何解釋其改變？根據命題一，我們可以提出兩項關於日本選制改革的假說：

假說一：中選區制的改革如果不和其他議題同時進入議程，提案將遭受挫敗。

假說二：中選區制的改革如果在一黨獨大時提出，提案將遭受挫敗。

我們可從日本的選舉制度改革史來檢證這兩項假說。自民黨成立不久後，鳩山一郎首相曾在 1956 年向國會提議將中選區制改爲小選區制。他的動機是要讓甫成立的自民黨能確保其多數的地位，以推動日本憲法第九條的修正案。但是這個企圖並沒有實現。[23] 另一次重要的選舉制度改革案，是田中角榮在 1973 年所提出的「小選舉區比例代表並立制」。其目的是要挽回自民黨逐漸喪失的選舉優勢。但是，這個提案也沒有成功。

一般都認爲，鳩山和田中的企圖之所以失敗，是因爲反對黨的抵制（Shiratori, 1995: 81; 降矢敬義，1994）。然而，由於自民黨在國會內始終都占有絕對多數的席次，這個理由不能成立。自民黨內部，必然也有相當多的議員反對改革。從命題一的角度，可以爲改革的挫敗提出另一個解釋：鳩山和田中在倡議小選舉區制的時候，並未帶入其他的議題。[24] 如前所述，中選區制是各黨派在選舉制度面向上唯一能找到的均衡點。因此，除非刻意導入其他因素，中選區制的穩定性極高。再者，改革案於自民黨一黨獨大時提出，減縮了提案者利用黨派矛盾進行談判的空間。如果強行推動小選舉區制，更有導致自民黨分裂之虞。這正是命題一的另一項要義：自民黨若要維持其優勢地位，就必須避免黨內在重大議題上出現分歧。我們在次節就會提到，自民黨之所以喪失政權，正是因爲選舉制度改革所導致的內鬥。

日本選舉制度改革的失敗史因而確證了上述兩項假說。至於中選舉區制爲何成爲當時唯一的共識，原因也不難理解：這是主張比例代表制者和小選舉區制者唯一能共同接

---

[23] 1919 年，在原敬內閣的努力下，日本眾議院亦曾通過選舉法修正案，實施小選舉區制。然而，這個制度不到幾年就被中選舉區制所取代。

[24] 所謂其他議題，可以是任何和權力重分配有關者，例如限制政治獻金、黨政職位分配等。一個可能的策略是，首相以政治職位化解某些派系對小選區制的抵制。以防堵金權政治的法案交換反對黨對選舉制度改革的支持，則是另一種策略。至於這種交換是否有必要，取決於新制度所帶來的好處是否大於自民黨領導者所付出的代價。

受的妥協方案。事實上，此一制度之所以在 1925 年被提出並長期持續，就是議會內大小黨派妥協的結果（堀江湛，1989：14）。

我們也可以從相反的方向來印證上述假說：第一，國會通過中選區制改革案時，必有其他法案被同時討論，或處於政權重組的狀態中。其次，改革成功時，國會處於多黨林立的局面。我們知道，日本的國會是在 1994 年初通過公職選舉法修正案的（詳見次節）。該案正是和其他三項有關政治改革的法案同時通過的。當時，也處於自民黨第一次失去政權，由反對黨組成多黨聯合政府主政的局面。這些現象都符合假說。那麼，選舉制度改革是如何和其他議題產生關連的？日本又如何從一黨獨大演變為多黨競爭？這些問題的答案，可說是分析中選區制改革的最終線索。以下，將分別論述之。

一、 選舉制度改革與政治改革的聯結

正如前述，中選舉區制在日本具有相當的穩定性。然而，也正因為長期使用此一制度，日本政治產生了體制性的危機。在此制度下，候選人汲汲於突顯個人功績，以在同黨相爭的局面中勝選。這造成兩個嚴重後果。一方面，由於候選人必須靠一己之力從事競選，導致選舉成本極高。另一方面，為增加當選機率，鞏固票源比擴充票源更重要。這迫使候選人和特定團體進行掛鉤，以承諾物質利益換取選票或政治獻金。再者，競選成本越高，國會議員就越需要鞏固其和特殊利益間的不當關係。兩者相乘的結果，就是惡名昭彰的金權政治。一般的日本國民，對此問題其實早有相當的體認。但有鑑於日本經濟持續成長，故尚能保持一定的容忍。

隨著日本經濟的衰退，選民的容忍程度也在降低。1988 年爆發的「瑞克魯特」事件，可以說是一個重要的臨界點。在本質上，這個事件其實和戰後日本一連串的金權醜聞並無不同。瑞克魯特是一家以出版就業資訊起家的企業；所謂的醜聞，是指其以未上市的股票賄賂政府官員及國會議員的事件。此一事件的嚴重性在於涉案人之廣、層次之高。除了至少有 54 名政界人物出現在賄賂的名單上之外，前後更有二位首相因此下台（許介鱗，1991：293-309）。涉案人廣及自民黨各派系乃至於部分反對黨的議員，媒體因此將之視為整個體系的貪污。果然，在 1989 年的參議院選舉中，自民黨遭受空前的慘敗；改革之論也甚囂塵上。

政治改革又是如何和選舉制度扯上關係的？要減輕金權政治的弊端，其實大可從立法規範政治獻金著手。事實上，輿論界也一直有人主張應限制對政治家個人的獻金，同時加強對政黨的補助。然而，將政治改革和選舉制度牽連在一起，卻和自民黨有密切的關係。自民黨的「政治改革委員會」在 1989 年 5 月所提出的《政治改革大綱》裡，明

確地將日本的政治腐化歸咎於中選舉區制，並建議代之以小選舉區制。有趣的是，這份大綱對於中選舉區制的批評雖然和一般的看法接近，卻並未解釋爲何替代方案爲小選舉區制而非比例代表制。日本的輿論界也自然將小選舉區制視爲改革的當然手段。

「選舉制度改革」與「政治改革」等兩大議題因而構成此一階段日本政治的主軸；政治勢力則劃分爲自民黨（包括盟友）及反自民黨兩大陣營，但自民黨內部的意見並不統一。根據第參節所提出的理論模型，在此情況下的選制改革並非不可能，但變動的空間有限，且結果對自民黨的領導階層有利。[25] 這也許就是自民黨以小選區制來應對改革要求的原因。自民黨可以有這樣的盤算：政治改革一旦和引進小選舉區制牽扯在一起，必然會受反對黨議員的抵制，改革也將因此擱淺。即使改革成功而必須對政治獻金進行更大的規範，小選舉區制還是對自民黨有利；左翼政黨也許就從此式微。換言之，以小選舉區制爲改革方案可以說是自民黨領導階層的「不輸之策」（dominant strategy）。

然而，出人意料的是，政治改革與選舉制度改革的連結也間接導致了自民黨的分裂。這些從自民黨分裂出去的精英亦偏好小選舉區制，但對於金權政治卻採取更積極的批判立場，以期爭取都會區選民的支持。相對而言，既有的反對黨雖然也批判金權政治，卻對選舉制度的改革採取保留態度。一個新的三角關係因而浮現，對於改革的路徑產生重要的影響。

二、 自民黨的分裂與改革契機

對於自民黨而言，瑞克魯特事件最大的傷害之一，就是黨內各大派閥幾乎都牽連在內。在幾乎無人可用，而各派閥又鬥爭不休的情形下，由河本派的海部俊樹在 1989 年 8 月繼任首相。河本派是一個繼承三木派的小派閥，向來以「清廉」自稱。海部一上台，即宣布將以政治改革爲主要使命，而輿論也給予相當支持。扮演改革提案者角色的，是以媒體代表爲主體的「第八次選舉制度審議會」。[26]

1989 年 11 月，海部內閣的第一份選舉改革提案出爐。其內容是所謂的「小選舉區比例代表並立制」，其中小選舉區對比例代表區的議席比是 300：171。在這種制度下，眾議院的議席被分成兩部分，分別由小選舉區制和名單式比例代表制選舉產生。由於兩

---

[25] 對自民黨領導階層而言，小選區制可以擴大其席次比例。然而，某些實力不強的自民黨候選人卻可能因此落選。因此，自民黨內對於選舉制度的偏好並不一致。

[26] 在此之前，審議會的代表來各政黨。第八次審議會之所以由媒體代表組成，除了有減少抗拒的作用外，也有拉攏媒體的意圖。在此之前日本的媒體一向反對選舉制度改革（世界臨時增刊，1994）。

種席次的產生互不相干,而小選舉區制所產生的席次之份量又重得多,這種制度可以說是偏向小選舉區制的混合制。[27] 許多的日本媒體,甚至直接簡稱其爲小選舉區制。

　　果然不出所料,這份提案遭受強大的反對。爲妥協起見,審議會在 1990 年 4 月將比例代表的席次提高爲 200。另一方面,海部政府也著手提案,限制對於政治家個人的政治獻金。然而,這些提案仍不能取得國會多數的支持。就在同年 8 月,波斯灣戰爭爆發。由於日本國會對海外派兵的問題反應遲緩,開始有人提出這樣的論述:中選舉區制不但造成國會內黨派林立,更導致議員僅關心選區利益而無心討論國政。如此下去,日本將在新的國際環境中失去應變能力。海部政府乃趁此氣氛在 1991 年 7 月向國會提出「關於政治改革之三法案」。其主要內容如下:1. 選舉制度改爲「小選舉區比例代表並立制」,其比例爲 300:171,選民投兩票、比例代表由一全國選區產生;2. 禁止對政治家個人獻金;3. 對政黨實行公費補助制度。不幸的是,在許多反對黨及自民黨議員的抵制下,這個提案胎死腹中。海部俊樹被迫辭職,而由宮澤喜一繼任首相。

　　海部的改革經驗再次驗證了前述假說:當自民黨控制國會多數時,由於其大多數的成員依賴政治獻金,改革必然被化約爲選舉制度的問題。如此一來,中選舉區制是唯一可以被各派接受的方案,使改革難以成功。然而,海部的挫敗並非全然徒勞無功。由於輿論對於國會反潮流的做法提出強烈的批判,部分自民黨議員感受到一個新的權力面向正在形成:批判自民黨將帶來選票。首先發難的是細川護熙。他在 1992 年 5 月宣布脫離自民黨,組成「日本新黨」。在 7 月的參議院選舉中,這個剛滿月的新政黨一舉獲得 8% 的選票,而各老牌政黨卻遭受慘敗。既得利益越是抵制改革,輿論的批判就越強,並吸引更多的議員以改革爲競選訴求。在接下來的一年內,政治改革就是沿著這個主軸進行的。

　　1992 年 8 月,爆發了所謂的「佐川急便」弊案。前自民黨副總裁,也是日本金權政治的代表人物金丸信,被控非法接受該企業的政治獻金。輿論要求改革的聲浪到了頂點,並要求設立政黨公費補助制度。然而,宮澤內閣卻仍然採取既有的應對方法。1998 年 3 月底,宮澤向國會提案,建議採用完全小選舉區制。如一般所料,這個議案遭到所有反對黨的抵制。然而,這個動作也爲自民黨的分裂譜下序曲。6 月 18 日,在野黨在眾議院大會中提出對宮澤內閣的不信任案。結果,此案在自民黨「改革派」議員投下贊成票的情形下獲得通過。就在宮澤內閣準備解散國會之際,自民黨羽田派的議員宣布脫黨組成「新生黨」。再加上前不久由部分自民黨脫黨議員所組成的「魁黨」

---

[27] 會中也有主張德國式混合制者。在此制下,選民投兩票,一票在小選區投人,一票在比例代表區投黨。政黨的席次乃依其所得票數按比例分配,但小選區的勝選者優先成爲各黨當選人。

表 1.2　1993 年眾議院選舉當選人所在選區之都市化程度

選區分類	公明黨	民社黨	共產黨	社會黨	自民黨	日本新黨	新生黨	全部
大都市停滯地區	12 (23.1%)	1 (5.6%)	6 (42.9%)	3 (4.2%)	15 (6.6%)	8 (16.3%)	7 (13.0%)	56 (11.0%)
大都市近郊地區	18 (34.6%)	3 (16.7%)	5 (35.7%)	11 (15.3%)	15 (6.6%)	20 (40.8%)	8 (14.8%)	82 (16.1%)
中都市商業地區	4 (7.7%)			5 (6.9%)	8 (3.5%)	2 (4.1%)	2 (3.7%)	21 (4.1%)
小都市工業地區	7 (13.5%)	5 (27.8%)	1 (7.1%)	11 (15.3%)	32 (14.0%)	3 (6.1%)	10 (18.5%)	73 (14.3%)
小都市周邊地區	7 (13.5%)	5 (27.8%)	1 (7.1%)	15 (20.8%)	53 (23.1%)	7 (14.3%)	7 (13.0%)	101 (19.8%)
半農村工業化區	2 (3.8%)	2 (11.1%)		19 (26.4%)	69 (30.1%)	7 (14.3%)	14 (25.9%)	117 (23.0%)
農村人口外流區	2 (3.8%)	2 (11.1%)	1 (7.1%)	8 (11.1%)	37 (16.2%)	2 (4.1%)	6 (11.1%)	59 (11.6%)
	52	18	14	72	229	49	54	509

資料來源：小林良彰（1985）。
說明：僅列出政黨提名當選人。

（sakigake），自民黨已經失去多數黨的地位。眾議院乃宣告解散舉行大選。

　　至此，三足鼎立的大勢已成。那麼，我們如何解釋所謂這些「改革派」議員的行為？其立場為何？從 1993 年 6 月的眾議院選舉結果中，不難看出一些端倪。表 1.2 將各黨當選人依其所在選區的都市化程度加以分類。此表明確顯示，這些從自民黨脫黨自立門戶的改革派當選人，相當集中在都市化程度較高的選區。相對而言，自民黨及社會黨的當選人，則呈現出明顯的鄉村化傾向。都市中產階級選民對現狀不滿，在日本不是新聞。他們成為金權政治主要的批判者，有幾個原因。首先，由於缺乏明確的組織歸屬，他們通常不是「利益誘導型」候選人鎖定的首要目標。其次，日本的選區劃分明顯偏差。這導致都市選民所投的票，價值不如鄉村選民。第三，都市選民必須負擔重稅及高物價以支付金權政治的成本。此外，由於教育程度較高、受媒體影響較深，他們也較可能成為所謂的「議題投票者」（issue voter）。至於這些改革派議員對選舉制度的態度，我們可以從表 1.1 找到一些線索。日本新黨及新生黨候選人以第一或第二高位當選者，比例遠超過其他政黨。這顯示出他們的改革形象受到廣泛的支持。在選舉制度上，

他們理應偏向小選舉區制（見表 1.1）。

選舉制度改革的條件，至此已趨成熟。我們可以約略將參與改革的主要角色及其立場敘述如下（不入斗智，1990；読売新聞社，1996）：

1. 自民黨：主要支持者來自非都會區及特殊利益團體。基本上對於政治改革（尤其是限制政治獻金）採取較消極的態度。成員對於選舉制度的態度，可能因為實力不同而成常態分配。但黨領導者，則隨著弊案的連連爆發而越發傾向於「單純小選舉區制」（富森叡兒，1993：151）。

2. 舊反對黨：以社會黨左派及共產黨為主。主要支持群在於勞工及部分薪水階級。反對金權政治，但對選舉制度改革採取消極態度，或希望引進比例代表制。

3. 革新政黨：這個集團的核心是日本新黨及新生黨，亦即從自民黨分裂出來的精英。我們也可將公明黨、魁黨及部分社會黨的派系包括在內。其支持者的核心為對政治現狀不滿的都市中產階級。大致而言，這個集團在反金權政治上和既有反對黨是一致的。但其潛在的意識形態可能是新保守主義。對於選舉制度，內部可能有歧異，但對外主張傾向於以小選舉區制為主的混合制。[28]

圖 1.3 顯示由權力分配及選舉制度改革所共同構成的議題空間。三大勢力在權力分配的面向（即底邊的三角形）上各占一頂點；任何兩黨的合作都可以改變分配的現狀。在選舉制度改革的面向上，舊有反對黨立場不同於主張小選區制的自民黨及革新政黨，因而具有較高的理想點。至於整個議題空間的現狀點，則是這樣定位的：就選舉制度而言，中選區制屬於「半比例代表制」，其位置因而介於舊反對黨與自民黨之間。就權力分配的面向來看，改革開始前的現狀應是自民黨壟斷權力。但拒絕改革將使自民黨失去相當的民意支持，權力分配的現狀因而不完全落在自民黨的理想點上。[29]

根據命題一，選舉制度的改革在此情況下是可能的。問題是，改革將遵循何種路徑，最後結果又如何？這是次節的課題。

---

[28] 在革新政黨中，以實現兩大政黨制為目標的新生黨及公明黨主張小選區比例代表一票制，日本新黨與魁黨則傾向兩票制（大嶽秀夫，1995：11）。所謂對外的態度，是以細川聯合政府的立場為基準。

[29] 正如第參節所言，權力重分配可能起因於各黨所獲支持的變化，也可能起因於聯盟重組。我們將現狀點界定為「選舉制度改革失敗的後果」，權力分配的現狀即取決於執政黨為改革失敗所付出的政治代價。政黨透過聯盟重組改變權力分配，可視為是對此一現狀的改變。

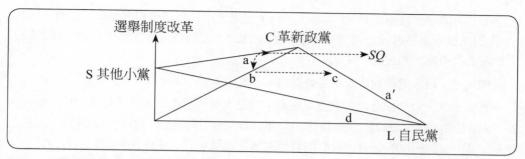

圖1.3　日本選舉制度改革的議題空間

陸、選舉制度改革的軌跡與日本政界的重組

　　根據命題二，選舉制度改革一旦成為權力重組的籌碼，則可能產生的新方案通常不只一個。在此情形下，議程設定權的歸屬就顯得很重要。議程設定者可以在可行方案中擇其所好者提交表決，其他黨派即使反對，也只能就此提案進行杯葛或翻案。因此，縱使新方案本身也是可被替代的，我們仍可描繪出一個制度改革的軌跡。[30] 以下，我們就針對日本選制改革的議程設定與演變軌跡進行分析。

　　日本是實行內閣制的國家，由多數黨所組成的政府享有議程的設定權。自民黨在黨分裂後，於 1993 年 6 月的眾議院選舉中失去多數黨的地位。儘管意識形態差距頗大，非自民及非共產的政黨仍在政治改革的共同目標下於 8 月組成聯合政府，並由日本新黨的細川護熙出任首相。革新政黨因而掌握了改革的提案權。在政黨的結盟實力方面，自民黨應該遠勝於舊有的小黨。聯合政府雖然掌握了眾議院的多數席次，卻因組成份子複雜、立場不一而削弱了行動力。為便於分析，我們以 L 代表自民黨，C 代表聯合政府，並以 S 表示其他小黨。三股勢力形成三種結盟的可能，並提供了至少三種改變現狀的方式：[31]

　　a 表示 {C, S} 聯盟：革新政黨連合其他小黨取得政權，降低選舉制度的比例性。

　　b 表示 {L, S} 聯盟：自民黨聯絡聯合政府以外的小黨組成在野聯盟，並主張縮減選舉制度改革的幅度。

　　c 表示 {C, L} 聯盟：聯合政府與自民黨合作通過小選區制。

---

[30]　命題二也指出，在權力重分配所形成的議題空間中，康氏贏家通常是不存在的。

[31]　關於這三個選項如何導出，請參見註 9。

　　上述各方案，在圖 1.3 中分別以 a、b、c 三點表示。在選舉制度改革的面向上，{C, L} 聯盟所提方案將最接近最完全小選區制，{L, S} 方案最接近比例代表制。我們提出下列關於改革軌跡的假說：

　　假說三：日本選舉制度改革之軌跡為 a → b → c。

　　推論如下。由於聯合政府掌握提案權，其最可能提出的改革方案是圖中的 a 點或 a′點。a 點是 SQ 在 SC 線段上的垂直投射。同理，我們可以找到 SQ 在 LC 線段上的垂直投射 a′ 點。a 點顯現的是聯合政府與舊反對黨在挑戰現狀時的最佳共識：兩者的權力皆擴大，而作為提案者的聯合政府則藉機將選舉制度的比例性降低。如果提案雖在 SC 線段上，卻高於或低於 a 點，另一方會產生公平性的質疑。a 點也顯示，小黨為了達到奪取自民黨政權的目的，可以容忍選舉制度作部分的調整（但離完全小選舉區制必有一段距離）。這也正是聯合政府內的原自民黨精英所必須妥協之處。依照同樣的道理，聯合政府也可以拉攏自民黨。若然，則 a′ 是最可能的選擇。但此一方案有一個相當大的問題：為拉攏自民黨，聯合政府必須與自民黨分享政權。這顯然有悖該政府在選前關於改革的承諾。因此 a 方案較 a′ 方案更具可能性。

　　然而，這並不表示 a 即是改革的結果。事實上，a 並非一康氏贏家方案。自民黨雖被排除在 {C, S} 聯盟外，卻可以聯合舊反對黨，提出替代方案 b。亦即，自民黨以抵制選舉制度改革為條件，拉攏可能在新制度下失去空間的小黨派。如果這種結盟成功，聯合政府甚至可能因改革失敗而倒台。但革新派並非無牌可出。如果真的發生這種狀況，聯合政府可以提議 c 方案來破壞舊勢力的聯盟。有趣的是，c 案其實更接近革新派的理想。c 案當然也可能被擊敗，而使過程不斷的循環下去，直到議題空間產生變化為止。

　　我們可以從實際的歷史過程來印證上述假設。革新政黨在 1993 年 6 月的眾議院選舉中得到大勝，並由細川護熙在 8 月出任首相，組成多黨聯合政府。標舉著「政治改革政權」招牌的細川內閣，在成立不久後即提出下列主張：小選舉區及比例代表區各選出 250 席，選民投兩票。此外，政府也準備提出「政黨助成法案」，嚴格規範政治資金的收取與運用。對於聯合政府的提案，自民黨果然不出所料地加以抵制，並準備在國會中提出替代案。此外，社會黨內部也出現批判選舉制度改革方案的聲音，聯合政府可以說面臨內外交攻的狀況。[32]

　　我們從表 1.3 即可看出各黨各派對於改革的分歧態度。表中所列的，是所謂「政治改革相關法案」中最引起爭議的部分。其中關於選舉制度改革的歧異，不但包括議席在

---

[32] 社會黨的困境充分反映了當時情勢的複雜性。就選舉制度而言，聯合政府的提案並不利該黨。但退出聯合政府，卻又使該黨失去參政空間（河野勝，1995）。

表 1.3　日本各黨派對政治改革的態度（1993 年 11 月）

政黨／派系	眾議院席次	參議院席次	對選舉制度之立場	對政治獻金之立場
自民黨	204	94	小選區比例代表並立制	每人可成立兩個政治獻金團體
			小選區 300 席比例代表 171 席	每人每年可接受 24 萬日圓捐獻
			一票制	對政黨補助不超過前年收入 1/3
			以都府道縣為比例區	禁止政治家個人接受政治獻金
自民黨改革派	13	5	小選區比例代表並立制	對政黨補助不設上限
新生黨	60	8	小選區 500 席比例代表 274 席	
日本新黨	52	15	兩票制	
魁黨、公明黨	52	24	以全國為比例區	
民社黨	19	11		
獨立派議員	5	0		
社會黨	71	56		
社會黨反對派	5	17	比例代表制或類似制度	禁止政治家接受政治獻金
共產黨	15	11		
獨立派議員	2	8		

資料來源：根據朝日新聞社（1994）整理。

不同制度間的分配，還有選民的投票數、比例區如何劃分等問題。這些因素都影響了選舉制度的比例性：減少比例代表的席次比、採一票制、或縮小比例區等手段，都可以擠壓小黨的空間。從表中，我們不難看出聯合政府想採取折衷方案的企圖。在規範政治資金方面，自民黨則明顯採取反動的立場。

　　為了預防自民黨從中作梗，細川首相主動妥協，將政府草案中的議席比修改為小選舉區 274 席、比例代表區 226 席。結果，修正後的政府提案分別在 11 月 16 日與 18

日獲得眾議院政治改革調整特別委員會及眾議院大會的通過（政界往來社，1994 年 2 月）。然而，改革並非就此完成。事實上，在眾議院大會表決時，各陣營就已出現分裂的狀況。在聯合政府方面，五名社會黨的議員對政府案投下反對票。在自民黨方面，則有 13 名議員贊成政府提案，而包括前首相海部俊樹在內的七名重量級人物則棄權（朝日新聞社，1994）。這些情況都為法案未來的命運投下陰影。

　　根據日本憲法，法案必須要得到參眾兩院的通過方能成立。聯合政府成立後，在參議院只擁有 252 席中的 131 席。這個比例只勉強過半數。參議院因而成為自民黨及其他小黨派進行翻案的新戰場。1994 年 1 月 21 日，參議院對政治改革相關法案進行記名表決。結果，在自民黨、共產黨，及部分社會黨議員的聯手下，政府法案以 12 票之差遭受否決。眾議院乃依憲法的規定，要求召開「兩院協議會」。然而，在 1 月 27 日召開的兩院協議會中，雙方卻不能達成任何協議。細川政府至此已經面臨信用破產乃至於倒台的危機。[33]

　　細川內閣唯一的出路，就是對自民黨讓步。1 月 28 日，在眾議院議長的斡旋下，細川首相和自民黨總裁河野洋平進行緊急會商。其結果如下：

1. 選舉制度：小選舉區比例代表並立制。其中小選舉區占 300 席，比例代表區占 200 席。選民投二票，一票投黨，一票投人。比例區與小選區席次分開計算，全國分為 11 個比例代表區。

2. 政治資金：自法案通過的五年內，容許企業或團體對政治家個人進行政治捐獻，但以一個團體為限，且每年不能超過日幣 50 萬圓。對政黨的公費補助，以前一年實際收支的 40% 為上限（林崎理，1994）。

　　就在細川與河野會談的翌日，參眾兩院通過了包括如上內容的政治改革相關法案。耗時六年的選舉制度改革，至此暫時告一段落。我們縱觀聯合政府成立後的整個改革過程，可以發現前述假設得到相當程度的印證。聯合政府先是為求拉攏社會黨及其他小黨，提出小選舉區比例代表各半的並立制，並主張完全禁止政治獻金。如此一來，不但搶奪了自民黨的政權，更斷了其資金來源（a 點）。但這個議案卻遭到自民黨及其他小黨議員的聯手抵制而在參議院擱淺。如果此舉成功，不但使選舉制度改革徒勞無功（即維持中選區制），更有迫使聯合政府垮台的可能（b 點）。細川首相為了保住政權，只

---

[33] 根據日本憲法第五十九條的規定，眾議院可以以三分之二的多數重新通過被參議院否決的法案（日本眾議院，1990：180-181）。但聯合政府顯然缺乏這樣的實力。因此，如果兩院協議會不能達成協議，政府提案形同被否決。由於選制改革是重大法案，此舉相當於對細川政府的不信任投票。

得向自民黨妥協，接受偏向於小選舉區的新制度，及放寬對政治獻金的限制。自民黨不但獲得對其有利的選舉制度，並充分展現政治實力（c 點）。

　　從最後的內容來看，日本國會所通過的改革法案很明顯地偏向自民黨的主張。然而，即使是這樣的讓步，仍不能保證改革的穩固及政局的穩定（因為結局仍非康氏贏家）。1994 年 6 月 29 日，發生了一件日本現代政治史上的大事：自民黨、魁黨及日本社會黨組成了聯合政府，並由社會黨左派的村山富市出任首相。媒體及學者一般都認為是權力意志超越了意識形態，才導致了這樣的怪異組合。其實，從本論文的觀點來看，這種結果並不令人意外。如前所述，最後通過的政治改革版本接近於圖 1.3 的 c 點。自民黨和左派政黨如果聯合，卻可以將結果轉移到圖中所顯示的 d 點。當然，由於改革法案已經通過，要立即將其修改或推翻的成本可能過高。然而，自民黨和社會黨在權力面向上所進行的交易卻是有效的。對社會黨的精英而言，獲得大臣的職位及出任首相，可以彌補他們在新選舉制度下必然萎縮的參政空間。對自民黨而言，此一「非神聖同盟」的作用不僅是奪回政權，更在於換得社會黨在許多重大議題上的讓步。[34]

柒、結論

　　本論文具有兩項理論意涵。其一，檢討新制度論這個新興的研究取向，並指出制度選擇是其不能忽略的課題。其二，將制度研究和「政黨重組」（party realignment）這個重要議題在理論上連結起來。本文認為，我們若要從制度論的角度處理制度選擇的問題，就必須考慮議題結構的演化及行動者角色的改變。然而，這兩者如何影響政黨重組的路徑，卻又受到制度性條件的制約。換言之，同樣的議題結構及偏好分布可能因制度的不同而產生迥異的政治後果，而同一個制度也可能因為議題的差別而產生完全相反的效果。當議題結構包含了制度改革的面向時，甚至可能導致制度的變遷。

　　以選舉制度為例，當同一制度因為使用過久而產生疲乏，甚至導致危機時，制度改革就可能成為整個改革論述的一環。若此連結亦為選民所認知，則政治精英就有動機推動制度選擇，而制度性條件亦將對政治勢力重組的軌跡發生影響。我們的分析也發現，權力集團的分化對於改革是十分重要的。以選舉制度來看，比例代表制比小選舉區制更容易造成利益的多元化，進而促成制度變遷。日本的「中選舉區制」屬於準比例代表

---

[34] 例如，村山自出任首相後，在日本的防衛、海外派兵、靖國神社參拜等問題上採取了迥異於社會黨一貫立場的態度（平野貞夫，1994：88）。

制，因此只要選民認知到此制和金權政治的關聯，就有部分的政治精英願意以選舉制度的改革爲訴求，組成新的政治勢力。因爲日本的改革精英大多從保守派分裂出來，更導致政黨重組過程的複雜。最後，選舉制度的改革將配合著政權重組而完成。

新選舉制度的實施，也重新界定了日本政治的賽權及遊戲規則。依照一般的看法，偏向小選舉區的新制度將有幾個效果：加速政權交替、使政黨取代候選人成爲選戰主角、及使政策辯論成爲選戰主軸（石川眞澄，1993）。在 1996 年 10 月 20 日首次採用新制度的眾議院選舉中，自民黨果然獲得大勝，社民黨（原社會黨）及魁黨等小黨則遭受毀滅性的慘敗。政黨和政策辯論在選戰中的角色的確有所提升，但離預期仍有相當的距離。多黨林立的結果，使政策辯論的焦點模糊，政治責任的歸屬不明，許多選民還是必須根據人的因素投票。不過，從長遠來看，政黨的合併只是時間的問題。屆時就有可能出現以政策爲本位的政治競爭。

在這樣的情勢下，新選舉制度的穩定性如何？根據選後民意調查，全日本有 43.6% 的民眾認爲應該採行修正後的現行制度，32.3% 的人主張恢復中選區制，只有 8.9% 的受訪者認爲應當維持現制（読売新聞社，1996：148）。[35] 選舉制度改革的民意基礎是存在的。然而，從本論文的觀點來看，改革的空間卻不大。現有選舉制度基本上有利大黨，小黨即使能因爲比例區的存在而進入國會，也不易掌控議程。選舉制度如果眞的要改，倒是有可能進一步減少比例區的席次。屆時，制度改革將更爲困難。正如美國及英國經驗所顯示的，儘管不斷有呼聲主張超越兩黨政治的架構，選舉制度改革卻一直不能進入主要的政治議程。唯一的出路，就是透過公民投票這種國會外的機制來改變小選區制。[36]

日本選舉制度改革的完成，也使台灣的立法院成爲全世界唯一由中選區制所產生的國會。同樣的制度改革是否可能在台灣出現？這當然牽涉到一些技術性的問題，例如變更選舉制度是否涉及修憲、立法院是否爲決策機關、議程掌控權的歸屬等。[37] 但從大局來看，制度改革需要主要政黨的協商，而世紀末的台灣正面臨多黨權力重組，則是不爭的事實。我們也有充分的理由相信，各黨派對於現行制度的評價不一，且各抱不同的改革主張。因此，現行中選舉區制的存廢，取決於該議題是否會被排入權力重組的議程中。若然，選舉制度最有可能在兩種情況下成爲利益交換的籌碼：政黨結盟（如成立聯

---

[35] 日本選民對小選區比例代表並立制的主要批判是其公平性。由於此制明顯有利大黨，使「死票」（即落選者得票）劇增。再者，小選區的候選人亦可出現在比例區的名單上，造成許多落選者的敗部復活。此次選舉的投票率只有 59%，爲戰後最低，反映許多選民對新制度的不滿。

[36] 如紐西蘭在 1993 年即透過公民投票將小選區制改爲比例代表制（Vowles, 1995）。

[37] 根據 Tsebelis（1995）的理論，決策的程序越複雜，越多機關擁有否決權，就越難改變現狀。

合政府）及其他制度的改革（例如修憲）。從日本經驗來看，利益交換的結果將使現行制度的比例性降低。不過，台灣的新制度究竟是小選區制和比例代表制的混合，還是降低選區規模的中選區制，仍取決於政黨間的協商和談判，以及各政黨的實力分布。

第二章

半總統制下的三角政治均衡[*]

壹、半總統制的定義

政治學界及憲法學界在論及中央政府體制的類型時，向來是以「內閣制」與「總統制」為兩大主軸。依據通說，內閣制的特徵在於行政權與立法權的合一，最高行政權掌握在總理的手中。在總統制下，行政立法權分立，最高行政權屬於總統（Sartori, 1997: 83-120; Lijphart, 1984: 46-66）。因此，一般人常以最高行政權是歸於總統或總理來判別其政體類型。然而，觀諸舉世各國，我們卻可發現許多國家元首（head of state）與政府元首（head of government）並非同一人。例如，德國、義大利、希臘等國就同時存在著作為國家元首的總統和政府元首的總理。在君主立憲的內閣制國家，國家元首也是君王而非總理。換言之，許多國家最高行政權的歸屬是雙元的，而不易歸為總統制或內閣制。

論者或許以為，上述國家的總統或君王僅是不具實權的虛位元首，不應成為我們判斷政體類型時的干擾因素。這種說法是有待斟酌的。在許多國家中（詳後），向國會負責的總理和擁有實權的民選總統共同分享政權。由於這些政體的普遍性及特殊性，我們不能僅將其視為總統制或內閣制的次類型或是兩者的混合。然而，這些政體本身是否構成一個獨自的類型？這個問題一直到了法國政治學者杜弗傑（Maurice Duverger）的手上才有初步的解答。杜弗傑很早即注意到《法國第五共和憲法》的特殊性，認為其同時具有總統制和內閣制的元素。1970 年，杜弗傑正式使用「半總統制政體」（semi-presidentialist regime）這個名稱來稱呼法國的憲政體制，並在其後（1974）將同樣的概念運用在其他幾個國家上。[1] 在 1978 年出版的《制衡君王》（*Echec au Roi*）一書中，杜弗傑將半總統制的概念體系化；1980 年的一篇論文更使這個概念受到學界和政界的矚目。他認為構成半總統制的形式要件有三：1. 普選產生的總統；2. 總統擁有相當的權力；3. 內閣掌握行政權並向國會負責（Duverger, 1980: 161）。

---

[*] 本文曾刊登於林繼文（編），《政治制度》（2000 年 7 月），頁 135-175，台北：中央研究院中山人文社會科學研究所。感謝中央研究院人文社會科學研究中心同意轉載。

[1] 關於杜弗傑對半總統制概念的提出與修正，請見 Bahro、Bayerlein 與 Veser（1998）及 Veser（1999）。

　　換言之，只要任何政體具有內閣制的要素，再加上民選實權總統的存在，即可適用杜弗傑「半總統制」的定義。[2] 儘管學界對於半總統制的名稱或界定仍然意見分歧，杜弗傑的定義仍可被視爲公分母。[3] 許多學者對於半總統制概念的討論，其實是在杜弗傑定義之上的細部修正（例如 Sartori, 1997: 131-135; Shugart and Carey, 1992）。就杜弗傑的定義來看，當今（2000 年）的半總統制國家至少有 30 個，其中大部分爲新興民主國家（Bahro, 1999）。[4] 半總統制的特徵並不能被總統制或內閣制的定義所涵蓋，也非總統制與內閣制之外的殘餘類別（residual category），因而構成其獨自的類型面向。

　　然而，杜弗傑的定義蘊含了兩個根本問題。第一，所謂「總統的實權」定義過於廣泛。這可能僅指被動的國會解散權或須得國會認可的總理任命權（例如愛爾蘭）。然而，總統的實權也可強到能主動解散國會，及自由任命總理（例如芬蘭）。這種差異性是否已經大到了使半總統制的概念過於空泛？若然，則半總統制作爲一種分析概念是不夠精確的。其次，杜弗傑自己也發現，半總統制憲法賦予總統的權力和總統實際擁有權力的大小並無明顯相關性。他在最後也只能將此差距歸因於傳統或環境等外生變數，或國會政黨組成等與半總統制無直接關聯的因素（Duverger, 1980）。若然，則半總統制作爲一種憲政體制的類型是無法獨自解釋政治運作的。

　　本論文的主旨，即在於重新審視半總統制的制度特性，及其對現實政治運作的影響。論文的結構如下。次節檢閱相關的文獻，歸納出其共同的問題。第參節闡述本文的主要觀點：杜弗傑對半總統制的定義仍是合理的，但須將總統的權力及國會對總理的支持度當作兩個主要變數，才會對現實運作有較好的解釋力。本節也運用賽局理論，將前述觀點操作化，模擬總統、總理、國會互動的三角均衡。第肆節探討代表性的半總統制個案，以印證前節的模型。第伍節總整理，重新釐清半總統制的類型及後果。結論部分則探討台灣在半總統制政體中的定位，及可能的憲政運作後果。

---

[2]　必須強調的是，總理向國會負責此一內閣制的特徵是半總統制的要素之一。由此產生的半總統制和內閣制仍是兩種不同的政體類型。

[3]　關於半總統制的各種定義和名稱，可參考吳東野（1996b：38，註 6）。

[4]　從這個定義，半總統制不包括總理不向國會負責的國家，例如南韓。根據 1987 年的南韓憲法第六十三條，國會僅能向大統領建議解除國務總理之職務，而無倒閣權。

貳、如何解釋半總統制的政治後果？

　　學界對於半總統制的界定方式雖不盡相同，卻並未超出杜弗傑的三項要件。[5]對半總統制的爭議，是環繞在其合理性及政治後果。同樣的定義為何會引起不同的評價？觀諸代表性的著作，我們可以發現兩種主要的論述形態。

　　第一種處理方式，是給予半總統制全稱式的讚許或否定。對半總統制的肯定意見可以美國政治學者薩托里（Sartori, 1997: 96）為代表：他認為半總統制較能應付分裂多數（split majority）的問題；拉丁美洲國家如果要放棄總統制，應以半總統制為替代制度。此外，杜弗傑本人也有類似的看法（1980）。他們的理由在於，半總統制使政權不至於（如內閣制般）為同一個多數黨所掌握，又可避免總統制下的僵局。對半總統制持負面看法者，則認為此制在總統和國會間權責不一致，而總統和總理間又有行政權劃分不清的問題。造成的後果就是缺乏對總統的制衡，以及總理角色的不明確（因同時向總統及國會負責）（Linz, 1990, 1994）。[6]同樣的兩極評價，也出現在台灣 1997 年的憲改辯論上。[7]贊成者的理由大致有二：半總統制可以同時滿足國家統合與民主化的目標，以及避免憲政僵局。[8]反對者的理由正好與此相對：半總統制將導致行政權的分裂，以及總統的專權。[9]也有學者指出，在半總統制下總統、國會及總理將因政治生態的變化而產生複雜的關係，造成政局不安（許志雄，1997：33）。

---

[5]　學界對於半總統制的爭議不在於定義本身，而在於哪些國家符合這些定義。杜弗傑即認為奧地利、冰島、愛爾蘭等國不算半總統制國家（Duverger, 1980: 167），因其總統沒有實權。但其所謂的實權，又不單指憲法所規定者。為避免混淆制度規範和制度後果，本文依據憲法條文的規定來判定半總統制國家，及總統的權力。至於總統的實際權力，則是本文的依變項。

[6]　林茲與史戴潘（Linz and Stepan, 1996: 279）亦曾指出「雙重首長制」所造成的僵局對於民主轉型不利。但他們並未對「雙重首長制」的種類做區分。

[7]　台灣的政界及與論界多使用「雙首長制」此一名稱。儘管雙首長制和半總統制的定義不盡相同（吳東野，1996b：39），本文不做此區分，而直接以「半總統制」指稱一般所謂的「雙首長制」。

[8]　代表性的贊成意見如下：化解憲政僵局（蔡政文，中國時報 12/20；蕭萬長，中國時報 4/27；蕭萬長，中國時報 12/17）；穩定聯合內閣，並在此情形下促進政黨紀律（蔡政文，中國時報 12/30）；總統有實權才符合民眾期待（田弘茂，中國時報 12/20）；節制立法院，防止立法懈怠（指解散國會權）（蕭萬長，中國時報 12/17）；總統受「直接民意」監督（蔡政文，自立早報 12/26）；兼顧國家整合與民主鞏固（5/30 民進黨萬言書）；國家主權象徵，又不直接介入行政，保持超然，可應付外患（李文忠，自立早報 5/21）；避免總統為虛位元首，解決國會亂象（許信良，自立早報 5/19）；充實民選總統職權，滿足社會期待（許信良，中國時報 5/2）；解決行政立法僵局（許信良，中國時報 5/2）。

[9]　主要反對意見為：原本即為雙首長制（陳儀深，5/21）；閹割國會、無制衡、超級總統制（民

　　如果憲政制度真的是影響政治後果的關鍵因素，同樣的半總統制就不至於引起如此歧異的評價。其實，就實際的運作後果而言，成功的半總統制政體（例如法國第五共和、芬蘭等國）與失敗的案例（如德國威瑪共和）差距也的確明顯。這使我們懷疑半總統制是否是一個有效的分析概念。對於半總統制的第二種論述方式，就是區分各種次類型，以解釋半總統制政體的不同政治後果。杜弗傑本人就曾以總統權力的大小來區別半總統制國家的不同，許多學者也有類似的做法（Veser, 1999）。但正如前所述，把總統權力大小視為變數並不能充分解釋政體運作的後果。所幸，我們不必因此即懷疑制度分析的效力，因為實權總統只是半總統制的構成要件之一。總理及國會的角色也是我們必須檢視的對象。政治學者舒格特及凱瑞（Shugart and Carey, 1992: 18-27）即曾根據總統與總理的權力對比，提出「總統總理制政體」（president-parliamentary regime）與「總理總統制政體」（premier-presidential regime）兩個半總統制的次類型，而廣為研究者所應用。[10] 在「總統總理制」下，總理及內閣閣員的任命與解職皆可由總統控制，總理因而同時對總統及國會負責。此外，總統並可解散國會，甚至享有立法權。相形之下，「總理總統制」下的總統則不能自由地任命閣員及解除其職務，總理僅向國會負責。

　　舒格特及凱瑞的分類比杜弗傑的定義更細緻。然而，他們的分類法是否具有較強的解釋力，仍有待檢驗。舉例而言，在冰島及奧地利，總統都可自由任命總理，也可解散國會，因此屬於總統總理制。但兩國實際上的運作卻非常接近內閣制。論者或可主張，即使總統具備強大的權力，其實際的運用並不一定能違背國會的意志。若然，其成因已不在於制度，而與總統總理制的定義無干。再以法國第五共和來看，同樣一套憲政體制也可能因為總統與總理所屬黨派的異同而有不同的結果。我們因而不能單從制度上的「總統總理制」來預測其政治後果。此外，兩位作者也指出，總統和總理間的權力劃分不清和總統權力過大可能都會導致不穩定（Shugart and Carey, 1992: 68）。但作者又認為，總統和總理權力劃分不清也可能在總理總統制發生。總理總統制和總統總理制因而可以產生相似的結果（Shugart and Carey, 1992: 24）。

　　以上的分析顯示，僅從總統與總理的關係還是不足以解釋半總統制政體的差異性。前述論著的共通性，是以總統權力的大小來預測政治後果。這種理解方式的不足使我們

　　進黨總統制派）；產生權責不符的總統（新黨）；行政權分裂、總統有權無責弱化國會、台灣社會無同時具備實施總統制與內閣制的社經文條件（民間監督憲改聯盟）；產生權責不符的總統（台大關心憲改聯盟／學術界反雙首長制連署；民間制憲聯盟）。

[10] 表面上，杜弗傑對半總統制的定義和舒格特及凱瑞的「總理總統制」相同。但其「總統總理制」的定義卻仍被杜弗傑定義所涵蓋。薩托里（Sartori, 1997: 132）即曾質疑舒格特及凱瑞的定義，並主張「總統總理制」與「總理總統制」皆為半總統制的次類型。

懷疑，總統的權力除了有大小不同外，是否也有性質的差異，或是使用時機的限制？由於半總統制下同時存在「總理／國會」、「總統／總理」及「總統／國會」三組關係，而總理與國會間的信任關係又構成此一制度的要件之一，我們不得不關切的問題是：總理與國會間的關係，會不會影響總統對國會及總理所施行的權力？國會的行為，是否也受到總統與總理關係的影響？簡言之，在半總統制的三角關係下，任一方的行動如何受到其他兩方互動的影響？

　　為了辨明權力使用的整體關連性，我們可以將總統權力分為主動權力（proactive power）及被動權力（reactive power）兩類。[11] 如果總統所行使的權力不以國會及總理互動的結果為依歸，這些權力就是主動的。反之，若總統權力的行使必須取決於國會與總理的互動結果，則權力再大也是被動的。有些權力的主動性不能僅以名稱取決，而須就憲法所規定的使用限制來判定。我們可以進一步將總統權力區分為政治性與政策性兩類。政治性的權力涉及總理的去留及國會的存續，一旦使用將造成權力重組。政策性權力則涉及總統對於政策形成的參與乃至於主導，但與權力結構的重組無關。根據權力的主動性與政治性，我們可歸納出四種半總統制下的總統權力類型（表 2.1）。

表 2.1　半總統制下的總統權力類型

總統權力	政治性	政策性
主動權力	自由任免總理；自由撤換總理；自由任免閣員；主動解散國會	主持內閣會議；緊急命令權；律令（行政命令）權
被動權力	任命國會同意之總理人選；接受總理之辭職；任命總理提名之新閣員；被動解散國會	否決國會通過之法案；將國會通過之法案交付公民複決

　　總統的目的若在主導決策，最有力的工具就是主動性的政治權力。然因政治性權力的行使涉及內閣乃至於國會的人事重組，所涉及的風險也最大：新總理或新國會可能更能配合總統，也可能正好相反。這種風險也受到總統民意支持度的影響：總統的支持度越高，就越能在政權重組中占上風，使新總理或新國會更接近其立場。相形之下，政策性權力雖然沒有這種風險，卻因必須和總理協調而降低了效力。如果總統只具有被動權力，則國會和總理的關係將決定總統運用權力的時機和方式。至於總統會使用何種權

---

[11]　一般在論及主動權力與被動權力時，多著重在總統的政策權（Mainwaring and Shugart, 1997）。本文則進一步將總統的政策權也考慮在內。

力，除了受限於制度規範外，也取決於總統對情勢的判斷。所謂的情勢，除了總統的民意支持度之外，也包括總統、總理及國會間的立場差距。總統、總理、國會三方基於制度與非制度性因素的考量所形成的互動模式，就是一種「三角政治均衡」。

我們可以將上列因素操作化，依據以下幾個變數及其關係來預測半總統制之下的政治均衡：1.總統權力的主動性，2.總統權力的大小，3.總統的民意支持度，4.總統、總理及國會的政策位置（policy position）。次節先透過賽局模型推演出幾個命題，第伍節再藉由個案研究來印證這些命題。

參、半總統下三角政治均衡之賽局模型

在分析上，我們可以把半總統制政體想像成一組三角關係：總理和國會間存在著屬於內閣制的信任關係，總統和總理間具有分享行政權的關係，總統和國會間的關係則取決於總理與國會的關係、總統權力的大小及總統與國會的立場差距。假定總統、國會及總理的目標都在於實現其政策立場。令 $L = \{1, 2, 3, ..., n\}$ 為國會，而 $L_m \subseteq L$ 為國會中的多數黨。L_m 可以是單一政黨，也可以是多黨聯盟。稱 $\beta_m \in \mathfrak{R}^k$ 為 L_m 在一 k 維議題空間中之理想點（idea point）。國會中的多數聯盟（majority coalition）可能不只一個。若然，則 β_m 可以為任何一個多數聯盟的理想點，我們的分析適用於任何一個多數聯盟。[12] 設總理所提之法案為 $\beta_g \in \mathfrak{R}^k$，則 $c = \|\beta_g - \beta_m\|$ 表示國會多數派與總理的政策距離。總統的政策立場則以 β_p 表示。$a = \|\beta_m - \beta_p\|$ 顯示總統與國會的立場差距，$b = \|\beta_g - \beta_p\|$ 則為總統與總理的差距。我們假設總統不可能提名一個他自己和國會都不喜歡的總理，因此 $a = \max\{a, b, c\}$。$c = 0$ 表示國會多數派與總理的立場完全一致，$b = 0$ 則顯示總統與總理的立場相同。

我們所要探討的，是半總統制的遊戲規則如何影響三者最佳行動策略的選擇，以及策略互動如何構成整體的政治均衡。除了三者的政策立場及國會對總理的信任度之外，影響賽局均衡的還有以下變數：

p：總統所擁有的主動權之大小，$0 < p < 1$。

---

[12] 多黨聯盟，乃至於單一政黨內部的立場都不必然一致。所謂的理想點，可以理解為多數聯盟經過協議後所達成的立場。更簡單的方法，是將此點視為多數派的中位方案（median voter）。如果這個協議可被推翻，就表示多個多數聯盟並存。由於我們的模型適用於任一多數聯盟，所導出的均衡解也可能是多重的。

s：總統和國會衝突時獲勝的機率，$0 < s < 1$。在本文中我們將其簡稱為總統的民意支持度。

δ：議題對總統之緊迫性，$0 \leq \delta \leq 1$。δ越小，總統延後解決問題時所蒙受的損失（利益折扣）越大。$\delta = 1$表示時間因素對於總統的利得全無影響。

上述變數所形成的各種均衡，即是半總統制的不同樣貌。以下所建構的，是一個根據半總統制規則所運作的有序賽局（sequential game）。共有九種可能的均衡路徑。分述如下（請參考圖 2.1）：

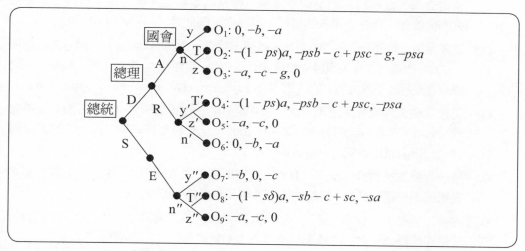

圖2.1　半總統制賽局之展開式

O_1：總統行使主動權介入決策（D），總理接受總統的立場（A），國會則接受總理的做法（y）。由於總統完全實現其立場，總理及國會則犧牲其部分立場，（總統、總理、國會）三者的獲利向量（payoff vector）可寫為 $(0, -b, -a)$。

O_2：總統行使主動權介入決策（D），總理接受總統的立場（A），但國會則反對總理的讓步（n），總統因而再次被動介入（T）。由於涉及總理與國會、總統與國會間的衝突，此一結果的利得分配受到許多因素的影響。對總統而言，制度性的權力越大，就越能取得優勢。然而，影響成敗的還有總統的民意基礎。如果總統徒有龐大的權力，卻全無民意支持，和國會抗爭（例如主動解散國會）將反而強化國會的力量。同理，支持度高的總統若無制度性權力的

配合，也無法施展其意志。因此，可將總統的利得寫爲 $-(1-ps)a$。由於國會和總統進行零和的政策競爭，其利得爲 $-psa$。這表示，只要總統制度性權力極小或是民意支持度極低（$p \to 0$ 或 $s \to 0$），獲勝的將是國會。至於總理，不論是總統或國會贏得抗爭，都必然犧牲某種程度的立場，並可能因爲失去國會信任而下台，付出 $-g$ 的代價。O_2 的利得向量因而是（$-(1-ps)a, -psb - c + psc - g, -psa$）。

O_3：總統行使主動權介入決策（D），總理接受總統的立場（A），國會斥拒總理的做法（n），但總統放棄再介入（Z）。由於遭到國會的抵制，總統又不再事後介入，此一局面的贏家是國會，輸家則是總統。總理除了要付出立場損失的代價外，還失去國會的信任。利得向量因此是（$-a, -c - g, 0$）。

O_4：總統行使主動權介入決策（D），總理不接受並訴諸國會（R），國會支持總理（y'），總統再次介入與國會相抗（T）。此一局面和 O_2 大致相同，但總理則因獲國會支持而不用付出 g 的代價，利得分配爲（$-(1-ps)a, -psb - c + psc, -psa$）。

O_5：總統行使主動權介入決策（D），總理不接受並訴諸國會（R），國會支持總理（y'），總統放棄再介入（Z'）。由於總統不再堅持立場，此局的贏家是國會，利得向量因而爲（$-a, -c, 0$）。

O_6：總統行使主動權介入決策（D），總理不接受並訴諸國會（R），但國會卻站在總統那一邊（n'）。結局爲總統大勝，利得爲（$0, -b, -a$）。

O_7：總統不主動介入決策（S），總理向國會提出其立場尋求支持（E），國會接受總理的提議（y"）。結果爲總理立場的實現，三者的報酬爲（$-b, 0, -c$）。

O_8：總統不主動介入決策（S），總理向國會提出其立場尋求支持（E），國會拒絕總理的提議（n"），總統被動介入決策（T"）。其結果又成總統與國會之爭，但總統因屬被動介入，其利得不再受制於 p，卻受到時間因素 δ 的影響。同理，國會與總理的利得取決於總統與國會的實力對比。最後結果可寫爲（$-(1-s\delta)a, -sb - c + sc, -sa$）。

O_9：總統不主動介入決策（S），總理向國會提出其立場尋求支持（E），國會拒絕總理的提議（n"），總統卻選擇不介入（Z"）。結果是國會的勝利，利得分配爲（$-a, -c, 0$）。

以上所刻劃的是一個有序（sequential）而訊息完備（perfect information）的三人賽局，在每一個訊息集（information set）中都只有一個決策結（decision node），每個路徑（path）也只能到達單一的訊息集，每個決策結亦是訊息分割（information partition）

和子賽局（subgame）的起點。爲便於分析，我們把經由路徑（1, 2, ... x）所到達的決策結記爲 $\Phi_{1, 2, ... x}$。舉例而言，Φ_{DAy} 就是到達 O_1 的路徑。基於賽局的有序特性，我們可以運用反向歸納法（backward induction）排除每個子賽局的劣勢策略（dominated strategy），進而找出整個賽局的子局完備均衡（subgame perfect equllibrium）。

在 $\Phi_{DAn 上}$，因爲 $-(1 - ps)a > -a$，所以總統選擇 T。由於 $-psa > -a$，國會在 Φ_{DA} 上應選擇 n。當總統走到 $\Phi_{DRy'}$ 時，由於 $-(1 - ps) a < -a$，應該選擇 T'。同理，國會在 Φ_{DR} 的選擇應爲 y'（支持總理）。基於這些前提，總統在 Φ_D 時應採取 R。換言之，只要總統主動介入政局，總理就應堅持立場並尋求國會的支持，國會也應支持總理。這也是以 Φ_D 爲起點的子局均衡。

如果總統不主動介入，總理和國會的關係又另當別論。在 $\Phi_{SEn''}$ 上，總統自然會選擇 T''（被動介入），因爲 $-(1 - s\delta) a > -a$。然而，國會是否因此在 Φ_{SE} 上選擇 y''（支持總理），卻是未定之數。關鍵取決於 $-c$ 與 $-sa$ 的大小。在狀況未明時，總統採取不主動介入的策略（S），可能得到的利得爲 O_7 的 $-b$ 或 O_8 的 $-(1 - s\delta)a$。因此，總統是否主動介入決策（D），取決於 $-(1 - ps)a$（在 O_4 的利得）與 b 及 $-(1 - s\delta)a$ 的比較。這些式子之間的關係，也決定了最後的均衡。所謂的均衡，記載了每一行動者在每一訊息集上的策略選擇。在最後的均衡中，我們不再複述子賽局中的優勢策略（dominant strategy），而專注於國會在 Φ_{SE} 的策略，以及總統在一開始的策略。可能的均衡有四，各有不同的構成條件。概述如下（請見圖 2.2）：

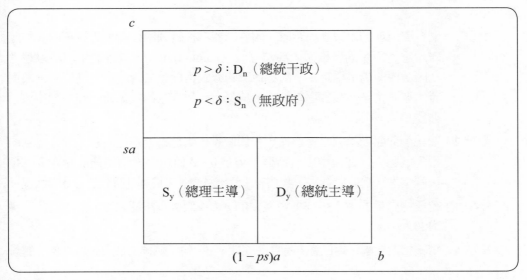

圖2.2　半總統制的賽局均衡與政體類型

結果 1：當 $c > sa$，$p > \delta$，D_n 為子局均衡。這表示總統若不主動介入決策，國會就不支持總理的立場，而總統選擇主動介入決策。

結果 2：當 $c > sa$，$p < \delta$，S_n 為子局均衡。這表示總統若不主動介入決策，國會就不支持總理的立場，但總統仍不主動介入決策。

結果 3：當 $c < sa$，$b > (1 - ps)a$，D_y 為子局均衡。這表示不論總統是否介入決策，國會都支持總理的立場，而總統主動介入決策。

結果 4：當 $c < sa$，$b < (1 - ps)a$，S_y 為子局均衡。這表示不論總統是否介入決策，國會都支持總理的立場，而總統不主動介入決策。

在上述結果中，前提條件所描述的是各半總統制國家的制度特性及政治情勢，均衡描述的則是半總統制運作的結果。然而，要將此一賽局模型運用在實證分析上，最大的障礙在於變數的不易測量。例如，要將總統的主動權量化，並和其他變數相乘或比較，就涉及不同變數是否可以共量（commensurable）的問題。因此，賽局模型提供給我們的是一個啟發式（heuristic）的分析起點，而非計量模型。根據賽局模型，我們預期半總統制的政體類型和各種變數存在某種關係。但我們對變數的估量則是以定性為主，並依此比較變數範疇間的相對次序，而非在絕對標準上的定量化。舉例而言，我們可以明顯地比較出不同政體下總統主動權的大小，但不能判斷其大小的程度。為降低主觀判斷的干擾，我們儘可能採用沒有爭議的標準，例如制度上對於總統權力的規定、內閣穩定度的制度性基礎（政黨體系、選舉制度、總理任命權等）、總體社會經濟指標等。具體言之，上述模型提供了下列四個變項（亦即本文的自變項）來探討半總統政體的可能運作後果：

變項1：國會與總理的政策立場距離。國會越能掌握總理的任命或去職，兩者的距離越短；國會的多數派內部越分歧（incoherent），兩者的平均距離越大（因為內閣越不穩定）。國會內部的分歧程度也受制於選舉制度。一般而言，單一選區比複數選區更能形成具有一致立場的多數派。在模型中，這個變項以 c 來表示。

變項2：總統所面臨的議題之緊迫性。我們假設，議題的緊迫性越強，延後行動的損失就越大。在模型中，這個變項是 δ。δ 值越小表示總統被動介入的損失就越大。為便於行文，我們以「危機社會」來簡稱 δ 值趨近於 0 的狀況。

變項3：總統主動權的大小，亦即模型中的 p。我們可以根據表 2.1 來估量此一權力的大小。

變項4：總統相對於國會的民意支持度（亦即 s）。除了總統的個人聲望之外，總統

選舉制度也是影響此變數的要因。採相對多數決選出的總統一般而言支持
基礎較弱。

這些變項的交互作用決定了半總統制不同類型。根據賽局模型所刻劃的各種均衡，
我們可以想像下列數種半總統制的政體類型（亦即本文的依變項）：

D_n：總統干政型。由於國會對總理的支持度低，總理不能成為決策中心。在此情勢
下，總統冒著和國會對抗的風險，主動介入決策而成為政策的發動者。由於
總統運用主動權的前提是內閣的低效能，我們將此種半總統制稱為總統干政。

S_n：無政府型。內閣同樣不能獲得國會的支持，但總統也不願介入。由於缺乏明確
的政策發動者，決策可能陷於無政府狀態。

D_y：總統主導型。總理獲得國會的支持，總統也積極參與決策。當總統與國會多數
派的政策立場接近時，總統與總理的分歧將更小。此時，總理只是總統的代
理人，國會也以對內閣的支持間接認可總統的主導角色。這種類型發生在總
統與國會多數派同黨時（總理也必為同黨）。但如果總統與國會多數派的政策
立場歧異大時，D_y 就可能意味著兩個行政中心爭奪政策主導權的雙元領導制。

S_y：總理主導型。國會支持總理的政策提案，總統也不主動介入決策，總理因而成
為政策制定的主導者。由於總統只扮演消極而儀式性的角色，這種類型也可稱
為準內閣制。

根據賽局模型，我們可以找出以上各種半總統制政體類型的成因，並將其歸納成以
下幾個命題（請參考圖 2.2）。

**命題 1：當國會對總理的信任度低，而總統所面臨的問題具有緊迫性時，結果為總
統干政。總統社會支持度越低，此種傾向越強。但總統若是主動權過小，
則可能陷入無政府狀態。**

根據結果 1，只要國會與總理的政策立場差距超過一定程度（sa），國會就不會支
持內閣的政策提案。如果情勢又有一定的緊迫性（$p > \delta$），即可誘發總統的主動干政。
這兩項門檻都是相對的。總統的社會支持度越弱（s 變小），國會就越有可能否決內閣
的政策提案，總統則越可能採取先發制人的行動。反推之，高聲望的總統可以阻嚇國會
的倒閣行動。其原因在於，國會一旦倒閣，即須面對改選的民意考驗，而總統聲望將成
為和國會相抗的主要指標。總統的民意支持度因而深刻地影響了和國會的策略。同理，
總統即使面對緊迫的情勢，也須有一定的權力才能主動介入政局。如果一個半總統制國
家處於危急狀態，總理失去國會支持，但總統又沒有權力介入決策，國家就會陷入決策
中心不明確的狀態（結果 2）。

命題2：當國會對總理信任度高時，總統主動權低或支持度低都可以導致總理主導。

當國會對內閣有相當的信任度時（$c < sa$），總統可選擇主動或被動介入決策。其態度則取決於幾個因素。根據模型，如果總統的主動權極小（$p \to 0$）或社會支持度極低（$s \to 0$），即會產生 $b < a \to 1$ 的結果。這表示總統應當選擇不介入決策而形成總理主導。同理，總理與總統的政策立場越接近（$b \to a$），也越容易導致此種後果。這個命題顯示，總統的制度性權力和實權並無必然的關連，總理主導制（或準內閣制）的原因可以是多重的。

總理主導制的國家須有以下特徵：總理任命須獲得國會的支持，且國會有穩定的多數。在這樣的國家中，如果總統不介入決策，總理即可以因為獲得穩定的國會支持而成為主導政局者。總統可能因為下列原因之一而選擇不介入決策。首先，總統若缺乏主動權，則即使有干政的企圖也無此管道。其次，總統若是社會支持度低，也會因為沒有對抗國會的本錢而不介入決策。不過，這兩項選擇的前提都是國會對總理的支持度高。如果總理不能獨得國會的支持，就會產生如命題1的結果。

命題3：當國會對總理信任度高時，總統主動權高及支持度高同時為總統主導的必要條件。

這個命題和命題2是一體兩面。如果許多因素都能個別導致總理主導制，總統主導制的形成就需要其反面條件的同時成立。具體言之，只有在總統有相當的主動權及高支持度時，才有可能滿足 $b > (1 - ps)a$ 的條件（因為 $a > b$）。此外，總統、總理及國會多數派若屬於同一政黨，也比較容易導致總統主導制。原因在於 a、b 都很小，$b > (1 - ps)a$ 的條件較易得到滿足。適用本命題的國家須具備下列條件：國會對內閣的信任度高、總統具有相當的主動權及民意支持度。國會對內閣的信任度受制於兩項因素：總理的任命是否需要獲得國會同意，以及國會的政黨結構。國會若無總理任命案的同意權，或是黨派過於分歧，都可能導致內閣的不穩，甚至誘發總統的干政。

肆、個案研究

上述分析指出，制度可以是影響政治後果的必要條件（necessary condition），卻很少是充分條件（sufficient condition）。換言之，要預測制度對於政體形態的影響，我們必須同時考慮社會分歧結構（social cleavage structure）、民意趨向、短期情勢等非制度因素。由於這些非制度因素經常變動，我們若只依制度特性就對各國的政體類型做分

類，必會產生誤差。但是，這也不意味我們就束手無策。本文所採取的策略，是觀察一個國家最具代表性的非制度特徵。對於可能的質疑，我們的辯解如右。第一，「最具代表性」的特徵並不能涵蓋所有的特徵。但以「眾數」（mode）或平均值來代表一個變數，本來就是社會科學的常用方法。如果一個國家在各階段有不同的代表性特徵，即應將之視爲不同個案。第二，對於什麼是「最具代表性」的特徵，可能見仁見智，沒有一定的看法。這是事實。然而，前述模型的用意，只是在於顯示「當制度條件 X 配合非制度條件 Y 時，結果爲 Z」這樣的邏輯。因此，當實際的非制度條件其實是 W（或有人如是主張）時，論述的邏輯還是一致的，我們也可根據結果來檢證非制度條件究竟爲何。

　　以下，我們根據十個主要的半總統制政體來檢證前節的命題。選擇這十個國家，是因其大多被杜弗傑、薩托里或舒格特及凱瑞等學者分析過。我們可以比較，不同的理論模型，是否會導致對同一個國家的不同預測。

個案一：【威瑪共和】

　　德國的威瑪共和（Weimar Republic, 1919-1933）是最原始的半總統制政體，也是印證**命題 1** 的最佳寫照。第一次世界大戰後的德國，經濟蕭條、社會動盪，又面臨巨大的國際壓力。德國總統所面對的，正是一個日漸惡化的危機社會。就制度而言，威瑪共和憲法以民選總統取代在第一次世界大戰後被罷黜的德皇，和總理共享政權。根據憲法起草人普魯斯（Hugo Preuss）的設計，實權總統不僅有填補德皇位置的象徵性功能，更可避免內閣制所造成的混亂政局。的確，由於社會利益的分歧，再加上採行以全國爲一選區且無任何門檻限制的比例代表制，威瑪共和的政黨體系極端分崩離析，所產生的國會（Reichstag）也極不穩定（蔡宗珍，1999）。根據威瑪憲法，總統可以自由任免總理，不受國會羈絆。這兩項因素相乘，造成總理和國會間的巨大嫌隙。[13] 威瑪憲法賦予總統有相當大的主動權：除了可以自由任免總理外，還可主動解散國會、頒布緊急命令及看守命令（care-take decree）、以及將法律付諸公民投票等。強權總統、無能國會與危機社會相加的後果，正如**命題 1** 所預料：從 1920 到 1930 年代初期，興登堡（Paulvon Hindenburg）總統不斷運用解散權以及緊急命令權，以應付層出不窮的內閣危機（Lepsius, 1978: 49）。隨著 1929 年經濟大恐慌的到來和總統社會支持度的降低，這種傾向更爲明顯：總理的政策不能得到國會的支持，國會則因左右勢力同時上漲而益發分崩離析。然而，正如**命題 1** 所言，總統干政與無政府只是一線之隔。危機的持續惡

---

[13] 用模型的變數來說，這就是因爲 c 過大而使國會採取 n 策略。

化，導致總統聲望的下跌，國會的反對派伺機起而代之。[14] 1933 年 1 月希特勒被任命為總理是這個過程的頂峰，但也宣告了威瑪共和的結束。

個案二：【俄羅斯聯邦】

和威瑪經驗足堪比擬的是當前的俄羅斯聯邦。自從 1989 年蘇聯解體後，俄羅斯經濟就一直處於危機狀態。目前（2000 年）的俄羅斯憲法，在 1993 年 12 月誕生於國會與總統對抗的硝煙戰火中。憲法規定總理向國會（主要是下議院，即 State Duma）負責，國會則由比例代表制與單一選區制分別產生各半的席次（Banks, Day, and Muller, 1997: 700）。和威瑪共和類似的是，社會經濟危機使得左右兩極端力量同時在俄羅斯上揚，處於其間的總理則兩面逢敵。此外，憲法對於總統權力的規定，更加深了國會和內閣的衝突。根據俄羅斯憲法第一百一十一條，當國會第三次拒絕總統所提名的總理人選時，總統即可解散國會。這使總統和國會處於相互威脅的狀態，總理則成為籌碼。即使不解散國會，俄羅斯總統還是有許多工具來宰制國會或主導政策：總統可決定政策方針、主持安全會議（Security Council）、發布律令、將法案付諸公決、否決法案、解除總理職務等（Finer, Bogdanor, and Rudden, 1996: 245-295）。我們的預測是：當國會左、右派的力量越是均衡地成長，俄羅斯總統就越有可能介入決策，並和國會對抗。最佳的證明，就是 1998 年葉爾欽（Boris Yeltsin）總統和國會在總理任命案上的數次抗爭。[15] 這種對抗的輸贏或在總統（如 1998 年 3 月的總理任命案），或在國會（如 1998 年 9 月的總理任命案）。但整個體制都將陷於總統和國會相抗的總統政制。

個案三：【波蘭】

1989 年 6 月波蘭共黨政權垮台後，新憲賦予波蘭總統相當大的權力，如外交國防權、律令權（需總理副署）、否決權等。但總理的任命則須得到國會（Sejm）的同意。波蘭因此成為半總統制國家。然而，波蘭在數年間經歷了數次制度變革，社會情勢也有所變化，其半總統制因而呈現多重樣貌。從共黨垮台至 1990 年 10 月，由於首任總統賈魯塞斯基（Wojciech Jaruzelski）缺乏正當性，決策權及政府組成都掌控在團結工聯（the Solidarity）手中，政體運作接近總理主導制。[16] 當瓦文薩（Lech Walesa）在 1990 年 12

---

[14] 1932 年 3 月的總統選舉為興登堡和希特勒的對決。但興登堡未能在第一輪投票取得半數，而有賴於第二輪投票方得勝選。

[15] 在 1995 年 12 月的國會大選中，左派和右派同時躍進。我們也預期，當總統個人力量變弱（例如健康問題）時，俄羅斯將陷入無政府型的半總統制。

[16] 賈魯塞斯基由國會以勉強過半的多數選出。以模型的語言來說，總統的社會支持度（s）很低，

月當選首屆的民選總統後，情況一變爲總統主導（因爲 s 增高，國會和總統又屬於同一多數，使 a 變小）。然而，這種局面維持不到一年，總統的經濟政策遭到國會抵制，團結工聯也面臨分裂。最嚴重衝突，發生在選舉制度改革上。國會企圖引進比例代表制，引起瓦文薩兩度動用否決權。然而，瓦文薩在這場鬥爭中失敗了。在 10 月的國會選舉中，比例代表制果然發揮了預期的效果：在進入國會的 29 個政黨中，沒有任何一個政黨得票率超過 13%。面對這樣的國會，瓦文薩企圖建立其自己的中間派聯盟，但並未成功（Wiatr, 1996: 106）。爲另尋出路，瓦文薩向國會提出憲法修正案，要求總統可以自由任免閣員，以及否決國會通過的不信任案。但這項企圖又胎死腹中。其結果正如**命題 1** 所預期，在總統干政與無政府狀態間擺動。這樣的危機，一直要等到 1992 年 12 月的憲改才有所轉機（詳後）。

此段期間的波蘭經驗反映了許多半總統制國家的困局：因爲社會分崩離析，所以人民才期待透過半總統制來強化領導。也正因高度的社會分歧使國會無能，總統才有介入的理由。換言之，形成總統干政型半總統制政體的主因是社會條件。當然，制度安排也扮演了一定的角色。如果說國會對總理的低信任度是總統干政的要件，這種低信任度可以被某種制度安排所強化。其中最具決定性的，就是總理及閣員的任命方式。如果總統可以自由任命、撤換總理或閣員，就有可能扶植違反國會多數意志的政府。若然，則即使國會內部分歧不大，還是可以導致總統的獨裁。

波蘭在 1992 年 12 月進行憲改，通過「小憲法」（1ittle constitution），或許就是想以制度改革來解決上述問題。[17] 整體而言，新法案使總統的權力受到相當的限制：總統固然可以提名總理，國會也可以在否決總統提名人選後選出自己的總理。總統的解散權也受到限制，須在國會對總理通過不信任案，卻無法選出新人選時方得施行之。此外，總統不能再主動撤換內閣（Wiatr, 1996: 108）。不幸的是，新憲法並未阻止總統介入政治的動作。1993 年 5 月，波蘭國會通過對於內閣的不信任案，但瓦文薩總統卻拒絕接受總理的辭呈，並將國會解散。在 9 月的選舉中，民主左派聯盟（Democratic Left Alliance, SDL）贏得 20.4% 的選票及 37% 的席次，波蘭農民黨（the Polish Peasant Party, PSL）則獲得 29% 的下院席次。整體而言，這次選舉使右派力量退潮，兩個主要的左翼政黨構成了一個穩定的國會多數，支持波蘭農民黨的波拉克（Waldemar Pawlak）出任總理。這個穩定的左派聯盟加深了總統和國會的嫌隙。舉例而言，1994 年 6 月，瓦文薩總統拒絕簽署國會放寬墮胎限制的法案。10 月，總理拒絕接受總統對

國會對總理的掌控良好（c 很低），結果因而爲總理主導。

[17] 正式名稱應是 1992 年「憲法法案」。

國防部長的撤換命令，國會則以壓倒性多數通過決議，要求總統不得再干政。1995 年 2 月，瓦文薩企圖解散國會，卻因為輿論的強烈反對而作罷。總統與總理的衝突，一直到 1995 年 11 月民主左派聯盟的克瓦斯紐斯基（Aleksander Kwasniewski）當選總統後才暫告一段落。

個案四：【斯里蘭卡】

　　由於宗教和族群的分歧與嚴重衝突，斯里蘭卡是一個典型的危機社會。1977 年，在賈耶瓦登（J. R. Jayewardene，1978 年當選總統）的主導下，斯里蘭卡國會進行修憲，將英國式的議會內閣制改為法國式的半總統制，以促進政治穩定與國家統合（Delury, 1987: 1009），1978 年並在此基礎上通過新憲。[18] 然而，和法國相較，斯里蘭卡總統的權力大得多。總統不但是國家元首，也是行政首長，甚至可以兼任閣員。國會雖可通過不信任案讓總理下台，總統卻可以自由任免閣員，並監督其施政。此外，總統還有兩項強大的權力。首先，總統可以宣布緊急狀態，中止國會運作。其次，總統可以將任何國會通過的法案交付公民複決（Shugart and Carey, 1992: 67）。因此，如果總統支持國會的少數派出任總理，卻遭受多數派的杯葛，總統還是有足夠的武器可用。斯里蘭卡採取一院制，由 169 名議員組成國會，國會議員的選舉制度則在 1978 年由單一選區改為比例代表制。國會原本應在 1983 年改選，但賈耶瓦登總統卻強行發動公民複決，將現任議員任期延長至 1989 年。我們或許可以這樣解釋賈耶瓦登的行動：在高度分歧的社會裡，比例代表制容易產生混亂的國會，總統所任命的總理難以受到國會支持。在面臨社會危機的緊迫情勢下，總統最佳的策略就是完全介入決策。凍結國會選舉只是比較極端的手段。根據**命題 1**，我們預期這種傾向會隨著總統危機感的增加及總統支持度的降低而增加。1988 年 12 月，原總理普瑞瑪達薩（Ranasinghe Premadasa）接替賈耶瓦登出任總統，但在選舉中只獲得 50.43% 的選票。上任後，普瑞瑪達薩立即解散國會，並任命並不具實力的維詰佟（Dingiri Banda Wijetunge）出任總理。不幸的是，總統的強勢領導並未化解斯里蘭卡的危機。1993 年 5 月 1 日，普瑞瑪達薩死於暗殺者的手中。

個案五：【芬蘭】

　　威瑪共和、俄羅斯共和國、波蘭、斯里蘭卡都屬於典型的危機社會。在這些國家中，我們可將總統干政理解為不得不然的結果。如果總統所面對的情勢並非如此緊急，其選擇又是如何？根據**命題 2** 與**命題 3**，當國會對於總理的信任度低時，總統的選擇取

---

[18] 關於斯里蘭卡實施半總統制的經驗，可參考 Zafrullah（1981）。

決於先行利益（即 δ 值）的大小。但這項利益是相對於總統的權力和支持度而言的。如果總統的主動權和社會支持度都很高，些微的先行利益即可引發總統的主動介入。芬蘭就是一個明顯的例子。芬蘭於 1917 年獨立，並在 1919 年以立法的形式訂立共和國憲法。根據憲法，芬蘭總統擁有強大的主動權：總統可主持國務委員會（Valtioneuvosto, Council of State），任命內閣閣員，不受限制地解散國會（Eduskunta），[19] 向議會提出法案，行使否決權（但國會可覆議），並擁有統帥權及外交事務主導權（Arter, 1987: 96-97）。在 1988 年之前，芬蘭總統是由 300 位選舉人所組成的選舉人團間接選出。[20] 1988 年選舉辦法改為兩輪制，如果第一輪有候選人獲得絕對多數選票即告當選總統，否則由選舉人團在第二輪投票選舉產生。但 1991 年修憲又將總統改為公民直選。芬蘭總統的社會支持度高，則和特殊的國際處境有關。在 1989 年之前，由於與蘇聯為鄰，芬蘭必須靈活地在東西方陣營間維持外交關係，總統在國防外交事務上的領導即顯得特別重要（周陽山，1995）。此外，芬蘭的快速工業化，也需要有效的領導（Delury, 1987: 333）。總統的重要性，可以從以下的證據看出：從 1946 至 1981 年，芬蘭只歷經了帕斯基威（J. K. Paasikivi, 1946-1956）與科寇能（Urho K. Kekkonen, 1956-1981）兩任總統，1973 年國會還以超過五分之四的多數通過特別法，讓科寇能總統連任四年，以維持和歐市間的自由貿易協定。1978 年，芬蘭六大主要政黨一致支持科寇能五度連任。科寇能的繼任人科維斯托（Mauno Koivisto）也相當有民意基礎，媒體甚至以「科維斯托現象」相稱（Delury, 1987: 333）。相較於總統穩定而有效的統治，芬蘭國會則顯得混亂而多變。戰後芬蘭的主要政黨數超過五個，是西歐民主國家中較多的，內閣的平均壽命卻只有一年多，則是各國中最短的（Lijphart, 1984: 83; Laver and Schofiled; 1991: 148）。穩定而有實權的總統加上紛亂的國會，使得芬蘭的半總統制也走向總統干政型。最明顯的例子，就是 1970 年代芬蘭國會的組成逐漸右傾，科寇能總統卻一直任命中間偏左的內閣。當然，和威瑪共和、俄羅斯等國相較，芬蘭的內外危機顯得並不嚴重。這也使芬蘭的半總統制看起來較為成功。此外，芬蘭總統的影響力並非完全來自於半總統制的制度。如果外交挑戰不再是主要議題，國會的凝聚力也有所提高，芬蘭就有可能轉化為總理主導制。

個案六：【葡萄牙】

葡萄牙的半總統制發展史和波蘭有兩點類似。首先，該制起源於獨裁政權的瓦解

---

[19] 但 1991 年修憲則規定總統須得總理同意方得解散國會。關於芬蘭總統與總理的關係，請參閱 Nousiainen（1988）。

[20] 芬蘭在 1988 年之前雖然採間接選舉總統，但結果仍難違反民意的偏好。我們若對杜弗傑的定義作較寬廣的解釋，芬蘭仍屬於典型的半總統制國家。

（1976年）。其次，半總統制歷經了制度與非制度因素的變化，而有不同樣貌。1976至1982年間的葡萄牙是典型的總統干政制。其因素包括三點。第一，1976年革命後的葡萄牙處於經濟衰退的危機狀況。第二，葡萄牙的內閣基礎不穩，從1976至1987年共舉行了五次大選，替換了十次內閣。第三，1976至1982年間葡萄牙總統擁有強大實權，如主持革命委員會（但不能主持內閣會議）、任免總理、解散國會、頒布律令等。這些都符合**命題1**的描述。1982年，葡萄牙進行憲改，修改了1976年憲法，廢除革命委員會（Council of the Revolution），並將原有的總統權力分配給不同的機關。修憲之後，總統不能再自由任免閣員；雖可否決法案，但國會可以覆議。總統的解散權行使也受到很大的限制，總統對於總理的任命案必須和國會各政黨諮商，閣員則是由總理提請總統任命。總理在就職後數日即必須向國會提出施政計畫，尋求國會的支持。如果施政計畫被國會否決，或是國會通過不信任案，總理即須下台。理論上，1982年憲政後的葡萄牙較接近**命題2**所描述的總理主導制。但葡萄牙的政黨體制則為總理主導制埋下了陰影。由於缺乏強勢政黨（strong party）（Laver and Shepsle, 1996: 69），葡萄牙的四個主要政黨很難形成有效的統治聯盟。其結果就是沒有內閣的壽命超過兩年（Gillespie, 1990: 242）。在此情況下，總統就會被迫介入，而有轉變為總統干政型政體的可能。[21]

個案七：【愛爾蘭】

愛爾蘭與修憲後的葡萄牙都符合**命題2**的前提。兩國的共同特徵在於，總理任命案需要國會的認可，總統也缺乏主動權。根據1937年通過的愛爾蘭憲法，總統由直選產生，總理則由總統任命。但總理的任命案須得到國會（Dail）的同意，總理也必是由多數黨領袖出任。總統雖可解散國會，卻須以總理提出請求為前提。除此之外，愛爾蘭總統並無其他權力。也因為如此，愛爾蘭的憲政運作和內閣制相當類似。

個案八：【奧地利】

奧地利現行憲法訂於奧匈帝國崩解後不久的1920年。根據憲法，奧地利聯邦總統（Federal President）可以自由任命聯邦總理（Federal Chancellor）（Bahro, 1999: 17），任命總理所提名的內閣閣員，以及依總理的請求解散國會。從憲法條文上來看，奧地利總統有相當的主動權。然而，根據憲政慣例，總統所任命的總理必然是下議院（Nationalrat）內最大黨的領袖。這種憲政慣例的形成和奧地利特殊的政黨結構有關。在1945至1966年間，奧地利國會是由奧地利社會民主黨（SPO）與奧地利人民黨

---

[21] 葡萄牙國會選舉採取比例代表制，增加了國會的不穩定性。1985年，恩內斯（Eanes）總統即曾以解散權為要脅，企圖阻止內閣的不斷改組。

（OVP）所組成的大聯盟（grand coalition）所掌控，兩黨所占國會席次比例高達90%以上。[22] 1966年人民黨在選舉中贏得過半的席次，首度組成一黨政府。在此後的幾次選舉中，則是由社民黨組成一黨政府。從1983年起，基本上又回復到社民黨與人民黨的兩黨大聯合政府（Banks, Day, and Muller, 1997: 52）。由於政黨結構十分穩定，總統能在組閣過程中發揮的影響力相當有限。內閣職位的分配，基本上只是反映政黨在國會中的實力（Muller, Philipp, and Steininger, 1996: 92）。杜弗傑認爲奧地利的半總統制形似內閣制（Duverger, 1980: 167），原因或許在此。然而，從以上的分析可知其成因並非全然是制度性的。同樣的制度，也曾在1933年導致獨裁制，乃至民主的崩潰。

個案九：【冰島】

冰島憲法是於1944年從丹麥獨立時透過公民投票建立的。一般的看法是，冰島總統僅扮演儀式性的角色，且對政府組成沒有影響力（Laver and Schofield, 1991: 64）。然而，就憲法條文來看，冰島總統對於總理的任命並不需要得到國會（Althingi）的同意，只要國會不通過不信任案，總理就無須辭職（憲法第十五條）。此外，總統也有充分的政策權。那麼，冰島在實際運作上爲何接近總理主導制？和奧地利不同的是，冰島國會內的黨派結盟並不穩定。戰後初期，掌握政局的是由獨立黨（the Independence Party）與社民黨（thc Social Democratic Party）組成的中間聯盟。之後的政治重心則往左偏移。1974年由獨立黨與進步黨（the Progressive Party）組閣，1978年變爲進步黨、社民黨與人民聯盟（People's Alliance）連合。1979年社民黨組成少數黨政府，卻在1980年被人民聯盟、進步黨與部分獨立黨議員聯手推翻。面對這種不穩定的局面，總統理應主動干預。根據冰島憲法，總統也不是沒有干政的空間。[23] 然而，實際狀況卻非如此。由此推論，冰島的總理主導制，必然有半總統制以外的因素。一個合理的解釋，是冰島特殊的修憲制度。在主要的民主國家中，只有冰島可以透過國會的簡單多數決來完成修憲（Lijphart, 1984: 189）。冰島總統如果主動介入決策和國會抗衡，國會只要通過修憲案即可削減總統的權力（Shugart and Carey, 1992: 72）。因此，冰島總統只有在國會本身也不能產生明確的多數意志時才有介入的理由和條件。

個案十：【法國第五共和】

根據命題3，當國會對總理的信任度高時，總統必須同時有強大的主動權及高支持

---

[22] 萊帕特認爲這種大聯合是基於對戰前經驗的反省而來的（Lijphart, 1984: 46-66）。

[23] 冰島總統也的確曾經因內閣難產的問題而介入。1983年索羅森（Gunnar Thoroddsen）總理要求解散國會並宣布去職，但三個主要政黨卻一直不能協調出組閣聯盟。最後，在總統（Kristjan Eldjarn）聲稱將任命無黨籍人士出任總理之後，進步黨和獨立黨才組成聯合政府（Banks, Day, and Muller, 1997: 364）。

度，才有可能主導政局。在主要的半總統制國家中，只有法國第五共和適用此一命題。
理論上，法國總統對總理的任命不必得到國會的同意，但在憲政慣例上新上任的總理都
會尋求國會的支持（張壯熙，1996：77）。[24] 此外，法國國會議員選舉由於採取兩輪投
票制（1986 年選舉除外），也鼓勵政黨的合併化和穩定化（Tsebelis, 1990: 187-232）。
這些因素強化了法國內閣的穩定度。在另一方面，法國總統則握有強大的權力。除了
任命總理及閣員外，法國總統還主持部長會議（Council of Ministers）、和總理及兩院
議長磋商後解散國民議會（National Assembly）、行使法律批審權、簽署議會通過之法
律、將法律提交公民複決、任命三分之一的憲法委員會委員、以及保有外交及國防政策
上的專屬領域（reserved domain）（Finer, Bogdanor, and Rudden, 1996: 213-244）。[25]

　　如果法國第五共和走向總統主導制，上列因素都是必要條件，但皆非充分條件。[26]
影響因素還有總統的社會支持度，及總統與國會多數派是否同黨。根據**結果 4**，如果總
統的社會支持度不高，而且總統與國會多數派不屬於同一政黨，結果將是總理主導。[27]
換言之，法國的總統主導制，除了須具備上述制度條件外，還須有支持度高的總統及
或是與總統屬於同一政黨的國會多數。總統支持度的高低隨時變動，總統選舉結果則
是最明確的指標。剛當選的總統可能挾著勝選的氣勢，勇於和國會對抗。反之，任期
中的總統則傾向謹慎行事。1981 年社會黨的密特朗（Francois Mitterrand）甫當選總
統，面對前任季斯卡（Valery Giscard d'Estaing）總統所遺留下來的右派國會，即曾在
1981 年 5 月行使解散權。1986 年 3 月，密特朗仍在第一次總統任內，右派政黨在國
民議會改選中重新掌握多數席次。然而，此次密特朗並未解散國會，而任命共和聯盟
（Rassemblement pour la Republique, R.P.R.）的席哈克（Jaques Chirac）出任總理，形
成法國憲政史上的第一次共治（cohabitation）。1988 年 5 月密特朗擊敗席哈克，成功
連任總統，便在數天後解散國會，重新讓左派變成國會多數。密特朗兩次解散國會的時
機，說明了總統支持度的重要性。如果總統在任期中貿然解散國會，則須負擔相當的風
險。最好的例子，就是 1997 年席哈克總統企圖解散國會以強化其支持基礎，卻造成左
派當家的反效果。其結果也成為最值得考驗的一次共治。[28]

---

[24] 法國總理還擁有兩項武器，增加了倒閣的困難度：信任投票制（confidence vote procedure）與
　　包裹投票（vote bloquee）（Huber, 1996: 3-7）。
[25] 就這些權力來看，法國總統並不像杜弗傑（1980）所說得那般缺乏制度性的實權。
[26] 在杜弗傑（1980）對七個半總統制政體的比較中，法國總統的實權最大。我們發現，的確也沒
　　有任何其他一個國家具備法國的這些條件。
[27] 理由如下：如果總統支持度極低，$s \to 0$ 將使 $(1-ps)a$ 趨近於 a，b 即可能小於 $(1-ps)a$。如果
　　國會與總統不屬於同一政黨，a 將變大，這種情形發生的機率更高。
[28] 傳統上，法國右派的正當性基礎在於國民主權，左派則強調於階級正義。因此，當右派掌握作

　　密特朗任內的兩次共治經驗也說明了總統與國會相對實力的重要性。在第一次共治時（1986 年 3 月至 1988 年 5 月），右派僅占國會 50.55% 的席次，且包括數個政黨。國會的相對弱勢使這次共治在衝突中發展，密特朗曾數次拒絕簽署席哈克政府所通過的法案，國會的立法效能也不彰（張壯熙，1996：79-80）。[29] 整體而言，此次共治仍有雙元領導的色彩。第二次共治（1993 年 3 月至 1995 年 5 月）的情形則有所不同。此時右派掌握了 77.6% 的席次，總理巴拉度（Edouard Balladur）的政治立場也較席哈克溫和。在第二次共治中，總統和總理的互動比前次平穩，政體運作也更接近總理主導制。

伍、總整理

　　由以上的分析可知，沒有單一因素能決定半總統制的運作後果。圖 3.3 將本文所探討的各項因素及其關係加以整理，共得出八項要素。如果我們把總統憲法權力的內涵列入考慮，變數將更為複雜。所幸，這些複雜的關係背後仍然有基本脈絡可尋。舉例而言，決定總統介入決策的主因是國會與總理的關係，總統的勝算則受到其社會支持度的影響。如果國會強力支持內閣，憲法又未賦予總統足夠的主動權，則不論其他變數如何，結果必是總理主導制。

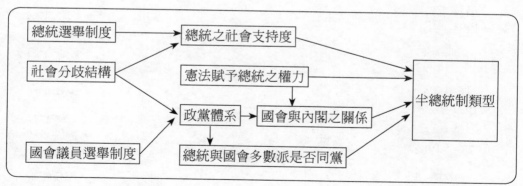

圖2.3　影響半總統制類型之因素

　　為國家主權象徵的總統職位，而左派控制作為社會利益代表的國會多數席次時，兩方就容易產生正當性的衝突。反之，若是左派擔任總統，右派控制國會（如密特朗時代的共治），兩者就較可能妥協。

[29] 即使如此，密特朗大致上還是傾向和席哈克妥協（Sartori, 1997: 125）。

　　根據個案研究，我們歸納出三項關於半總統制政體類型的基本命題。表 2.2 對十個個案的整理，則印證了這些命題。

表 2.2　半總統制類型及其成因

個案	國會對總理的支持度	總統主動權	是否為危機社會	半總統制類型
奧地利（1945 年迄今）	高	大	否	總理主導
冰島（1944 年迄今）	高	大	否	總理主導
法國第五共和共治期間	高	大	否	總理主導
葡萄牙（1982 年迄今）	高	小	否	總理主導
愛爾蘭（1937 年迄今）	高	小	否	總理主導
威瑪共和（1919 至 1933 年）	低	大	是	總統干政
俄羅斯聯邦（1993 年迄今）	低	大	是	總統干政
波蘭（1991 至 1992 年）	低	大	是	總統干政
斯里蘭卡（1977 年迄今）	低	大	是	總統干政
葡萄牙（1976 至 1982 年）	低	大	是	總統干政
芬蘭（1945 年迄今）	低	大	否	總統主導
波蘭（1990 至 1991 年）	高	大	是	總統主導
法國第五共和非共治期間	高	大	否	總統主導
波蘭（1993 至 1995 年）	高	小	是	總統主導

一、總統主動權的大小和半總統制類型沒有明確的關係

　　如個案分析所示，冰島、奧地利及法國第五共和（共治時期）都賦予總統相當大的制度性權力，但其運作結果卻接近內閣制。[30] 修憲（1992 年 12 月）後的波蘭，總統權力受到相當的限制，但並未減低其干政的企圖。杜弗傑將此種落差歸因於歷史文化因素，我們則更明確地指出這些因素如何影響半總統制的運作。如果國會多數黨（聯盟）的凝聚力高，總統也未面臨緊急狀況，總理主導制是可以和實權總統並存的。反之，當總統面臨緊急狀況，而總理又不受國會支持時，就可能迫使其逾越憲政規範，主動干預政局。

二、總統干政型的半總統制政體有類似的成因

　　儘管總統的制度性權力和政體類型沒有絕對的關係，某些特定的類型卻有共通的成因。在我們所檢視的個案中，共有五個總統干政型政體：威瑪共和、俄羅斯聯邦、修憲前的波蘭、斯里蘭卡，及 1976 至 1982 年的葡萄牙。這些個案具有三項共同特徵：危機社會、內閣不穩與實權總統。[31] 這三項特徵也有著關聯性：危機社會的分歧結構通常很複雜，由此而產生的政黨體系亦傾向分裂化。在國會沒有明確多數派時，內閣被推翻的機會也變大。政局不安加上社會危機的深化，使一般人更期待總統的強勢領導，總統本身也因情勢危急而有介入決策的動機。實權總統的干政因而具有其必要性與正當性。

三、危機社會不可能產生總理主導制

　　個案分析也顯示，總統干政式的半總統制只發生在危機社會，而總理主導制只發生在非危機社會。因此，如果總統干政和總理主導代表了半總統制的兩個對立類型，那麼最能解釋兩者差異的不在於總統權力的大小，而在社會條件。[32] 我們也發現，在總理主

---

[30] 有學者認為，奧地利、冰島等國的總統行政權力有限，故基本上為議會內閣制（周陽山，1996：56）。然而，這是就總統的實權而言。事實上，以憲法所規定的權力而言，冰島與奧地利總統的權力並非半總統制政體中最小的。

[31] 蘇聯解體後，許多前蘇聯共和國和東歐國家（如立陶宛、馬其頓、賽爾維亞、卡薩克斯坦、摩達維亞、羅馬尼亞、烏克蘭、亞美尼亞、斯洛維尼亞、克羅埃西亞等國）亦採取半總統制。其在制度設計上都給予總統相當的實權（Bahro, 1999），因此可以以俄羅斯共和國與波蘭為代表。

[32] 本文的總理主導制類似舒格特及凱瑞（Shugart and Carey, 1992）所說的「總理總統制」。但我們的分析顯示，總理總統制的成因並非完全取決於憲法的規定。

導制的政體中，國會對於內閣的支持度都較高，不論其選舉制度是否為比例代表制。其可能的理由在於，非危機社會的分歧度低，政府只要站在中位選民（median voter）的立場，就有可能獲得多數的支持。只要國會支持總理，總統想要介入的困難度就會提高（請見**命題 3**）。

陸、結論

　　杜弗傑在 1980 年提出「半總統制政府」時，曾將其形容為「一種新的政體模型」（a new political system model）。不論就學術上或實務上來看，這都是相當有企圖心的提法：半總統制不但是一種新的分析概念，也為制度選擇提供了一種新的可能性。然而，事實的情況卻不盡如杜弗傑所願。作為分析概念，半總統制的範圍過大，經驗指涉相互矛盾，學界對其概念多有爭議（吳東野，1996a：73-77）。作為實際的政體模型，半總統制被批評為權責不清，製造僵局（Linz and Stepan, 1996: 278-279）。

　　實情果然如此嗎？上述兩種批評，其實是互不相容的。如果半總統制的定義過於含混，我們就不能輕易地將其運作上的問題歸咎於制度本身。如果半總統制有共同的定義，我們就須解釋威瑪共和為何失敗，而法國第五共和如何能成功。本論文的目的就是在解決這個難題。我們發現，杜弗傑發展出半總統制的概念有助於我們理解總統制與內閣制以外的許多政體，但其定義蘊含了多種憲政運作的可能性。我們將杜弗傑所說的「總統的實權」進一步劃分為兩個變數：總統對總理的任免權，及總統在決策上的主動權。總統對總理的任免權影響了國會與總理間的政策距離，乃至於國會對內閣的支持度。當國會不支持總理時，總統主動權的大小決定了總統是否介入。此外，我們也考慮了總統的社會支持度、國會黨派結構、社會危機的程度等因素如何影響總統的選擇。結果發現，某種政體運作可以由不同的因素組合所造成，同樣的制度條件也可能導致不同的政體類型。然而，就實際的案例來看，「總理主導型」與「總統干政型」的半總統制有著明顯不同的構成因素，是否為危機社會則是兩類型的主要差別所在。

　　總統干政型的半總統制和危機社會密切相關，並不是一個偶然的現象。危機社會通常伴隨著社會力的高度分歧化，因此需要類似內閣制的機制來代表各種利益，以避免總統制之下的僵局。然而，由此產生的國會較難支持一個穩定的政府，改革也無法順利開展。在危機無法解決的情況下，期待實權總統的主動介入來提供有效的政治領導，是一個自然的現象。我們甚至可以大膽提出這樣的假說：對民主轉型國家而言，半總統制比純粹的內閣制或總統制更有吸引力；而一旦採用此制後，總統干政是最有可能的後果。

對許多學者而言，總統干政型政體存在著若干病態現象。第一，其前提為國會與內閣的對抗。其次，總統干政若不能獲得有效制衡，即有走向總統獨裁制之虞。所幸，就本文的分析來看，這種困局是有幾種方法來化解的。最直接也最重要的手段，就是強化國會對內閣的支持度。具體方法包括：賦予國會對於總理任命案的同意權，以及改革選舉制度，形成穩定的多數。其中又以選舉制度改革最為關鍵。選舉制度如果能促使國會形成穩定多數，就不必擔憂國會以同意權威脅總統，因為總理必然出自此一多數派。如果再能適度地強化總統的正當性基礎（例如透過總統選舉制度的安排），並賦予其一定的政策介入權，就有可能走向總統主導制。如果總統的作為有重大爭議，社會支持度就會將低，總理主導制將起而代之。

最後，對於 1997 年修憲之後的台灣，本文提供了一個可能發展路徑的參考座標。此次修憲刪除了立法院對於行政院長任命案的同意權（原憲法第五十五條），並賦予總統被動解散立法院的權力，使台灣符合半總統制的定義。[33] 根據本文的邏輯，我們藉由兩個變數來預測半總統制在台灣的可能後果：行政院長與立法院的關係如何？當立法院不支持行政院長時，總統有無介入的空間和理由？

首先，基於幾點理由，我們不預期立法院給予行政院充分的政治支持：1. 未來立法院極可能沒有任何政黨掌握過半的席次，不論總統任命何黨人士（包含無黨籍）出任行政院長，其他黨派都可能以正當性不足而杯葛其施政。換言之，取消立法院之同意權固然可以解決行政院長的任命問題，卻可能在多黨不過半的情形下削弱其正當性。2. 台灣特殊的選舉制度（多席次單記非讓渡投票制，single nontransferable vote under multi-member district）造成立法院派系林立、政黨紀律不彰，政府提案要獲得通過的成本很高。

不過，我們並不預期立法院會以倒閣的方式來對抗行政院：在當前的選舉制度下，候選人個人的競選成本極大，連任失敗率也相當高，而倒閣卻意味著改選。因此，倒閣多數形成不易。如此一來，修憲賦予總統的被動解散權就無用武之地。問題在於，如果立法院以倒閣以外的方式對抗行政院（如杯葛預算案、法案之審查），總統有無介入的空間？就其原始設計來看，《中華民國憲法》其實並未賦予總統實質的行政權。目前之所以認為總統有行政權，是長期實行《動員戡亂時期臨時條款》，而總統又身兼執政黨主席的結果。目前雖然已經廢除臨時條款，臨時條款機構卻藉修憲而合憲化：根據憲法

---

[33]　也有學者認為，修憲前台灣已具有「雙首長制」的憲法架構（薛化元，1997）。然而，1997 年修憲前行政院對立法院的負責關係並非十分明確，即使形式上有雙重行政中心，仍不完全符合半總統制的定義。

增修條文第二條第四項，「總統為決定國家安全有關大政方針，得設國家安全會議及所屬國家安全局，其組織以法律定之。」[34] 論者或許以為此一條文將總統的權力限制在國家安全方面，因此不和行政院長衝突。然而，台灣最可能發生危機的領域，正在國家安全。對於結果，我們可以想像兩種可能性。首先，如果行政院做出重大的大陸政策決定，但卻被立法院所否決，總統即可透過國安會直接做出決策。其次，如果立法院支持行政院的大陸政策，但內容不為總統所喜，總統還是可以獨行其是，但須面對和行政院的衝突。不論情形為何，行政院在國家安全的領域都沒有主導權。如果國家安全成為台灣的主導性議題，憲政運作的基本樣態即取決於立法院的黨派組成：當總統、立院與行政院長同黨時，結果為總統主導；當總統所屬政黨在立院非為多數時，結果為總統干政（如果行政院長偏向總統）或雙元領導（如果行政院長偏向立法院）。對於國家安全以外的議題，結果將是總理主導制（如果立院支持行政院）或無政府狀態（如果立院不支持行政院）。[35] 基於我們對未來立院黨派生態的假定，最有可能的結果就是國家安全事務上的總統干政，以及其他事務上的無政府狀態。這兩種後果都有令人憂懼之處。從本文的觀點來看，最重要的改革手段有二：透過修憲或釋憲，釐清總統和行政院在國家安全事務上的權責劃分；透過選舉制度改革，強化立院形成穩定多數派之能力。[36] 至於這兩項改革有無可能進行，則是將來的研究課題。

---

[34] 關於修憲後行政權分裂的問題，請參考黃昭元（1998：194-200）。
[35] 因為總統在這些事務上沒有主動權。當然，總統可能以執政黨主席的身分而間接指導行政院長的施政。
[36] 湯德宗（1998：18）亦曾主張，半總統制的國家為避免運作上的困擾，應明確劃分總統與總理的職權，並確立總理向國會負責的原則。依本文的觀點，這種改革對總統干政型政體尤其重要。

A Veto Player Theory of Policymaking in Semipresidential Regimes: The Case of Taiwan's Ma Ying-jeou Presidency[*]

Two national elections held in early 2008 reshaped Taiwan's political landscape. In January, the election for the members of the Legislative Yuan (parliament), adopting for the first time a mixed-member majoritarian system, changed the multiparty system into one-party dominance. The Kuomintang (KMT) became a dominant party by winning 81 of the 113 legislative seats, while the then ruling Democratic Progressive Party (DPP) returned with only 27 seats. Two months later, the KMT's presidential nominee Ma Ying-jeou won the presidential election by securing 58.45% of the popular vote. These elections replaced the divided government under former president Chen Shui-bian, a DPP leader, with a unified government. It was believed that a unified government should make President Ma a supreme political leader and the DPP a toothless opposition party.

I. Troubles in the Backyard

What has happened since Ma took office on May 20, 2008, defies both expectations. The DPP, although holding less than a quarter of the legislative seats, has been exerting a much greater influence.[1] More puzzling is the executive-legislative dissonance. Liu Chao-shiuan, the first premier appointed by President Ma, stepped down on September 10, 2009. Liu stayed

---

[*] Reproduced from [Lin, Jih-wen. "A Veto Player Theory of Policy Making in Semi-Presidential Regimes: The Case of Taiwan's Ma Ying-jeou Presidency." *Journal of East Asian Studies* 11(3): 407-435, 2011], with kind permission of Cambridge University Press.

[1] The DPP's influence is manifested more by its capacity to delay the passage of executive bills than to realize its own goal. One possible cause is the KMT's incoherence, a topic I examine in this article. The DPP also benefits from the legislative rule that, in the second reading stage, the Legislative Yuan has to reconsider a bill if more than ten legislators make the request.

in office for 478 days, which was shorter than the average of the DPP premiers. At the local level, lukewarm grassroots support resulted in misfortunes for the KMT in the 2009 county magistrate and city mayoral elections and the legislative by-elections.[2] Some attributed Ma's predicaments to his personal leadership style or the unfavorable environment but cannot fully explain the *variance* in his policy performances. I show in this article that Ma's decisions on some policies are quite consistent and persistent but on others are volatile; sometimes the KMT stands firmly by his side, sometimes the KMT does not seem to exist.

I also explain why a unified government may encounter intraparty dissonance by applying the veto player theory to Taiwan's semipresidential system, in which a popularly elected president can single-handedly appoint a premier who is accountable to the parliament.[3] This constitutional design—known as a president-parliamentary system—makes the premier a representative of the president rather than a leader of the parliament. Accordingly, the agenda setter—the actor presenting "take it or leave it" proposals to the other veto players (Tsebelis, 2002: 2)—is either the legislature or the president. The legislature sets the agenda if it moves in the final stage of policymaking and can revise the proposals presented by the other actors; the president is the agenda setter if he can discipline the legislators in his party and the legislature is not entitled to amend an executive proposal. In the following section, I review related literature and explain why the veto player model offers helpful insights. A model in the third section shows that the legislature, as a collective veto player, has the last-mover's advantage when it is entitled to revise an executive proposal, and that the two executive heads are more likely to be incongruent if a policy has to be deliberated by the legislature. This argument is confirmed by the hypothesis-based case studies presented in the sub-sequent two sections. Finally, I highlight in the conclusion the contribution of this article to the study of semipresidentialism in general.

---

[2]　In the county magistrate and city mayoral elections, the DPP obtained a historically high vote share. In the thirteen by-elections held so far, the KMT claimed victory in only three races, while the DPP took nine seats, in addition to one taken by an independent candidate. For details, see http://www.cec.gov.tw (accessed March 16, 2011).

[3]　For the original definition of semipresidentialism, see Duverger (1980); for a broader definition, see Elgie and Moestrup (2007).

II. Studies of Policymaking in Semipresidential Regimes

A natural starting point to explain President Ma's dilemma is to examine the presidential-legislative relations. Many studies argue that when the president is a key decisionmaker, policymaking is affected by whether the president and the legislative majority belong to the same party.[4] Obviously, this theory cannot adequately explain Taiwan's situation, because President Ma, the leader of a unified government, has been experiencing legislative challenges to his important policies. An alternative explanation is that the governing party in presidentialist countries is less disciplined than its counterparts in the parliamentary system (Linz and Valenzuela, 1994: 35), and Taiwan's case is closer to the former type. Such a view neglects the fact that in Taiwan, it is the premier who is accountable to the parliament and that the constitution gives the president only limited powers. Even if the president is considered a de facto executive head, as in Taiwan, policymaking in a semipresidential regime is more complicated than that in a presidential regime.

The second approach pays attention to the variance of constitutional systems. Robert Elgie (2001a) extends the concept of divided government to different constitutional systems and distinguishes between presidentialism and semipresidentialism. For semipresidentialism, a government is divided if the government fails to command a legislative majority or a party opposed to the president has a legislative majority; in the latter case, the prime minister may not be the president's subordinate (Elgie, 2001a: 10-12). Elgie's definition implies a triangular relationship between the president, the legislature, and the prime minister, an important characteristic of semipresidentialism (Duverger, 1980; Elgie, 1997, 2004; Pasquino, 1997).

Although a triangular perspective is more in line with a semipresidential regime, existing works are often unitary or dyadic; they focus either on the powers of the president (Shugart and Carey, 1992; Frye, 1997; Metcalf, 2000; Roper, 2002; Siaroff, 2003; Beliaev, 2006) or the executive-legislative relationship. Some studies on semipresidentialism do underline its dual-executive feature—namely, the division of the administrative powers between the president and the prime minister (Elgie and Machin, 1991; Baylis, 1996; Wu, 2000b; Kirschke, 2007;

---

[4] The "divided government" approach is based predominantly on US experience. For the most representative works adopting this approach, see Mayhew (1991) and Fiorina (1996a).

Tavits, 2008; Samuels and Shugart, 2010b), but how to consider the executive-legislative relationship concurrently remains problematic. What we need is a theory that accounts for the relationships between the president, the prime minister, and the legislature simultaneously.

Even a triangular analysis can be complicated by the idiosyncratic conditions of a particular regime. For example, studies assuming Taiwan's premier to be a subordinate of the president neglect the fact that the constitution detaches the president from the Executive Yuan (the equivalent of parliamentary government) so that the presidential command of ministers is most likely informal and irregular; the president lacks veto power and relies on the Executive Yuan to interact with the Legislative Yuan. Meanwhile, Taiwan's legislators, although empowered to dismiss the premier, are not allowed to concurrently hold a government post, and none of Taiwan's major parties is led by the legislators. Under-the-table bargaining plays a crucial role in legislation, thereby reducing the influence of parties; the importance to win the personal vote in the legislative elections further weakens party discipline. These features are essential to understanding the real dynamics of Taiwan's constitutional politics and therefore should not be ignored.

In sum, what we need is a theory that satisfies the following conditions. First, the theory should consider the executive-legislative relationship and the dual legislative relationship at the same time. Second, the theory should take into account the preferences of the actors; otherwise we cannot explain why policy outcomes may vary under the same institutional settings.[5] Last, the theory should pay attention to idiosyncratic conditions that affect policymaking. This theory should map the interaction among the major constitutional actors to the set of policy outcomes and treat the idiosyncratic conditions as constraints of actions.

The veto player theory (Tsebelis, 1995, 2002) satisfies these conditions for several reasons. First, this theory can deal with any number of actors and is thus useful for a complicated constitutional system like semipresidentialism. Second, the veto player theory is based on the spatial preference that measures utility by the distance between a policy position and an actor's ideal point. Third, idiosyncratic conditions can be captured by the veto playing

---

[5]   A triangular model taking into account the preference of each actor can shed light on how to categorize the subtypes of semipresidentialism (Shugart and Carey, 1992; Elgie, 1999; Roper, 2002): constitutional arrangement constrains to what extent the actors can realize their goals, while policy preference determines what their goals are.

structure of a regime, such as the number and policy preference of the veto players and the sequence of their actions. Still, the veto player theory has to be modified to be applicable to Taiwan. This is the focus of the next section.

III.　A Veto Player Model of Taiwan's Policymaking

A veto player is an actor whose agreement is needed to change the status quo. Some non-veto players (such as individual legislators) can form a collective veto player (e. g., a legislature). The propositions of the veto player theory are straightforward: the status quo is changeable only if the veto players reach a consensus, so the capacity of a political system to produce policy change increases only if the number of veto players decreases, the ideological distance among veto players shortens, and the collective veto players become less cohesive (Tsebelis, 2002: 19-63).

Applying the veto player theory to semipresidentialism not only expands the scope of this theory but also generates new theoretical insights.[6] According to the veto player theory, the agenda setter is the government in the parliamentary system and the legislature in the presidential system. What I show here is that for semipresidentialism, the agenda setter varies by the subtype and nature of a policy. For a president-parliamentary system in which the prime minister represents the president rather than the parliament, the agenda setter is the parliament if it can revise a bill. But the president sets the agenda if he controls the governing party and the legislators are not entitled to change a government policy.

These advantages aside, the veto player theory does not discuss whether the policies replacing the status quo are by themselves replaceable. To know if a new policy is "in equilibrium," we need to embed the concept of veto player in the noncooperative game

---

[6] When first introduced (Tsebelis, 1995), the constitutional systems covered by the veto player theory did not include semipresidentialism. Indeed, the veto player theory has been applied most widely to study parliamentary democracy (Tsebelis, 1994, 1999; Thayer, 1996; O'Malley, 2006), presidentialism (Tsebelis and Aleman, 2006; Croissant, 2003), or both (Andrews and Montinola, 2004). Only when the veto player theory is applied to a large cross-country dataset are some semipresidential countries included (for example, see Cunningham, 2006). For the veto player approach of semipresidentialism, see Elgie (2004: 326-328).

theory. What we are looking for is Nash equilibrium—policy outcomes that will not be changed further. To see the properties of a veto playing game, consider a set of veto players who move sequentially in a multidimensional space to make a decision. In this space, every policy proposal can be represented by a point, and the shorter the distance between a policy proposal and one's most preferred outcome the higher the payoff. A veto player in a semipresidential system can be any player who can stop a policy from being realized. For example, if an important policy is unrealizable without the president proposing it, the government implementing it, and the legislature approving it, the three actors are all veto players.

For important policies, it is reasonable to assume the players to have perfect information over the actions taken by the previous players. The policy initiator, if seeking to change the status quo, moves first to select a point in the issue space as his or her policy proposal. The remaining players can be divided into two subsets. The first subset contains players who are only allowed to accept or reject the proposal proposed by the preceding player. The second subset comprises players who can accept, reject, or revise a proposal. The following equilibrium indicates the most general result of this game (see Appendix for a formal illustration).

The Veto Player Equilibrium: In equilibrium, a policy replacing the status quo should make all veto players better off; the player who has the greatest capacity to maximize his or her utility is the one who can revise the proposals and moves *last*.

The first part of this claim is easy to understand: any veto player can reject a proposal that makes him or her worse off. The intuition of the second part of this proposition is the last-mover advantage: a player who can revise the proposals can always choose from the adoptable alternatives the one that maximizes that player's utility. It follows that if several players have this capacity, the last mover has the greatest advantage by being able to revise the proposal made by the others and no one can change that decision.

This proposition can be used to study any constitutional system and is particularly useful for a complicated system like semipresidentialism. Suppose policymaking in this system starts from the executive (the president or the premier, who may or may not be from the same party) making a proposal to the legislature, which may or may not revise the proposal. Two corollaries follow the equilibrium:

Corollary 1: A policy replacing the status quo will be closer to the ideal point of the legislative body when the legislators can revise a policy proposal than if they cannot.[7]

Corollary 2: When policymaking involves the agencies controlled by the president and the premier, the power of the legislature to revise policy proposals increases the probability of the two executive heads being incongruent.

Corollary 1 is a different way to depict the equilibrium. Corollary 2 shows that when the legislature moves last and revises an executive proposal, the premier has to adjust his stance, which may be incongruent with the president's initial proposal.

To derive from the above propositions verifiable hypotheses, we need to consider distinctive features of Taiwan's political system. First, Taiwan's president is less powerful than many of his counterparts in other semipresidential countries—he does not have veto power, does not participate in cabinet meetings, and cannot actively dissolve the Legislative Yuan. However, the president has been seen by the people as the paramount leader; presidential elections held since 1996 have further given the president the mandate to crystallize his campaign promises as government policies. The president appoints the premier without legislative consent and can dismiss the premier, making Taiwan's semipresidential system president-parliamentary (Shugart, 2005). Taiwan has never experienced the French-style cohabitation, and the premiers are usually the president's subordinates.

Second, the Legislative Yuan appears to be less powerful than its parliamentary counterparts. Taiwan's legislators cannot concurrently hold government positions and are thus detached from the policymaking process. Nor is it easy for the Legislative Yuan to revise policies that are not embodied as laws or budgets.[8] Given these constraints, the legislators are unlikely to be the initiator of important policies. But the president or the premier can hardly discipline the legislators of their party without paying a political price. The major reason lies in the importance of the personal vote. Partly due to the long history of using the single nontransferable voting under the multimember district, an electoral system encouraging the

---

[7] According to the veto player theory, the decision a collective veto player makes is volatile because majority rule creates unstable results. From the perspective of noncooperative game theory, however, the collective veto player must include a player whose proposal cannot be revised further. The ideal point of the collective player is determined by this player.

[8] For the powers of the Legislative Yuan, see the Legislative Yuan Functioning Act, http://db.lawbank.com.tw/FLAW/FLAWDAT01.asp?lsid=FL000290 (accessed April 2, 2011).

personal vote (Carey and Shugart, 1995), Taiwan's legislators have been working hard to maintain a personal connection with their constituents. Such a campaign culture persists after the electoral system was changed to a mixed-member majoritarian system in 2005. In fact, the personal vote has become even more critical in some constituencies because the new system gives candidates the incentive to garner support from nonpartisan voters. For this reason, many legislators pay more attention to constituency services than to party platform, and members of the same party may hold different issue positions. Penalizing a dissentient legislator who has strong local support runs the risk of losing that seat.[9] Party discipline is also restrained by legislative rules. Roll call is not mandatory in the Legislative Yuan, and under-the-table bargaining is quite common. Both features make it possible for the legislators to exert their influence beyond the oversight of their parties at almost any stage of the legislative process.

The cited conditions suggest that, for most important policies, the president, the premier, and the Legislative Yuan are the veto players, for they require the initiation of the president, the substantiation of the Executive Yuan, and the consent of the Legislative Yuan. Legislators from the ruling party opt to challenge the Executive Yuan because they are alienated from the policymaking process but unconstrained by party discipline. The following hypotheses show the application of the propositions to Taiwan:

> *Hypothesis 1* (*Legislative Power*). When the KMT legislators do not fully endorse an executive proposal, the power to revise a government bill increases the capacity of the Legislative Yuan to change the government position.

> *Hypothesis 2* (*Executive Incongruence*). When the making of a policy involves the joint effort of the president and the premier, the probability of the two taking different issue positions is increased if the policy is to be revised and adopted by the Legislative Yuan.

Both hypotheses result from the equilibrium of the veto player model. Hypothesis 1 posits that the Legislative Yuan, if allowed to revise executive proposals, can force the government to adjust its original position; the government faces no such pressure if the legislature does not have this power. Hypothesis 2 extends Corollary 2 to Taiwan: if the

---

[9]　A related reason is the timing of elections. In the 2008 elections, the presidential coattails were significantly restricted because the legislative election was held before the presidential election.

president, the premier, and the Legislative Yuan move in sequence and the legislative majority can compel the premier to modify his position, the positions of the president and the premier may appear to be incongruent. The same logic implies that the president will dominate policymaking if the Legislative Yuan is not allowed to revise an executive proposal.

To see how these hypotheses capture the reality, we need to determine what constitutes an important policy. On the second anniversary of Ma Ying-jeou's presidential inauguration, the Research, Development and Evaluation Commission (RDEC) of the Executive Yuan published a report assessing to what extent the president's campaign promises had been fulfilled.[10] Apparently, these promises cannot all be important. In this article, I use the RDEC list as a base and select from it the ones that Taiwan's major mass media have headlined as important policies. I have added policies not covered by the RDEC because their importance could not have been anticipated by Ma when he campaigned for the 2008 presidential election—these events are either accidents or policies that captured the media's attention after unexpected controversies arose. Multiple sources are used to code these policies so that partisan bias can be minimized.[11]

The variables of the hypotheses are operationalized in the following ways:

1. The Legislative Yuan is entitled to revise an executive proposal if this policy is related to the making of a new law or an amendment to an existing law. The Legislative Yuan has no power to revise a policy if it results from executive decrees or regulations; this scenario includes the instance in which the Legislative Yuan can only pass or reject a government bill as a package but cannot change its content.

2. The president and the premier hold incongruent policy positions if both (or the agencies under their control) are responsible for the making of a policy but reveal inconsistent positions over time. The president is certainly mindful of the important

---

[10] See http://www.rdec.gov.tw/ct.asp?xItem=4527780&ctNode=12232&mp=100 (accessed March 16, 2011) for the report of the RDEC.

[11] The following are the major sources of data (all accessed December 2, 2010): *United Daily News*, http://udn.com/NEWS/main.html; *Taipei Times*, http://www.taipeitimes.com; Democratic Progressive Party, http://www.dpp.org.tw; Kuomintang, http://www.kmt.org.tw; National Policy Foundation, http://www.npf.org.tw; and Citizen Congress Watch, http://www.ccw.org.tw. For the English translation of laws and amendments, see the Laws and Regulations Database of the Republic of China, http://law.moj.gov.tw. Case studies are based on the same sources.

policies, but his personal remarks or opinions do not necessarily constitute dual executive policymaking. Dual executive policymaking is operationalized by the president and the premier (or the agencies under their control) formulating and presenting their proposals when a policy is being made. A strict criterion will be used when the involvement of one of the executive heads cannot be ascertained.

3. The KMT's legislators do not fully endorse the executive if the party's legislative leaders (the speaker or the secretary of the KMT caucus) or a group of KMT legislators openly question the executive about its policy proposals.

These policies and their features are reported in Table 3.1. As the table shows, the final outcome is consistent with the executive proposal in some cases but not in others. Two reasons explain the consistency: first, the legislative majority and the executive have congruent preferences; second, some KMT legislators have an incentive to adjust the proposals but are not allowed to do so. By contrast, executive-legislative incongruence always results from a significant number of KMT legislators modifying executive bills that are amendable. To be more specific, out of the twenty-nine cases, twenty-one (72.4%) are laws or amendments revisable by the legislators, thirteen (44.8%) see incompliant KMT legislators, at least fourteen (48.3%) involve dual executive decisions, and the KMT and the DPP clash on twenty-one (72.4%) of these policies. The most common type has these features: legislation needed, bipartisan difference, incoherent KMT, and dual-executive decision. This is the policy type that characterizes Taiwan's semipresidential system: legislators of the ruling party do not always stand by their leaders in the executive, and the policy positions of the two executive heads are not always consistent.

The question is how the hypotheses can be tested most appropriately. Straightforward as it may seem, a quantitative test of the hypotheses has some limits. First, the number of cases is small and most variables are dichotomous, both of which make it hard to estimate the quantitative relationship among the variables. Second, a quantitative correlation does not necessarily specify the choices made by the veto players. For these reasons, I use here a hypothesis-based case study to link choices and outcomes. Unlike a quantitative analysis based on a large number of randomly selected cases, case studies do not estimate the parameters of a statistical model depicting the relationship among variables. Instead, case studies examine whether the expected links between choices and outcomes appear in different cases.[12] The validity of a hypothesis increases with the number of cases satisfying its prediction.

Table 3.1 Important Policies in the First Half of the Ma Ying-jeou Presidency

Policy	Proposal revisable by legislators?	Partisan difference?	KMT incoherence?	Dual executive decisions?
Direct cross-strait charter flights	No	No	No	Yes
Relaxing quota for mainland visitors	No	No	No	Yes
Participation in World Health Assembly (WHA)	No	Yes	No	Yes
Amendment to the Organic Act for Executive Yuan	Yes	Yes	No	No
Abolishment of capital punishment	Yes	No	No	No
Amendment to the National Pension Insurance Act	Yes	No	No	No
Amendment to the Employment Insurance Act	Yes	No	No	No
Amendment to the Assembly and Parade Law[a]	Yes	Yes	Yes	No
Amendment to the Labor Insurance Act	Yes	No	No	No

(continued)

---

[12] For the analytical advantages of a case study, see Gerring (2004).

Policy	Proposal revisable by legislators?	Partisan difference?	KMT incoherence?	Dual executive decisions?
Allowing mainland Chinese students to study in Taiwan	Yes	Yes	No	Yes
Adjustment of the health insurance premium rates	Yes	Yes	Yes	No
Amendment to the Income Tax Act	Yes	Yes	Yes	No
Amendment to the Estate and Gift Tax Act	Yes	Yes	No	No
Amendment to the Local Government Act	Yes	Yes	Yes	Yes
Cross-strait financial supervision memorandum of understanding	No	Yes	No	Yes
Consumption voucher	Yes	No	No	No
Amendment to the Offshore Islands Development Act	Yes	Yes	No	No
The Economic Cooperation Framework Agreement[a]	No	Yes	Yes	Yes
Amendment to the Civil Code	Yes	No	No	No

(continued)

Policy	Proposal revisable by legislators?	Partisan difference?	KMT incoherence?	Dual executive decisions?
Relaxing the regulations on business trips to Taiwan by mainland Chinese	No	Yes	No	Yes
Swine flu and H1N1 control	No	Yes	Yes	No
Statute for Industrial Innovation; Statute for Upgrading Industries	Yes	Yes	Yes	Yes
Importation of US beef[a]	Yes	Yes	Yes	Yes
Relieving the victims of Typhoon Morakot[a]	No	Yes	Yes	Yes
Absentee voting system[a]	Yes	Yes	No	No
Amendment to the Civil Servants Evaluation Act	Yes	Yes	Yes	Yes
Amendment to the Computer-Processed Personal Data Protection Act	Yes	Yes	Yes	No
Farm Villages Revival Act	Yes	Yes	Yes	Yes
Establishment of the Anti-Corruption Commission	Yes	Yes	Yes	Yes

Note: a. These cases are policies not covered by the RDEC Report.

The following two sections select the cases according to the two hypotheses and count the number of cases that satisfy or falsify the predictions. Two notes of research design should be explained here. First, depending on the nature of the dependent variable, the independent variables of the veto player model can be measured in various ways. Since both hypotheses are related to the changeability of executive proposals, a categorical measurement to test them will suffice. Second, the different dimensions of the same case can be analyzed to test different hypotheses, and policies receiving unanimous support from the KMT's legislators are not suitable to test these hypotheses.[13]

A. Hypothesis 1: Legislative Power

Hypothesis 1, postulating the impact of legislative power on policymaking, can be tested when the legislative majority and the executive have disagreements. It follows from this hypothesis that legislative influence should be stronger on the policies that the legislators can revise than on the cases that they cannot. Table 3.2 shows whether the cases fit the expectation. The cases are divided into two types by whether the Legislative Yuan can revise an executive proposal (Type 1a) or not (Type 1b). For the eight cases in which the Executive Yuan proposed a bill for the Legislative Yuan to deliberate, the legislators made significant changes in seven of them. For the two cases in which the Legislative Yuan was not entitled to make revisions, the disgruntled KMT legislators could not but accept these policies as they were. Overall, the percentage of cases satisfying Hypothesis 1 is quite high. The following are the details of the making of these policies.

(A) Type 1a-1: Amendment to the Assembly and Parade Law. The controversy over the amendment to this law concerns the degree to which assemblies and parades should be regulated. The issue was more complicated than it appeared: during the period 2000-2008, the DPP was the ruling party and is now in control of many local governments, while some supporters of the KMT can be on the side of the protesters. When Ma was elected president, the positions taken by different actors on this issue reflected their attitudes toward the Executive Yuan's policy. This law, established in 1988 right after martial law

---

[13] The following analysis will exclude the amendment to the Civil Servants Evaluation Act, because it has been drafted by the Examination Yuan rather than the Executive Yuan.

Table 3.2 Cases in Hypothesis 1

Type number	Policy	Focus of executive-legislative disagreement	Result
1a-1	Amendment to the Assembly and Parade Law	Degree to which regulations on assembly and parades should be relaxed	Regulations in the amended law were more relaxed than what MOI proposed.
1a-2	Amendment to the Local Government Act	Whether township officeholders can continue their jobs and receive remunerations	Amended law and government bill were significantly different on both issues.
1a-3	Amendment to the Income Tax Act	Whether tax exemption of military and school employees should be abolished	Amended law kept the tax exemptions intact.
1a-4	Adjustment of the health insurance premium rates	Whether to adopt the new formula of health insurance premium rate that is based on household incomes rather personal incomes	The original DOH proposal was rejected by the Legislative Yuan.
1a-5	Importation of US beef	What parts of the cow should not be imported	Amended law imposed stricter restrictions than the Taiwan-US protocol.
1a-6	Amendment to the Computer-Processed Personal Data Protection Act	Whether to give mass media more responsibility for the transgression of individual privacy	Responsibility of mass media was not included in the amended law as some KMT legislators wished.
1a-7	Establishment of the Anti-Corruption Commission	Whether to establish the Commission under MOJ; whether the Commission should investigate corruption and vote buying	Vote buying was not mentioned in the law passed by the Legislative Yuan.
1b-1	The Economic Cooperation Framework Agreement	How the agreement should be approved; which items should be included in the Early Harvest Program	ECFA voted on as a package. No discussion allowed on Early Harvest Program.
1b-2	Swine flu and H1N1control	Whether medical insurance should cover vaccine produced by Adimmune	DOH maintained its decision on the coverage.

was lifted in Taiwan, became an issue when the protests against the visit of Chen Yunlin, nominally the chairman of the Association for Relations Across the Taiwan Straits (ARATS) and substantively a representative of the People's Republic of China (PRC), resulted in serious clashes between the police and the protesters. In reaction to the public's concern, the Executive Yuan proposed in December 2008 an amendment to this law that would change the regulation of a rally from "permission by police" to "registration to police" before one could be held. Contrary to the Executive Yuan's proclamation that this amendment marks a great step forward because the role of the police is changed from an ex ante approver to a regulator of the rally activities, many social activists lashed out at the new law because it gives the police too much power to halt or penalize a registered rally. Social pressure pushed the KMT's caucus leader to adjust the amendment, and the Executive Yuan agreed to cancel the power of the police to dissolve a rally before it is held and shorten the registration deadline from five days to three days before a rally is to be held.

(B) Type 1a-2: Amendment to the Local Government Act. As explained above, the importance of the personal vote in Taiwan's legislative elections makes legislators heavily dependent on local politicians to garner grassroots support. Legislators are therefore sensitive to laws or regulations that may affect the status of the local officeholders. Amendment to the Local Government Act became an issue when five of Taiwan's municipalities were to be upgraded to special municipalities in 2011. Several positions can be identified concerning how this act should be amended. First, some legislators naturally requested that the township heads of these metropolitan areas be appointed as the district chief administrators of the special municipalities and the members of the township assembly be appointed as the district councilors of the special municipalities. Second, there was public concern for the legitimacy to maintain the positions of these local politicians. If the township heads were to be automatically appointed as the district chief administrators (and assembly members as the councilors) in the special municipalities, they would come to hold public office for a period of nine years since they were first elected in 2005—a long tenure beyond the tolerance of many people. Third, the Executive Yuan's position was somewhere in between. According to the original plan of the Ministry of the Interior (MOI), the township heads should be elected in 2009 and serve a five-year term until 2014, and the township assembly members should be made the district councilors without remuneration. It turns out that the MOI's proposal, although favoring the incumbent local officeholders, failed to convince KMT legislators who thought that the local officeholders should keep their jobs and that all township assembly members should be on the government's payroll. The power of the legislators is evidenced by the final proposal approved by the Legislative Yuan in February 2010, which stated that the township heads should be appointed as the district chief administrators unless they have committed a felony or have served two terms and that township assembly members to be made district councilors have no salary but can be reimbursed when they attend district meetings. Evidently, the legislators gained the upper hand in their bargaining with MOI.

(C) Type 1a-3: Amendment to the Income Tax Act. The focus of this amendment is the abolishment of the tax exemptions of the military personnel and teachers. This is a significant issue involving not only income redistribution but also the support bases of political parties. Several attitudes can be found. First, in Taiwan, professionals working in the military and schools are more likely to support the KMT than the DPP.[14] The KMT legislators, especially those supported by voters who work in the public sector, have been hesitant to change the status quo. Second, for this same reason, the DPP is a strong opponent of the tax exemption policy. Third, in contrast to the people working in the military and schools, who enjoy stable and above-average incomes, those suffering from economic recession tend to associate the KMT with what they see as an unjustifiable tax policy. Fourth, for exactly the same reason, President Ma has been planning to modify this policy. In August 2008, the minister of finance remarked that he was quite optimistic about the abolishment of the tax exemptions of people working in the military and schools; in June 2009, the Executive Yuan submitted to the Legislative Yuan a bill planning to revoke these tax exemptions as of 2011. The Income Tax Act was indeed amended by the Legislative Yuan in June 2010, but the tax exemptions of military personnel and schoolteachers remained intact. This result shows again that the Legislative Yuan is an effective veto player when it has the power to revise an executive proposal that some members of the ruling party disfavor.

(D) Type 1a-4: Amendment to the health insurance premium. Very few policies affect as many people as the health insurance premium does, and very few legislators dare to endorse a reform that increases the premium rate. The position of the Department of Health (DOH) on

---

[14] According to a survey conducted by the TVBS network for the 2004 presidential election, about 66% of military, government, and school employees voted for the KMT candidate, which was much higher than the KMT candidate's actual vote rate of 49.9%. See www.tvbs.com.tw/FILE _DB/files/yijung/200404/yijung-20040414111305.pdf (accessed March 21, 2011).

the premium rate can be explained by its concern over the National Health Insurance deficit. According to the DOH's proposal for the "second generation of National Health Insurance," the reform focused on changing the basis of the premium rate from personal income to household income, because rich people's wealth may not be reflected in their personal income. On March 8, 2010, Yaung Chih-Liang, then minister of DOH, even pledged to resign if the DOH's proposal was not carried out. For their part, the legislators were fearful of the backlash caused by raising the premium rate, especially when DOH had not yet demonstrated its ability to curb the waste of the health insurance resources. On April 29, 2010, the Social Welfare and Environmental Hygiene Committee of the Legislative Yuan passed resolutions demanding DOH to publicize the financial model of the National Health Insurance reform, to hold public hearings, and to establish a National Health Insurance fund. Not surprisingly, some endorsers of these resolutions were members of the KMT. The most serious blow to DOH was nothing other than the health insurance premium passed by the Legislative Yuan on January 4, 2011, in which it did not even consider using household income as the basis of the health insurance premium. Seeing his core proposal rejected, Yaung immediately resigned after the law was passed.

(E) Type 1a-5: Importation of US beef. As a renowned journalist put it, this issue provoked a "collective riot" among KMT legislators (Wang [王健壯], 2010). However, very few people—Ma included—expected the serious repercussions of this event. When Ma was inaugurated in May 2008, President Lee Myungbak of the Republic of Korea was troubled by a strong social protest against his decision to lift the ban on US beef imports. Cautioned by the South Korean experience, Ma remarked that when importing US beef, Taiwan should follow the standards of the World Organization for Animal Health. This statement signaled Ma's underestimation of the domestic backlash that would challenge his legitimacy. When DOH announced that imports of US beef would be resumed by the end of October 2009 because Taiwan and the United States had signed the import protocol, many legislators, including the leader of the KMT caucus, immediately issued statements protesting the decision.[15] On the surface, their disapproval came from the public's anxiety over mad cow disease, which had

---

[15] Formally, the protocol is called "Protocol of Bovine Spongiform Encephalopathy (BSE)-Related Measures for the Importation of Beef and Beef Products for Human Consumption from the Territory of the Authorities Represented by the American Institute in Taiwan (AIT)." See http://www.fda.gov.tw/files/site_content/D058_1.PDF (accessed March 21, 2011).

been linked to US beef. That might be the government's attribution of the public grievance, as evidenced by its repeated emphasis on the infinitesimal possibility of mad cow disease occurring. As it turned out, this technical explanation failed to alleviate the public's anger; in fact, a referendum drive demanding public approval of US beef imports was initiated. It turns out that, for this case, the legislators could demonstrate their dissatisfaction by amending the Act Governing Food Sanitation. According to the latest act and the resolutions attached to it, both passed by the Legislative Yuan on January 5, 2010, US cows over thirty months old, ground beef, beef offal, and other beef parts such as skulls, eyes, and intestines shall be barred from entering Taiwan, the government should abide by the result of a proposed referendum on beef imports, and legislators and the government should resist pressures from countries disagreeing with the amendments. While the amended act may have violated the Taiwan-US beef import protocol, the president still has to promulgate it as a law.

(F) Type 1a-6: Amendment to the Computer-Processed Persona Data Protection Act. This case is important in that it demonstrates a limit of the legislative power when an amendment may undermine the electoral fortune of some legislators. To be more specific, this event reveals how the mass media can prevent the legislators from passing an amendment that may put the freedom of speech at stake. The Personal Data Act, proposed by the Ministry of Justice (MOJ), sought to extend the protections on personal data. The focus of the debate concerns whether the mass media should be held accountable when they are suspected of infringing on one's privacy. While the old act was quite specific about the likely transgressors of personal privacy (including the mass media), the bill proposed by MOJ describes the likely transgressors in unspecific terms. When deliberating this bill, some KMT legislators proposed that the mass media should be obliged to inform and seek consent from the involved persons before collecting or publishing their personal data. Such a move was justified by the worry that Taiwan's media sometimes deliver false alarms that may transgress personal privacy or defame the persons involved. The legislators' proposal immediately incurred a strong protest from the mass media, arguing that this amendment would impinge on freedom of information and hinder the media's investigation of corruption scandals. This concern, announced consistently by media with different partisan affiliations, delegitimized the legislators' attempt to revise the MOJ bill. The amendment finalized in April 2010 exempted the media from having to inform and seek consent from individuals before collecting personal data "if their report serves the public interest." It should be noted that the final amendment was still different from what MOJ proposed. It is social pressure rather than government dominance that explains the legislative backdown.

(G) Type 1a-7: The Anti-Corruption Commission. Anticorruption is a valence issue on top of the agenda of most politicians. The motivation to take anticorruption actions is especially strong for Ma, who defeated the corruption-embroiled DPP in the 2008 presidential election. Ma's attempt would soon backfire because instances of corruption under the KMT's presidency do not appear to be in decline. Legislators relying on political donations to win their position may also be cautious about stricter anticorruption measures. Setting up an anticorruption commission was initiated by President Ma in July 2010 after a series of corruption scandals involving the police and judiciary called into question the credibility and legitimacy of the government. While very few people doubted the seriousness of these events and Ma's determination, some KMT legislators—including a caucus leader—thought Ma's plan to set up the commission under MOJ unnecessary and redundant. Legislative pressure explains the watering down of Ma's plan. What Ma envisioned in July 2010 was a commission with the power to investigate corruption of public servants and vote buying of elected officeholders, but the draft submitted by MOJ to the Legislative Yuan said nothing about vote buying. Even so, intra-KMT disagreements kept the Legislative Yuan from passing the MOJ version immediately. When the Legislative Yuan eventually adopted the organic law of the anticorruption commission in April 1, 2011, it was more than eight months after Ma initiated the issue.

(H) Type 1b-1: The Economic Cooperation Framework Agreement (ECFA). In contrast to the above cases, the legislative review of the ECFA demonstrates the restricted influence of the legislators if they can only accept or reject an executive proposal but cannot change its content. The ECFA is a framework for trade agreements between the governments of the Republic of China (ROC, Taiwan) and the PRC, with the purpose of reducing tariffs and commercial barriers between the two sides. For President Ma, completion of the ECFA has become one of his most important policies, and he has been supervising the negotiations. The ECFA was signed on June 29, 2010, in Chongqing by Chiang Pin-kung, chairman of Taiwan's Strait Exchange Foundation (SEF), and Chen Yunlin, president of ARATS, and approved by the Executive Yuan on July 2. For the proponents of the ECFA, this agreement is necessary for Taiwan to sign free trade agreements (FTAs) with other countries, without which Taiwan would be marginalized. For those who doubt the political intentions of Beijing, the ECFA will further lock Taiwan into the PRC economy; Taiwan's signing of FTAs with the other countries, even if possible, must be approved by Beijing. Without a doubt, the KMT and the DPP are on opposite sides of the debate.

It would be wrong, however, to assume that the legislative majority would immediately approve the ECFA in the form in which it was signed. First, some KMT politicians have personal interests in mainland China. The Early Harvest Program, the core of the ECFA, determines which goods or services shall benefit from this agreement.[16] It is unlikely that the ECFA would satisfy all legislators. Some items included in the ECFA were susceptible to adjustment had the legislators the power to revise the ECFA. The second controversy was how the Legislative Yuan should review the ECFA. While the DPP insisted that the ECFA should be reviewed article by article, the Executive Yuan proclaimed that the ECFA is like a treaty and should be reviewed as a package. In between, Wang Jin-pyng, speaker of the Legislative Yuan and a leading KMT politician, had his own view. Wang quoted the interpretation of the Grand Justice and remarked that, due to the special situation across the Strait, the ECFA should be seen as an agreement rather than a treaty. Accordingly, how the ECFA is to be reviewed should be decided by the Legislative Yuan. The executive, seeing Wang's contention as a personal opinion rather than a jurisprudential argument, remained quite intransigent. In the end, Wang proposed a compromise on July 7 that the ECFA could be discussed article by article but could not be revised when it was reviewed in committee. The ECFA was approved by the Legislative Yuan on August 17, 2010, in the form in which it was signed. It is clear from this case that the Legislative Yuan may become a rubber stamp if the content of a proposal is not revisable.

(I)　Type 1b-2: Swine flu and H1N1 control. This was an unexpected event that seriously undermined the executive's credibility. Even so, the Legislative Yuan had no legal instrument to redress the DOH decisions that some legislators found problematic. The major controversy concerns whether National Health Insurance should cover a vaccine made by a government-funded biotech company. The Legislative Yuan had little role to play in this decision because DOH was authorized by the National Health Insurance Act to make decisions about medical insurance coverage. Although the Act also demands that the DOH's decisions be monitored by the Supervisory Board, the coverage decisions are usually technical and beyond the expertise

---

[16]　For how the relatives of some KMT leaders invest in China, see Tian [田習如] (2010).

of the legislators. Also due to the technicality of pandemic control, the legislators are usually ill informed; they question DOH only if distressful events take place. This is what happened in this case. The H1N1 vaccine campaign was launched by DOH starting in late 2009. The DOH's credibility declined sharply with the rise of the fatality rate of people receiving the vaccine produced by Adimmune, a government-sponsored Taiwanese company. To aggravate the situation, the price of the Adimmune vaccine rose by 18% after DOH decided that the National Health Insurance would cover the Adimmune vaccine. Popular discontent compelled many legislators, many of whom were from the KMT, to shift their anger to the minister of DOH. Even a member of the Control Yuan volunteered to investigate whether there was collusion between the government and Adimmune. Despite the blame the officials in charge received, DOH did not change this health insurance coverage decision.

To summarize this section, the capacity of Taiwan's legislators to revise executive proposals does give them considerable influence on policymaking, as stated in Hypothesis 1. As illustrated in the next section, legislative power also impacts another feature of semipresidentialism─the congruence of the two executive heads.

B. Hypothesis 2: Executive Incongruence

Semipresidentialism differs from other constitutional systems by its dual executive design, hence the likelihood of executive incongruence. What Hypothesis 2 posits is how this problem may be induced by the legislative power. This section also divides the cases involving dual executive decisions by whether the legislators have the power to adjust executive proposals (Type 2a) or not (Type 2b). As shown in Table 3.3, legislative power exposes the inconsistency between different government agencies in three out of the four cases. The two cases for which legislation is not needed both see the persistence of executive cohesion. The following are the details of these cases.

(A) Type 2a-1: Amendment to the Local Government Act. I discussed the content and importance of this case (Type 1a-2) when explaining how legislative power changed the proposal submitted by the Executive Yuan. Not addressed was the vague term *executive*, which is composed of various agencies controlled by different administrative heads. In this section, I show how, in the drafting of this policy, legislative influence and social pressure forced different agencies to adjust their positions, thereby exposing the incongruence in the

Table 3.3 Cases in Hypothesis 2

Type number	Policy	Roles played by different government agencies and their positions	Legislative role
2a-1	Amendment to the Local Government Act	1. MOI (EY): Township heads would be elected in 2009 for a five-year term; township assembly members would be appointed as district councilors without remuneration. 2. KMT secretary general: Township assembly members would serve one more term with research fund. 3. President: district councilors should be appointed according to original MOI proposal; township heads charged with treason or felony cannot be transferred as district chief administrator.	Some KMT legislators requested MOI to change its proposal.
2a-2	Importation of US beef	1. NSC and MOFA (president) were in charge of the signing of Taiwan-US Beef Importation Protocol. 2. DOH (EY) was in charge of food sanitation; minister claimed that the beef to be imported is safe.	Regulations imposed by the revised act were stricter than the protocol; DOH had to follow the act.
2a-3	Statute for Industrial Innovation	1. MOF(EY): Set a 20% business income tax; agreed to reduce it to 15% for multinational corporations when pressured by legislators. 2. President: Business income tax should be 20%.	A KMT legislator proposed to tax the multinational corporations at 15% and the domestic enterprises at 20%.
2a-4	Farm Villages Revival Act	1. President actively pushed for the passage of the act; his position was reflected in the EY bill. 2. EY proposed a NT$150 billion revival fund to be allocated over ten years.	EY maintained its position (hence executive congruence), but KMT legislators added all additional resolution that the government should prepare another NT$50 billion after the revival fund is used up after ten years.

(continued)

Type number	Policy	Roles played by different government agencies and their positions	Legislative role
2b-1	Relieving the victims of Typhoon Morakot	1. President was in command of the armed forces in charge of emergency relief. 2. NSC and MOFA (president) decided whether to accept international relief support. 3. Premier was in charge of the Missions of Central Disaster Prevention and Protection Council.	The KMT legislators, despite their criticisms on the government's relief effort, found no way to change the government's disaster relief policy.
2b-2	The Economic Cooperation Framework Agreement	1. President led the negotiation with the PRC government and coordinated different agencies. 2. NSC, MAC (president), MOEA, and MOF (EY) were responsible for the signing of the ECFA.	LY voted on the ECFA as a package and passed it as signed.

executive. At least two executive players can be identified. First, as mentioned in the previous section, the original plan of MOI was to have the township heads elected in 2009 serve a five-year term until 2014, township assembly members would become district councilors without remuneration, and only some township heads could be appointed as district chief administrators. Second, President Ma was deeply concerned with this issue as well but lacked official channels to voice his policy proposal. Ma therefore relied on then KMT secretary-general King Pu-tsung, his trusted friend, to negotiate with MOI and the legislators. Responding to the objections of some KMT legislators to the MOI's proposal, King proposed in January 2010 a new formula: the township assembly members could serve one term as district councilors and receive NT$45,000 as their "research fund," and township heads could serve one term as district chief administrators. MOI accepted this deal and claimed that a research fund is not equivalent to salary. This deal raised serious doubts that the legislators would not be serving their own interests, forcing King, MOI, and the KMT legislators to renegotiate. This time Ma gave clear instructions that township heads accused of corruption, rebellion, treason, or participation in organized crime should not be transferred as district chief administrators; that the appointment of the district councilors should follow the MOI's original proposal; and that no research fund should be paid to the district councilors. Clearly, legislative power and social pressure explain the inconsistent positions taken by different executive players.

(B) Type 2a-2: Importation of US beef. This issue shows not only the impact of legislative power (Type 1a-5) but also how Taiwan's semipresidentialism works—the making of this policy involved at least the National Security Council (NSC), the Ministry of Foreign Affairs (MOFA), and DOH. MOFA claimed that the Executive Yuan can simply notify the Legislative Yuan of a signed protocol that it does not consider a treaty. The importance of NSC in the negotiations is evidenced by the roles played by Su Chi, then secretary-general of NSC. On November 5, 2009, Su alerted the Legislative Yuan of the unwanted consequences if the negotiations with the United States were to be restarted; on February 11, 2010, he suddenly resigned. Su's role indicates that high politics beyond the reach of the Executive Yuan were involved when the importation of US beef was to be relaxed. DOH's reaction to the public outcry corroborates this conjecture. The original position of DOH, announced on October 23, 2009, was that the beef to be imported in accordance with the Taiwan-US protocol was safe; when confronted by the outraged legislators a few days later, DOH promised that the imported beef would not include viscera and ground meat. DOH's shifting attitudes discloses its passive and subsidiary role in the making of this policy. Eventually the Legislative Yuan revised the Act Governing Food Sanitation to restrict the imports of US beef. Like it or not. DOH is obliged to follow this law. In comparison with the stances held by MOFA and NSC, DOH's adjusted position leaves the impression that the government has not been able to maintain a consistent position on this issue.

(C) Type 2a-3: Statute for Industrial Innovation. Ma was elected in 2008 with the mandate to rescue Taiwan's economy from recession. Although cutting the tax rate of some industries is an expedient strategy to attract investment, President Ma has had to consider the financial deficit and social injustice that this policy may cause. While some people agreed that taxes should be reduced for industries conducive to Taiwan's economic growth, the controversy is over the amount of the tax cut. The adoption of this statute involves dual executive efforts, because President Ma was deeply concerned with this issue and gave straightforward instructions for how much the business income tax should be reduced. The original plan of the Executive Yuan was to set up a 20% business income tax. When reviewing this bill in October 2009, a KMT legislator proposed to tax multinational corporations (MNCs) at 15% and domestic enterprises at 20%. Amid the criticism that this proposal favored big corporations, the Executive Yuan agreed to tax MNCs at 15%. It was President Ma who insisted that the Executive Yuan should persist in the 20% tax rate to prevent the popularity of his administration from dropping. This case shows how a single KMT legislator can create an inconsistency between the president and the premier.

(D) Type 2a-4: The Farm Village Revival Act. This case differs from the previous three in that public pressure prevented the legislators from arousing executive incongruence. President Ma has been paying considerable attention to the reconstruction of Taiwan's rural villages because the agricultural sector is vulnerable to closer economic ties across the strait, one of his most important goals. It is in this context that President Ma gave instructions to the Executive Yuan for how the farm villages should be rebuilt. The focus of the Farm Village Revival Act was the amount of financial resources that was to be devoted to the rebuilding of the farm villages. While the DPP criticized this act as a vote-getting tactic of the KMT, some KMT legislators felt dissatisfied with the amount of money the Executive Yuan drafted. In July 2010, the Executive Yuan proposed to the Legislative Yuan an NT$150 billion revival fund that is to be allocated over ten years. When reviewing this bill in committee, some KMT legislators planned to raise the amount to NT$200 billion. It was the public outcry against this request that kept the Executive Yuan from backing down to the legislators. Although the act was adopted as it was proposed, the Legislative Yuan still added a resolution that the government should prepare another NT$50 billion to help reconstruct the farming villages after the revival fund was used up after ten years. Had social pressure been weaker, the legislators could have created an executive dissonance.

(E) Type 2b-1: Relieving the victims of Typhoon Morakot. Most observers would agree that that this event marked the decline of Ma Ying-jeou's popularity. From the perspective of Hypothesis 2, this case demonstrates the inability of the Legislative Yuan to modify the decision made by the two executive heads even if the premier was ultimately held accountable. When Typhoon Morakot hit Taiwan on August 6, 2009, the landslides it caused killed hundreds of people instantly, and serious economic losses followed. Given the severity of the catastrophe, what the executive leaders did on August 8 seemed intolerable. Premier Liu was away from the Missions of Central Disaster Prevention and Protection Council that he should have been in charge of, and the general secretary of the Executive Yuan was having a midnight snack with his father-in-law. Their inattentive attitudes outraged the public, urging some KMT politicians to hold Premier Liu accountable. Eventually the Liu cabinet resigned on September 7, 2009. Aside from the premier's responsibility, the president also played an important role. To begin with, only the military forces have the capacity to relieve the victims of a calamity effectively, and the president is the commander in chief. In fact, President Ma was criticized after the Morakot disaster for declining to issue the decree of emergency that would have given the military the authority to command the relief efforts. Moreover, NSC was believed to be responsible for the rejection of US support, although it was MOFA that took the direct blame. In any case, MOFA and NSC are both under the president's supervision, making the Morakot disaster relief a clear case of dual executive decisionmaking. The Legislative Yuan did approve the Post-Morakot Reconstruction Special Regulation *after* the disaster, but the bill focused on the postdisaster relief work rather than the accountability of the agencies controlled by the president. What we see from this case is the removal of officials rather than a change in the policy of disaster relief when the legislature is excluded from the policymaking process.

(F) Type 2b-2: The ECFA. This case shows that the inability to revise the ECFA not only constrained the legislative power (Type 1b-1) but also prevented the executive agencies from taking inconsistent positions. The very title of the ECFA suggests that the Ministry of Economic Affairs (MOEA), the Mainland Affairs Council (MAC), and NSC were the indispensible actors, and President Ma was the dominant decisionmaker. It would be interesting to see whether the constrained legislative power helped the government maintain a coherent policy. As a matter of fact, it is difficult for the executive agencies to reveal inconsistency—all government officials emphasized the importance of the ECFA but none disclosed its contents until the agreement was signed. The fact that the Legislative Yuan passed the ECFA in the form in which it was signed by no means implies that the KMT legislators wished to see its contents intact. As already explained, most legislators would have liked to adjust the Early Harvest Program in accordance with their own interests. The result could have been quite different had they had the power to revise its contents.

In sum, case studies in this section largely confirm Hypothesis 2; all but one of the cases show that executive congruence is undermined when legislators intervene. The case defying this expectation, the farm village revival fund, suggests that the executive heads are more likely to be congruent when public opinion is on their side.

IV. Conclusion

The likelihood of executive-legislative gridlock under semipresidentialism is usually higher than that under parliamentarism because premier survival in the former system may depend more on presidential support than on parliamentary confidence. Semipresidentialism is also distinguishable from presidentialism because the president and the cabinet ministers may disagree on important policies. To depict the complicated dynamics of semipresidentialism, I modify this article the veto player theory and derive two hypotheses: when the legislature is empowered to revise executive proposals, the government tends to concede; when policymaking involves the two executive heads, legislative power can generate inconsistency between the president and the premier.

These hypotheses are confirmed by case studies on Taiwan's policymaking in the Ma Ying-jeou presidency. Among the cases in which the KMT legislators did not fully support the executive but enjoyed the freedom to amend the executive proposal, all but one saw the Legislative Yuan making significant changes to the executive bill. Only in the amendment of the Computer-Processed Personal Data Protection Act were the legislators prevented from modifying the executive proposal to their advantage. In contrast, the cases in which legislative power could not be used tell a different story. Concerning the control for swine flu and H1N1, the KMT legislators who questioned DOH's decision on medical insurance coverage had no way to overrule it. The KMT legislators endorsed ECFA as a whole but had no leverage to express their redistributive concerns when voting on this agreement as a package. These events show that the Legislative Yuan is a powerful collective veto player if they are allowed to revise executive proposals. Otherwise, the executive can set the agenda in such a way that the legislative majority cannot but agree with the government's policies.

The same logic implies that the president and the premier are more likely to display different policy positions when the legislature is entitled to revise executive proposals. Out of the four cases in which the decision was made by the two executive heads and the Legislative Yuan could revise executive proposals, three indicate executive incongruence. There is no sign of dual executive incongruence in the two contrasting cases in which the Legislative Yuan had no power to alter executive policy.

Although limited in number, the cases presented in this article do show that the KMT government is often challenged by and yields to its members in the Legislative Yuan.

Such a problem is exacerbated by the separation of the lawmakers from the policymaking process, which will not occur in parliamentary democracies. Another weakness of the current policymaking system is the gap between formal and informal powers. The president, seen by most as the primary leader, lacks the constitutional powers to control the administrative agencies. President Ma has to rely on nonconstitutional mechanisms (such as the ruling party) to coordinate government actions and the executive-legislative relationship. Having the president making decisions behind the premier makes Taiwan's semipresidential system less accountable than the parliamentary or presidential systems, especially if the participation of the lawmakers is restricted. No wonder some legislators felt alienated and used their power to veto executive decisions.

At the theoretical level, I question in this article the presumption that presidents in the president-parliamentary regimes are powerful. Prime ministers surviving on the trust of the president rather than the confidence of the parliament lack the legitimacy to associate important policies with a confidence motion. The platform of a politically dominant president usually defines the important policies of his country, but if policy implementation requires legislation but the president cannot effectively discipline the legislators in his party, the eventual content of these policies is finalized by the legislature rather than the president. In their turn, the legislators have the power to undermine the unity of the dual executive system unless the president depends on decrees to rule. The Taiwanese experience can thus be generalized to study other semipresidential regimes.

Appendix: A Policymaking Game

Suppose the alternatives of a policy constitute a compact Euclidean issue space, and a group of veto players $N = \{V_1, V_2, \cdots V_i, \cdots V_n\}$ move sequentially to choose an alternative in the issue space. The players evaluate policy alternatives by the Euclidean distance—that is, for player V_i with ideal point v_i, the utility of outcome x is $u_i(x) = -\|v_i - x\|$, which is maximized when $v_i = x$. Designate $W_i(x) = \{y: y \neq x, u_i(y) > u_i(x)\}$ as the set of alternatives preferred by V_i to x.

V_1, the policy initiator, can select any point in the issue space as his proposal. The remaining players can be divided into two subsets. The first subset, N_r, is composed of players who can reject or revise a proposal; the second subset, N_s, contains players who can only accept or reject a proposal but cannot revise it. Thus defined, $V_1 \in N_r$.

The game is of perfect information: all players observe the move taken by the preceding players. V_1 starts the game by choosing a point in the issue space as his proposal. Seeing V_1's proposal, V_2 can accept (or revise if $V_2 \in N_r$) or reject the proposal; the game stops if V_2 rejects V_1's proposal. The process continues likewise until V_n, the last mover, makes his decision. The Nash equilibrium of this game is either q, the status quo, or a policy outcome replacing q.

Theorem. Let V_r be the last mover of N_r The subgame perfect equilibrium is (1) q if $\exists V_i \in N$, $v_i = $ q or $\cap W_i(q) = \varnothing$ or (2) $k_r^* \neq$ q such that $k_r^* \in \cap W_i(q)$ for $\forall V_i \in N$ and $\|k_r^* \text{-} v_r\| \leq \|k_r'\text{-}v_r\|$ for $k_r' \in \cap W_i(q)$.

Proof. If $v_i = $ q for some player, he can unilaterally stop the game. If $v_i \neq$ q for $\forall V_i \in N$, consider the following scenarios.

First, if $k_r^* \notin \cap W_i(q)$, then $\exists V_i \in N$, $v_i = $ q, a contradiction.

Second, a game of perfect information can be solved by backward induction. Consider two cases.

Case 1. Suppose $V_n \in N_r$. Then V_n can choose k_r^*, the point in $\cap W_i(q)$ that gives him the highest utility.

Case 2. Suppose $V_n \in N_s$. and $V_{n-1} \in N_r$. Then V_n will accept V_{n-1}'s selection of k_{n-1}^* because $k_{n-1}^* \in W_n(q)$. If $V_{n-1} \in N_s$, then the process continues until V_r appears and chooses k_r^*, the point in $\cap W_i(q)$ that gives him the highest utility. QED.

Corollary 1. $V_i \in N_r$ maximizes his utility if he moves last.

Corollary 2. V_1 maximizes his utility if no other player can revise his proposal.

第四章

The Endogenous Change in Electoral Systems: The Case of SNTV[*]

I. Duverger's Law Revisited

The relationship between electoral systems and party systems has attracted a large number of studies with a high level of theorization. Most notably, Duverger's hypothesis on the impact of electoral systems on party systems is so well received that some scholars regard it as evidence that politics can be studied scientifically (Riker, 1982). Duverger himself claims it to be sociological law that "the simple-majority single-ballot system favors the two-party system" (1963: 217). A related proposition posits that "the simple- majority system with second ballot and proportional representation (PR) favors multipartism" (Duverger, 1963: 239). To explain his theory, Duverger points out the mechanical factor—that the threshold of exclusion is high under the simple-majority single-ballot system—and the psychological factor—that voters are tempted to forsake candidates nominated by the minor parties. It follows the same logic that multipartism emerges easily under PR because its low winning threshold gives voters less incentive to sacrifice minor parties. One can make a general statement that electoral systems, by generating a particular kind of strategic choice, are exogenous determinants of party systems.

However, we can also analyse the relationship between electoral systems and party systems from the reverse direction. Colomer (2004, 2005) shows that it is the number of parties that explains the choice of electoral systems rather than the other way round. Boix (1999) demonstrates that when a two-party system faces a strong challenge from new parties, lawmakers are given the incentive to introduce a proportional system so that the old parties can still hold some seats even if candidates nominated by the new parties rank higher; in contrast, the old parties can rely on a majoritarian system to monopolize the legislative seats if the challengers are not strong enough to be elected under this system. Speaking more

[*] Reproduced from [Lin, Jih-wen. "The Endogenous Change in Electoral Systems: The Case of SNTV." *Party Politics* 17(3): 365-384, 2011], with kind permission of SAGE Publishing.

generally, electoral systems will change when political parties, wishing to gain more seats under an alternative electoral system, can form a winning coalition to change the existing institution (Benoit, 2004). Party systems can thus be seen as a variable that explains the change in electoral systems.

What, then, is the causal relationship between electoral systems and party systems? How do we explain their changes? A typical solution is to accept Duverger's propositions about the influence of electoral systems on party systems and ascribe the change in electoral systems to idiosyncratic factors. This view is to ignore the possibility that the changes in electoral systems and party systems are indeed correlated but that neither is the real cause of the other. It is possible that the same variable explains the impact of electoral systems on party systems, as well as the stability of party systems on the changeability of electoral systems. We can build a theory of endogenous change in electoral systems if a factor satisfies the following conditions: first, it is induced by the electoral system but varies over time; second, within some range, this factor helps consolidate a particular party system that reinforces the electoral system; and, third, when this factor moves beyond a certain range it can precipitate the formation of a new party system and motivate some political parties to change the electoral system. This endogenous factor may explain why electoral systems shape party systems and how electoral systems are chosen by political parties.

The question, of course, is what this factor is. In this article, I attempt to show that voters" choices can be endogenized to explain the changeability of electoral systems. This model will then be used to account for the persistence and demise of the single non-transferable vote electoral system (henceforth SNTV) that was used for decades in Japan and Taiwan.[1] In both cases, SNTV coexisted with one-party dominance for a period of time, but was abandoned *after* the dominant party failed to win a majority of seats and lost control of government. Intriguingly, some major proponents of electoral reform in both cases were large parties and politicians who came from these parties. These puzzles can be explained by the endogenous dynamics of electoral system change. SNTV is self-reinforcing if a dominant party can monopolize political power, maintain steady economic growth and deliver private benefits to a majority of voters. But the same process is also self-undermining, because economic development inevitably increases the anonymity of voters and it becomes difficult

---

[1]   Other than Japan and Taiwan, SNTV has also been used, for shorter periods of time, in South Korea, Jordan, Vanuatu and Afghanistan at the national level.

for the dominant party to garner votes in this way. Strong dissatisfaction with SNTV led to a push for a change of party system, which made it possible for some politicians and political parties to profit by adopting a new electoral system.

The next section gives a detailed description of the theory of endogenous institutional change and how it can be applied to study the change in SNTV. Focusing on the variation in voters" choices and the party system they induce, the subsequent three sections discuss the relationship between SNTV and one-party dominance, why multipartism gradually evolved under SNTV and how SNTV was abandoned in multiparty bargaining. The concluding section extends the same theory to other electoral systems and explains why the endogenous change in majoritarian and PR systems, although possible, is much less likely to take place (Katz, 2005).

II.　A Model of the Endogenous Change in SNTV

It is tempting to use the same set of variables to explain the persistence of and change in an institution. When analysing the consequences of an institution, causes of institutional change are usually seen as parameters—factors assumed to be constant to describe a particular institutional environment. By contrast, theories of institutional change tend to take a historical perspective and study the evolution of an institution over time (Hall and Taylor, 1996; Thelen, 1999) rather than the persistence of the institution. To integrate the two approaches, we need to endogenize parameters as variables in a theoretical model.[2] A parameter that can be endogenized must have some variance so that it can be treated as a variable; to be meaningful, the endogenized variable should be correlated with other variables in the model, inparticular those related to the institution itself. When these conditions are met, the functioning of an institution can change the endogenized parameters, which will in turn affect the stability of the institution.[3]

---

[2]　Greif and Laitin (2004) call these parameters "quasi-parameters".

[3]　It is theoretically and empirically important to solve the endogeneity problem before constructing a model of institutional change. A theory of endogenous institutional change uses fewer variables to explain a wider range of phenomena. In statistics, the negligence of the endogeneity problem may lead to a correlation between independent variables and the error term.

For several reasons, a vital parameter that should be endogenized to explain the change in electoral systems is the choice voters make in the elections. First, a voter's choice is affected by the electoral system – this is in fact the basic assumption of Duverger's propositions. Second, at the aggregate level, voters' choices (and the party system they entail) may vary under the same electoral system if we view Duverger's propositions as probabilistic statements. It is possible for majoritarian or proportional systems to generate party systems that are different from what Duverger hypothesized. For example, multipartism may arise if voters do not have complete information about candidates' odds of winning; multipartism may not exist if vote distribution among parties attending PR races is unequal. Third, politicians and political parties have an incentive to adopt an electoral system in which they perform best, and a key component of their utility function is the choices voters make. Voters' choices, which may generate self-reinforcing or self-undermining effects on the electoral system, are thus an essential variable in the study of the change in electoral systems.

A probabilistic interpretation of Duverger's propositions implies that the likelihood of majoritarian or proportional systems being self-reinforcing is high because under both systems most voters are likely to vote as Duverger suggested. Challengers of the majoritarian systems are rarely as strong as the incumbents, while proportional systems make it easy for anti-majoritarian parties to dominate the legislature. An interesting possibility is for a majority party to persist under a proportional system. If the majority party owes its majority status to this electoral system, the electoral system will be stable if voters do not alter their choice. When an endogenous force gradually reduces the vote-share of the majority party, however, the proportional nature of the electoral system creates a centrifugal tendency that can fracture this party, and the emerging multipartism can undermine the support for this electoral system.

SNTV is exactly this kind of electoral system. To see why, consider the features of this electoral system and how they affect voters' choices. By definition, SNTV is almost identical to the single-member simple plurality system—in both systems voters cast one ballot for a specific candidate, votes received by a candidate cannot be transferred to others, and seats are allocated by plurality rule. The only difference between the two systems is district magnitude—it is 1 in single-member simple plurality rule and usually greater than 1 in SNTV. However, this small difference is large enough to make single-member simple plurality a typical example of a majoritarian electoral system and SNTV a proportional system (Lijphart, Pintor, and Sone, 1986). With multiple winners to be elected, the threshold of exclusion in SNTV decreases as the district magnitude increases. Under SNTV, since voters can cast only one non-transferable vote for a specific candidate, the candidates need only a small percentage of the votes to be elected, but candidates nominated by the same party tend to compete with each other to garner the votes of the party's loyal supporters. To win, a candidate's best strategy is thus to provide private benefits to a specific group of voters and reinforce this base of support through personal connections.[4]

This incentive structure increases the difficulty of predicting the kind of party system that SNTV is most likely to entail. Although Reed (1990) has shown that, according to Duverger's law, the effective number of candidates competing under SNTV tends to be district magnitude plus 1, the question of how many parties these candidates represent remains unanswered. Two possibilities exist. On the one hand, the low winning threshold of SNTV favours the representation of small parties. On the other hand, the importance of securing personal votes gives some candidates an incentive to assemble a dominant party that monopolizes political power. To figure out which party system is most likely to result from SNTV, consider this problem as an evolutionary competition between two types of party-builder. First, when no politician has the resources to form a dominant party in charge of producing and delivering private benefits, the most likely outcome is a multiparty system characterized by intense inter-party competition. Now suppose economic development allows some politicians to assemble a majority party commissioned to produce and deliver private goods to the majority of voters. A dominant party formed in this way enjoys tremendous advantages over its opponents because it can help its candidates consolidate their personal votes while the other parties are suffering from centrifugal competition. It should be noted that two conditions are necessary for a dominant-party system to maintain its competitiveness: first, the economy must be developed to such a degree that enough surplus can be turned into private goods; and, second, the supporters of the dominant party must be recognizable so that the party can evenly distribute the benefits among its supporters and prevent its candidates from engaging in a fratricidal battle. When these conditions are satisfied, the dominant party will have a strong incentive to keep SNTV intact. Thus, a dominant party capable of producing and providing private benefits to a majority of voters is endogenized to make SNTV self-reinforcing.

---

[4] For the incentive to cultivate a personal vote under different electoral systems, see Carey and Shugart (1995). According to these authors, SNTV is the system where candidates have the strongest incentive to cultivate personal votes. Grofman (2005) also finds SNTV one of the most candidate-centred electoral systems.

However, the same process will gradually reduce the political support for the dominant party. Economic growth tends to increase the mobility and anonymity of the population, both of which weaken the ability of the ruling party to recognize who benefits from the private goods. Meanwhile, urbanization usually follows economic growth, and urban dwellers not only shoulder a heavy financial burden to furnish private goods but are also sensitive to corruption scandals involving the ruling party. As a result, the longer the dominant party rules, the harder it is for this party to increase its vote-share by distributing private goods. The proportional nature of SNTV encourages some voters to shift their support to parties that challenge the legitimacy of one-party dominance. Eventually, the ruling party will no longer be able to win a majority of seats and the party system will change from one-party dominance to multipartism. The declining electoral strength of the formerly dominant party gives its leaders an incentive to reduce the proportionality of the electoral system so that the party's seat-share can be increased. At the moment of electoral reform, leaders of the dominant party and critics of one-party dominance are, for different reasons, both interested in changing the electoral system, and the emerging multipartism gives them a chance to form reform coalitions.

An important question is whether the endogenized party system can both reinforce and undermine the electoral system. With some reasonable assumptions, we can show that a dominant-party system reinforces SNTV for a period of time and then starts undermining it. Consider the probability of a randomly selected voter voting for the dominant party. His decision is determined by how much he expects to gain from the private goods provided by the dominant party and the cost he has to shoulder. Designate $B > 0$ as the average value of the benefit the dominant party prepares for each of its supporters, $p > 0$ the probability of this voter receiving this benefit, and kB ($k \in [0, 1]$) the average cost to be shouldered by each voter. Assume B and p to be functions of time, denoted as t, and k a constant. The probability of a randomly selected voter voting for the dominant party is thus $V(t) = p(t)B(t) - kB(t)$.

The shape of this function is determined by the right-hand-side variables. If the dominant party is able to keep the economy growing, B is expanding over time with a decreasing growth rate, thus $B'(t) > 0$ and $B''(t) < 0$. The urbanization accompanying the economic growth gradually increases the difficulty for the dominant party to identify a randomly chosen voter, thus $p'(t) < 0$. As a probability, $p(t)$ may look like a logistic function with $p'(t) < 0$ and $p''(t)$ changing over time. It can easily be shown that, given these assumptions, $V(t)$ is most likely a concave function that increases to its maximum and then starts decreasing. The dominant party may lose the majority of votes after $V(t)$ becomes smaller than 0.5.[5]

This model explains why SNTV, regarded by many as an undesirable system, could persist for a considerable period of time before it is abandoned. According to Shugart (2001: 38), SNTV is an "extreme" electoral system in the intra-party dimension. This system is highly candidate-centred, encourages factionalism rather than policy debate among parties and nurtures money politics at the price of government deficit. Highly unpopular, these outcomes created a strong demand for reform. Some reformers wished to replace SNTV with an alternative system that enhances political responsibility and the efficiency of decision-making, while some others were genuinely devoted to sweep away corruption, and some politicians feared that blocking the reform would endanger their political careers. These "act-contingent" considerations (Reed and Thies, 2001: 153) played critical roles when SNTV was about to be changed, yet dissatisfaction with the electoral system may not be sufficient to fulfil the reform unless the reformers can deprive the ruling party of its majority status. As implied by the model, electoral reform is possible only when the dominant party is no longer able to win majority support by providing pork and private benefits to its supporters. The dominant party was able to achieve this goal exactly because the consequences of SNTV were regarded by the critics as undesirable. By endogenizing party system (as a result of voters' choices) in this way, we explain why SNTV could persist for decades despite the strong criticisms it incurs over time, and why some reformers come from the party to be reformed.

The following analysis examines how the endogenous change in SNTV unfolds in reality. In the next section I study the relationship between one-party dominance and SNTV in Japan and Taiwan, the only two countries that used this system to select their national lawmakers for a considerable period of time, and examine how the outcomes of this electoral system affect the electoral fortunes of the dominant parties. The subsequent sections address how the formerly dominant parties manipulated the agenda in multiparty bargaining and introduced majoritarian-leaning mixed-member systems.

---

[5] Differentiating V to t, we have $V'(t) = p'(t)B(t) + p(t)B'(t)$, so the second derivative of V to t is $V''(t) = p(t)B''(t) + 2p'(t)B'(t) + p''(t)B(t)$. Since $p(t)B''(t) < 0$, $2p'(t)B'(t) < 0$, $B(t) > 0$, and $p''(t)$ is very unlikely to be a large positive number, $V''(t)$ is most likely negative. If so, $V(t)$ is a concave function that reaches its maximum when $p'(t)B(t) = p(t)B'(t)$.

III. SNTV and One-party Dominance

SNTV was used longest in Japan, even though the origin of this electoral system may lie somewhere else.[6] The electoral system in modern Japan experienced several changes, but SNTV—including the so-called large district system—was used most of the time since the nation began to hold elections in the 1890s.[7] Between 1902 and 1993, 33 out of 34 House of Representatives (Lower House) general elections used SNTV.[8] It is believed that SNTV factionalized Japan's political parties (Ramseyer and Rosenbluth, 1997: 10-12), which helped strengthen the capability of the country's developmental state.

Taiwan began to use SNTV in the local elections of 1936, when the island was under Japanese occupation. Most likely, the colonial government introduced this system because it used in Japan at the same time. The Kuomintang (KMT) inherited the same system when it immigrated to Taiwan after the Japanese left. After that, SNTV became the principal electoral system used in Taiwan's legislative elections. Although Taiwan's partial re-election of national legislatures did not begin until 1969, and it took another two decades for popularly elected delegates to dominate national legislative bodies, the Taiwanese people are familiar with SNTV—in fact, they have little experience with other electoral formulas. Five general elections of the Legislative Yuan (the parliament) took place under SNTV between the first complete re-election of 1992 and the abolishment of this system in 2005.[9]

The history of SNTV in Japan and Taiwan reveals several common features. To begin with, the electoral histories of these two countries suggest that SNTV does not necessarily coexist with one-party dominance. In Japan, four Lower House elections were held under

---

[6] Soma (1986: 43) points out that the 1881 Brazilian Constitution already used a "median-sized electoral system", which is what SNTV is called in Japan.

[7] When Japan held its first Lower House election in 1890, the electoral system was a combination of 214 single-member seats and 43 SNTV seats elected under two-member districts. SNTV under a multi-member districts system was introduced in 1900 and was used until 1993. The only exception is the Lower House election of 1946, which used a limited vote. See Grofman et al. (1999: 5-8).

[8] Including the elections of 1920 and 1924, when the district magnitudes were temporarily reduced to one to three members.

[9] Before SNTV was changed, Taiwan's status quo system was actually a mixed one: 176 seats were elected under SNTV, and the other 49 were distributed by PR. Since the PR seats were allocated by the parties' SNTV vote-shares, most people considered the system to be SNTV.

SNTV between 1947 and 1955 (the year when the LDP was established), and each of them saw the fragmentation of the conservative and the leftist camps. Taiwan's authoritarian regime owed more to the Cold War than to its electoral system. Nevertheless, SNTV does help reinforce a dominant-party system when the following conditions are satisfied: a sustainable economic growth that allows the ruling party to allocate resources in a suboptimal way, the capacity for the ruling party to identify who the beneficiaries of their private benefits are, and a conservative but practical platform that prevents ideological dispute from splitting the ruling party apart. Japan and Taiwan both satisfy these conditions.

In both countries, the birth of the dominant party was hastened by the Cold War. The United States, as the leader of the capitalist camp, pressured political elites in these countries to boost their economies so that the seed of communism could be extinguished. In response, the US offered not only a huge number of orders for goods to be produced by the East Asian countries, but also a wide market for these goods. It is thus not coincidental that these East Asian countries both witnessed statist developmentalism. Through the help of their electoral systems, the governing parties were able to penetrate rural areas and incorporate local elites by their ability to provide private goods and to coordinate intra-party competition. Also thanks to SNTV, the economic planners of these countries were able to make long-term plans because most elected politicians would rather spend time serving their local constituents than debating with policymakers.

The dominant party does not need to have a coherent ideology, but must be capable of allocating resources in such a way that its members can consolidate their personal votes. To achieve this goal, the party provides its legislators with favours that benefit a particular set of voters. These private benefits include government-funded pork-barrel projects, legislation or government policies favourable to special interest groups, extra-legal lobbies, and so on. In return, legislators receive from these constituents handsome financial contributions, which are vital to their electoral success. When the election comes, the dominant party nominates the optimal number of candidates and coordinates competition among its nominees, while the beneficiaries of private goods garner votes for their legislative agents.[10] Thus, SNTV gives

---

[10] To coordinate among its nominees, this party must ensure that its votes are allocated evenly so that the party's seat-share can be maximized. For the coordination function of political parties in elections, see Cox (1997: 242-244).

the dominant party and their supporters incentives to establish a reciprocal relationship. In the eyes of critics, this is a clientelist relationship that encourages corruption.

As explained above, the capacity for the ruling party to maintain a particularistic connection with its supporters declines with socio-economic changes, which in turn undermine the political support for SNTV. While votes generated by private goods decline with economic growth and the accompanying urbanization, the number of voters who are sure to shoulder the financial burden of one-party dominance does not decrease. The proportional nature of SNTV encourages the disgruntled voters to shift their support to the challengers of one-party dominance and its unwanted consequences. As displayed in Figures 4.1 and 4.2, the two dominant parties are indeed suffering from a long-term decline of vote-share and seat-share despite an upswing for a short period of time.[11]

If the misfortune of the dominant party comes from its declining capacity in resource allocation, the lost votes are more likely to be taken over by new parties rather than old opposition parties—in the latter case, the shift of support involves ideological conversion and is thus quite costly. Since urbanization increases the mobility and anonymity of voters, it is very likely that some new parties are organized by urban-based politicians protesting the corruption of the dominant party, and that some of their leaders are renegades from the ruling party. It turns out that, in both Japan and Taiwan, the declining seat-share of the ruling party was contributed to mainly by intra-party split, and the division was associated with the nature of the constituents the politicians represent.

In Japan, the New Liberal Club (NLC) was founded in 1976 by LDP mavericks discontent with the scandal-embroiled LDP and the failure of the LDP to address the needs of urban voters. Most likely, the supporters of the NLC were predominantly urban conservatives who were disappointed with the LDP's corruption. As shown by Tanaka (2005: 112), the vote-share of the NLC in the 1976 House of Representatives election increased with the degree of urbanization of the electoral district, which is in direct contrast to the LDP's pattern.[12]

---

[11] Even after considering the seat bonuses received by large parties, SNTV is still fairly proportional. For the seat bonuses of the LDP and the KMT, see Cox and Niou (1994).

[12] Although the NLC was formed in protest against the corruption under the LDP's governance, it behaved more like a faction within the LDP than a fully fledged party. For this reason, the LDP still managed to maintain its status as the governing party even though it did not hold the majority of seats between 1976 and 1986.

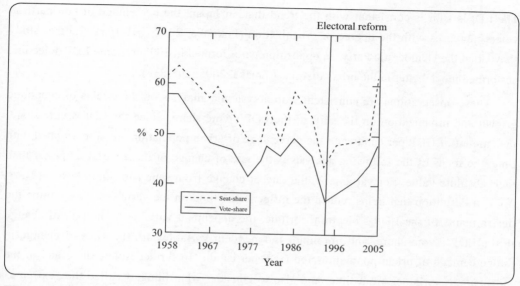

Figure 4.1 The LDP's Vote-shares and Seat-shares

Data source: 1955-1993, Ishikawa (1995); 1996-2005, Ministry of Internal Affairs and Communications
(*sōmushō*).

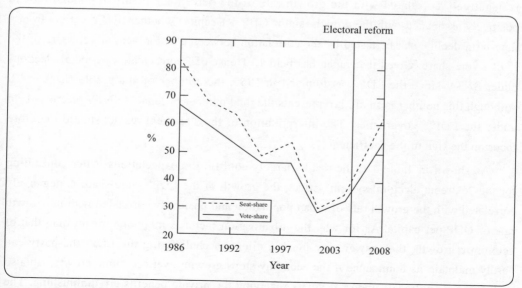

Figure 4.2 The KMT's Vote-shares and Seat-shares

Source: The Central Election Commissions (Zhongyang xuanju weiyuanhui).

The LDP's split is consistent with the trend that, in Japan, the percentage of non-partisan voters increases with the degree of urbanization (Fukuoka, 2001: 101-103). Another study shows that the Democratic Party, an opposition party formed in 1998 by some LDP defectors, performed much better in the urban districts (Tanaka, 2005: 208-238).

These observations are consistent with a systemic analysis on the effects of economic growth and urbanization on the shift of the LDP's vote-share. Since the LDP's vote-share, the amount of GDP per capita and the percentage of urban population are all correlated with time, the focus of the following analysis is the rate of change of these variables rather than their absolute value. For variable X, the rate of change from time t to time $t + 1$ is $(X_{t+1} - X_t)/X_t$, a definition that helps reduce the influence of time on the variables. To examine the determinants of the LDP's electoral fortune, the dependent variable is the rate of change in the LDP's vote-share, and the major independent variables are the rates of change in the percentage of urban population and GDP per capita. To further isolate the effect of the independent variables from time, and also to consider what Shugart called the "extreme" electoral system factor, the model uses election year as another independent variable.

If the electoral performance of the LDP is indeed affected by economic growth and urbanization, the expected findings should be that the increase of the LDP's vote-share is negatively correlated with the growth rate of the percentage of urban population and positively associated with the growth rate of GDP per capita. Whether SNTV suffers from a long-term decline can be tested by the correlation between election year and the rise of the LDP's vote-share. Given that Japan has held 13 House of Representatives general elections under SNTV since the LDP was founded in 1955, the number of analysable cases is 12. Although this number is small, it represents the total number of Japan's SNTV elections held under the LDP's governance. The interpretation of the statistical results should therefore focus on the sign of the coefficient.

As shown in Table 4.1, the results largely confirm the expectations. After controlling for the "extreme electoral system" effect, the growth of the LDP's vote-share is negatively correlated with the growth rate of urban population and positively correlated with the growth rate of GDP per capita. As for why the urbanization factor is more significant than that of economic growth, the answer may lie in a dilemma challenging the LDP: the party can hardly maintain its dominance if the economy stops growing, yet economic growth can also undermine its political support if voters receiving the private benefits are diminishing. The key is to deliver the benefits to the voters when the economy is growing.[13] That may be why urbanization displays a greater impact.

Table 4.1 Determinants of the Shifts in the LDP's Vote-share

	Coefficients	Standard error	*p*-value
Constant	1383.434	646.314	0.065
Changes in urban population percentage between elections	-5.361	2.398	0.056
Changes in GDP per capita between elections	0.489	0.435	0.294
Election year	-0.695	0.325	0.065
Adjusted R^2	0.247		

Data: GDP per capita comes from the Center for International Comparisons at the University of Pennsylvania at: http://pwt.econ.upenn.edu; urban population comes from World Bank/HNPStats database at http://go.worldbank.org/N2N84RDV00 (populations of 1958 and 1959 are estimated by projecting the trend between 1955 and 1960).

Note: Number of observations = 12. The cases are all of Japan's House of Representatives elections where the shift of the LDP's vote-share can be calculated.

In Taiwan, five legislative elections were held under SNTV when the Legislative Yuan was open for total re-election. The degree of freedom of these cases is not enough for a multivariate analysis of the change in the KMT's vote-share, yet indicators can still be found to demonstrate the impact of urbanization on the party's declining electoral strength. Just like the LDP, the KMT's electoral misfortune can be attributed to the formation of splinter parties. In 1993, the New Party (NP) was founded by a group of KMT defectors. In a similar fashion, James Soong, a former KMT secretary-general who joined the 2000 presidential race as an independent candidate, assembled the People First Party (PFP) in 2000 after he

---

[13] When the growth rate of GDP per capita is dropped out, the *p*-value of the growth rate of urban population becomes 0.054, which is very close to what Table 4.1 displays. This shows the robustness of the urbanization factor.

lost the election.[14] As in Japan, supporters echoing these criticisms were more likely to live in the urban areas than in the countryside. For the KMT, it was difficult to compete with these splinter parties in places beyond the reach of its clientelist network. The evidence is the KMT's electoral performance in the urban districts: before the NP was founded, the KMT received 49.9% of the votes cast in Taiwan's metropolises in the 1992 election; in 2001 that percentage dropped to 23.5.[15] Between 1992 and 2004, the KMT's average vote-share was 35.3% in the metropolis districts and 43.5% in the other districts. With the progress of Taiwan's urbanization, therefore, the KMT gradually lost control of the Legislative Yuan.

The data presented above show that the demise of the dominant-party system is endogenous to SNTV—the longer these parties depend on the delivery of private benefits to garner votes, the smaller the number of voters who can receive these benefits, a trend continuing until the dominant party no longer holds a majority of seats. The moment when the formerly dominant party loses control of government is the best time for a new electoral system to be adopted. With the shift of government power, multipartism gives all political parties the opportunity to promote their own favourable electoral formula, making mixed-member systems the most likely outcome of compromise. The next two sections give detailed accounts of how SNTV was replaced by mixed-member majoritarian systems in Japan and Taiwan.

IV. New Preferences for Electoral Systems

When the party system under SNTV gradually shifts from one-party dominance to multipartism, parties of various sizes have to consider their electoral fortunes under different electoral systems. While small parties still find the low winning threshold of SNTV attractive, large parties—in particular the formerly dominant party—seek to increase their seat-share by adopting a less proportional system. The reshaped preferences of political parties give electoral reformers and the formerly dominant party the chance to realize their goals.

---

[14] For a study of the consequences of SNTV in Taiwan, see Moon (1997).

[15] The metropolis constituencies include the cities of Taipei, Kaohsiung and Taichung. To see Taiwan's electoral outcome, check the website of the Central Election Commission, http://www.cec.gov.tw/.

We begin by examining the attitudes of the dominant party towards electoral reform. Although electoral reformers tend to ascribe corruption to one-party dominance, the dominant parties had long responded to public criticism by proposing electoral reform. As early as 1956, just a year after the LDP was founded, Japan's Prime Minister Hatoyama Ichiro tried but failed to introduce plurality rule. After the scandal-marred Lower House election of 1960, the Diet established the first Electoral Reform Advisory Council. This Council, and the ones that followed, proposed electoral systems with low proportionality, including pure plurality or mixed systems that assign a high weight to single-member seats. Another prime minister who endeavoured to advocate a new electoral system was Tanaka Kakuei. Facing deteriorating LDP electoral performance, in 1973 Tanaka proposed changing the system into a mixture of single-member and PR, but the proposal was again rejected. Appeals for electoral reform rose again after the outbreak of the Recruit Cosmos scandal of 1989 and the Sagawa Kyubin scandal of 1992. Unlike the precedent cases, this time the LDP was losing its control of Japan's Diet, as indicated by the party's loss of its majority in the 1989 Upper House election. In 1993, the LDP failed to grab a majority of seats in the Lower House election after large numbers of its legislators defected and joined the new parties before the election. This proved to be a critical juncture in Japan's electoral reform.

Taiwan travelled down a very similar path. The KMT came up with a proposal for electoral reform in 1995, when the party almost lost its legislative majority but won all seats in districts where only one winner was to be elected. KMT Premier Lien Chan immediately proposed replacing SNTV with a majoritarian-leaning mixed system. The KMT made the same proposal in the National Development Conference, a non-official roundtable on constitutional reform held in December 1996, and since then has stuck to the same proposal. As in Japan, these majoritarian-leaning proposals were not adopted because they would reduce the odds of winning for many legislators, especially those in the KMT who depended on clientelist networks to win. Also similar to the LDP, the inability of the KMT to disengage from money politics gradually undermined the party's legitimacy. Eventually, the Legislative Yuan election of 2001 deprived the KMT of its majority status.

Interestingly, the collapse of one-party dominance turned out to be a critical moment of electoral reform. The success of the electoral reform and the content of the new system depend on the preferences of other parties. In general, a party's attitude towards electoral reform is affected by the share and concentration of its votes. A party prefers a majoritarian electoral system if it expects to receive a high vote-share in its strongholds; a party supports proportional systems if it is unlikely to be the top winner in most districts. The plurality party thus favours a majoritarian-leaning system because its candidates are most likely to rank highest in such a system. This logic certainly applies to the LDP and the KMT when they were dominant, yet intra-party resistance prevented them from adopting the majoritarian systems. The downfall of one-party dominance and the loss of political power cleared the obstacles for these two parties—now a majoritarian institution becomes their life-preserver, and party members who do not favour electoral reform have a harder time justifying their disagreement to the new electoral system.

The other parties are more reluctant to accept a majoritarian-leaning system unless they are able to be the top vote-getters in their constituencies. A good example is Japan's coalition government, which took political power from the LDP after the election of 1993. The coalition government was mandated by the Japanese voters to accomplish political reform, yet the constituent parties—including the Japan New Party (JNP), the Renewal Party (RP), the New Party Harbinger (NPH), the Clean Government Party (CGP) and some members of the Japan Socialist Party (JSP)—did not share a unified preference for electoral systems. Among these parties, the most enthusiastic proponents of a mixed-member majoritarian system were the JNP and the RP, and this attitude can be explained by the structure of their vote bases. Organized by politicians who dubbed themselves reformers, the RP and the JNP were highly popular when they were founded. Ozawa Ichiro, the leader of the RP, hoped a majoritarian electoral system could facilitate party turnover and strengthen political leadership. Meanwhile, many of his reformist allies were confident in their ability to win in single-member elections. This confidence was based on the fact that, in the general election of 1993, many candidates nominated by the JNP and RP were elected as the top vote-getters.

The same logic accounts for the attitude of Taiwan's political parties towards electoral systems. Accompanying the KMT's decline was not only the formation of its splinter parties but also the expansion of the Democratic Progressive Party (DPP), the KMT's major rival. The electoral preference of the DPP shifted with the party's varying electoral strengths. At the beginning, the DPP proposed a mixed-member proportional system at the National Development Conference. Then the DPP's nominee, Chen Shui-bian, won the presidential elections of 2000 and 2004, and the party also won many single-member races held at the county level. In March 2002, President Chen issued a report announcing that the electoral system should be changed to a mixed-member majoritarian system. The DPP then followed this formula until SNTV was abandoned in 2005. Unlike Japan, where the LDP has always been the majority party, Taiwan saw competition between the KMT and the DPP to become the largest party. In fact, equal strength makes it easier for these two parties to reach a consensus on electoral reform. The results of the Legislative Yuan elections held in 2001 and 2004 suggest that both parties could benefit from a majoritarian-leaning electoral system. The data from the 2001 election show that the winners in the DPP had a higher probability of ranking highest than those in the KMT and other parties. In 2004, the KMT and the DPP reversed their positions—the KMT had more candidates ranked highest than the DPP did, although both parties performed better than the other parties. Most likely, the difference between the KMT and the DPP in these two elections was caused by nomination error, a problem that would not take place in a majoritarian system.

Taiwan's minor parties are much less confident in their capability to nominate the top vote-getters, and thus advocate proportional systems such as the mixed-member proportional system or even modified SNTV. The PFP, even when reaching the apex of its strength, was still a small party holding no more than 21% of the legislative seats. The Taiwan Solidarity Union (TSU) had proposed halving the size of the Legislative Yuan rather than changing the electoral system. Given its small size and lack of popular politicians, the TSU had no reason to support a majoritarian-leaning system.

A notable feature of the new preference profile is that, in both Japan and Taiwan, the dominant party lost its seat-share steadily and gradually rather than suddenly, giving it the freedom and leverage to craft its preferred electoral system. The next section examines how the formerly dominant parties in Japan and Taiwan manipulated the electoral reform and schemed to create a majoritarian-leaning mixed system.

V. Multiparty Bargaining in Electoral Reform

The moment when the dominant party loses its governing status is the best time for electoral reform—the party has little to lose if discipline is to be enforced to adopt an electoral system that can increase the party's seat-share, and the longer it waits, the smaller its political influence. Yet the shift of political power creates another problem: when no party controls a majority of seats, what new electoral system is most likely to be adopted?

The answer depends on the complexity of the reform issues and the bargaining power of political parties. If electoral reform is more complicated than simply choosing an alternative system to replace SNTV, decision-making is intrinsically unstable.[16] Electoral reform, therefore, becomes a bargaining game among the political parties over multiple issues. In comparison with other parties, the formerly dominant parties (and parties of their size) enjoy greater bargaining power because they are large enough to veto decision-making. In Japan, the coalition government controlled a majority of seats only in the Lower House, while the LDP was able to boycott the reform bills in the Upper House; in Taiwan, the KMT and the DPP were both large enough to veto the three-quarters majority needed to adopt a new electoral system.

To be more specific, Japan's electoral reform is much more complicated than just whether or not to dump SNTV.[17] It was quite obvious that a majoritarian-leaning system would decrease the seat bonus of most parties. Parties promoting such a system must therefore combine the choice of electoral systems with some other issues that are attractive to small parties. In Japan, SNTV was considered to be a source of corruption, making it natural for agenda-manipulators to mingle the choice of new electoral systems with some anti-corruption measures. If these bills are to be voted on together, parties of different sizes can all find an issue position that makes them better off than the status quo. There are usually multiple alternatives to replace the status quo, compelling different coalitions to bargain over the possible alternatives.

Given the goal of the three major groups—the LDP, the coalition government and the leftist parties—and the seats they controlled, three coalitions were most likely. First, the new parties and the leftist parties could coalesce to wrest power from the LDP. The coalition government could bestow some portfolios to the socialist members, or cooperate with the latter to pass anti-corruption bills. The problem with this coalition was that the partners did not share a common position on the electoral system, the spotlight of Japan's reform. The second possibility was that the new parties could align with the LDP to change the electoral

---

[16] For a formal analysis of the instability of decision-making in a multidimensional issue space, see McKelvey (1976).

[17] For other accounts of Japan's electoral reform and its result, see Christensen (1994), Shiratori (1995) and Reed and Thies (2001).

system. The problem is how the former LDP members could justify their collaboration with the party they had defected from; collaborating with the LDP would also restrain the influence of the new parties. Lastly, the LDP and the old opposition parties could cooperate to prevent the new parties from becoming dominant.

The coalition government, mandated to test its credibility as a political reformer, became the initiator of electoral reform. In September 1993, the newly established coalition government prepared the following proposal: 1. in the Lower House election, each voter would cast two ballots; 2. 250 seats (of the Lower House) were to be elected in the single-member simple plurality districts and 250 in the PR districts; and 3. political donations were to be restricted. The LDP opposed this proposal and attempted to offer a better deal to some members in the government. In response, the government adjusted the number of the plurality and PR seats to 274 and 226 before the proposal was to be sent to the Diet. The House of Representatives passed the revised bills on 18 November 1993.

Japan's bicameralism gave the LDP the chance to exert its bargaining power.[18] Right after the House of Representatives passed the reform bills, the bills were rejected by the House of Councillors, and members of the LDP played crucial roles in the obstructive coalition. Facing a possible setback of the government's major campaign promise, Prime Minister Hosokawa held an emergency meeting with the LDP President on 28 January 1994. Finally, a deal with the following content was agreed upon: 1. each voter could cast two ballots; 2. 300 seats would be elected by the single-member simple plurality rule, in addition to 200 seats allocated in 11 PR blocks; 3. each year a politician would be allowed to accept a donation of 500,000 yen from one company for five years; and 4. public financing of party activities would be introduced. The two Houses recognized this agreement the next day. Compared with the government's original proposal, the adopted electoral system is much closer to what the LDP wanted.[19] The LDP clearly benefited from its bargaining power.

Like Japan, Taiwan's electoral reform involved several issues. Since most people

---

[18] In Japan, a bill is not passed if the House of Councillors rejects it, unless the House of Representatives passes the bill again by a two-thirds majority. This rule does not apply to the designation of prime minister or to the budget.

[19] This, however, was not the end of the story. On 30 June 1994, the LDP, the Japan Socialist Party and the NPH formed a new government and selected a left-wing socialist as the prime minister. Strange as it may seem, this is exactly what the above analysis predicted.

had little knowledge about the details of electoral systems, electoral reform in Taiwan was advocated by populist appeal—halving the size of the Legislative Yuan, a slogan responding to the widespread discontent with the legislators. Again, it was the political elite who linked the change of electoral system with the streamlining of the Legislative Yuan. This strategy also made a constitutional amendment a necessary step to accomplish electoral reform, because the size of the Legislative Yuan was stipulated in the constitution. According to the rules of constitutional amendment (before 2005), the Legislative Yuan had to pass a constitutional amendment proposal with the support of at least three-quarters of the lawmakers, followed by the approval of the popularly elected National Assembly. This rule made the KMT and the DPP the only two parties that could veto a reform proposal, for no other party held more than a quarter of the legislative seats.

The critical catalyst that put the issue of electoral reform on Taiwan's political agenda was the presidential election of 2004. This was a competitive race, and crediting the failure of institutional reform to the rival was a useful strategy to prevent undecided voters from voting for the other side. This momentum was captured by the proponents of Taiwan's legislative reform, who promised to penalize the defenders of the status quo electoral system. Fear of retaliation explains why the Legislative Yuan endorsed the electoral reform right before the legislative election of 2004.

Recognizing that electoral reform is unavoidable, Taiwan's political parties struggled to control the reform agenda to ensure that the outcome satisfied their demands. While the KMT and the DPP hoped to institute a majoritarian-leaning system, the TSU was only interested in reducing the size of the Legislative Yuan. The PFP faced uncertainty: some of its members performed quite well, but the party as a whole was small and did not have concentrated vote bases. Due to these concerns, small parties wanted constitutional amendments to be put to the vote separately so that they would be in a better position to reject the new electoral system. Since the DPP and the KMT were both interested in adopting a majoritarian system, they collaborated to set a rule that all these constitutional amendments must be voted on as a package. On 23 August 2004, the Legislative Yuan proposed constitutional amendments to halve the size of the Legislative Yuan and define a mixed-member majoritarian system. Out of the 113 members of the Legislative Yuan, 73 seats would be elected in local constituencies by the single-member simple plurality rule, six seats would be chosen by aboriginal districts and the remaining 34 seats would be allocated by closed-list PR. Each voter would cast two ballots, one for a candidate and one for a party. The voters then elected the delegates of the National Assembly on 14 May 2005. With the KMT and the DPP winning 83.8% of the seats, the National Assembly approved the constitutional amendments on 7 June 2005. Since the constitutional amendments were passed as a package, minor parties still gained something, such as halving the size of the Legislative Yuan and the very high threshold for constitutional amendment that the anti-Taiwan independence parties desired.

That is how SNTV became history in Japan and Taiwan. The post-reform parliamentary elections in both countries clearly indicate that large parties were the winners in the electoral reform. As illustrated in Figure 4.1, the seat-share of the LDP under Japan's new mixed-member majoritarian system not only grew rapidly but was also significantly higher than its vote-share. Most stunning is the 2005 election of the House of Representatives, where the LDP gained 47.77% of the district votes and 38.18% of the PR votes but won 67.67% of the seats. Taiwan is a similar situation. In the Legislative Yuan election of 2008, when the mixed-member system was first used, the KMT grabbed 71.68% of the seats by obtaining 53.50% of the district (and aboriginal) votes and 51.23% of the PR votes.

VI. Conclusions

Despite their differences in many dimensions, Japan and Taiwan share a very similar experience in the change of their electoral systems. For decades, both countries had used SNTV and were governed by a dominant party relying on allocating private benefits to consolidate their legitimacy. Eventually, both countries replaced SNTV with a majoritarian-leaning mixed-member system that helped the formerly dominant party regain their power. The purpose of this article is to explain the changeability of SNTV by examining its relationship with the party system.

In contrast with the studies that use SNTV to explain what happens under this electoral system, this article posits that the consequences of SNTV—in particular voters' choices for parties—will in turn affect the stability of this electoral system. SNTV is self-reinforcing if it allows a dominant party to transfer the fruits of economic growth to the private benefits of its supporters, yet the more the dominant party depends on this strategy the more likely for the accompanied social change to undermine its support basis, hence the stability of SNTV.

When one-party dominance collapses, political parties are given the freedom to promote their favourite electoral systems by forming reform coalitions, but the gradualness of the decline of the dominant-party system gives the formerly dominant party the leverage to set the reform agenda. That is why the result of the electoral reform favours the formerly dominant party.

In this way, this article helps answer some theoretical questions. First, it explains why an "extreme" electoral system like SNTV can persist for decades: the stability of this electoral system is correlated with the capacity of a dominant party to deliver private benefits to the majority of voters, and this capacity varies with the outcomes of one-party dominance under SNTV. Second, it explains when the act-contingent considerations can precipitate the abandoning of SNTV: given the self-undermining forces inherent in SNTV, reformers are most likely to fulfil their goals when the change of party system gives them the chance to form winning coalitions.

By uncovering the endogenous dynamics of electoral system change, this article also sheds some light on the relationship between electoral systems and party systems. SNTV is peculiar in that it allows one-party dominance to persist, even though it also favours the representation of minor parties. The proportional nature of SNTV implies that, as soon as the dominant party is unable to satisfy the majority of voters, one-party dominance will be superseded by multipartism, followed by a reform of the electoral system. Voters' choices and the party system they created can be endogenized to explain why other electoral systems appear to be self-reinforcing. Under the majoritarian systems, voters are motivated to forsake the challengers of the status quo electoral system; under the proportional systems, parties attempting to reduce the proportionality of the electoral system often face the opposition of smaller parties. The prevalence of majoritarian or proportional systems around the world probably explains why the interactive relationship between electoral systems and party systems is rarely treated as a single issue.

第五章

The Consequences of Constitutional Systems on Party Systems[*]

I. Is the Mixed-Member Majoritarian System Creating a Two-Party System?

For the competitors of a legislative election, winning a seat is only the first step toward sharing political power. How powers are distributed depends on the constitutional arrangement of executive-legislative relations, but studies on electoral systems are largely legislative-centric. An executive-centric theory of electoral systems plays an important role in filling this gap. Japan and Taiwan are perfect cases—they traveled a similar path of electoral reform but are distinguishable by constitutional systems. The following analysis explains why these two cases are worth comparing.

The first reason is the *similarity* of Japan and Taiwan compared with the global pattern. From a comparative perspective, the Asian model deserves special attention. As pointed out by Reilly (2007a, 2007b), the Asian experience is characterized by a decrease in proportionality, while the trend in the rest of the world is just the opposite.[1] If an increase in proportionality results from the fragmentation of the party system, the best justification of the Asian model of electoral reform is the expectation of a more efficient and stable government. Indeed, the introduction of a majoritarian-leaning electoral system is likely to

---

* Reproduced from [Lin, Jih-wen. "The Consequences of Constitutional Systems on Party Systems." In *Mixed-Member Electoral Systems in Constitutional Context: Taiwan, Japan, and Beyond*, eds. Nathan F. Batto, Chi Huang, Alexander C. Tan, and Gary W. Cox. Ann Arbor: University of Michigan Press, pp. 52-72, 2016], with kind permission of University of Michigan Press.

[1] One should not equate the decrease in proportionality with the shift from proportional representation to a majoritarian system (see Reilly, 2007b: 1359). In Reilly's cases, Cambodia switched from closed-list PR to the closed-list PR with the highest average method, Indonesia changed from closed-list PR to open-list PR, the Philippines substituted plurality-block with MMM, and Thailand replaced block vote with MMM. Only in South Korea, Japan, and Taiwan was there a change from the single nontransferable vote (SNTV) to MMM.

improve government stability as it will reduce the number of parties (Duverger, 1964a; Rae, 1971; Lijphart and Grofman, 1984). Another effect of a majoritarian-leaning electoral system is that it facilitates power turnover when an election is competitive: when only one winner is to be elected, a party gains no seats at all if it falls one vote short of the winning party. By creating a larger seat swing, a majoritarian-leaning system makes it easier for the voters to hold the ruling party accountable. Within the Asian model, Japan and Taiwan are good cases to compare.[2] Both countries are in East Asia and are embedded in a political culture that emphasizes personal connections; both traveled down a similar path of electoral reform and saw a decrease in the number of parties.

The second reason is their difference in executive-legislative relations. As the dependent variable, small parties play a more important role in Japan than in Taiwan, and the effective number of parties in Taiwan is decreasing faster than it is in Japan (Jou, 2009). We thus have two cases of the "most similar system design" to compare. The question is how to link the party system to the constitutional system, the independent variable of this chapter.

As Huang, Kuo, and Stockton (2016) detail in chapter 1, small parties─those that ranked third or lower in legislative elections─have fared far better in Japan than in Taiwan. There are some differences in the Japanese and Taiwanese mixed-member majoritarian (MMM) systems, but Huang, Kuo, and Stockton conclude that these variations cannot fully account for the differences in the fates of small parties in the two systems.

This chapter argues that the differing constitutional systems, not the differing electoral systems, are the most important source of the contrasting fates of small parties. If the electoral system determines the winning threshold of each electoral district, the rule of portfolio allocation specified by the constitution affects the incentive for legislators elected in different constituencies to join a national political party. The major hypothesis of this chapter is that MMM does make it harder for weaker candidates to win in each district,

---

[2] The Republic of Korea (South Korea) also abandoned SNTV (two-member district) in 1988 and replaced it with MMM, under which the voters could cast only one ballot. (The Republic of Korea shifted to a two-ballot system in 2004). Unfortunately for this volume, South Korea's electoral reform took place at the same time that this country transitioned to democracy, making it difficult to untangle the effects of electoral reform and democratization. For details, please see Brady and Mo (1992) and Mo and Brady (1999). In addition to the three East Asian cases, Afghanistan, Vanuatu, and Jordan have also had experience with SNTV for their national elections.

but whether the winners across all districts are from two parties still depends on how the executive offices are distributed. Given Japan's parliamentary system, prime ministers are elected by the Diet. Legislators can thus bargain with the prime minister by threatening to defect from the ruling party—splinter parties are sometimes formed in these circumstances. In contrast, Taiwan's executive offices are allocated by the president without legislative participation, giving legislators elected in different districts a strong motivation to stay in the national parties. Another complication is the legislative process: while Taiwan has a unicameral legislature, the Diet of Japan includes the House of Representatives (HR) and the House of Councillors (HC), with the latter mandated to approve the policy bills proposed by the prime minister. It has been pointed out that bicameralism—especially using different formulas to elect the delegates of the two chambers—strengthens the leverage of small parties because intercameral agreement is needed to adopt a bill (Hammond and Miller, 1987; Riker, 1992; Brennan and Hamlin, 1992; Tsebelis and Money, 1997; Heller, 2001; Druckman and Thies, 2002). The influence of Taiwan's small parties on policy making is limited because its unicameral legislature does not give them the chance to reject government bills.

How the head of state, the head of government, and the legislature interact with each other in Taiwan and Japan is presented in Table 5.1. It is clear that the major difference between the two constitutional systems is the rule of portfolio allocation: Taiwan's premier and ministers are appointed by the president, the de facto supreme leader, without legislative participation; the Japanese prime minister is designated from among the members of the Diet by a resolution of the Diet before he appoints his cabinet ministers. Taiwan's small parties have little role to play in the unicameral legislature, whereas Japan's bicameralism gives large parties an incentive to include nonpivotal small parties as coalition partners so that the latter can help adopt the government bills in the upper house. How these constitutional systems are related to the number of parties will be discussed later.

In the next section, we will show how the role of political parties in portfolio allocation is defined by the constitutional system and how Riker's size principle can be used to derive hypotheses. Sections three and four will examine how party politics interact with the constitutional systems of Taiwan and Japan, and how small parties have different capacities in the allocation of executive positions. Section five concludes by addressing the general implications of this study and how the number of parties may be affected by constitutional designs.

Table 5.1 The Constitutional System in Taiwan and Japan

	Taiwan	Japan
Head of state	President: de facto leader	Emperor: symbolic head
Appointment of head of government	Premier is appointed by president without legislative consent; ministers are appointed by president at premier's recommendation.	Before appointing the cabinet ministers, prime minister is designated by the Diet with the HR playing the decisive role.
Legislature	Unicameralism. Legislative Yuan can pass vote of no confidence in premier and veto policy proposals.	Bicameralism. The HR can pass vote of no confidence in prime minister, HC can veto most policy proposals.

Source: Author's analysis of the constitutions of the two countries.

II. The Role of Political Parties in Portfolio Allocation in Different Constitutions

Political parties coordinate both in elections and in the distribution of executive offices (Shugart, 1995; Cox, 1997; Hicken, 2009). In elections, the electoral system is the key determinant of what a party can do. If an electoral system requires the candidates nominated by the same party to compete for the same set of voters, the party should nominate an optimal number of candidates; if a party nominates only one candidate, coordination should take place before the election starts. Thus, the shift from SNTV to MMM marks a great transformation in the electoral roles of parties. Even so, maximizing its presence in the legislature is just the first kind of coordination work a party has to undertake. Once elected, legislators have to think about how to make the best use of their influence over portfolio allocation, which is the real goal of many politicians. In democracies, portfolio allocation is an important way to make policy changes (Budge and Laver, 1986). Since the number of ministerial positions to be distributed is fixed, the "minimal winning coalition" principle holds: every member in the winning coalition should make itself pivotal, so that each can maximize its share of the portfolios, hence its influence over the policies to be implemented by the ministry (Riker, 1962). This principle implies that the size of the coalition and the parties in it should both be minimal because unnecessary members will reduce the share each can get.

The constitutional system defines what a minimal winning coalition is. The Japanese constitution makes every party a potential pivot. The highest executive power is held by the prime minister, who is designated by both chambers of the Diet—with the HR playing the decisive role—and then formally appointed by the emperor.[3] The power of Japan's small parties is enhanced by its bicameralism in two ways. First, it is easier for a small party to win a seat in the HC elections because the electoral system mixes 48 national PR seats with 73 SNTV seats. Second, Japan's bicameralism is almost symmetric because the HC can veto most bills proposed by the prime minister, which will in turn put the prime minister's leadership at stake. Small parties can thus exchange their legislative veto power for political resources. Nevertheless, Japanese prime ministers do not always want to invite small parties to join their cabinets because of a trade-off between policy making and portfolio allocation. The prime minister can compromise with the small parties without allocating any position to their members. Whether a small party wishes to join the cabinet also depends on how much the prime minister needs its support to pass legislation.

Taiwan's constitutional system arranges the allocation of ministerial positions differently. Taiwan's premier is appointed unilaterally by the popularly elected president, leaving no role for the political parties to play. According to the constitution, cabinet ministers are selected by the premier, but, in practice, they are handpicked by the president. Although the legislators can launch a censure motion against the premier by rallying majority support, such a move is quite unlikely because it will put the jobs of the legislators at risk. What the president has to keep in mind is whether the legislature is controlled by an opposition majority. If this is the case, the legislators may use their veto power to prevent government bills from being adopted.

Another concern is the electoral system. Under SNTV, major parties nominate multiple candidates in most districts, the legislators tend to deliver resources to a particular group of voters, and the parties are usually factionalized. Particularist distribution of government

---

[3]　Sometimes the ruling party has an effective majority when it is just a few seats away from holding the majority of seats and can cooperate with the independent legislators to pass bills. If the ruling parties are unable to create an effective majority, the typical solution is to form a coalition government controlling the majority of seats in the HR.

resources is prevalent in both MMM and SNTV, but the targets of the pork may differ. It is quite common for single-member district systems to encourage pork-barrel bills targeting the undecided voters in the competitive districts rather than just a particular set of constituents. Moreover, legislators elected under MMM are supposed to represent the whole constituency, giving them the incentive to choose policy stances different from those of the central government. A shift from SNTV to MMM thus decreases the incentives for internal factionalization. Nevertheless, there is a major difference between Taiwan and Japan. In Taiwan, the directly elected president creates more pressure for Taiwanese legislators to align their campaign appeals with a major national party, but Japanese legislators are freer to tailor their messages to the local district, perhaps even to the point of representing a third party.

We can now hypothesize how the partisan composition of the Taiwanese and Japanese cabinets is affected by their respective constitutional systems. First, Taiwan does not have a tradition of coalition government, and political parties have a limited influence on cabinet formation. This affects both big parties and small parties. Small parties should be shut out of the cabinet almost entirely. However, this does not mean that members of the president's party will monopolize all seats in the cabinet. The president can appoint ministers as he sees it, and he may choose to appoint a significant number of nonpartisan figures to the cabinet. Tavits (2008: 43) has argued that directly elected presidents have a preference to name nonpartisan ministers to demonstrate their status as the head of state.[4] The incentive to appoint nonpartisan ministers is particularly strong when the president is leading a minority party. Rather than opting for a single-party minority cabinet, which might cause gridlock, or a multiparty majority cabinet, which might weaken the president's leadership, the president may prefer to appoint nonpartisan ministers to depoliticize the cabinet and convey the image of the president as leader of the entire country. Critically, while nonpartisan ministers may help the president dampen opposition from other parties in the legislature or appeal to a wider segment of the electorate, they are not representatives of or responsible to opposition parties. Alternatively, if the primary threat to the president's power comes from factions within his own majority party, he may be more likely to emphasize his role as head of the party and prefer to appoint fewer nonpartisan ministers. The percentage of nonpartisan ministers can

---

[4]　There is also empirical evidence showing that presidential regimes are much more likely to appoint nonpartisan ministers than their parliamentary counterparts, with semipresidential regimes in between (Amorim Neto and Samuels, 2010: 14).

thus give clues to the influence of the president on cabinet formation.

In sum, there is no need to test the number of parties in Taiwan's cabinets, because ministers are predominantly from the president's party or nonpartisans.[5] Rather, nonpartisan ministers play a much more important role in highlighting the president's role in ministerial appointment. *Thus, we expect that, in Taiwan, the percentage of nonpartisan ministers is higher 1. in divided government than in unified government and 2. when MMM is the electoral system than when SNTV was used.*

Second, political parties in Japan should exercise a greater influence on cabinet formation than their Taiwanese counterparts, for the Constitution of Japan requires the prime ministers to be elected by members of the Diet. Since most cabinet ministers are concurrently legislators, we can examine how the number of parties in the cabinet can be explained by the key variables.[6] *The number of parties in the cabinet should increase when the cabinet is not in control of the upper house.* Further, if MMM accelerates the turnover of parties in power, prime ministers should have less confidence that they will be able to maintain a majority in the HC. Thus, *we expect the number of parties in the cabinet to rise after electoral reform.* The logic behind these hypotheses is that the bargaining power of small parties is increased if the probability of the prime minister encountering bicameral deadlock becomes higher. The second test operationalizes the prime minister's influence in cabinet formation in a slightly different way. *We expect the percentage of ministers from the prime minister's party to decrease when the party of most cabinet members does not hold the upper house majority or when MMM is used,* because these factors will weaken the leadership of the prime minister for the reasons already discussed.

The difference in constitutional systems permeates other political arenas. If legislators play different roles in the allocation of executive offices, the voters' expectations of them should also diverge. Taiwan's legislative elections have become highly presidentialized and focus on the debate over national identity issues between the two largest parties.

---

[5] The number of ministers from parties allied with the president is negligibly small. Additionally, Taiwan's ministers cannot concurrently hold a legislative position, which gives the president a strong justification to handpick the nonpartisans.

[6] Coalition government is a normal practice in a parliamentary system. Although some cabinet positions are kept for nonpartisan ministers, most ministers are either from the prime minister's party or the parties of the coalition partners.

MMM reduces Taiwan's effective number of parties to less than two because the number of presidential candidates is usually two. Japan lacks a centralized national leader, and legislative candidates can compete on constituency issues, some of which may be related to the national division among the political parties while others are local in focus. Since the constituency cleavage plays an important role in Japan, we expect the effective number of parties to be higher than in Taiwan.

What we see above are theoretical models with rich empirical implications. In the next two sections, we will demonstrate how the constitutional system affects the portfolio allocation in the two cases, and therefore the number and power of small parties. We will discuss Taiwan first because the evolution of its party system shows clearly the power of the constitutional system despite the intervening variables that a young democracy usually faces.

III. How Taiwan's Unicameral Semipresidential System Intermediates the Impact of Electoral Reform

To validate the claim that MMM has reduced the number of parties but variations in the constitutional system give political parties different roles to play, this section will describe how Taiwan's unicameral semipresidential constitution has strongly depressed the influence of political parties on cabinet formation and given the president a great deal of freedom to fill executive offices.

Taiwan's constitution is parliamentary by design but highly presidential in practice.[7] The seven constitutional reforms enacted since 1991 endeavored to make the president's de facto powers constitutional by stipulating a popularly elected president; they further enhanced the president's power by removing the Legislative Yuan's power to confirm the presidential appointment of the premier. The Legislative Yuan can pass a vote of no confidence in the

---

[7]　The president's role in the original constitution is close to a symbolic head of state. The highest administrative organ, the Executive Yuan, is headed by the premier rather than the president (Art. 53). The presidential appointment of the premier should have the consent of the Legislative Yuan (Art. 55); a premier failing to veto a legislative resolution "shall either accede to the Legislative Yuan's view or tender his (her) resignation" (Art. 57). The president appoints the cabinet ministers on the recommendation of the premier and cannot attend the weekly meetings of the Executive Yuan.

premier but the premier cannot initiate a snap election (Lin, 2011c).[8] Before 2000, executive congruency gave the president the power to dismiss the premier, making Taiwan a president-parliamentary regime (Shugart and Carey, 1992; Shugart, 2005). The president dominated the appointment of the premier even when the government was divided (2000-2008). Based on this practice, no popularly elected president has consulted the legislature when appointing a premier or his cabinet ministers.

By this design, the president appoints and dismisses the cabinet ministers with the latter's accountability to the legislature in mind. The ways in which the legislators hold the cabinet accountable include a vote of no confidence—which is rarely considered—and the blocking of executive proposals—which is often applied. When explaining the president's decision in portfolio allocation, MMM is also an important factor because the majorities represented by the president in the whole nation and the legislators in the MMM districts may be incongruent. To ease the pressure from MMM and opposition parties, *we expect the percentage of nonpartisan ministers in the cabinet to follow this order: MMM plus divided government > SNTV plus divided government > MMM plus unified government > SNTV plus unified government.* We do not make the number of parties in the cabinet as a variable because the cabinets are predominantly composed of the president's party and nonpartisans rather than the nonpresidential parties.

Given the limited influence of Taiwan's small parties on cabinet formation, we will directly examine how the aforementioned variables affect the president's role in portfolio allocation. Table 5.2 shows how much the president dominates cabinet formation by the percentage of ministers from his party.[9] Counting the change in electoral systems and the president's majority status, the data include several possible divisions, with the "MMM plus divided government" type thus far absent. Since the percentage is a continuous variable and the independent variables are categorical, we run a One-Way ANOVA by the following groupings: 1. whether a president leads a unified or a divided government, 2. electoral

---

[8]　These designs did not fully realize the proclaimed goals, as the high threshold of constitutional amendments required cross-partisan collaborations.

[9]　Due to Taiwan's authoritarian history, many people formally joined the Nationalist Party (Kuomintang, KMT) but later allowed their membership to lapse. We thus define party membership by one's active position in the party hierarchy. Party members are those who had a seat in the central committee, held a paid job in the party bureaucracy, or represented the party in an election.

Table 5.2 Partisan Profile of Taiwan's Cabinet Ministers

	Party	Premier	Premier party	Term begins	Ministers from president's party	Whether largest party controls majority (= 1)
Lee Teng-hui	KMT	Hau Pei-tsun	KMT	6/1/1990	95.24%	KMT = 1
Lee Teng-hui	KMT	Lien Chan	KMT	2/27/1993	98.31%	KMT = 1
Lee Teng-hui	KMT	Siew Wan-chang	KMT	9/7/1997	96.30%	KMT = 1
Chen Shui-bian	DPP	Tang Fei	KMT	5/20/2000	24.32%	KMT = 1
Chen Shui-bian	DPP	Chang Chun-hsiung	DPP	10/6/2000	26.47%	KMT = 1
Chen Shui-bian	DPP	Yu Shyi-kun	DPP	2/1/2002	44.74%	DPP = 0
Chen Shui-bian	DPP	Hsieh Chang-ting	DPP	2/1/2005	62.16%	DPP = 0
Chen Shui-bian	DPP	Su Tseng-chang	DPP	1/25/2006	55.56%	DPP = 0
Chen Shui-bian	DPP	Chang Chun-hsiung	DPP	5/21/2007	51.43%	DPP = 0
Ma Ying-jeou	KMT	Liu Chao-shiuan	KMT	5/20/2008	66.67%	KMT = 1
Ma Ying-jeou	KMT	Wu Den-yih	KMT	9/10/2009	47.22%	KMT = 1
Ma Ying-jeou	KMT	Chen Chun	KMT	2/6/2012	34.21%	KMT = 1

Source: Yu and Zhu [余克禮、朱顯龍] (2001), Guoshiguan Zhengjiaochu [國史館] (1994, 1998, 2001), Liu [劉國銘] (2005), Liu [劉維開] (1994), and the *United Daily News* online database (http://udndata.com/library/), accessed March 19, 2012.

Note: The number of ministers is person-time. Whether a minister comes from a particular party depends on whether he/she is (was) a member of the central committee or receives (received) paid jobs from the party, or represented the party in the elections.

systems, and 3. the three presidential periods. For 3, a reasonable hypothesis is that President Lee Teng-hui had the highest percentage of ministers from his own party because he led a unified government with legislators elected under SNTV; the lowest percentage should be found under the Chen Shui-bian presidency, as Chen never assembled a majority cabinet, especially when the Kuomintang (KMT) dominated the Legislative Yuan. Standing in between, Ma Ying-jeou's strategy represents the presidentialized unified government that MMM produces.

The results in Table 5.3 validate the hypotheses. Overall, the average percentage of ministers from the president's party is 58.55. If the percentages of ministers from the president's party are compared according to whether the president controls the legislative majority or not, the "yes" and the "no" groups have an average of 72.3% and 44.1%, respectively. It is evident that divided government forced President Chen to appoint more nonpartisan ministers to water down the cabinet's DPP makeup so as to decrease the likelihood of his policies being rejected by the Legislative Yuan. If the data are compared according to the electoral system, the "SNTV" group has 61.6% and the "MMM" group has 49.4% on average. Finally, if the average percentages for the three presidents are compared, the "Lee period" is 96.6, the "Chen period" is 44.1, and the "Ma period" is 49.4. All One-Way ANOVA tests show the expected sign, and the differences between the three presidents are not only statistically significant but also larger than the other two comparisons.[10]

The cabinets headed by premiers appointed by President Ma are a salient illustration of the dominance of the president—as the head of state rather than the chairperson of the ruling party—in cabinet formation. Ma's KMT has held a clear majority of legislative seats throughout his two terms in office. However, Table 5.3 shows that the percentage of ministers from the president's party, already low in 2008 compared to those of President Lee, has

---

[10] The president's approval rate can be another factor affecting the appointment of ministers. Presidents with high popularity are less likely to face obstruction from the legislature (Neustadt, 1990; Kernell, 1997). Both President Chen and President Ma saw severe declines in their approval ratings over their time in office. The percentage of nonpartisan ministers has steadily increased under Ma as his ratings declined. Chen appointed a significant number of nonpartisan members after he was elected in 2000 to ease worries about Cross-Strait stability. As these fears eased, the number of nonpartisan members increased, but it decreased during his second term as his approval ratings dropped. Relative to his two successors, President Lee enjoyed much higher approval ratings, and the percentage of nonpartisan ministers in his cabinets was much lower.

further decreased in the intervening years.[11] Ma's preference for appointing nonpartisan scholars and civil servants as ministers reflects his ambivalence regarding the partisan composition of the cabinet. Given the KMT's dominance in the legislature, Ma must have minimized the role of political parties when forming his cabinets.

Table 5.3 One-Way ANOVA for Partisan Compositions of Taiwan's Cabinets

		Mean	Variance	Sig.
Compared by presidential majority	No	0.441	0.024	0.052
	Yes	0.723	0.078	
Compared by SNTV or MMM	SNTV	0.616	0.084	0.516
	MMM	0.494	0.027	
Compared by presidents	Lee	0.966	0.000	
	Chen	0.441	0.024	0.002
	Ma	0.494	0.027	

Source: Author's calculation.

The strong influence of the president on portfolio allocation extends to elections. Two effects can be observed. The first is that Taiwan's presidential elections may have a contamination effect on legislative elections.[12] If the two elections are held concurrently or within a short period of time, voters may use information from the highly prominent presidential race to make their decisions in the less salient legislative race. Since the presidential race encourages supporters of small parties to vote strategically, they may apply the same logic to legislative elections regardless of the strength of the small party's local candidate. Presidential elections thus intensify the Duvergerian obstacles[13] facing small

---

[11] Premier Jiang Yi-Huah (2013-), the successor of Chen Chun, did not renew his KMT membership until he was about to be appointed premier. Very few of Jiang's ministers are active KMT members.

[12] Batto, Kim, and Matukhno (2016) make a similar argument about how presidential races contaminate legislative elections.

[13] For detailed examinations of Duvergerian logic, see Huang, Kuo, and Stockton (2016), Wang, Lin, and Hsiao (2016).

parties in district elections. The second effect concerns cleavage structure. Campaigning dominated by the presidential race will restrain the capacity of small parties to articulate their favorite issues. In Taiwan, small parties are forced to stand with a particular camp first of all and then distance themselves from that camp's leading presidential candidate. In the legislative election of 2012, James Soong, the leader of the People First Party, was the only presidential candidate who claimed that Taiwan should eventually be reunified with the mainland. The Taiwan Solidarity Union, at the opposite extreme, was quite insistent that Taiwan's independent sovereignty should not be infringed upon. So the two small parties could be clearly identified by their positions on national identity. That helped these small parties to consolidate their PR seats, but the overall effect was limited. What MMM does is to sharply decrease the influence of the small parties when the campaign issues are set by the large parties.

IV. How Japan's Bicameral Parliamentary System Intermediates the Impact of Electoral Reform

Taiwan can be seen as a baseline when we turn our attention to Japan, a country with a longer experience of democracy under a stable constitutional system. When compared with Taiwan, Japan's cabinet formation is dominated by legislative parties, giving electoral systems a more important role to play. We expect to see that *the number of parties in the cabinet increases and the percentage of ministers coming from the prime minister's party decreases after MMM is introduced, especially if the cabinet does not hold the majority of seats in the HC.*

A review of Japan's Constitution will be helpful here. Japan's prime minister shall be designated by the Diet before he appoints the cabinet ministers. According to Article 67 of the Constitution, disagreement between the two chambers about the designation of the prime minister is eventually determined by the HR. According to Article 69, the HR can pass a resolution of nonconidence in the prime minister or reject a confidence motion proposed by the latter—after which the prime minister must resign—but the prime minister can also actively dissolve the HR and call for an early election. No such relationship exists between the prime minister and the HC, but the latter can veto bills passed by the HR—except prime minister designation, treaty, and budgetary bills—unless the government can pass them a second time by a two-thirds majority in the HR.

In sum, Japan's bicameral parliamentary system strengthens the bargaining power of the small parties when the prime minister's party is unable to control the HC. Small parties can win seats in the HC and boycott government bills even if they are weak in the HR. Since MMM tends to create larger seat swings in the elections of the HR, the prime minister becomes less confident that he will control the majorities of both chambers. Nevertheless, it is optional whether the prime minister will expand the coalition to control the majority of the HC, for reasons already explained in the theoretical section.

We use Japan's portfolio allocation to test the hypotheses concerning the role of the small parties. Table 5.4 displays the partisan composition of Japan's cabinets, including the percentage of ministers from the prime minister's party and the number of parties (nonpartisan included) in the cabinets. When determining the size of the cabinet, the denominator is the number of ministers rather than their positions because a minister may concurrently hold more than one position. Note that we do not count control of the HC before 1955 because that period saw a tumultuous realignment of Japan's party system, making it difficult to measure the partisan composition of the cabinets. We should also focus on cabinets formed by prime ministers heading the largest party, otherwise the coalition governments will by nature be oversized.

Table 5.4 Partisan Profile of Japan's Cabinet Ministers

Prime minister	PM's party	Term begins	Number of non-PM parties	Ministers from PM's party	Cabinet always controls HC	MMM
*Shigeru Yoshida (I)	JLP	5/22/1946	5	32.26%	0	0
*Tetsu Katayama	JSP	5/24/1947	4	39.29%	0	0
*Hitoshi Ashita	DP	3/10/1948	3	46.67%	0	0
*Shigeru Yoshida (IIa)	DLP	10/15/1948	2	77.78%	0	0
*Shigeru Yoshida (IIb)	LP	6/28/1950	4	44.26%	0	0
*Shigeru Yoshida (IIb)	LP	10/30/1953	3	79.17%	0	0
*Shigeru Yoshida (IIb)	LP	5/21/1954	1	93.33%	0	0
Ichiro Hatoyama (a)	JDP	12/10/1954	1	85.00%	0	0

(continued)

Prime minister	PM's party	Term begins	Number of non-PM parties	Ministers from PM's party	Cabinet always controls HC	MMM
Ichiro Hatoyama (a)	LDP	11/22/1955	1	90.91%	0	0
Ichiro Hatoyama (a)	LDP	11/22/1956	1	94.74%	0	0
Tanzan Ishibashi	LDP	12/23/1956	1	95.00%	0	0
Nobusuke Kishi	LDP	2/25/1957	1	94.59%	0	0
Nobusuke Kishi	LDP	6/12/1958	1	97.73%	0	0
Hayato Ikeda	LDP	7/19/1960	1	95.24%	1	0
Hayato Ikeda	LDP	12/8/1960	1	98.33%	1	0
Hayato Ikeda	LDP	12/9/1963	1	97.30%	1	0
Eisaku Sato	LDP	11/9/1964	1	98.55%	1	0
Eisaku Sato	LDP	2/17/1967	1	98.04%	1	0
Eisaku Sato	LDP	1/14/1970	1	97.78%	1	0
Kakuei Tanaka	LDP	7/7/1972	1	95.45%	1	0
Kakuei Tanaka	LDP	12/22/1973	1	98.11%	1	0
Takeo Miki	LDP	12/9/1974	1	92.11%	1	0
Takeo Fukuda	LDP	12/24/1976	1	95.35%	1	0
Masayoshi Ohira	LDP	12/7/1978	1	95.45%	0	0
Masayoshi Ohira	LDP	11/9/1979	1	91.30%	0	0
Zenko Suzuki	LDP	7/17/1980	1	97.56%	1	0
Yasuhiro Nakasone	LDP	11/27/1982	1	91.67%	1	0
Yasuhiro Nakasone	LDP	12/271983	1	98.28%	1	0
Yasuhiro Nakasone	LDP	7/221986	1	95.83%	1	0
Noboru Takeshita	LDP	11/6/1987	1	95.35%	1	0
Sosuke Uno	LDP	6/3/1989	1	95.45%	1	0
Toshiki Kaifu	LDP	8/10/1989	1	95.65%	0	0
Toshiki Kaifu	LDP	2/28/1990	1	97.56%	0	0

(continued)

Prime minister	PM's party	Term begins	Number of non-PM parties	Ministers from PM's party	Cabinet always controls HC	MMM
Kiichi Miyazawa	LDP	11/5/1991	1	95.65%	0	0
*Morihiro Hosokawa	JNP	8/9/1993	7	18.18%	0	0
*Tsutomu Hata	JRP	4/28/1994	6	39.13%	0	0
*Tomiichi Murayama	SDP	6/30/1994	3	24.44%	0	0
Ryutaro Hashimoto	LDP	1/11/1996	3	54.55%	1	1
Ryutaro Hashimoto	LDP	11/7/1996	1	97.56%	0	1
Keizo Obuchi	LDP	7/30/1998	3	84.09%	0	1
Yoshiro Mori	LDP	4/5/2000	3	80.00%	0	1
Yoshiro Mori	LDP	11/7/2000	3	82.35%	0	1
Junichiro Koizumi	LDP	4/26/2001	4	79.49%	0	1
Junichiro Koizumi	LDP	11/19/2003	2	82.86%	1	1
Junichiro Koizumi	LDP	9/21/2005	2	90.91%	1	1
Shinzo Abe	LDP	9/26/2006	2	88.89%	1	1
Yasuo Fukuda	LDP	9/26/2007	2	84.38%	0	1
Taro Aso	LDP	9/24/2008	3	75.00%	0	1
Yukio Hatoyama	DPJ	9/16/2009	3	83.33%	0	1
Naoto Kan	DPJ	6/8/2010	2	88.10%	0	1
Yoshihiko Noda	DPJ	9/2/2011	2	82.22%	0	1

Source: Toshio (1990), Shiratori (1986, 1987), Kyofu (1996), and Naikaku seido hyakujunen kinen shi henshu iinkai (1996). In addition, the partisan composition of cabinets formed after MMM was introduced can be found at the website of the major newspapers.

Notes: 1. Members of cabinet includes ministers, the chief secretary, and commission chairpersons. Nonpartisans are seen as one party when counting the non-PM parties. 2. Ministers holding concurrent positions are counted only once. 3. Whether a cabinet always controls the HC is determined by the whole term of a prime minister. For this reason, "0" may include prime ministers with interrupted majority supports from the HC. 4. Prime ministers indicated by an asterisk (*) are not from the LDP or the DPJ and are excluded from analysis, except the first cabinet of Ichiro Hatoyama, who became the first LDP prime minister in November 1955. Cabinets resulting from party switching are also not counted. 5. A coalition government is defined by whether the cabinet includes at least two parties (nonpartisans excluded).

We will use the screened data to display the role of the small parties. Since the dependent variable is continuous, we run two parts of a One-Way ANOVA to test if the means are different as a result of the categories we choose. The first hypothesis is to see whether the number of parties in the Japanese cabinet varies by whether 1. the cabinet parties hold the majority of seats of the HC and 2. the electoral system for the HR is MMM. For the second part of the hypotheses, we will use the same categories to test how much the average percentage of ministers coming from the prime minister's party makes a difference. This is the opposite dimension of a similar variable.

The empirical data are shown in Tables 5.5 and 5.6. The results largely confirm our expectation. What we see from the first half of Table 5.5 is that the number of small parties in the cabinet goes up when the cabinet fails to have continuous control of the upper house. The implied message is interesting: the more the cabinet is unable to control the upper house, the greater the bargaining power of the small parties because they can threaten the prime minister and boycott his policy bills. By the same logic, the small parties lose their pivotal positions if the ruling party can unilaterally control the two chambers. The second half of Table 5.5 delivers a similar message in an even clearer way. Under SNTV, the prime ministers would leave a countable number of positions for the nonpartisans rather than for the small parties because the latter are dispensable.[14] The adoption of MMM changed the strategy of portfolio allocation because the fear of losing power in an MMM race made the collaboration with some small parties inevitable, even if the number of the nonpartisan ministers remains the

Table 5.5 One-Way ANOVA for the Number of Coalition Parties in Japan's Cabinets

		Mean	Variance	Sig.
Compared by whether the coalition parties always control the upper house	No	1.762	0.991	0.050
	Yes	1.250	0.303	
Compared by SNTV or MMM	SNTV	1.000	0.000	
	MMM	2.500	0.577	0.000

Source: Author's calculation.

---

[14] All Japanese cabinets have nonpartisan ministers. Since we count nonpartisans as a group, whether they are seen as a constituent part of the cabinets makes no statistical difference.

same. The underlying cause is that a majoritarian-leaning electoral system like MMM renders the undecided voters decisive and compels the prime minister to be mindful of the parties representing their interests.

Table 5.6 One-Way ANOVA for the Ratio of Ministers from PM's Party in Japan's Cabinets

		Mean	Variance	Sig.
Compared by whether the coalition parties always control the upper house	No	0.891	0.005	0.160
	Yes	0.929	0.010	
Compared by SNTV or MMM	SNTV	0.953	0.001	
	MMM	0.824	0.009	0.000

Source: Author's calculation.

For the second part of the hypothesis, we use the percentage of ministers from the prime minister's party to test the effects of the same set of variables. Note that Japan's parliamentary rule requires the prime ministers to be elected by the Diet, with the HR playing the decisive role. The denominator is therefore "the ministers from the parties of the prime minister and the small parties in the cabinet." The average percentage of ministers from the prime minister's party when the cabinet has continuous control of the upper house is 92.9%, which is higher than the 89.1% when it lacks continuous control. This result suggests an interesting dynamic: the prime minster's influence on cabinet formation declines when the cabinet fails to control the upper house. A likely cause is that bicameral deadlock weakens the prime minister's position in his cabinet. If so, electoral reform should have a significant impact because MMM is supposed to promote policy debates among political parties. Indeed, 95.3% of the ministers are from the prime minister's party when SNTV is used; this is reduced to 82.4% after MMM is introduced. In this sense, electoral reform enhances the bargaining power of the small parties on policy making even though their representatives are reduced in number.

To highlight the growing influence of Japan's small parties, consider the example of the cabinet organized by Prime Minister Yukio Hatoyama (2009-2010). Hatoyama's Democratic Party of Japan (DPJ) gained 308 of the 480 seats (64.17%) in the HR election of 2009 but still invited the heads of two small parties to join his cabinet: Shizuka Kamei from the People's New Party (PNP) as the minister of state for financial services and minister of state for postal reform, and Mizuho Fukushima from the Social Democratic Party (SDP) as the minister of state for consumer affairs and food safety, social affairs, and gender equality. Especially noteworthy is Fukushima, who was a member of the HC at that time. The DPJ chose to offer cabinet positions to the two smaller parties and they chose to accept them because there was a degree of policy congruence among the three parties, making it easier for them to garner support from the upper house to form a temporary majority. However, the alliance was fragile, and Fukushima resigned her position in 2010 over the issue of the Marine Corps Air Station Futenma.[15] When the degree of policy congruence was high, the SDP was able to use its position in the upper house to win a cabinet seat; when the degree of policy congruence decreased, the SDP decided to withdraw from the cabinet and dampen the credibility of the Hatoyama cabinet. Thus this example neatly illustrates the opportunities small parties are afforded in Japan's constitutional system as well as the trade-offs among cabinet portfolios, policy positions, and support in the parliament that large parties much consider.

Japan's party system is further fragmented by its parliamentary elections. Because Japan lacks a central leader, MMM reduces the differences between political parties and gives some politicians a reason to establish their own parties. For many voters, the party platforms are intangible—at least more intangible than real politicians—and contenders in each constituency tend to embody their ideas through their personal image or social connections. One trend has been the formation of small parties by politicians who are not very different from their fellows in the parties from which they originated. Such a trend is further endogenized by the fact that the new electoral system is conducive to regime turnover (at the national and local levels). This helps explain why some local potentates have an incentive to defect from their parties as long as they have a chance of winning the seat. Thus, the lack of a centralized leader makes some small parties powerful enough to grab the SMP seats.

Nevertheless, MMM is not exactly an SMP system: the latter gives electoral contenders much less motivation to build their own parties, whereas the former creates contamination

---

[15] The U.S. base on Okinawa has been controversial because the military base is close to a populated area and creates noise pollution. The base is also a reminder that, when the Second World War came to an end, Okinawa suffered from the most deadly strike launched by the United States.

effects that small parties can utilize to gain some seats. Taiwan also adopted MMM, but the role of its small parties is much less salient than that of small parties in Japan. As we have seen, this difference cannot be fully accounted for by the design of the electoral system. It is the constitutional system that explains the varying amounts of bargaining power of the small parties.

V. Conclusion

Few topics can be studied as rigorously and fruitfully as those concerning electoral systems. Concepts like the threshold of winning and effective number of parties apply to all electoral systems and are well recognized in the literature. MMM, by giving priority to single-member district competitions, is expected to decrease the number of parties. This expectation finds support in Japan and Taiwan, both of which shifted their electoral systems from SNTV to the majoritarian-leaning MMM systems. Although the effective number of parties is smaller when measured in relative terms, the absolute number of parties in Japan is always higher than that of Taiwan, leaving a puzzle to be explained.

This chapter takes an executive-centered approach to answer this puzzle. A theory of portfolio allocation suggests that a constitutional system instituted with more players who can veto the appointment of the head of government, and hence portfolio allocation, makes small parties more influential. Exogenously imposed, the rule of portfolio allocation gives small parties an endogenous interest in breaking away from the large parties in and after the legislative election. This theory explains why Japan's bicameral parliamentary system creates bargaining power for Japan's small parties, and why Taiwan's unicameral semipresidential system makes the small parties much less effective than the president when executive offices are to be arranged. Furthermore, Japan's parliamentary system gives some electoral competitors the justification to run a campaign at the district level because the party platform is less visible than a real candidate. The chances of Japan's small parties receiving seats are thus higher than those of their counterparts in Taiwan.

The partisan composition of cabinets in Taiwan and Japan corroborates this argument. For Taiwan, we expect the percentage of nonpartisan ministers to be increased by MMM and the president's inability to control the Legislative Yuan, for both will increase the likelihood of the executive proposals being rejected, and nonpartisan ministers can buffer such pressure. The One-Way ANOVA dividing the data by three Taiwanese presidents offers a significant count of the percentages of nonpartisan ministers. That is, Taiwan's constitutional system makes the president the paramount leader subject to the different degrees of legislative distrust of the executive officers, for which electoral reform plays an important role. Small parties are almost entirely cut out of cabinet positions, as the semipresidential system denies them any opportunity to negotiate for ministerial posts. In Japan's parliamentary system, the HR approves the appointment of the prime minister and the HC can veto most policy bills. Since the prime minister should receive majority support from the HR, whether the cabinet also controls the HC becomes a major determinant of the cabinet's partisan composition. We expect the number of parties in the cabinet to increase and the percentage of ministers from the prime minister's party to decline when the cabinet fails to control the upper house majority. If MMM reduces factionalism and speeds up power transitions, we expect the electoral reform to increase the number of parties in the cabinet and decrease the percentages of ministers from the prime minister's party. These hypotheses are confirmed, and the effects of MMM are especially impressive.

Comparing the partisan compositions of the cabinets of the two countries, we find Japan to have far more ministers from the prime minister's party than Taiwan has ministers from the president's party. The weights of the other parties are high in Japan while Taiwan's president tends to ill the executive positions by selecting ministers without partisanship or those from his party instead of parties with similar ideologies. This result supports the theory of portfolio allocation.

Taiwan and Japan are specific cases with general implications. We can make a further generalization by considering the two extreme possibilities: 1. a unicameral presidential system where the president heads the government and is the only agent responsible for portfolio allocation, and 2. a multichamber parliamentary system where the appointment of ministers has to be agreed to by the political parties in all chambers. In the first case, the number of nonpartisan ministers should be high; in the latter, political parties play decisive roles in cabinet formation and the number of ministers from the prime minister's party depends on to what extent the prime minister controls the chambers. What electoral reform does is to alter the number of parties the political leader can choose from rather than the rules regulating portfolio allocation. That is why we need to consider the electoral system and the constitutional system together to explain a country's party system.

憲政制度與半總統制

主題導讀

林繼文的半總統制研究

吳玉山

　　在林繼文教授對政治學熱情而又理性的研究當中，半總統制占有非常重要的地位。[1] 其原因顯然是由於台灣在 1990 年代初進入民主時期，因此像所有的新興民主國家一樣，必需要進行政治制度的抉擇，這裡包括憲政體制和選舉制度，而又以憲政體制最為核心。林教授是於 1996 年回國進入中央研究院中山人文社會科學研究所服務，隔一年我國就進行了最重要的第四次修憲（即修改《中華民國憲法》增修條款），建立了總統直選、而作為最高行政機關首長的行政院長又要率領內閣對立法院負責的半總統制。究竟這種介於總統制和內閣制之間的憲政體制會怎樣地運作，對於我國是不是合適，這些都是研究政治制度的人所必然關切的重大議題。由於林教授是採用理性抉擇的方法論，又以「單記不可讓渡投票制」（SNTV）的選舉制度作為博士論文的主題，因此他對於半總統制的研究就展現了兩個必然的特點。[2] 第一是沿用理性抉擇的分析途徑，第二是探討憲政體制如何和選舉制度配套，又會產生怎樣的結果。在這兩方面，林教授都著述甚豐，為國內的研究樹立了標竿。

　　所謂半總統制是一種揉合了總統制和國會制核心特徵的憲政體制，一方面總統透過人民直選而產生，因此具有很高的威望和合法性，有可能因為獲得了人民的託付而要求主導政事，另一方面總理又帶領內閣對國會負責，因此國會可以用不信任投票迫使總理和內閣去職。半總統制因為同時讓總統和國會都由民選產生，因此具有雙重的民主合法性，而為絕大多數的新興民主國家採行。可是另一方面，這樣的制度不可避免會產生總統和總理之間權力分際不清楚的現象，同時總統會和國會爭奪對於政府的掌控。我國從1997 年第四次修憲後便進入了半總統制，因此我國學者對於此種制度具有很大的研究興趣，也產生了大量的研究成果，其中林教授就是一位指標型的人物。

---

[1]　在林教授豐富的各類型著作當中，主要是處理了幾個主題：憲政體制、選舉制度、數量方法，和兩岸關係。其中就期刊論文和專書論文而言，憲政體制（半總統制研究）占了 22%，僅次於選舉制度居第二位；而在研討會論文方面，憲政體制則佔有 34%，居第一位。

[2]　林教授的博士論文題目是 "Consequences of the Single Non-Transferable Voting Rule: Comparing the Japan and Taiwan Experiences"（University of California, Los Angeles, 1996）。

　　我們可以從制度的上、中、下游，也就是制度的抉擇、運作，和影響這三個面向來看林教授對於半總統制的研究。林教授在制度抉擇的方面曾運用空間模型分析在李登輝總統主政下，台灣修憲成功的原因，是議題的多面向化，於是國民黨主流派和民進黨在「政府體制改革」和「本土化」的兩大議題之間，可以進行合作，從而獲得修憲所必須的超級多數（Lin, 2002）。沿著這個思路在理論化上更進一步，林教授又在 International Political Science Review 所刊出的 "How Are the Powers of the President Decided? Vote Trading in the Making of Taiwan's Semi-Presidential Constitution" 當中，採用了「選票交易」理論（vote-trading theory）來解釋 1997 年修憲的妥協是如何達成的（Lin, 2017）。這一篇較新的作品是本書中所選刊的（見第六章）。

　　所謂「選票交易」理論來自對於立法行為的研究。在立法時，有可能看似不相干的議題會被包裹到一起，而民意代表之間則進行對這些議題的選票交易，從而達成對交易雙方而言都比不交易更有利的結果。林教授把這個理論運用到九七修憲的過程當中，主要目的是解釋為什麼我國憲法在當時採用了一種很特殊的半總統制，一方面給予總統對於行政院長的單獨任命權（毋須獲得立法院的同意），一方面又僅給予總統對於立法院的被動解散權（僅有在立法院通過對於內閣不信任案的情況下才能夠解散立法院）。此種半總統制的憲法規定和半總統制的標竿國家法國第五共和比較起來，就可以看出其運作的困難之處。在法國第五共和，總統有對於總理的主動任命權，也有對於國會（國民議會）的主動解散權，所以當新總統上台，而府會不一致時，總統必然會解散國會，訴求民意，並讓民意來決定新的內閣組成。此時通常總統黨會在新的國會選舉中獲勝，從而解決府會不一致的問題。而在台灣，由於總統並沒有主動的國會解散權，因此面對府會不一致的新任總統，就算擁用有新民意的支持，仍然不能夠改變國會的組成。而國會中的多數黨，也因為害怕喪失席次，因而不會倒閣，其結果就是府會的僵持。如果像法國一樣給總統足夠的權力，或是不給總統閣揆的單獨任命權、也不給他國會的主動解散權，這兩種做法都會帶來較好的憲政運作表現。那麼，為什麼台灣會出現一方面對總統賦權、一方面又限制總統權力的制度安排呢？這就是國民黨和民進黨進行「選票交易」的結果。

　　對兩黨而言，有三個主要的議題可以加入交易包裹：行政院長的任命（現狀即需要立院同意、不需要立院同意）、國會的解散（現狀即無法解散、主動解散、被動解散），和台灣省政府的處理（現狀即維持、取消、精簡）。有兩個均衡是可能的：「行政院長不需要立法院同意而任命、被動解散、精簡省府」和「行政院長不需要立法院同意而任命、主動解散、取消省府」。雖然主張台灣獨立的民進黨希望能夠取消省府，但是因為外在壓力（美國與對岸），所以國民黨堅持僅能精簡省府（精省），於是民進黨

也就只能夠同意給總統被動解散國會權，雙方乃在第一個均衡上達成妥協，透過選票的交易，完成了第四次的修憲。這就是我國的半總統制憲法對於總統又賦權、又限權，並造成日後府會僵局的原因。

　　在解釋了 1997 年修憲成功的原因之後，林教授又比較了 1997 與 2015 年的修憲情境。在他於 *Taiwan Journal of Democracy* 所發表的 "Taiwan's Semi-Presidential System Was Easy to Establish but Is Difficult to Fix: A Comparison between the Constitutional Reform Efforts of 1997 and 2015" 中指出這兩個修憲情境都是由國民黨和民進黨所主導、兩個政黨對於總統是否有權單獨決定閣揆人選均有不同的立場、而二者在若干其他議題上卻有其共識，那麼為何在 1997 年雙方能夠合作修憲成功，但是在 2015 年雖然修憲之說甚囂塵上，卻無法達成共識，讓修憲案在立法院中獲得絕對多數同意通過，這就成為一個值得研究的比較案例（Lin, 2016b）（見本書第七章）。[3] 在這裡林教授提出了一個重要的觀點，即當「樞紐行為者」（pivot）對修憲各相關議題的偏好是可分的時候（separable preferences），修憲較易成功，相反地，如果偏好是相互交纏的（nonseparable preferences），則修憲便不易成功。[4] 在 1997 年國民黨和民進黨對於修憲的各主要議題（行政院長的任命、不信任投票、立法院的解散、省府的精簡 / 廢止）均持可分偏好，因此最終能夠透過選票的交易來達成修憲的共識，成功地將台灣引入了半總統制。到了 2015 年，由於受到之前服貿爭議、太陽花學運和馬王政爭等重大事件的影響，國內又掀起了一波修憲的風潮。此時的主要議題包括行政立法關係（是否回復立院對於閣揆的任命同意權），降低選舉年齡與不在籍投票，修改比例代表制的 5% 門檻，考監兩院存廢與降低修憲門檻，以及人權和其他議題。雖然在修改選制和人權議題上兩大黨有達成共識的可能（這主要是學術界和小黨的主張），但是修憲最後還是被國民黨對於降低選舉年齡和不在籍投票的交纏偏好所阻礙了。對國民黨而言，降低選舉年齡只有在通過不在籍投票的情況下才能夠被接受，而在 1997 年修憲的時候兩黨並沒有在主要議題上出現類似的偏好交纏的現象。由於國民黨的堅持，因此在 2015 年兩黨主導修憲時出現了功虧一簣的結果。

　　在以上的兩篇論文當中，林教授用「選票交易理論」和「樞紐行為者的偏好是否

---

[3]　固然在兩個情境當中，修憲的第二步並不相同，也就是在 1997 年修憲案經過立院全體委員四分之一提案、四分之三出席投票、四分之三多數同意通過後，是要送交國民大會來複決，而到了 2015 年，由於國民大會已經不存在，由立院所通過的修憲案是需要交由公民複決，如果通過上次總統大選時選民人數的過半同意則為通過。

[4]　偏好交纏的意思是指一個人對於一套選項的偏好繫於對於另一套選項的偏好；偏好可分是指對於各套選項的偏好是相互獨立的（Lacy and Niou, 2013）。

交纏」解釋了為何國民黨和民進黨能夠在 1997 年達成修憲的共識，將台灣帶入半總統制，但是而卻無法在 2015 年複製當年的經驗，進行成功的修憲。這些都是制度上游（制度抉擇）的研究。制度的框架一旦確定，究竟會如何運行，這就是制度中游的問題。在這一方面，林教授對於台灣的半總統制進行了個別和跨國比較的研究。他發現雖然台灣的半總統制師法法國，但是卻和法國的「共治」傳統大相逕庭。在府會不一致（也就是總統黨無法掌握多數）的情況下，台灣的總統會任命本黨人士擔任行政院長，法國卻會邀請反對黨領袖組閣。對於台法運作半總統制的差異，林教授經由賽局推導出一個頗為創新的看法，就是總統在與總理（行政院長）不同黨派的情況下所能夠保有的權力，是一個關鍵的變項。

林教授在《東吳政治學報》所發表的「共治可能成為半總統制的憲政慣例嗎？法國與台灣的比較」當中，試圖解釋為什麼在台灣和法國當總統任命總理時都不需要獲得國會的同意，然而當國會由反對黨（聯盟）控制時，法國的總統會任命反對黨（聯盟）的領袖為總理，因而產生左右共治，而台灣的總統卻不會做這樣的動作（林繼文，2009a）（見本書第八章）。此種現象並非由憲法所規定，而是一種由競爭性的政治菁英所共同構築的憲政慣例。在經由形式模型推演後，發現造成兩國憲政慣例差異的主要原因在於總統的專屬權力和國會的選舉制度。由於《法國第五共和憲法》賦予總統相當大的權力（例如國防外交的特權、主持部長會議、可拒絕簽署行政法令、可主動解散國會），因此即使總統同意共治，他仍然具有相當的政策影響力；而台灣的總統由於憲法權力較小，因此無法期待在共治的情況之下仍然能夠保持相當的影響力。質言之，就是由於共治的成本較小，所以法國總統同意共治的誘因比台灣的總統大。就選舉制度而言，法國的「兩輪多數決選制」比台灣的「單記非讓渡投票複數選區制」所帶來的席次擺動率為大，這使得總統高度重視民意，而法國的民意又贊成共治，這就提高了總統接受共治的動機；相對地台灣的選制比例性高，民意又支持總統主導內閣組成，因此台灣總統接受共治的誘因便較低。透過這樣制度和理性抉擇的分析，本文解釋了為何法國會出現共治的憲政慣例，而台灣在類似的情況之下卻沒有，這是一個關於半總統制實際運作樣態的研究。

當制度已經決定，並且以一定的模式運作後，便會產生影響，這就是制度下游的範疇。台灣的半總統制從 1997 年開始運作，在次類型當中很明顯地是屬於總統權力較大的「總統國會制」（president-parliamentarism）（Shugart and Carey, 1992）。[5] 此種次類

---

[5] 根據 Shugart 與 Carey（1992），半總統制可以區分為總統權力較大的「總統國會制」（president-parliamentarism）和國會權力較大的「總理總統制」（premier-presidentialism）。二者主要的差異點是總統是不是能夠將總理解職，從而使得總理除了需要面對國會的不信任投票之外，還要

型一般被認為會給予總統較大的權力，而又對民主存續和政治穩定不利。不過究竟台灣在實際運作「總統國會制」時會產生什麼樣的結果，卻是需要在經驗中加以探詢的。以往在這一方面的經驗研究集中在總統黨在國會中是否占有多數帶來的影響，也就是以「府會一致性」作為主要的自變項，來觀察對於民主表現所造成的結果。然而這樣的做法是事先假設一旦總統黨居於國會多數，就不會有政事推行不順利的問題（但是可能造成總統威權專斷）。林教授藉著考察馬英九總統第一任期的施政表現，卻發現了一個重要現象，即「總統國會制」下的總統即使在府會一致的情況下也未必很有權力，他可能會受到國會中同黨議員的強力挑戰。林教授的這篇研究論文 "A Veto Player Theory of Policymaking in Semipresidential Regimes: The Case of Taiwan's Ma Ying-jeou Presidency" 於 2011 年發表在 *Journal of East Asian Studies*。他準確地觀察到馬英九總統的執政困局，並且以理論的深度來加以分析。這個困局到了馬總統的第二任期就演化成一系列的危機，包括服貿爭議與太陽花學運，從這裡我們可以看出林教授觀察與分析的精確。

　　林教授對馬總統執政困局的研究是採用他的論文指導教授 George Tsebelis 所發展出的「否決者理論」（Veto Player Theory）。否決者是指任何對於現狀的改變均需要獲得其同意的行為者，而在否決者當中，下最後一手的行為者（last mover）具有最大的優勢，成為「議程設定者」（agenda setter）。在不同的憲政體制當中，否決者的數目與採取行動的先後順序都有所不同，而半總統制的情況最為複雜。若是總統國會制，則如果總統可以控制執政黨、而國會又不能夠改變政府政策（例如行政命令或只能為可否決議的法案），那麼總統是議程設定者；然而一旦總統無法控制執政黨的議員、而國會又可以改變政府的政策（即有空間可以大幅修政府的法案），則議程設定者變成是國會。馬總統的執政困局就是來自於雖然他是總統國會制下面對府會一致有利態勢的總統，但因為無法控制立法院中的國民黨委員，因此在立法院可以修改政府政策的法案中，便經常遭受同黨議員的抵制，使得其施政困難，並進而造成總統和行政院長之間的意見不一致。林教授在檢視馬總統執政初期的立法表現時，清楚地點出了這個現象。由於我國憲法雖然給予總統相當的權力，使其得以控制行政院長，但是總統對於國會的控制卻僅能夠仰賴執政黨的非正式機制，所以一旦此一機制失靈，總統便陷於左支右絀的境地。

　　然而為何國民黨的立委會和馬政府有不同的意見？這是因為第一、我國的憲政體制規定立法委員不得兼任官吏，因此造成立法和行政部門的隔閡，而與內閣制的國家大相逕庭。此種狀況使得國會議員經常無法獲得參與決策過程的機會，而對於政府的法案缺

面對總統的解職威脅，因而形成「雙重負責」（double accountability）。在「總統國會制」中總統有這樣的解職權，而在「總理總統制」中的總統卻沒有。

乏認同感與支持的熱情。第二、我國的選舉制度和選舉文化非常強調立法委員和選區的聯繫，選民投票的候選人（而非政黨）取向也很強。這使得立委必須積極地經營選區，而黨紀便不容易維繫。最後是記名投票並非議事常態，因而更弱化黨紀。因此在馬總統的第一任期，就可以看出來國民黨的立委一旦有可以修改政府議案的機會，便會大肆修改，讓總統無法控制。在林教授的這篇論文發表三年後，服貿爭議與太陽花學運爆發，其關鍵的原因就是府會一致下馬總統的施政困局。

　　憲政體制也會對於政黨體系產生影響。林教授在鮑彤（Nathan Batto）等人所編著的 *Mixed-Member Electoral Systems in Constitutional Context: Taiwan, Japan, and Beyond* 中撰寫了 "The Consequences of Constitutional Systems on Party Systems"，比較了台灣和日本在「內閣職位分配」（portfolio allocation）上的不同表現，認為其根源是兩國不同的憲政體制，並將之用來解釋為什麼日本的政黨絕對數目始終高於台灣。傳統上學術界總習慣於用選舉制度來解釋政黨體系，這篇論文則打破了這樣的傳統思路，而認為憲政體制也具有很強的解釋力。由於台灣和日本都將其國會選舉制度從「單記不可讓渡投票制」（SNTV）改成「以單一選區為主的兩票制」（MMM），因此二者在改革前後都具有類似的選制，而他們在政黨體系上的不同之處就不能夠歸之於選制的不同。又由於兩國在政治制度上最大的差異就在於憲政體制，台灣是以總統為權力核心的半總統制，而日本則是典型的內閣制，所以要解釋二者政黨體系的不同，最可能的原因就是存在憲政制度當中。

　　這裡的關鍵變項是不同憲政體制下的「內閣職位分配」模式。在台灣的半總統制當中，總統具有對於內閣職位分配的極大權力，而且不會受到國會的掣肘，與總統制下類似。這會反映在無黨籍的內閣閣員數目當中，而他們就是總統施展組閣權力的結果。在擁有兩院內閣制的日本，閣員的分配主要是看眾院中各政黨的比例，不過由於參議院仍然具有相當的立法職能，因此一旦首相的政黨在參院中無法掌握多數時，也需要在內閣中增加各政黨的代表數目。內閣的職位分配既然有不同的模式，對於想要入閣的人而言，是否加入與支持小黨便有不同的考量。在台灣小黨對於入閣完全沒有談判的地位，但是在日本卻有相當大的議價空間，也因而增加其存在的條件。在選制改革之後，雖然兩國國會中的有效政黨數目都減少了，但是由於憲政體制所決定的內閣職位分配模式不同，因此日本小黨的絕對數目還是比台灣的多，從而形成兩國政黨體系不同之處。

　　制度的影響未必是僅僅是憲政體制所造成的結果，通常憲制和選制會經由互動，從而決定政治制度所產生的影響。在憲制與選制的配套方面，林教授 2006 年在《選舉研究》的「政府體制、選舉制度與政黨體系：一個配套論的分析」是個經典（見本書第九章）。他認為過去經由「其他條件不變」（*ceteris paribus*, other things being equal）

的前提所得出的研究結論是有很大問題的，因為那些研究通常是把各種經由孤立研究後所得出的因素相加，認為就是制度配套的結果，而沒有考慮到這些因素彼此是互動的，他們彼此間會產生「化學變化」，而這不是能夠線性地來加以捕捉的（林繼文，2006）。這一篇論文的背景是 2005 年我國通過了第七次修憲，往減少比例性的單一選區（MMM）和兩黨制跨進了一大步。此種新選制搭配強勢總統，將會對政治穩定會造成什麼影響，成為大眾所關切的議題。此一問題顯然不能夠從憲制與選制各自對政治穩定的影響來看，而後予以加總，而必須看到兩種體制互動的化學變化，也就是當府會一致時會產生高效行政，而分立政府時則會出現嚴重的對抗與僵局，也就是「大好大壞」的結果。林教授在文中又點出「選舉時程」的關鍵重要性，而這些都被日後的發展所證實了。

林教授除了藉由發表論文來推進半總統制的研究前沿之外，更在國內與國際半總統制的學術社群當中扮演著關鍵的角色，產生了重大的影響。從 2010 年開始，中央研究院政治學研究所與國內的研究型大學合作，每年舉辦一次「半總統制與民主」學術研討會，林教授從第一屆到第八屆，每屆必與。[6] 所擔任的角色包括一次主題演講、四次主持、六次評論、並參加四次圓桌論壇。中研院政治所又在 2003 與 2008 年舉辦了兩次的半總統制國際研討會，林教授也竭力支持，並參與會後專書的出版（Lin, 2011c）。[7] 此外，由跨院校學者所組成的「半總統制研究群」為了精進研究方法，曾經邀請林教授進行專題講座。[8] 總而言之，在國內半總統制與憲政體制的研究上，林教授是極為重要的推手，產生了極大的貢獻。[9]

林教授對於半總統制的研究創新精深，其特點自然是運用理性選擇與形式理論，透過數量與邏輯推理，來達致其研究結論。[10] 但是林教授的憲政研究並非僅關注「理性」

---

[6] 「半總統制與民主」學術研討會的第一屆在台灣大學舉行，是由中研院政治所與台灣大學政治系合辦，以後各屆分別在東海大學（第二屆）、台北大學（第三屆）、東吳大學（第四屆）、中山大學（第五屆）、中正大學（第六屆）、東海大學（第七屆）、中山大學（第八屆）舉行。第九屆研討會於文化大學舉行時（2018 年 5 月 12 日），林教授已經過世（2018 年 1 月 2 日）。

[7] 這兩次在中研院舉行的半總統制研討會是 Conference on Semi-Presidentialism and Nascent Democracies（2003）和 Conference on Semi-presidentialism and Democracy: Institutional Choice, Performance and Evolution（2008）。

[8] 林教授擔任半總統制講座所談的題目是 "Database: Why, What & How"。

[9] 為了紀念林教授對半總統制研究的貢獻，在他過世後四個多月所舉行的第九次半總統制與民主學術研討會便以「第九屆半總統制與民主暨林繼文教授紀念研討會」為名，並從歷屆會議論文中選出最優者，頒發「林繼文教授紀念獎」。這是國內第一個以紀念林教授為名的學術研討會與紀念獎項。

[10] 關於這一塊在台灣政治學中的發展，可參閱謝復生、林繼文（2013）。

的一塊，而是帶有很大的「感性」成分。這可分爲兩個部分來說，第一是驅動他研究憲政體制的形成、運作和影響的，主要就是他的家國關懷，是他從學生時代就投身的民主運動，和希望爲台灣尋覓最合適的憲政體制。第二個感性的部分，是即使他採用理性選擇的典範，卻對於個人的價值偏好高度敏感，並對人文學的充分尊重。他說「如果沒有對於個人偏好的深入描述、不能對行動意義進行人類學式地體悟，或無法像歷史學家般掌握人在進行抉擇時的進退維谷，理性選擇所提供的解釋就會是貧弱的，甚至是虛假的」（林繼文，2005：95）。這種認識是何等深入，而這種願意擁抱不同典範、不同方法的襟懷，又是何等寬廣。在檢視林教授半總統制的研究成果時，對此實在無法不再三致意，深表欽佩之忱。在林教授的身上，我們眞是看到了政治學者結合「理性」與「感性」的最佳典範。

第六章

How Are the Powers of the President Decided? Vote Trading in the Making of Taiwan's Semi-presidential Constitution[*]

I. Introduction

All semi-presidential systems have a popularly elected president who appoints a premier to head the cabinet, and a parliament that can hold cabinet ministers accountable by proposing a vote of no confidence in the premier (Elgie, 2007). Under this general principle, two subtypes can be derived from the relationship between the president, the premier, and the parliament. In the first subtype, the president can unilaterally choose the premier and dissolve the parliament without a vote of no confidence being passed. Thus the president takes the lead and can test his/her credibility in a snap parliamentary election. In the second subtype, the appointment of the premier requires legislative approval and the parliament cannot be dissolved without the premier being sacked first, so the majority party (or coalition) in the parliament plays the determining role. Most semi-presidential regimes have adopted one or other of these two formulas.

Nevertheless, some exceptions exist and deserve further exploration. A good example is Taiwan, in which the president chooses the premier without legislative confirmation but cannot actively dissolve the parliament. Under this system, the parliament is unlikely to pass a vote of no confidence, as the president can either name another unpopular premier or dissolve the parliament and put all the legislators out of a job. The best evidence for this can be found in 2000, when Taiwan experienced its first transfer of power. The newly elected president, Chen Shui-bian of the Democratic Progressive Party (DPP), was inaugurated on May 20 at a time when the parliament was still dominated by the Kuomintang (KMT, the nationalist

[*] Reproduced from [Lin, Jih-wen. "How Are the Powers of the President Decided? Vote Trading in the Making of Taiwan's Semi-Presidential Constitution." *International Political Science Review* 38(5): 659-672, 2017], with kind permission of SAGE Publishing.

party). The first premier chosen by President Chen was Tang Fei, a retired general. Chen appointed Tang without any prior negotiation with the opposition-controlled parliament as he thought Tang's background as a member of the KMT would reduce parliamentary resistance. It turned out that not even Premier Tang could resolve the divergent positions taken by Chen and the opposition majority on the construction of a fourth nuclear power plant in Taiwan. Besieged from both sides, Tang resigned after only 136 days in office, to be succeeded by premiers who were members of the DPP. Most likely, this experience taught Chen that a DPP premier would both enhance the unity of the government and be unlikely to be subject to a vote of no confidence, as that would lead to the dissolution of the parliament.

Chen attracted some criticism for subsequently refusing to select premiers from the opposition party, the course of action taken by French presidents whenever an opposition alliance holds a majority in the National Assembly. Although the French constitution exerted a considerable influence over the making of Taiwan's semi-presidential system (Cabestan, 1997), Chen's critics over-looked the fact that the French president can dissolve the National Assembly before the premier is unseated. It is easy to see what the relationship is between the sharing of executive powers and the president's power to dissolve the parliament. Whenever a French president finds that power sharing is no longer necessary, he/she is free to dissolve the National Assembly and make French voters the ultimate arbiters. The chain of accountability is broken if a president does not have power of dissolution—there would be no snap election unless the premier is unseated, but legislators have little incentive to pass a vote of no confidence that might endanger their own seats. So the relationship between the executive and the legislature in Taiwan does appear puzzling. What is the explanation for Taiwan's constitutional choice?

In an attempt to answer this question, this article will focus on the president's powers to appoint the premier and dissolve the legislature discussed above. In the following empirical analysis, we do not use the well-known typology proposed by Shugart and Carey (1992: 23-24) because the president's power to dismiss the premier is not a commonly defined constitutional arrangement.[1] In a cross-national comparison, we should start from

---

[1]　The typology we construct here is close to but different from the one that Samuels and Shugart (2010a) fine-tuned. According to their definition, in a president—parliamentary regime, the premier is dually accountable to the president and the parliament; in a premier—presidential regime, the premier is formally accountable exclusively to the parliament and not to the president.

what is stipulated in most constitutions.[2] In the next section it will be demonstrated that the arrangement regarding the powers of the president in Taiwan is different from the arrangements in France and most other semi-presidential regimes. We will then try to ascertain whether vote-trading theory can be used to solve the Taiwan puzzle.

II. Taiwan's Position among the World's Semi-presidential Systems

A brief examination of the world's semi-presidential constitutions reveals that the Taiwan case is unusual. Individual scholars produce different lists of semi-presidential regimes, among which Siaroff (2003) is a detailed count based on the powers of the president.[3] To ensure that we do not include presidents whose power to appoint the premier is only symbolic, we add a condition that the president should also play a central role in government formation (Siaroff, 2003: 204). To ensure that the constitution is effective, we focus on democracies in which transition of power is normally peaceful.

Siaroff lists thirty-eight semi-presidential democracies. We find that in most of these cases presidential powers are designed in a consistent way: a president can appoint the premier without legislative confirmation and dissolve the parliament with little constraint, or he/she can do neither of these things. Using these institutional powers as screeners, the following regimes (ordered alphabetically) appear to be headed by a strong president with constrained dissolution power:[4]

1. Finland (1956-1994). In this period, the Finnish president was active in the selection of premiers. Under the 1919 constitution, the president could dissolve the parliament after some conditions were met.

2. Mozambique. Under the constitution, the president, as head of state, appoints and dismisses the premier but is also the head of government. The president may dissolve

---

[2]　Passive dissolution power is different from a president having active dissolution power but not using it—the former is an institutional constraint while the latter comes from a calculated action.

[3]　For a detailed discussion of the different varieties of semi-presidentialism, see Roper (2002).

[4]　We use Elkins, Ginsburg, and Melton (2014) to verify the coding of Siaroff (2003).

the assembly if it rejects the government's program and he/she may then call for a new legislative election.

3. Peru. Under the constitution, the president appoints and removes the premier. While the 1979 constitution allowed the president to dissolve the congress after it had censured cabinet members three times, the current (1993) constitution reduces this to two times.

4. Russia (after 1993). The president's appointment of the premier of the Russian Federation must be agreed to by the State Duma (parliament); if the nominated premier is rejected three times, the president can dissolve the parliament or appoint another premier.

It is, in fact, debatable whether Finland and Mozambique are genuine semi-presidential regimes at all, as before 1994, the Finnish president was indirectly elected, and in Mozambique, the president is also the head of the government. Peru and Taiwan appear similar, even though the Peruvian constitution allows the parliament to censure the cabinet two times; a similar argument can be made for Russia. When compared with most of the semi-presidential regimes, Taiwan's constitutional design does seem to be exceptional.

As will be explored in the next section, Taiwan's current semi-presidential system may have been shaped by the trading of votes on issues involving the arrangement of constitutional powers and Taiwan's idiosyncratic sovereignty status. We will first review the literature on constitutional choice and then address the likely contribution of vote trading.

III. How the Issue of Vote Trading in Taiwan's Constitutional Reform Can Enrich the Literature

When we investigate the general nature of constitutional choice, several theories are worth considering. The classification of constitutional systems is a popular approach, but it is typically concerned with the consequences of the choice rather than the bargaining that takes place before that choice is made.[5] Constitutional study is another frequently used

---

[5] Representative works on comparative constitutional systems are to be found in Goodin (1996), Lijphart

methodology but the emphasis is mainly normative rather than empirical. The puzzle at the heart of this article—why did Taiwan choose this particular constitution?—should be seen as an empirical question. Among the empirical studies, historical institutionalism stresses not only the micro dynamics but also the macro transformations of constitutional change. Nevertheless, this approach focuses more on path-dependent specificities than on the overall pattern of constitutional choice.[6] What we need is a general theory that can account for a particular case like Taiwan.

In a case study with general implications, an abnormal example (an outlier) deserves special attention because its deviation from the overall pattern may point to directions in which the theory can be modified. Vote-trading theory, which has been widely applied in legislative studies, is a likely example of such a theory. Vote trading refers to an agreement made between at least two legislators to vote strategically on at least two issues to produce an outcome better than the one that could be achieved by voting sincerely. Vote trading shows how seemingly unconnected issues can be decided together.[7] In the making of a semi-presidential constitution, executive–legislative relations and some unconnected issues may be voted on as a package the outcome of which may undermine the consistency of the former. Most research on constitutional choice seems to have missed this possibility.

Many studies of constitutional reform in Taiwan employ the jurisprudential or historical approaches. Among the few empirical studies on the subject, Higley, Huang, and Lin (1998) discusses the pre-1997 negotiations and depicts them as an "elite settlement." What this study does not anticipate is that as soon as the National Assembly was convened in 1997, the provisional agreement faded away as political reality set in. Missing from these studies is the formation of the issue package in the 1997 constitutional revisions. The issues voted on together with the rearrangement of constitutional powers were important but also peculiar to Taiwan, and they can be used to explain the atypical result of Taiwan's constitutional reform. Without inquiring how the issue package was formed, one could easily describe the 1997

---

[6] (1999b), Sartori (1997), Samuels and Shugart (2010a), and Tsebelis (2002). For studies of constitutional change from the perspective of historical institutionalism, see Broschek (2010, 2011), Filippov and Shvetsova (1999), Immergut (2005), Jung and Deering (2015), McFaul (1999), Pierson (1996), and Solum (2008).

[7] Vote trading and logrolling are sometimes used interchangeably. For a definition of vote trading, see Stratmann (2008: 372).

reform as an "opportunity lost" in the overhauling of Taiwan's constitutional system (Noble, 1999).

In brief, the issue voted on together with the rearrangement of constitutional powers originated from Taiwan's sovereignty status, and this is a circumstance unlikely to occur in other semi-presidential constitutions. The Constitution of the Republic of China (ROC), as its title suggests, was promulgated in 1947 (when a civil war was raging in China) and implemented in Taiwan and its offshore islands after the mainland was taken over by the People's Republic of China (PRC). The fact that the constitution was only effective in a limited area was justified by two mechanisms: the Temporary Provisions Effective during the Period of Communist Rebellion that gave the executive branch unlimited powers; and the retention of a proportion of unelected legislators representing mainland Chinese constituents. As time went by, the leaders of the authoritarian regime gradually died off, allowing an opportunity for political reform. The first revision of Taiwan's constitution took place in 1991 during the presidency of Lee Teng-hui when the Temporary Provisions were terminated. Lee had been vice president under President Chiang Ching-kuo, the KMT strongman. When Lee, a native Taiwanese, succeeded Chiang in 1988, he attempted to institute direct presidential elections in an effort to expand his power base beyond the limits imposed by the conservatives in the KMT. At that time, the ROC constitution stipulated that for a constitutional amendment to be adopted, it had to win the approval of at least three-quarters of the membership of the National Assembly. Given the number of its National Assembly delegates, the KMT was able to achieve this goal for the first three constitutional revisions it introduced. However, in the 1996 elections, the KMT's seat share was reduced to 54.79%, meaning that it had no choice but to collaborate with the DPP.[8] In contrast to the KMT, the DPP questioned the very legitimacy of the ROC constitution—how could a constitution designed for the whole of China be applicable to Taiwan? In electoral races, most voters have no problem distinguishing between the two parties by their divergent stances on Taiwan's national identity. How then could these two parties collaborate to amend the ROC constitution?

Taiwan's constitutional reform was a sensitive issue because the external community—the PRC in particular—presumed that a new constitution could only be made by a new nation.

---

[8]　For Taiwan's election results, see the Central Election Commission, http://db.cec.gov.tw/histMain. jsp?voteSel=19960301A9 (accessed October 5, 2015).

Understandably, international pressure precluded a completely new constitution. For the DPP, therefore, the main problem was how to modify the ROC constitution in such a way as to manifest Taiwan's de facto independence. Two strategies were available: first, to have the ROC president popularly elected by the people of Taiwan; second, to reorganize Taiwan's constitutional structure—especially in terms of its administrative levels, which signified that the island was a part of China—so that it looked more like an independent country.

With regard to the first strategy, it happened that direct presidential elections were also what Lee wanted. Note here that having a popularly elected president does not necessarily create a presidential system. In the mid-1990s, the DPP felt that it had more chance of increasing its number of legislative seats than it did of winning a presidential election. In these circumstances, the only way out was semi-presidentialism, a hybrid of presidentialism and parliamentarism. There are many types of semi-presidentialism, and the DPP could choose the one most conducive to the party's growth. The KMT, on the other hand, wished to maximize the president's powers within the semi-presidential framework. As for the second strategy, the DPP wanted a reformed constitution that looked like a new constitution and the KMT attempted to substantiate the president's administrative powers. The best target was therefore the Taiwan Provincial Government, the existence of which indicated that Taiwan was no more than a "province" of China. If the Taiwan Provincial Government could be abolished, Taiwan would be closer to an independent country in name. Note that these two objectives could be handled separately. To analyze how the two parties teamed up to amend the constitution by combining these issues into an issue package, we need the help of vote-trading theory.

Before applying this theory, two things have to be clarified. First, the chairpersons of the KMT and the DPP, as the leaders of the bargaining teams, were mandated to set the agenda. Hsu Hsin-liang, the DPP's chairperson at that time, was surrounded by party members who would have preferred an alternative constitutional system; some of them strongly criticized the KMT's proposal to give the president the power to actively dissolve the legislature. Hsu's job was to set an agenda that most DPP politicians could accept even though they might still have reservations. Lee Teng-hui's position was more fragile—the KMT was divided between his supporters who endorsed the idea of direct presidential elections and anti-Lee members who opposed the expansion of the president's powers.

The second point that must be clarified is that there was a reason for the two parties to converge on the issue of the Taiwan Provincial Government. While the constitution purported to apply to the whole of China, the jurisdiction of the ROC after it retreated to Taiwan was almost identical to that of the Taiwan Provincial Government. Naturally, the DPP endeavored to abolish the provincial government (Chao, Myers, and Robinson, 1997: 674), a symbol of the idea that the ROC still represented the whole of China. For Lee, the then governor of Taiwan Province, James Soong, was becoming a menace, but the most Lee could do was to halt elections for the Taiwan Provincial Government.

The DPP was attempting to use the constitutional reform to highlight Taiwan's de facto independence, but Lee's primary goal was the consolidation of his executive power. The two party chairpersons therefore made the "Taiwan Provincial Government" and the "appointment of the premier" indispensable elements of the issue package. As a reassurance, a National Development Conference (NDC) was held in December 1996, awaiting the National Assembly to approve its proposals. Whether the tentative settlement reached at the NDC could be carried over into the constitutional revision was another story.

By revealing the mechanism of vote trading, we will show in the next section how the arrangement of constitutional powers was affected by unrelated issues, and how bargaining can lead to multiple outcomes. In this way, vote-trading theory not only answers the question we raised but enriches the literature of constitutional choice.

IV. A Model of Vote Trading

Vote trading is an important topic in legislative studies (Buchanan and Tullock, 1962; Mueller, 1997). Since constitutional choice also involves decision-making by vote, the theory of vote trading can be immediately applied to it. Most public choice theories ask how vote trading affects the final decision. In particular, Schwartz (1977: 999) proves that when at least some of the issues can be decided upon independently and when there exists a feasible outcome not dominated by any other, then that outcome will automatically be chosen in the absence of vote trading. An implication of this statement is that if preferences are nonseparable (i.e., cannot be measured independently), vote trading may occur and create an unstable decision.[9]

These models of vote trading leave some important questions unanswered. The first is which analytical tool should be used. Cooperative game theory, a widely used tool for the study of vote trading, focuses on coalition formation rather than commitment to the agreement reached by a coalition. In contrast, the equilibrium concept in non-cooperative game theory is designed to handle the enforceability problem.[10] This article will use the non-cooperative game as the analytical tool because enforceability is one of the essential issues in vote trading. Second, the higher the threshold for passing a resolution, the more difficult it becomes to change the status quo. The ability to change the status quo is thus an important issue under the qualified majority rule. This is also a matter of practical importance because constitutional revisions usually involve multiple issues and qualified majority rules. Third, Tullock (1959) and Riker and Brams (1973) have shown that vote trading may create Pareto inefficient outcomes. From the perspective of citizens of a country, social optimality is a critical issue in their evaluation of constitutional choice. These are all problems that a model of vote trading should take into account.[11]

To cope with these problems, the following propositions are derived from the equilibrium of a non-cooperative game of vote trading. Here we define an "issue package" as the set of issues that must be voted upon at the same time. For vote trading to happen, the voters must identify at least two issues to form an issue package. Two voting results on an issue package are inconsistent if they differ on at least one issue even if votes on the other issues are the same. Proposition 1 specifies the conditions of vote trading, and Proposition 2 demonstrates how the preference order of the status quo determines the likelihood of vote trading.

Proposition 1: If preferences are separable for all issues in the issue package and players can reach an undefeatable decision to replace the status quo, vote trading will not happen.

What this proposition says is that if no alternative can defeat the best choice of issues

---

[9]　For an application of (non)separable preferences, see Lacy and Niou (2000a).

[10]　An illustrative example is the prisoner's dilemma: in the cooperative game, "mutual defection" will not occur because it is Pareto dominated; in the non-cooperative game, "mutual defection" is the *only* equilibrium because "defection" is the strictly dominant strategy.

[11]　Aside from a few exceptions, earlier studies on vote trading are largely theoretical. For empirical works, see Finke (2009), Kau and Rubin (1979), and Stratmann (1992, 1995).

in the issue package, which must exist because preferences are separable, then no group in the decision-making body can choose any other option that would increase the payoff for any member.[12] Conversely, vote trading may happen if preferences on some issues are nonseparable or the players cannot reach an undefeatable decision to substitute the status quo. An implication is that voting in line with one's principles on the separable preferences may still result in the absence of consensus, and the status quo will not be changed. On this occasion, players with separable preferences are encouraged to trade their votes to obtain a Pareto optimal outcome.

Note that Proposition 1 applies to all types of majority rule, and the probability of a player being included in a winning coalition increases with the threshold of decision-making. A player who is needed by all the winning coalitions to adopt a resolution—who may or may not exist—is called a *pivot*. The following proposition addresses the relationship between vote trading and the preference of the pivot.

Proposition 2: If vote trading happens when preferences are separable, then the status quo across all issues in the issue package is not the best choice for any pivot.

To understand why this is the case, consider a pivot who contradicts this proposition and has the status quo on a particular issue in the issue package as his/her second choice.[13] In these circumstances, the pivot's best choice must be a change in the status quo on this issue. We cannot exclude the possibility that sincere voting by this voter will create an inconsistent voting result for this issue package, so that the status quo will be kept intact. The only way to prevent vote trading from happening is to have the status quo across all issues as a pivot's best choice, in this way he/she can unilaterally veto any change.

Note that this proposition suggests that "if vote trading happens, then the status quo across all issues in the issue package is not the best choice for any pivot" is a necessary condition of vote trading. Since we know that vote trading took place in Taiwan in 1997, we have to show that the status quo in the issue package could not have been the best choice of either the KMT or the DPP. Also note that this proposition applies to any issue package no matter how the weights are determined across issues. Therefore, this proposition can be used

---

[12] If preferences on every issue are separable, then the best choice of each issue is tantamount to the best choice of the issue package, but the converse may not be true.

[13] The status quo ranked below the second choice can be proven to have the same effect.

to tackle the issue package on which the weight of issues varies by pivots. These points will be elaborated in the next section.

V. Vote Trading in the Making of Taiwan's Semipresidential Constitution

To apply vote-trading theory to Taiwan, we will first define the reform issues and the status quo, and then identify the stances of the reformers on these issues. To rephrase the core question: is the status quo across all issues in the issue package the top choice for the KMT and the DPP?

A. Issues

We learn from Proposition 2 that the satisfaction of the stated condition does not imply that vote trading will take place on all issues. For instance, for an issue position seen by all pivots as the best choice, trading votes is unnecessary; it is also pointless to cast a strategic vote to support options at the bottom of one's preference list.[14] Excluding these alternatives, there may still be multiple tradable issues which necessitate the agenda setter deciding the order of voting. The chairpersons of the two parties have to establish a consensus acceptable to their intraparty and interparty partners.

Official archives reveal the following issues to be important to the chairpersons of the two parties (for the references and details of the bargaining, see Table 6.1):

1. Vote of no confidence: whether to allow the parliament to unseat the premier by a vote of no confidence.

2. Appointment of the premier: whether to allow the president to appoint the premier without legislative confirmation.

3. Dissolution of parliament: whether to allow the president to dissolve the Legislative

---

[14] Details of the 1997 constitutional reform are to be found in *Guomin dahui huiyi shilu* (Meeting records of the National Assembly), Vol. 16-18: http://lis.ly.gov.tw/nacgi/ttsweb?@0:0:1:dbini/ lymeetingdb@@0.6962012632289616 (accessed October 5, 2015).

Yuan (parliament); if yes, whether the president has to wait until a vote of no confidence is passed.

4. Legislative powers: whether to give members of the Legislative Yuan the powers to investigate, audit, hold hearings, and impeach the president and vice president.

Table 6.1 Issue Stances

	Kuomintang (KMT)	Democratic Progressive Party (DPP)
Vote of no confidence	· 19/12/96: Legislative Yuan (LY) should have vote of no confidence (VNC) · 26/6/97: Agreed to the restriction that VNC and dissolution cannot be used within the first year after the LY's election	· 21/12/96: LY should have VNC · 23/4/97: DPP insisted on VNC even if LY is not allowed to confirm the appointment of the premier · 26/6/97: With some intraparty disagreement, agreed to the restriction that VNC and dissolution cannot be used within a year after the LY's election
Dissolution of parliament	· 19/12/96: Executive Yuan (EY) can dissolve LY · 12/4/97: President can actively dissolve LY · 10/6/97: Consensus reached on passive dissolution	· 26/4/97: President can only passively dissolve LY · 10/6/97: Consensus reached on passive dissolution
Appointment of the premier	· 19/12/96: President can unilaterally appoint the premier · 21/3/97: President can unilaterally appoint the premier · 26/6/97: Consensus reached that president can unilaterally appoint the premier	· 9/6/96: DPP strongly opposed Lien Chan continuing as premier and asserted that LY should reconfirm the appointment of the premier · 26/6/97: Consensus reached that president can unilaterally appoint the premier
Legislative powers	· 21/6/97: KMT agreed to give members of LY the power to impeach the president in exchange for the removal of LY's power to confirm the appointment of the premier	· 19/12/96: Members of LY should have the powers to impeach, investigate, and audit · 21/6/97: Members of LY have the power to impeach the president

(continued)

	Kuomintang (KMT)	**Democratic Progressive Party (DPP)**
Reconsideration of legislative resolutions	· 11/4/97: EY's request for reconsideration should be maintained even if VNC is adopted · 26/6/97: Consensus reached that LY's threshold for overriding EY's request for reconsideration should be lowered from two-thirds to absolute majority	· 25/4/97: LY's threshold for overriding EY's request for reconsideration should be lowered from two-thirds to absolute majority · 26/6/97: Consensus reached that LY's threshold for overriding EY's request for reconsideration should be lowered from two-thirds to absolute majority
Electoral systems	· 22/12/96: Size of LY should be increased to 200 and term to 4 years · 12/4/97: Term of LY should be extended to 4 years · 26/6/97: Consensus reached that presidents should be elected by a runoff system	· 22/12/96: LY election should use mixed-member proportional (MMP) system; terms of LY and president should be the same; NA should be abolished · 25/4/97: LY election should use MMP · 26/6/97: Some DPP members questioned the consensus that presidents should be elected by a runoff system
Taiwan Provincial Government	· 19/12/96: Taiwan Provincial Government should not be abolished · 26/6/97: Consensus reached that Taiwan Provincial Government elections should be suspended	· 19/12/96: Taiwan Provincial Government should be abolished · 26/6/97: Consensus reached that Taiwan Provincial Government elections should be suspended
Cross-Strait relations	· 22/12/96: One country, two political entities	· 22/12/96: Taiwan is an independent country; political entity is equivalent to a country

Notes: The NDC was convened between December 23 and December 28, 1996. The NA was convened to carry out revision of the constitution between May 5 and July 18, 1997.

Sources: *Central Daily News, United Daily News, United Evening News, Central News Agency*, and *Guomin dahui* (1998).

5. Reconsidering legislative resolutions: whether to lower the legislative threshold for repassing a resolution which the government has demanded to be reconsidered.

6. Electoral systems: whether the constitution should define the electoral systems for the presidential and legislative elections; if yes, what the electoral systems should be.

7. Taiwan Provincial Government: whether to downsize or to abolish the Taiwan Provincial Government.

8. Cross-Strait relations: whether to set up an extra-constitutional council to handle cross-Strait affairs.

Of these issues, cross-Strait relations are extra-constitutional, electoral systems may or may not be constitutional, and the Taiwan Provincial Government is not constitutional unless its relationship with the central government is to be adjusted.[15] Vote trading would affect the functioning of semi-presidentialism if a vote of no confidence, the appointment of the premier, and the dissolution of the parliament are addressed together.

B. Preferences

To verify Proposition 2, we will examine whether any pivot ranks the status quo across all issues in the issue package as his/her favorite choice. Another condition of Proposition 2 is that sincere voting cannot defeat the choice of strategic voting. These conditions will be tested later.

The issue stances of the two parties can be traced back to the first direct presidential election held in 1996. The most pressing issue for Lee, who had just won the election, was the power of the Legislative Yuan to approve the appointment of the premier. The blocking of Lien Chan, Lee's handpicked premier, by the Legislative Yuan in 1996 explains why Lee wanted to exclude legislators from the process of cabinet formation. Thus, "appointment of the premier" was the most critical issue for Lee. Moreover, Lee preferred the president to have active rather than passive dissolution power, with the status quo as the last choice (Noble, 1999: 105). The DPP put the greatest emphasis on abolition of the Taiwan Provincial Government, which would eliminate a symbol of the ROC as the representative of the whole

---

[15] The original constitution stipulated legislative confirmation of the appointment of the premier (Art. 55), the reconsideration threshold (Art. 57), and the legal status of the provincial governments (Art. 112).

of China.[16] On the "dissolution of parliament" issue, the DPP's chairperson preferred passive to active dissolution, with the status quo as the last choice, because the party seemed to have little chance of winning a presidential election in the 1990s.

On the issue of "vote of no confidence," there was a strong bipartisan consensus. Under semi-presidentialism, a vote of no confidence can coexist with a strong or a weak presidency, and was thus acceptable to both parties. On "legislative powers," the DPP sought to expand them, and the KMT agreed as long as the DPP would endorse the exclusion of legislators from the appointment of the premier. As for "reconsidering legislative resolutions," there was disagreement at first, but the two chairpersons quickly agreed to reduce the threshold from a two-thirds majority to an absolute majority. "Electoral systems" and "cross-Strait relations" were dropped from the agenda because the two parties held incompatible positions.

C. Vote Trading

The following list summarizes the most critical issues and the possible alternatives (as indicated by the numbers):

1. Appointment of the premier: (1) status quo, (2) no confirmation.
2. Dissolution of parliament: (1) status quo, (2) active dissolution, (3) passive dissolution.
3. Taiwan Provincial Government: (1) status quo, (2) abolish, (3) downsize.

There were other issues as well, but these three represented the major concerns of the two pivots. We want to demonstrate that vote trading was possible even with these three issues. Issues 1 and 2 should have been deliberated after there was bipartisan consensus on the "vote of no confidence," and their combination determined the subtypes of Taiwan's semi-presidential system. In contrast, issue 3 had nothing to do with the rearrangement of constitutional powers and could be addressed independently. However, the DPP placed the greatest emphasis on issue 3 and insisted that it must be included in the issue package if the constitution was to be amended.

---

[16] If issues have equal weight, further equilibria may emerge. Issues with different weights may thus reduce the cost of bargaining.

Table 6.2 Preferences of the Kuomintang (KMT) and the Democratic Progressive Party (DPP) on the Key Issues.

Issues	Preferences	KMT	DPP
Appointment of premier	1. SQ (confirmation needed) 2. No (no confirmation)	2 > 1	1 > 2
Dissolution of parliament	1. SQ 2. Active dissolution 3. Passive dissolution	2 > 3 > 1	3 > 2 > 1
Taiwan provincial government	1. SQ 2. Abolish 3. Downsize	3 > 2 > 1	2 > 3 > 1

Source: Author's count.

Note: "SQ" = "status quo", ">" = "preferred to".

Table 6.2 displays the preferences of the two parties. It shows clearly that vote trading happened while the two pivots ranked the status quo as their least favorable choice on the critical issues. In the following, Result 1 deals with the social optimality of the consensus the two parties could have reached; Result 2 says more about the impact of these two equilibria on Taiwan's constitutional system.[17] For the purpose of this article, the key question is whether vote trading mismatches the power and accountability of Taiwan's president.

Result 1: "No confirmation, passive dissolution, downsize the Taiwan Provincial Government" and "no confirmation, active dissolution, abolish the Taiwan Provincial Government" are Pareto efficient equilibria.

The first step is to verify that these two outcomes are in equilibrium. The stances of the two parties will first meet at "no confirmation, passive dissolution, downsize the Taiwan Provincial Government," the KMT's second choice and the DPP's sixth choice, or "no confirmation, active dissolution, abolish the Taiwan Provincial Government," the fourth choice of both. Accordingly, if the two parties adopt one of these two outcomes, neither has the incentive to adjust its strategy because the payoffs are sure to decrease. Second, regarding

---

[17] Some other consensuses may also be Pareto efficient, but they are not the best consensus the two pivots can obtain.

their Pareto optimality, we can see from the ranking of their preferences that no other equilibrium improves the payoff of both pivots, or at least increases the payoff of one pivot and keeps the payoff of another pivot constant, apart from the two outcomes described here.

Result 2: "No confirmation, passive dissolution, downsize the Taiwan Provincial Government" and "no confirmation, active dissolution, abolish the Taiwan Provincial Government" are both the result of vote trading, but only the former does not permit the president to dissolve the parliament before a vote of no confidence is passed.

According to Proposition 2, both equilibria reflect the necessary conditions of vote trading. "No confirmation, active dissolution" allows the president to unilaterally appoint the premier and actively dissolve the parliament, which means that the president takes the greatest administrative responsibility and can ask the electorate to arbitrate when the premier is no longer supported by the parliament. But the status of the Taiwan Provincial Government complicated the negotiations. Expecting that the KMT would at most downsize the Taiwan Provincial Government, the DPP turned down the KMT's proposal for the power of active dissolution. Yet both parties still found "no confirmation, passive dissolution, downsize the Taiwan Provincial Government" to be better than no change at all. That is why the KMT, although it favored giving the president active dissolution power, supported the DPP's request for "passive dissolution," and the DPP, although it wished to maintain the confirmation power, had the incentive to endorse the KMT's demand for "no confirmation." If there had been no external constraints preventing the two parties from abolishing the Taiwan Provincial Government, the chain of accountability would have been maintained in a more consistent way.

We saw at the beginning of this article that "no confirmation, active dissolution" is what is stipulated in the French constitution. Taiwan could have created a similar arrangement if the KMT had been willing to abolish the Taiwan Provincial Government in exchange for the DPP's support for giving the president active dissolution powers. The first occasion on which the two parties might have made such a deal was during the NDC. President Lee had won a second term in 1996, so at the time of the NDC power succession was an imminent problem. Lee's attempt to limit support for Governor Soong coincided with a campaign for independence by the DPP; that explains why the NDC put equal emphasis on the Taiwan

Provincial Government and the rearrangement of constitutional powers.[18]

For this reason, votes could have been traded between the independence-leaning DPP and the power-seeking KMT to abolish the Taiwan Provincial Government and create a constitutional system that would allow the electorate to make the ultimate decision. Had this been the case, the DPP would have been more willing to compromise on the president's active dissolution powers because its chances of winning a presidential election were positively correlated with the credibility of Taiwan independence. It was external pressure that made this prospect less likely. The KMT's hesitation also explains why the end of the NDC marked the beginning of the constitutional reform and the resolutions adopted in the latter were different from the decisions taken by the former. Before the NDC, the DPP insisted that the premiership be reconfirmed and sought to strengthen the powers of the legislature as an instrument of checks and balances. Above all, the powers of the Legislative Yuan would have been enhanced if the dissolution of parliament had to be preceded by the passage of a vote of no confidence. Unfortunately, the calculations made in the 1997 revision of the constitution deprived Taiwan's voters of a mechanism for identifying who is accountable in a snap election. The shrewd behavior of the two party chairpersons may have created loopholes in Taiwan's semi-presidential constitution.

VI. Conclusion

We have demonstrated in this article how Taiwan's semi-presidential system mismatches the power and accountability of the constitutional actors. Most seriously, although the president dominates the formation of the government, he/she is not allowed to call for an early parliamentary election and ask voters to speak out. There are two other systems that would obviously be preferable. The first is a system in which the president takes the lead in that he/she can appoint the premier without parliamentary confirmation and dissolve the parliament before the premier is unseated so that voters are mandated to judge who is accountable. In

---

[18] According to Chao, Myers, and Robinson (1997: 679), the DPP had insisted that the Taiwan Provincial Government should be abolished throughout the NDC. Some would even argue that the subsequent constitutional reform was carried out in order to resolve the Taiwan Provincial Government problem. See http://www. haixiainfo.com.tw/80-3377.html (accessed October 5, 2015).

the second, the premier would have the upper hand as he/she represents the majority in the legislature and the president could only dissolve the parliament after a vote of no confidence had been passed. Most semi-presidential regimes have adopted one of these two designs. Taiwan is an exception, and we cannot explain why this is the case without understanding how its sovereignty status is connected with bargaining over constitutional reform.

The issue of Taiwan's sovereignty was exemplified by the direct presidential election—the electorate consisted of citizens living in Taiwan and its offshore islands but the president was elected to represent the whole of China. The DPP, constrained by the framework of the ROC constitution, attempted to revise this constitution to make Taiwan more like an independent country. That meant that the existing rules governing constitutional amendment had to be followed. Although they had very different ideas about Taiwan's national identity, the KMT and the DPP teamed up in 1997 to revise the constitution. Vote trading took place because Lee Teng-hui was trying to exclude legislators from playing a part in the appointment of the premier and the DPP wanted to abolish the Taiwan Provincial Government. This transaction produced an innately flawed semi-presidential system.

Using reform of Taiwan's constitution as a special case, this article proposes a new method for studying the general nature of constitutional choice. When dealing with multiple issues, vote trading is frequently used and can be applied to any voting body. Given the large number of issues and the qualified majority rules that are often involved in the choice of a constitution, minority interests will have a certain amount of leverage that enables them to influence the final outcome. We have also shown that the non-cooperative game is a useful tool for unravelling the mechanism of vote trading when no rule enforces the consensus reached by the voters. Moreover, the qualified majority rule increases the chances of a voter being a pivot, and vote trading may occur if all the pivots find issues on which the status quo is not the best choice.

There are other implications as well. Questions arise as to how negotiations may help to achieve an eventual equilibrium and how the reform process is conditioned by the rules of decision-making. There is also an important normative question: who should be the decision-makers when a constitution is to be made or amended? We have seen how elected delegates may trade their votes on different issues to prevent gridlock, even though the package that is eventually negotiated may not function well. If a referendum or another independent agency had been required to ratify the constitutional revisions, there is a good chance that the current semi-presidential system would have been rejected. Indeed, the rules of constitution making affect the content of the constitution, so the former are as important as the latter.

Taiwan's Semi-Presidential System Was Easy to Establish but Is Difficult to Fix: A Comparison between the Constitutional Reform Efforts of 1997 and 2015[*]

I. The Puzzle

Democratization and constitutional revisions can come in tandem if new social forces unleashed by the former choose rules to institutionalize their ideas. Taiwan, a nascent democracy, experienced seven constitutional revisions between 1991 and 2005, rendering a reform every two years. Especially noteworthy are the constitutional reform of 1997, when direct presidential election and parliament's vote of no confidence were combined to establish Taiwan's semi-presidential system, and the attempted revision in 2015, which failed to reform this constitutional system. Both of the reform efforts focused on the adjustment of executive-legislative relations, both were dominated by Taiwan's two largest parties, the Kuomintang (KMT) and the Democratic Progressive Party (DPP), and both saw the two political camps attempt to reach a consensus on some issues.[1] Given the similar institutional environments in 1997 and 2015, why was there a difference in the outcomes of the reform efforts?

Although the body responsible for the approval of legislative proposals for constitutional amendments was changed in 2005 from the National Assembly to the public, the legislative stage for constitutional amendment was the same in 1997 and 2015. It seemed that the inability to adopt any amendment in 2015 was induced by the incompatibility of legislators'

---

[*] Reproduced from [Lin, Jih-wen. "Taiwan's Semi-Presidential System Was Easy to Establish but Is Difficult to Fix A Comparison between the Constitutional Reform Efforts of 1997 and 2015." *Taiwan Journal of Democracy* 12(2): 39-57, 2016] with kind permission of Taiwan Foundation for Democracy.

[1] Constitutional revisions in Taiwan affect not only domestic interests but also external actors. For instance, when commenting on Taiwan's constitutional reform, an international publication viewed it as a spin away from the "one country, two systems" model proclaimed by the People's Republic of China (PRC). See Wu and Gold (2015).

positions on issues.[2] Without a doubt, the political parties held different views on whether the appointment of the premier should be confirmed by the parliament, but this difference existed in 1997 as well. In both reform efforts, the constitutional decision makers shared consensus on some issues, so why did the common ground in 1997 lead to the establishment of semi-presidentialism, but in 2015 fail to result in passage of *any* proposal? This is an intriguing question, for consensus on some issues can lead to effective resolutions, even if legislators hold different positions on other matters.

The fundamental question is the definition of "issue positions." The main argument of this essay is that, even if a consensus seems to exist regarding some issues, preferences concerning individual issues may not be fixed; rather, they may vary according to how positions on issues are packaged. By this logic, the preferences of the 1997 reform effort concerning important issues can be evaluated independently, but those of the 2015 effort are mutually dependent. To verify this argument, the essay first examines the redefinition of issue positions and highlights its contribution to the literature. The essay then discusses the formation of partisan positions and explains why the results of the two constitutional reform efforts were divergent. The essay concludes by pondering the role of democratization in diminishing space for cooperation.

II. What Are Separable Preferences?

Constitutional reforms seek to change the status quo, and almost all constitutional choices are adopted by voting for concerns listed on an agenda. Many theories have studied the rules for both voting and agenda-setting, but very few of them have applied these concepts to constitutional choice. Yet, two elements are essential to the theory of constitutional choice: the threshold for adopting an amendment and the nature of the positions on issues. The threshold ranges between simple majority rule to unanimous rule, and the difficulty to change the status quo increases with the number of votes needed to pass a resolution. The nature of

---

[2] Since we are comparing the same country over different time periods, many factors should be treated as parameters, such as the political culture that is dominated by respect for the educated class and the importance of personal connections in political life. Even the "five constitutional powers" principle embodied in Sun Yat-sen's doctrine remains unchanged.

the positions on issues is more complicated and must be explained in detail.

An issue is a matter to be discussed with the others, whereas positions on an issue are chosen through one's subjective will. The major question is whether a person can have a fixed preference regarding an issue no matter in which package of issues it is embedded.[3] Represent preferences as utilities and let $u_i(x_i)$ be the utility on issue i. Then preferences are separable if, and only if,

$$u(x) = u_1(x_1) + u_2(x_2)... + u_m(x_m)$$

for m issues, so that the increase (decrease) of $u_i(x_i)$ will monotonically increase (decrease) $u(x)$; preferences are nonseparable if we cannot derive such an equation.[4] If a voter has a nonseparable preference regarding the issues, the preferences concerning the package of issues are nonseparable. This argument has been formalized as the following theorem. In reference to separability of preferences, Schwartz states that, "when at least some of the issues can be decided upon independently and when there exists a feasible outcome not dominated by any other, then that outcome will automatically be chosen in the absence of vote trading (1977: 999)." In other words, if a constitutional reform aimed to adjust the status quo and preferences were separable, sincere voting would achieve this goal. Conversely, for the status quo to be unchangeable, even if consensus seemed to exist (when only issues favoring its passage were evident), nonseparable preference would be a necessary condition.

How the theorem can be extended to constitutional modifications with veto players is our major concern. To facilitate analysis, players whose agreement is needed to pass a resolution are labeled the "pivot".[5] Two factors are correlated with the changeability of the status quo. First, the key determinant is the separability of preferences. When preferences are

---

[3]　Separable preferences almost never have been used to study constitution making. For one of the few exceptions, see the use of nonseparable preferences toward the limit of European integration in Finke (2009). Other works tend to presume that the players have separable preferences so that the spatial model can be applied. See Steunenberg (2004).

[4]　Understanding an issue by its context is similar to but not exactly the same as nonseparable preferences, unless the former implies the change in preferences by contexts. The (non)separable utility is a generalization of the (non)separable preferences of binary choices. For the definition of separable preferences of binary choices, see Schwartz (1977); Lacy and Niou (2000a). For the relationship between these two concepts, see Nakamura (2009).

[5]　In Taiwan's case, a pivot makes a decision until a strong intraparty disagreement arises. In this sense, no formal rule is used to constrain the pivot's decision making.

nonseparable, the barrier to a successful reform is much greater than if the preferences are separable. Second, using the concept of utility, payoffs may vary by issue. This factor has little effect on the stability of the status quo, but it affects setting the agenda (i.e., the order in which issues are to be discussed). The cost of a reform is reflected in the establishment of the agenda—otherwise no one would be interested in controlling the sequence of discussions. Consequently, we postulate the following hypothesis:

> *When the cost of constitutional reform is not zero, the higher the percentage of issues with nonseparable preferences and the lower the payoffs of issues with separable preferences, the less likely for the status quo to be changed.*

The next question is how the above hypothesis may enhance our understanding of the theories of constitutional choice. The following section elaborates further upon this topic.

III. Theories of Constitutional Choice

Focusing on questions concerning constitutional choice, this section explores the theoretical implications of the separability of preferences. Before addressing the works on constitutional choice, a distinction must be made between separable preferences and issue linkage. Issue linkage is an analytical tool in negotiation theory which asserts that the discussion of two or more issues is a bargaining strategy that may increase the probability of reaching an agreement.[6] For example, dilemmas in collective action can be solved by adding another issue that may persuade the potential free riders to collaborate. It is true that, in this essay, some issues are linked when a choice is to be made. However, issue linkage does not imply nonseparable preferences. That is, issue linkage is a necessary step to having a nonseparable preference, but the two concepts are different. Issues can be linked even when the preferences are separable.

Several general theories can be considered concerning empirical studies on constitutional choice. To begin with, interest in political institutions revived in the 1980s at the ebb of institution-free behavioralism. As symbolized by the book, *Bring the State Back In*, students

---

[6]　For a recent review of issue linkage and empirical tests of whether this strategy is effective, see the articles published by Poast (2012, 2013a, 2013b).

began to notice the indispensable role of political institutions (Evans, Rueschemeyer, and Skocpol, 1985). "Historical institutionalism" analyzes political institutions as a source of individual power but also as a constraint on the exercise of this power. As for how an institution is chosen, historical institutionalism tends to be cautious and explains institutional formation by path dependency (the future is conditioned by what has happened before) and critical juncture (events that may disrupt the equilibrium of the current situation).[7] The question is: Can we use historical institutionalism to make predictions for what types of constitutions are likely to emerge, especially for those outside a travelled path? Later, the essay explains how preferences matter in answering this question.

The rational-choice-based new institutionalism is the flip side of historical institutionalism. An institution by definition is supposed to be stable. In particular, a constitution should endure for as long as possible so that actors can have long-term expectations of how others will behave. Accordingly, while historical institutionalism is good at explaining institutional change, rational-choice-based new institutionalism usually is used to interpret the effects of a stable institution. In keeping with the "structure-induced equilibrium" metaphors (Shepsle and Weingast, 1981), one aims to maintain a fixed institution in order to study the behavior it produces; even if there are multiple institutions to be studied, the focus tends to be on comparative statistics concerning the consequences of a specific institution rather than on why a particular institution was chosen. One even can argue that the more stable an institution (such as a constitution), the harder to explain its change. Endogeneity is another problem stemming from the approach of keeping institutions intact. For example, it is well known that electoral systems shape party systems (Duverger, 1963), an argument provoking many empirical tests. But can the causality be reversed? A party may choose a majoritarian electoral system precisely because it is likely to dominate the parliament (Boix, 1999; Colomer, 2005). Both approaches are exacerbated by the assumption that institutions do not change. For the purpose of this essay, therefore, the key question is how to study the changes in a constitution by what the constitution produces. We will come to this point later.

In the meantime, discussions about the choice of constitutional systems arise.[8] The

---

[7]　For the formalization of path dependency, see the overview by Rhodes, Binder, and Rockman (2006).

[8]　Some of the most well-cited studies in constitutional choice belong to this type. For example, Sartori (1997), Lijphart (2012), Tsebelis (2002), Samuels and Shugart (2010b)。

first type of argument assumes an "engineering" perspective and addresses the likely consequences of a particular institutional arrangement. Linz (1990) started the debate: the presidential system is a danger because the winner takes all, leaving no political status for the defeated candidate. Lijphart (2012: 105-109) also cast some doubt on the presidential system because it could place the leader of a plurality group in power. Some scholars have refuted these arguments, and have thought that the electoral system plays a more critical role than constitutional systems regarding unwanted consequences (Horowitz, 1990). Moreover, the most typical winner-takes-all system can be found in the United Kingdom, a country that has adopted the pure parliamentary system, because the majority party controls almost all political powers (Mainwaring and Shugart, 1997). As for semi-presidentialism, a hybrid of presidentialism and parliamentarism, the subtypes are so complicated that we cannot easily attribute its advantages or problems to presidentialism or parliamentarism (Sartori, 1994; Elgie, 2005). Again, we are not certain why a country selects a particular constitutional system and whether the "normative values" and the "partisan positions" are linked, let alone are we certain about the separability of preferences.

　　The theories reviewed above all pay inadequate attention to the final stage of constitution making: how votes are aggregated and by which rules. These will have a tremendous effect on the collective choice. It is here that preference structure plays an important role. First, while historical institutionalism tends to be vague about *ex ante* expectations of institutional arrangement, preference structure may help to narrow unlikely paths. From the separability of preferences, we also can distinguish between the likelihood of sincere or strategic voting when a choice is being made. Whether a constitutional choice reflects the true preferences of the reformers is a critical lesson of democracy. Second, regarding rational-choice-based new institutionalism, the tendency to observe the effects of an institution forces a theorist to keep the latter unchanged. What we can do is to apply the concept of "quasi-parameters"—changes that appear to be parameters in the short term but variables in the long run (Greif and Laitin, 2004: 639). We have shown that nonseparable preferences resist change in the status quo, but that sometimes leaders who set the agenda may raise new and important issues with separable preferences that can upset the status quo. In this way, whether an institution is changeable depends on our horizon. Third, the selection of constitutional systems can be studied in a similar way. Bargaining over the final decision suggests the coexistence of several feasible outcomes. Whether the pivots have nonseparable preferences plays a decisive role. Presenting a nonseparable preference is a useful strategy for those who prefer maintaining the status quo to accepting alternatives proposed by the other parties. Conversely, smooth adoption of a reform suggests that the preferences are separable on the most critical issues.

In summary, preference structure is a minute illuminator enlightening the grand theories of constitutional choice. As long as constitutional choice is made by voting, the separability of preferences affects how individual positions can be aggregated into a collective decision. On this basis, the following sections validate the hypothesis that the separability of preferences matters by comparing Taiwan's constitutional reform efforts of 1997 and 2015. Before setting the stage for these reforms, we discuss how democratization has shaped the issue preferences of the key players.

IV. Formation of the Issues

Despite the high frequency of Taiwan's constitutional revisions, some common goals have been shared by the political parties across time.[9] After the first direct presidential election in 1996, the Kuomintang, under the chairmanship of Lee Teng-hui, sought to maximize the president's powers, while the Democratic Progressive Party and the other opposition parties sought to augment the powers of the legislature, or parliament (Legislative Yuan). Nevertheless, the DPP also supported direct presidential election because Taiwan's residents would constitute the electorate, a significant symbol of independent sovereignty.

While the KMT remained the largest party in the 1990s, the National Assembly election

---

[9] These constitutional reforms and their major accomplishments are the following: 1. 1991: definition of the electoral systems for the elections of the national legislative bodies and the two political entities across the Taiwan Strait; 2. 1992: election of the president of the Republic of China by residents living in the country's free area; 3. 1994: direct election of the president of the Republic of China by the people residing in the country's free area, and removal of the premier's countersignature for personnel appointed by the president; 4. 1997: removal of the parliament's confirmation power for the appointment of the premier and downsizing of the Taiwan Provincial Government; 5. 1999: definition of both the electoral system for and the size of the National Assembly; 6. 2000: redefinition of the electoral system and powers of the National Assembly; and 7. 2005: change of the electoral system for the election of the Legislative Yuan. Accordingly, only the 1997 reform dealt with a significant adjustment of executive-legislative relations.

held in 1996 made the DPP a veto player because the passage of amendments required the support of three-quarters of the body. The only compromise the two parties could achieve was a constitutional system combining the features of presidentialism and parliamentarism. A change in Taiwan's constitutional system was an immense project, involving vital matters such as the parliament's vote of no confidence, appointment of the premier, the president's power to dissolve the parliament, and the legislative threshold to override an executive veto. Other concerns included the status quo of the Taiwan Provincial Government (TPG), the jurisdiction of which was essentially equivalent to that of the Republic of China (ROC), and electoral systems for legislative elections. On the basis of the direct election of the ROC president, the KMT endeavored to remove the parliament's confirmation power over the appointment of the premier and to give the president active power to dissolve the parliament. Given its strength at that time, the DPP was able to assume positions opposite those of the KMT. As will be elaborated later, the two pivots agreed to abolish the parliament's confirmation power over the appointment of the premier, but did not allow the president to dissolve the parliament unless, first, the premier had been dismissed.

In 2000, the DPP's nominee, Chen Shui-bian, won the presidential election by gaining a plurality (but not a majority) of the votes, while the KMT remained the parliament's majority party. According to the constitutional reform of 1997, the president could not dissolve the parliament unless the premier first had been unseated. However, the legislators preferred to keep the existing premier in office because the parliament had no power to confirm the appointment of the next premier. To minimize the probability of divided government, some regarded the timing and formula to elect the legislators important. In the constitutional reform of 2005, Taiwan switched from the single nontransferable vote (SNTV) under the multimember district system to the mixed-member majoritarian (MMM) system and extended the term of the legislators from three years to four, hoping that the majoritarian-leaning electoral system and the simultaneous electoral timing would reduce the chances of a minority government.

Constitutional revision turned out to be more complicated than expected. The first unified government under the new electoral system was formed in 2008. Hong-Ming Chen and Jung-Hsiang Tsai [陳宏銘、蔡榮祥] (2008) discovered that executive-legislative incongruence under President Ma Ying-jeou, Chen Shui-bian's successor, remained prevalent. Hong-Ming Chen [陳宏銘] (2012: 48-49) also found that, although the president, rather than the premier, officially was the proposer of major policy under Taiwan's semi-presidential constitution, in reality, the president's legislative influence was limited because it was the premier who faced the parliament. Lin (2011b) demonstrated that the parliament could create dissonance between the premier and the president because the executive and legislative powers were separated, and the president did not hold veto power. Such studies point to the innate defects of Taiwan's semi-presidential constitution: the president, as the primary decision maker, can neither chair the cabinet meeting nor actively dissolve the parliament. By this design, a serious coordination problem hinders communication between the executive branch of the government and the parliament, even though both may be controlled by the same party.

The cross-Strait agreements signed between Taipei and Beijing are a litmus test for the executive-legislative tension under the unified government. The KMT government sought to minimize legislative oversight of the Economic Cooperation Framework Agreement (ECFA), signed on June 29, 2010, and suggested that the Legislative Yuan only could accept or reject, rather than revise, this agreement. Although ECFA was passed as a framework agreement, subsequent agreements were more controversial. In Ma's second term as president, the Cross-Strait Agreement on Trades in Services (CSATS), a follow-up agreement to ECFA, aimed to liberalize investment by service industries across the Strait. Again, the executive branch insisted that the parliament could not have an item-by-item vote on the CSATS, with the rationale that the rejection of a single article might place the entire agreement at risk. When a KMT legislator attempted to move promptly on CSATS, the student-led Sunflower Movement erupted on March 18, 2014. That students could occupy the parliament for twenty-three days revealed that the legislators—some of whom perhaps were from the KMT—were dissatisfied with the government's behavior.

The Sunflower Movement also opened the gate for constitutional reform. Concerns included restoring legislative power to confirm the appointment of the premier, lowering of the voting age, and updating the constitution's human rights list, among other objectives. As will be explained in the next two sections, the success of constitutional reform is strongly affected by whether partisan preferences regarding the important issues are separable.

V. The 1997 Constitutional Reform

This section examines in detail the 1997 issue preferences of the KMT and the DPP to determine whether they were separable. We would expect that, even when taking into account the cost of constitutional reform, amendments still would have been passed if the preferences regarding important issues were separable. However, as will be demonstrated in the next section, separable preferences do not necessarily lead to successful constitutional reform if the issues are of minor importance to the pivots.

Taiwan's 1997 constitutional reform was a significant event because it marked the establishment of the semi-presidential system, following Taiwan's first direct presidential election in 1996. As the two pivots prepared to establish the semi-presidential system, the most vital issue to the KMT was the president's direct control of the premier. Prior to the 1997 reform, presidential appointment of the premier had to be approved by the parliament. The most critical issue for the DPP, an independence-leaning party, was not so much the selection of a constitutional system as it was the status of the TPG—abolishment or significant downsizing of this administrative unit could help to normalize Taiwan as a country. The KMT wished to downsize (rather than abolish) the TPG and allow the president to actively dissolve the parliament (before dismissal of the premier by the Legislative Yuan), whereas the DPP hoped to abolish the TPG and permit the president to dissolve the Legislative Yuan only if a vote of no confidence to dismiss the premier first were passed (passive dissolution).

To probe the bottom lines of the political parties, the National Development Conference (NDC, 國家發展會議) was convened in December 1996. The major points of debate included presidential appointment of the premier; the parliament's vote of no confidence regarding the premier; dissolution of the Legislative Yuan; the powers and functions of the Legislative Yuan and the National Assembly; public referenda; the sizes and terms of the Legislative Yuan and the National Assembly; the electoral systems to govern future elections; cross-Strait relations; and the TPG. Basically, the 1997 constitutional reform effort followed the issue agenda of the NDC. Among the multitude of proposals raised in this reform effort, four were especially critical and suffice to demonstrate the adoptability of the issues. These issues and the respective alternative positions held by the pivots are listed below.

1. Appointment of the premier: (1) maintain the status quo, or (2) remove the Legislative Yuan's confirmation power.

2. Vote of no confidence: (1) maintain the status quo, or (2) enable the Legislative Yuan to pass a vote of no confidence to dismiss the premier.

3. Dissolution of the Legislative Yuan: (1) maintain the status quo, (2) permit the president to dissolve the Legislative Yuan before passage of a vote of no confidence to dismiss the premier (active dissolution), or (3) permit the president to dissolve the Legislative Yuan only following a vote of no confidence to dismiss the premier (passive dissolution).

4. TPG: (1) maintain the status quo, (2) downsize the TPG (halt the elections for the Governor and Provincial Council of the TPG) and simplify its organization, or (3) abolish the TPG.

Although all of these matters were important, the one with the highest utility for the KMT was appointment of the premier. For the DPP, it was the TPG. In other words, the pivots had to place these two concerns on the bargaining table.

Table 7.1 shows clearly that, for both pivots, preferences were separable because, no matter how the issues were considered, the ordinal sequence of the utilities remained the same. Notice that "the dissolution of the Legislative Yuan" was linked with "the Legislative Yuan can pass a vote of no confidence." Since the two pivots had little disagreement regarding the parliament's ability to sack the premier, the focus was on the timing of the president's dissolution of the parliament.

Even after taking into account the cost of the reform, the separable preferences of the critical issues still could lead to a changeable status quo.[10]

Since the two pivots engaged in vote trading across their critical issues, the benefits received by each side should have been higher than that from sincere voting. In fact, the importance of their traded issues *enlarged* the total gains because of the addition of the TPG issue. Meanwhile, the enlarged space for consensus increased the necessity of agenda-setting.

---

[10] Also see Buchanan and Tullock (1962), Mueller (1997)。

Table 7.1 Preferences on the Agenda of the 1997 Constitutional Reform Effort

Issue	KMT	DPP	Note
Appointment of Premier	1. Remove confirmation power 2. The status quo	1. The status quo 2. Remove confirmation power	Most critical concern of the KMT
Vote of no confidence	1. Yes 2. The status quo	1. Yes 2. The status quo	If a vote of no confidence is passed, the parliament can be dissolved
Dissolution of parliament	1. Active dissolution 2. Passive dissolution 3. The status quo	1. Passive dissolution 2. Active dissolution 3. The status quo	
TPG	1. Downsize 2. Abolish 3. The status quo	1. Abolish 2. Downsize 3. The status quo	Most critical to the DPP

Source: A summary of the *Central Daily News*, the *United Daily News*, and the *Central News Agency*.
Note: Numbers indicate preference order revealed at the beginning of the negotiation.

Why did the TPG issue facilitate the establishment of the semi-presidential system? It is because the KMT could not agree with the DPP's goal to abolish the TPG, thereby leading to greater concessions on the other issues. Except for the KMT's insistence on the removal of the parliament's confirmation power, the DPP made gains on other issues such as the president's passive dissolution power regarding the parliament and the lowering of the parliament's overriding threshold. Eventually, both pivots found the final result better than retaining the status quo.

The 1997 constitutional reform indicates that changing the status quo hinges more on the separability of preferences than on the complexity of issues. To test the flip side of the hypothesis, the next section uses the constitutional reform of 2015 to gauge the impact of nonseparable preferences.

VI. The 2015 Constitutional Reform Effort

Taiwan's experience with a semi-presidential system—especially between 2008 and 2016—shows the flaws of institutional design irrespective of the dividedness of government. Since the constitutional revision efforts held in 1997 and 2015 had almost identical legislative procedures, it is worthwhile to study whether the abortive reform in 2015 had something to do with the nonseparable preferences of the key issues.

The mismatched power and accountability under Taiwan's constitutional system can be seen in the communication problem occurring among the president, the premier, and the parliament. The Sunflower Movement took place exactly when the personal relationship between the president and the speaker of the Legislative Yuan soured and no channels could institutionalize the negotiations between the two sides. As could be expected, the demand for constitutional reform rose again. The major proposals covered three areas: 1. executive-legislative relations, 2. voting age, and 3. human rights and other issues. As discussed above, the KMT and the DPP may have taken different stances on executive-legislative relations, but that did not imply a lack of consensus on the other issues.

The formal proposal for constitutional revisions was launched by thirty-seven legislators from the KMT, the DPP, the Taiwan Solidarity Union (TSU), and the People First Party (PFP) in a December 12, 2014 press conference, two weeks after the KMT suffered a disastrous defeat in the local elections.[11] These legislators assembled a Constitution Amendment Committee in the Legislative Yuan (CACLY, 立法院修憲委員會).[12] On December 17, 2014, a DPP legislator proposed updating the human rights articles in the constitution and lowering the voting age to eighteen; the same legislator also suggested that the threshold to amend the constitution should be lowered (*Liberty Times* [《自由時報》], 2014; Tai [戴雅真], 2014). On January 15, 2015, the KMT proposed restoring the legislative power to confirm the appointment of the premier, while the DPP proposed that the president should have the active power to dissolve the Legislative Yuan.[13] After the political parties finished drafting their

---

[11]　For the signatures, see Chen and Chen [陳彥廷、陳慧萍] (2014).

[12]　For the organization of the CACLY, see *Organic Regulations of Committee on Constitution Amendment Committee, Legislative Yuan* [立法院修憲委員會組織規程]: http://www.ly.gov.tw/02_introduce/0204_comm/intro.action?comtcd=29 (accessed June 25, 2016).

[13]　The DPP's proposal regarding the president's dissolution power was based on the advice of a scholar.

proposals, the constitutional reform effort was launched in the Legislative Yuan on March 4, 2015.

The following list enumerates the major issues and the stances taken by the political parties. A party's position is defined by what was formally stated in the documents prepared by the CACLY, even though intraparty noises might still have existed.[14]

1. Human rights. When the Constitution of the ROC was adopted on January 1, 1947, the scope of human rights was much smaller than what it was in 2015. This issue of protecting expanded human rights was initiated by scholars working on this topic and endorsed by the DPP (Fu [符芳碩], 2015).[15] This was an issue for which the other parties (such as the KMT) lacked good reasons to voice their disapproval.

2. Voting age. Most democracies have used age eighteen as the start of the voting age. Eric Chu, the KMT's chairperson at that time, asserted that the KMT's top priority was to lower the voting age to eighteen (Chiu [邱珮文], 2015).

3. Absentee voting. As the KMT expressed it, enlarged suffrage should include not only young persons between eighteen and twenty years old, but also people living temporarily outside their voting districts.[16] The KMT justified this reform as a global trend, whereas the DPP did not think a constitutional amendment was needed to achieve this goal.

4. The confirmation power of the parliament on the appointment of the premier (Tseng [曾盈瑜], 2015). Initiated by the KMT, the justification for this reform was that the

---

In response to the KMT's proposal to restore the Legislative Yuan's power to confirm the appointment of the premier, the DPP made a counter-proposal that the president must be able to dissolve the Legislative Yuan prior to passage of an ensure motion, which would make Taiwan's people the ultimate arbitrator in a snap election (Liu [劉康彥], 2015).

[14] Since no roundtable was held to address the 2015 constitutional reform effort, the proceedings of CACLY have been used to identify the positions of the political parties. See CACLY, 2015, http://www.ly.gov.tw/02_introduce/0204_comm/business/businessFolderList.action?comtcd=29&id=46981&itemno=02082900 (accessed July 3, 2016).

[15] In this public hearing, a scholar complained that only one public hearing was held concerning human rights.

[16] There are many types of absentee voting. For the KMT's proposal, see a legislator's opinion in a public hearing, "Report of Public Hearing no. 3 and 4 of CACLY [立法院修憲委員會公聽會報告，第三場及第四場]" May 1, 2015: http://www.ly.gov.tw/saveAs.action?comtcd=29&fileName=201505041720270.pdf (accessed June 25, 2016).

best means to fulfill the constitutional requirement of the premier's responsibility to the parliament was to let the appointment of the former be confirmed by the latter. For this reason, the KMT placed considerable emphasis on this reform (Tseng [曾盈瑜], 2015). The DPP, on the other hand, was hesitant to approve this revision, claiming that this change might produce a conflict between the premier and the president and blur the lines of political accountability.

5. The threshold to amend the constitution. Initiated by the DPP, the current threshold required an amendment to be proposed by a three- quarters legislative majority and approved by more than half of the electorate in the most recent presidential election. The DPP sought to reduce the threshold, without specifying the exact formula.

6. Electoral system. This reform reflected the dissatisfaction of the small parties regarding the current electoral system not only because of its single-member simple plurality tier but also because of the 5% threshold needed to obtain seats in the proportional representation (PR) tier. Owed to the disgruntlement of Taiwan's small parties, a proposal was raised to decrease the threshold to 3%, to which neither the KMT nor the DPP voiced their disagreement.

7. The status of the Control Yuan and the Examination Yuan. The DPP considered these two institutions redundant, but the KMT refused to abolish these institutions (DPP [民主進步黨], 2015).

No doubt there were disagreements between the two pivots on many issues. But some issues appeared to be negotiable, such as voting age and changes to the electoral system. Given the existence of consensus on some issues, the factor that prevented the KMT and the DPP from acting on these areas is worth explaining. First we summarize the issue positions, then explore the likely answers.

Table 7.2 reports the positions of the two pivots on the most important issues. It is quite obvious that the KMT did not have a separable preference regarding "voting age and absentee voting." "Absentee voting" was more preferable to the KMT than "no absentee voting," and the party claimed that "18 years old, plus absentee voting" was its formal proposal. If "18 years old and no absentee voting" was the worst choice for the KMT, then we have the rank of preferences shown in Table 7.2. "No absentee voting" ranked higher than "absentee voting" for the DPP. For the DPP, "18 years old, with no absentee voting" was the best option, and "20 years old, with absentee voting" was the worst. It is debatable how the DPP ordered

Table 7.2 Issue Preferences on the Reform Agenda in the 2015 Constitutional Reform Effort

Issue	KMT	DPP	Note
Human rights	1. Add 2. The status quo	1. Add 2. The status quo	An issue initiated by scholars
Voting age and absentee voting	1. 18 years old if absentee voting is passed 2. 20 years old if absentee voting is passed 3. 20 years old if absentee voting is not passed 4. 18 years old if absentee voting is not passed	1. 18 years old if absentee voting is not passed 2. 20 years old if absentee voting is not passed 3. 18 years old if absentee voting is passed 4. 20 years old if absentee voting is passed	Critical issues for the two pivots; KMT's positionis conditional on absentee voting; DPP insisted that absentee voting should be defined by law rather than the constitution
Threshold of constitutional amendment	1. The status quo 2. Reduce	1. Reduce 2. The status quo	An important issue for the DPP
Electoral systems	1. Reduce to 3% 2. The status quo	1. Reduce to 3% 2. The status quo	An issue of concern to small parties
Control Yuan and Examination Yuan	1. The status quo 2. Abolish	1. Abolish 2. The status quo	

Source: Author's summary of existing studies or government archives.

Note: Numbers indicate preference order revealed at the beginning of the negotiation. The second and third preferences of the DPP's positon on "voting age and absentee voting" can be switched, but the KMT's preferences remain nonseparable.

the remaining two alternatives, but the result does not change the KMT's nonseparable preferences on "voting age and absentee voting." Therefore, the nonseparable preferences could prevent the two pivots from reaching a compromise. Given this structure, it is unlikely that the KMT would have "delinked" the two issues. Regarding the confirmation power of the parliament, another critical concern, the KMT and the DPP held contradictory stances. They also held opposing views on whether the threshold to amend constitutional revisions should be reduced and whether the Control Yuan and the Examination Yuan should be abolished. The only hope was that human rights concerns and a reduction of the threshold to gain PR seats were separable preferences, which might produce some degree of consensus about revising the constitution.

After the CACLY sent its proposal to the "Consultation Mechanism Among Political Parties" (朝野黨團協商)[17] on June 16, 2015, no concessions were made to adopt any revisions because the KMT caucus insisted that the votes on lowering the voting age and absentee voting must be made together (Su [蘇方禾], 2015). But why was it that the consensuses on human rights and the reduction of the threshold to obtain PR seats were not turned into proposals for constitutional amendments? Two possibilities exist.

First, issues advanced by legal scholars and small parties were far from the core interests of the two pivots, despite their seemingly separable preferences on these issues. Consensuses on these issues were thus insufficient to cover the cost of persuasion regarding constitutional reform. Moreover, had these two issues been modified and turned into proposals for constitutional amendments, the two pivots would have had to explain to the public why compromise could not also be extended to issues on which they seemed to share consensus. Second, it is also possible that the pivots were not genuinely in support of reform in the two areas—when one side was reluctant to show ardent support for change, the other side might follow. Of what we are certain is that nonseparable preferences regarding critical issues prevented the pivots from revising the status quo in the 2015 constitutional reform effort.

---

[17]　Taiwan's two major parties plus significant small parties, each with at least five members of parliament, are given seats at the negotiation table in this body. The rule of decision is consensus, which gives even the smallest party with five members of parliament a veto power in this "consultation" process.

VII. Conclusion

The constitutional reform efforts of 1997 and 2015 warrent comparison. In the legislative stage, they were identical in procedure but divergent in content—a semi-presidential system was successfully established in 1997, but could not be renovated in 2015. Cultural and institutional factors can be only parameters; we need to show how the stances of the two pivots, which was the major variable, were different. This essay highlights a concept commonly addressed by legislative studies but rarely mentioned in the literature concerning constitutional choice: the separability of preferences. This study shows that separable preferences explain the outcomes of constitutional revisions when the preferences are not affected by other concerns to which they are compared. The variant weights placed on issues on the agenda do not matter much regarding change to the status quo, but have a role in agenda-setting: when persuasion and negotiations involve some cost, issues of minor importance may be kept intact, even if there is consensus to change them.

In 1997, the two pivots had separable preferences on critical issues of constitutional reform, giving them the incentive to modify the status quo, even in light of the considerable cost of negotiation. Introduction of the seemingly irrelevant TPG issue further enlarged room for cooperation. The vital issues of the two pivots were different but not in conflict, allowing the separable preferences on these issues to be traded and to produce a better outcome than if both had made their sincere choices.

However, vote trading mismatched power and accountability regarding Taiwan's semi-presidential system, and pressures to alter the system gave rise to the constitutional reform effort of 2015. The KMT, expecting the 2016 presidential election to be a tough race, yearned for reinstitution of the parliament's confirmation power. Tsai Ing-wen, the DPP's presidential nominee at that time (and always the front-runner in opinion polls), had been hesitant to give this power to the legislators. For the KMT, lowering the voting age was linked with absentee voting, creating a nonseparable preference unfavorable to collaboration. Although the two pivots seemed to have reached a consensus to update the list of human rights and reduce the threshold for small parties to obtain a PR seat, these issues were not significant enough to compensate for the cost of bargaining. Ultimately, no amendments were made to the constitution.

The comparative study of two constitutional reform efforts with almost identical legislative backgrounds has broad implications. Regarding the study of constitutional choice empirically, the structure of the actors' preferences illustrates an important dimension that could have an important effect on the final choice. The separability of preferences is nothing new—it has been widely used to study legislative behavior and vote trading in legislative studies. If constitutional choice is made by voting, this concept can be applied immediately. Variables of preference structure also can bridge theories of historical institutionalism, rational-choice-based new institutionalism, and constitutional classification. In the context of these general theories, issue structure clarifies why some institutional reforms are possible and others impossible, even when the parameters look the same. From this perspective, Taiwan is a special case of a general theory of preference separability.

We also learn from this essay how the preferences of the constitutional decision makers might be shaped by the process of democratization. At the beginning of democratization, common distaste for the authoritarian past might have unified different factions and pushed their representatives to write a new constitution. In Taiwan's case, the chairs of the DPP and the KMT both supported direct presidential election, with the DPP hoping it would demarcate the boundary of a sovereign state, and the KMT envisioning such election consolidating the regime's legitimacy. By proposing an alternative solution to power succession, the conservatives became a minority. Once the two pivots found that a semi-presidential system was the only compromise, other issues were raised to satisfy the demand of each side. Especially interesting was the topic of the TPG, which was only remotely correlated with the constitutional system but nevertheless was placed on the negotiation table to broaden the scope of cooperation.

Although the loopholes of the constitution were basically institutional, presidential elections forced the political parties to adopt a partisan perspective regarding the necessity for reform. Issues raised by the KMT mostly related to its chance of winning the 2016 presidential election, such as the linkage between voting age and absentee voting and the restoration of the parliament's confirmation power. The DPP, on the other hand, was cautious about the KMT's proposals. Although a consensus was forged on human rights and the threshold to obtain PR seats, these two proposals were far from the core interests of the two pivots. The contrasts between 1997 and 2015 show the importance of understanding Taiwan's constitutional reforms in the context of its democratization.

第八章

共治可能成爲半總統制的憲政慣例嗎？
法國與台灣的比較[*]

壹、半總統制下的競爭者可能形成共治慣例嗎？

　　半總統制（semi-presidentialism），是日漸受到注意的憲政體制，採行此一體制的國家也日漸增多。根據 Maurice Duverger（1980: 166）的定義，半總統制的要件包括：民選且具有相當權力的總統，以及掌管政府且需得國會信任的總理。此種特性，使半總統制和議會內閣制與總統制具有本質上的差異。[1]在總統制之下，政府官員無須因爲失去國會信任而下台；在內閣制之下，總統爲間接選出，而且只具有象徵性的權威。簡言之，半總統制下的總統可能擁有實權，又任命需對國會負責的總理，所以具有雙首長制（dual-executive system）的特性。總統和總理具有何種關係，因而成爲理解半總統制的核心議題。半總統制國家的實質最高領袖，可能是作爲國家元首（head of state）的總統，也可能是作爲政府首長（head of government）的總理（台灣稱爲行政院院長）。如果總統是實質的政治領袖，又可依政府是否由國會多數黨（或聯盟）組成，區分爲多數政府或少數政府。總統主導的少數政府，可能造成朝野僵局；由總理組成的多數內閣，可以和總統共享權力，也可能造成行政權內部的衝突（Kirschke, 2007）。

　　要瞭解這些錯綜複雜的可能性，法國與台灣是值得比較的案例。主要理由有二。第一，法國自 1959 年第五共和成立以來，一直採行半總統制，台灣則是在 1997 年憲改後進入半總統制國家的行列；法國和台灣的總統任命政府首長，都不需要得到國會的同意，內閣職位是否分配給國會的多數黨派，取決於總統對政府首長的選擇。在半總統制

---

[*]　本文曾刊登於《東吳政治學報》，第 27 卷第 1 期（2009 年 3 月），頁 1-51。感謝東吳大學《東吳政治學報》同意轉載。

　本文接受國科會專題計畫（NSC96-2414-H-001-025）的補助。感謝匿名審查人對論文的指正，所有文責由作者自負。

[1]　Duverger 特別強調，他是以憲法的內涵來界定半總統制。其他對半總統制的定義，往往將憲法與實務混合，因而與 Duverger 的定義不完全一致，涵蓋的國家也不盡相同。例如，Sartori（1997: 131-132）對半總統制舉出五個要件，尤其強調總統與總理需分享行政權，而兩者的權威處於動態的均衡狀態。Elgie（2007: 6）爲半總統制下的定義，只有兩個條件：民選總統與向國會負責的總理。按照 Elgie（2007: 9）的計算，這樣的國家在 2007 年共有 55 個。

的民主國家中，總統可以獨享行政首長任命權的國家不多，除了法國和台灣，大約只有奧地利、冰島、芬蘭（2000 年之前）、納米比亞（Namibia）和馬利共和國（Republic of Mali），其中奧、冰、芬三國為多黨制國家，通常在選後才能確定國會多數由哪些政黨組成，納米比亞迄未出現國會多數與總統不同黨派的情況，只有馬利勉強可以比擬法國。[2] 反觀法國，左右界線清晰，台灣則是藍綠涇渭分明，且都出現過總統所屬陣營和國會多數不一致的情況。第二，法國第五共和的總統，不論屬於左派還是右派，都在另一陣營贏得國民議會（L'Assemblée nationale）多數席次後，任命該陣營的領袖為總理，從無例外。[3] 台灣的情形剛好相反：2000 與 2004 年民主進步黨（民進黨）的陳水扁贏得總統選舉，前後共任命八屆行政院院長，組成的都是不能掌握立法院（國會）多數席次的少數內閣。[4] 我們可以說，當總統與國會多數不同黨時，法國的左右共治已經成為超越憲法規範的憲政慣例（constitutional convention）；台灣的民主化歷程較短，憲政發展的走向具有多種可能性，但一再出現的少數政府，至少可以顯現共治的障礙何在。[5] 問題是，我們如何解釋兩者的差異？

　　法國每次的左右共治，都發生於特殊的歷史情境，但是連續出現相同的統治模式，更是值得我們注意的課題。尤其重要的是，法國的共治，並沒有清楚憲法的依據，所以可以看成是政治菁英自行建構的憲政慣例。所謂憲政慣例，是指憲法沒有明文規範，但卻為相關機關所共同遵守的憲政規則。以半總統制為例，共治所涉及的對象，正是主要的政治競爭者，亦即總統和反對黨領袖。在法國，選舉競技場上激烈競爭的對手，為何能在沒有憲法規定的情況下建構共治的慣例？台灣的困難又在哪裡？下節的文獻檢討將

---

[2]　嚴格來說，法國在 1962 年改採公民直選總統後才符合 Duverger 對半總統制的定義。某國是否民主，是以「自由之家」（Freedom House）是否將其列為自由國家來認定。馬利的情況和法國比較類似，會在結論部分提及。

[3]　法國向來以左、右來區分政黨，並以左右來判斷何方掌握多數。左右兩邊，各自包括一些政黨。第五共和仍有數次的少數政府出現，但都沒有發生在非總統聯盟掌握國民議會多數席次的情形下，而是因為總統陣營內的有些政黨不願意加入內閣。關於法國第五共和總理，請參閱 Site de Premier Ministre（2009）。

[4]　其中張俊雄前後擔任三屆行政院院長，游錫堃擔任兩屆行政院院長。唐飛雖為國民黨籍，但因組閣未經政黨協商，所以並不代表國民黨。屆別乃以院長個人請辭或內閣總辭為區分（行政院，2009）。

[5]　左右共治是不是慣例，端看慣例的定義而定。如果憲政慣例是重複出現，且具實質約束力的憲法實踐，三次共治的確符合這個條件。或有論者質疑，法國總統選擇共治乃不得已的作為，所以不見得具有憲政慣例的性質。這個觀點的問題在於，以行動者的主觀意願作為憲政慣例的判準會有認定上的困難。政治菁英選擇遵循某些憲政慣例，當然可能是因為某些壓力或利益考量所致，但這並不表示他們的選擇是非自願的。本文在討論法國案例時，會討論左右共治的慣例性質。

說明，「慣例形成」是研究共治不可或缺，但又較不受注意的課題，而既有關於慣例的研究則欠缺實證的理論基礎。循此，第參節建構關於共治慣例的理論模型，並將其用在法國與台灣的案例上。由於憲政慣例涉及同一憲法實踐（constitutional practice）的重複出現，理論模型將慣例的形成視爲具有時間性的重複賽局。根據模型，可以發現總統的專屬權力和國會的選舉制度，是影響賽局均衡的主要因素。第肆和第伍節，根據理論模型所推演出的命題，解釋法國爲何能產生共治的慣例，並說明台灣不利於共治的條件。[6]

貳、如何研究共治慣例的形成？

　　半總統制是橫跨憲法學與政治學的課題，自從 Maurice Duverger（1980）將這個概念介紹給英文世界後，產生了非常多的相關研究，其中當然包括許多對於法國憲政體制的討論。然而，對於法國第五共和爲什麼會出現三次左右共治，研究卻相對有限。歸納既有文獻，大致可以舉出以下幾種對於共治原因的解釋。首先，半總統制被視爲左右共治的先決條件（Poulard, 1990: 244-249; 徐正戎，2001：8-14）。在半總統制之下，總統必須任命對國會負責的行政首長（總理），然因總統和國會議員都由人民直選產生，總統所屬政黨（或聯盟）可能和掌握國會多數席次的政黨不同，所以總統是否會任命能代表國會多數意志的人士擔任總理，成爲重要的憲政課題。這種看法，的確指出共治的必要條件，但是共治並非半總統制國家的普遍現象，所以半總統制顯然也不是充分條件。對此，歷史傳統可能提供某些線索。以法國爲例，第三、四共和都採行議會內閣制，所以由國會多數黨派組閣似乎是理所當然的結果（Huber, 1996: 28-29; 湯德宗，1998）。反觀台灣，雖然《中華民國憲法》具有「改良式內閣制」的特色，但行憲以來的憲法實踐卻大多是一黨政府。法國的議會制傳統，的確使「多數內閣」具有很高的正當性。不過，第五共和之所以賦予總統相當大的權力，正是要改善議會制之下的混亂與低效能，而 1986 年第一次共治之前，法國都是由右派掌握總統職位和國會議會多數，總統也都被視爲最高的政治領袖（Poulard, 1990: 248）；法國的首次共治，仍須超脫第五共和成立以來 28 年總統主導的傳統。共治，應該還受到其他因素的影響。

　　第三種對於共治成因的解釋，是新舊民意的交替。由於總統和國會議員是透過不同的選舉產生，當兩者的任期不同，總統很可能會在任內遭遇國會議員選舉（Elgie, 2001b: 113-118）。如果國會議員的選舉產生不同於總統所屬陣營的新多數，總統爲了

---

[6] 國內關於半總統制的研究相當豐富，但比較法國與台灣半總統制的研究則不多，例如 Wu（2000b）、徐正戎（2001）、Liao 與 Chien（2005）、蘇子喬（2006）。

回應新民意,即應讓新國會多數組閣,以符合半總統制的憲政精神(Poulard, 1990: 255-256; Cole, 1994: 41; Thody, 1998: 111-112; 張壯熙,1996:78;徐正戎,2001:8-17)。這個看法的延伸意涵是:如果總統罔顧國會多數,仍然任命少數黨人士出任總理,國會即應對政府提出不信任投票。從憲政規範的角度來看,總統任命的總理的確應該獲得國會多數議員的支持。不過,從實然面觀之,新民意不見得能約束總統對組閣的影響力。在半總統制的國家中,總統選舉和國會選舉時程不一的國家不少(包括台灣),但法國式的左右共治並非常態(陳宏銘、蔡榮祥,2008:169-173),顯然受到其他因素的影響。關鍵問題,在於國會選舉所產生的「新民意」是否強大到足以讓總統願意釋出組閣權。Skach(2005: 93-117)認為,鞏固的多數對法國的半總統制產生重大影響。問題是,法國的國會多數為什麼鞏固?所謂的「多數」,又是以何種形式展現?

　　也有學者直接針對法國的共治進行研究,嘗試從當事人的角度解釋共治的形成。其中受到許多學者注意的是第一次共治,亦即 1986 年右派取得國民議會選舉過半數的席次,社會黨籍的總統密特朗(François Mitterrand)任命右派的共和聯盟(Rassemblement pour la République, RPR)領袖席哈克(Jacques Chirac)為總理。關於密特朗為何做出此一決定,許多研究者都提到了前述的「新民意」,但也有學者認為他的目標在於贏得即將於 1988 年舉行的總統選舉。當時密特朗的第一任總統任期只剩兩年,所以選擇與國會的右派多數共存,有助於其在兩年後的總統大選勝選。此外,席哈克的目標也在兩年後的總統大選,而擔任總理職位,是邁向總統之路的重要條件(Ardant and Duhamel, 1999: 7; Poulard, 1990: 257-259)。同樣的情況,也發生在第三次共治上。[7] 1997 年,席哈克總統解散國民議會,結果由左派贏得過半席次,他遂任命社會黨領袖喬斯班(Lionel Jospin)為總理。當時,席哈克也面對 2002 年的總統選舉,而喬斯班正是其主要競爭對手。這個情境,和 1986 年的情況很類似,所以「維持總統的影響力,贏得總統選舉」很可能也是席哈克和喬斯班共治的原因。此外,席哈克自己是第一次共治的主角之一,不太可能違背自己和密特朗立下的先例。第三次共治長達五年(1997-2002),占了席哈克第一任總統任期(1995-2002)的大部分時間。從政治菁英的角度來思考,的確可以讓我們更瞭解共治的形成過程,但也帶來新的問題:共治為什麼有利於總統競選連任?將政府交給未來的競爭對手,是否會阻礙總統實現其政策?

　　法國的共治並沒有憲法根源,在第一次共治之前,學界對於密特朗會如何面對由右派掌握的國會,看法並不一致,席哈克則認為應由密特朗自己決定(Harrison, 1986:

---

[7]　第二次共治(1993-1995)發生在密特朗第二任總統的後期。1993 年,右派在國民議會選舉中大勝,贏得超過八成的席次,密特朗總統遂任命 RPR 的巴拉度(Édouard Balladur)為總理。

101-102）。事實上，在 1986 年國會選舉之前，席哈克對於共治的態度也不明確，他最後接受共治還是因爲總統選舉的考量（Friend, 1998: 97-98）。所以，我們可以把法國的左右共治，看成是由主要的政治競爭者所共同形塑的憲政慣例。法國著名的憲法學者 Ardant 和 Duhamel 即曾指出，法國的共治之所以能夠延續，是因爲遵循憲法和慣例：「如果共識有助於共治，共治也有利於共識的產生（1999: 10）」。[8] 問題在於，以爭取政權爲目標的政治菁英，爲何要在選舉前追求共識，並形成具有拘束力的慣例？

　　關鍵在於憲政慣例的形成機制，也就是相互競爭的政治菁英，爲何願意在無法可循的情況下建構共同遵循的規則。從憲法本身的角度來看，所有的明文規定都可能有不合時宜或曖昧不明之處；彌補成文憲法未盡之處的，正是憲政慣例。[9] 所有國家都有某些憲政慣例，以被當成內閣制典範的英國爲例，根本就沒有成文憲法，該國最爲人所熟知的憲政規則，幾乎全爲慣例（Lijphart, 1999b: 9-30）。[10] 美國雖有成文憲法，但許多重要的憲政規則仍爲不成文的慣例。[11] 憲政慣例雖然如此重要，對於憲政慣例的研究卻大多以規範取向爲主，亦即關注「憲政慣例是什麼、應該具有何種條件、應否建立憲政慣例」，而非回答「憲政慣例如何形成」這種經驗性的問題。這種規範分析，也出現在台灣的憲政研究上。憲法學研究的規範特性自不待言，即使是憲政分析，也常出現應然面的論述，主張台灣應該建立符合雙首長制的憲政慣例（陳志華，2002；林濁水，2002），或組成多數政府（黃德福，2000；高朗，2001；周育仁，2002）。規範面的分析，有助於釐清憲政慣例的性質，但難以解釋法國共治的成因。

　　所以，要理解法國左右共治如何形成，我們必須先建構實證理論，回答「競爭性的政治菁英爲何要共同構築憲政慣例」這個問題。如果我們把憲政慣例界定爲「具有重複性，且能讓政治行動者自覺受到合理限制的先例（precedent）」（Jennings, 1959: 136），核心問題就在於先例的創造。[12] 而既然憲政慣例是不依賴法條即能自我執行的規

8　用新制度理論的概念來說，這種共識是一種能「自我增強」的規則形塑過程：政治菁英如果在某個時間點選擇共同遵循某個規則，則這個規則在日後被遵守的機率會更高。

9　司法機關（例如憲法法庭）雖然可以透過釋憲來解決憲政爭議，但必須以既有憲法爲範圍。司法機關，通常採取被動的立場來釋憲，難以主動解決憲政爭議。

10　例如：首相由下議院多數黨領袖出任、君主不能拒絕簽署由上下院通過的法案、只有首相才能建請君主解散國會、君主同意首相解散國會之提議、預算案由下議院提出，以及上議院同意下議院所提之預算案等。關於英國的憲政慣例，見 Bagehot（1867）、Bryce（1905）、Marshall（1984）、Brazier（1988）。

11　例如：各州選舉人團將所有選舉人票投給相對得票最高的總統候選人、總統可以不經參議院許可即將經其同意任命的官員解職、國會不得改變最高法院法官人數等。見 Gerhardt（2000）。

12　台灣的憲法學者和大法官會議，認爲憲政慣例要符合三個條件：時間的持續性、主觀的確信以及以法規形式存在。見陳慈陽（2004：56）以及大法官第四一九號釋憲文。

約，我們可將第一次的共治視爲總統和在野黨領袖經過理性判斷所互動出來的先例。若然，最適合的理論框架就是將慣例視爲「協調賽局」（coordination game）的均衡。[13] 這個觀念，源自經濟學者 Thomas Schelling（1960）的「焦點理論」（focal point theory）和哲學家 David Lewis（1969）對慣例的研究。[14] 簡單來說，所謂的協調賽局，是指行動者可以透過採取一致的策略而使彼此得利。由於協調賽局存在多重均衡，行動者爲了追求對彼此皆有好處的結果，會找尋焦點或建立慣例，以確信彼此會採取一致的行動。我們可以用 Lewis 的理論來描繪慣例在協調賽局中所扮演的角色：假設某個雙人賽局有「妥協」與「對抗」兩個純粹策略的納許均衡（pure-strategy Nash equilibria），而且兩位參賽者在前一種均衡的報酬高於後一種均衡的報酬。但兩人若要妥協，必須相信對方會採取妥協的策略，而且相信對方也有同樣的信念。這種共同信念，常因某些初始情境（initial condition）而產生，例如某些被雙方同時認知的制度條件乃至歷史傳統。

　　政治學者 Russell Hardin 延伸了 Lewis 的概念，展開一系列關於憲法形成的研究。對 Hardin（1989, 1999）而言，憲法和一般法律或契約最大的不同在於憲法的最高位階性：契約不可違背法律，法律不可違背憲法，而憲法之上卻別無他法。基於這種特性，憲法必須基於制憲者的共識而存在，而制憲者之所以要訂立憲法，正是爲了要解決其協調困局。[15] 憲法如此，憲政慣例更是如此，所以我們可以借用類似的理論來理解共治的形成。不過，Lewis 和 Hardin 等人的理論，仍然存在一個盲點：憲政慣例，涉及同一憲法實踐在時間上的延續，但是兩人的研究皆未考慮時間因素。所以，我們可以構思具有延續性的賽局，模擬共治慣例的形塑過程，以推論有利於共治形成的因素。

　　總結以上分析，可以歸納出幾個解釋共治成因的方向。第一，半總統制的確是共治的必要環境，但因許多半總統制國家沒有發生共治，所以我們只能將憲政體制當成參數，並找尋能夠解釋共治與否的解釋變數。第二，先例不可能建立在眞空狀態，必然受到歷史發展的影響，但歷史傳統往往是多元的，有些有利於共治，有些則不利，必須加以區分。第三，在半總統制下，由國會選舉所呈現出來的新民意是否對現任總統構成共治壓力，要看其展現形式和強度。第四，針對法國共治的研究顯示，不管是密特朗總統或是席哈克總統，都以維持其政治影響力爲目標；對在野聯盟領袖而言，擔任總理亦有

---

[13] 某些研究憲政慣例的著作，也採取這樣的分析模型，如 Jaconelli（1999, 2005）。

[14] 關於 David Lewis 的理論，除了 Lewis 的原著，也可參考 Cubitt 與 Sugden（2003）。

[15] Hardin（1989, 1999）認爲，憲法和一般契約另一項不同，在於後者通常爲了解決「囚犯難題」（Prisoner's Dilemma）而訂，而憲法則以處理協調問題爲主。在單回合的「囚犯難題」中，「彼此背叛」是唯一的均衡，而且是唯一不屬於「帕雷圖最適」（Pareto optimal）的結果。爲了解決這個困境，外來的強制力是唯一的手段。下文將對這個看法提出修正。

助於提升其政治權力，所以我們可以假定「維持或擴大政治影響力」是共治當事人的目標。第五，共治涉及最高政治菁英的互動，有時間的延續性，而當事人可以自行決定是否維持共治狀態，所以可以看成憲政慣例的建構過程。

　　整合以上論點，我們可以提出以下的研究假定。第一，總統和在野黨領袖的行動是被解釋項，他們的互動決定共治是否發生。總統和在野黨領袖的目標，應該是維持甚至擴大其政治影響力；當其面臨選舉時，則以勝選爲目標。共治持續的時間越長、重複的次數越多，越能使共治成爲憲政慣例。第二，主要的解釋變項之一，是憲法賦予總統和總理的職權。行動者爲了達成前述目標，必須維持對於各項政治事務的影響力。對總統而言，共治對其憲法權力的削弱程度越輕，共治就越可能成爲合理的選擇；對在野黨領袖而言，掌握政府越有助於其政策的實踐、越有助於其資歷的積累，接受共治的可能性就越高。除此之外，憲法給予總統主動結束共治的權力越大（例如主動解散國會或解除總理職務），總統應該越願意採行共治。第三，民意對於政治菁英的支持程度，是另一個重要的解釋變項。民意受到諸多因素的影響，除了政黨認同與意識形態，還有對於政府與競選者的評價，而後者又受制於民眾是否支持共治。影響民意的另一項重要因素，是民意的呈現方式。一項合理的假設是，國會的選舉制度比例性越高，國會選舉呈現出的民意就越接近原本的民意分布狀態，但若選舉制度的比例性低，則會擴大民意分布中「眾數」（mode）所占的份量，並因此增加民意在不同選舉中的震幅（swing）。

　　以上的假定若能成立，不但可以補充既有對於法國共治的研究，還可幫助我們解釋台灣爲什麼沒有走向共治。根據 Liao 與 Chien（2005）的研究，台灣之所以沒有發生共治，主要原因在於台灣向來爲一黨政府，欠缺雙首長的經驗，而立法委員的改選成本高，則使立法院不容易通過對少數政府的倒閣案。我們可以用同樣的變數來觀察法國經驗，確認這些因素的可靠度。除此之外，比較法國與台灣的經驗，可以幫助我們瞭解政府組成背後的憲政脈絡，釐清分立政府（divided government）與少數政府（minority government）的異同，對相關的實證研究應該有所裨益。[16] 以下，將先說明本論文的理論模型與待證假設。

---

[16] 台灣學者大多從執政者的黨籍和議會多數黨是否相同來界定少數政府的存在，且較常使用「分立政府」的概念。分立政府和少數政府不盡相同，總統制和半總統制下的政府組成型態也有差異。關於台灣少數政府的研究，請見吳重禮、王宏忠（2003）、吳重禮、楊樹源（2001）、吳重禮、黃紀、張壹智（2003）、吳重禮、徐英豪、李世宏（2004）、黃紀、吳重禮（2000）、廖達琪、洪澄琳（2004）等。關於半總統制之下的少數政府，請參閱高朗（2001）、沈有忠（2005）、陳宏銘（2007）。

參、理論模型

承接前節的文獻分析，本節提出以下的理論模型。第一個議題，涉及誰是建構共治慣例的行動者。在法國與台灣的半總統制下，總統是主要的政治行動者之一，對其所屬政黨或聯盟擁有重要的影響力。在野黨（聯盟）通常也有領導人，其影響力取決於陣營內部對他的支持。我們可以將總統和在野黨（或在野聯盟，以下簡稱在野黨）領袖視為主要的政治行動者，兩者相互競爭，但也可能選擇共治。由於共治涉及政治菁英的理性判斷，我們可以建構以總統和在野黨領袖為參賽者的賽局。第二個議題，是模型的適用性。為符合法國和台灣的情況，假設總統任命總理無須國會同意，而在野黨已經取得國會多數席次。在此情況下，總統有權決定是否任命反對聯盟領袖為總理，而後者可以決定是否接受此項任命。當在野黨領袖接受總統任命為總理，即是共治的起點，共治的時間持續越久，越可能演變為憲政慣例。為探討時間對於菁英行動的影響，以下將建構無限延伸的重複賽局（infinitely repeated game），模擬兩位參賽者的策略選擇。

為了便於說明，我們先界定參賽者在賽局第一回合的行動選項和互動結果。假設總統和在野黨領袖在每一階段都有兩種行動選項：合作（C）或不合作（D）。在賽局的第一回合，雙方的互動決定共治是否能成立，其互動共有四種可能的結果：

CC：共治。總統任命在野黨領袖為總理，在野黨領袖接受總統的任命，雙方都採取合作的行動。

CD：總統有共治意圖，但在野黨領袖不願意，所以共治不成立。此時，總統將面對在野黨在國會的反對力量。[17]

DC：在野黨領袖有合作意願，但並未被總統任命為總理，所以也非共治。此時，因為在野黨領袖有合作意願，所以即使未擔任總理，反對總統的強度應該沒有前一種情況來得大。

DD：相互抗衡。總統不任命在野黨領袖為總理，在野黨領袖亦無意和總統妥協。此時，由於雙方各自堅持立場，總統雖然掌握行政權，但將面臨在野多數在國會的反對，在野黨雖然掌握國會多數，但不能控制政府。

總統與在野黨領袖在這四種情況下的報酬，受到幾個因素的影響。首先，對總統而

---

[17] 有關法國的共治研究，一直以「共治」或「總統辭職」為總統的兩個選項，忽略了其他的可能性，例如少數政府。如果總統選擇辭職，則一切回到原點，由改選後的總統和在野黨領袖重新展開賽局。從經驗上來看，1988 年密特朗主動解散國會，改選後右派雖然沒有贏得多數席次，但共產黨並未加入社會黨內閣，所以出現三位組成少數內閣的總理。

言，與在野黨領袖共治的代價，在於降低對政策的影響力。總統之所以可能選擇共治，動機在於選民的支持，而這種支持有助於總統維持其威信（甚至總統選舉的勝選）。同理，如果在野黨代表的是明確而嶄新的多數民意，總統不任命代表這個多數的領袖爲總理，可能導致所屬政黨在選舉上的失利，甚至減損總統本身的威信與正當性。對在野黨領袖而言，與總統共治可以提升他的政策影響力並爭取更多選民的支持，但風險在於和敵對陣營的總統妥協，可能有損其原本的政策目標。最後，如果總統和在野黨領袖相互對立，等於形成分立政府的態勢，總統掌握行政權但不能得到國會支持，在野黨掌握國會多數但只能杯葛政府政策。簡言之，作爲民選的政治菁英，總統和在野黨領袖關注的焦點在於選民支持和政策影響力。

爲便於分析，下列參數描繪總統和在野黨領袖對這些因素的考量。表 8.1 所顯示的，是構成重複賽局的階段賽局（stage game）。[18] 此一正規式（normal form）的參數定義如下：

k：在共治狀態下雙方的權力。對總統而言，k 表示任命在野黨領袖爲總理之後所保有的權力；對在野黨領袖而言，k 表示擔任總理職位後取得的權力。

g：在對方採取合作態度的情況下，堅持立場所獲之利益。對總統而言，g 表示控制政府，且未遭遇在野黨強力反對時的利益；對在野黨領袖而言，g 表示在野黨領袖未擔任總理，無須負擔政治責任，而總統又採取妥協態度時的利益。

m：總統和在野黨領袖表現出合作態度時所獲得的民意支持。假設只有採取 C 行動時方能獲得 m。

h：總統和在野黨領袖相互抗衡時所得之利益，其中又以忠誠選民的支持最爲重要。

表 8.1　憲政慣例的階段賽局

	C	D
C	$k+m, k+m$	m, g
D	g, m	h, h

資料來源：筆者自製。

---

[18] 這個賽局不一定是對稱的（symmetric），賽局的參數也可依參賽者區分。以下爲了敘述的方便而不進行這樣的區分。

上列參數，受到諸多因素的影響，說明如下：

k：對總統而言，在共治時期究竟能保留多大權力，和憲法賦予總統的職權有密切關連。最極端的情況是，憲法賦予總統極大的專屬權力（即無須其他憲政機關同意即可運用之權力），總統可以隨時解除總理職務並介入日常政務運作，甚至可以透過命令（decree）來執行其政策。另一個極端是，總統只有象徵性的權力，欠缺參與日常政務的管道，無法發布行政命令，也無法解除總理的職務。另一個影響 k 的因素，是總統本身的正當性。除了個人因素，總統選舉制度是影響總統正當性的原因之一：在兩輪投票制下，總統必須取得過半選票才能勝選，正當性應該高於在相對多數決選制下未獲過半選票當選的總統。對總理而言，內閣越是以總理為中心、其所統領的政黨越受其控制、總理在黨（或聯盟）內的地位越鞏固，k 的值應該越高。

g：由於總統和總理的憲法職權是固定的，所以影響此一參數的主要原因是政治性的。依常理，g 會隨著總統和總理的政策立場差距而擴大。換言之，總統和總理在共治時期需要讓步的空間越大，雙方就越有脫離共治的誘因。這也表示，當總統與總理所屬陣營處於競爭狀態時，g 很可能大於 k。

m：影響民意的因素相當多。以民眾對政府組成的態度而言，受到歷史傳統的影響很大。以法國而言，因為有第三、四共和的經驗，所以民眾對於國會多數黨派組成政府應該不陌生，甚至可以因此支持共治。除了民眾的既有態度，民意的呈現方式也很重要。一般而言，政黨屬性較弱的選民較易同時表達對不同政黨政治菁英的支持或否定，而多數決選制比較容易讓這些選民影響選舉結果。

h：總統若與在野黨領袖抗衡，通常較能得到黨派屬性較強的選民支持，所以 h 的大小和這類選民在政治競爭中扮演的角色有關。政治聯盟之間的意識形態或政策立場差距越大，h 當然也越大。

如果賽局只進行一個回合，均衡取決於以上參數的大小。如果 $h > m$，DD 永遠是一個純粹策略的納許均衡，無論其他參數的大小為何。如果 $g > k + m$，D 成為最上策（strictly dominant strategy）；如果 $k + m > h$，此一賽局成為囚犯難題：即使共治對雙方的利益都高於其他結果，均衡還是相互對抗。如果 $k + m \geq g$，則 CC 成為另一個純粹策略的納許均衡，賽局成為前述的協調賽局。此時，雙方有共治的誘因，但不能排除相互對抗的可能。

不過，共治是持續的過程，總統和在野黨領袖的互動，不會僅限於總理任命此一事件。所以，我們可以用延伸賽局來描繪共治的持續。當在野黨領袖被任命為總理後，總

統和總理仍然處於既競爭又妥協的狀態，而且會以對未來的預期決定其行動策略。總統的考慮因素包括：總統的影響力會不會被總理限縮？如果會，總統能否主動結束共治？如果總統決定和總理攤牌而在野黨也以杯葛總統法案回報，對何者的選舉有利？總理的考慮和總統類似，例如：總統是否會阻礙其施政？若然，是否應該辭職？如果提早改選總統或國會議員，對誰有利？在每一階段的賽局，雙方都可以決定是否要維持相互妥協的策略，還是要結束共治。

　　在多回合的賽局中，總統和總理的策略和前述階段賽局是不同的。我們可以用無限延伸的重複賽局來描繪參賽者的計算。所謂重複賽局，是指重複進行表 8.1 所描繪的階段賽局。重複賽局之所以無限延伸，有可能是賽局眞的沒有止境，但也可能是因爲參賽者無法在賽局開始時判別賽局何時結束。以半總統制國家爲例，總統和國會議員都有任期，所以賽局必有止境，但因總統和在野黨領袖都可隨時終止賽局，所以雙方無法預知終局何時發生，只能以機率猜測之。[19] 重複賽局的報酬，是每個階段賽局的總和。對參賽者而言，越後面發生的事情越不確定，在其總報酬中所占的比重也越輕。我們以 $d \in (0, 1)$ 來表示「折扣率」（discount rate），亦即因爲時間而減損的利益。假設某位參賽者在每一回合都得到報酬 x，且 $t = 1, 2, \cdots$ 爲時間點，則其總報酬就是 $x + xd + d(xd) + \cdots = x(1 + d + d^2 + \cdots) = x/(1 - d)$。

　　回到表 8.1 所描繪的階段賽局。共治持續的時間越長，總統和總理就越有可能使其憲法實踐變成爲憲政慣例。我們可以這樣想像這種長期均衡的具體樣貌：假設總統在某日任命在野黨領袖爲總理，總理所組成的政府，對總統採取妥協的態度，總統對政府政策的干預也有所節制，則只要這種相互妥協的情況持續一天，賽局就重複一次；時間持續越久，相互妥協就越能被看成是憲政慣例。因爲這個均衡屬於所有參賽者的共同認知，所以能夠約束他們的行動。反論之，如果有參賽者在任一回合選擇 D（對抗），即表示互信受到破壞，賽局中止。從賽局的觀點來看，參賽者選擇持續妥協，原因並不僅在於妥協的象徵意義，更在於持續妥協帶來的利益高於對抗。基於這個道理，我們可以推論以下的命題：

命題 1：若 $(k + m) \geq g\,(1 - d)$，參賽者在所有的時間點都採取 C 行動爲子賽局均衡。

　　說明：如果參賽者在所有時間點都採取 C 行動是此賽局的子賽局均衡（subgame perfect equilibrium），則兩位參賽者在任意時間點採取 C 行動的報酬不能小於片面改採

---

[19] 關於無限延伸的重複賽局，詳見 Axelrod（1984）。延伸賽局如果有清楚的終點而且爲所有參賽者所認知，參賽者可以透過逆向歸納（backward induction）選擇其最佳策略。

D 行動的報酬。以任意時間點爲起點，永遠採取 C 行動的報酬是 $(k + m)(1 + d + d^2 + \cdots)$ $= (k + m)/(1 - d)$，若在另一參賽者行動不變的情況下改採 D 行動，則會在此時間點獲得 g，但在接下來的時間點因爲賽局結束而沒有任何報酬。所以，子賽局均衡存在的條件是 $(k + m)/(1 - d) \geq g$，亦即 $(k + m) \geq g(1 - d)$。

命題 1 指出可以讓共治成爲子賽局均衡的條件。必須說明的是，子賽局均衡不見得只有一個。事實上，一開始就相互對抗，也是一個子賽局均衡，原因在於對抗將使賽局中斷，即使參賽者預備好在其他的訊息集（information set）採取妥協的行動亦然。這兩種子賽局均衡的並存，顯示先例的重要性。當命題 1 的前提成立時，如果有參賽者在一開始就採取合作的態度，即有可能促成相互妥協的良性循環。但如果有參賽者在一開始就採取對抗行動，卻能導致相互對抗的惡性循環。話雖如此，重複賽局和單回賽局（one-shot game）畢竟還是有本質上的差異。命題 1 適用於所有符合其前提的賽局，包括囚犯難題。在單回的囚犯難題賽局中，相互妥協對所有參賽者都好於相互對抗，但後者卻是唯一的納許均衡。在重複的囚犯難題賽局中，參賽者卻可能在滿足命題 1 的前提下相互妥協。[20] 所以，即使是處於囚犯難題的敵對菁英，還是有可能在重複賽局中演化出合作的關係。我們可以證明，在某些條件下，共治具有演化上的穩定性：

命題 2：若 $(k + m) > g(1 - d)$，則參賽者在所有的時間點都採取 C 行動，是能夠防禦突發對抗的穩定演化策略。

說明：令 x 與 y 爲兩個策略選項，$\pi(y, x)$ 表示在其他參賽者採取 x 策略的情形下，某參賽者從 x 策略突變爲 y 策略的報酬，餘類推。根據演化賽局理論，如果 x 是能防禦 y 突變的「穩定的演化策略」（evolutionarily stable strategy），則 $\pi(x, x) > \pi(y, x)$ 或 $\pi(x, x) = \pi(y, x)$ 且 $\pi(x, y) > \pi(y, y)$。在本賽局中，$(k + m)/(1 - d)$ 是參賽者隨時都採取 C 行動的報酬，g 則是某參賽者在他人不變的情況下改採 D 行動的報酬。由於 $(k + m)/(1 - d) > g$ 滿足上述條件，故得證。[21]

上述兩個命題顯示，在其他參數不變的情況下，總統和總理持續維持共治的可能性，會因爲 k、m、d 的增加而增加，並隨著 g 的增加而減少；這樣形成的共治，也具有時間上的延續性。依據之前對模型參數的說明，可以推論以下的實際意涵：

總統在共治時的權力越大、選民對於共治的支持度越高、總統和國會選舉越鼓勵向

---

[20] 所以 Axelrod（1984）將無限延伸的重複賽局視爲解決囚犯難題的方式。不過，Axelrod 所建構的重複賽局並未規定只要有人採取 D 行動賽局即告終止，和本文所描繪的賽局規則不同。

[21] 關於穩定演化策略的定義與說明，請參考 Maynard 與 Prince（1973）。

心競爭、總統和國會議員的任期越長、總統與在野黨政策立場差距越小，越有可能建立共治的憲政慣例。

在這些變數中，總統和在野黨的立場差距因社會分歧、執政者乃至國家而異，但其他因素則大多和憲政設計和選舉制度有關。在制度因素中，總統與國會議員的任期最容易辨認，但其他變數則需要進一步運作化：

1. 共治時期的總統權力既然以維持總統的影響力為目的，最重要的觀察面向應該在於總統參與日常政務的權力；然因共治的可能性也受制於總統是否能隨時結束共治，亦應觀察總統的預備性權力，尤其是解散國會權和緊急命令權等。

2. 選民對共治的支持程度，可以透過民意調查探知；我們亦可透過國會席次的擺動幅度，顯現國會選舉如何影響民意的呈現和變動。

3. 關於總統和國會選舉的競爭模式，已經有許多文獻探討選舉制度是否促進向心競爭，我們可以將這些研究運用到法國和台灣的案例上。

如果本節的理論成立，法國第五共和總統的權力應該高於中華民國總統，民眾支持共治的程度也應該高於台灣；在選舉競爭方面，兩國的總統選舉都採單一選區制，但法國的國會選舉制度應比台灣更能鼓勵向心競爭。以下兩節，將分別就總統的權力和選舉競爭來比較法國和台灣的差異。

肆、法國與台灣總統權力的比較

總統權力受到許多因素影響，包括總統是否受到國會多數黨（或聯盟）的支持、總統職位的正當性以及總統的憲法職權等。其中總統是否得到國會多數支持，取決於國會選舉結果（詳見下節），總統職位的正當性則受到總統選舉制度的影響。法國採取兩輪投票制，總統必定取得半數以上的選票方能勝選，具有一定的正當性。台灣採取相對多數決制，2000 年陳水扁以不到 40% 的選票贏得總統選舉，使反對陣營一直挑戰其正當性；2004 年選票雖然剛好過半，但因為槍擊案而使泛藍陣營質疑其正當性（鄭夙芬、陳陸輝、劉嘉薇，2008；張佑宗，2006）。這樣的差別，使法國第五共和的總統比較容易扮演憲法第五條所賦予的仲裁者角色。[22] 再就憲法賦予總統的職權來看，大多數的總

---

[22] 本文所提及的《法國第五共和憲法》條文，引自徐正戎（2002）的中文翻譯。該憲法為 2000 年修憲後之版本，但本文所引用的條目和早先的憲法相同。

統制或半總統制國家，都賦予總統作為國家元首的一些權力，並以總統為軍隊統領。但光靠這些權力，總統可能仍是象徵性的虛位元首。對總統實權影響比較大的，是實際參與政務的權力，可以略分為以下幾類：第一，總統的專屬權力，亦即不需要其他憲政機關（尤其是總理）配合即可行使的權力；第二，和政府運作和政策制訂有關的權力；第三，與國會有關的權力。這些權力，又可依行使的時機，分為日常性的權力和預備性的權力。以下，我們根據這個分類來比較法國與台灣的差別。

　　首先，兩國憲法都賦予總統在國防外交事務上的特權。《法國第五共和憲法》第五條規定：「總統維護憲法之遵守。由其仲裁，保障公權力之正常運作及政府之延續。總統維護國家獨立、領土完整與國際條約之遵守。」這個條文，等於是讓法國總統成為國家的護衛者，論者因此認為國防外交屬於總統的「保留領域」（domaine réservé）。必須說明的是，法國憲法也規定了總理在國防外交事務上的職責，所以國防外交不能算是總統的專屬權力。[23] 此外，對於國防外交相關法令的制訂，總理仍享有副署權。憲法雖然有這樣的規定，但處於共治中的總統並不難在國防外交事務上取得優勢。舉例而言，當密特朗在 1986 年任命席哈克為總理時，一開始拒絕了席哈克所提名的外交部長和國防部長（Skach, 2005: 111），之後任命的外交部長和國防部長，並不具有明顯的黨派色彩，而且與總統配合度高（Cole, 1994: 116）。密特朗之所以能在國防外交事務上占有上風，除了憲法的規定，也和第五共和成立以來總統在相關事務上扮演的主導地位有關。此外，法國在歐盟扮演的重要角色，也給予總統很大的政治空間，並與憲法和總統選制賦予總統的正當性結合。這樣的條件，有助於密特朗在共治中維持其影響力。事實上，密特朗很清楚憲法賦予他的權力。在 1986 年國會選舉前，預見失敗的密特朗表示，不論國會改選結果為何，選後總統仍將保有憲法解釋權、仲裁權、緊急命令權、外交國防指揮權等；1993 年國會選舉前，密特朗再次提出類似的的說法（Portelli, 1999: 60-61）。在第二次共治期間，密特朗也透過外交事務（如波灣戰爭、歐盟發展）取得很大的影響力。

　　《中華民國憲法增修條文》第二條則有這樣的規定：「總統為決定國家安全有關大政方針，得設國家安全會議及所屬國家安全局，其組織以法律定之。」憲法本文雖然無此規定，但此一增修條文等於是將總統作為國家安全決策者的憲法實踐合憲化。再加上台灣特殊的外交與兩岸處境，很難想像民選總統會在（可能的）共治中失去關於國家安全的決策力。問題的關鍵，在於總統如何實現其國家安全的政策目標。這個問題，涉及

---

[23] 《法國第五共和憲法》第二十條規定，「政府指揮行政機關及軍隊」，第二十一條則提及，「總理指揮政府施政，負責國防」。

總統在政府運作中扮演的角色，以下提出說明。

　　總統若要在共治期間維持影響力，應確保其主要政策得以實現，並防止政府推行違反其理念的政策。要達到這些目的，光靠國家元首的權威或總理在表面上對總統的尊重是不夠的，總統必須實際介入政策的訂立和執行。關於此點，法國和台灣具有明顯的差異。《法國第五共和憲法》賦予總統幾項與行政事務相關的權力，其中最重要的是憲法第九條的規定：「共和國總統主持部長會議。」短短幾個字，卻產生相當大的影響。因爲總統主持部長會議，所以必須被告知政務和會議議程（通常透過總統的秘書長和總理的秘書長傳遞訊息）。以實際運作經驗來看，共治時期週一、週二總統舉行和國防部長與外交部長的會談，週三主持部長會議之前，則和總理會談（Ardant and Duhamel, 1999: 14-16）。這樣的日程設定，使總統可以保持對重要政務的瞭解，縱使不能直接指揮內閣閣員，仍然增加了總統設定議程以及影響政策的能力。

　　法國總統的另一項權力，是行政法令的簽署權。第五共和憲法第三十八條規定：「政府爲執行其施政計畫，得要求國會授權，在一定之期限內，以行政法令之方式規範原屬法律範疇之事務。」憲法第十三條又規定：「共和國總統簽署部長會議所決議之行政法令及命令。」所以總統影響政策的另一項權力，就是拒絕簽署行政法令，迫使政府將這些法令交付國會表決（Ardant and Duhamel, 1999: 23）。拒絕簽署行政法令，不見得能讓總統直接影響政策內容，卻給予總統較大的談判空間。密特朗清楚知悉這項權力，在第一次共治剛開始的 1986 年 3 月，他公開表示「不會簽署無助於既定社會政策的行政法令」（Poulard, 1990: 257），而他的確在兩次的共治期間都採取了這樣的行動（Portelli, 1999: 67-68）。例如，1986 年 6 月 14 日密特朗即曾拒簽席哈克所提的私有化行政法令，迫使席哈克將法令送交國會審查。這樣做的好處，在於維持共治的局面但不至於讓席哈克執行違反社會黨基本價值的行政法令（Cole, 1994: 42）。[24]

　　相較之下，《中華民國憲法》賦予總統的行政權是相當有限的。憲法第五十三條規定，「行政院爲國家最高行政機關」，第五十八條規定：「行政院設行政院會議，由行政院院長，副院長，各部會首長及不管部會之政務委員組織之，以院長爲主席。行政院院長，各部會首長，須將應行提出於立法院之法律案，預算案，戒嚴案，大赦案，宣戰案，媾和案，條約案及其他重要事項，或涉及各部會共同關係之事項，提出於行政院會議議決之。」這兩個條文清楚顯示，總統無法參加行政院會議，而該會議卻是議決重要法律案、預算案之會議。《中華民國憲法》並未規定立法院可以授權行政院發布行政法令，總統也就無法利用簽署權來影響政策制訂。相反地，憲法第三十七條規定，「總統

---

[24] 關於法國第一次共治期間總統和總理在行政事務上的互動，請參考張壯熙（1996：78-80）。

依法公布法律，發布命令，須經行政院院長之副署，或行政院院長及有關部會首長之副署」，彰顯行政院作爲最高行政機關的權責。[25] 這些憲法條文顯示，台灣總統之所以被看成實質的行政首長，很可能是因爲長期處於一黨政府之下，透過政黨使行政院院長居於總統之下；1996 年之後的總統直選以及 1997 年修憲後總統可以直接任命行政院院長，雖然進一步強化「總統爲主、行政院院長居次」的印象，但並未同擴充總統的行政權。這也表示，一旦台灣出現共治，由在野黨來組成內閣，總統對政策的影響力可能會大幅縮減。

　　最後，半總統制國家的總統通常也擁有某些「預防性」的權力，其中又以解散國會權和緊急命令權最具代表性。解散國會權所要預防的，是政府失去國會信任後的憲政危機；緊急命令權，通常是要加強政府應付重大危機的效能。在這兩項權力上，法國和台灣都有不小的差異。關於解散國會權，《法國第五共和憲法》第十二條有這樣的規定：「共和國總統於諮詢總理及國會兩院議長後，得宣告解散國民議會。全國大選應於國民議會解散後二十日至四十日內舉行之。國民議會在選舉後第二個星期四自行集會。此集會如在國會正常會期外舉行時，其會期爲十五日。國民議會因解散而改選後一年內，不得再予解散。」根據此一條文，法國總統幾乎可以隨時解散國民議會。雖然該條文規定總統在解散國民議會前要諮詢總理和國會兩院議長，但後者並沒有副署權。所以，總統可以主動解散國會而終止共治，等於是給共治加了一道保險。必須說明的是，法國總統的主動解散國會權具有多種用途，終止共治只是其中之一。如果共治的經驗是成功的，總統就沒有必要在共治期間主動解散國會。[26] 所以，主動解散國會權是一種預防性的權力。

　　關於緊急命令權是，《法國第五共和憲法》第十六條有這樣的規定：「當共和國制度、國家獨立、領土完整或國際義務之履行，遭受嚴重且急迫之威脅，致使憲法上公權力無法正常運作時，共和國總統經正式諮詢總理、國會兩院議長及憲法委員會後，得採取應付此一情勢之緊急措施。總統應將此事詔告全國。此類措施須以在最短之期間內，恢復憲法上公權力之正常運作爲目的。憲法委員會就此應被徵詢。國會應自動集會。總

---

[25] 因應總統任命權的調整，增修條文第二條修正了行政院院長的副署權，「總統發布行政院院長與依憲法經立法院同意任命人員之任免命令及解散立法院之命令，無須行政院院長之副署」。

[26] 密特朗和席哈克都曾主動解散國會，但是理由不一定在於結束共治。密特朗在 1981 年當選法國總統時，國會多數是由右派掌控，他乃解散國會，結果光是社會黨即已贏得多數席次。密特朗在 1988 年第二次解散國會，正處於左右共治的時期。選舉結果，左派仍然取得多數席次，但社會黨並未一黨過半。席哈克在 1997 年解散國會，結果因爲左派贏得多數席次，所以任命社會黨的喬斯班爲總理。

統在行使緊急權力期間，不得解散國民議會。」此一條文顯示，法國總統所享有的緊急命令權，遠較其他民主國家為大（Gross and Ní Aoláin, 2006: 197）。不過，如其名稱所示，緊急命令權並非日常性的權力。從法國第五共和的歷史來看，只有戴高樂（Charles de Gaulle）總統曾在 1961 年動用緊急命令權，壓制阿爾及利亞的兵變。法國的經驗，顯現緊急命令權的功能在於「預防與威嚇」（徐正戎，2002：142）。[27] 不過，也正因為緊急命令權具有預防與威嚇的功能，所以是總統的最後一道防線。

與法國第五共和相比，《中華民國憲法》賦予總統的預防性權力是相當有限的。就總統的國會解散權來看，增修條文第二條有這樣的規定：「總統於立法院通過對行政院院長之不信任案後十日內，經諮詢立法院院長後，得宣告解散立法院。」根據此一條文，台灣的總統只能在立法院通過對行政院院長的不信任投票案之後才能解散立法院，無法隨時透過解散國會、提早改選來產生新多數。之前也提到，《中華民國憲法》賦予總統的行政權相對有限，如果總統不滿意由在野黨控制的行政院，並無法透過主動解散國會來結束共治狀態。總統的另一條路是解除行政院院長的職務，但中華民國總統是否能任意解除行政院院長的職務，仍是有爭議的課題（湯德宗，1998）。

再看總統的緊急命令權，《中華民國憲法》第四十三條的規定是：「國家遇有天然災害，癘疫，或國家財政經濟上有重大變故，須為急速處分時，總統於立法院休會期間，得經行政院會議之決議，依緊急命令法，發布緊急命令，為必要之處置，但須於發布命令後一個月內提交立法院追認。如立法院不同意時，該緊急命令立即失效。」增修條文第二條則規定：「總統為避免國家或人民遭遇緊急危難或應付財政經濟上重大變故，得經行政院會議之決議發布緊急命令，為必要之處置，不受憲法第四十三條之限制。但須於發布命令後十日內提交立法院追認，如立法院不同意時，該緊急命令立即失效。」很明顯地，《中華民國憲法》賦予總統的緊急命令權，比法國第五共和小很多。以動用緊急命令權的條件而言，上述憲法條文規定的基本上屬於經濟變故或自然災害等「不可抗力」（force majeure）因素，而未提及憲政危機、國家安全等事項。以使用緊急命令權的程序而言，總統需得行政院會議之決議方能發布緊急命令，我們甚至無法將緊急命令視為中華民國總統的專屬權力。再以緊急命令的施行期間來看，上述條文明白規定發布命令後十日內提交立法院追認，而立法院對於緊急命令也有否決權。所以，對

---

[27] 戴高樂的確徵詢了憲法委員會，而某些委員對於此舉是否妥當持有保留意見，但他仍然發布緊急命令。此外，憲法第十六條並未提及緊急命令權的行使期限，其他憲政機關，也無法監督或終止總統使用緊急命令權。事實上，阿爾及利亞事件僅持續大約一個月即結束，但戴高樂動用緊急命令權的時間卻長達五個月。有學者因而認為戴高樂在行使緊急命令權的期間，是「憲政獨裁者」（Skach, 2005: 105）。

台灣的總統而言，緊急命令權的效用是相當有限的。[28]

除了總統權力，影響共治可能的另一項因素是總統任期。如前節理論所示，總統的任期越長，越能從長遠的角度思考共治的後果。法國第五共和總統任期，在 2000 年修憲之前是七年（後改為五年），是歐美民主國家中最長的。第五共和國憲法對於總統的連任次數沒有規定，如果依慣例連任一次則總長度可達 14 年。[29]當密特朗或席哈克就任總統時，至少有七年的任期，稀釋了共治所可能對總統造成的影響。反觀台灣，總統任期只有四年（增修條文第二條），可連任一次，幾乎是法國的一半。在短短的四年間，如果行政院由控制國會多數的在野黨掌握，而這個多數又不太可能會倒閣，勢必影響總統的施政空間。

總結本節的分析，法國總統的權力高於台灣總統，任期也比台灣總統長得多。根據前節的理論模型，總統在共治中的權力越小，越可能失去對政策的影響力，也就越沒有採取共治的誘因。《法國第五共和憲法》賦予總統相當大的權力，不因共治而消失，也使密特朗和席哈克不至於因為共治而失去總統權威。從同一角度，我們不難想像陳水扁在當選總統時對行政院院長人選的考量。他以不到四成的選票當選總統，面對國民黨一黨占有立法院多數席次，卻拒絕國民黨所要求的「黨對黨」內閣人事協商。他表示，全民政府不等於聯合政府，清流共治也不等於國、民兩黨共治。他還用了一個生動的比喻：不能讓國民黨「軟土深掘、整碗捧去」（彭威晶，2000）。黨對黨協商，結果不見得是國民黨取得組閣權，但從陳水扁的處境思考，他的顧慮不是全無道理：如果行政院院長由國民黨的領袖出任，閣員大部分也屬國民黨籍，總統沒有他們的配合很難執行他的國家安全政策，也無法透過參與行政院會議參與決策；如果總統和行政院院長發生衝突，既難以迫使行政院院長辭職，也無法解散國會重新改選。相較之下，一黨政府雖然容易造成僵局，對陳水扁而言卻是比較安全的選擇。

---

[28] 除此之外，法國和台灣總統在其他面向上也有明顯差異。例如，法國總統享有法律審批權（Elgie and Griggs, 2000: 32-41），還可發動公投，而中華民國總統沒有法律批審權，也只能在特殊情況下發動防禦性公民投票。法國總統的批審權，法源是第五共和憲法第十條：「共和國總統對於國會通過之法案，於送達政府後十五日內公布。在此期限內，總統得就該法案之全部或部分條文要求國會覆議，國會不得拒絕。」

[29] 2008 年修憲明確規定總統任期為兩任。

伍、選舉競爭對共治的影響

　　根據模型，民意是影響共治可能性的另一向要因。共治的主角，都是民選的政治菁英，不但擁有憲法所賦予的職權，也要面對選民的考驗；他們本身是總統選舉的參選者，也要領導所屬陣營贏得國會選舉。法國第一次共治的主角密特朗和席哈克，都以贏得 1988 年的總統選舉爲目標；到了 1997 年，共治的主角換成席哈克和喬斯班，而兩人也是 2002 年總統選舉的主要競爭者。就發生共治的時機而言，則和國會選舉的結果有密切關連。第參節的理論模型顯示，民意對共治的支持程度以及民意的呈現方式，都會影響總統對共治的態度。如果民眾支持共治，採行共治的總統和總理就能在未來的選舉中得到更多選民的支持；如果國會選舉呈現出的新民意既清楚又強大，抵擋這個新民意的總統就會付出政治代價。以下的分析，就以這兩點作爲比較法國與台灣的主軸。

　　關於法國民眾對共治的態度，Gérard Grunberg（1999）的研究提供了詳細的說明。他針對法國民眾從 1986 到 1998 年對共治的態度進行調查，發現對共治抱持正面態度的選民至少都有五成，抱持負面態度的最多三成；從時間軸來看，1986 年 5 月對共治保持正面態度的受訪者有 51%，無意見的有 20%，到了 1998 年 10 月，對共治保持正面態度的受訪者上升到 66%，無意見的則下降到 11%。由此可見，法國人民已逐漸將共治視爲慣例，而且大多抱持正面態度。再以共治當事人的民調支持度來看，第一次共治時密特朗持續領先席哈克，顯示共治有助其勝選；第二次共治時密特朗不連任，支持度也較巴拉度總理爲低；到了第三次共治，席哈克總統和喬斯班總理的民意支持度都相當高（Grunberg, 1999: 92-93），顯示共治有助於雙方當事人提升其支持度。Richard S. Conley 的實證研究也發現，密特朗和席哈克在共治期的聲望都比非共治時期高；對總理而言，共治期間的民意支持度高於非共治時期（Conley, 2006: 573-574, 580），顯示共治對總統總理都有好處。有學者指出，民意對共治的支持，使密特朗與席哈克都不願意提早結束第一次共治（Friend, 1998: 103）。

　　從選民的角度來觀察，法國民眾的投票行爲，受到候選人評價很大的影響。法國雖然左右界線分明，意識形態上的左右和政黨認同也影響選民的投票抉擇，但決勝關鍵不見得在這些因素。Guy Michelat（1993: 65-66）觀察 1960 到 1980 年代的法國選舉，發現大部分的法國選民可以辨認自己在左右光譜上的位置，但也有三成左右選民選擇「中間」。1980 年代初期，法國發生了政黨重組的現象（Martin, 2000），到了 1980 年代後期，出現一批年輕、受過高等教育且具獨立性的「新選民」，在 1988 年的總統選舉扮演決定性的角色（Elgie and Griggs, 2000: 133-135）。研究法國選舉的學者發現，某些選民之所以能夠獨立於左右意識形態之上，和他們對候選人的評價有關。Roy Pierce

（1991）對 1988 年法國總統選舉的研究顯示，在控制了選民自我的左右認知以及政黨認同後，候選人評價仍對投票抉擇產生重要的影響力；在第二輪投票，候選人評價的統計顯著性甚至高於選民的左右認同和政黨認同。Jay K. Dow（1999）研究 1995 年的總統選舉，發現選民的投票抉擇不僅受到意識形態的影響，也和候選人在重要議題上的態度有關。由於總統選舉只有一人可以當選，即使大多數的法國選民有左右和政黨的認同，但在左右競爭激烈的選舉中，競選者仍須爭取根據候選人評價來投票的選民。也因為如此，競選者難以忽視民眾對於共治的高支持度。

總統不僅在總統選舉面對選民的考驗，更因國會選舉的結果而面對新民意。就此而言，法國的國民議會選舉制度，使新民意能以清晰而強大的方式展現出來。法國第五共和，採用「單一選區兩輪投票制」（single-member majoritarian system in two rounds；或稱 two-ballot majoritarian system）選舉國民議會議員。此一選舉制度規定，國會議員選舉若有候選人得票數超過選區所有票數的一半以及所有有效選民四分之一以上者當選。如果沒有候選人得票超過這兩個門檻，則所有得票率超過所有有效選民 12.5% 以上的候選人進入第二輪投票；若只有一名候選人超過此一門檻，則第一輪投票得票次高者亦進入第二輪投票。第二輪投票，以得票最高者為當選人。[30] 此一選舉制度被視為「多數決選制」（majoritarian electoral system），對法國的政黨體系和國會運作產生幾項重大影響。第一，每次的國民議會選舉，都由左派或右派政黨取得半數以上的席次，使國會具有非常清楚的多數，無須另外組成聯合政府。雖然左、右兩派內包含不同的政黨，但基本上兩方陣營是鞏固的；在選舉時，兩方政黨多已建立選舉聯盟，避免因為票源分散而使敵對陣營贏得選舉（Thiébault, 2000: 498-502）。第二，單一選區制帶來很大的席次擺動（seat swing）。單一選區制只選出一位當選者，採用兩輪投票，當選的門檻更高。由於得票接近半數的政黨不見得能當選，政黨的得票率和席次率往往有很大的差距，多數聯盟很容易在選舉中喪失多數，而少數聯盟卻可能透過選舉變為多數，因此造成席次的大幅擺盪。這種情況，對總統和在野黨都產生重大影響。

圖 8.1 顯示法國第五共和歷次國民議會選舉的席次分布。從圖中可以清楚看出席次的大幅擺動。值得注意的是，從 1981 到 2002 年，每次國民議會選舉都使多數席次在左右陣營間替換，而這段期間剛好就是發生三次共治的時期。在 2002 年之前，總統任期七年，國民議會議員的任期五年，所以總統必然會在任內遭遇國會改選。由於總統與

---

[30] 1986 年曾經改為比例代表制，但隨後又改回原制。關於法國國民議會選制的介紹，請參考 Inter-Parliamentary Union（2008）。

國會議員改選時間不一致，新產生的國會多數不見得與總統同黨派。[31] 所以，如果國民議會選舉產生清楚而具有凝聚力的多數聯盟，而產生此一多數的國會選舉又新於總統選舉，彰顯的民意也就新於總統選舉所呈現的民意。如果總統忽視這個新多數，很可能導致統治困境，對想要競選連任的總統更是不利。有學者甚至認為，法國的「非同時選舉時程」（non-concurrent electoral cycle）是促成左右共治的主因（Elgie, 2001b: 113-115）。根據前述分析，這個看法應該修正為：非同時選舉時程和單一選區制，使總統和國會政黨都清楚認知多數民意所在，進而增加左右共治出現的機率。

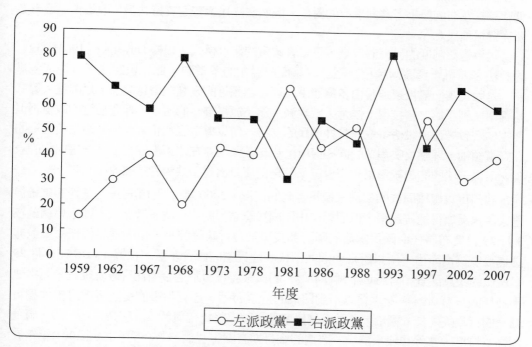

圖 8.1　法國第五共和國民議會選舉的席次分布
資料來源：1959-1997（Thiébault, 2000: 499）、2002-2007（Ministère de l'Intérieur, 2009）。

---

[31] 總統選舉和國會選舉如果同時舉行，或國會選舉在總統選舉後舉行，總統當選者和國會多數屬於同一政黨的機率比較高。同理，如果兩種選舉舉行的時間差距越大，總統與國會多數不同黨的機率就越高。見 Shugart 與 Carey（1992: 206-225）。

　　要得知法國國民議會席次的擺幅究竟有多大，我們可以用左、右陣營為單位，計算國民議會選舉的席次擺動率（average seat swing）：將某陣營在某次選舉的席次率減去前次選舉的席次率，並取絕對值。計算結果顯示，左派聯盟從 1962 到 2007 年的平均的席次擺動率是 20.3%，右派聯盟則是 19.7%。大約兩成的擺動是相當大的，足以讓掌握國會多數的聯盟在接下來的選舉失去多數，並讓敵對陣營贏得多數，而 1980 年代以降的選舉真的呈現這樣的趨勢。對總統和反對聯盟而言，掌握這些移動的選票，就等於是掌握多數國會席次的關鍵，總統當然也無法忽視這些流動的選票。前面已經提到，擺動於左右之間的選票，很可能和候選人評價有關，而這些選票既然較不受制於意識形態，就應該是左右的競爭者共同爭取的對象。既然法國民眾普遍支持共治，政治菁英沒有必要違背這種民意。

　　國會選舉制度的另一個效應，是影響政黨的競爭模式。根據 Duverger（1963: 239）的說法，「單一選區兩輪投票制」容易促成溫和的多黨制。此一選制之所以造成多黨制，是因為第一輪投票通常由多黨競爭，理念越相近的政黨競爭越激烈，以圖進入第二輪選舉。到了第二輪投票，候選人數驟減，為了贏得唯一的席次，理念相近的政黨不但要團結一致，還要設法爭取陣營外選民的支持，所以導致溫和化。作為共治主角之一的在野黨領袖，理應反映選舉的向心競爭，和總統共治並在政策上妥協，就是趨中化的表現。所以，法國的總統選舉和國會選舉，是促使政治對手共治的重要原因。

　　我們可以根據同樣的架構來檢視台灣的情況。2000 年 3 月 18 日民進黨籍的總統候選人陳水扁贏得總統選舉，但面對由中國國民黨掌握的立法院多數席次。陳水扁總統在 3 月 29 日宣布將任命國民黨籍的國防部長唐飛為行政院院長，但因為這個任命案並非透過政黨協商產生，所以唐飛內閣並不代表國民黨的國會多數。根據 TVBS 在 3 月 29 日所做的民意調查，有將近半數（48%）的民眾認為唐飛適合擔任行政院院長，認為他不適任的只有 24%。陳水扁以不到四成的選票勝選，卻有半數的受訪者認可由他獨自任命的行政院院長，顯示大多數台灣民眾還是習慣將總統與行政院院長視為一體。唐飛的高支持度，當然和陳水扁處於勝選的蜜月期有關，我們若將時間點拉到 2001 年年底立法委員選舉前，即能更清楚呈現台灣民眾對於政府組成的態度。TVBS 在 8 月的民意調查顯示，有六成的民眾贊成組成聯合政府，但這並不代表民眾支持由在野黨組閣。在被問到如果聯合政府是由兩黨組成民眾的偏好為何時，有半數（50%）受訪者的選擇是「國民黨、民進黨」，回答「國民黨、親民黨」（即泛藍陣營）的，只有 28%；如果聯合政府不限於兩個政黨時，仍以回答「國民黨、民進黨」的受訪者最多（30%），其次為「國民黨、民進黨、親民黨」（19%），回答「國民黨、親民黨」的，只有 10%（TVBS 聯合調查中心，2001）。換言之，認為政府應包括執政黨的選民，遠多於認為

應由在野多數組成政府的選民。這樣的認知結構，使「政府組成」議題很難進入台灣的選舉議程。即使候選人評價對選民的投票抉擇具有一定的影響力（鄭夙芬、陳陸輝、劉嘉薇，2005），政府組成也不見得是評價候選人的主要指標。

台灣的總統任期四年，立法委員任期三年（2005 年修憲前），所以立法委員選舉也可能呈現新民意。然而，台灣立法委員選舉所帶來的席次擺動相當有限。台灣的立法委員選舉，長期採用「單記非讓渡投票複數選區制」（single nontransferable voting under multi-member district, SNTV-MMD），後來在 2005 年修憲改為並立式單一選區兩票制（mixed-member majoritarian system）。在 SNTV-MMD 之下，每位選民投票給一位候選人，候選人得票最多者當選，而選區的應選名額通常多於一人。如此簡單的選舉制度，卻造成許多獨特的後果。首先，由於候選人所得的票數不能轉讓給別的候選人，而大黨通常又在同一選區提名超過一位以上的候選人，導致同黨相爭，甚至黨內派系。其次，為了要和黨內其他提名人競爭，候選人通常會和特定背景的選民建立個人關係，這種關係可能是候選人和特定選民之間的特殊利益，或是特定（通常也比較極端）的政治意識形態。對立法者而言，在選區建立和特定選民的特殊關係，比通過符合公眾利益的法案更有助於其連任。第三，SNTV-MMD 具有一定的比例性（proportionality），小黨也容易存活，但國會議員仍然需要政黨來協調利益的分配和選舉的提名；能替提供候選人特殊利益的政黨，仍能維持一定的規模。這些後果，深刻影響政治菁英的競爭模式。

先看立法委員選舉如何影響席次變化。在台灣，通常將政黨分為支持台灣獨立的泛綠陣營，包括民進黨與台灣團結聯盟，以及反對台灣獨立的泛藍陣營，包括國民黨、親民黨與新黨。總統是否掌握國會多數席次，也是從兩個陣營所擁有的席次來判斷。作為一種比例性的選舉制度，SNTV-MMD 下的席次擺動率比單一選區制小得多。圖 8.2 顯示兩大陣營從 1992 年立法院全面改選，到 2008 年立法委員選舉的席次分布。國民黨雖然曾因分裂成其他泛藍政黨而喪失部分席次，但兩個陣營的國會席次基本上沒有大幅度的變化。在使用 SNTV-MMD 選舉立法委員的 1992 到 2004 年期間，泛綠陣營的席次擺動率是 4.4%，泛藍則為 4.9%，比法國小很多。從長期的觀點來看，立法院的多數席次始終為泛藍陣營所控制，不因立法委員選舉而有改變。對陳水扁總統而言，即使任命國會多數領袖為行政院院長，恐怕也難以改變這種席次分配的狀態。

SNTV-MMD 對於台灣的政黨體系和政黨競爭也帶來深刻的影響。首先，此一選制降低政黨的團結度，也常使同一聯盟內的政黨處於緊張狀態。在選舉制度中，SNTV-MMD 的個人化程度最高（Carey and Shugart, 1995），競選者為了要和同黨候選人區隔，往往要耗費大量資源建立個人的支持網絡，理念相近的政黨，也成為彼此的勁敵。

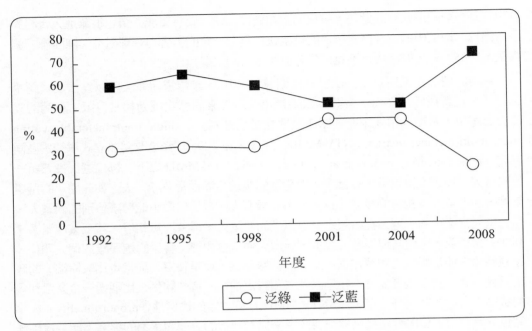

圖 8.2　台灣立法選舉的席次分布
資料來源：由筆者自行整理繪製（中央選舉委員會，2009）。

其次，因為 SNTV-MMD 之下的競爭高度個人化，改選成本極高。第三，因為選區服務是候選人爭取選票的重要手段，現任者不見得比地方人士更具競爭力。以 2001 和 2004 年的選舉為例，大約有至少三分之一的當選者不是現任立法委員。這幾種後果相加，使立法院欠缺制衡少數政府的能力：如果國會要通過對行政院院長的不信任投票案，同一陣營的政黨必須行動一致（Wu, 2005a）；又因為總統依憲法可以在不信任投票通過後解散國會提早改選，所以立法委員往往因為改選成本高和連任率低而不願意贊成倒閣提案。陳水扁在 2000 年當選總統，未與各黨協商即任命唐飛為行政院院長，即有人提議倒閣，但此一提案並未被接受。日後，雖然親民黨也曾建議倒閣，但並未獲得國民黨的支持。既然少數政府被倒閣的機率極低，總統採取共治的壓力也就小很多。

陸、結論

　　半總統制下的敵對政治菁英，為何能在無法可循的情況下建構共治的慣例？本文以法國的三次左右共治為案例，並以台灣為對照組，嘗試回答這個問題。本文假定政治菁英都希望能維持其影響力，而為達到此目的，必須儘可能運用其憲法權力並爭取選民支持。透過理論模型的推演和經驗資料的分析，我們發現兩個有利於共治慣例形成的條件：第一，選民透過國會選舉送給政治菁英清楚的訊息，使總統意識到只有正面回應此一新民意才能延長其政治生命。第二，憲法如果賦予總統足夠的權力（尤其是無須總理配合的專屬權力），使其不至於因為共治而喪失影響力，總統任命在野黨領袖為總理的動機就會增強。法國第五共和符合這些條件：由絕對多數選出的總統被憲法賦予仲裁者和國家防衛者的任務，享有國防外交的特權，主持部長會議，可以拒絕簽署行政法令，也可主動解散國會；國民議會的選舉，因為選舉制度的因素，使左右陣營都面臨席次大幅變動的可能；對總統而言，新民意既強且大，而且多數選民對共治抱持正面態度。這些條件，使密特朗的共治具有很高的可能性與可行性，而他也的確立下了共治的先例。反觀台灣，並未出現如同法國的條件：總統由相對多數選出，不能主動解散立法院，即便可以調解五院爭議但不能參加行政院會議，雖然可以制訂國家安全大政方針但需要行政院配合才能實行；立法委員的選舉制度造成競選成本高、連任率低，連帶降低倒閣的可能性，但選制的比例性又使政黨席次變動有限，即使新民意出現也不容易對總統造成壓力。

　　這些發現，不但幫助我們瞭解憲政慣例如何形成、法國為何出現共治以及台灣為何難以出現共治，也提示了一個半總統制研究的重要課題：當總統可以獨自任命總理時，為什麼有些國家可以出現共治，有些卻產生少數政府？憲政傳統和憲政文化當然具有一定的影響力，但本論文也指出制度因素的重要性，而同樣的制度可以遍存於不同國家。[32] 為瞭解法國的共治模式是否也出現在其他國家，我們需要尋找滿足以下條件的半總統制國家：總統享有獨自任命總理的權力以及主動解散國會權、國會選舉採取單一選區制、總統黨籍曾和國會多數黨（聯盟）不同。在民主的半總統制國家中，只有非洲的

---

[32] 2005 年修憲後，台灣的立法委員選舉改採並立式單一選區兩票制。理論上，此一選制應能降低國會的政黨數，並增強政黨在國會扮演的角色。在 2008 年總統大選期間，國民黨候選人馬英九曾提及，「組閣尊重國會多數」；民進黨候選人謝長廷也說，「組閣找國民黨協商，兩黨共治」。馬、謝兩人是否會實現其諾言，我們不得而知，但至少表示新選制造成的政黨體系變化，是總統思考組閣問題時的重要變數。關於兩位總統候選人的言論，請參考張菁雅、彭顯鈞（2008）、王貝林（2008）。

馬利共和國符合這些條件。[33] 馬利共和國的總統任命總理無須國會同意，可在與總理與國會議長諮商後解散國會，並享有與法國總統類似的緊急命令權；該國的國會議員選舉，也採單一選區兩輪投票制。[34] 馬利從 1992 年採行此一體制以來，有十年的時間由同一陣營掌握總統職位和國會多數，和 1981 年之前的法國第五共和類似。2002 年選出的馬利共和國總統 Amadou Toumani Touré 並無清楚的黨派屬性，而其任命的總理所組成的政府則包含大多數的國會黨派。馬利的情況和法國的共治仍有相當的差距，只有一位超黨派總統和包納國會多數政黨的政府並存，也還不能算慣例。不過，以一個貧困、沒有議會制傳統的國家而言，馬利的經驗在新興民主國家中是相當獨特的，顯示制度設計可能扮演了重要的角色。反觀台灣，雖然具有一定程度的民主化，也比馬利富裕很多，但始終處於總統主導的統治模式；在少數政府時期，總統雖然仍被認為是最高政治領袖，但難以突破行政立法僵局和菁英之間的對抗。本文比較法國和台灣，正是要顯現既有的制度設計如何影響菁英互動以及新慣例的建立。

---

[33] 非民主的半總統制國家，制度對行為者的約束有限。大多數的半總統制國家採取比例代表制選出國會議員，而行單一選區制的半總統制國家，總統很少享有獨自任命總理的權力。

[34] 馬利的國會選舉制度是以政黨名單為投票對象，和法國略有不同。馬利共和國憲法全文請參考 Constitution Finder（2009）。

第九章

政府體制、選舉制度與政黨體系：一個配套論的分析[*]

壹、制度配套的化學變化

政治制度包含不同的面向，如中央政府體制、選舉制度、政黨體系，國會制度，官僚制度、司法體系、中央地方關係、軍文關係以及國家的經濟角色等（Rothstein, 1996: 135）。許多經驗研究都是以特定制度為對象，界定其特質與後果；關於制度選擇的辯論，也多集中在其中某些面向上。例如，很多探討中央政府體制的學者，認為除了美國以外的大多數總統制國家都有政局不穩的情形，所以內閣制比總統制優越（Linz, 1990, 1997）。[1]關於選舉制度的討論亦然：非常多的研究，都將焦點集中在小黨在不同制度下的生存機會，並以此推估選舉制度和政黨體系的關係。[2]關於其他制度的研究，大致也是針對特定面向中的制度類型進行定性與分析。

但是，這樣的研究取向，時常碰到難以解釋的案例。例如，同樣實施內閣制，同樣處於二次戰後的蕭條，為何英國和法國的憲政經驗有巨大的差距？英國從 1945 到 1957 年間只換了兩位首相，而法國第四共和（1947-1959）在同樣長的時間內卻有 22 位總理。同樣採取總統制，美國經驗為什麼迥異於拉丁美洲或菲律賓？再就選舉制度來看，雖然學者對於制度的席次分配效應有很高的共識，但卻很少有人能明確指出其憲政後果。同樣因為採取單一選區制而形成兩黨制的英國和美國，政治風貌就有很大的不同。

---

[*] 本文曾刊登於《選舉研究》，第 13 卷第 2 期（2006 年 11 月），頁 1-42。感謝政治大學選舉研究中心《選舉研究》同意轉載。

[1] 有趣的是，某些不同意此種觀點的研究，也是把總統制和內閣制當作對立的概念，主張總統制不一定比較差（如 Horowitz, 1990）。也有學者認為新興民主國家採取總統制乃反映社會需求（Fukuyama, Dressel, and Chang, 2005），所以只能用其他制度（如憲法法庭）來彌補其弊端。在台灣，憲政辯論如果涉及中央政府體制，也常出現「內閣制好還是總統制好」的思維方式（如盧瑞鍾，1995）。

[2] 在政治學中，選舉制度是少數能達到高度精確化且解釋力很強的研究課題，許多經典也以此主題聞名，如杜弗傑（Maurice Duverger）（1969）、Rae（1971）、Grofman 與 Lijphart（1986）、Taagepera 與 Shugart（1989）、Cox（1997）、Colomer（2004）等。

英國過去兩百多年來,歷屆政府只有兩次因爲不能獲得國會的信任而下台。[3] 反觀美國,總統因爲和國會意見不一而動用否決權,幾乎是憲政常態。

有人因此認爲制度本身不足以解釋憲政運作。一個常見的說法是,眞正影響憲政運作的關鍵是文化。持此看法者可以宣稱,法國第四共和與同時期英國的憲政運作之所以差異很大,乃因法國政治文化強調理念實踐,英國政治文化重視現實經驗;美國的總統制比拉美上軌道,是因爲美國的市民社會比較成熟。這種說法其實很難反駁,因爲憲政文化和憲政運作可能根本就是同義詞。當我們說某國的憲政文化成熟,自然預設該國不會發生重大的憲政衝突,反之亦然。所以,憲政文化可能是因,也可能是果。再者,如果我們只觀察特定國家在某時間內的憲政運作,憲政文化就沒有變異性(variance),不能當作解釋變數。

如果我們還是想從制度論的角度來進行解釋,另一種方法就是將不同的制度面向配套起來看。研究配套,最常見的有兩種模式:第一種,乃找出不同制度面向的共通性,並以各制度在面向上的定位,描繪制度配套的樣貌。由於此法並不改變原有制度面向的性質,所以是一種「物理變化」的配套論。在相關論著中,最有名的例子就是 Lijphart(1999a)的民主體制模型。他認爲各種制度面向都可以用「多數決型」(majoritarian)或「共識決型」(consensus)來歸類,例如內閣制、兩黨制、單一選區制和單一國家制(unitary state)都接近多數決型;總統制、多黨制、比例代表制和聯邦制則屬於共識決型。Lijphart 運用因素分析抽繹出兩個主軸,並把不同國家的位置標示出來。透過此法,Lijphart 的確能將複雜的民主體制放在統一的座標上來比較。然而,這種模式不見得能解釋民主體制的運作後果。Lijphart 在 1984 年的著作建構了這種模式(Lijphart,1984),但並未解釋其政治或政策後果。他在 1999 年修訂版中嘗試比較兩種民主類型,並認爲共識決體制在總體經濟發展上並不比多數決型遜色,而在人權、福利等民主品質的指標上超越多數決型(Lijphart, 1999a: 258-300)。這樣的比較,在統計上的意義可能不大:所謂「不遜色」,可能是因爲作者的模型解釋力弱;而民主品質指標,和共識型體制都強調多元代表性,兩者在意涵上高度相關。

Lijphart 的模型有一個預設:如果一個民主體制在各面向上都表現出明顯的共識型特性,其制度配套一定也是最具共識型的,多數決型的情形亦然。然而,這不一定符合現實經驗。例如,美國的憲政體制長久以來都是總統制和兩黨制的配套,但其運作情況卻會因一致政府(unified government)或分立政府(divided government)而有很大

---

[3] 一次是 1924 年保守黨的 Baldwin 首相,另一次是 1979 年工黨的 Gallaghan 首相。

的差異。[4] 此外，某些制度彼此配套後，可能會喪失在原本制度面向上的特質。例如，當多黨制和總統制放在一起時，可能有利於總統的權力擴張（Duverger, 1964b: 411; Mainwaring, 1993; Mainwaring and Shugart, 1997）；反之，議會內閣制之下的多黨制具有多元代表的性質，但會縮短政府壽命。所以，總統制下的多黨制和內閣制下的多黨制，特質並不相同。要處理這個問題，我們必須思考制度配套的「化學變化」，亦即配套對制度在原有面向性質的改變。這就是研究制度配套的第二種模式。

本文的主旨，乃是以選舉制度和中央政府體制為主軸，探討其配套所可能產生的「新變種」。這兩個主軸，正是 Sartori（1997）建構其「憲政工程學」（constitutional engineering）的骨幹，也是許多新興民主國家憲政選擇的關鍵項目。所以，這兩個制度配套後究竟可能產生何種後果，是一個相當重要的問題。在下一節，本文將澄清基本概念，並建構分析模型。第參節提出五項基本假定，尤其關注選舉制度、社會分歧和政黨體系間的關係。根據這些假定，第肆節推演出五個命題，顯現選舉制度和政府體制搭配的可能後果，並以行政和立法的選舉時程為分析重點。第伍節將研究發現運用到第七次修憲後的台灣，根據命題預判未來可能出現的憲政後果。

貳、制度配套的分析模型

如果制度配套可能產生非預期的變化，我們的分析應先從不同制度面向的排列組合開始。以政府體制和政黨體系而言，第一步應是先劃分這兩個面向的類別。[5] 為方便說明，我們用最簡單的二元法來進行分類。假設中央政府體制可以劃為分立與合一兩型，政黨體系可分為兩黨與多黨兩類（見表 9.1）。後者即如字面所示，前者則表達行政權的來源。所謂合一，是指行政與立法同源。以內閣制為例，人民投票選出國會議員，再由國會多數黨（或聯盟）組成政府，而政府隨時要接受國會信任投票的考驗。同理，分立是指行政立法兩權不同源。例如，總統制國家的總統和國會乃透過不同選舉產生，

4　所謂分立政府，應該是指總統在國會面對另一多數黨。所以，總統所屬政黨非為國會多數，並不是分立政府的充分條件。如果國會屬於無任何政黨過半的多黨制，應稱為少數政府（minority government）或非多數政府（non-majority government）。如果總統在國會搭建多黨聯盟，可稱為聯合政府（coalition government）（Shugart, 1995: 327）。但也有學者認為分立政府包括無政黨過半的情況（Elgie, 2001a）。本文採取前一種界定，以對概念作更細緻的區分。

5　政黨體系和選舉制度雖然高度相關，但並不相同。次節將會探討政黨體系如何受到選舉制度和其他條件的影響。

兩者不能決定彼此的去留。半總統制國家兩種成分都有，因為總統任命的行政首長（總理）要得到國會的信任，但總統本身又是人民選出。其位置要看具體憲政規定，如果總理基本上受制於國會而非總統，則接近合一型，如果總統才是實質行政領袖，則趨近分立型。

表 9.1　憲政體制與政黨體系的可能配套

行政立法關係　＼　政黨體系	二黨	多黨
合一	一黨統領行政立法：英國	多黨聯盟執政：西歐
分立	一致或分立政府：美國	總統建構多數聯盟：拉美

資料來源：筆者自行整理。

　　表 9.1 呈現的是極簡型的制度配套模式，[6] 其他的配套，或有更多的制度面向，或有更細的制度分類。如前節所述，要探討制度配套的化學變化，我們必須找到關於制度運作的一套理論，然後將這套理論配置到各種排列組合上。在比較制度研究中，Tsebelis（1995, 2002）的「否決者理論」（veto player theory）是常被引用的分析架構。此一理論認為，不管政治制度為何，應該要先找出其決策過程中的否決者及其政策偏好；所謂政治制度，基本上只是在規範否決者的數目。[7] 這套理論的要旨是，否決者越多或否決者間的偏好歧異越大，現狀就越難改變。我們如果將憲政運作定義成行政部門和立法部門達成一致決策的機率，則主要的解釋變項就是兩者是否為否決者。如果行政和立法部門都是否決者，而且兩者立場歧異很大，就易使決策陷入僵局，甚至引發憲政危機。

　　如果大多數的決策都要由行政部門執行甚至提案，行政部門就是否決者之一。所以，問題的關鍵在於國會政黨的分化程度及其偏好差距。圖 9.1 用二維的歐氏空間（Euclidean space）來描繪行政部門與國會黨派的偏好分布。在此空間中，每位行為者都有其最想達到的政策目標（稱為理想點，ideal point），距離此點越遠表示效用越低，

6　Duverger（1964a: 206-207）曾經建構類似的分類，他是以總統制／內閣制與兩黨制／多黨制為指標，分出四類政體。相較之下，表 9.1 的「行政立法分立」涵蓋的不止總統制，也包括半總統制。而 Duverger 認為兩黨總統制可以運作的很好，但未深入探討分立政府的狀況。

7　某些體制沒有形式上的否決者（如多黨聯合政府）。即使如此，Tsebelis（2002: 38-63）認為我們可以把這些非否決者的整體視為「集體否決者」（collective veto player），並用同樣的邏輯分析政策穩定。

再假設現狀位於所有行動者的帕雷圖集合（Pareto set）中。[8] 我們要回答的問題是：在不同的制度配套下，改變現狀的可能性大小爲何？圖 9.1 中的灰色區域，就是各種制度配套的現狀改變力。[9] 一個合理的推論是，在內閣制之下，政府越難改變現狀，就越難長期執政；在總統制之下，府會關係越緊張，政府越難以改變現狀。

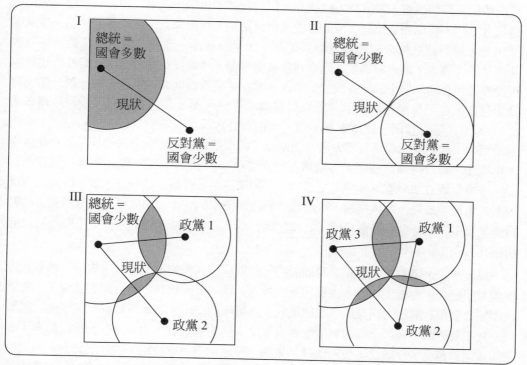

圖 9.1　四種制度配套的現狀改變力（灰色區域）
資料來源：筆者自行整理。

圖 9.1 的分析如右。在總統制或實權半總統制下，我們以總統的理想點來代表行政部門。如果是內閣制或虛位半總統制，則由組成政府的政黨來代表政府立場。首先，我

8　選項 X 若爲帕雷圖集合的元素，即表示無任一其他選項 Y 可以不減損所有決策者在 X 的利益，並至少讓一人更好。帕雷圖集合外的選項對所有決策成員都是不利的，所以現狀應會移動至此集合內。

9　在空間模型中，所有可能改變現狀的替代方案構成「勝集」（winset），亦即不同行動者意欲替代現狀方案的交集。圖 9.1 的灰色部分即爲勝集。

們分析總統制或實權半總統制的情況，當行政立法分立且爲兩黨制時，有兩種偏好分布的可能。第一種狀況（I），是總統所屬政黨爲國會多數（即一致政府）。此時總統和其政黨的政策目標一致，該政黨又掌握國會多數，所以總統是唯一的否決者，改變現狀的能力很強。在行政立法合一和兩黨制的配套下，執政黨必須是國會多數，所以情形也是如此。第二種狀況（II），是總統所屬政黨非爲國會多數（即分立政府）。此時，所有決策都要得到國會多數支持方能成立，但行政部門也是否決者。由於現狀已位於兩個否決者之間，所以完全沒有改變的可能。用白話說，行政和立法處於僵局。第三種狀況（III），是行政立法分立和多黨體系並存。如果沒有任一政黨掌握國會多數，而行政部門又是否決者，則政府必須在國會建立多數聯盟，才能推行其政策。此時改變現狀的可能性是存在的，但小於一致政府的情況。其次，若爲內閣或虛位半總統制，即便有總統存在，也不具備否決能力，所以只有兩種可能。第一是國會由單一政黨取得多數（I），第二是沒有單一政黨掌握多數，而由聯合政府控制政府（IV）。在圖 9.1 的四個類型中，此兩者的現狀改變力居於前兩位。如果把各種制度配套改變現狀的可能性作大小排序，可以得到這個結果：兩黨行政立法合一 = 兩黨一致政府 > 多黨行政立法合一 > 多黨行政立法分立 > 兩黨分立政府。[10] 同樣是兩黨行政立法分立，現狀改變力可能最高，也可能最低。這些推論，可以延伸到任何多維的空間：由於現狀位於行動者的帕雷圖集合中，而行動者最多三個，其理想點和現狀必定處於二維的空間上，所以可以適用圖 9.1 的推論。[11]

　　以上所述，是制度配套和政府效能的一般原理，我們的確發現，中央政府體制和政黨體系配套後，會產生和原本性質相異的效應。例如，同樣在二維空間的情況下，多黨內閣制改變現狀的能力略高於多黨總統制；在單維的情形下，多黨總統制甚至會引起僵局。其主要原因，在於不同的制度配套會產生不同的否決者，而否決者的數目越多，政府的效能就越低。反論之，要將此種抽象的一般原則運用在特定的制度配套上，即須說明各種制度的性質爲何，所規範的否決模式爲何。事實上，行政立法是否合一以及政黨體系的分化程度，都涉及決策受到幾個機關或組織的控制。中央政府體制，通常是由憲法所規範，也比較好辨認，但是影響政黨體系的因素就複雜多了，如果我們考慮各種可

---

[10] 如果議題空間是單維（one-dimensional）的，結果和圖 9.1 稍有不同：因爲現狀位於帕雷圖集合，所以一定在總統和國會反對黨之間。不論反對黨的數目爲何，結果都是無法改變現狀的僵局。

[11] 如果行動者超過三個，就不見得能用二維的空間來描繪其理想點的分布。McKelvey（1976）的定理已經證明，在多維的空間中，只要 Condorcet 點不存在，任何的結果都可透過某種議程設定而達成，現狀一定可以被改變。這和現狀在單維空間不能被改變，形成明顯對比，也和圖 9.1 的發現類似。

能的因素，再同時考慮中央政府體系的類別，可以推得許多關於政府效能的命題，這是以下兩節的主題。

參、關於選舉制度與政府體制的一些基本假定

制度配套涉及多種力量的交互作用，其原理不見得顯而易見。但我們可以從既有文獻出發，歸納一些廣被接受的事理（stylized facts），將其當作建構制度配套理論的假定。關於政黨體系，影響至鉅的是選舉制度，但諸如選區劃分、社會分歧等因素，也扮演重要角色。所謂選舉制度，又包含行政首長與國會議員的選舉。以下提出五項相關假定，其中第一、二項敘述國會多數黨存在的制度條件，第三項說明議題結構的一般性質，第四項和元首直選的政治效應有關，第五項歸納有關選舉週期的研究發現。

假定一：在其他條件不變的情況下，選舉制度比例性（proportionality）越高，政黨數目就越多，也越不容易由單一政黨掌握國會多數。

研究選舉制度的學者，大多認為選舉制度的比例性是形塑政黨體系最重要的因素之一。所謂比例性，簡單來說，就是政黨得票率和席次率之間的轉換函數（Taagepera and Shugart, 1989: 67-69; Lijphart, 1994）。得票率和席次率越接近，選舉制度的比例性就越高；兩者的差距越大，選舉制度的比例性越低。比例性最高的狀況，是每位選民都投票給自己且所有選民都當選；比例性最低的狀況，是某政黨只差一票就拿到半數選票，但沒有贏得任何一席。後者，只有在單一選區制才會發生。更一般性地說，選區應選名額越低，比例性就越低。[12] 基於此理，單一選區不利小黨。反過來說，如果選區的應選名額高，小黨容易生存，當然不容易由單一政黨取得半數以上的國會席次。[13] 研究選舉制的學者常用「有效政黨數」（effective number of parties）來描繪一國的政黨分化程度，當其他條件不變時，選舉制度的比例性和有效政黨數成正比。我們還可延伸此一概念，定義「有效國會政黨數」（effective number of legislative parties），來討論政黨體系和憲政運作的關係。[14]

---

[12] 令應選名額為 M，則任一政黨或候選人得票率高於 $1/(M + 1)$ 即確定能獲得至少一席。實際門檻當然不會這麼高，但也和 M 成反比。

[13] 必須強調的是，比例代表制並不排除由單一政黨取得國會多數席次的可能，只是機率遠比單一選區制小。比例代表制（尤其是應選名額低者）亦非多黨制的必要條件，如奧地利的比例代表制就和兩大黨制並存。

[14] 命題三將對有效政黨數進行比較詳細的討論。有效政黨數的公式是 $1/\sum V_i^2$，有效國會政黨數的

假定二：當國會選舉的比例性低時，全國分歧與區域分歧越一致，越容易由一黨掌握國會多數。

所謂應選名額，是以選區來計算的，有效政黨數，當然也是以選區爲範圍。所以，選區和全國的有效政黨數相同，表示兩者的選民分布和投票行爲是相似的。反之，如果各選區的選民分布有重大差異，即使每個選區的有效政黨數都反映其應選名額，在全國層次的有效政黨數仍應高於選區有效政黨數的平均值。最極端的狀況，是選民有強烈的地域主義，所以如果採用單一選區制，獲勝者可能正是代表該地域的政黨，在全國的層次造成多黨化。[15] 依此理，只有當全國分歧與區域分歧一致時，單一選區制才能產生兩黨制，進而使單一政黨掌握國會多數。

假定三：單面向的議題空間比多面向的議題空間更容易產生穩定的多數決。

如果我們能把決策者對議題的偏好排列在一個單維的數線上，即產生單面向的議題空間。根據「中位選民定理」（median voter theorem）（Downs, 1957），若議題空間爲單面向且決策乃以多數決進行，中位理想點是唯一的均衡，而且永遠存在。[16] 然而，在多面向的議題空間中，均衡存在的可能性微乎其微（McKelvey, 1976）。這個假定的功能，在於說明同樣的政黨體系，可能會因爲議題面向的差異而表現出不同的現狀改變力。

假定四：在民主體制中，國家元首的直接民選是其能成爲實質行政首長的必要條件。

在民主國家，國家元首若是由人民直接選舉產生（通常爲總統直選），即表達人民對國家最高領導人的授權。如果此時總統本身也具有很大的憲法權力，他應該就是最高的行政首長；如果總統在憲法上的權力有限，其實質影響力取決於民意的歸屬而可能有大有小。如果民眾面對的是效能不彰的國會，民選總統就很有可能成爲直接對選民負責的實質領袖。相對地，在公民文化成熟的社會中，民選總統有可能扮演象徵性領袖的角色，而讓體制趨於內閣制。反論之，間接選舉產生的國家元首，除了欠缺人民的直接授

公式是 $1/\Sigma S_i^2$，其中 V_i 與 S_i 分別表示政黨 i 的得票率和議席率。

[15] 最明顯的例子，是採用單一選區相對多數決制的印度。雖然印度的國會選舉乃由兩大聯盟競逐，但聯盟內部的構成政黨數目相當多。某些學者也發現，族群分布是選舉制度和政黨體系重要的中介變項（Mozaffar, Scarritt, and Galaich, 2003）。

[16] 必須說明的是，此處的決策規則乃是將所有的理想點相比，試圖找出能不被其他選項替代的選項。對本文而言，這種規則描繪的是國會的決策。若將 Downs 的模型用在選舉競爭，而參賽者的目標在於極大化選票，參賽者的數目就會影響均衡存在與否。

權，也可能受其投票者（如國會議員）所操控，不太容易成為實質的行政首長。[17]所以，直接民選應是總統成為實質行政首長的必要條件，而非充分條件。從實際經驗來看，總統制國家的元首和行政首長原本就是同一人，所以沒有爭議。芬蘭、冰島、愛爾蘭和奧地利都有直選總統，但當前其總統權力大多是象徵性的，所以可歸為象徵總統式的半總統制國家。必須強調的是，此一假定只限用於有競爭性選舉的國家，在尚未民主化或處於民主化初期的國家，國家元首可能是實質的政治領袖，不論其產生方式為何。例如，巴基斯坦常被認為是總統制的國家，但其總統乃由間接選舉產生。很多內閣制國家（如英、日），其實都曾經歷過世襲君主權力很大的歷史階段。

假定五：若國會選舉制度的比例性低且主要政黨獲票能力接近，則行政立法兩權改選的間隔時間越長，越容易出現分立政府。

國會議員選舉制度的比例性越高，產生一黨過半的機率越低。[18]反之，國會選舉制度的比例性如果很低，雖不保證導致兩大黨制，但由一黨掌握多數的機會就高得多。問題是，如果國會席次乃由兩大黨分享，行政首長（如總統）所屬政黨在什麼情況下可以掌握國會多數？從經驗資料看，許多研究都有這樣的發現：當總統與國會同日改選，或國會在總統選舉後很快改選，出現總統政黨掌握國會多數席次的機率較高（Shugart and Carey, 1992: 263）；反之，如果總統選舉和國會選舉非同時進行，出現分立政府的情形較多。[19]

探究行政與立法選舉如何受到其先後順序的影響，就是所謂「選舉時程」（electoral cycle）的問題。[20]之所以會出現前述模式，可能有兩種原因。第一，選民對於政府的施政評價，常常會隨著時間而下滑（Shugart and Carey, 1992: 244; Shugart, 1995; Jones, 1995: 118）。政府剛上台的時候，背負著人民期待但尚未遂行其政策，故

---

[17] 關於總統直選和憲政體制的關係，請參考王業立（2001a）。

[18] 單一選區制若採多輪投票制，小黨就有生存空間（Duverger, 1969），也降低國會由單一政黨取得多數的機率。所以，此處所謂的單一選區制以相對多數決制為主，而大多數施行單一選區制的國家也的確採行此制。不過，如果行政首長和採行比例代表制的國會同時改選，會降低後者的競爭政黨數（Shugart and Carey, 1992: 206-207）。

[19] Shugart 與 Carey（1992: 220）的資料清楚地驗證了這些假設：採用相對多數決制的國家，有效國會政黨數高於採取比例代表制或多輪投票制的國家，而同時選舉則可減低國會的有效政黨數。

[20] 關於選舉時程的劃分模式，請閱 Shugart 與 Carey（1992: 206-225）。除了影響政府組成的形態，選舉時程對總統與國會的關係還有另一種影響：如果總統後於國會選舉，即可宣稱其掌握最新民意，增強其主導政府形成的動機。反之，如果國會選舉在總統選舉之後，而多數又和總統不同黨，總統就較難主導政府形成。

多享有一定的蜜月期，隨著政府施政的開展，某些選民會發現成效不如預期，因此降低對政府施政的滿意度。當然，為了防止此種情況的發生，行政部門常會在選前一段時間推出刺激景氣的政策，形成所謂的「政治經濟週期」（political business cycles）。某些尋求連任的行政首長還可運用現任優勢，提升其競爭優勢。但若這些手段不能彌補民意的喪失，執政黨很可能會在首長選舉之後的國會選舉中失去國會多數，導致分立政府。美國的期中選舉（midterm election）就常常有這種效果。第二種解釋更直接：民意的變動具有時間性，所以間隔兩場選舉的時間差越長，越可能出現非共時性，進而導致分立政府。

　　一個有趣的問題是，如果在國會議員選舉之後不久進行總統選舉，對於府會的政黨分布會有什麼影響？這個情形不會出現在美國，因為非同時選舉和同時選舉的輪替時間是固定的，都是兩年，而這正是兩種選舉最大的時間差距。但如果某國行政、立法改選時程不一致，甚或任期不一，就可能出現國會改選完不久後改選總統的情況。為了便於分析，我們假定主要的選舉競爭者只有兩個政黨，而其實力接近。此時的關鍵因素是總統選舉對國會選舉的「磁吸效應」，間隔兩場選舉的時間越長，兩場選舉的磁吸效應越弱、選民的投票抉擇差異越大，國會選舉就越具有「期中選舉導致分立政府」的可能。反之，在總統選舉之後不久舉行國會選舉，非常可能產生所謂的「衣尾效應」（coattail effect）：新任總統多享有一段蜜月期，且尚無施政表現可供評價，選民在選擇國會議員時的依據和總統選舉不會差太多。有人將此種情況稱為「蜜月選舉」（honeymoon election）（Shugart and Carey, 1992: 263-264）。同理，如果國會選舉先於總統選舉，但兩者時間差距很短，總統候選人已進入短兵相接的階段，國會選舉即可能成為總統選舉的前哨戰，甚至可視為總統選舉的一部分，其效果也會近似同時選舉。[21]

　　必須說明的是，上述論點隱含了幾個假設：第一，國會議員選舉制度的比例性低。如果國會議員選舉制度比例性高，使國會多數非為單一政黨所能掌控，則無所謂分立政府存在；第二，選民在同時選出總統和國會議員時，投票行為基本上是一致的；[22]第三，競爭者實力接近。如果競爭者實力有相當差距，非同時選舉不見得會導致分立政

---

[21] 如果選民已經知道國會議員選舉的結果，是否會影響其在總統選舉的投票行為？這要看兩種選民的比例：制衡論者與效率論者。前者會希望選出不同黨的總統來約束國會，後者希望透過一致政府來提升效能。這兩類選民的比例，相當程度取決於政黨對立的程度，政黨對立越嚴重，制衡論者就越少。

[22] 同時選舉比較能產生一致政府的另一原因，在於總統選票和國會議員選票由同一批動員者所聚集，而總統選舉的議題更會主導國會選舉（Samuels, 2004）。對參選國會選舉的候選人而言，與同黨的總統候選人一起競選乃勢所必然。同理，首長選舉和國會選舉若採取不一樣的制度，就會對動員方式與投票行為產生不同的影響，進而減低一致政府出現的機率。

府。試想，倘若總統支持度低到已經沒有連任的希望，而選民在之前的國會選舉已經懲罰過執政黨，則下一回的總統選舉可能導致另一政黨主政下的一致政府。反之，如果執政黨的支持度很高，則即使隨著時間的演變而喪失某些支持，仍可維持一致政府的態勢。

肆、有關憲政配套的五個命題

　　前述假定大致根據既有研究總結而成，雖未直接回答本文所關注的問題，但已提供足夠的線索。本節探討這些假定之間的邏輯關連，推演有關中央政府體制和選舉制度配套的五個命題。其中命題一、二說明國家元首產生方式和選舉制度配套之後果，命題三、四、五則以特定的政黨體系和社會分歧為前提，探討元首產生方式與政治穩定的關係。

命題一：直選元首若具有實權，且國會議員選舉制度的比例性低，則政府改變現狀的能力為最高或最低，同時選舉則可提升此一能力。

　　根據假定四，民主國家的元首若要擁有實權，必須透過直接民選產生。但是，國家元首具有實權，並不保證可以遂行其政策，關鍵在於國家元首是否受到國會的支持。他可透過不同的方法來爭取國會支持，例如直接訴諸人民或利用國際壓力等，但主要的工具仍在政黨。政黨除了甄拔人才、形成政策，更是選舉和國會中的主角，在選舉時，很少有選民能清楚認識候選人的背景或政策主張，更何況其政見，所以，候選人所屬政黨的形象和基本立場，就成為吸引選民的主要因素。在國會中，如果沒有政黨，數百位議員難以議事或協商，所以，政黨可說是協助國會議員集體行動不可或缺的組織。在一定的憲政制度下，單一選區制比複數選區制更能增強政黨黨紀，因為政黨必須傾全力支持一位候選人方能勝選。[23] 此外，單一選區制也更容易使單一政黨控制國會多數。如前節（圖 9.1）所述，總統所屬政黨如果是國會多數黨，行政立法受到同一政黨所控制，將有很強的現狀改變力。[24] 反之，如果國會是由反對黨掌握多數，直選總統和國會將處於

---

[23] 同樣實施單一選區制，內閣制的黨紀可能比總統制更強。原因在於內閣制若不能維持黨紀，行政部門很可能會失去政權，而總統制則無此問題。總統即使不能得到同黨議員支持，也不至於喪失權力。美國政黨的黨紀不如英國強，主要是採行總統制和聯邦制的緣故。

[24] Jones（1995: 161）即主張，如果要提升總統制國家的穩定度和效能，應該讓總統選舉採取相對多數決，且讓總統和國會選舉同時舉行，但國會選舉應採比例代表制。最後一點的理由，或許

分立狀態，兩者政策理念不同，又是總統選舉的主要競爭者，妥協的空間不大，非常容易發生僵局。

在主要的民主國家中，美國是驗證這個命題的最佳案例。雖然許多研究都指出，美國的施政表現並不因一致政府或分立政府而有明顯的差異（Mayhew, 1991; Brady and Volden, 1998; Fiorina, 1996b; Krehbiel, 1998），但這可能是模型設定或是變數測量的問題。[25] 例如，如果我們以法案通過率或預算赤字為依變項，就無法辨認當中所發生的府會對抗。如果我們把行政部門當作否決者，所謂的法案或預算案應和該部門的重大政策有關，或至少由該黨議員所提案，否則，反對黨只要掌握國會多數，自然可以通過執政黨所不樂見的法案，即便行政部門可以抵制此類法案的執行。[26] 所謂的僵局，應該是指行政立法兩權在重大法案上的爭議，以美國的憲政環境而言，此種爭議應可從總統是否動用否決權看出。有許多研究顯示，處於分立政府的美國總統運用否決權的機率高於一致政府時（Carter and Schap, 1987; Dearden and Husted, 1990; Shields and Huang, 1995）。以否決權作為標準，當然也涉及變項選擇的問題，不過，否決權的運用預設行政權和立法權意見的差異，和其他以法案審查為對象的研究仍有不同。在半總統制下，總統不見得有否決權，但是我們仍可用同樣的邏輯找尋分立政府之下兩權相抗的證據（例如內閣的存續時間，見命題五）。同時選舉既然可以降低分立政府出現的機率，也就能夠減緩分立政府所造成的僵局。

命題二：在一定的社會分歧下，若國家元首非由直選產生，政府的現狀改變力與國會政黨的分化程度成反比。

根據假定四，民主國家之元首如果非由直接民選產生，幾乎都是虛位元首，所以會以內閣制的方式運作，如果政府無法改變現狀，就會因為不能實現其競選承諾而喪失國會的支持，進而減損其壽命。如果國會存有穩定的多數，政府必須得此多數支持才能存活；反之，國會若無穩定多數，政府的存續可能因多數聯盟的更替而受影響。根據前述分析（圖 9.1），在內閣制之下，國會政黨分歧度越高，現狀改變力即越弱。以大多數

就是要避免分立政府所形成的僵局。Jones 也認為，同時進行相對多數決總統選舉和比例代表制國會選舉可以讓總統掌握國會多數。對此論點可能需要謹慎的評估：某些國家的國會政黨乃依循特定的社會分歧而劃分，不見得會被總統選舉帶著跑。若然，國會的多黨化仍不可免。

[25] Cheibub（2002）的研究涵蓋了更多國家，也有類似的發現。然而，這樣的發現仍可能是模型設定的問題。事實上，在跨國比較方面，這些問題更為明顯。前述 Lijphart 對於共識型與多數決型民主體制的跨國比較，也有類似的問題。

[26] 如果這個邏輯成立，我們應可在不同政黨分別掌控參、眾議院多數時，觀察到法案通過率的降低。Rogers（2005）證實了這種假設。

是多黨內閣制的西歐國家而言，一般都認為多黨制是政治不穩定的主要原因，而同質性高的兩黨制，則被認為是有利穩定的政黨體制（Lipset, 1963）。

這是從理論推得的結論。在經驗上，要瞭解政黨體系究竟如何影響施政能力，必須進行跨國比較（可參考 Lijphart, 1999a; Lane and Ersson, 1999; Muller and Strom, 2000），而這是一項艱鉅的工作，變數的選擇和測量都會影響檢測，而跨國比較更須考慮社會、經濟、文化與民主程度的差異。另一個難題，是個案的數目通常太少，但是需要控制的變數卻很多，為了避免誤導，必須慎選自變項，排除測量上有爭議或實質上無關的因素。比較簡單的做法，是挑選社會經濟發展程度相近，但政治制度不同的國家進行比較。以命題二而言，西歐應該是最能符合各種要件的地區之一：這些國家大多都是老牌的民主國家，社會經濟發展程度相當，但政治體制則有差異，有兩黨／多黨與內閣制／半總統制的差別。

表 9.2 是針對 16 個西歐的經濟合作發展組織（Organization for Economic Cooperation and Development, OECD）國家所進行的線性迴歸分析。依變項乃借用 Lane 與 Ersson（1999: 303）的政府存續力（government durability）來顯示政府受到國會支持的程度，時間為 1946 至 1997 年。這個變數是這樣界定的（Lane and Ersson, 1999: 301-302）：政府存續的定義是內閣領袖和組成政黨都沒有變動，存續力則是政府存續的月份除上政府所能存在的最長月份再乘上 100。例如，如果內閣總理最長只能任職五年，而其實際任期為 48 個月且其間內閣都是由同樣的政黨組成，則其存續力是 80。由於個案數目少，在解釋變項方面限於以下幾項：1. 1970 至 1995 的人均 GDP（Lane and Ersson, 1999: 24）；2. 有效國會政黨數（Lijphart, 1999a: 312）；3. 是否為半總統制國家（1 = 是，0 = 不是）。人均 GDP 顯示的是社會發展程度，有效國會政黨數表達政黨的分化程度，半總統制與否則和是否有直選元首有關。[27] 此一分析並未將社會分歧列為解釋變項，是因為本文關切的是社會分歧的向度（dimensionality），但既有研究無法顯示此一變數。[28] 如果命題二成立，應該可以看到有效政黨數和政府存續力的負相關。從表 9.2 的確可以看出，每增加一個有效國會政黨單位，政府存續力就縮短 11.69，而這個相關是顯著的；換言之，三黨制的政府存續力比兩黨制低超過 10%。

---

[27] 人均 GDP 乃為 1970、1990 與 1995 三年的 Purchasing Power Parities（PPP）平均值，半總統制與否則以是否有直選總統為標準。

[28] Lijphart（1999a: 80-81）條列了 36 個國家在各分歧上的強度，並以其總和為向度。Lane 與 Ersson 則計算了這些國家在宗教、族群與階級上的分歧度。這兩項指標都無法顯示不同分歧之間的相關性，例如，假設某個國家有明顯的階級和族群衝突，則其分歧面向可能因為兩者無關而為 2，也可能因為兩者高度相關而接近 1。

表 9.2　對 16 個西歐國家政府存續力的解釋

自變項	迴歸係數	標準差	t	p
常數	74.722	23.636	3.161	0.008
人均 GDP	0.002	0.001	1.046	0.316
有效國會政黨數	-11.693	4.038	-2.896	0.013
是否為半總統制	-9.307	7.429	-1.253	0.234
Adjusted R^2 = 0.340，N = 16，p is two-tailed.				

資料來源：筆者自行整理。

命題三：單一政黨取得國會多數的機率越高，實權總統越不能增進政府的現狀改變力。

　　這個命題為第一、二項命題的邏輯延伸。根據命題一，一國若有民選的實權元首，有可能因為和國會多數不同黨而形成分立政府；命題二則認為，如果一國沒有民選的實權元首，現狀改變力將和政黨體系的分化程度成反比。依此道理，如果國家元首只有象徵性的地位，兩黨內閣制的現狀改變力最強。如果直選元首具有相當實權且掌握國會，其現狀改變力和兩黨內閣制差不多；如果屬於分立政府，就比兩黨內閣制低很多。所以，當國會多數由一黨掌握，現狀改變力不會因為實權元首而增加，反而可能因為分立政府而降低。

　　要檢證這個命題，必須要解決兩個問題。首先，比較對象的國家元首權力要有差距，但須處於類似的社會經濟條件，否則影響政府效能的可能不是政治制度，而是社會條件；其次，必須找到指標來描述「單一政黨過半的機率」。關於前者，可以用經濟條件（如 GDP）來當作控制變數；後者，則可以用「有效國會政黨數」來測度單一政黨過半的機率。這兩個變數存在某種數學關係：假設國會有 N 個政黨，因為有效政黨數是 $P = 1/\Sigma S_i^2$，所以 P 的極大值發生在 N 個政黨席次完全相等時。如果其中某個政黨的席次率 $S_1 \geq 0.5$，則 P 在其餘政黨席次均等時極大化，而此時 $P = 1/[S_1^2 + (1 - S_1)^2/(N - 1)] = (N - 1)/(NS_1^2 - 2S_1 + 1)$。我們可以用這個公式來描述 S_1 和 N 對 P 的影響：當 $S_1 \geq 0.5$ 時，P 的極大值會隨著 N 的增加而增加，隨著 S_1 的增加而減少。一般而言，N 很少超過 6，S_1 也不容易高過 0.6。如果 N 以 5 計，則 P 的極大值在 $S_1 = 0.5$ 時為 3.2，在 $S_1 = 0.6$ 時為 2.5。至於 P 的最低值，必然是在 N = 2 時產生，所以 $S_1 = 0.5$ 時 P 的極小值為 2，$S_1 = 0.6$ 時 P 的極小值為 1.92。總結來說，若 N = 5 且 $S_1 = 0.5$，P 介於 2 和 3.2 間，平均為 2.6；當 S_1 為 0.6 時，P 介於 1.92 和 2.5 間，平均為 2.21。所以，除非政黨數目

極少，P 應該介於 2 到 2.6 之間。一黨過半當然也可能和更高的 P 並存，不過此時 N 要很大，一大多小，在民主國家並不常見。

　　依照命題三，屬於兩黨制的國家，會因國家元首是否擁有實權而有不同的現狀改變力。如果考慮到制度的差異性和社會經濟發展的類似性，OECD 國家應該還是最佳的案例，這些國家的元首權力大小不同，但行政首長都要獲得國會信任方能存活，所以可以從政府存續力探知其施政效能。[29] 表 9.3 條列了 16 個 OECD 國家的政黨體系和政府的存續力。嚴格說來，這些國家只有英國和奧地利屬於兩黨制（P 小於 2.5）。兩黨制的國家，無黨過半的機率非常低，其餘國家單一政黨過半的機率則隨著有效政黨數的增加而下滑。表 9.3 的資料，呈現出兩項有意義的訊息。第一，英國和奧地利的政府存續力都高於平均值甚多，奧地利雖有直選總統，但其地位是象徵性的。第二，所有擁有實權半總統制的國家，如葡萄牙、法國、芬蘭，其政府存續力都遠低於總體平均，雖然某些內閣制的國家政府壽命也不長，但原因可能在於政黨體系的分化（見命題二）。這樣的結果，算是部分印證了命題三。要更完整地檢測此一命題，需能找到兩黨制和半總統制搭配，但政府存續力很短的國家。一個有趣的問題是，為什麼西歐難以找到這種民主政體？原因之一，或許正是要避免此種配套可能引發的憲政衝突。

命題四：當社會分歧趨向單面化時，直選的實權元首不會增加現狀改變力。

　　根據假定三，如果國會黨派反映社會的單面向分歧，則此分歧的中位選項（median position）是唯一能以多數決達成的結果，不論選舉制度和政黨體系為何，也不論主張此一方案的黨派是否控制國會多數。如果一國採取內閣制，政府必須接受此一結果方能存活。但直選的實權元首不見得支持此一方案，而將增加府會發生衝突的機率。要檢證這個命題，需要尋找同樣處於單面向分歧，但憲政體制不同的國家進行比較。在以上 16 個西歐國家中，分歧面向少於 2 的有英國、奧地利與愛爾蘭三國（Lijphart, 1999a: 80-81）。[30] 這三國有幾個共同的特色：中央政府體制都為內閣或趨近內閣制的半總統制；三者的政府存續力都相當長；三國的有效政黨數都小於 3。這驗證了命題四的一部分預期：如果國家沒有直選的實權元首，則政府的存續力取決於內閣是否能支持主要社會分歧的中位選項。因為主要行政權掌握在行政首長（總理或首相）手裡，所以內閣必須支持此一選項才可能得到國會的信任。事實上，當有效政黨數少時，執政黨非常有可能已經包含了支持中位選項的議員。

---

[29] 因此，我們無法用同樣的標準比較同樣是兩黨制的美國和英國。

[30] 如前所述，如果分歧議題的數目超過 2，則實際向度可能因不同分歧的相關性而更低。但如果分歧議題的數目小於 2 甚至等於 1，則無所謂相關性的問題，向度應即為分歧議題數。

表 9.3　政黨體系與西歐國家政府的存續力

國家	政府平均存續力 （1946-1997）	有效國會政黨數 （1945-1996）	是否爲半總統制[*]
英國	53.6	2.1	否
奧地利	63.9	2.5	是
西班牙	67.0	2.8	否
愛爾蘭	58.0	2.8	是
德國	66.2	2.9	否
瑞典	63.2	3.3	否
葡萄牙	33.9	3.3	是[*]
盧森堡	70.9	3.4	否
挪威	53.2	3.4	否
法國	21.2	3.4	是[*]
冰島	55.4	3.7	是
比利時	37.9	4.3	否
丹麥	42.2	4.5	否
荷蘭	60.3	4.7	否
義大利	19.8	4.9	否
芬蘭	29.7	5.0	是[*]
總平均	49.8	3.6	

資料來源：筆者自行整理。
說明：＊表示總統有實權（Duverger, 1980）。

　　但是，這三個國家在中央政府體制上的差異不大。在其他的西歐國家中，有直選實權總統的法國和芬蘭，但其社會分歧向度皆大於 2，不適合驗證此一命題。其他區域或有單向分歧的社會（如加拿大、澳洲、紐西蘭等），但因多採內閣制而不適合比較；其餘採總統制或半總統制的單向分歧社會，則多因社會經濟發展程度和西歐有所差距，而難以相提並論。既要滿足憲政體制的差異，又要有相應的社會經濟發展程度，大概只有美國可堪比較了。根據 Lijphart（1999a: 81）的觀察，美國的社會分歧是單面向的，因

爲美國實行總統制，行政首長任期固定，無法由政府存續力來觀測政治穩定。不過，從美國總統運用否決權的時機看來（見關於命題一的討論），可以清楚得知分立政府對美國憲政運作的衝擊。相較之下，英國的兩黨內閣制幾乎沒有遭逢因倒閣而提早解散的危機。所以，同樣是兩大黨制的單向分歧社會，社會經濟發展程度又很類似，英美的差異應該和憲政體制有密切的關係。在單向分歧的社會，如果要維持政治穩定，只能採用議會內閣制，或是讓直選元首只扮演象徵性的角色。後者，在許多新興民主國家是難以達成的。

命題五：在多黨制半總統制下，國家元首越能主導政府組成，少數政府出現的機率就越高。

　　一個國家可能因爲高比例性的選舉制度、地域分歧或多面向分歧而產生多黨制，使國會難由一黨取得多數（假定一、二、三）。此時如果是內閣制，政府組成的問題比較單純：如果社會分歧是單向的，執政黨不論是否掌握多數，都必須支持中位選項方能存活，否則隨時可能被倒閣；如果分歧是多面向的，則執政黨必須建構多數聯盟方能得到國會信任，但此聯盟並不穩定。若爲總統制，總統固需國會多數的支持才能遂行其政策，但政府組成的權力屬於總統，國會難以干涉閣員的任命；如果是半總統制，總統會根據制度的差異而有不同的策略選擇。第一，如果總統對行政首長的提名受制於國會，而國會對於發動不信任投票又沒有太大的顧忌，其效應就會類似內閣制。第二，如果總統對行政首長的任命有自主權，而國會又憚於倒閣，則總統會考量其本身的選民壓力與國會生態而做出權衡。總統的理念距離中位選項越遠、國會的黨派越分歧，總統越有可能任命少數總理，如果此時的社會分歧是多面向的，政府改變現狀的能力會介於兩黨內閣制和分立政府之間（見圖 9.1）。

　　我們可以回到西歐 16 國的經驗來檢視此一命題。表 9.4 採取和表 9.2 同樣的個案，依變數和自變數也大致相同，但將「是否爲半總統制」改換爲「元首權力」。此一變數的登錄方式爲：凡是沒有直選元首的國家爲 0，虛位半總統制者爲 0.5（包括奧地利、愛爾蘭與冰島），其餘則爲 1。[31] 將表 9.2 與表 9.4 相比，可以發現兩項值得注意的結果。

---

[31] 其中需要說明的個案有芬蘭和葡萄牙。芬蘭的憲政體制歷經多次變遷。在歷史上，芬蘭總統曾享有很大的權力：總統可主持國務委員會（Valtioneuvesto）、任命內閣閣員、不受限制地解散國會（Eduskunta），向議會提出法案，行使否決權（但國會可覆議），並擁有統帥權及外交事務主導權。1991 年修憲後，規定總統須得總理同意方得解散國會，約束了總統權力；2000 年的新憲更確立總統的象徵地位。因爲芬蘭憲政的內閣制化是近十多年的事，表 9.4 仍將芬蘭總統權力登錄爲 1。葡萄牙曾爲威權統治的國家，但在 1982 年修憲，廢除革命委員會，總統不能再自由任免閣員；總統雖可否決法案，但國會可以覆議。雖然如此，有鑑於葡萄牙長期的威權

其一，「有效國會政黨數」的解釋力幾乎未變，而且仍是最顯著的；其次，我們可以從顯著下降的 p 值看出，「元首權力」比「是否為半總統制」更有解釋力。雖然模型解釋的是政府的存續力而非組成方式，但少數政府的壽命比多數政府的壽命更短，應是合理的推斷。

表 9.4　憲政體制與政府存續力：西歐 16 國

自變項	迴歸係數	標準差	t	p
常數	78.532	21.390	3.671	0.003
人均 GDP	0.001	0.001	0.777	0.452
有效國會政黨數	-10.686	3.730	-2.865	0.014
元首權力	-17.166	8.560	-2.006	0.068
Adjusted R^2 = 0.441，N = 16，p is two-tailed.				

資料來源：筆者自行整理。

伍、國會改革與台灣的憲政發展

如果前述命題可以成立，我們即可根據一個國家的中央政府體制、選舉制度、選舉時程以及社會分歧，判斷其憲政運作的情形。前節藉由美國與 16 個西歐國家的案例驗證相關命題，發現有效政黨數和國家元首權力在統計上和政府存續力相關，本節藉由對台灣個案的研究，更進一步地描繪這些因素如何影響憲政運作，以呈現統計相關背後的因果機制。首先，我們需對台灣的憲政體制和選舉制度進行說明。

台灣自 1980 年代末期進入選舉民主（electoral democracy）的年代，迄今已經歷了七次憲法修改和三次總統直選。1997 年的修憲引入立法院對行政院長的信任投票機制，並取消立法院對行政院長任命案的同意權，再加上已經存在的總統直選，台灣進入半總統制的時代。在國會（立法院）議員的選舉制度方面，長期採取獨特的「複數選區單記非讓渡投票制」（single nontransferable voting under multi-member district,

---

統治，仍將其總統權力登錄為 1。若將葡萄牙登錄為 0.5，對統計的結果也沒有太大的影響。

SNTV-MMD）。[32] 因為此一制度的當選門檻低，有學者將其視為「半比例代表制」（semiproportional system）（Lijphart, Pintor, and Sone, 1986）。儘管如此，SNTV-MMD 不一定導致多黨體系。就長期採用此制的台灣和日本而言，反而是以一黨獨大為主。根據台灣的中央政府體制和政黨體系，我們可以區分出幾個不同的憲政配套階段：1. 自 1997 年至 2000 年 5 月，為國民黨同時掌握行政權和立法權的一致政府時期；2. 從 2000 年 5 月到 2002 年 1 月，民進黨取得總統職位，但國民黨仍為立法院多數，屬於分立政府時期；3. 從 2002 年 1 月迄今，總統仍為民進黨掌握，但立法院沒有單一政黨過半，是為少數政府時期。這三個階段，剛好符合本文所陳述的三種政府組成形態。根據前述理論，我們可以比較台灣在這些階段的差異，並展望國會議員選舉制度改變後的發展趨勢。[33]

綜合前述命題，這三個階段政府的現狀改變力應該是一般政府 > 少數政府 > 分立政府。[34] 我們可以從內閣存續時間和立法結果來印證這個猜測。表 9.5 條列了台灣行政院長的任期天數，並註明其就任時的政府形態。必須先說明的是，以台灣的情形而言，國會從來沒有成功倒閣過，而一些重大的政治變動反而會帶動內閣改組，例如新總統就職或新國會開議。即使考慮這些因素，表 9.5 的數字還是可以佐證我們的假設。如果我們將過去 13 年六位行政院長的任期做比較，並依據政府是否分立，以及國會是否有單一政黨掌握半數以上席次做為分類標準，可以歸納出三個類別。[35] 院長平均任期天數，果然如同之前的預測，一致政府最高，少數政府次之，分立政府最低，而其差距非常顯

---

[32] 在此選制下，每位選民投一票給特定候選人，候選人得票不能轉移，在選區應選名額為 M 的選區，得票最高的前 M 名候選人當選。除了台灣以外，長期運用 SNTV-MMD 選舉國會議員的國家，只有日本和南韓，但這兩個國家已經改變此一制度。

[33] 從民進黨開始取得縣市執政權後，台灣縣市常有民進黨員擔任縣市長，議會則由國民黨掌握多數的情況。對此現象，國內有某些研究者採用「分立政府」的概念來探討各種相關問題，諸如概念的適用性（吳重禮，2000、2001）、其投票之成因（吳重禮、王宏忠，2003；吳重禮、徐英豪、李世宏，2004）、對府會運作的影響（黃紀、吳重禮，2000；吳重禮、黃紀、張壹智，2003；吳重禮、楊樹源，2001；廖達琪、洪澄琳，2004）等。對於第七次修憲後的台灣，我們可以對分立政府的概念作更細緻的定義。台灣地方議會選舉採用的是複數選區單記非讓渡投票，選民的投票行為和地方首長選舉不見得一致。再者，中央政府屬於半總統制，而縣市長則類似總統制下的總統。我們要回答的問題是，在中央出現的分立政府，和地方性的分立政府有何異同？國會（議會）是否由單一政黨掌握多數，對府會關係有何不同的影響？地方議會的黨紀比較弱，而修憲後中央層級的黨紀應會很強，這兩者有何不同的影響？

[34] 嚴格地說，台灣至目前為止尚未採取偏向單一選區制的立委選制，所以分立政府與少數政府的差別應該不大。不過，國民黨在 2001 年立委選舉之前仍掌有國會多數，和之後無黨過半的情況仍有所不同。

[35] 本文寫作期間蘇貞昌院長仍在任內，故不列入計算。

表 9.5　台灣行政院長的任期天數與政府形態

形態	行政院長	任期	天數	平均
一致政府	連戰	1993 年 2 月 27 日至 1997 年 1 月 9 日	2,636	1,814
	蕭萬長	1997 年 1 月 9 日至 2000 年 5 月 20 日	992	
分立政府	唐飛	2000 年 5 日 20 日至 2000 年 6 月 10 日	139	311
	張俊雄	2000 年 6 月 10 日至 2002 年 1 月 2 日	482	
少數政府	游錫堃	2002 年 1 日 2 日至 2005 年 1 月 20 日	1,095	733
	謝長廷	2005 年 1 月 20 日至 2006 年 1 月 25 日	370	

資料來源：筆者自行整理。

著。[36] 我們發現，立法院改選後的新會期或是新總統上任時都會改組行政院，但這並非改組的必要條件。通常，總統會依據內閣的施政表現決定是否留任院長，除非總統換人。施政表現相當程度受到府會關係的影響。[37] 所以，表 9.5 的確反映國會對內閣的支持程度。

　　再就法案審查的過程來看，已有學者指出不同立法院屆期之間的差別。盛杏湲（2003）發現，行政院在一致政府時期（1999 年 2 月至 2000 年 5 月）提案通過的平均天數少於執政黨（國民黨）提案所通過的天數，而在分立（含少數）政府時期（2000年 5 月至 2002 年 12 月），行政院提案的通過天數高於國民黨提案的天數。在一致政府時期，行政院提案的通過率是 72.7%，到了分立政府時期，比例驟降至 38.5%。整體而言，一致政府時期的法案通過率是 67.7%，分立政府時期卻只有 47.5%。黃秀端（2003）採用同樣的時期劃分，發現在一致政府時期，執政黨（國民黨）在立法院所有的記名表決中，共有 98.99% 的獲勝率，而民進黨執政後，獲勝率跌至 34.38%（第四屆）及33.70%（第五屆）。這些數據清楚顯示，行政和立法兩權的一致或分立，對於立法過程有重大影響，不管從內閣存續力或立法效能來看，分立政府時期的政治穩定都是低於一致政府時期的。

---

[36] 表 9.5 和預期相符，但尚未能呈現完整的資料。台灣仍未出現國民黨執政的分立（少數）政府，或民進黨執政的一致政府。

[37] 唐飛就是最明顯的例子。陳水扁總統任命國民黨籍的唐飛擔任行政院長，原本就是考慮到國民黨在國會的多數席次，但這仍無法避免行政院和立法院在重大法案上的爭議。唐飛的辭職，就是因為陳水扁總統在停建第四核能廠的事件上，和國民黨主張續建的立場不能相容。

　　這種困境，是否可以透過制度變革來改善？從 1991 年開始的七次憲政改革，主軸大致為中央政府體制的調整和國會制度的改革。國會改革包括立委席次的變動和選舉制度的改革，因為事涉立法委員的利害，一直拖到 2005 年才有成果。2005 年 6 月 7 日，任務型國民大會以 249 票贊成、48 票反對的票數，複決通過了立法院在 2004 年 8 月 23 日所通過的憲法修正提案。其要項為：1. 由人民複決立法院所提出之修憲案或領土變更案（第一條）；2. 複決立法院修憲提案的通過門檻為總選舉人半數以上同意（第十二條）；3. 立法院提出之正副總統彈劾案，由憲法法庭審理；4. 自第七屆起，立法委員席次減半為 113 席，任期四年，保障婦女名額占不分區至少一半，區域立委 73 人，每縣市至少一人，全國不分區及僑居國外國民依政黨名單投票選舉（第四條）。其中至關緊要的是第四條：2007 年年底的立委選舉，台灣將以所謂的「並立式單一選區兩票制」，以單一選區制選出 73 名區域代表，並以全國為選區的封閉式名單比例代表制選出 34 名代表，再加上六席原住民代表，共計 113 席。[38]

　　由於修憲條文規定廢除國民大會，將來修憲要透過人民複決，而其通過門檻為總選舉人半數以上同意，所以在可見的未來，憲法的修改將比第七次修憲更困難。我們甚至可以假設，單一選區兩票制和半總統制就是未來台灣憲政架構的兩大主軸，分別規範國會議員的產生以及行政部門的權責。根據假定一，選舉制度比例性越高，政黨數目就越多，也越不容易由單一政黨形成穩定多數。反之，如果要形成兩大黨制，傾向單一選區制的選舉制度是重要條件。台灣的新選舉制度給予相對多數決單一選區制很高的比重，社會分歧則以國家認同為主導，泛綠、泛藍的票基雖有南北差異，但並未形成區域政黨，所以我們有理由相信將來會趨向兩大黨制。[39] 問題是，這對將來的憲政運作會產生什麼影響？

　　根據命題一，若直選元首具有實權，則行政和立法兩權同時透過單一選區制改組，

---

[38] 許多人以「日本式」單一選區兩票制稱呼台灣的新國會議員選舉制度。事實上，在實施並立式單一選區兩票制的國家中，日本是極少數採取高比例單一選區席次的國家。1994 年日本修正其選舉制度時，單一選區定為 300 席，占總席次 500 席的三分之二；後來總席次減為 480 席，比例略增為 62.5%。以台灣而言，73 名單一選區席次共占總數 113 席的 64.6%，比重比日本更高。再加上立法院委員總數的減半，論者大多以為新制不利小黨。關於各種不同的單一選區兩票制及其運作後果，請參閱 Shugart 與 Wattenberg（2001）。

[39] 以日本而言，2005 年 9 月眾議院大選後，自民黨以區域 48% 以及比例 38.2% 的得票率共獲 296 席，占眾議院 480 席的 61.7%。這種情形，非常可能在台灣發生。第一，台灣單一選區制的比例比日本更高；第二，台灣和日本一樣，都沒有明顯的地域主義，所以符合假定二；第三，日本欠缺明顯的對立主軸，競選者的選舉訴求共同性很高，而台灣因為國家認同的分歧，候選人有明顯區隔（詳見假定三），選民有很強的政黨認同投票動機。所以，台灣走向兩大黨制的可能性應該比日本更強。

可使現狀改變力變得很低或很高，同時選舉則可提升此能力。依據憲法，中華民國總統的行政權相當有限，例如：必須經由行政院長提名才能任命行政院部會首長、不能出席行政院院會、不能主動解散國會、只有在特殊狀況下才能發動防禦性公民投票等。總統雖然掌有國家安全大政方針的制定權，但國家安全會議的編制極小，必須依賴行政院相關部會的配合才能施行政策。[40] 然而，大多數的台灣人民，不管其政黨傾向為何，多認為中華民國總統是實質的最高行政首長，儘管依憲法最高行政機關是行政院。台灣自1996年迄今，已進行三次總統直接選舉，每次都將台灣民主政治的發展帶入新階段，大多數的政黨也都將競逐總統大位看成攸關政黨生存的關鍵，再加上台灣民主政治強烈受到兩岸關係的影響，在可見的未來總統都不太可能虛位化。

總統當然是透過單一選區制選出的，而台灣所用的相對多數決制，更會讓競爭趨向兩大黨化，所以，影響未來憲政發展的關鍵因素就是國會多數和總統是否屬於同一政黨。依據假設五，行政和立法兩權同時透過單一選區制改組，產生一致政府的機率比非同時選舉高。那麼，台灣未來的選舉究竟比較接近同時選舉，還是類似期中選舉？根據第七次修憲的結果，台灣未來將出現一種「先國會後總統」的選舉時程。修改後的憲法第四條規定，立法委員自第七屆起任期四年，為符合憲法規定「立法院會期，每年兩次，自行集會，第一次自二月至五月底，第二次自九月至十二月底」的規定，立委改選時間必須在就任前的前一年年底，或最晚不能超過次年年初。再以總統來看，任期四年，就職日為5月20日，所以選舉日期為就任年之3月。[41] 依此時程，除非立法院尚未屆滿任期就被解散，或是有另一次修憲改變總統或立委任期，從下屆立委改選開始，立委選舉都是在總統選舉的前三個月舉行，而且此一模式會持續下去。

假定五對於同時選舉的效應已經有詳細的說明。非同時選舉若要導致分立政府，需

---

[40] 以法國為例，其總統可以主動解散國會、發動公民投票、主持國務會議，甚至可以拖延法案的簽署。

[41] 根據1997年通過的憲法增修條文第二條，總統任期四年。因為之前的總統都是在5月20日就職，所以之後的總統也需在同日就職方能符合憲法規定。換言之，除非修憲，總統就職日是不能變動的。即使能夠調整選舉時程，還有其他的問題要克服。依照慣例，內閣都會在總統改選和國會改選後總辭。假設同時選舉一併更換了行政和立法部門的執政黨，理論上，行政院必須在國會產生新的多數黨後辭職，但是新總統就職後卻還得辭一次。比較可行的做法，應是由新多數黨組閣，新總統就任後仍留任同一行政院長，但是否需經辭職的動作，卻仍有爭議。如果同時選舉仍導致分立政府，問題會更複雜：第一，假設國會多數黨改變，總統仍為同黨所勝。理論上，行政院長必須總辭，以彰顯國會黨派結構的改變，但是他卻可能和新當選的總統屬於同一政黨，呈現另一種正當性的基礎。第二，假設國會多數黨未變，總統卻由另一黨勝選。此時如果行政院長留任至新總統就職，就會形成長達四個月的看守內閣，此時舊有的內閣和國會能否通過重大的法案或預算？法理上是可以的，但是正當性卻會有問題。

要幾個條件的配合，例如主要競爭者實力的接近、國會選舉距離總統選舉有一定時間距離等。第一個條件尚難預料，但第二個條件則可由選舉時程得知。以台灣而言，國會選舉和總統選舉只隔三個月，非常可能成為總統選舉的前哨戰，此時總統選舉的候選人早已確定，且已進入議程設定的競逐戰。假設主要競爭者的實力接近，我們可以從兩方面來評估總統選舉對立委選舉的磁吸效應。首先，區域部分的立委採取單一選區制，同黨不可能提名一人以上，再加上總統候選人此時已進入短兵相接的階段，大多數政黨提名的立委候選人都必須和該黨總統候選人並肩作戰。一方面，總統候選人的知名度高於立委候選人，所以後者很可能要搭前者的便車；另一方面，各黨也多會提名具有地方實力的立委候選人，所以總統候選人會以其知名度和擁有地方實力的立委候選人互相拉抬。在此情勢下，總統選舉的議題應會帶引立委選舉，沒有總統候選人站台的立委候選人，勢必難以當選。若然，選民對於總統候選人的評價，應會影響其在立委選舉的投票抉擇。

總統選舉固然會深刻影響立委選舉，但後者的結果會先揭曉。在立委選舉落敗的政黨，有無可能利用這個結果，鼓勵其支持者在總統選舉「翻盤」？如果主要競爭者實力非常接近，這種可能性不是沒有，但是機率並不高。第一，國會選舉的得票率一般而言會比總統選舉低。[42] 立委選舉的敗者，當然希望未投票的選民中有人會在總統選舉時投票給該黨，但是立委選舉的贏家也會對其潛在的支持者發出類似的訴求。立委選舉是在每個選區進行，即使有爭議或弊端，也不容易激勵選民大規模的出來翻盤。所以，投票率的差距不見得對敗者有利。第二，某些選民可能是「制衡者」，不希望看到國會和總統被同一政黨所控制，所以會在總統選舉時改變投票對象。此種策略如果能影響總統選舉結果，除了競爭者實力必須非常接近外，制衡論者的數量也不能太少。以台灣而言，如果將來朝向兩大黨制演進，社會又以國家認同為主要分歧，會有幾項重要的後果：政黨會有一定的理念差距並影響其支持者；[43] 黨紀會增強，連帶強化選民的政黨認同：國會受制於此分歧，阻礙跨黨聯盟的建構。這些因素，都會減低制衡選民的數目。

另一個重要的問題，是小黨在這種選舉時程下的生存策略。如果 Duverger 法則能

---

[42] 以台灣而言，1996、2000 與 2004 年總統選舉的投票率分別為 76.04%、82.69% 及 80.28%，1998、2001 與 2004 年立委選舉的投票率則為 68.09%、66.16% 及 59.16%。詳見中央選舉委員會網站，http://www.cec.gov.tw/。

[43] 根據中位選民定理，如果只有兩個政黨在相對多數決中競爭，兩黨都應趨向中間選民。但這個理論常被經驗否證，原因之一，可能是政黨的得票並非均勻分布在各選區。以台灣而言，歷次選舉已形成「北藍南綠」的態勢，而各選區在國家認同面向上的中位並不一致，所以，藍綠政黨在此議題上的立場也不會相同。

夠成立，以相對多數決進行的總統選舉和區域立委選舉應以兩大黨爲主要競爭者，小黨沒有勝選的機會。但是台灣未來的立委選舉制度並非全然的單一選區制，得票率很低的黨，仍有機會贏得以比例代表方式分配的 34 席全國不分區席次。要取得選民的政黨票，小黨可以採取兩項策略：第一，提醒策略性選民他們的第二票（政黨票），可以作爲他們在區域選舉放棄該黨的補償。第二，小黨甚至也可推出總統候選人，一方面替立委選舉的候選人造勢，另一方面威脅和其立場相近的大黨。當大黨實力相近時，小黨的選票對總統選舉仍可發揮關鍵作用。小黨採取此一策略，可迫使大黨做出某些讓步（如職位分配、政策調整等），也可促使選民將政黨票投給該黨。

即便如此，小黨的席次率仍會比目前滑落許多。一個在全台灣有 10% 實力的小黨，能贏得三到四席的全國不分區席次，就已經相當不錯了，要在單一選區勝選，困難更大。所以，台灣的政黨體系，應該會朝向兩大多小發展，由單一政黨掌握國會多數的機率應該比目前更高。此外，台灣的區域立委選舉改採單一選區制，政黨只能提名一人才能勝選，會促使政黨強化其黨紀，防止黨的分裂。從台灣行政首長（如總統、縣市長）選舉的經驗可以得知，分裂的政黨很少有勝選的機會，因爲當選門檻高，脫黨或跳黨參選者也不像在複數選區制下那麼容易當選。但實質上，政黨有可能在某些地區受制於具有地方實力之人物，形式上黨是團結的，但權力卻可能地方化。此外，全國不分區採用封閉式名單比例代表制，且由人民的政黨票決定當選席次，政黨的影響力勢必比目前更重，黨紀的強化，還可以提升反對黨發動不信任投票的動機，增加制衡行政部門的工具。

在政黨數目減少、黨紀變強的趨勢下，台灣未來的政府效能，相當程度取決於國會多數是否和總統同黨（命題一），如果出現分立政府，效能會比目前更低。根據之前關於選舉時程的分析，出現此種情況的機率並不是很高。由於國會選舉和總統選舉時間非常接近，再加上國會選舉的輸家不容易在總統選舉翻盤，贏得國會選舉多數席次的政黨很可能也是總統選舉的獲勝者。有趣的是，這顯然不是修憲者有意設計的結果。第七次修憲，一方面回應社會壓力而改革立法委員的選舉制度，另一方面將立委任期調整成四年，以求與總統一致。爲了滿足這些需求，必然導致三個月內進行兩次大選的情況。就選舉花費而言，這是浪費的，因爲同時選舉更能形成一致政府，而成本更低。如果這種選舉時程能促成一致政府的形成，只能說是意外的收穫。第七次修憲還爲台灣未來的憲政改革設下了一道很高的公民複決門檻。因爲這個門檻規定在憲法裡，所以要降低這個門檻就得修憲（也就是要達到這個門檻）。在可見的未來，半總統制和單一選區兩票制即將成爲台灣的憲政主軸，而台灣的府會關係也將邁入新的階段。

陸、結論

　　政體變遷（regime transformation）是民主化最重要的步驟，通常也伴隨著憲政體制的調整。憲政選擇是複雜的過程，除了涉及最高統治權的產生方式，還要考慮行政權的劃分、國會的功能、國會議員的選舉、政黨體系的重塑、文官體制的建立、司法體系的屬性、中央與地方關係等許多項目。本文的目的，就是從制度配套的觀點，思索憲政選擇和政黨體系以及選舉制度的關係。對此問題，既有研究大多採取兩種研究策略：第一，以 Arend Lijphaft 爲典型的是「加法」途徑。他用某種共通的指標替個別制度定性，然後將每個制度的特性加總，以判定整個憲政體制的性質。對 Lijphart 而言，這個共通的指標就是個別制度在「共識決 vs. 多數決」上的位置。第二，以 George Tsebelis 爲代表的是「減法」途徑。他從各種制度之下抽釐出更根本的性質，並涵蓋所有的制度。對 Tsebelis 而言，這個性質就是否決者的數目。不管是加法還是減法，目的都是要分析制度配套的後果。但是，加法難以分析配套以後的化學變化，例如，多黨制比兩黨制更接近共識決，但是配到總統制後，反而讓總統更威權。減法可以幫助我們瞭解制度運作的原理，但是卻也掩蓋了制度細節，例如，總統制和半總統制下的分立政府都有兩個否決者，但前者表現在府會僵局，後者卻是以總理爲總統的代理，兩者的性質不見得相同。

　　本文採取的是「乘法減法並用」的策略：把配套所產生的結果當作一個新類型（乘法），並利用否決者理論分析其性質。這樣既可以推得一般命題，又可關照制度細節。根據分析，在行政與立法合一的中央政府體制下，政府效能的確和政黨體系的分化程度成反比，而此一命題也由西歐國家內閣的存續力得到證明。但若由人民直接選出具有實權的國家元首，政黨體系的影響就必須和選舉時程一起考慮。如果總統和國會同時透過比例性低的選舉制度選出，產生一致政府的機率較高；在同樣的制度配套下，國會選舉若和總統選舉有一定的時間差，很可能產生很不穩定的分立政府。這點，從美國經驗可以得到清楚的驗證。修憲後的台灣，也是實權總統搭配比例性低的國會選制，然因國會選舉與總統選舉十分接近，出現一致政府的機率應高於分立政府。若爲半總統制和多黨體系的配套，總統權力越大越容易形成少數政府，但其現狀改變力仍高於分立政府。從這些命題，我們的確發現無法單從政黨體系或總統權力來判定憲政運作的情況，而須將其搭配起來觀察。

　　這樣的分析架構，可以幫助我們重新審視比較制度研究。我們可以約略將世界上的民主政體這樣歸類：美國的兩黨總統制和英國的兩黨內閣制，雖然被很多人當作民主典範，卻是異例。西歐國家大多爲多黨內閣制，拉丁美洲國家則多屬多黨總統制；從理論上來說（命題五），後者沒有前者穩定，從經驗而言，恐怕也是如此。比較值得注意的

是這些區域以外的新興民主國家，在中央政府體制和選舉制度上都有很大的變異性，值得進一步研究。我們發現，具有實權總統而又採行低比例性國會選制的國家，其實並不多，以當前的亞洲國家而言，大概只有南韓和修憲後的台灣可以歸入此類（Hicken and Kasuya, 2003: 133）。[44]

　　南韓的行政領袖是民選總統，任命需要得到國會同意的總理，而其國會選舉則採混合制，以單一選區選出 243 席，以比例代表制選出 56 席，其低比例性和未來的台灣類似。但其總統任期五年，國會任期四年，選舉時程沒有規律性，總統選舉和國會選舉也不見得互相影響。以選舉時程而言，和未來台灣最類似的應是俄羅斯聯邦。俄羅斯也是半總統制的國家，其「國家杜馬」（State Duma，下議院）也是四年一任，選舉時間在總統之前。以最近一次的選舉時程而言，國家杜馬的選舉時間是 2003 年 12 月 7 日，總統選舉則是 2004 年 3 月 14 日。在這次國會選舉中，最大的贏家是「聯合俄羅斯黨」（United Russia），共贏得 119 席比例席次與 102 席單一選區席次，總席次為 221，幾乎為總席次的半數。這個政黨的宗旨，其實就是支持普丁（Vladimir Putin）總統，在 2004 年的總統選舉中，形式上為無黨籍的普丁，以 71.2% 的超高得票率贏得選舉，俄羅斯聯邦因此乃由一致政府所統理，雖然對某些人而言這已接近威權統治。[45] 未來的台灣會不會走向俄羅斯模式，值得關注，而本文提供了某些預測的判準。

---

[44] 1994 年以前，菲律賓的制度和美國非常類似，都以相對多數決單一選區制選出總統和國會議員。菲國自 1995 年以後改採混合制選出國會議員。

[45] 在比較俄羅斯案例時，必須注意到幾個和台灣不同之處。第一，該國的政黨體系較弱，政黨分合變動大，所以有時難以從政黨名稱判斷其與總統候選人之關係。第二，俄羅斯的比例代表席比重比台灣高許多，所以小黨的生存空間也較大，由單一政黨取得過半席次並不容易。第三，該國總統選舉採取兩輪投票制，也和台灣不同。當前俄羅斯的選舉制度是由前總統葉爾欽（Boris Yeltsin）在與國會衝突的 1993 年以行政命令頒布，並於 1995 年完成立法。關於俄羅斯選舉制度的演變，請參考 Moser 與 Thames（2001）。

選舉體制

主題導讀

林繼文與選舉研究

吳親恩

壹、前言

　　林老師的作品在選舉研究這一塊，最大的重心是在於選舉制度的選擇上，即政黨會選擇比例性比較高的選制，例如比例代表制，還是比例性比較低的選制，例如單一選區多數決。這裡選出兩篇代表性的文章來討論。他假定政黨的選擇是建立在理性選擇的基礎上，即執政黨會思考其選舉實力，來選擇對其最有利的選舉體制。且在選舉制度選擇中，林老師將之放在民主發展程度的框架裡面來討論，關切民主轉型與民主發展對選舉制度的影響。另外一篇收錄的文章則是討論一個更根本的問題，即威權政體中選舉制度在什麼情況下會出現，這篇文章除了關切經濟發展與歷史脈絡等因素之外，也關心外在國際環境的影響。除了討論在什麼樣的結構下政黨會偏好哪一種選舉制度之外，林老師也關切政黨在不同選區的參選決定，所以本書包括另一篇文章，討論給定選舉體制是單一選區並立制下，小型政黨的參選行為。以下簡單介紹這幾篇文章的主要研究問題與發現，以及這些發現對於政治學選舉研究領域的意義。

貳、選舉制度變遷

　　關於選舉制度與政黨體系之間的關係，是比較政治學中一個非常重要且持續討論的議題。「選舉制度為何變遷？理論與檢證」這篇文章即討論這個主題（林繼文，2015b）。從杜瓦傑的討論開始，他指出比例代表制有利於多數黨的持續，單一選區多數決制有利於兩黨制。不過後來有許多的研究指出因果關係可能是相反。Colomer（2005）指出選舉制度跟政黨體系之間的因果關係是另一個方向，他指出大黨若能夠有支配國會的實力，會傾向於選擇多數決選制，如果是一個國家存在多黨制的話則傾向於選擇比例代表制。Boix（1999）則是比較動態的觀點，認為兩黨體制中，若新興挑戰者實力堅強，兩大黨會增加選制的比例性，以避免席次大幅喪失，但是若新的挑戰者羽翼

未豐，兩大黨會減少選制的比例性，以能繼續壟斷席次。

　　不過既有關於選舉制度與政黨體系間關係的研究，主要以西方民主國家為主，對於新興民主國家的選舉制度選擇則並未涵蓋，作者在這一篇文章中將新興民主國家的例子也納入，在實證的範圍與理論的視野上都有重要的擴展。也因為研究將新興民主國家納入，國家在政治發展上的歧異度增加，所以本文非常巧妙的利用這個機會，將民主化程度納入分析，觀察這個因素對於選制選擇的影響，而且本文同樣是採取比較動態的觀點，分析不同條件下執政黨的選舉制度選擇。政治學界將選制變遷放在民主化的階段來觀察是非常少有的，選制變遷與民主化兩個議題的研究大部分是各自獨立的，將這兩個議題有機的連結在一起，讓我們可以理解在不同的民主發展中，對於選制選擇的思考邏輯並不完全一樣。

　　作者指出統治者會思考要採行哪一類的選舉制度，若反對黨勢力較小，無法與執政黨抗衡時，則執政者會優先選擇多數決選制，以防止新政黨獲取席次。進一步依照一個國家的民主的進展來討論，在新興民主國家中，如果現狀是多數決選制，執政者會繼續偏好維持多數決選制；但相反的若現狀是比例性比較高的選制，並不會變成多數決選制。而在亞洲國家中，則相對比較有可能從比例性較高的選制轉為多數決選制。另外新興民主國家中因為族群分歧程度較高，所以常常會偏好採行比例代表制，之後往往也就缺乏足夠的誘因要調整為多數決的選制。

　　之後作者綜合討論了兩種選制變遷與政黨體系之間另一個方向的因果關係，他指出在有族群分歧的國家裡面，在新興民主國家中，當選制從多數決選制轉為比例代表制之後，因為這些國家原來就是比較有族群分歧的社會，所以有效政黨數目本來就比較多，因此選擇轉向比例代表制，政黨數目並不會因此而大幅增加。但是另外一方面，當某些外生的因素發生，造成了一個國家的選制從比例代表制轉為多數決選制，有效政黨數目的確是會出現明顯的降低，這樣的預期符合了杜瓦傑的假設。

　　經過這些清晰的討論，可以看出選制與政黨體系間的影響作用，兩個方向均可能成立。一個動態的變遷過程中可以看出，選制變遷不是一個實驗室裡面的選擇，而是鑲嵌在特定的政治經濟歷史背景下，因此，必須考慮這些背景因素的制約作用。在這樣的理解下，文章討論民主發展以及分歧程度對選制選擇的影響，這兩者本身都是重要的結構性變數，忽略掉這些因素的話，事實上是無法正確的看出選制變遷的脈絡，特別是其中政治人物的計算考量。

參、政黨的選制比例性偏好

　　"Looking for the Magic Number: the Optimal District Magnitude for Political Parties in d'Hondt PR and SNTV" 本篇文章討論選區規模偏好中政黨的計算（Lin, 2003），這一篇與前一篇研究選制變遷的文章兩者有呼應的關係，前一篇比較是實證上的討論，本篇則是理論上的探討。Taagepera 與 Shugart（1989）的討論裡面，指出選區席次增多時，選舉的比例性會增加，大黨可以獲得的超額席次也會跟著減少。在選舉制度中選區規模（即每個選區應選席次）的偏好上，從政黨的領袖的角度來看，決定於選票轉換成席次的比例，文獻認為大黨比較偏好較小的選舉席次規模，小黨比較偏好較大的選舉席次規模，但是給定政黨的得票情形，政黨會偏好多大的選舉席次規模，以讓獲得的席次比例最大化呢？這個問題可以用精確的數學推導來得出嗎？林老師的這篇文章，就是要解決不同規模的政黨所偏好的選區規模是多少這個問題。

　　既有對於選票轉換成席次比例的討論主要都是從立方定律（Cube law）的方法來觀察，但這個方法是一個經驗法則，並沒有個體的推論基礎在裡面，因此這篇文章要建立以個體為基礎的推論，討論 d'Hondt 與 SNTV 兩種選制下政黨的選區規模偏好。作者將是否會當選的包含門檻（inclusive threshold）跟排除門檻（exclusive threshold）帶進來討論。依照這兩個門檻模型得出的選票與席次轉換比例，與使用立方定律得出來的結果幾乎一樣。接著，以包含門檻跟排除門檻為基礎，計算出影響政黨選舉席次規模偏好的得票比例區間。而因為包含門檻同時考慮參選政黨的數目，政黨得票的分布以及政黨在複數選區中的提名策略等因素，所以這個新的得票比例區間，也包含了這些資訊。以此作者推論給定政黨的得票情形，政黨會偏好多大的選舉席次規模，也就是政黨的最適選區規模，以最大化其席次比例。這個模型指出，對一個中型的政黨來說，其得票處於這個政黨得票比例的區間中時，會偏好多席次的選區。而當政黨的選票比例比這個區間的上界還高時，政黨就會希望選區規模越小越好，最好是單一選區多數決，但是如果政黨選票實力低於這個區間的下界時，其就會希望選區規模越大越好。

　　在文章的最後一部份，作者進一步使用模擬的方法，探討政黨得票比例變化對選區規模偏好的可能影響。發現當優勢政黨的支持度出現變化時，優勢政黨對於選區規模的偏好會大幅變化，特別是一個優勢政黨如果其主導的地位出現動搖時，即有很強的挑戰者出現時，其會特別擔心選區規模的議題，這時優勢政黨不會再執著於選區規模很小的選制，其偏好的選區規模將會大幅的增加。

肆、威權體制中選舉的出現

"Political Development in the 20th Century Taiwan: State-Building, Regime Transformation and the Construction of National Identity" 這篇文章是林老師與朱雲漢老師合寫，探討台灣民主制度與選舉制度的出現（Chu and Lin, 2001）。本文從歷史的角度來討論，整體性的描述台灣的政治發展，政治發展中一個很大的重心在於選舉制度的發展。日本以及國民黨統治的政權，在本地台灣人來說都是外來的，雖然國民黨政權同時有一批外省移民一起來台灣，但是對其他大部分的台灣人來說國民黨是一個外來的統治政權，作者們討論兩個威權體制中選舉體制出現的原因。相當程度兩個時期都可以見到，當主要的社會階級因為經濟發展開始壯大之後，他們會希望有更多的政治參與。在日本統治時期因為日本本土經濟的發展，使得日本對台灣的稻米的需求增加，當台灣的地主階級經濟富裕之後，其子女有機會受到很好的教育，爾後發起了多次鼓吹增加政治參與的社會運動。

在議會請願運動的努力，以及日本國內政治氛圍的開放，有了成果。雖然議會請願運動鼓吹設立台灣議會，後來日本政府只允許地方層級的議員選舉，半數的州庄街政府的議員由選民直接選舉產生，每四年改選一次，1935 年開始舉行第一屆的選舉，這成為台灣歷史上第一次的選舉，而且也是地方自治的開端。不過只舉行兩屆，就因日本對外發動戰爭而中斷。

在國民政府統治台灣之後施行威權統治，但是同時在縣的層級以及省議會的層級允許地方政治菁英來參與選舉，推動這些選舉的目的一部分是為了有一個民主的外衣，另外就是鞏固政權的正當性基礎，但是過程中藉著對於社會的控制，以及侍從主義的特殊利益給與和買票，維持了對於選舉的勝利與對地方菁英的控制。但是隨著國民政府出口導向經濟政策的成功，使得私人經濟力量不斷的增長，特別是一些中小型的企業也逐漸的成長，加上國際的政治體系的衝擊，包括退出聯合國以及美中的和解，為維持統治的正當性以及緩解來自民間的壓力，國民政府最後被迫逐漸地開放中央層級的立法委員選舉，最後進而全面開放中央民代改選，以及最後的總統直選。此外因為政府必須依賴稅收以及軍隊人員的補充，所以對台灣本土社會的需求更加重視，而且選舉變成是一個管道與場域，讓台灣的本土的政治菁英與民間力量可以集結，不斷的擴大對於政治參與的要求。

台灣在日本統治與國民黨統治時期的政治參與擴大，很大程度可以看到現代化理論的體現，特別是國民黨統治時期的政治參與擴大更為明顯。隨著經濟的發展，民間社會逐漸成長，一方面更具有追求自由平等的意識，一方面經濟上更加獨立，故起而追求政

治的開放。但是儘管如此，外來的環境因素的重要性也不能忽視，日本大正時期的政治開放，為地方議會選舉的開放開了綠燈，但是進入昭和時期的戰爭動員，短暫的政治開放戛然而止。台灣面對的國際環境壓力，也是民主改革的重要背景之一，國民黨政府藉著改革開放來維持統治的正當性。這或許也提供中國民主改革前景的思考，雖然現今中國的國民所得已經超越台灣與南韓當初民主化的 8,000 美元所得，且在民意調查中，民眾的整體民主價值在東亞國家中已屬中等，許多高所得者或是對所得分配不滿者也偏好推動政治改革，但社會似乎絲毫無法突破國家的掌控，中國大陸的國家太大，國際壓力無法扮演重要的角色，加上西方國家近幾年的經濟危機，反而更依賴中國的市場，儘管中國是一個依賴高負債融資來成長的模式，但卻是許多國家仰賴的市場。所以國際環境因素是一個重要背景因素。

林老師的文章中，也指出認同的問題，因為台灣兩次面對的外來政權，其建構的國家認同與本地原居民的國家認同往往不一致。日本統治時期的台灣社會發動的議會請願運動不純粹只是爭取民主的運動而已，也含有認同的問題，因此造成路線的選擇，其中一個路線是究竟要不要選擇強化台灣自己的認同。如果弱化台灣人的認同，則可以強調台灣是日本的一部分，自然應該獲得更多的公民參政的權利；但是另一方面，若他們強調台灣的認同的話，則很可能會失去日本人中支持同化者的支持。從比較的角度來看，因為當時只有地方議會選舉，且選舉的時間短，所以認同問題並未具體浮現，但若是全島層級的選舉，且選舉的次數增加，認同議題勢必成為主要的政治爭辯焦點。到了國民黨統治時期，認同的問題就更重要，國民黨的大中國的思想，與本土興起的台灣自決思想間產生的衝突，這樣的一個對於認同的對立，在國民黨統治初期即已經浮現。但是當時的選舉只侷限於地方層級的選舉，加上政治控制比較嚴密，到了 1970 年代開始開放中央民代改選，認同議題即在選舉中浮現，到了解嚴之後，認同議題更是立即超越階級議題，成為接下來 30 年，台灣選舉競爭中的主軸，究竟是要選擇台灣自決，期待未來建構一個台灣國，還是維持現狀，保留一個大中國的概念架構，在未來中國民主化之後，保持統一的可能性，這樣的衝突後來就一直持續下去。

伍、小黨在並立制下的參選策略

「以輸為贏、小黨在日本單一選區兩票制下的參選策略」（林繼文，2008）這一篇文章討論了一個很有趣的議題，就是在採取單一選區域比例代表並立制的國家中，小黨只有參加比例代表制才有機會當選，但實際情形中，小黨會同時會選擇也參與單一選區

的選舉，原因為何，以及小黨會在哪些選區參選，兩個都是很有趣的問題。在混合選制下政黨的參選行為，學界討論的不多，這是一個很有趣的議題。單一選區混合選制是指同時採用單一選區與比例代表制，而其中常提到的是並立制，即分別使用單一選區與比例代表制，兩者的席次各自獨立計算。

　　因為同時有單一選區與比例代表制，選民的投票意向在這兩票間往往互相影響，在這樣的影響下政黨的提名會同時考慮兩種體制下得票的關聯性，以決定其是否同時參與選舉。學界對於小黨是否參與單一選區的選舉，主要是討論的是感染效應，也就是小黨參與單一選區藉此拉抬其在比例代表選區的聲勢（Gschwend, 2007）。作者提出感染效應的另一種可能因素的補充，即小黨參與單一選區選舉，因為知道選民基於策略性考量，在單一選區不投給這些小黨，但是為了補償的心理，在政黨得票的部分則會投給小黨，這樣的機制可以說是一種反向的策略性投票。進一步作者也討論究竟小黨會是在哪些選區推出候選人，如果小黨在所有的選區都推出候選人，可能力有未逮，所以小黨會在比較有希望的選區參選，但究竟是那些選區，既有理論並未有清楚的說明。

　　作者發現小黨會選擇在策略性選民密度比較高的地區，同時在單一選區與比例代表選區推出候選人。作者發現當區域選區的領先者當選的次數越多，代表其可能掌握的社會網絡越強，民眾進行策略性投票的比例會降低。另外如果區域選區的領先者是來自政治世家，則可能會擁有較強的社會連結，民眾進行策略性投票的比例也會降低。另外都市化程度較高的選區，傳統社會網絡與侍從體系均較弱，選民比較會自主投票。小黨參與單一選區的選舉通常是為了提升其政黨票，而非真的想要贏得單一選區的選舉。這幾個因素都可以來預測，選民是否會進行策略投票。另外作者也發現，政黨本身的特性，也會影響其是否能夠藉著參選單一選區來拓展政黨票，理念型的政黨，如共產黨，地方實力較弱，比較無法藉由參選單一選區來提升政黨票，但是民主黨的參選人許多前身是自民黨的議員，其在區域選區有比較強的實力，比較有特定的地域連結，藉著參選單一選區比較可能增強其在比例代表制部分的得票。

　　從這裡作者進一步討論另外一個影響小黨獲取席次的關鍵，是比例代表選區的劃分情形，日本將全國的劃分為 11 個比例代表制選區，因此小黨可以選擇在某些特定的比例代表選區集中火力爭取不分區的席次，也就是採取以輸為贏的策略，在這些區域中的單一選區提名候選人。但以台灣來說，因為全國只有一個不分區選區，所以小黨無法集中火力，在某些較有可能當選的地理區域爭取席次，因此這限制了小黨的勝選機會，使得小黨在台灣幾乎沒有生存的空間。這樣的比較是很有意義的觀察，未來若要修法來提高小黨的代表機會，除了調降當選得票門檻之外，增加比例代表制的選區數目，也會是一個重要的方向。

陸、選舉預測市場

　　衆人的集體智慧是不是比專家的意見更能夠做出正確的判斷，一直是一個廣受討論的問題。各種市場金融市場的交易結果，例如股市與期貨指數，是否能正確反映市場的價格，也一直是社會科學經常討論的課題。另外像是維基百科也是衆人的參與，其結果某種程度也反映出一種衆人對歷史詮釋理解的均衡。衆人智慧的正確性這個問題，最早從康多賽（Condorcet）的陪審團理論（Jury theorem）開始（Mueller, 2003），孔多賽認爲，假定每個陪審員做出正確決定的比例大於五成，當陪審團人數增加時，集體會做出正確決定的機率會趨近於 1。孔多賽的問題關懷，其實是關於多數決體制是否能夠做出正確的判斷，還是會淪於群衆的無知與盲目的決定。而衆人集體來預測未來發生的政治與經濟事件是否出現，並不是在做決策，但同樣是在體現集體智慧，而且這類型事件能夠檢證集體智慧的程度更高，因爲事件是否發生是很清楚的，而陪審團判定的案件內容是否眞的發生，以及投票是否選出好的政府領導人，有時很難正確的評估。

　　未來事件交易所就是讓參與者來買賣未來發生事件的合約，參與者可以判斷該事件未來的情勢，以及未來可能發生的影響變數，來進行買賣，然後我們就可以依照買賣合約的價格，來預測某個事件是否會發生，這個類似期貨市場的交易機制，整合各方面的資訊，來對來進行預測，在政治學的最常見的應用，就是那個候選人是否會當選，以及其得票的比例。「台灣選舉預測：預測市場的運用與實證分析」這篇文章即是討論這個問題（童振源等，2009）。雖然限於篇幅，這篇文章並沒有收錄到本書中，但是是一篇非常重要的文章，因爲這是這篇文章是台灣第一個探討選舉預測市場的實證分析，對於這個議題有開創性的意義。文中介紹未來事件交易所的運作方式與實際買賣結果的準確度，實證資料案例部分探討 2006 年的台北北高市長選舉預測、2008 年的第七屆立法委員選舉預測、以及 2008 年總統選舉預測等等。預測的內容包括了誰會當選，以及各縣市誰最高票，某一個候選人的全國得票率，以及在各縣市的得票率等等。

　　未來事件交易所是集合衆人之力來預測未來的結果，在孔多賽的理論之中如果陪審團的數目增加的時候，對於判決做出來正確的決定的機率，就會跟著增高，或者簡單來說，是三個臭皮匠勝過一個諸葛亮，雖然台灣的未來交易並沒有金錢上的交易或獎品的交易，因爲參與人數多，使得預測事件發生情形的正確機率增加，交易結果顯示對事件的發生與否的預測頗爲準確。

　　當然未來事件交易所在選舉預測上提供的資訊，若能跟其他的方法進行互補會更好。傳統的民調成本比較高，雖然精準度不見得更好，但是它可以針對受訪者的背景跟行爲進行分析，這樣可以更瞭解一些學術上的問題，因此未來交易市場與傳統民調兩者

是可以互相補充。另外未來事件交易所本身是一個網路時代的分析工具，在社群媒體興起之後，民眾可以透過網路來表達意見的管道更加多元，每天都有非常多的資訊在臉書、twitter、instagram 或者是電子論壇裡面進行發言，對這些電子網路與社群媒體的分析，可以瞭解政治支持的情形。所以值得我們進一步的去探討與分析，是否網路聲量高的候選人在民調的資料中會比較高，且在未來事件交易所得預測出來的當選機率比較大，這之間的一致與不一致的關係非常值得進一步研究，林老師團隊的研究開創了這方面一個新的課題，值得政治學界未來繼續探討。另外，選舉預測市場的決定其實跟選制本身有密切的關係，因為在從文章裡面可以看出來，目前進行選舉預測市場的都是單一選區，如果在複數選區裡面，如 SNTV 選制下或多黨體系的比例代表制中，選民很難進行選舉預測。這某種程度跟孔多賽的投票悖論（the voting paradox）有關。在投票的時候，若選擇的對象超過兩個，則民眾的集體偏好是有循環性的，例如有 ABC 三個選項，一部分民眾認為 A 選項最優，一部分民眾認為 B 選項最優，一部分民眾認為 C 選項最優，則沒有一個明確的贏家。也就是選擇的對象超過兩個時，民眾要做決策時的難度大增，增加了選舉預測市場預測的複雜性。

柒、結論

從林老師這幾方面的貢獻可以看出，老師在選舉研究領域的確是台灣這方面研究的重要開創者之一，不管是對於選制的選擇、選制與政黨體系之間的關係、小黨的參選策略與威權體制中選舉制度的出現，以及選舉預測市場的研究，都是這幾個研究領域的先驅。透過這幾篇的討論，也可以知道林老師選舉研究作品的幾個特色。首先林老師的作品通常都具有比較的視野，即使是專門討論日本的文章，也會將日本與台灣兩地的差異帶進來，進行比較，讓我們可以知道國家之間的異同。其次，林老師的研究提醒了我們制度本身的作用，都是鑲嵌在歷史與文化的背景裡面，我們必須要去理解這些歷史與政治文化因素的作用，才能夠正確的理解制度的影響。當然林老師在選舉研究中的這幾個主題，也提供了未來的研究方向，特別是林老師擴展了選制研究的研究對象範圍，從西方成熟民主國家，擴展到包括新興民主國家，所得到的發現擴展了既有的理論，這是開拓台灣選舉研究國際能見度的重要方向。

另外在研究方法上，他的討論最根本的是基於理性的考量，在裡面並沒有道德的成份，和任何先驗的價值在裡面，都是基於個體基礎進行客觀的分析。但是在個體的理性計算之外，他也很重視行為者所在的歷史與文化結構，以此來進行分析更能夠有效的進

行推論。最後林老師的作品也符合 EITM 的精神，就是先有個體基礎的理論推導，然後有統計的實證分析。因此，除了深入的理論探討之外，林老師在選舉實證資料方面的收集所下功夫也非常深，使得寫出的文章更紮實深入。這部分的資料分析，現在林老師已無法繼續進行，但希望能有林老師的學生或其他學術同儕，能接手努力，期待看到得到更多令人驚艷的研究作品。

Political Development in 20th-Century Taiwan: State-Building, Regime Transformation and the Construction of National Identity[*]

Yun-han Chu and Jih-wen Lin

In the 20th century, Taiwan has experienced two cycles of regime evolution, during which the Japanese colonial regime and the Nationalist émigré regime consecutively dominated its political history each for about half a century.[1] The two regimes, each wrestling with the challenge of subordinating the native society to its authoritarian rule, vision of nation-building and state-building agenda, travelled a comparable trajectory of institutional adjustment and adaptation. Each had shifted its heavy reliance on extensive use of coercive measures during the installation stage to selective co-optation, and to limited electoral opening as the incumbent elite tried to consolidate and partially institutionalize its rule. Both met with strong societal resistance as they tried to suppress the indigenous cultural identity and impose a cultural unity between the ruler and the ruled through state-sponsored cultural programmes. Both were initially highly autonomous and insulated from the native society, but over time the interests of the state elite became more enmeshed with the native elite, who turned out to be the indispensable intermediary for effective social control. Both regimes, at the zenith of their rule, exhibited exceptional effectiveness in organizing popular compliance

---

[*] Reproduced from [Chu, Yun-han, and Jih-wen Lin. 2001. "Political Development in the 20th Century Taiwan: State-Building, Regime Transformation and the Construction of National Identity." *The China Quarterly*, 165, 102-129, 2001], with kind permission of Cambridge University Press.
We thank Lung-chih Chang, Tun-jen Cheng, Louis Edmond, Steve Goldstein, Joseph Wu, and Rwei-ren Wu for their helpful comments and suggestions for revisions.

[1] For our analysis, a political regime is defined as an ensemble of patterns that determines the methods of access to the principal public offices; the characteristics of the actors admitted to or excluded from such access; the strategies that actors may use to gain access; and the rules that are followed in the making of publicly binding decisions. See Schmitter and Karl (1991).

and allegiance, controlling and mobilizing the society, and regulating political participation, elite recruitment and access to the policy-making process. Both fundamentally transformed Taiwanese society through state-building and state-sponsored modernization projects. For that reason, both regimes were also substantially transformed by the very society they governed as the incumbent elite came to encounter a steadily more politicized society and a more resourceful as well as diversified native elite. Thus, the state's transformative capacity in socio-economic modernization was both an important source of the regimes' legitimacy and their eventual undoing.

The two cycles of regime evolution, despite their comparability, produced substantially different outcomes in terms of the development of political society[2] and the construction of collective identity. Towards the end of colonial rule, the aspiration of the native Taiwanese for a limited home rule was only partially fulfilled. Under the KMT rule, in contrast, a "national political system" gradually took root in Taiwanese society and the citizenship was redefined in full accordance with the state's de facto territoriality. At the close of colonial rule, there was no tangible social support for a political struggle for national sovereignty and Taiwan had not yet emerged as a self-contained political community with a distinctive political identity. In stark contrast, with the demise of KMT authoritarian rule came a vibrant Taiwanese nationalist movement with growing and broad-based social support. The popular aspiration for an independent Taiwan became increasingly crystallized and cohesive at the close of the 20th century. Most significantly, with the indigenization of the KMT power structure, the state was eventually converted from a cultural agent of Chinese nationalism into an incubator of a "re-imaged community" based on a new Taiwanese identity.[3]

This article sets out to analyse the transformation of the two émigré regimes and the formation of Taiwanese identity—the two developments that principally defined the political experiences of the Taiwanese people in the 20th century—and their mutual influences. The two cycles of regime evolution are considered in terms of the initial historical conditions for their installment, the strategies that the incumbent elite employed to consolidate and partially institutionalize its rule, and the political processes as well as the changing structural

---

[2]　Political society refers to the arena in which a political community specifically arranges itself for political contest to gain control over public power and state apparatus. On the concept of political society in a democratic setting, see Linz and Stepan (1996).

[3]　The expression "imagined community" is adopted from Anderson (1991).

conditions that led to their eventual transformation. The article explains why the two regimes employed a different mixture of political co-optation (versus suppression), social integration (versus segregation) and economic inclusion (versus exclusion) at various stages of their rule in terms of the constraining and enabling structural conditions, the nature and level of threats to their political security, and their state-building and nation-building agenda. In acting, they made mistakes and generated unintended consequences, in some instances changing their very identity below the level of consciousness.

For each political cycle, special attention is paid to how different aspects of Taiwan's state-building process constrained the historical path of both regime transformation and the development of new political identities. The article investigates how the state politicized society by tightening state-society relations and by caging its subject on to a "national political terrain."[4] In particular, the growing dependence of society on the state for its capacity to provide a coordinating framework, regulatory regimes and supportive infrastructures for the emerging capitalist economy made the latter a growing object of political contention as more local social groups and classes tried to shape state actions to suit their own interests. Next, it examines how the colonial boundaries, socio-economic segregation and hierarchical political order provided the key conditions for the formation of modern ethnic and national identity, and how the modern state, which possessed the most encompassing material and symbolic infrastructure for the construction of a social and cultural entity more homogeneous internally and more distinctive externally, became instrumental in the development of full-blown national identity.[5]

Taiwan's unique history of modern state-building also prompts an investigation of how the process of indigenization and consolidation of a "transplanted state" influenced regime evolution and the development of new political identities. The twin processes provide the necessary conditions for a dependent, subordinate and non-sovereign political unit to evolve into an independent and self-contained sovereign entity with a distinctive national identity.

The article examines the bargaining and mutual accommodation between the local and incumbent elites within the broader context of state-building and changing state-society

---

4 For the notion of "social caging, " see Mann (1993: 61).

5 For the view that the establishment of national identity should be understood as an explicit political project pursued by elites, see Gellner (1983).

relations. It identifies the force behind the formation of new political identities, which were shaped by the inherited pre-modern myths, memories and symbols, deliberate projects pursued by political elites, and the unintended consequences of the state-building process. The incumbent state elite designed and pursued their state-building project in accordance with their knowledge and vision of state-building, on the basis of the existing state apparatus they inherited, and in response to the need for controlling their domestic political environment and to the security and economic imperative imposed by the larger international context.

I. The Evolution of the Japanese Colonial Regime (1895-1945)

In 1885 the Qing government declared Taiwan a province and appointed Liu Mingchuan its first provincial governor (xunfu). Liu was assigned a difficult mission: to modernize the island and make it a blockhouse against foreign incursion of China. However, Taiwan, as a frontier settlement for poor Chinese immigrants, had been tossed aside by Chinese governments for centuries.[6] For much of the Qing period, the island was governed by absentee Mandarins based primarily in Fujian, who spent little time on the island and regarded Taiwan as a chaotic and plague-ridden periphery.

Thus depreciated, Taiwan was ceded to Japan through the Treaty of Shimonoseki in April 1895 after the Sino-Japanese war. The Japanese took over Liu's truncated business of modernization, but within a very different political framework. The challenge faced by the Japanese was twofold. On the one hand, armed resistance must be crushed for the colonial government to be installable.[7] On the other, incorporating some 2.5 million Chinese immigrants politically, economically and culturally into the emerging Japanese imperium remained a daunting task. Opinions varied over how the new colony should be managed.

---

[6] For an analysis of how Taiwan was incorporated into the Chinese empires, see Winckler (1983).

[7] With the withdraw of the Qing officialdom, the remaining officials waged their feeble resistance by declaring the founding of the Taiwan Republic (Taiwan minzhu guo) in May 1895, which was the first modern republic in Asia, but lasted for less than five months. Nevertheless, armed revolt continued for another two decades.

To many of Japan's colonial theorists, who were conversant with Western colonial thoughts and experiences, the colonized people belonged to an inferior race and should be acculturated through guidance. The colony was separate from the homeland, and should not be governed as its prolongation.[8] However, the Western model does not fit into Japan and Taiwan nicely. Geographical proximity and racial affinity between the Japanese and the residents of Taiwan allowed the colonial rulers to chain the new colony closely to the homeland, implying a more equal treatment of the colonized people.

This dilemma was reflected in a report presented by Hara Takashi, an under-secretary of the Foreign Ministry, to the Bureau of Taiwan Affairs in 1896. He outlined two alternatives of colonial policy, assimilation or non-assimilation, and asserted the first one. Under his "principle of homeland extensionism" (naichi enchō shugi), the Taiwanese should be treated equally as Japanese. This policy, though not officially denied, turned out to be impractical. The occupation of Taiwan was dominated by political and military considerations, under which the Taiwanese were treated as potential challengers rather than as equal citizens. In addition, the Japanese did not find Taiwan's climatic and sanitarian environments favourable to large-scale emigration. With a handful of colonizers clustering in the cities, the assimilation policy was simply unrealistic.

The colonizers were thus left with only one viable option: to build an elite-steered colonial state that was penetrative and efficient. It is generally agreed that the major architect of this scheme was Gotō Shinpei, the civil administrator (minsei chōkan) of Kodama Gentarō who was the fourth Taiwan governor-general (sōtoku) in 1898. A German-trained medical doctor, Gotō was keenly aware of the racial difference between the Taiwanese and the Japanese, and adopted the "biological principle" to guide colonial rule. This premise was that the Taiwanese are biologically distinguishable from the Japanese, and must be governed according to local conditions. Under this policy, extensive surveys were conducted between 1898 and 1903 on Taiwan's geography, land, traditional customs and population. These investigations helped the colonial government to usurp unclaimed properties, reassign land ownership, implement tax reform, monopolize key industries and reach financial independence.[9]

---

[8] For more detailed analysis, see Peattie (1984).

[9] As a result, the Taiwan colonial government became the richest property-owner on the island. By the

Taiwan's regime structure was transformed under the same principle. Basically, the colonial government kept Taiwan's social structure intact,[10] but subjected it to close surveillance. With an extensively built police network that was fused with the traditional *baojia* system, the government infiltrated every corner of Taiwanese society,[11] while itself remaining well protected and imperious. Based on Law No. 63 (adopted by the Imperial Diet in 1896), the Taiwan governor-general can issue law-like decrees and remain unchecked by any other institution.[12]

As the biological principle triumphed, a conundrum arose. Although discriminated against by the Japanese government, the Taiwanese lived under Japan's jurisdiction and must have an identity in the Japanese imperium. In accordance with the Treaty of Shimonoseki (Article 5), Taiwanese residents were allowed to choose nationality in the first two years of occupation. Only a few thousand left for China, and the remainder became Japanese subjects. Even so, the Taiwanese far from enjoyed complete Japanese citizenship. They were excluded from the government and representative bodies, did not even hold partial suffrage, were vulnerable to police abuse, and had no right to serve in the military.[13]

It was the First World War that compelled Japan to re-examine its colonial policies. In the Japanese homeland, the moribund oligarchic system finally gave way to the parliamentary parties, a transition that created both competition and chaos. Economically, Japan experienced

---

end of Japan's colonial rule, 66.8% of Taiwan's land was state-owned. See Taiwan sōtokufu [台灣總督府] (1945: 501).

[10] The Taiwan colonial government not only preserved the literati-gentry class, but also sponsored meetings for Chinese poem composition, and conferred a "gentleman's badge" to collaborators.

[11] In 1905, there were 4,817 police officers in Taiwan, each taking charge of an average of 617 native Taiwanese. In 1905 the total number of public servants was only 13,207. See Taiwan sōtokufu (1946), *Tōkeisho* [Statistical Books] of each year, complied by the Xingzheng zhangguan gongshu [Office of the Administrator-General] in *Taiwansheng wushiyinianlai tongji tiyao* [Statistical Summary of the Taiwan Province in the Past 51 Years], Taipei: Xingzheng zhangguan gongshu, pp. 352, 1321. This density was higher than those in other Japanese colonies. For the police system in colonial Taiwan, see Chen (1984).

[12] Although the governor-general's decree must be approved by the advisory council (hyōgikai), the procedure is mainly ritualistic because the governor-general appointed the council members. For the evolution of Taiwan's legal system in the Japanese colonial period, see Wang [王泰升] (1997: 183-230).

[13] In 1905, only 0.28% of the native Taiwanese served in the government, in contrast to 17.4% of the Japanese. See Xingzheng zhangguan gongshu [台灣省行政長官公署] (1946: 134).

a temporary boom when the Europeans withdrew from their Asian colonies during the war. Economic expansion boosted Japanese demand for rice, for which Taiwan was the major supplier, and helped incubate a commercialized landholding class in Taiwan. In keeping with their rising economic status, the landed class wanted more political autonomy and launched various political movements. This time they were armed with modern ideologies, such as democracy and self-determination, that the colonial government could not easily counteract with violence.

In the meantime, Taiwan had become much more accommodating to the Japanese than two decades earlier, and Japanese was no longer a foreign language to Taiwan's educated class.[14] Armed resistance was totally eradicated, and Japan's international status was affirmed by its participation in the war. By September 1918, with Hara Takashi now Japanese prime minister, a major transformation of colonial policy was on the way. In March 1921, the Hara cabinet proposed the "Law concerning the ordinances to be enforced in Taiwan" (usually called Law No. 3) to replace Law No. 31.[15] With this, the laws of the Japanese homeland were in principle to be enforced in Taiwan, under the condition that the Taiwan governor-general's law-making power was to be recognized.[16]

Institutionally, the structures of local government and the Taiwan government were both renovated. Since 1919, the office of the Taiwan governor-general was no longer assumed by military officers. Other institutional changes deprived the civil governor-generals of the omnipotence enjoyed by their predecessors. First, the military power of the Taiwan colonial government was redirected to the Taiwan army commander. Since the governor-general and the army commander had different homeland supervisors and career interests, a potential conflict loomed, and actually broke out in wartime.[17] Secondly, the governor-general must

---

[14] In 1920, the percentage of Japanese in Taiwan was almost triple that in 1905, while the number of Japanese working for the colonial government declined sharply, see Xingzheng zhangguan gongshu [台灣省行政長官公署] (1946: 136).

[15] Law No. 31 replaced the previous law in 1907, the only difference being that the governor-general's decrees could no longer violate Japanese laws.

[16] Incidentally, Law No. 3 was almost identical to the law plan that Hara once proposed based on assimilation policy. For the relationship between Hara Takashi and Japan's colonial policy-making, see Meitetsu (1980).

[17] In pre-war Japan, the ultimate source of military command was the Japanese emperor, whereas the ministers of army and navy took charge of the military administration. The Taiwan governor-general

accept interrogations of the Diet members, and share his power with the chief administrator. Thirdly and most importantly, as a backbencher in the cabinet, the governor-general was fettered by Japan's chaotic domestic politics. As a result, nine civil governor-generals of different partisan backgrounds served between 1919 and 1936.[18]

Although none the powers that checked the colonial government rested on native Taiwanese, the anti-government elite did find a greater leverage to affect policy-making. As long as public opinion in the Japanese homeland was divided, the Taiwanese elite, now fluent in Japanese, could find their sympathizers. It turned out that the real challenge for the Taiwanese leaders was how to balance between two strategies that were contradictory though both justifiable. By playing down their own identity and instead stressing that they were also Japanese citizens, the Taiwanese could ask for equal civil rights. Alternatively, they could emphasize their distinctiveness, but with the risk of losing the support of Japanese assimilationists. Self-determination and equal citizenship were both desirable goals, but not obtainable at the same time.

On the other side, the Japanese colonizers also hovered between assimilation and non-assimilation policies. Strategic interaction between the two groups thus created an interesting dynamics of identity politics. When Lin Hsien-t'ang, a prominent Taiwanese leader, espoused the strategy of "equalization through assimilation" and organized the Taiwan Assimilation Society (Taiwan dōkakai) in 1914, the colonial government ordered it to dissolve. When the Japanese government finally shifted to homeland extensionism in the early 1920s, the Taiwanese were no longer satisfied with assimilation. With the formation of the Taiwan Cultural Association (Taiwan bunka kyōkai) in 1921, the anti-government movement soon shifted to an emphasis on Taiwan's peculiarity and petitioned for the establishment of a parliament for Taiwan. Although implicit, the underlying assumption of the petition movement was the ethnic distinction of the people of Taiwan.

In retrospect, the aims of the counter-elite and the colonial government were rarely in tune, even though both sides once pursued compatible goals. Still, the nascent ethnic

---

was supervised by the Bureau of Taiwan Affairs headed by the prime minister (1895-1929) or the minister of colonial affairs (since 1929).

[18] Thus, the average term for each governor-general was two years. By contrast, seven governor-generals served between 1895 and 1919 (each stayed 3.6 years in average), and three served between 1936 and 1945 (3.3 years in average).

consciousness never made its way to a full-fledged nationalistic movement, because of the friction in other issue dimensions. To the conservatives, their interests could be better represented in a Taiwanese parliament than in the Japanese Diet, where they were destined to be a minority.[19] Their emphasis on Taiwan's identity was therefore highly strategic. Interestingly, the radicals also viewed the identity issue strategically. The Taiwan Communist Party (formed in 1928) asserted "Taiwan racial independence" and "establishment of the Republic of Taiwan," but only in so far as the republic was a communist one.

Thus the issue of national identity did not even surface when the anti-government movement suffered from internal schisms and gradually dissolved. By the mid-1930s, even the moderate petition movement was quenched. Disintegrated and defenceless, counter-elites of different camps faced a tough choice on national identity again. For the radicals, the problem was where to seek asylum after they were forced to go underground or abroad. Communist parties in Japan and China provided different opportunities and each held their own visions of nation building. The landed class had no choice but to accept the government's assimilation plan in exchange for security.

This dilemma came to an unexpected solution as war became imminent. By the mid-1930s, Japan was on the brink of a total war with China, and Taiwan bad been transformed from a supplement to Japan's capitalist development into a factory of military supplies. With the upgrade of Taiwan's strategic values, measures were taken to strengthen the mobilization capacity of the colonial government. The exact measures involved a series of institutional transformations, developed in line with the assimilation policy. Especially notable is the institutional reform on self-government in 1935, a year after the petition movement ended. According to the new laws, province (shu) and city (shi) councils were given the power to make decisions that the executives could overrule. Partial and limited elections were introduced to select half the members of the city, street (kai), and village (shō) councils, who then elect half the members of the provincial councils.[20] Through several local elections held between 1935 and 1945, the Taiwanese leaders were fully incorporated into a new system in

---

[19] *Taiwan minbao*, December 12, 1926.

[20] The electoral law adopted the multi-member district single nontransferable vote system, still in existence today. As the law imposed strict constraints on the right to vote, the percentage of eligible voters was very low. Nevertheless, it was enough to include most landlords and professionals, hence the elite class.

which they could participate but not dominate. Many of the anti-government elite not only joined the election and got elected, but also participated in other collaborative organizations in the years to follow (Chen and Lin [陳明通、林繼文], 1998).

When Japan found the battlefield in the Chinese mainland a quagmire and tried to break out through the sea, Taiwan's role was changed into a naval military base. The colonial regime was transformed again, leaving a deep mark on identity formation that was to exert a traumatic imprint after the war. Kobayashi Seizō, a retired navy admiral who became the 17th governor-general in 1936, outlined three policies for the colonial government: to "Japanize" the Taiwanese people, to build military industries and to turn Taiwan into a base for southward advance.

Kobayashi's assumption of office marked a new phase of regime transformation: the restoration of the military governorship. Unlike their counterparts in the early occupation period, however, the wartime military governor-generals no longer ruled by the biological principle, but implemented the assimilation policy in an assertive way. With the movement of "converting (the colonial people) into the imperial subjects" (kōminka, that is "Japanization"), the colonial government enforced the adoption of Japanese customs, religion, language and even names. The number of school children accepting Japanese education rose sharply during this period, indicating the progress of the movement. Classical Chinese was totally removed from the curriculum in 1937 and all private schools for Chinese education were banned in 1940, whereas the percentage of Taiwanese pupils in elementary schools rose to 71.17% by the end of the war (Taiwan sōtokufu [台灣總督府], 1945: 39).[21]

Meanwhile, native society was fully politicized to ensure the success of the new policies. Not only was the colonial government turned into a command post, but also every street corner was caught in the war machine. At the top of the state apparatus hierarchy was the governor-general, served by the navy admirals between 1936 and 1944 and sharing power with the Taiwan army commander. Both posts received commands from their homeland superiors, and clashed when Japan's marine and continental strategies came into conflict. The military, even in wartime, had a limited and cryptic presence on the island. It was the police who carried the baton for the colonial state and kept watchful eyes on the native communities. To the ordinary Taiwanese, the police formed the major interface between the colonial government and their neighbourhoods.

---

[21]　For the impact of Japanese education, see Tsurumi (1977).

The colonial government intensified its penetration into local communities as Japan enlarged its battlefront. In 1940, it installed the "Public Service Association of the Imperial Subjects" (kōmin hōkōkai) to promote the movement of spiritual mobilization. Headed by the executive of each administrative level, the Association monitored even minute details of the everyday life of ordinary Taiwanese. Taiwanese elites, including many who had participated in the anti-government movement a decade earlier, had no choice but to assist the Association as local agents.

By the end of the Second World War, the colonial government had been enforcing assimilation policies for more than two decades. The impact on identity formation, however, varied across age and social class. For the old and uneducated, the Japanization movement came too late to lead their socialization. Aged gentry with a Chinese education might find the Japanization movement an embarrassment, but had to remain submissive to protect their class interests. The younger members of the local elite, irrespective of their earlier response to colonial rule, were apt to think and act like their Japanese counterparts. They could detect the politics behind the Japanization movement but were also sensitive to political risks and, when no other alternatives existed, chose to become collaborators. The most vulnerable target of the Japanization movement turned out to be the social marginals who reached their adolescence during the war. The Japanese imperium gave these youngsters not only hopes but also education and job opportunities. It is therefore not surprising that the aborigines became the most loyal warriors of the Japanese imperium, even though their tribes were ruthlessly demolished in Musha (Wushe) in 1930.

Overall, the state of national identity in Taiwan around the end of the Second World War was nebulous, but several elements remain evident. With a shared resentment of colonial rule and the development of a common social space, sub-ethnic categories gave way to the concept of Taiwanese (*Taiwanren*) in public discourse. Still, few people questioned their Han Chinese identity. Politically, Taiwan residents lived with their (partial) Japanese citizenship with little difficulty. It is groundless to declare the Japanization movement a big success, just as it is impossible to extract from the inchoate Taiwanese consciousness a firm base of national identity. For both sides, identity formation had been a highly politicized process. The colonizers designed their policies along two dimensions: to use force or not, to assimilate or not. The Taiwanese elite also wandered between two identifies: a secondary Japanese who enjoys some political powers, or a non-Japanese who is disenfranchised. The final outcome was determined by the strategic interaction between the two sides and the constraints each faced.[22]

Despite the precarious state of national identity in the late colonial period, one thing is certain: the regime in Taiwan had been completely transformed, from one based on repressive mechanisms[23] into one relying on information superiority.[24] The colonial infrastructure was inherited by the Nationalist government after the war, and played crucial roles in the KMT's regime instalment. It was the unsolved issue of national identity that pushed Taiwan into another turbulent cycle of nation-building.

II. The Evolution of the Nationalist Émigré Regime (1945-1996)

With Japan's unconditional surrender in August 1945, Taiwan was once again war booty. Under a plan drawn up by Allied leaders, the island was retroceded to China, now under the Nationalist government. The retrocession was virtually pre-ordained to have tragic consequences, as the Chinese on the mainland and the native Taiwanese had experienced distinctively different modern state-building and nationalist struggle over the previous half century. The social, political and cultural gaps between the two groups were huge. The island had experienced a protracted period of stable social and economic development and, as a consequence, was more modern than most of the Chinese mainland. The whole island

---

[22] A way to see the strategic nature of the Japanization movement is to compare Taiwan and Korea. In Korea, the movement was promoted more intensively but incurred a more negative response. See Chou (1996).

[23] During the final phase of armed resistance, 1,435 persons were gaoled under the Decree of Bandit Punishment. Since the Decree was replaced by the Security Maintenance Law, the number imprisoned was reduced to less than 100 each year. See Xingzheng zhangguan gongshu [台灣省行政長官公署] (1946: 494-495).

[24] The colonial regime underwent gradual evolution and expansion. The ratio of Taiwan residents to government officials was 230 in 1905 and 99 in 1940. In the meantime, the number of divisions in the Taiwan colonial government tripled (Xingzheng zhangguan gongshu [台灣省行政長官公署], 1946: 348-349, 354). The Taiwan government also centralized the control of the mass media in the last days of its colonial rule.

shared a unified system of administration, law, education, commerce and agriculture under a repressive and ubiquitous colonial state. The colonial boundaries and rules were instrumental in shaping a shared sense of social space and identity among the residents of Taiwan. Colonial rule had also introduced new cultural values and world views, under which Taiwan was accorded a semi-peripheral status superior to China within the Japanese imperium. In particular, the second-generation islanders groomed under the colonial rule had acquired a sense of history and cultural identity intrinsically different from the historical consciousness of mainland Chinese.

The abrupt ending of colonial rule turned the world upside down for a great majority of the native Taiwanese elite, whose newly acquired language and cultural skills and political credentials were suddenly degraded into a potential liability under a returned Chinese regime. The Nationalists took over the island without a carefully-prepared retrocession plan as Taiwan was only a sideshow to their granter effort to recover all of China after the war. The new administration under the administrator-general and garrison commander Chen Yi paid little attention to the aspiration for equality of the disoriented native elites. Mainlanders and half-mountains[25] were favoured over native Taiwanese in filling up the vast government vacancies left behind by the Japanese. The economy deteriorated rapidly. Taiwan's resources were siphoned off to the mainland by the Nationalists to fuel their military struggle with the Communists and by corrupt carpetbaggers to enrich themselves. The transmission of hyper-inflation from the mainland to Taiwan had a devastating impact on the war-torn island economy. Also, a myriad of disputes erupted over the confiscation of the assets formerly owned by the Japanese.[26] By the time a large number of frustrated and jobless Taiwanese conscripts from South China and South-East Asia returned in late 1946 and early 1947, the island was already at boiling point.

On 28 February 1947, a single event of police brutality sparked an island-wide popular uprising (Lai, Myers, and Wei, 1991). The Nationalists responded with a harsh military crackdown. Thousands of native Taiwanese, including numerous well-educated and well-

---

[25] Half-mountains (or *banshan*) were viewed by the native as token Taiwanese who had spent the war years in China and were recruited by the Nationalist government. For the origins of half-mountains and their role in post-War retrogression, see Jacob (1990).

[26] A major source of the dispute arises from the token transfer of assets from private Japanese to their native Taiwanese friends on the eve of the hand-over.

respected social elites, were persecuted and purged. Many lives were also lost as a result of internal strife among faction-based security and intelligence organs during the crackdown. After the incident, the Nationalists made some attempts to placate the local people. They upgraded Taiwan from a special military, zone to a province and called for immediate local elections. Chiang Kai-shek also replaced Chen Yi with Wei Tao-ming, a civilian. But these measures were too late and too little.

The tragic event had a profound and lasting effect on the Taiwanese people. It became a lightening-rod event that constantly reminded them of their "common sorrow." It transfigured a latent Taiwanese nationalism into a burgeoning independence movement, launched first by the native elites who went into exile in Japan after the incident. This lasting scar also complicated the efforts by the Nationalists to reconstruct a cultural and ethnic unity between the mainlanders and native Taiwanese through state-sponsored resinicization programmes in later years. The only tangible benefit of the incident to the Nationalists was that it drove a generation of politically conscious social elites into self-imposed political passiveness. The political acquiescence of the native elites created the conditions for a sweeping three-phased land reform, which was first introduced in 1948 to pre-empt communist insurgence in the countryside and, inadvertently, laid the foundation for post-war economic reconstruction and a more equitable pattern of economic growth.

When Chiang Kai-shek retreated from mainland to Taiwan with his mainlander followers and million-strong troops around the end of 1949, everyone, including the Truman administration, anticipated that his days were numbered as the Chinese Civil War was entering its final stage. Then, however, came another dramatic twist for the people of Taiwan. The outbreak of Korean War on 25 June 1950 suddenly extended the lease on the life of the Nationalists for another half century. The resumption of U.S. military and economic aid helped the Nationalist state apparatus and armed forces stay afloat. Soon after the formal partition of Vietnam in 1954, the United States institutionalized its security commitment to Taiwan by signing the U.S.-ROC Mutual Defence Treaty. Thus, a new security demarcation in East Asia gave the Nationalists a historic chance to consolidate a one-party authoritarian regime on new social soil.

The post-1949 KMT authoritarianism was constructed on a quadripartite foundation—an elaborate and centralized party apparatus, a system of extra-constitutional legal arrangements and emergency decrees, a controlled electoral pluralism implemented at the local level, and structural symbiosis between the party and the state. Learning from his disastrous defeat on the mainland, Chiang Kai-shek responded to the challenge of political reconstruction with an ambitious party reorganization plan, officially launched on 5 August 1950.[27] Factionalism in the security and intelligence apparatus was eliminated. The system of political commissars for the military was re-established. Between 1950 and 1952, party leadership was drastically re-composed. Hierarchical party organs were installed at all levels of the state apparatus and representative bodies. Party cells reached into all organized social sectors, such as labour unions, youth groups, religious groups, professional associations, business associations, farmers' associations, women's associations, schools and mass media.

Party membership grew by more than 150% between 1950 and 1954, from 168,719 to 403,260 (one KMT member for every ten adult males). It was concentrated disproportionally in the military and state bureaucracy (especially at the level of central government), in the urban social sectors, and among the mainlanders, who still accounted for 73.6% of total membership (Lin, 1998: 75-77). This indicated that penetration of the party apparatus into the countryside and among the native Taiwanese was relatively weak during the initial phase of regime installation. Nevertheless, the party reorganization of the early 1950s created a structure of personified power centralization anchored on the paramount leader, secured a stable, homogeneous and non-competitive process of elite recruitment, and laid the organizational foundation for the KMT to establish its hegemonic presence in society.

The KMT's re-organizational task was made easier by the proclamation of a general state of siege on Taiwan on 19 May 1949. The imposition of martial law greatly expanded the scope of power of Taiwan garrison command and suspended the protection of civil rights guaranteed in the 1947 ROC Constitution.[28] Furthermore, many important provisions of the constitution were replaced or superseded by the so-called "Temporary Articles" and a series of special legislation under the rubric of "During the Period of Mobilization and Combating Rebellion." Together, they threw the country into a permanent state of emergency. These

---

[27] For an excellent analysis of the political background of the party reorganization plan, see Lin (1998: ch3).

[28] The mainlander elite chose freezing, not abolishing, the 1947 Constitution. For them, the ROC Constitution is irreplaceable because it is the quintessential legal embodiment of the one-China principle. It was adopted when the Nationalist government still exercised effective governance over a majority part of China, including Taiwan, and was internationally recognized by all major powers.

extra-constitutional arrangements were steadily expanded during the 1950s and 1960s (Hu, 1987). In their final form, they provided the president with extensive emergency powers, invalidated the two-term limit on presidency, suspended the re-election of the three national representative bodies—the National Assembly, the Legislative Yuan and the Control Yuan—extended the tenure of their incumbent members for life, and deferred the election of provincial and municipal heads indefinitely.

The KMT introduced elections for township head, county/city council and country/city magistrate in 1950, and popular election for the Taiwan Provincial Assembly in 1954 to incorporate a diversified local elite into the process of party-building and to provide the authoritarian system with a modicum of democratic façade. The KMT leadership discovered a proven formula for controlling a limited popular electoral process by employing the old trick of "divide-and-rule." At the grass-roots level, existing patron-client networks were incorporated into the party structure. Within each administrative district below the provincial level, the KMT nurtured and kept at least two competing local factions striving for public offices and other electoral offices in many quasi-state organizations, such as farmers' associations and irrigation associations, and more importantly, for a share of region-based economic rents in the non-tradable goods sector to be distributed by the party-directed local spoils system (Bosco, 1994).

The local factions and central party leadership developed a mutual dependence. On the one hand, the smooth functioning of the vote-buying mechanism, irregular campaign practices and the local spoil system depended on the indulgence of the various state regulatory and law-enforcement agencies, which were under the influence of the party. On the other hand, the patron-client networks helped the party to extend its reach into local communities. Also, the fierce competition among the factions crowded out opposition candidates in local elections. On top of this, the central leadership could claim the overall electoral victory delivered by disparate local factions. Thus, the combined mobilizing strength of the KMT party and the local factions virtually without exception delivered more than two-thirds of popular votes and three-quarters of seats in all elections, especially the more significant country magistrate and Provincial Assembly elections, for more than three decades until the political opening of the late 1980s (see Table 10.1).

From the very beginning, there existed a structural symbiosis between the party and the state. This manifested itself at three levels of state-building. First, it meant a fusion of party

Table 10.1 Local-Factions and KMT Shares of Votes and Seats in Provincial Assembly and County Magistrate/City Mayor Elections (1954-1994)

Year	Taiwan Provincial Assembly elections				County Magistrate/ City Mayor elections			
	KMT's share of votes (%)	KMT's local factions' share of seats	KMT's share of seats	Total seats	KMT's share of votes (%)	KMT's local factions' share of seats	KMT's share of seats	Total seats
1954	68.8	27	48	57	71.8	17	19	21
1957	67.8	28	53	66	65.0	16	20	21
1960	65.4	29	58	73	72.0	16	19	21
1963	68.0	32	61	74	-	-	-	-
1964	-	-	-	-	73.1	16	17	21
1968	75.5	27	60	71	72.4	15	17	20
1972	68.9	23	58	73	78.6	9	20	20
1977	64.1	32	56	77	70.4	7	16	20
1981	70.3	25	59	77	59.4	12	15	19
1985	69.8	34	59	77	62.6	13	17	21
1989	64.0	30	55	77	56.1	13	14	21
1993	-	-	-	-	47.3	8	13	21
1994	51.0	26	48	79	-	-	-	-
Average	66.7	39.08%	76.78%	-	66.2	62.83%	82.74%	-

Source: Data provided by the Political System and Change Workshop, Department of Political Science, National Taiwan University.

and state, in both organizational and personnel terms. Secondly, it meant mutual dependence between the two over key functional areas. The party provided the only coordinating mechanism among disparate arms of the state. It also helped maintain the ideological coherence of state through a system of elite recruitment and training programmes for the appointment and promotion of senior government officials and military officers. In addition, the party regulated the access of social actors to the state. On the other hand, the party relied on the resources and coercive power of the state to preserve its institutional prerogatives and to squash any attempt to form an alternative power bloc. Under the rule of martial law, the security authority was prepared to suppress even a hint of political stirring. The state privileged the party in controlling the organizational bases for interest intermediary. The party dominated the selection of leadership for all state-sanctioned corporatist organizations and provided the only organizational link across different social sectors. The party also relied on a vast array of state-owned enterprises to cushion the economic security of loyalist mainlander followers.

Thirdly, symbiosis meant that the legitimacy of one-party authoritarianism was ultimately tied to the legitimacy of the state structure. The justification for a system of extra-constitutional legal arrangements and emergency decrees and the revolutionary mandate of the KMT party were both founded on the so-called "one-China" principle, which sustained the claim that there is only one China, Taiwan is part of China, and the ROC government is the sole legitimate government representing the whole of China. The mismatch between the ROC's *de jure* jurisdiction (China) and *de facto* one (Taiwan) was meant to be transitory. This precarious sovereign claim turned out to be the most unsettling legitimating pillar for the émigré regime. First, the sovereign status of the ROC faced the challenge of the PRC's conflicting claim and its unceasing threat of forced retrocession. Both Beijing and Taipei sought an exclusive representation of all of China in the international community. The ROC's precarious sovereign status, for an extended period following the outbreak of the Korean War, was sustained essentially by American hegemony. It was the United States-initiated international recognition, including membership of the United Nations and a seat on Security Council before 1971, that elongated KMT's fictional sovereign claim until the end of 1979.

The initial structural characteristics as well as institutional arrangements of the one-party authoritarianism had profound implications for its adaptation, evolution and eventual transition. First, the political security of the émigré regime was highly susceptible to pressure from the international system, especially a redirection in American China policy and/or the PRC's reunification strategy. External developments and interventions defined a number of critical junctures for its evolution. The steady consolidation of the North-East Asian security demarcation during the 1950s was the driving force behind the shift in the raison *d'être* of the Nationalist state from "recovering the mainland" to "building the anticommunist bastion (Taiwan)." During the 1958 Quemoy and Matsu crisis, Chiang Kai-shek succeeded in rejecting the American demand to abandon the offshore islands, but he was eventually persuaded to give up any plan for waging military operations on the mainland under intense pressures from the Kennedy administration in 1961-1962 (Harding, 1992: 32-33). As a consequence, the KMT leadership had to update its historical mission, from anti-communist crusade to securing the island's self-defence, international standing and economic prospect.

The American intervention was also instrumental in the economic reforms of the early 1960s, which set the island on a path of export-oriented industrialization. It took an American threat to reduce the aid package to expedite the centrepiece measure, the 19-point programme of economic and financial reform, through the bureaucracy in 1960 (Jacob, 1996: 134-135). The success of export-oriented industrialization defined a new arena for co-operation between the émigré regime and the native society, gradually shifted economic power from the state to the private business community, and created a new outward-looking business elite comprised primarily of owners of small and medium-sized enterprises.

A crisis of international legitimacy provided the initial impetus for the demise of authoritarianism and eventually transition to democracy. The PRC-U.S. rapprochment in the early 1970s pulled the rug from under the feet of the KMT leadership. The official one-China principle crumbled amid diplomatic setback, the loss of the UN seat to the PRC in 1971 and de-recognition by major allies throughout the 1970s. The de-recognition crisis was immediately followed by a series of peace overtures initiated by Communist China starting in 1979. In the early 1980s, the *détente* atmosphere in the Straits began to melt down the siege mentality among the public and weakened the rationale for retaining martial law. The KMT leadership felt compelled to respond to the crisis by enhancing its own democratic legitimacy at home through a steady opening of the electoral process. Opening of elections to national representative bodies was first instituted in 1972, and it was expanded in 1980 and again in 1989.[29]

---

[29]　For an narrative account of the gradual electoral opening, see Chu (1992: ch3).

Finally, in the transition to a post-Cold War era, the political and territorial integrity of many existing states was seriously challenged. In many instances, the international community was receptive to claims of rights to self-determination, autonomy or secession. At the same time, the emerging structural configuration of the Asia-Pacific security order has made more room for Taiwan's diplomatic manoeuvring as the long-term goals of China, as the major power aspirant, would be potentially in conflict with that of a defending hegemony (the United States) and a regional rivalry (Japan). These developments have evidently lifted the hopes of the pro-independence camp and shifted internal debate in favour of an independent Taiwanese statehood (Chu and Lin, 1999).

As it turned out, the structural symbiosis between party and state was as much a source of strength as a root of vulnerability for the KMT regime. As the transplanted state deepened its dependence on Taiwanese society for fiscal revenue, and supply of military conscripts and rank-and-file state personnel, the incumbent elite necessarily became more susceptible to local demand and concern. With the steady drain of American aid after the early 1960s, the incumbent elite was compelled to place more emphasis on local economic accumulation. The Nationalist government launched its military conscription in Taiwan as early as 1951, but the real reproduction crisis began to surface when most mainlander soldiers reached decommission age in the early 1960s. For the professional officer corps, large-scale replacement by native Taiwanese came much later as the military academies recruited more rigorously from the offspring of the mainlander veteran families, and the native Taiwanese consciously avoided military careers. But the trend of increasing indigenization was inevitable and accelerated over time. For the state bureaucracy, native Taiwanese accounted for 56.5% of the overall civil service and only 37.3% of the civil servants working for central government in 1959. By the end of 1991, their percentage in the overall civil service was 71% and among those working for central government, 66.2%.[30] The indigenization of the state necessarily transformed the profile of the KMT membership and eventually the outlooks of the party leadership.

Practising a functional sovereign state on Taiwan over time had by itself done more damage than anything else on the official one-China claim. When the Nationalists moved

---

[30] Civil servants include bureaucrats, public school teachers and state-owned enterprises employees. See *Statistical Bulletin of the Ministry of Civil Service*, various years.

their capital from Nanjing to Taipei in 1949, they essentially endowed Taiwan with a *de facto* sovereign status. Growing political and ideological cleavage between Taiwan and the mainland further confused a local population already disenchanted with the concept of Chinese reunification. Long-term separation across the Taiwan Straits also precipitated the assimilation of the mainlander group steadily into local society. Finally, recurring war-preparation against possible PRC aggression fostered alienation from mainland China and a shared sense of destiny between the mainlander and native Taiwanese. The jurisdictional boundaries and legal order set by a *de facto* sovereign state quietly fostered a popular aspiration for a separate statehood. Thus, the KMT's nationalistic vision was in fact undermined by the intrinsic mismatch between the *de jure* state structure and its actual practice of a sovereign state on Taiwan over more than four decades.

Another important source for the transformation of one-party authoritarianism was the inherent contradiction between the political imperative to limit electoral pluralism and the success in state-sponsored economic modernization. First, the nature and significance of the electoral mechanisms were bound to change amid rapid socio-economic transformation. They were transformed from a sideshow to the authoritarian order into a primary legitimating device. During the 1960s and 1970s, local elections steadily evolved into a major institution to assimilate emerging economic and social forces into the political system, and an indispensable vehicle for the political ascent of the native elite.

Secondly, as the legitimating function of the electoral mechanism rose, the power equation between the party leadership and local factions gradually shifted in favour of the latter. Unfortunately, the KMT could not find viable alternatives to local factions in mobilizing electoral support. A deliberate effort by Chiang Ching-kuo to replace them with young native cadres groomed by the party in the early 1970s met with stringent resistance and was eventually abandoned.[31] At the same time, the leverage of the party over local factions declined as the local administrative apparatus and quasi-state organizations were increasingly staffed by native bureaucrats affiliated with local factions. Thirdly, the social transformation brought about by the rapid industrialization and the accompanying demographic changes

---

[31] This policy backfired in the 1977 election, in which an unprecedented number of dissidents were elected to the Provincial Assembly because the defiant local factions refused to support party-nominated candidates. See Chen (1995).

tended to enhance the mobilizing capacity of opposition candidates. The opposition found a growing number of ready ears among an increasingly politically conscious and economically secured middle-class electorate and among the economic laggard groups.

By the late 1970s, a new cohort of post-war generation political opposition emerged. Unlike most of the previous independent candidates, who had no national political aims, or the vocal mainlander dissidents of the 1960s,[32] whose influence was largely confined to the intellectual circle, the new opposition established political identity as well as built electoral support on a platform emphasizing democratic reform and Taiwanese identity. This development lead to a major breakthrough in the local election of 1977, in which a loosely coordinated opposition group, *Tangwai*, literally outside the (KMT) party, made considerable gains in contesting local offices and Provincial Assembly seats. In the vigorously contested election of the Taoyuau county magistrate, a riot in Chungli stopped the KMT local officials from vote-rigging. In retrospect, the Chungli incident epitomized the beginning of a protracted demise of the authoritarian regime. The restraining of the KMT leadership in the use of coercive measures during the incident helped the opposition to overcome an important psychological threshold. Thus, the 1977 election set in motion a drive to form an island-wide alliance among the opposition candidates based on an updated belief about the vulnerability of the regime. The momentum of the opposition movement was temporarily disrupted by the arrest of some *Tangwai* leaders in the aftermath of the Kaohsiung (Formosa) Incident of December 1979. But *Tangwai* soon regrouped and renewed its drive to form a quasi-party after the 1983 supplementary legislative election. This time the opposition movement was reinforced by a mushrooming of social movements, representing all kinds of socio-economic laggard groups and newly awakened environmentalists and consumer rights activists. The social movements of the 1980s loosened the firm grip of the authoritarian state on the civil society and provided a mobilized soil in various social sectors for the political opposition to take root (Chu, 1994). Finally, on the eve of the 1986 election, a new opposition party, the Democratic Progressive Party (DPP), was declared in defiance of the official ban.

The one-party authoritarianism also suffered from its internal weakness. The KMT's power structure, like any other dictatorship-for-life, was liable to succession crises. Many

---

[32] The vocal mainlander dissidents of the 1960s were best represented by many of the associates of the *Free China Journal*. See Huang (1976).

institutional mechanisms might cease to function properly without the paramount leader. When power transferred from Chiang Kai-shek to his oldest son, Chiang Ching-kuo, in the late 1960s, the succession was initially relatively smooth as Chiang Ching-kuo had been groomed by his father for the post for well over two decades. Nevertheless, without the historical stature of his father and foreseeing the legitimacy crisis of the regime, Chiang tried to broaden his social support by recruiting more native Taiwanese to the party and state leadership and upgrading the industrialization process with largescale infrastructure projects. This culminated in his decision to nominate Lee Teng-hui, a native, as the vice-president and his official successor in March 1984. A succession crisis loomed after Chiang's deteriorating health became publicly known in 1985. During the last few years of his tenure, he initiated a series of political reforms to prevent a future deeper crisis. His decision to tolerate the forming of the DPP in 1986 and the subsequent announcement, only a week after the birth of the DPP, of his intention to lift martial law and many long-time political bans, were a watershed in Taiwan's regime transition. They essentially pushed the process of authoritarian breakdown over the point of no return.

However, the incumbent-initiated political liberalization was initially intended to be a directed political change. The KMT and the KMT-affiliated local factions still retained enormous electoral resources. In addition, the party continued to enjoy a firm grip on the organized sectors of the civil society and had under its direct control substantial financial and media resources, giving it a certain flexibility in responding to the opposition's demand for democratic reform (Lin, 1999). It was further helped by the fact that society had little divisive socio-economic cleavage which might be exploited by the opposition and translated into polarized political cleavage. This strengthened the hands of the incumbent elite in setting the limits on the scope and speed of democratic reform.

The passing Chiang Ching-kuo in January 1988 hastened the breakdown of the one-party authoritarian rule. The built-in succession mechanism put Lee Teng-hui in charge of political reform. The intra-party power struggle between the so-called mainstream and non-mainstream factions (Tien and Chu, 1994) inadvertently accelerated the trend of Taiwanization, provided the impetus for abandoning the KMT's core commitment to Chinese nationalism, partially checked the natural tendency of the entrenched incumbent elite to restrict the scope of democratic reform, and facilitated ideological accommodation with the opposition on the issue of democratic reform and national identity. On his way to power consolidation, Lee skillfully shifted the burden of defending the orthodox lines─defending the extra-constitutional arrangements amid a global wave of democratization, insisting on the one-China principle when virtually all major nations had shifted their diplomatic recognition to the PRC, and upholding a Chinese identity in the wake of a re-emergence of Taiwanese identity─to his rivalry.

The accumulation of animosity and distrust simply hardened the resolve of Lee and his allies to accelerate the trend of Taiwanization and speed up institutional reforms, especially in the direction that would effectively undermine the power base of his rivals. After the abolition of the Temporary Articles in May 1991 and three phases of KMT-directed constitutional revision in the first half of 1990s, most of the legal obstacles that hindered a normal functioning of representative democracy were removed. The December 1992 Legislative Yuan election brought in a new parliament wholly elected for the first time by the people of Taiwan. It was also the first time that the KMT formally surrendered its governing position to a democratic contest, and signalled the end of the mainlanders' dominance in national politics. Han Bei-tsun was forced to resign from the premier post after the election and, as a consequence, the non-mainstream faction was thoroughly marginalized from the power centre (Mao and Chu, 1996). From this point on, Lee enjoyed the full control of the state as well as the party apparatus. He introduced more constitutional change to move the system away from parliamentarianism to semi-presidentialism and redefine the cultural orientation of the state, from cultivating Chinese identity to endorsing the burgeoning Taiwanese consciousness.[33]

Lee has accomplished two seemingly impossible tasks. First, he engineered a graceful extrication from one-party authoritarianism, making Taiwan the only Third Wave democracy in which a quasi-Leninist party not only survived an authoritarian breakdown but capitalized on the crisis to its advantage. Secondly, he helped construct a new foundation for the legitimacy of the ROC state structure without violent internal polarization and external military intervention. Lee was able to refurbish the KMT's electoral dominance by moving the centre of electoral gravity away from representative bodies to executive offices (Chu, 1999). He was able to harness the independence zeal with a gradual defection from the one-

---

[33] In his most revealing interview with Ryōtaro Shiba, a well-known Japanese writer, in autumn 1994, Lee spoke of "the misery of being a Taiwanese," implying that Taiwan has, for hundreds of years, been ruled by different foreign regimes and never got a chance to determine its own fate. This widely-cited line came very close to a tacit endorsement for the principle of self-determination.

China principle and with a sensible alternative to the pursuit of *de jure* independence by launching a concerted diplomatic effort to join the United Nations and its related agencies since 1993 and promoting the so-called "Republic of China on Taiwan" formula that anchors on a two-China model, culminating in his announcement of "special state-to-state" relation in July 1999. Toward the end of 1990s, a new consensus on consolidating the sovereign status of the ROC on Taiwan emerged (Chu and Lin, 1999). Recurring political participation under a democratic regime helped develop a sense of collective consciousness among the people, transforming the term "Taiwan" from a geographic unit to a political community and the term "Taiwanese" from an ethnic term for native Taiwanese to a civic term for citizens of Taiwan. Most significantly, through indigenization and democratization, the society managed to transform the raison *d'être* of the state in a fundamental sense. The state was re-engineered to foster the growth of Taiwanese nationalism and to consolidate the "re-imagined community" both at home and in the international system.

III. Conclusion

Contrasting the two regime cycles. The milestones of Taiwan's political development in the 20th century are highlighted in Table 10.2. During both regime cycles, new developments in the international system as well as redirections in the policies of great powers in the region generated the most important impetus for change at all major junctures of regime evolution and transformation. Bat over time, the unintended consequence of modern state-building exerted the most profound impact on state-society relations. Initially the incumbent's state-building project was driven by the security and survival imperatives as well as the incumbent elite's nationalistic vision. But as the state became more dependent on the native society for essential resources, it faced the task of local capitalist accumulation. Towards the end of both cycles, the native society invariably gained greater access to government positions and decisions through broadened scope of citizenship and expanded avenues of interest articulation, political representation and recruitment. Also, both regimes were compelled to look for a way out of their imminent legitimacy crisis. In the case of Japanese rule, the process of regime transition did not get the chance to run its full course as it was abruptly truncated by the post-Second World War settlement. In the case of the KMT rule, the

Table 10.2 Milestones in Taiwan's Political Development (1895-1999)

Year	Major political issues	Taiwan's international status	Legal-institutional framework; government structure	Important policies	Representative bodies; opposition parties
1895	Armed resistance. Transition between social systems. Infrastructure building. Monopoly system.	Special legal zone in the Japanese Imperium.	Law No. 63. Decree of Bandit Punishment (1898). Military governor-generals.	Biological politics of Gotō Shinpei. Extensive investigations. Infrastructure building.	Government-appointed Councils.
1907 1918	Nationalization of unclaimed land. Subjugation of aborigines. Establishment of sugar industry.		Law No. 31. Decree on Police Authority.		
1921 1922 1927 1928 1930	Non-violent political movements. Competition between rice and sugar crops.		Civilian governor-generals. Military power transferred to the Taiwan Army Commander. Law No. 3.	Assimilation policy. Homeland extensionism.	Taiwan Cultural Association (1921). People's Party of Taiwan. Taiwan Communist Party. Alliance of Self Government.

(continued)

Year	Major political issues	Taiwan's international status	Legal-institutional framework; government structure	Important policies	Representative bodies; opposition parties
1934 1935 1938	Turning Taiwan into war base.		Wartime-legal system. Military governor-general.	Japanization movement. Military industrialization.	Partially elected local Councils. Limited suffrage. SNTV.
1944		Scheme to normalize Taiwan's administrative status.	Compulsory conscription applied to Taiwanese.	Wartime mobilization.	
1945 1946	Political and economic takeover in factional strifes and cultural rift.	A province of the ROC	Administrator-General. ROC constitution. The Five Powers constitutional structure.	Violent suppression of riots.	Elections for Village and Township Representatives.
1948			ROC constitution frozen by the Temporary Provisions.		Elections for County/ City Councils and County/City magistrates.
1949 1951	Settling down of the émigré regime. Cold War. US aid. Political and economic stabilization. PRC's military invasion.	De jure a province of the ROC; de facto an independent state.	Martial Law suspended. Freedom of speech and association. Party state under CKS.	Land reform (~ 1953). Four-year economic plan (1953). Encourage of Foreign Investment Regulations (1954). Repression of unyielding elites. Building of patron-client network.	
1954			Law on Police Authority revised to authorize Police intervention of civic life.		

(continued)

Year	Major political issues	Taiwan's international status	Legal-institutional framework; government structure	Important policies	Representative bodies; opposition parties
1969	End of US aid. Diplomatic isolation and legitimacy crisis.		National Security Council.	Programme of Economic and Financial Reform (1960). Economic Processing Zone (1966).	Elections for the supplementary members of the National Assembly and the Legislative Yuan.
1973	Challenge from ethnic Taiwanese.		CCK chaired the KMT (1975) and assumed presidency (1977).	Ten Major Construction Plan (1973). Taiwanization policy. The Hinchu Industrial Zone (1980).	
1979	US recognized PRC. The Formosan Incident. Upsurge of social protests.				
1986					Democratic Progressive Party.
1987	PRC's economic opening. Cross-strait interaction. Impetus of Taiwanization and democratization.		Martial law lifted.	Travel to the mainland allowed.	

(continued)

Year	Major political issues	Taiwan's international status	Legal-institutional framework; government structure	Important policies	Representative bodies; opposition parties
1988			Lee Teng-hui chaired the KMT and assumed presidency. Party formation permitted. Law on Police Authority abolished. Temporary Provisions terminated.		
1989 1990	Post-Cold War new world order. Faction-circumscribed political competition. Money politics and corruption.			National Affairs Conference (1990).	
1991		De facto recognition of the PRC through the terminations of the Temporary Provisions and Period of Mobilization.	Criminal Code Art. 100 revised.	Six Years Construction Plan.	
1992 1993				Plan to restore UN membership. Koo-Wang Talk.	Complete re-election of the Legislative Yuan. New Party.
1996 1999	PRC's military threat. Strategic alliance between the US and the PRC. Economic integration with the PRC.	Lee Teng-hui's remark on the special state-to-state relation with the PRC.	Lee Teng-hui directly elected president. Post-Lee power transition.	Lee's Taiwanization policies.	Direct presidential election.

incumbent elite exercised a graceful extrication from one-party authoritarianism with an early adoption of the Taiwanization policy and an orderly multi-phased installment of democratic reform. Finally, a step-wise consolidation and indigenization of a modern sovereign state structured the path of regime evolution and laid the material and structural foundation for the development of nationalist aspirations beyond the comprehension of the incumbent elite.

The regime cycles, despite their underlying similarities, produced substantially different outcomes in terms of the development of political society and the construction of collective identity. At the end of colonial rule, home rule remained an aspiration, not a political reality; Taiwan had not yet emerged as a self-contained political community with a distinctive political identity, and the native elite had not yet forged a coherent nationalist vision among themselves. In contrast, under KMT rule, the electoral avenue was eventually expanded to allow full representation of the island's citizens in an emerging national political system and access by the native elite to all principal public offices through open multi-party competition; Taiwan emerged as a closely bound community with a distinctive ethnic, cultural and historical identity.

The two regimes were never equal. In the first instance, the overwhelming influence of the Japanese colonial legacies to a great extent preordained the KMT regime to follow a different path of regime transformation and the mainlander elite to confront formidable local resistance to its nation-building agenda. Next, the KMT took Taiwan as a province and used direct rule, while Japan took it as a colony and used indirect rule. Also, there were significant differences in the nature and progress of indigenization and consolidation between the two externally-imposed states. The Japanese colonial state, for most of its existence, used the interstate system as a subsidiary of the modern Japanese nation-state and was never under any pressure to undertake a fully-fledged indigenization strategy, not even during the height of the Pacific War when the island colony was expected to be fully self-reliant.[34] In contrast, the transplanted Nationalist state, which was at first principally manned by the minority mainlander group, was forced to adopt a full-blown indigenization strategy as it was totally cut off from its home base, territorially confined to the island, confronted with an acute reproduction crisis in the recruitment of state and military personnel, barred from instituting

---

[34] For instance, the colonial state introduced universal conscription, a watershed event on its movement toward indigenization, as late as January 1945.

a *de jure* apartheid between the mainlander and native Taiwanese by its own notion of Chinese identity and citizenship, and steadily more dependent on successful local economic development for meeting its military and fiscal requirements. At the same time, while the sovereign status of the transplanted Nationalist state was never firmly constituted within the post-1949 interstate system, over time other sovereign states increasingly engaged Taiwan as a *de facto* sovereign state in functional if not strictly legal terms. The consequences of full indigenization of a transplanted state and the long-term practice of a functioning sovereign state were perhaps beyond the comprehension of the émigré elite. In time, the indigenization process blurred the artificial divide between the local (provincial) and national politics and thus redefined the political terrain on which the émigré and native elites engaged with one another, compelled the state to redefine the scope of citizenship in closer accordance with the *de facto* territoriality, and subtly undermined the official one-China claim while fostering popular aspiration for an independent statehood.

While the Nationalists suffered from a much more fragile international legitimacy from the very beginning, their rule was more advantageously cushioned by an elaborate party apparatus that had been firmly in place well before the island became fully industrialized. This apparatus, with its intermediary function between the state and native society, helped the incumbent elite assimilate the newly emerged socio-economic elite into the political system, controlled the scope of political contestation in electoral process, and harnessed the politicizing effect of capitalist development. However, there was a limit to the working of party apparatus in obstructing the growth of the political opposition and in retarding the emergence of a civil society amid rapid socio-economic transformation.

Taiwan at fin-de-siècle. Taiwan in the 20th century has been transformed from a loosely governed peripheral province and frontier settlement for Chinese immigrants under China's imperial administration, into a centrally administered and semi-autonomous colony under a modern Japanese state, and into a self-contained sovereign entity under a transplanted Nationalist party-state. Over the century, the people of Taiwan have also lived through a tortuous search for their collective identity. They have been enmeshed in a century-long struggle with state-sponsored cultural programmes, from "desinicization" at the early stage of colonial rule, to "Japanization" at the subsequent stage, and to "re-sinicization" under the KMT rule. Despite many inherent tensions and contradictions, in the second half of the 20th century there was a clear trend towards a growing aspiration for a separate Taiwanese identity in both cultural and political terms.

At the end of the century, Taiwanese society is moving away from a state-centric and state-dominant mode of state-society interaction. With the installation of democratic institutions, society is now able to arrange for political contest to gain control over public power and state apparatus. With the stunning defeat of the KMT in the year 2000 presidential election, the resiliency of Taiwan's new democracy has passed its last test. But the emerging consensus over national identity is by no means consolidated. Into the next century, the people of Taiwan will continue to wrestle with competing claims to their political allegiance and cultural identity. The deepening of economic interdependence between Taiwan and mainland China, the settlement of an increasingly larger number of Taiwanese businessmen and migrants in the mainland,[35] and the emergence of a Mandarin-based media industry across the Straits will certainly complicate the consolidation of Taiwanese identity. Most fundamentally, an elite-orchestrated Taiwanese nation-building project will inevitably run into a head-on collision with a state-orchestrated Chinese nationalism on the mainland, putting the security and well-being of the Taiwanese people at grave risk.

---

[35] According to the internal document of Mainland Affairs Council, it is estimated that there are currently at least 200,000 Taiwanese expatriates living in China.

第十一章

Looking for the Magic Number: The Optimal District Magnitude for Political Parties in d'Hondt PR and SNTV[*]

I. Introduction

The seat-vote relationship and the impact of district magnitude have been two themes central to the study of electoral systems. The seat-vote relationship indicates how many votes it takes to win a seat, or how many seats can be obtained given a particular vote share won by a political party. District magnitude, the number of seats to be elected in a district, is in fact a major variable in the seat-vote function. It is well known that larger district magnitude increases the proportionality of the seat-vote relationship (Taagepera and Shugart, 1989: 113), and that the seat bonus of large parties decreases as district magnitude increases (Sartori, 1968).

District magnitude is such a decisive factor that some scholars see it as the principal dimension that spans other methods of classifying electoral systems. Sartori (1968), for example, puts the single-member district system and large district proportional representation (PR) systems on the same continuum by considering their district magnitudes. Cox (1991) has suggested that plurality systems can be further distinguished by their district magnitudes, and has demonstrated the "equivalence" between the single non-transferable vote (SNTV) system and the d'Hondt PR system.[1]

Since the proportionality of electoral systems goes up with district magnitude, it is generally believed that large parties prefer smaller district magnitudes and vice versa. The

---

[*] Reprinted from [*Electoral Studies*, 22(1). Lin, Jih-wen. "Looking for the Magic Number: the Optimal District Magnitude for Political Parties in d' Hondt PR and SNTV" pp. 49-63, copyright (2003)], with kind permission of Elsevier.

[1] Not all scholars accept this continuum. Nohlen (1984b), for example, argues that plurality and PR are two incompatible principles of representation.

problem comes when one tries to be exact. How large must a party be to make the single-member district system its first preference? Parties of what size will find the ideal PR system most favorable?[2] Fundamentally, can we predict a party's ideal choice of electoral systems by knowing its size? Is a party either going to prefer the single-member district system or the ideal PR system? Are "median-sized" systems always the result of a compromise?[3]

A key to these questions lies in the optimal district magnitude for political parties of various sizes, even though many other variables also matter. Formally put, district magnitude m is optimal for a party with vote share v if these two variables render an expected seat share s that cannot be further increased by changing m. Our major task is therefore to establish a function $s(m, v)$ and examine whether a maximum exists for s.

Without doubt, efforts have been made to build a seat-vote equation containing these variables. In the next section, I first review the famous cube law that specifies a particular relationship between s, v and m. After pointing out the limits of the cube law, I propose a new model in the subsequent section. A test of the model using the electoral data in Finland and Taiwan will also be provided. I then use this seat-vote equation to find the conditions under which a maximum for s exists. On the basis of these analyses, the concluding section will address some important issues in electoral reform.

II. The Cube Law Revisited

Formulated originally to predict the seat-vote relationship in two-party elections, the cube law is perhaps the most well-known seat-vote equation. The name cube law originates from the equation $s_K/s_L = (v_K/v_L)^3$, where K and L stand for two different parties. The model

---

[2] Under the ideal PR system, the seat share equals the vole share. Such a system rarely exists in reality, but can nevertheless be the ideal system for a party.

[3] In reality, district magnitude is only one of the factors that determine seat allocation. The same district magnitude can produce different seat allocations when the division of votes or the number of candidates vary. A party calculating its optimal district magnitude can only make reasonable *assumptions* about these factors, because the election is yet to take place. This article assumes rational nomination and captures other factors by a variable λ. Even this variable can be given an exact estimate under some assumptions.

has been modified by many scholars, among which Taagepera (1986) gives the most general formulation.[4] In the Taagepera model, the seat share of party K in multi-seat PR elections will be:

$$s_K = v_K^n / \sum v_i^n, \tag{1}$$

where $n = (\log V / \log DM)^{1/M}$, V, D and M designate respectively the total number of votes, the total number of districts, and the district magnitude.

Reed (1996) has demonstrated that this model predicts the Japanese election admirably well. Apart from its empirical achievement, however, the model itself raises several problems to be discussed. First, the model is rather complicated. With x parties running, $x + 3$ variables are needed to predict a party's seat share.[5] Second, a link is missing between the cube law and some other important aspects of electoral studies. On the one hand, the cube law does not specify any behavioral assumptions because it adopts the "physics-style" approach. A theory without actors as such would invite some criticism, especially from the rational choice approach (see Reed, 1996 for example). On the other hand, the cube law does not incorporate the concept of threshold, on which numerous theoretical and statistical studies on the seat-vote relationship are based. These studies have defined the threshold of inclusion (representation) as the minimum vote share that can earn a party a seat, and the threshold of exclusion as the maximum vote share that may be insufficient to win a seat under the most unfavorable conditions (Lijphart, 1994: 25). With m seats to be elected in a district, the seat share of a party is 0 if its vote share is below the threshold of inclusion, and is at least $1/m$ if its vote share is above the threshold of exclusion. Eq. (1), however, implies that $s_K = 0$ if and only if $v_K = 0$, manifesting no threshold effect.[6]

Discussions above suggest what an improved seat-vote equation should look like. First, the calculation of expected seats should be based on behavior assumptions about the parties or candidates. Second, the model should reveal the threshold effect of electoral systems. Third, the model should employ the minimum number of variables and remain applicable

---

[4]　See also Taagepera and Shugart (1989: 156-172) for more detailed discussions.

[5]　Or $x + 2$ variables when the formula is applied to a single district ($D = 1$). Taagepera further reduces the equation into $s_K = v_K^n / [(v_K^n + (N-1)^{1-n}(1 - v_K)^n]$, where N is the effective number of parties, by assuming that party K faces $N - 1$ other parties of equal size.

[6]　This is a mathematical statement. In reality, a party still wins no seat if $v_K > 0$ but $ms_K < 0.5$ when we round off the number of seats to the nearest integer.

to the maximum number of cases. If possible, it should use variables at the district level to help achieve this goal and prevent the ecological fallacy from happening.[7] The next section attempts to build such a model, and will compare its predictive power with that of the cube law. Whether the model implies an optimal district magnitude can then be studied.

III. The Threshold Model

The following seat-vote equation embodies the preceding ideas in the most straight-forward way:

$$s_i(m, v_i) = \begin{cases} 0 & \text{if } v_1 \leq t_1 \\ 0 < s_i < 1 & \text{if} \quad t_1 < v_i < t_2 \\ 1 & \text{if } v_i \geq t_2 \end{cases} \qquad (2)$$

where s_i and v_i indicate the seat share and vote share of party i in a district of magnitude m, and t_1 and t_2 denote the threshold of inclusion and the exclusion threshold for winning all seats.[8] Accordingly, the seat share below t_1 and above t_2 is $0/m = 0$ and $m/m = 1$. With a vote share in between, a party has some chance to win $1 \leq k < m$ seat(s), creating a seat share of $0 < k/m < 1$. The particular seat-vote equation thus derived will be named the *threshold* model to characterize its foundation.

The reader should be reminded that t_2 is a generalization of what is commonly called the threshold of exclusion, above which a party is guaranteed to win one seat. We can specify the functional form of the threshold model as soon as the thresholds of inclusion and exclusion are identified. The present article will focus on electoral systems in which the exclusion threshold is $1/(m+1)$ (Grofman, 1975; Lijphart, Pintor, and Sone, 1986; Taagepera and Shugart, 1989). A notable system that has this threshold is the d'Hondt PR (Rae, Hanby, and Loosemore, 1971; Rae, 1971).[9] The single nontransferable vote (SNTV) can have the same threshold if political parties seek to maximize their expected seat share, have precise

---

[7]　Sankoff and Mellos (1972), for instance, criticize a nation-based model for tending to overlook the concentration of votes.

[8]　Henceforward, small letters are used to designate variables at the district level.

[9]　Grofman (1999: 319) suggests the same exclusion threshold for the single transferable vote.

expectations of the distribution of vote support, and can allocate their total vote equally among their nominees (Cox, 1991: 121). The parties must also nominate the optimal number of candidates to keep their votes from being wasted (Cox and Rosenbluth, 1994). For SNTV, these assumptions furnish the behavioral foundation of the threshold model and yield outcomes of seat allocation that are in equilibrium: because the seat-vote function is based on the optimal vote division, no party can move from that state and improve its electoral performance. The model to be characterized below is thus not mechanical, but founded on the premises of rational choice.

IV. The Exclusion Threshold for Winning All Seats

For a variety of electoral systems, and most notably for the d'Hondt PR, the exclusion threshold for winning k seats is $k/(m+1)$ (Rae, 1971: 193; Lijphart, 1994: 26). It can be further extended to define the exclusion threshold for winning *all* seats:

$$t_2 = \frac{m}{m+1}.$$

$$(3)$$

In a single-member district election ($m = 1$), winning half of the total votes ($t_2 = 0.5$) assures victory. The threshold approaches 1 when m becomes very large, confirming the intuition that it is more difficult for a party to monopolize all seats when district magnitude increases.

It should be emphasized that t_2 is simply the threshold across which a party takes all seats *for sure*. In reality, it may require fewer votes for a party to win all seats. However, we do not expect such a thing to happen *all* the time. The average seat share to be expected when $v < t_2$ is therefore less than 1.

V. The Inclusion Threshold

In contrast to t_2, which depends solely on district magnitude, t_1 is harder to define. Also termed the threshold of representation, t_1 is the minimum vote share necessary to earn a party its first seat, based on the most favorable condition in terms of how the other parties divide their votes (Lijphart, 1994: 25). In theory, the inclusion threshold cannot be higher than the exclusion threshold, but can be as low as 0 when all losing parties (candidates) receive no vote at all. Still, many scholars have worked on various formulae to give an estimate of the most likely threshold above which a party can win its first seat. For example, Rokkan (1968: 13) has proposed $1/(m+n-1)$ (n being the number of parties running in a district) as the threshold of inclusion for the d'Hondt PR.[10] Taagepera and Shugart (1989: 117) have picked $50\%/m$ and call it the *average threshold*. Lijphart (1994) has calculated $\dfrac{50\%}{m+1} + \dfrac{50\%}{2m}$ as the *effective threshold* and later (1997: 74) modified it to $75\%/(m+1)$.

All these thresholds are functions of district magnitude, the key variable that this article studies. They differ from each other because of the intervening variables such as the number of competitors, the distribution of vote, and nomination strategy (for SNTV). To be parsimonious but general, I define the inclusion threshold as:

$$t_1 = \lambda/m, \tag{4}$$

where λ captures all the intervening factors. Thus defined, t_2 is lowered by the decrease of λ or the increase of m. In accordance with other characterizations of the inclusion threshold, the second order derivative of m to t_1 is positive in Eq. (4). Since the inclusion threshold cannot be higher than the exclusion threshold, $0 \leq \lambda/m \leq 1/(m+1)$ and thus $0 \leq \lambda \leq m/(m+1) < 1$. It also follows that $t_1 \to 0$ as $m \to +\infty$.

While the negative impact of district magnitude on the inclusion threshold is well known, λ embodies factors that are exogenous to the electoral system, and can be estimated through empirical investigations. The value of λ can also be theoretically interesting. For instance, $\lambda = 0.5$ if we apply Rokkan's inclusion threshold and make the Duvergerian assumption that $n = m + 1$ (Reed, 1990; Cox, 1994). Still, the variance of λ does not change the prediction of s very much as long as the focus is on multiseat elections.[11] It is m that stands out as the most determining variable in the seat-vote equation.

---

[10]　The same inclusion threshold is suggested by Taagepera (1998: 406) for the district level.

[11]　In a five seat district, for example, $t_1 = 0.08$ if $\lambda = 0.4$ and $t_1 = 0.12$ if $\lambda = 0.6$. Such a shift is big enough for λ, in contrast to the small increase of t_1. In general, the impact of λ shrinks as m increases.

VI. The Seat-vote Equation

As indicated by Eq. (2), the threshold model requires that $s = 0$ when $v = t_1$, $s = 1$ when $v = t_2$, and $0 < s < 1$ when $t_1 < v < t_2$. These conditions make the commonly used logistic function inapplicable: with s as the dependent variable, the range of the logistic function is $(0, 1)$ when the domain is $[0, 1]$. The problem to be solved is therefore how to let $s(m, v)$ pass two points $(t_1, 0)$ and $(t_2, 1)$, with the two thresholds characterized as in Eqs. (3) and (4).

I take the straightforward assumption that the function connecting $(t_1, 0)$ and $(t_2, 1)$ is linear, and give two justifications. First, no study so far has demonstrated that a particular non-linear function describes the reality better. Even if it is to be used, we have no clue to determine the shape of the non-linear function. Second, a linear function is a safe approximation of whatever non-linear relationships there might be: we do know that s increases with v, even though the speed may not be constant.

On the basis of the linear assumption and the thresholds specified above, I plug in two points $(\lambda/m, 0)$ and $\left(\dfrac{m}{m+1}, 1\right)$ into a linear function $s = \alpha + \beta v$ and rewrite s as a function of m and v. The result is that, for $v \in \left(\lambda/m, \dfrac{m}{m+1}\right)$,

$$s(m, v) = \frac{\lambda m - vm^2 + \lambda - mv}{\lambda m + \lambda - m^2}. \tag{5}$$

Two properties of Eq. (5) are worth exploring. First, the negative relationship between λ and s indicates that the decrease of λ makes it easier for all parties to win their first seat. Nonetheless, since the total number of seats remains unchanged, the lowering of the inclusion threshold brings more benefit to the small parties than to the larger ones. Second, it can be shown that, for all vote shares between the two thresholds, the threshold model predicts a seat share that is never less than what a party is guaranteed to gain. To see this, suppose $v = k/(m+1)$ and demonstrate that $s(m,v) \geq k/m$. Since $s\left(m, \dfrac{k}{m+1}\right) = \dfrac{\lambda m + \lambda - mk}{\lambda m + \lambda - m^2}$ and $k \leq m$, it is easy to see that $s\left(m, \dfrac{k}{m+1}\right) - \dfrac{k}{m} \geq 0$. Therefore, although the model is built upon two thresholds, the predictions in between do not violate the basic assumptions.

With Eq. (5), we are ready to examine the relationship between m and s. As this is a complicated issue that deserves special attention, I will leave it for a separate section. Before exploring its theoretical implications, it will be helpful to inspect how well the threshold model explains the seat-vote relationship in the real world.

VII. Empirical Test for the Threshold Model

Eq. (5) cannot only be manipulated to derive the optimal district magnitude, but also used to predict a party's seat share given its vote share and the district magnitude. The discrepancy between prediction and reality then tells the fitness of the threshold model. This section selects two recent elections to fulfill this task. The first is the Finnish parliamentary election of 1999, where d'Hondt PR is used to allocate 200 seats in the 15 constituencies (average magnitude = 13.3). The second case is Taiwan's Legislative Yuan election of 1998, which employs SNTV in 29 districts for 168 seats (average magnitude = 5.8). By their variant district magnitudes and the absence of legal threshold, these two cases illuminate well the impact of district magnitude on seat allocation.[12]

To validate the threshold model, it is not enough to find an insignificant probability of the specified variables being unrelated to the dependent variable. Instead, we must demonstrate how the model, as defined by Eqs. (2) to (5), predicts the actual seat share won by major political parties in the electoral districts.[13] The method that serves this purpose is not the standard significance test, but a straightforward comparison between the actual and predicted seat shares.

In addition to the percentages of correct predictions, a scatterplot of the actual and predicted seat shares can indicate the sources of missed guesses. For instance, the threshold model underestimates the parties' seat-gaining capacities if the predicted seat shares lie below the line of a perfect prediction. To give a more exact measurement of the goodness of the fit, I calculate the bivariate correlation coefficients between the actual seat share (s_{actual}) and the predicted seat share ($s_{predicted}$). The model yields a perfect prediction if, in the equation $s_{actual} = \alpha + \beta s_{predicted}$, $\alpha = 0$, $\beta = 1$, and R-square = 1. The variance and value of these coefficients

---

[12] District magnitudes in Japan, for example, are usually less than five and thus much less variant.

[13] The purpose of the following test is to show how to operationalize the model, and that it actually works in two eases embedded in very different political environments. More cases have to be included to reduce the selection bias of the test.

disclose further the overall pattern generated by the threshold model.

The test is operationalized as follows. First, I set $\lambda = 0.5$ and hence $t_1 = 1/2m$ to make seat share determined only by district magnitude and vote share. As explained already, this value has theoretical implications and marks the median of the possible values of λ. Most important, the reader can verify by conducting the same test that a slight adjustment of λ produces almost no change of the prediction. Second, in correspondence with Eq. (2), the seat share of party i is set to be 0 if $v_i \leq 1/2m$ and 1 if $v_i \geq \dfrac{m}{m+1}$. For a party in between, its vote share in a district and the magnitude of that district are plugged into Eq. (5) to render its seat share. The seat share is then multiplied by district magnitude and rounded off to the nearest integer to find the number of seats a party is expected to gain under the threshold model. To see whether the threshold model improves the cube law, I conduct the same test using Eq. (1) and setting $D = 1$ for each district. The procedure is applied to nine parties in Finland and three parties in Taiwan in all electoral districts.[14]

Several remarks can be made about the testing results presented in Tables 11.1 and 11.2. For the Finnish case, both models predict considerably well, with the cube law model closer to the perfect fit. This is not a surprising result: the average district magnitude is much higher in Finland than in Taiwan, making $\lambda = 0.5$ an overestimation for Finland. We can measure the actual inclusion thresholds for the Finnish elections and produce a much more accurate prediction. For the Taiwanese case, it is apparent that the threshold model predicts better. Although the R-squares in both models are almost identical, coefficients in the cube law model suggest that it has underestimated the seat share of leading parties. As for why both models work better for the Finnish case, two conjectures are plausible. First, due to its higher average magnitude, the Finnish system is quite proportional and produces a predictable seat share distribution. Second, political parties competing under SNTV must solve the vote division dilemma and nominate the optimal number of candidates. The threshold model has assumed rational nomination, which can be difficult to follow sometimes and bring unnecessary loss of seats. The cube law does not even make these assumptions.

---

[14] We can of course run the same test for the other minor parties in Finland and the independent candidates in Taiwan. But the result will not be significantly changed because their vote shares are generally too low to give them any seat.

Table 11.1 Empirical Tests of the Threshold Model and the Cube Law Model, Finland 1999

	The threshold model	The cube law model
Intercept	0.08	-0.004
Slope	1.123	1.039
R-square (adjusted)	0.953	0.956
Number of cases	135	135
Number of correct predictions (%)	98 (72.6%)	115 (85.2%)

Table 11.2 Empirical Tests of the Threshold Model and the Cube Law Model, Taiwan 1999

	The threshold model	The cube law model
Intercept	0.057	0.045
Slope	0.954	0.821
R-square (adjusted)	0.719	0.704
Number of cases	83	83
Number of correct predictions (%)	60 (72.3%)	57 (68.7%)

It should be fair to conclude that the threshold model performs as successfully as the cube law by using much fewer variables. With the threshold model, a party can estimate its expected seat share in an electoral district by simply knowing its vote share. Other variables like λ can be fitted to yield a more accurate prediction, but the institutional variable m will prove to be more consequential. The threshold model is thus useful to the analysis of electoral system reform. Party i can compute the maximum of s_i as a function of m and v_i and determine its position on the selection of district magnitude. It is this issue that I now turn to.

VIII. The Optimal District Magnitude

With the threshold model affirmed by empirical test, we are ready to check whether it implies any optimal district magnitude for political parties. An alternative possibility could be that the expected seat share increases or decreases monotonically with the district magnitude, such that a party is either going to support the single-member district system or the ideal PR system, but nothing in between.[15]

The solution is a typical problem of optimization with constraints. Simply put, we are to examine the first and second order conditions of $s(m, v)$, i.e., to find the conditions under which m maximizes s given v and λ. The result is the following theorem:

THEOREM. *For $m > 1$ and $0 < s_i < 1$, $m^* = \dfrac{\lambda(1 - v_i) + \sqrt{\lambda^2(1 - v_1) - \lambda v_i^2}}{v_i - \lambda(1 - v_i)}$ maximizes $s_i(m,$*

v_i) if $\dfrac{\lambda}{1+\lambda} < v_i < \dfrac{3\lambda}{1+4\lambda}$.

The calculation is given in Appendix. In plain language, this theorem says that *a median-sized party will find a particular multi-member district its best choice*, if the median-sized parties are those with a vote share between $\dfrac{\lambda}{1+\lambda}$ and $\dfrac{3\lambda}{1+4\lambda}$. It can be demonstrated that s decreases monotonically with m when v is higher than $\dfrac{3\lambda}{1+4\lambda}$ and increases monotonically with m when v is lower than $\dfrac{\lambda}{1+\lambda}$. In the former case, a party should like the district magnitude to be as small as possible, while in the latter case the district magnitude should be as large as possible. When the size of a party is between the boundaries, $m^* > 1$ becomes its optimal district magnitude.

The theorem suggests that λ affects not only the existence and value of m^*, but also the definition of a median-sized party. As illustrated in Figure 11.1, the boundaries that define a median-sized party, to which $m^* > 1$ exists as its optimum, range between $(0, 0)$ (when $\lambda = 0$) and $(0.5, 0.6)$ (when $\lambda = 1$). Despite this variance, however, it is unlikely for λ to deviate from the median value (0.5) very much. Consider a typical case where λ should be low: suppose $m = 10$ and $t_1 = 0.05$. Since $\lambda/m = 0.05$, $\lambda = 0.5$. λ is increased to 0.6 when $t_1 = 0.06$, and lowered to 0.4 when $t_1 = 0.04$.

---

[15] In such a case, the first (partial) derivative of s to m will never be zero.

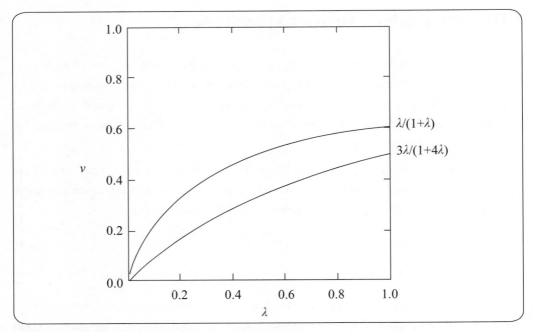

Figure 11.1 The Definitions of Median-sized Party as a Function of λ

In addition to the reasons already mentioned, other properties make $\lambda = 0.5$ a case that deserves special attention. First, $\lambda = 0.5$ implies that $t_1 = 1/2m$. This is equivalent to the "average threshold" proposed by Taagepera and Shugart. According to the authors, regardless of district magnitude, the number of parties, and the allocation rules, the average of inclusion and exclusion thresholds is in most cases close to $50\%/m = 1/2m$. Second, $\frac{\lambda}{1+\lambda} = 0.33$ and $\frac{3\lambda}{1+4\lambda} = 0.5$ when $\lambda = 0.5$. These parameters are intuitively interesting: a "dominant" party which grabs more than half of the votes will always find the single-member district its first preference, while a "small" party which gains less 1/3 of the votes should want the district magnitude to be as large as possible. The "median-sized" parties in between will find some "median-sized" district the most favorable choice.

We can thus use $\lambda = 0.5$ as a typical case to illustrate how parties of different sizes determine their optimal district magnitude (Figure 11.2). For instance, with a vote share of 0.42, the expected seat share can be maximized to 0.44 when the district magnitude is 4.06 (or 4 in terms of the nearest integer). The expected seat share will be lowered to 0.41 when m is decreased to 2, and drops drastically when m is reduced to 1.

More generally, two interesting observations can be made from the theorem and Figure 11.2. First, a district magnitude higher than the optimum is less harmful to the median-sized parties than one that is lower. The expected seat share approaches v when m increases, but suddenly slumps to 0 when m drops to 1. It is thus safer for a party with an unstable vote basis to run in a multi-member district than in a single-member district. Second, the preference of the median-sized parties over district magnitude tends to vacillate. According to the theorem, the optimal district magnitude soars from 1 to infinity when v drops from $\dfrac{3\lambda}{1+4\lambda}$ to $\dfrac{\lambda}{1+\lambda}$. As shown in Figure 11.1, the maximum difference between these two values is 0.179, when $\lambda = 0.323$. A 10% vote swing can thus change a party's preference over district magnitude

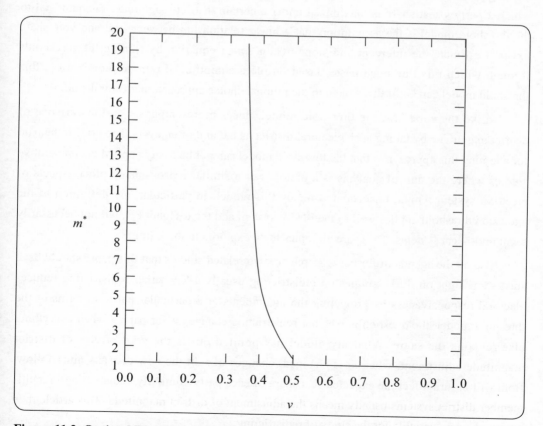

Figure 11.2 Optimal District as a Function of Vote Share ($\lambda = 0.5$)

radically. Parties declining from a dominant position (i.e., $v > 0.5$) will be especially sensitive to the adjustment of district magnitude. For smaller parties, it will be safer to stick to larger district magnitudes, even though a chance of upward swing exists.

IX. Conclusion

This article proposes a model to link three central themes in the study of electoral systems: the seat-vote relationship, the threshold of representation, and the effects of district magnitude. My strategy is simply to build a new seat-vote equation on the basis of the existing proposals of effective thresholds. Through this model, I establish the conditions under which a party's seat share is maximized under a certain district magnitude. Fundamental to the threshold model is the assumption that a linear relationship between seat and vote share exists. I estimate the intercept and slope of this linear equation by finding the thresholds through which this line must pass. Based on the assumption of rational nomination, this threshold model can be further linked to the rational choice approach in electoral studies.

Unlike the cube law, the threshold model places more emphasis on the variance of district magnitude by taking each electoral district as the unit of analysis. The price to be paid for adopting this approach is that the threshold model can not be easily applied to comparative studies where the unit of analysis is a nation. For a similar reason, many other aspects of electoral system remain unaccounted for by this model. In particular, my definition of the exclusion threshold applies well to the SNTV system and the d'Hondt PR, but not necessarily to all multi-seat systems. These are all topics to be explored in the future.

Also on the agenda of further research are two related studies that this paper should have shed some light on. First, studies on redistricting usually ask whether redistricting reduces electoral responsiveness by protecting the incumbents or a particular party. In terms of the threshold model, the question is whether redistricting changes v_i for party i when everything else remains the same. What my model has pointed out is the *dual* effects of district magnitude adjustment: when m is changed, changes of v in the new districts must follow. Both will in turn affect the expected seat share of each party. Similarly, redistricting in multi-member district systems usually means the adjustment of district magnitude. This article thus proposes a new variable for the study of redistricting.

Second, the present study addresses an important issue for the choice of electoral systems: the relationship between the size of a party and its preference over district magnitude. The findings in this article go far beyond the common perception that larger parties prefer smaller district magnitudes. I have established two thresholds above and below which a party should find the single-member district system or a pure PR system the ideal choice. For median-sized parties, a particular district magnitude is most favorable. However, these parties are likely to be uncertain about the optimal magnitude, which shifts drastically with a slight change in a party's strength. The most interesting case to be studied is the ruling party whose typical vote share is roughly 50%. It is very likely that the vote share of a party can decline from 50 to 45% in a single election, but the optimal district magnitude for this party will be lowered from 1 to 3. When there is no dominant party ($v > 50\%$) in a single-member district system, the increase of district magnitude becomes an attractive proposal for all parties. In any event, the threshold model can be used to predict the mostly likely compromise on district magnitude as soon as the typical vote share of each party becomes stable.

Appendix: Proof of the Theorem

Examining the first order condition in Eq. (5), we have:

$$\frac{\partial s}{\partial m} = \frac{-\lambda v m^2 - 2\lambda v m - \lambda v + \lambda m^2 - v m^2 + 2\lambda m}{(\lambda m + \lambda - m^2)^2} \tag{A1}$$

$$(i) = 0 \Leftrightarrow \lambda m^2 + 2\lambda m - v\lambda m^2 - 2v\lambda m - \lambda v - v m^2 = 0 \tag{A2}$$

From Eq. (A2), $v = \dfrac{\lambda m(m+2)}{(1+\lambda)m^2 + 2\lambda m + \lambda}$. I shall call v and m satisfying this condition v^* and m^*. It can be verified that $\dfrac{\partial v^*}{\partial m^*} < 0$. Since $m > 1$, it follows that $v^* < \dfrac{3\lambda}{1+4\lambda}$. Based on the same reason, $\lim\limits_{m \to +\infty} v^* = \dfrac{\lambda}{1+\lambda} < v^*$.

Now examine the second order condition:

$$\frac{\partial^2 s}{\partial m^2} = \frac{-2\lambda v m^3 + 2\lambda m^3 - 2v m^3 + 6\lambda m^2 - 6\lambda v m^2 - 6\lambda v m + 2\lambda^2}{(\lambda m + \lambda - m^2)^3} \tag{A3}$$

Since $m > 1$ and $\lambda/m \leq 1/(m+1)$, $\lambda(m+1) < m < m^2$ and thus $(\lambda m + \lambda - m^2)^3 < 0$. Therefore, Eq. (A3) < 0 if and only if

$$v < \frac{\lambda m^3 + 3\lambda m^2 + \lambda^2}{(1+\lambda)m^3 + 3\lambda m^2 + 3\lambda m}. \tag{A4}$$

It is easy to see that Eq. (A4) is always true as long as Eq. (A2) is satisfied. Accordingly, the test for the second order condition establishes that $s(v^*, m^*)$ is a local maximum with the given constraints, in so far as $\frac{\lambda}{1+\lambda} < v_i < \frac{3\lambda}{1+4\lambda}$.

With Eq. (A2), we can also write m^* as a function of v^*. From Eq. (A2), we obtain two roots for m^*. That is,

$$m^* = \frac{\lambda(1-v) \pm \sqrt{\lambda^2(1-v) - \lambda v^2}}{v - \lambda(1-v)}.$$

For these two roots, it can be demonstrated that $\frac{\lambda(1-v) - \sqrt{\lambda^2(1-v) - \lambda v^2}}{v - \lambda(1-v)} < 1$. To see this, let $L = \lambda(1-v) - \sqrt{\lambda^2(1-v) - \lambda v^2} - [v - \lambda(1-v)]$, show that $maximum\ L < 0$:

$$\frac{\partial L}{\partial v} = \frac{\lambda\sqrt{(\lambda+2v)^2} - (2+4\lambda)\sqrt{(\lambda^2(1-v) - \lambda v^2)}}{2\sqrt{\lambda^2(1-v) - \lambda v^2}} \tag{A5}$$

If we let Eq. (A5) $= \frac{\lambda}{1+\lambda}$, $v = \frac{\lambda^2 - \lambda - 2}{2} < 0$. Since $\frac{\partial v^*}{\partial m^*} > 0$, $v^* > \frac{\lambda}{1+\lambda}$, and $\frac{\lambda^2 - \lambda - 2}{2} < 0$, $maximum\ L < 0$.

Consequently, $m^* = \frac{\lambda(1-v) + \sqrt{\lambda^2(1-v) - \lambda v^2}}{v - \lambda(1-v)}$ is the only solution that meets the requirement that $m > 1$. As demonstrated already, the relationship satisfies the constraints if and only if $\frac{\lambda}{1+\lambda} < v_i < \frac{3\lambda}{1+4\lambda}$. QED.

第十二章

以輸爲贏：小黨在日本
單一選區兩票制下的參選策略[*]

壹、單一選區兩票制對小黨的影響

　　過去十多年來，結合單一選區制和比例代表制的混合選制（mixed-member electoral system）成爲一股新興潮流，爲許多國家所採用。混合選制，又可依分配席次的方法，區分爲以比例代表制政黨票爲分配基準的聯立式（mixed-member proportional system），以及分開計算單一選區和比例代表選區席次的並立式（mixed-member majoritarian system）。後者，在中文世界常被稱爲「並立式單一選區兩票制」。[1]在採取並立式單一選區兩票制的國家中，又可依照單一選區席次相對於比例代表席次所占的比重，衡量其是否傾向於多數決選（majoritarian electoral system）。觀諸近年來採取混合選制的國家，可以發現日本、台灣與南韓等東亞國家，都是由原本的「單記非讓渡投票複數選區制」（single nontransferable vote under multi-member district, SNTV-MMD）改採並立式單一選區兩票制（Reed, 2003: 22-23），而且都是以單一選區相對多數決制選出大部分的國會席次。[2]相較於其他在過去十多年進行選制變革的國家，東亞國家的特殊性在於其變遷路徑是由傾向於比例性的 SNTV-MMD，轉化爲傾向於多數決選制的並立式單一選區兩票制。[3]這種選制改革的路徑，透過對政黨體系的重塑，深刻影響了這些國家的政治發展。

---

[*] 本文曾刊登於《選舉研究》，第 15 卷第 2 期（2008 年 11 月），頁 37-66。感謝政治大學選舉研究中心《選舉研究》同意轉載。

　本論文的完成，要感謝兩位匿名審查人所提出的寶貴意見，蔡佳泓、若畑省二與吳博群在論文寫作過程中給予的協助，以及沈有忠、陳鴻鈞與吳佩眞對論文資料的蒐集整理。所有的文責，由作者自負。

[1] 所謂「並立式單一選區兩票制」是台灣一般的用法，在日本稱爲「小選區比例代表並立制」。英文之所以將並立制稱爲 mixed-member majoritarian system（多數決混合制），是爲了表示該制接近單一選區制；聯立式在英文稱爲 mixed-member proportional system（比例性混合制），乃是要彰顯該制以政黨票來等比例地分配席次。關於混合選制的名稱與意涵，請參考 Shugart 與 Wattenberg（2001: 13-17）。

[2] 韓國一直到最近兩次國會選舉才改採單一選區兩票制。之前雖然採行混合制，但選民只能投一票。

[3] Reilly（2007b）認爲，亞洲國家的選制改革大部分都有這樣的特性。日本、台灣與南韓的案例，尤其明顯。

選舉制度影響政黨體系，是學界的共識。所以，傾向於多數決選制的混合制究竟會形塑何種政黨體系，成為一個重要議題。一個直觀的看法是，並立式單一選區兩票制中單一選區席次所占的比例越重，小黨越難贏得國會席次。法國學者 Maurice Duverger 很早就提出關於選舉制度的「杜弗傑法則」（Duverger's law），認為單一選區相對多數決制傾向促成兩黨制。他後來又延伸出「杜弗傑假說」（Duverger's hypothesis），認為比例代表制對小黨較為有利（Duverger, 1963: 217, 1972: 23-32）。其他學者亦提出類似意見（Lijphart, 1999b: 165），或更進一步主張選區的應選名額越小，對小黨越不利（Sartori, 1968; Taagepera and Shugart, 1989: 113）。[4] 所以，傾向於多數決選制的混合制不利小黨，似乎是難以避免的結果。

然而，混合選制和純粹的單一選區制畢竟有本質上的差異。[5] 即使混合選制是以單一選區制為主，小黨還是有可能透過比例代表制獲得一定的席次。要得知小黨如何在傾向於多數決選制的並立式單一選區兩票制下贏取席次，日本是相當值得探究的案例。日本的混合選制與台灣及南韓類似，大部分的席次由單一選區選出。日本迄今舉行過四次單一選區兩票制的眾議院選舉，在 1996 年的大選中，500 個議席分別以單一選區相對多數決選出 300 席，以比例代表制選出 200 席；其後國會席次減為 480 席，單一選區仍維持 300 席，比重為 62.5%。[6] 單一選區雖然占了這麼大的比重，日本的小黨仍能獲得一定的國會席次。以日本眾議院的有效政黨數（effective number of legislative parties）來看，四次選舉之後分別是 2.94、3.18、2.56 與 2.23，顯現小黨在國會占有一定比例的席次。[7] 日本選舉累積了豐富的資料，使我們可以探討小黨如何在偏重單一選區制的混合選制下贏得國會席次。

在並立式單一選區兩票制下，小黨獲得比例代表席次的機率遠高於在單一選區制中勝選。然而，日本的小黨不僅參與比例代表的競爭，更在許多單一選區參選。如果小黨的目的在於獲取比例代表制的政黨票，為何要參與單一選區的選舉？許多研究發現，小黨在區域選舉的得票率和其比例代表區的得票率具有很高的相關性（Cox and Schoppa,

---

[4]　政黨體系當然也受到其他因素的影響。例如，社會分歧（social cleavage）的面向越多，政黨的數目通常也越多（Amorim Neto and Cox, 1997; Lijphart, 1999b: 87-89; Ordeshook and Shvetsova, 1994）；從經驗上來看，情況也是如此（Moser, 1999）。不過，當我們研究對象是同一個國家時，社會分歧的結構已經固定，因而能比較不同選舉制度對政黨體系的影響。

[5]　除了並立制和聯立制，混合選制還包含其他的分類方式。請參閱 Massicotte 與 Blais（1999）；Shugart 與 Wattenberg（2001）。

[6]　大部分採取並立式單一選區兩票制的國家，兩種選制所占比重相差不大，請參閱 Shugart 與 Wattenberg（2001: 20-21）。所以，台灣和日本是少數以單一選區制為主的國家。

[7]　令 S_i 為 i 黨在國會所占席次的比例，則有效國會政黨數為 $1/\sum S_i^2$。

2002; Ferrara and Herron, 2005; Herron and Nishikawa, 2001; リード，2003；Reed and Thies, 2001: 385-386; 水崎節文、森裕城，1998），所以小黨是否參與單一選區選舉似乎與其區域實力有關。然而，觀察這些區域選舉，卻可發現小黨得票離當選仍有相當距離，並和其比例代表區的得票有一段差距。小黨選擇參與單一選區的競爭，究竟要達成什麼目的？單一選區和比例代表制的得票差，又具有何種意涵？小黨會在所有的單一選區參與選舉嗎？如果答案爲否，哪些單一選區較能吸引小黨參選？

有些理論認爲，單一選區選舉和比例代表制選舉之間有互動關係，所以政黨參選區域選舉是爲了拉抬比例代表制的得票。這就是所謂的「感染效果」（contamination effects）理論。本文的目的，在於解釋這套理論背後的機制，並藉此探討一個感染理論尚未能妥善回答的問題：小黨參與單一選區選舉，是否具有選擇性？本文主要的論點爲：小黨的確可以透過參與單一選區的選舉，鞏固甚至提高其比例代表制的政黨票，但這並不代表小黨會參與所有單一選區的競爭。小黨之所以能藉著參與單一選區選舉來提升比例代表得票，乃因其能反向操作 Duverger 所說的策略性投票：如果某小黨參與單一選區競爭，某些選民可能因爲策略考量而不會投票給這個政黨，所以產生補償心理，進而更願意將政黨票投給這個小黨。這是一種「以輸爲贏」的保險策略。不過，小黨實力可能有地域之別，策略選民的數量也因選區而異，所以小黨應該選擇其實力較強，但策略選民數目也較多的選區參選，方能獲得最大參選效益。所以，策略選民密度越高的區域，小黨越有動機參與單一選區的競爭，進而導致參選人數的增加。小黨的參選策略，仍有許多有待分析的問題，是本文可以補充既有文獻之處。透過這個問題的答案，我們更能瞭解小黨如何在並立式單一選區兩票制下贏得國會席次。

要驗證上述「補償心理」假說，我們可以檢視和策略投票有關的因素是否影響參與單一選區選舉的候選人數目。如果答案是肯定的，就表示小黨是否參與單一選區選舉不單只是反映其選區的實力，更與策略投票者的聚集度有關。爲了驗證這個理論，本文將分析日本過去四次單一選區兩票制選舉所有的選區資料。次節先探討相關研究，並說明本文的貢獻。第參節，將闡明前述理論，並說明資料來源與統計模型。第肆節爲實證分析，將從不同面向說明策略投票如何影響單一選區選舉參選者的數目。結論部分，將比較日本與台灣的差別，指出台灣以全國作爲唯一的比例代表區，是小黨難以存活的主因之一。

貳、單一選區制與比例代表制在混合選制下的互動

　　所謂的混合選制，是指同時使用單一選區制與比例代表制的選舉制度。其中的並立制，是指分別用兩種選制選出當選者，獨立計算當選席次（王業立，2001b：32-38）。關於並立選制如何影響有效參選人數以及有效政黨數，一種估計方式是假設單一選區與比例代表互不影響，並分別計算兩制可能導致的後果再予以加總（盛治仁，2006；謝相慶，1999）。然而，許多研究指出，混合選制不單純只是單一選區制和比例代表制的折衷，對有效參選者的影響也不僅是兩制的加總。混合制之下的單一選區和比例代表，具有相互影響的「感染效果」（Ferrara and Herron, 2005; Gschwend, 2007; Herron, 2002; Herron and Nishikawa, 2001; Nishikawa and Herron, 2004）。[8] 在此效果下，政黨的提名必須考量兩種選制的互動，兩種選制下的得票率也有關連，所以我們無法把單一選區和比例代表的競爭切開來觀察。要瞭解小黨透過何種參選策略來擴大其在混合選制下的生存空間，我們必須對此一選制下的互動效果有更深入的瞭解。

　　產生「感染效果」的原因有很多種。例如，政黨基於選制因素而進行的結盟，即可能使兩種選制的結果產生互動。由於混合制包含了兩種選制，政黨可以建立協議，某些政黨參選區域選舉，其他政黨參與比例代表制選舉，使結盟政黨共蒙其利。另一種政黨結盟的形式，是政黨聯合提名，但讓不同政黨在不同單一選區參選，以免分散票源。政黨結盟，一方面避免政黨在區域選舉衝突，另一方面卻可利用參選區域選舉而提升其政黨票，所以使政黨在單一選區得票和比例代表選區得票出現正向關係。不過，若要從結盟理論來探討小黨在單一選區兩票制下的參選策略，還要回答一個根本的問題：政黨結盟，究竟是不是普遍存在的現象？對小黨而言，參與政黨結盟是否一定能提升其席次？Ferrara 與 Herron（2005）指出，混合選制越是傾向於多數決制，越會促使政黨進行選前結盟。然而，觀察實際的情況，卻可以發現日本的選前政黨結盟和這樣的預期有若干差距。以 1996 年的眾議院大選為例，根據讀賣新聞的調查，在 300 個單一選區中，只有 80 個選區出現政黨結盟（比率為 26.7%），其類型共有 13 種，但大部分都涉及兩大黨（自民黨、新進黨）和其他政黨的結盟；小黨間的結盟，只有三種（読売新聞社，1999：35）。在大黨與小黨的結盟模式中，大黨其實在絕大多數的單一選區都有提名，所以這種結盟其實是大黨不希望小黨參選，以免分散票源。可以想像，在許多單一選區，參與選舉的小黨是沒有進行政黨結盟的。其實，小黨不論是否與它黨結盟，大多只

8　對於政黨體系不穩定的國家而言，選舉制度的比例性和政黨體系更是欠缺清楚的關連（Moser, 1999; Moser and Scheiner, 2004）。

會參與部分單一選區的選舉。所以，問題的核心在於小黨是否能選擇適當的選區參選，以提升其席次。既有文獻，對此問題很少著墨。

另一個可能導致「感染效果」的原因，在於日本特殊的「重複提名制」（dual candidacy）以及隨之而來的「惜敗率」設計。所謂重複提名，是指政黨可以讓單一選區的候選人也出現在比例代表的名單上。在日本，政黨可以將好幾個人放在比例代表名單上的同一個順位。如果這些人也參與了單一選區的選舉但是都落選，而且無法全部分得比例代表的席次，則與單一選區當選人票數比率越接近的候選人越優先分配比例代表的席次。如果有人因此分配到比例代表席次，等於是「敗部復活」而當選。所謂惜敗率，就是重複參選者在單一選區得票與該選區勝選者得票的比率。這樣的制度設計，使某些候選人有很強的動機同時參與兩種選舉，在區域的部分，即使不能勝選還是要衝高得票率。此一制度，也使某些選民願意投票給難以在區域選區勝選的候選人，以增加其獲得比例代表席次的機會。重複提名和惜敗率的制度設計，其實鼓勵小黨進行另一種「犧牲打」的參選策略：小黨提名某些比例代表制名單上的候選人參與單一選區選舉，明知其勝選無望，卻可藉區域候選人打開政黨知名度，並藉此增進其比例代表的政黨得票。在重複提名的單一選區，選民比較可能投票給小黨的候選人；在沒有重複提名的選區，選民比較可能犧牲小黨的候選人。無論是哪種情況，選民都要進行策略投票的計算。所以，選擇策略選民聚集度比較高的選區參選，是小黨的上策。

感染效果，對兩種選制的選舉結果也有所影響。例如，小黨若是爲了要衝高比例代表制的選票而參選區域代表，可能導致某些選區參選人數增加，進而降低區域當選者的當選票數。如果某政黨採取重複提名策略，可能使其政黨比例代表的名單具有濃厚的區域色彩，進而排除其他類型的候選人。由此可知，不論單一選區制與比例代表制如何相互「感染」，我們都難以將兩種選制下的政黨參選策略或選民投票行爲分開處理。以政黨的參選策略爲例，Reed（2003）曾對 1996 和 2000 年日本眾議院大選進行跨時分析，結果發現政黨是否參與小選區的選舉，會影響其比例代表制的選票。有學者甚至認爲，混合制鼓勵小黨參選，容易形成多黨制，使該制下單一選區的有效候選人數介於純粹的單一選區制和比例代表制之間（Nishikawa and Herron, 2004: 762-766）。

兩種選制在混合制下的互動性，不只影響政黨體系，還涉及複雜的分裂投票（split-ticket voting）問題。關於分裂投票，許多理論是建立在採用同樣制度的兩種選舉上，例如以「制衡執政者」的概念來解釋美國期中選舉分裂投票的研究（Alesina and Rosenthal, 1995），比較的基準就是同樣爲總統選舉和國會選舉所採用的單一選區相對多數決制。在台灣，分裂投票的比較對象往往是同時舉行，但選制不同的選舉，例如採

用單一選區相對多數決制的縣市長選舉，和使用SNTV-MMD的縣市議員選舉。[9]相較之下，混合制卻是同一場選舉採行不一樣的選舉制度。在混合制之下，雖然單一選區制比較容易誘發策略性投票，競選者也比較不容易採取激進的競選策略，但投票和競選行為不完全只受到單一選區制的影響。[10]例如，混合制不但會增加單一選區的參選者數目並影響競選者的競選策略，也可能因為許多政黨同時參與比例代表制的選舉，而使競選趨於離心（centrifugal）（Cox and Schoppa, 2002）。更重要的問題，在於如何區別混合制之下的分裂投票和策略性投票。從總體資料上來看，兩者都表現在同一區域兩種選制得票數的差距上。分裂投票理論可將這種差距歸因於選民的偏好，策略投票理論則可從「選票效用極大化」的假設解釋同一個現象。要釐清兩者的關係，最好能以個體資料探討選民偏好與投票行為的關係。如果暫時沒有這種資料，我們可以間接以總體資料觀察與策略性投票有關的變數，是否能解釋同一政黨在兩種選制下得票差距。如果答案是肯定的，即表示小黨可以選擇策略選民比較多的地方參選，以增加其比例代表的席次。

綜合以上的分析可知，混合選制下的單一選區制和比例代表制具有複雜的互動關係。不論形成這種互動關係的原因是政黨結盟、重複提名還是策略投票，小黨都不太可能參與所有單一選區的選舉，而須選擇選民自主性較高、策略選民比較多的選區參選，才能鞏固其比例代表制的政黨選票。既有研究已經發現，在日本的單一選區兩票制之下，某些選民有策略性投票的行為（Reed, 1999; 王鼎銘等，2004；黃紀、王鼎銘、郭銘峰，2005）。本文延伸這個發現，試圖辨認策略選民較多的所在地，並以此解釋小黨的參選策略。這樣的研究設計，同時觸及混合制之下兩種選制的互動、策略性投票、分裂投票、小黨的參選策略等議題，對既有文獻有一定的補充作用。本文也將說明，小黨能否實現此種「以輸為贏」的策略，和比例代表席次的選區劃分有關。比例代表區越是和單一選區接近，小黨越能操作此種策略並提升其政黨票；反之，如果比例區的數目少，甚至只有一個，則小黨即使能衝高政黨票，仍很可能因為選票被「稀釋」到全國而無法贏得任何席次。

---

[9] 關於台灣的分裂投票研究，請參考洪永泰（1995）及黃紀、張益超（2001）；關於分裂投票的研究方法，請見黃紀（2001）。

[10] 混合制之下的策略投票，不一定是犧牲小黨。Ferrara（2004）即指出，在聯立式的混合選制下，策略選民有可能在比例代表選舉中犧牲大黨的名單。

參、理論模型與其經驗意涵

　　爲了更清楚說明本文的理論內涵與待證假設，我們需要界定一些重要的概念。首先，本文所指稱的小黨，是指候選人在單一選區中支持度排名在第二位以下的政黨。假設某單一選區共有 n 位候選人參選，而所有選民都對這些候選人有清楚的偏好。我們可以將這 n 位候選人的支持度排序寫成 $V = (v_1, v_2, v_3, ...v_n)$，$v_1 \geq v_2 \geq v_3... \geq v_n$，$\Sigma v_i = 1$。[11] 根據杜弗傑法則，某些選民爲了極大化其選票的效用，會放棄沒有當選希望的候選人，而將選票集中在前兩位候選人之一上。依此理，我們可以將策略性投票之後的選票排序寫爲 $W = (w_1, w_2, w_3, ...w_n)$，$\sum w_i = 1$。令 k 爲 W 之排序，則 $k \leq 2$ 時 $w_k \geq v_k$；當 $k > 2$ 時 $w_k \leq v_k$。所謂小黨，就是指單一選區候選人排在 $k > 2$ 以下的政黨。對小黨 i 而言，v_i 與 w_i 分別代表其支持者中非策略選民與策略選民所占的比例，所以 $w_i - v_i \leq 0$ 即爲該黨在單一選區因爲策略投票所遭受的損失。在並立式混合選制之下，該黨可以吸引策略選民的政黨票，以補償這個損失。

　　混合選制下的策略選民，因爲考量選票效用而不會在單一選區中投票給小黨，但在比例代表制中則可能支持小黨。相較於策略選民對選票效用的考量，非策略選民之所以會不論成敗地投票給其最偏好的候選人，有可能是因爲重複提名制使然，但更有可能是爲了要回報得自這些候選人的恩惠（patronage）。對於小黨而言，參選的主要目的應該是爭取策略選民的政黨票，所以必須估算選區內有多少策略選民，再決定是否在單一選區參選。如果某個單一選區大部分的選民都不會進行策略投票（例如受到恩庇體系的影響），參選是不合算的。反之，選區內的策略選民越多，小黨越容易得利，參選選舉的小黨也應該越多。

　　問題是，小黨如果不參與單一選區的選舉，難道就拿不到策略選民的政黨票嗎？關鍵在於策略選民如何形成其偏好，以及如何做出棄保的決定。選民若能具備關於候選人支持度的清楚排序，是因爲他們對於候選人已經形成固定的偏好排序，並享有關於勝選機率的完全訊息。若然，小黨參選單一選舉的效用的確很低，因爲選民的政黨偏好會反映在其政黨票的投票抉擇上。然而，現實上選民的偏好和訊息幾乎不可能是充分的。策略選民往往需要從政黨得到一些訊號，才能做出合理的投票抉擇。對參選政黨而言，如何傳遞對其有利的訊號給選民，則是致勝的關鍵。小黨，特別是剛成立的小黨，很難只靠黨綱或理念來爭取選民支持。在此意義下，參選單一選區，等於是在打政黨廣告，形

11　我們不能假定非策略選民一定是誠實的偏好表達者。在日本的重複提名制之下，非策略性選民可能是爲了要讓其支持之候選人贏得比例代表席次而在區域選舉投票給這位候選人。

塑選民的偏好排序。此外，如果一個小黨不參與單一選區的選舉，選民可能根本無法估量其獲勝的機率，遑論策略性地「放棄」這個政黨。因此，如果某個小黨參與單一選區的選舉，策略選民就有可能認識其存在；如果這些選民在單一選區放棄這個政黨的候選人，就更有可能在比例區投票給這個政黨。在此情況下，策略選民的比例越高，小黨參與單一選區選舉的動機就越強（雖然其相對利益也越低）。

所以，我們可以將影響小黨參選策略的主要因素，歸納爲以下的命題：

當策略選民對於候選人偏好與候選人當選機率的訊息不充分時，小黨有動機參與單一選區選舉，以提升策略選民將政黨票投給該黨的機率，而選區內策略選民所占比例越高，參選的候選人越多。

要估算選區內策略選民的數目，最直接的方法是針對選民進行調查，瞭解其候選人偏好與投票抉擇。不過，要針對所有的選區取得這樣的資料，幾乎是不太可能的事情。若無此資料，我們仍可根據某些總體資料，進行間接的推論。首先，選民是否會策略投票，與選區的某些集體特性有關。一般文獻較少從集體行動的角度來分析策略投票，但策略投票要發生效果，必須要有足夠的選民採取同樣的行動。所以，選民是否會策略投票，不但受到個人偏好和訊息的影響，也和他們覺得其他人會不會策略投票有關。選區若有實力很強而選票不易流失的參選者，等於是給策略選民一個訊號，表示策略投票的效果不大；當大多數選民有同樣的感覺時，策略投票的人數當然很少。基於此理，以下情況是不利策略投票的：第一，領先者當選的次數越多（越資深），越表示其掌握其他候選人所欠缺的當選條件；其次，領先者如果來自政治世家，即表示其擁有較強的社會連結，許多選民可能接受過該家族的恩惠。反之，都市化程度越高的區域，選民越不受傳統社會網絡或恩庇體系的包圍，也越能自主投票，所以都市選民比較容易預測彼此會策略投票。這些訊息都是公開的，所以容易成爲選民判斷策略投票效用的重要線索。

除了上述變項，我們還可以根據投票紀錄，建構與策略投票難易度相關的變項。根據杜弗傑法則，在單一選區制之下，選票會向支持度第一、二名的候選人集中。在訊息不充分的狀況下，選民雖然不見得辨認得出前兩名的候選人，但選票仍會向較有當選希望的候選人集中。爲瞭解選區整體的選票轉移現象，我們可以比較實際參選人數（the actual number of candidates）和有效參選人數（the effective number of candidates）的差別。[12] 有效候選人是以候選人的得票率來計算，所以兩者差距越大，越表示選票向特定候選人集中。我們可以將實際參選人數除以有效候選人數，並將這個數值定義爲 AE 率

---

[12] 定義 V_i 爲 i 候選人的得票率，則有效候選人數的公式是 $1/\Sigma V_i^2$。選票越集中在少數候選人上，有效候選人數越低。

（the ratio of the actual to the effective numbers of candidates）。AE 率越大，越表示選票集中在少數候選人上，也顯示選區有較多的策略選民。[13] 所以，我們預期 AE 率和實際參選人數具有正的相關性。針對這種相關性，一個可能的疑問是：有效候選人數和實際候選人數可能具有正向的關係，所以 AE 率和實際候選人數的相關，是否只是變項本身的相關，而和策略投票無關？有效候選人數和實際候選人數是否有正相關，有待資料檢驗，但即使這種正相關存在，AE 率卻不見得和參選人數有明顯的關係，兩者甚至還可能存在負的關係。[14] 我們並沒有充分的證據顯示這兩個變項的正相關，是變項本身的特性所造成的。

此外，如果小黨參與單一選區選舉是爲了增加其比例代表區的席次，我們還可以考慮另一個自變項：比例區的應選名額。日本的比例代表席次劃分爲 11 個選區選出，每個選區的應選名額不一。[15] 比例區的應選名額越高，排除門檻（threshold of exclusion）就越低，小黨也越容易分得席次。所以，應選名額越高的比例區，小黨參與其中單一選區競爭的效益越強，也越容易導致參與單一選區選舉人數的增加。

總結以上的分析可知，選民的策略投票動機越強、比例代表區的排除門檻越低，小黨越願意參與單一選區的選舉，參選的小黨數目也越多。在我們進行實證檢驗之前，還要回答一個問題：這樣的理論有沒有內在矛盾？單一選區參選人數的增加，是否會降低小黨「以輸爲贏」策略的效果？小黨想從策略選民吸納的政黨票，會不會因爲分食者眾而變得稀少？若然，我們還能不能以參選人數爲依變項？策略選民人數有限，參選人數增多的確可能減弱小黨的參選誘因。不過，如果小黨參選單一選區選舉的眞正目標在於提升比例代表區的政黨票，參選人數的多寡應該不會影響小黨的策略選擇。原因在於「以輸爲贏」是小黨的上策（dominant strategy）：即使小黨所能吸納的補償性政黨票

---

[13] 另一個可能的指標，是 Cox（1997: 85）提出的 SF 率（the ratio of the second to the first loser's vote total），亦即落選第二名得票數除上落選第一名得票數的比率。Cox 認爲，如果杜弗傑法則是正確的，那麼落選第二名應該沒有選票，所以 SF 率應該等於 0。要得到這個推論，必須假設所有選民都有關於候選人的充分訊息。事實上，選民的訊息不可能是充分的。再者，如果候選人超過三人，策略性投票不見得會讓落選第二名完全沒有選票。以日本的眾議院選舉而言，共產黨幾乎在所有的單一選區參選，更使我們不能只透過落選第一、二名的得票來測量策略性投票的程度。

[14] 舉個最極端的例子，變項 x 和 $x-k, x>k>0$ 有完全的正線性相關，但兩者比率 $x/(x-k)$ 和 x 之間卻有非線性的關係，而且 $x/(x-k)$ 越大 x 就越小。由於實際候選人數不可能小於有效候選人數，我們可以把 x 想像成前者，把 $x-k$ 想像成後者。所以，認爲 AE 率會製造出和實際候選人數的正相關，並不正確。

[15] 這 11 個比例代表區是以地域劃分的，包括：北海道、東北、北關東、南關東、東京都、北陸信越、東海、近畿、中國、四國、九州。

隨著參選人數的增加而減少，只要政黨票的利益超過競選成本，參選仍比不參選好。如果參選者的數目多到使某些小黨的利益低於成本，這個小黨自然會退出選舉。所以，實際上存在的參選者數是一個均衡狀態。

　　為了檢證關於小黨參選策略的理論，本文以「單一選區的參選人數」為依變項，以和策略選民比重有關的因素為主要的解釋變項。分析的對象是日本採用單一選區兩票制的四次眾議院大選，舉行時間分別在 1996、2000、2003 與 2005 年。統計模型以單一選區為分析單位，單位數共計 1,200 個。資料來源如下：

1. 以選區為單位之選舉結果：日本選舉結果的正式公告，是由該國總務省自治行政局選舉部所發布，目前可從該部網站取得 2003 與 2005 年選區層次的資料（日本總務省自治行政局選舉部，2007）。1996 與 2000 年的選舉資料，分別採用讀売新聞社（1999）與宮川隆義（2000）編纂的資料（詳參考文獻）。為確保資料的正確，四筆資料都與朝日新聞刊載的資料對照，並確定無誤。朝日新聞的資料來自 1996 年 10 月 21 日、2000 年 6 月 26 日、2003 年 11 月 10 日與 2005 年 9 月 12 日。這些資料包括所有參選人之姓名、黨籍、當選次數與選票數等。

2. 世襲當選人：名單由上田修一的網站取得（上田修一，2006）。[16]

3. 都市化程度：所謂的都市化程度，是以各單一選區人口集中地區的人口比例（DID 人口比）所推算出來的。在日本，這是衡量都市化程度的主要指標，而 DID 人口比又是根據日本總務省統計局所出版的國勢調查（普查）紀錄來計算。[17] 在四次選舉中，有五個選區經歷重劃並改變名稱。這些選區的都市化指標，是以該當選區自治體在 2000 年所屬選區作為界定標準。

4. 比例代表區資料：同選區資料，由總務省自治行政局選舉部、讀売新聞社（1999）、宮川隆義（2000）與各選舉年朝日新聞取得，包括比例區的應選名額、政黨得票率與當選人名單等。

根據這些資料，界定以下變數：

1. 參選人數：每個單一選區的參選人數。

2. 世襲當選人：當選者是否出身政治世家；1 表示是，0 表示不是。

---

[16] 這個網站還包括所有世襲當選人在日本新選制下的競選紀錄。

[17] 本資料由東京大學先端科學研究技術研究中心（東京大学先端科学技術研究センター）菅原研究室的菅原琢先生所蒐集計算而來（菅原琢，2004）。

3. 當選次數：當選者曾當選國會議員之次數。[18]

4. AE 率：實際參選人數除以有效候選人數的比率。

5. 都市化：數值 1、2、3、4、5，數字越大表示選區的都市化程度越高。

6. 比例區席次：單一選區所屬比例區之平均應選名額。

根據之前的分析，與參選人數具有負向關係的自變項應該包括世襲當選人的存在以及當選者的當選次數；和參選人數具有正向關係的變項則有 AE 率、都市化程度以及比例代表區席次。

爲選擇妥當的統計方法來驗證上述假說，我們應先檢視資料的性質。絕大多數的選區都出現在四次選舉中，某些候選人也參加過一次以上的選舉，但由於我們並不假設選舉和選舉之間具有關連，所以可以把每次選舉當成獨立的事件，而無須將之視爲時間序列的資料。[19] 所以，這 1,200 個分析單位，可以看成合併橫斷面（pooled cross-sectional）的資料。作爲依變項的參選人數，最小值是 1，最大值在理論上是無限大，所以不能將其看作一般的常態分布。爲考慮依變項分布的特性，我們將以 1 爲變項左側的分界，使用「截尾式迴歸法」（truncated regression）來進行分析。該方法假設依變項的分布是截尾式的常態分布，以最大概似估計（maximum likelihood estimation）來估計自變項的相關性。我們之所以選擇這個統計模型，是因爲一般最小平方法（ordinary least square, OLS）線性迴歸的依變項數值範圍趨近無限值，而截尾式迴歸的依變項的分布只存在於某個數值範圍內。如果我們用 OLS 線性迴歸來分析截尾式的依變項，會造成殘差項的期望值不等於 0，並可能和自變項相關，不但降低估計值的一致性，也違反了 OLS 線性迴歸的假定。

肆、影響小黨參選的因素

在進行統計分析之前，我們先描述一些與選舉有關的重要資料，以從實質面來觀察日本這四場單一選區兩票制選舉的大致輪廓。首先說明依變項的分布狀況。以四次單一選區參選人數的分布來觀察，中位數（median）是 3，眾數（mode）也是 3。由於共

---

[18] 資深國會議員不一定能選贏，參選的資深議員也可能超過一位。不過，每個選區的情況不同，我們將目標鎖定在當選者的當選次數，是爲了便於跨選區的比較。

[19] 某些理論認爲選舉之間是有關係的。例如，某些高票落者，若參與次回選舉，則當選機率會增高。由於本文是以選區爲分析單位，暫時無須考慮此一問題。

產黨幾乎在每個單一選區參選，這個結果並不令人意外。然而，參選人數的平均數卻是 3.73，表示部分選區的參選人數遠超過 3。本文的目的，就是要瞭解這些選區為何能吸引小黨參選。其次，我們要清楚辨認哪些政黨是小黨。我們若將小黨定義為在某選區內支持度排名在第二名以下的政黨，全國層次的小黨不見得是選區層次的小黨。一種最極端的狀況，是全國性的小黨在地方是大黨，而全國性的大黨在地方則有大有小。為瞭解日本眾議院選舉的情況，表 12.1 描述四次大選參選政黨的提名人數。依該表所示，作為最大政黨的自由民主黨（自民黨），在絕大多數的單一選區都有提名候選人，作為第二大政黨的新進黨（1996 年）或民主黨（其餘三次選舉），在單一選區的提名率則逐漸提升，和自民黨不相上下。比較有趣的是日本共產黨，幾乎在所有的單一選區參選。[20] 除了前述政黨，其他政黨的提名則具有選擇性，在單一選區的提名比例有高有低，但都沒有超過一半。

為瞭解哪些政黨是所謂的小黨，表 12.2 根據得票率來計算這些政黨在選區中的排名。結果顯示，比較知名的全國性大黨，和其他政黨果然有所差別。以自民黨為例，大部分的提名人都得到最高票，而排名第二以下的候選人則相對較少。曾經是第二大黨的新進黨，在 1996 年也大多擠進前兩名。從 2000 年起爬升到第二大黨的民主黨，在大部分的選區也都維持在前兩名，不過勝選率比自民黨低了很多。其他政黨，幾乎都排名在第二名以下。比較特殊的是公明黨，勝選率非常高，在最近兩次選舉甚至接近全勝，顯示該黨在全國雖小，但在其票倉選區則是大黨。[21] 在無黨籍候選人（無所屬）方面，部分參選者具有當選實力，但落選者也不少。整體而言，大部分的政黨在全國和地方都是小黨。撇開共產黨不計，這些小黨包括民主黨（1996 年）、自由聯合、社會民主黨、先驅新黨（新党さきがけ，1996 年）、自由黨（2000 年）、保守黨（2000 年）、保守新黨（2003 年），以及一些更小的黨派。

這麼多政黨參與單一選區的選舉，對選舉結果有沒有影響？圖 12.1 的直方圖描繪了這 1,200 個選區當選者的得票率。這個圖形近似常態分布，平均值非常接近 50%，而

---

[20] 日本共產黨歷來的選舉方針，都是在所有的單一選區參選。在日本的小黨中，這個方針是獨特的，卻也讓該黨付出一定的代價。2007 年 9 月該黨中央委員會會議決議要調整這個方針，改以比例代表區為該黨的主要目標，單一選區則只提名較有實力的候選人。如此一來，日本共產黨和其他小黨就很類似了。日本共產黨網站，對此調整有所說明：「選挙方針見直し、なぜ？」（日本共産党中央委員会，2007）。

[21] 公明黨（英文名稱為 New Komeito 或 New Clean Government Party）於 1964 年創立，和宗教團體創價學會關係密切。該學會有數百萬會員，具有很強的組織動員力量。公明黨歷經分合，曾於 1996 年解散，分裂成公明新黨與公明黨，幾天之後公明新黨解散，組成新進黨，但新進黨也在 1997 年底解散。目前的公明黨是結合了幾個小黨派重組而成的。

表 12.1　日本眾議院大選政黨在單一選區之提名人數

1996 年

政黨	日本共產黨	自由民主黨	新進黨	民主黨	自由連合	無所屬	社會民主黨	新社會黨	諸派	新黨さきがけ	民改連	改革クラブ	小計
提名數	299	288	235	143	88	85	43	37	28	13	2	4	1,261
百分比	99.7	96.0	78.0	47.7	29.3	28.3	14.3	12.3	9.3	4.3	0.7	1.3	100

2000 年

政黨	日本共產黨	自由民主黨	民主黨	自由連合	無所屬	自由黨	公明黨	保守黨	無會派	諸派	改革クラブ	小計
提名數	300	271	242	123	79	61	18	16	9	5	4	1,199
百分比	100.0	90.3	80.7	41.0	26.3	20.3	6.0	5.3	3.0	1.7	1.3	100

2003 年

政黨	日本共產黨	自由民主黨	民主黨	無所屬	社會民主黨	保守黨	公明黨	無所屬の會	自由連合	諸派	小計
提名數	300	277	267	86	62	11	10	8	1		1,026
百分比	100.0	92.3	89.0	28.7	20.7	3.7	3.3	2.7	0.3		100

2005 年

政黨	日本共產黨	民主黨	自由民主黨	無所屬	社會民主黨	公明黨	新黨日本	國民新黨	諸派	無所屬（自）	小計
提名數	290	289	275	68	38	9	6	6	4	2	989
百分比	96.7	96.3	91.7	22.7	12.7	3.0	2.0	2.0	1.3	0.6	100

資料來源：日本總務省自治行政局選舉部，各年。
說明：百分比＝政黨提名數÷300。

表 12.2 日本眾議院大選政黨在單一選區之排名分布

	第一名	第二名	第三名	第四名	第四名以下	全部
1996 年						
新進黨	95	118	20	2	0	235
自由民主黨	170	96	20	2	0	288
日本共產黨	2	22	160	103	12	299
民主黨	17	32	56	35	2	143
新社會黨	0	1	7	7	22	37
自由連合	0	3	7	32	46	88
社會民主黨	4	8	13	9	9	43
無所屬	9	15	10	16	35	85
諸派	0	1	0	4	24	28
新黨さきがけ	2	6	0	3	2	13
民改連	1	1	0	0	0	2
2000 年						
自由民主黨	177	89	4	1	0	271
自由黨	4	11	11	29	6	61
日本共產黨	0	18	198	69	15	300
自由連合	1	2	11	52	57	123
民主黨	80	133	24	3	2	242
無所屬	15	16	9	19	20	79
公明黨	7	8	3	0	0	18
保守黨	7	7	1	1	0	16
社會民主黨	4	14	30	17	6	71
改革クラブ	0	1	2	1	0	4
無會派	5	1	2	1	0	9
諸派	0	0	1	0	4	5

（接下頁）

	第一名	第二名	第三名	第四名	第四名以下	全部
2003 年						
民主黨	106	149	12	0	0	267
自由民主黨	167	107	3	0	0	277
日本產黨	0	5	229	61	5	300
無所屬	11	11	23	24	17	86
社會民主黨	1	20	22	16	4	62
諸派	0	0	1	1	2	4
公明黨	9	1	0	0	0	10
無所屬の會	1	3	2	1	1	8
保守新黨	4	4	3	0	0	11
自由連合	1	0	0	0	0	1
2005 年						
民主黨	52	214	23	0	0	289
自由民主黨	219	65	6	0	0	290
日本共產黨	0	0	221	49	5	275
諸派	0	0	0	2	0	2
無所屬	19	12	13	14	10	68
社會民主黨	1	7	13	14	3	38
國民新黨	2	1	2	1	0	6
國民	0	0	1	3	0	4
無所屬（自）	0	0	1	0	1	2
新黨日本	0	0	5	1	0	6
公明黨	8	1	0	0	0	9

資料來源：日本總務省自治行政局選舉部，各選舉年。

這個百分比正是單一選區制之下能確保當選的排除門檻。[22] 根據參選者數和當選門檻的分布狀況,我們可以推論策略選民的確存在,使小黨的選票向領先群集中。[23] 這個結果也顯示,小黨參與單一選區的競爭,主要還是為了要提升其政黨票,而非贏得單一選區的選舉。

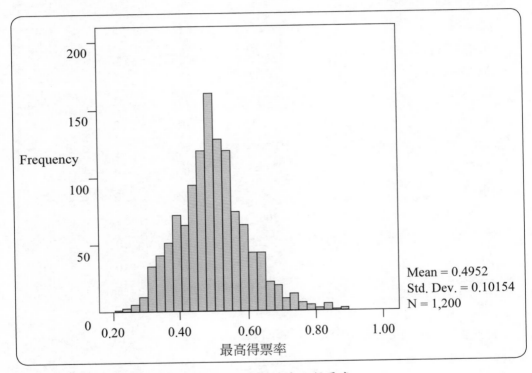

圖 12.1　日本單一選區兩票制眾議院選舉獲勝者之得票率

　　這四次選舉以及參選政黨的特性,顯示本文所描述的情況的確存在:相當多的小黨參與單一選區的選舉,但只在某些選區參選;其目的不在贏得選舉,而在提升其比例代表區的得票。為了瞭解這些選區的性質是否符合理論預期,我們以截尾式迴歸來檢測單

---

[22] 在應選名額為 m 的情況下,排除門檻是 $1/(m + 1)$。在單一選區制之下 m = 1,所以只要拿到一半的選票就可確保當選。

[23] 不過,迴歸分析仍顯示參選人數越多,當選者的得票率越低。

一選區參選人數與各解釋變項的關係。變項間的預期關係已如所述，其中「都市化」這個指標，需要進一步說明。要建構日本眾議院選舉每個單一選區的都市化指標，必須先對構成選區的自治體進行調查，而日本的國勢調查每五年才舉行一次，所以我們不可能估算每次選舉的選區都市化指標。本文所使用的資料乃根據 2000 年的國勢調查結果所計算，剛好位於四次眾議院大選的中間，所以可以看成四次選舉的平均值。爲謹愼起見，也爲了瞭解這個變項的影響力，我們先將都市化變項排除，觀察其他變項對參選人數的影響，接下來才放入都市化指標，比較其變化。

　　表 12.3 是排除都市化指標的截尾式迴歸。統計結果顯示，此模型的 Wald 卡方值爲 487.52，表示所有係數皆爲 0 的機率極低，整體模型在統計上的相關性相當顯著。就個別自變項而言，對被解釋項的影響力都符合理論預期：有效候選人與實際候選人差別越大（AE 率越高）、比例代表區平均應選名額越多，單一選區的候選人就越多；當選者當選次數越多，參選人數就越少；當選者若是世襲議員，更讓參選人數減少 0.35。這些自變項的係數，在統計相關上都達到非常顯著的水準。

表 12.3　對單一選區參選人數的截尾式迴歸分析（不含都市化程度）

參選人數	Coef.	Std. Err.	z	P > |z|	[95% Conf. Inteval]	
世襲當選人	-0.3452818	0.0543898	-6.35	0.000	-0.4518839	-0.2386797
當選次數	-0.0550562	0.0081402	-6.76	0.000	-0.0710107	-0.0391018
AE 率	2.105107	0.102236	20.59	0.000	1.904728	2.305486
比例區席次	0.0169983	0.0036767	4.62	0.000	0.0097921	0.0242046
常數	0.7263148	0.1705161	4.26	0.000	0.3921095	1.06052
sigma						
常數	0.8232106	0.0173787	47.37	0.000	0.7891491	0.8572722

Limit: lower = 1	Number of obs = 1194
upper = +inf	Wald chi^2(4) = 487.52
Log likelihood = -1451.2181	Prob > chi^2 = 0.0000

資料來源：根據上田修一（2006）、日本總務省自治行政局選舉部（各選舉年）、宮川隆義（2000）、朝日新聞（各選舉年）與読売新聞社（1999）之原始資料計算。

　　其次，我們將都市化指標放入模型。因爲我們只有根據 2000 年的國勢調查所建構

的都市化指標，若要將這筆資料用在四次選舉的每個選區，必須假設都市化的變動不大或是等距變動（就統計分析而言，兩者是一樣的）。截尾式迴歸分析的結果如表 12.4，和表 12.3 相當接近，顯示其他自變項的影響力沒有受到太大影響。根據表 12.4，Wald 卡方值上升不少，表示選區都市化指標增進了整體模型的統計相關性。個別自變項和參選人數的關係仍符合理論預期，其係數在統計相關上也具有很高的顯著性。與表 12.3 的結果相比，比較明顯的改變包括：「世襲當選人」的相關性稍微減弱、係數的絕對值略降；當選次數的係數稍降；比例區平均應選名額的相關性變得比較不顯著。至於 AE 率，變動的幅度相對較小，顯示策略投票的因素仍然非常重要。表 12.3 與表 12.4 的差異，透露重要的訊息。很明顯地，一個選區的都市化程度，和領先群的特性有密切的關係。由兩表的差異可以推知，高都市化的選區較少出現世襲當選人，當選者比較不資深，比例代表區的平均應選名額也比較高。當我們放入都市化變項後，截距比不放入都市化變項低了將近 0.65。這個差距，可以理解成都市化的效應。

表 12.4　對單一選區參選人數的截尾式迴歸分析（含都市化程度）

參選人數	Coef.	Std. Err.	z	P > |z|	[95% Conf. Inteval]	
世襲當選人	-0.2424628	0.0511017	-4.74	0.002	-0.3426202	-0.1423054
當選次數	-0.0394698	0.0076538	-5.16	0.000	-0.054471	-0.0244686
AE 率	2.273492	0.096	23.69	0.000	2.085336	2.461649
都市化	0.2322692	0.0171541	13.54	0.000	0.1986477	0.2658906
比例區席次	0.0052418	0.0035185	1.49	0.136	-0.0016542	0.0121379
常數	0.1660463	0.1469472	1.13	0.258	-0.121965	0.4540576
sigma						
常數	0.7651528	0.0160788	47.59	0.000	0.733639	0.7966666

Limit: lower = 1	Number of obs = 1188
upper = +inf	Wald chi^2(5) = 743.91
Log likelihood = -1358.8474	Prob > chi^2 = 0.0000

資料來源：根據上田修一（2006）、日本總務省自治行政局選舉部（各選舉年）、宮川隆義（2000）、朝日新聞（各選舉年）與読売新聞社（1999）之原始資料計算。

以上分析顯示，在單一選區兩票制之下，小黨的確可以選擇適當的單一選區參選，

以鞏固甚至增加其政黨票。一如理論所預期，這些選區比較少出現世襲或資深的參選者，選舉競爭也比較激烈。基於這些特性，這些選區的選民比較有誘因將選票轉移給較有可能勝選的候選人，成爲所謂的策略選民。[24] 這些選區的選民，通常也比較沒有傳統的包袱，較少受到現任議員的恩惠。所以，小黨如果在這些選區參選，一方面較易贏得選民支持，另一方面卻常因實力不足而在選舉時被策略選民所放棄。如果是單純的單一選區制，小黨很可能就完全被犧牲掉；但在單一選區兩票制之下，策略選民卻可以用其政黨票來彌補被犧牲掉的小黨。所以，小黨在這些選區參選，雖然難以在區域勝選，卻可以藉此鞏固其政黨票。

這些對小黨有利的選區，通常都市化的程度比較高。主要的原因，在於高都市化的區域不利恩庇體系的發展，使政治世家難以依靠此一體系長期壟斷議席。此外，在都市化程度高的地區，選民的流動性和匿名性都高、人口密度高但欠缺面對面的溝通，使候選人難以透過特殊利益或社會網絡來鞏固票源。再者，都市化程度通常和媒體的影響力成正比，而依賴傳統方式贏取選票的候選人不見得是媒體名人，當然也比較不容易在都會區長期壟斷議席。反觀小黨，卻可利用這些對傳統議員不利的因素爭取選票。一方面，選民的流動性高、策略選民的數目多，小黨有較好的機會爭取選民的政黨票；另一方面，小黨可以提名雖然欠缺傳統地盤，但形象鮮明的候選人，吸引都會選民的注意，甚至以批判執政黨或其他大黨爲主要訴求，爭取不滿現狀的抗議票。在單一選區兩票制之下，這種抗議票很容易變成小黨的政黨票。小黨在這些單一選區的得票，有些時候因爲重複提名的因素而比單純的策略投票高，但在大多數的情況下仍低於比例代表區的得票；兩者的差距，有相當的部分仍是由策略投票所引起的。

以上的分析，解釋了爲什麼自民黨的地盤以鄉村型選區爲主，而新近成立的政黨（包括許多小黨）卻大多在都會區發跡、茁壯。既有文獻大多強調自民黨乃透過特殊利益的輸送和分配取得優勢（Ramseyer and Rosenbluth, 1997: 38），而鄉村地區的社會結構有助於此種模式的形成。對自民黨而言，都會選民的流動性高，使其難以依賴個人式的特殊利益連結獲取選票，進而降低都市選民投票對象的穩定性。小黨如果能吸引這些選民的注意，就有可能贏得席次。關於都市化與日本選民投票行爲的關係，已有實證研究證實，都市化的程度越高，選民的非黨派屬性越強（福岡政行，2001：101-103）；

---

24 我們可以用另一個指標佐證參選人數與策略投票的關係。依照杜弗傑法則，在單一選區相對多數決下，策略投票會使選票往前兩名候選人集中。依此理，我們可將每個選區的最高票除上第二高票，其比率越接近 1，越表示第二名越可能吸納了策略選票。如果策略選民比例的增加導致參選人數的增加，那麼參選人數和第一、二名得票比應該具有負相關。經檢測 1,200 個單一選區的相關資料後發現，這兩個變項的確出現非常顯著的負相關。

也有學者發現，在 1996 年的選舉中，自民黨的得票率隨著都市化程度而減少，但是民主黨──當時的第三大黨──的情形恰巧與自民黨相反，在接下來幾次的眾議院選舉，也有同樣的趨勢（田中善一郎，2005：208-209、222-223、238）。針對這些現象，本文提供了一個補充解釋：鄉村地區的結構，有利於特定政治家族建構穩固的地盤，不利小黨的挑戰，也欠缺策略投票的空間；同理，都會區不利恩庇結構的發展，選民的流動性和自主性高，所以具有很大的策略投票空間。由於都會選民不見得對新政黨有充分的訊息，所以小黨可以在這些地區參選，雖然難以在單一選區勝選，但可以藉此傳遞政黨形象，並利用策略選民的補償心理，鞏固或增加其政黨票。

伍、對小黨獲利空間的估算

　　如果日本的小黨的確如本文所述，以參與單一選區的選舉來鞏固其政黨票，就表示小黨在單一選區的支持度越高，越能換得支持者的補償性政黨票；反之，單一選區如果沒有小黨的支持者，該黨當然也就無法獲得補償性的政黨票。雖然小黨在單一選區的得票率會因為策略投票而無法反映其實際的支持度，但策略選民畢竟人數有限，所以單一選區和比例代表的選票應該具有正相關。我們一旦找出這種關係，即可估算小黨可以透過參選單一選區選舉換得多少政黨票。要進行這種估算，一項最直接的資料就是政黨在兩種選制下的得票率。我們預期的發現是，單一選區制得票率越高的政黨，在比例代表制下的政黨得票率也越高，而同一政黨在兩制下得票率的差別，應該和策略性選票的數量成正相關。

　　日本眾議院選舉劃分了 300 個單一選區，比例代表部分 1996 年有 200 席，之後減為 180 席，分為 11 個區域選出。由於兩種選制的選區大小差很多，為便於比較，我們先找出每一個比例代表區所包含的單一選區，並計算每個政黨在這些單一選區的平均得票率，再與該政黨在該比例代表區的得票率相比較。圖 12.2 以單一選區平均得票率為橫軸、比例代表區得票率為縱軸，其中每一點代表某次選舉中的一個政黨在兩種選制下的得票率。此圖顯示，政黨在比例代表區的得票率，和政黨在區內單一選區的平均得票率具有明顯的線性關係。以 OLS 線性迴歸，求得兩者的關係為：政黨比例區得票率 = 5.58 + 0.68 政黨單一選區平均得票率（N = 279, R-square = 0.89, s.e. = 0.015）。這個迴歸分析顯示，兩種得票率的線性關係雖然明確，卻非等比例。[25] 這條迴歸線，和「單

---

[25] 圖 12.2 透露出一個有趣的訊息：對單一選區得票率趨近 0 的政黨而言，比例代表區得票率的變異性最大。這表示某些小黨純粹只靠比例代表獲得席次。

一選區得票 = 比例代表得票率」這條線有個交會點：17.41%。我們可以這樣詮釋這個線性關係和這個交點：一個政黨如果不參選單一選區選舉（或參選但得票率為 0），仍有可能獲得 5.6 左右的比例代表選票；單一選區得票率每增加 1%，比例代表區的選票就增加 0.68%；當政黨在單一選區得票率大於 17.41% 時，比例代表制的得票率低於單一選區的得票率，當政黨在單一選區得票率小於 17.41% 時，比例代表制的得票率高於單一選區的得票率。所以，如果政黨要從單一選區得利，至少要能在單一選區獲得 17.41% 的選票。如果本文所假設的策略投票和補償效應的確存在，適用的對象就是在單一選區得票小於 17.41% 的政黨。

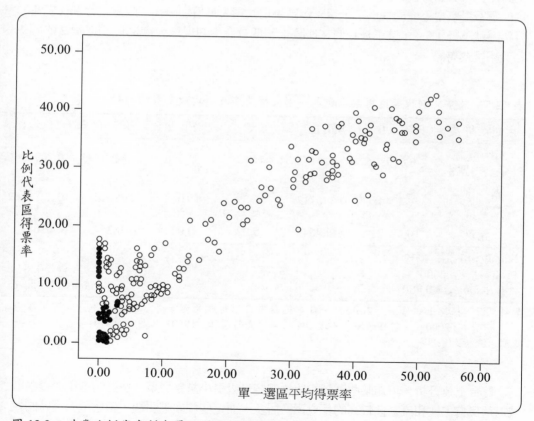

圖 12.2　政黨比例代表制與單一選區制得票率之關係

圖 12.2 不只顯示小黨的單一選區得票率低於比例代表得票率，更呈現兩者清楚的

線性相關。這種關係，顯示兩種選舉制度有系統性的關連。為進一步說明這種關連和策略性投票的關係，我們進行以下的檢測：在政黨單一席次得票率不變的情況下，單一選區候選人數的增加，是否會降低政黨的比例代表得票率。前節已經說明，小黨為了增加政黨票，會在單一選區參選，但隨著參選人數的增加，這種策略的效果也會降低。反論之，如果圖 12.2 所顯示的線性關係只單純反映兩種選制不同的比例性，參與單一選區的候選人數就應該不會改變參選政黨的比例代表得票率。我們將政黨單一選區平均得票率和單一選區平均參選人數當作自變項，以政黨比例代表區的得票率為依變項，求得線性迴歸的結果如表 12.5。該表顯示，即使放入參選人數這個自變項，政黨單一選區得票率對比例代表制得票率的影響仍然是一樣的，但參選人數卻有非常明顯的效應：在政黨單一選區得票率不變的情形下，單一選區平均候選人每增加一人，政黨在比例代表區的得票率就下降 1.3%。這正是我們在理論上預期會發生的現象，也說明了圖 12.2 的關係和策略投票有關。

表 12.5　政黨比例代表區得票率與單一選區得票率及參與政黨數的關係

比例區得票率	Coef.	Std. Err.	t	P > |t|	[95% Conf. Inteval]	
單一選區平均得票率	0.679806	0.015122	44.87	0.000	0.6499773	0.7096346
單一選區平均候選人數	-1.304486	0.546712	-2.39	0.018	-2.380741	-0.2282302
常數	10.49722	2.089648	5.02	0.000	6.383543	14.61089

Number of obs = 279
Prob > F = 0.0000　　　　　　　　　　　　　　　　　　　　F(2,276) = 1026.38
Adj R-square = 0.8807　　　　　　　　　　　　　　　　　R-squared = 0.8815

資料來源：根據上田修一（2006）、日本總務省自治行政局選舉部（各選舉年）、宮川隆義　　　　　　（2000）、朝日新聞（各選舉年）與読売新聞社（1999）之原始資料計算。
說明：分析對象限於小黨。

綜合上述分析，可知某些區域的確比較容易吸引小黨參與單一選區的選舉。這些區域以選民自主性和流動性較高的都會選區居多，而這些傾向越明顯，參與單一選區的競爭者就越多。在競爭者眾的情況下，能否選擇妥當的單一選區參選，就成為小黨致勝的關鍵。然而，這也表示小黨的策略會受到其政黨屬性的限制。某些小黨較能提名具有地域色彩、但又不足以當選的候選人參與單一選區選舉，以訴諸該地選民的補償心理。但

如果一個小黨全靠理念吸引選民注意，且欠缺具有地域連結的候選人，能吸引到的大約就是理念型的選票，能換得的補償性政黨票也比前者少。我們可以從實際的選舉過程，觀察不同類型的小黨如何利用參與單一選區選舉來提升其政黨票。觀察的焦點，是日本第一次採用單一選區兩票制的 1996 年眾議院大選。當時自民黨甫經 1993 年選舉的大挫敗，力圖透過此次選舉重掌執政權，許多新政黨則企圖取代自民黨成為執政黨。在非自民黨中，新進黨在此次選舉共贏得 95 席單一選區的席次（表 12.2），是第二大黨。其餘政黨可看作全國性的小黨，其中最值得比較的是剛成立的民主黨，和老牌的日本共產黨。兩黨的政黨票得票率只差了大約 3%，但是所獲得的比例代表制席次卻差了 11 席（占比例代表席次的 5.5%）。如果本文的論點成立，這種差異很可能是因為民主黨的特性，使其比共產黨更能吸引單一選區選民的補償票。

民主黨是由菅直人、鳩山由紀夫等人於 1996 年組成，目標是聚集不滿自民黨與新進黨的第三勢力。[26] 在 1996 年的眾議院選舉中，該黨僅獲得 17 席單一選區席次（占 300 席的 5.7%），但得到將近 900 萬的政黨票（16.1%）以及 35 席比例代表席次（占比例代表席次的 17.5%）。民主黨在都會區吸收了大量選票，但其主要訴求並非清楚的理念，而是「反兩大黨」。許多民主黨的領導人來自自民黨，具有特定的地域連結，連帶使其得票也產生地域差別。反映在民主黨的比例代表得票率上，可以高到北海道的 31.8%，也可以低到九州的 10.8%。該黨在 11 個比例區的得票率有很大的差異，標準差高達 6.2%。相較於民主黨，日本共產黨則是完全不同類型的政黨。如其名所示，該黨有非常清楚而特殊的理念——共產主義，個別政治人物的影響力相對較弱。共產黨清楚瞭解其議席來自比例代表區，但在單一選區的部分採取全額提名的策略，希望能在各地宣傳政黨理念。在 1996 年的眾議院選舉中，共產黨僅獲得二席單一選區席次；在政黨票的部分，該黨獲得超過 720 萬票（13.1%），但只得到 24 席（占比例代表席次的 12%）。以 11 個比例區得票率的標準差來看，共產黨只有 2.9%，遠低於民主黨。民主黨和共產黨的票基差異不大，但民主黨總共獲得 52 個席次，共產黨只有 26 席，剛好是前者的一半。很顯然地，小黨的特性影響其參選策略，也造成獲取席次的差別。

不論是從總體資料還是政黨個案來分析，我們得到的結論是一致的。在單一選區難以贏得席次的小黨，必須仰賴選民的政黨票，才有機會贏得國會議席。要達到這個目的，小黨必須標舉鮮明的旗幟，強化選民的認同；對剛成立、欠缺傳統根基的小黨而言，這種宣傳更是重要。再者，小黨應選擇特定的單一選區參選，一方面打政黨形象廣

---

[26] 該黨和 1998 年 4 月成立的民主黨（Democratic Party of Japan）不同。前者被稱為舊民主黨，後者則是結合了幾個小黨派（包括舊民主黨）而組成的政黨。

告，另一方面塑造某些策略選民的補償心理，爭取他們的政黨票。小黨要能夠完成這些策略，必須將資源投注在特定的選區，以提升這些選區的政黨票。日本將比例代表選舉分爲 11 個區域進行，剛好滿足了小黨「集中火力、以輸爲贏」的需求。反過來說，如果日本沒有劃分比例代表的選區，小黨就難以施展這種策略，所能獲得的席次勢必減少。以 1996 年的民主黨爲例，在全國總共獲得 16.1% 的政黨票，如果比例代表席次完全按照比例分配，只能分到 32 個席次，少於其眞正取得的 35 席。[27] 共產黨因爲參與了每一個單一選區的選舉，得到的選票也普遍分配到不同選區，所以獲得的比例代表席次（24 席）剛好就是該黨得票率（12%）乘上 200 席。這個例子，清楚說明小黨參選策略對其勝選機率的影響。

陸、結論

　　過去十多年來，單一選區兩票制之所以被許多國家採用，原因之一是由於該制包含了單一選區制與比例代表制，可以滿足不同政黨的需求。對新興民主國家而言，這種混合選制更是民主化初期最容易妥協出來的選擇。但是，這種折衷方案並不必然能滿足小黨的需求。如果單一選區兩票制是以並立方式運作，而且以單一選區制選出大部分的席次，小黨的生存空間將受到大幅限制。然而，我們也不能直接推論小黨在此一選制下完全沒有機會贏得議席。在採用並立式單一選區兩票制的國家中，日本雖然以單一選區制選出將近三分之二的眾議院席次，但小黨在該國舉行的眾議院大選中，仍能贏得相當數量的席次，而且原因並不只是日本沒有設立政黨的法定當選門檻。

　　對小黨而言，混合選制中的比例代表席次應該是其參選的主要目標，但如何達成此一目標卻有賴於妥當的參選策略。由於日本採取重複提名制，某些小黨可以透過此一制度提升其單一選區的得票，但整體而言許多選民仍會在單一選區選舉中犧牲沒有勝選希望的小黨。如何促使這些沒有在單一選區投票給小黨的策略選民將其政黨票投給小黨，成爲致勝的關鍵。本文延伸了杜弗傑法則，認爲小黨可以在特定的單一選區參選，策略性地被潛在支持者放棄並塑造其補償心理，以增強其獲得這些選民政黨票的機率。這些選民通常自主性較高，比較不受恩庇體系的束縛，當然也比較可能支持新興政黨，並成

---

[27] 事實上，就算是比例代表制也不可能完全等比例地分配席次。以 1996 年的眾議院選舉爲例，作爲第一、二大黨的自民黨和新進黨，得到的比例代表席次超過其政黨得票率，連帶減少其他政黨所能分配到的席次。

爲策略投票者。以其居住地來看，這些選民住在都會區的機率應該高過非都會區，其人數越多，小黨越有動機參與單一選區選舉，並導致參選人數的增加。

　　本文以單一選區參選人數作爲依變項，並以影響策略投票的相關因素爲主要的解釋變項，印證了前述理論的預期：策略投票傾向越明顯（即實際參選人與有效參選人差距越大）、都市化程度越高、勝選者當選的次數越少、比例代表區平均應選名額越多，參選人數就越多；當選者如果出身政治世家，則會降低參選人數。這些發現，清楚顯示小黨會選擇策略選民較多的地方參選，而避開存在政治世家或資深議員的選區。日本將比例代表分爲 11 個地區選出，使小黨能選擇對其有利的選區參選，進而提升該區域的政黨票。這些研究發現，不但說明日本的小黨爲何能在單一選區兩票制下獲得部分席次，也解釋了爲什麼日本新舊政黨的分布有城鄉差異。

　　日本在單一選區兩票制下的經驗，可以作爲比較研究的基準。在採取同類型選舉制度的國家中，台灣是最值得與日本進行比較的案例。台灣在國會選舉中所採取的並立式單一選區兩票制和日本十分類似，但小黨的命運卻相當不同。台灣在 2008 年 1 月 12 日首次實施了並立式單一選區兩票制的選舉，在 113 個立法委員的席次中，73 席以單一選區相對多數決產生，34 席全國不分區席次依比例代表制分配，其餘六席原住民席次則以 SNTV-MMD 選出，單一選區所占席次爲 64.6%（日本在 2000 年之後爲 62.5%）。[28] 國民黨和民進黨在此次選舉共囊括 108 席，占總席次的 95.6%。曾經在台灣民主化過程中扮演重要角色的台灣團結聯盟與新黨，並未獲致任何席次；連曾經是國會第三大黨的親民黨，也僅獲得一席原住民席次。[29] 小黨在台灣的單一選區兩票制之下，幾乎沒有生存的空間。

　　有人或許以爲，日本的單一選區兩票制並未設立政黨當選門檻，而台灣規定了 5% 的法定門檻，所以日本有小黨的空間，台灣則沒有。的確，除了國民黨與民進黨，其他政黨並未在台灣 2008 年的立法委員選舉中取得 5% 以上的不分區得票。不過，台灣的小黨無法贏得席次，仍然受到其他因素的影響。首先，日本許多取得比例代表制席次的小黨，在比例代表區所獲得的得票率遠高於 5%，例如前述民主黨和共產黨，但這些政黨的整體席次率卻有相當的差距。這表示，法定門檻不是影響小黨席次率的唯一因素。其次，不論是否設有法定的當選門檻，所有選舉制度都存在實際的當選門檻。

---

[28]　台灣的單一選區兩票制，已經規定在憲法之中。見《中華民國憲法增修條文》第四條。憲法也規定，憲法之修改，須經立法院立法委員四分之一之提議，四分之三之出席，及出席委員四分之三之決議，提出憲法修正案，並經選舉人投票複決，有效同意票過選舉人總額之半數方爲通過。修憲門檻如此之高，在可見的未來，台灣的國會選舉都不容易改採其他的選制。

[29]　關於此屆立法委員選舉的選舉結果，請參閱「選舉資料庫」（中央選舉委員會，2008）。

根據 Lijphart 的公式，若 m 為應選名額，則實際當選門檻大約為 1/2m（Lijphart, 1994: 27）。以日本的比例代表區來看，門檻最高的是應選名額七席的四國，門檻為 7.1%；門檻最低的是應選名額 33 席的近畿，門檻為 1.5%。台灣的全國不分區有 34 席，未劃分選區，所以實際門檻是 1.5%。[30] 換言之，跨越實質門檻，是小黨獲得席次的必要條件。第三，比例代表選舉是否劃分選區，對小黨的參選策略有重大影響。日本劃分了 11 個比例代表區，所以小黨（尤其是具有區域色彩者）可以選擇支持度較高的單一選區參選，以鞏固該區域的政黨票。反觀台灣，所有的比例代表席次全放在同一個選區，使小黨無法依其特性選擇適當的選區參選。以台灣 2008 年立法委員選舉的全國不分區票數分布來看，新黨在台北市的得票率高達 9.4%，在台北縣為 5.8%，基隆市則有 6.1%。如果北台灣被劃成一個比例代表區，新黨不但能得到超過 5% 的票數，還可贏得一定的席次。依照本文的理論，如果新黨能在單一選區參選，或許更能提高該黨在此區域的政黨得票。[31] 總結日本與台灣的差異可以發現，雖然兩國採取相當類似的混合選制，但一些細部因素仍對小黨產生重大影響。這些因素，也應列入制度選擇的考慮。

　　日本的小黨雖然找到了某些生存策略，終究難以逆轉並立式單一選區兩票制對政黨體系帶來的重大影響。這種傾向於單一選區制的混合選制，畢竟還是對大黨有利，甚至可能促成兩黨制的形成。當政治資源逐漸被大黨壟斷，小黨的空間是否會跟著縮小？在日本，小黨的支持者是否會連政黨票都改投第二大黨，以更快速地讓自民黨下台？小黨過度集中在特定選區參選，是否造成惡性競爭，削減其選票？在生存不易的情形下，小黨領導人是否覺得併入大黨較為合理？從日本四次眾議院大選的資料看來，的確已經看到某些跡象。這四次大選，每個選區的平均參選人數依序是 4.20、4.13、3.42 與 3.30，表示日本的有效政黨數正在減少。不過，這畢竟是一個漸進的過程，對該國的小黨而言，單一選區兩票制並未完全剝奪其政治空間；被視為不利小黨的單一選區席次，甚至可以成為小黨爭取比例代表席次的跳板。這點，是值得其他國家小黨參考之處。

30　對政黨而言，要考慮的不只是當選門檻，還有當選票數。台灣的實質門檻雖然低，但乘上總票數後，還是相當高。

31　新黨在 2008 年立法委員選舉，完全沒有提名候選人參與單一選區的選舉。

第十三章

....

選舉制度爲何變遷？理論與檢證*

....

壹、選舉制度和政黨體系的因果關係

選舉制度（以下簡稱爲選制）影響政黨體系，是眾所周知的因果推論。早在五十年前，法國學者 Maurice Duverger（以下簡稱杜弗傑，以符合慣用法）就指出，單一選區相對多數決選制（single-member simple plurality system，或稱 first past the post）能促成兩黨制，而單一選區兩輪投票制（two-ballet system，又稱 two-round system）和政黨名單比例代表制（party-list proportional representation）有利多黨制。[1] 杜弗傑認爲，這種因果關係來自機械效應（mechanical effect）和心理效應（psychological effect）：前者是指不同選制的當選門檻有差異，後者是說選民會隨著當選門檻的高低而決定是否犧牲某些候選人或政黨（Duverger, 1963: 248）。以單一選區相對多數決選制爲例，因爲只有一人可以當選，所以選民會將選票集中在前兩名的候選人上，以避免浪費選票；政黨名單比例代表制的當選門檻低，選民無須集中選票在兩大黨上，所以容易形成多黨制。杜弗傑的假說不但有清楚的因果機制，也符合理性選擇的假定：選民爲了極大化選票的效用，間接對政黨體系產生影響。William Riker 因此把杜弗傑假說當成政治科學的範例，探討如何透過經驗研究來修正這個假說，而此一假說也的確對政治科學產生深遠的影響。[2]

----

* 本文曾刊登於《問題與研究》，第 54 卷第 3 期（2015 年 9 月），頁 1-29。感謝政治大學國際關係研究中心《問題與研究》同意轉載。

[1] 關於選制的分類，請見第參節。

[2] 所謂杜弗傑法則，或稱「社會學法則」（the sociological law），是針對單一選區相對多數決選制而言。「杜弗傑假說」（Duvergerian hypotheses），則包括比例代表制和兩輪投票制。本文以「假說」來通稱杜弗傑對於選制後果所提出的命題。有關 Riker 的評論，請參閱 Riker（1982）、Grofman、Blais 與 Bowler（2009）的評論。Riker 認爲，杜弗傑所提的「心理效應」，假設選民期待選票能影響選舉結果，但這種影響力應該極低，使投票成本高於效益，所以難以解釋策略投票。Riker 認爲，選民投票是基於偏好而非選票效用，而政治菁英的獻金則是促成兩黨制的重要原因。這個論點是否能修正杜弗傑假說，仍有討論的空間。依照 Riker 的邏輯，若將投票視爲對稱賽局，則在他人投票的狀況下，投票的成本大於效益，所以應該不會去投票。可是這種狀況並非均衡：如果所有人都這樣計算，將導致投票率爲 0；此時，任何一人投票都可主導全局。但這也不是均衡：依此理，投票率應會增加，但這又會降低每票對最後結果的影響。所以，最後的投票率是混合策略的均衡。至於政治菁英的操作，通常會以能勝選的政

　　杜弗傑假說，有這樣的潛在意涵：如果選制符合國會政黨的利益，國會政黨就會保護既有選制。[3] 是否如此，Joseph M. Colomer 提供了另一種解讀：選制和政黨體系的確有相關性，但杜弗傑法則把因果關係弄反了（Duverger's law upside down）。他以理論模型和 87 個國家的選舉資料庫，顯示選制是既存的政黨所選擇，所以多黨制會選擇比例代表制；大黨若能支配國會，則傾向於選擇多數決選制。[4] Colomer 的解釋有其道理，但不見得有悖於杜弗傑假說。例如，某政黨之所以選擇單一選區相對多數決制，可能正因為此一選制有利兩黨制的形成。要讓兩派意見對話，可以進行兩項工作。第一，政黨選擇對其有利的選制，可能正是因為選制會保護特定的政黨體系，所以選制和政黨體系互為因果。第二，我們可以將杜弗傑假說視為機率的形態。杜弗傑在陳述他的假說時，本來就用了機率式的陳述。這表示，杜弗傑的假說雖有解釋力，但不能排除某些例外。這些例外的比例雖低，但從歷史和全球的框架來看，卻也累積了一定的數量。這些預期之外的政黨體系是否會改採對其有利的選制？如果答案是肯定的，就表示 Colomer 的理論是合理的，但若新選制所造成的政黨體系符合杜弗傑假說的預期，也證成了這個假說的有效性。簡言之，政黨體系成為選制變遷的「內生變因」（endogenous factor）。

　　將選制變遷歸因於政黨抉擇的「內生論」，可能引發一些爭論。懷疑者認為影響選制變遷的因素複雜，和政黨體系不見得有關，選制改革者的訊息也可能不足，制約了變遷的路徑。我們可將這種看法稱為「外生性」（exogenous）理論（Rahat, 2004; Renwick, 2010）。由此，我們可以歸納兩派有關選制變遷的理論：[5]

　　1. 內生論：原本作為選制後果的政黨體系，成為改變選制的主因。

黨為對象，但這是另一個變項，而非對心理效應的否證。關於投票效益的討論，另一篇重要的文獻是 Riker 與 Ordeshook（1968）。

[3] 例如，如果單一選區相對多數決制有利兩黨制，那麼兩黨就會阻礙小黨進入國會；如果比例代表制有助於小黨贏得議席，小黨就會反對大黨壟斷議席。但仍有著作質疑杜弗傑假說對於政黨體系的預測，例如加拿大或印度。出現這些反例，可能是因為選區的有效候選人不見得等同於全國的有效政黨數。關於加拿大的例子，請參閱 Blais（2008）。關於印度的例子，請參閱 Ziegfeld（2012）。

[4] 事實上，Colomer 並非這個說法的原創者。根據 Taagepera 與 Shugart 的研究，Lakeman 與 Lambert、Grumm 和 Lakeman 都曾指出，單一選區制下的多黨化，是形成選制轉變成比例代表制的主因。研究選制和社會分歧的先驅者 Rokkan 也認為，既有政黨在二十世紀初受到新興勞工階級的威脅，才將選制改為政黨名單比例代表制。關於上述討論，請參閱 Colomer（2004: 247）、Taagepera 與 Shugart（1989: 148）、Lakeman 與 Lambert（1955）、Grumm（1958）、Lakeman（1984）以及 Rokkan（1970）。

[5] Colomer 和杜弗傑的理論處理實然面的問題。關於應然面的選制改革，請參閱 Norris（1997: 310-311）。

2. 外生論：選制變遷成因複雜，沒有固定範圍，和政黨體系也沒有直接關連。

「內生論」以機率式來顯現杜弗傑假說，並以該假說預期之外的政黨體系來解釋選制變遷。就「外生論」而言，影響選制變遷的成因沒有固定範圍，只能歸納可能的原因。對這兩派選制變遷理論的驗證，涉及研究方法。個案研究法的長處在於重視選制變遷的細節，但受限於個案數目，不容易得出具有理論意涵的通則。比較研究法擴大了個案數，可以同時顧及細節和理論意義，但必須進行一些簡化。本文的重點之一，在於以新興民主國家的經驗來檢證以先進民主國家為基準的選制變遷理論，所以範圍較廣，但也可能會有些誤差。面對這個問題，最好的方法就是盡量擴展個案的數目，將誤差視為統計模型上的殘差值，並觀察哪些變項可以橫跨大量的資料而具有統計上的顯著性。基於這個考慮，本文的實證研究，是以最新的全球選制資料庫為對象。實證分析將顯示，在多數決選制下，如果沒有政黨掌握國會多數席次，選制變遷的機率的確相當高，而比例性選制的變革主要受到外生因素的影響，和政黨體系沒有直接關係；比例性選制通常產生不利選制變革的多黨制，而多數決選制下的政黨數分布相當偏斜，所以多數決選制的變遷率高於比例性選制。這些發現，釐清了相關研究的爭辯：選制變遷究竟起於內生因素還是外生因素，和選制本身有關。

次節先檢討相關文獻，探討既有研究如何分析不同的選制變遷模式。為了要讓理論推演更細緻化，第參節先處理選制分類的問題，並定義什麼是多數決選制和比例性選制。第肆、伍節將主要變項操作化，並進行假設檢證。結論部分，會說明如何根據本文的發現進行個案研究，以彌補量化研究所忽視的細節。

貳、選制變遷的相關研究

選制並不容易改變（Nohlen, 1984a: 217-218）。檢視相關文獻，也可以發現研究選制後果的多，探討選制變遷成因的少。這種現象，和杜弗傑的假說有關。由於該假說意涵選制的穩定性，政黨體系可視為選制的均衡後果（Rae, 1971; Grofman and Lijphart, 1986; Lijphart, 1990; Taagepera, 2007）。這個看法，很接近「新制度論」（new institutionalism）的精神：制度要長久運作，才能累積足夠的證據顯現其後果。在「選制不變」的假設下，有些學者更進一步地根據應選名額、選區數目、有效當選門檻（effective threshold）、議會規模甚至社會分歧等相關因素來解釋選制在各層面上的影

響。[6] 由此，學者認爲選制影響政黨的大小以及競選策略；[7] 更有研究者認爲，杜弗傑假說不僅能解釋單一選區相對多數決選制和政黨名單比例代表制下的政黨體系，也可以用在其他的選制，例如單記非讓渡投票制（single nontransferable vote, SNTV）、單記可讓渡投票制（single transferable vote）、排序投票制（alternative vote）乃至政黨名單比例代表制。[8] 這些研究不但聯繫了政黨體系和選制的關係，更大大拓展了選制研究的範圍。

即便選制是穩定的，但若把杜弗傑假說看成機率的形式，例外就可能引發變遷。當觀察值變多時，選制變遷的個案數目將隨之上升，解釋的必要性也相對提高。對前述的「內生論」而言，選制所塑造的政黨體系，不見得都包含想維持既有選制的政黨，有些政黨甚至可能組成聯盟來改變選制。那麼，什麼樣的政黨會想改變選制？按常理，政黨越大（小），越支持多數決選制（比例性選制）（Lijphart, 1984; Benoit and Hayden, 2004; Colomer, 2004: 3）。Boix（1999）從這個角度，發展出政黨對選制偏好的動態理論：在多數決選制下，形式上爲兩黨制的國家若面對強敵挑戰，有可能增加選制的比例性以防止席次喪失，但如果新政黨還不足以與其抗爭，則會維持原制以防杜新政黨獲取席次。不論是 Colomer 還是 Boix，都是從政黨的角度出發，以席次極大化來解釋選制的偏好和變遷。

選制變遷的外生論，如何看待「政黨席次極大化」的假定？以下先說明外生論的要旨，再談內生論如何處理前者的疑問。[9] 在瞭解爭議所在後，即可思考如何修正和檢證這些理論。

第一，變遷外生論重視實際發生的選制變革過程，認爲選制變遷常源自和政黨體系沒有直接關連的因素，例如歷史、族群分歧、地域主義、公民投票、憲政規則、國際壓力、學習效應乃至既有選制的失靈等（Benoit, 2002: 38）。對此派論者而言，不同行動者的偏好互異，對選制有認知上的限制，也使「政黨席次極大化」的假定看來太單純。[10] 我們不難想像，此派學者對歷史細節的重視，超過對一般理論的興趣。

---

[6] 關於應選名額因素，請參閱 Benoit（2001: 203）。關於議會規模因素，請參閱 Taagepera 與 Ensch（2006: 761）。關於社會分歧因素，請參閱 Amorim Neto 與 Cox（1997）。

[7] 有關政黨大小如何影響選制偏好，請參閱 Diwakar（2007: 539-540）、Taagepera（2007）。關於競選策略，請參閱 Cox（1990）、Carey 與 Shugart（1995: 424-432）、Grofman（2005: 737-738）。

[8] 關於單記非讓渡投票制，請參照 Grofman 等（1999）。關於單記可讓渡投票制，請參照 Bowler 與 Grofman（2000）。關於排序投票制，請參照 Horowitz（2004）。關於政黨名單比例代表制，請參照 Slinko 與 White（2010）。

[9] 有關研究選制變遷的方法論，請參閱 Rahat（2004）、Renwick（2010）。

[10] 例如，Rahat（2004: 471-475）就認爲理性選擇途徑不能解釋以色列在 1990 年代的選制改革。

　　第二，針對這些疑問，內生論者可能有這樣的回應。首先，內生論者不一定都假定有關政黨席次分配的訊息是均等分布的。如果黨內有某些人掌握較充分的訊息，即可傳遞給其他同志（Colomer, 2005: 8）。再者，觀察值的大小也很重要。如果研究者僅針對單一國家作個案研究，的確可能發現不少和政黨體系無關的因素。但內生論者不見得都以少數國家為案例，而各國的外生因素可能也不盡相同，所以可以用增加觀察值的方法，查考政黨體系是否在各國都是影響選制變遷的重要變項。[11] 建構選制的資料庫，就是增加觀察值的常見方法（Leyenaar and Hazan, 2011: 448）。

　　第三，另一種回應外生論的方法，是指出政黨和選制改革交易成本的關係。政黨是政治運作的核心，而外生因素常會增加選制改革的交易成本，所以外生因素越多，選制就越不容易改變，但也越容易在改革發生時顯現政黨的作用。[12] 舉例而言，某些國家規定，選制改革如果要成案，需要國會超多數支持或兩院皆同意，所以單有國會過半的贊成尚不足以變更選制；對某些新興民主國家而言，政黨制度化的程度低，或有較多的地域衝突，也可能阻礙選制的變革。在這些例子中，「表決多數」、「低政黨制度化」和「地域衝突」都是外生因素，通常會讓現狀更難改變，但選制一旦改革，就可能顯現政黨體系的作用。

　　到底哪種說法成立，需要實證檢驗。如果檢證的結果可以幫助我們修改理論，這種理論可稱為理論模型（theoretical model）。理論模型的目的，在於藉由一套假定來推論因果機制，以幫助我們詮釋實證研究的發現，並藉著誤差值來修改理論假定。在建構選制變遷的理論模型時，可以假定政黨以極大化席次為目的，然後推論政黨在什麼情況下會對選制變遷有影響，什麼情況下不會有影響；對於後者，我們可以設定某些外生因素，並判別此種情況的發生機率。

　　建構理論模型的目的既然在於接受檢證，即應注意資料的範圍，以降低命題的偏誤。就既有文獻來看，Colomer 的資料庫包含 87 國的 219 次選舉，Boix（1999）乃以 23 個民主國家的 32 個選舉法規為分析單位，Lijphart（1994）將範圍限於 27 個民主國

其中的關鍵問題，在於對選制的認知。游清鑫（2012）發現台灣選民對單一選區兩票制的認知不高，但隨著投票時間的接近而提升。

[11] 一般而言，樣本平均值的變異量會隨樣本觀察值的增加而下降，所以即便是個案研究，也應該注意觀察值的多寡，請參閱 King、Keohane 與 Verba（1994: 70）。

[12] 關於外生因素和交易成本，請參閱 Dunleavy 與 Margetts（1995: 7-24）。在外生因素中，公民投票是少數可以加速選制變革的手段。紐西蘭就是透過公民投票，在 1993 年直接將單一選區相對多數決制改為聯立式單一選區兩票制。請參閱 Vowles（1995）、Gallagher（1998）、Sakamoto（1999）。

家，Renwick（2010）更只挑選四個先進民主國家作為比較案例。這些國家的民主化程度雖高，卻並非全球各國的典型；其選制變遷是否具有代表性，也仍待檢證。[13] 將範圍擴及其他國家不僅能增加觀察值的數量，還有幾個好處：1. 近三十多年的資料，包含誕生於第三波民主化潮流中的國家，使我們能將新國家的選制變遷經驗和經典理論對比；[14] 2. 新興民主國家施行競爭性選舉的日程較短，甚至可能還在實驗某些新的選制，而這些經驗可以和成熟民主國家的早期經驗相互比較；3. 某些國家雖有選舉，但仍處於威權體制，使我們得以觀察這些國家的領袖是否偏好特定的選制。本文採取 IPU PARLINE 資料庫對選制的定義。在這筆資料庫中，扣掉資料不全或無法歸類的國家或選舉，總共包含 170 個國家和 907 次國會選舉，平均每國 5.34 次。這些數據顯示，本文所要運用的資料庫，觀察值高於既有文獻，樣本也較無區域限制。國會選舉的結果是否可信，可能因民主化程度而有別；本文採取的方法，是將國家自由度和民主化程度列為自變項，所以每個係數都是控制其他變項之後所得的估計值。自由度和民主化程度是否影響選舉，可以從這兩個變項的係數看出。

　　本節檢視兩派選制變遷的文獻，並推演理論模型。模型假定政黨以極大化席次為目標，但並不認定政黨體系就是解釋選制變遷的主要變項。重點在於解析政黨在什麼時機可以組成改變選制的聯盟，什麼時機不行，且讓選制變遷受到外生因素的影響。外生因素是無法窮盡的，但至少可以考量與選舉競爭有關的變因，例如民主政體的特性以及國會的角色等。本文也假定，威權體制的國家較易出現少數菁英操弄選制，新興民主國家較常發生離心競爭，亞洲國家較重視群體價值。為了便於建構理論模型和操作實證檢驗，下節先界定選制變遷的定義，並討論如何替選制分類。

參、選制的變遷方向與類別

　　選制之所以發生變遷，常常是因為既有選制不符合政黨利益。所以，要判定選制變遷的方向，就要瞭解不同選制如何影響大小政黨的席次分配。在研究選制變遷之前，

---

[13] 以西歐為主的選樣，也使許多研究高度集中在多數決選制轉為比例代表制的變遷路徑上。這種路徑是否普遍存在，需要進一步的檢驗。

[14] 從長期的觀點來看，選制和政治菁英的利益應會相互增強，導致選制的穩定化。所以，當前仍處於大幅變動的新興民主國家，可以對照上世紀初的歐洲國家。當時歐洲因為勞工階級的興起，某些國家從單一選區制轉變為比例代表制，某些則否。關於這些國家的選擇，請參考 Boix（1999）。

要先定義選制的類別，才能瞭解什麼樣的變化算是選制變遷。但既有的選制分類，並不容易回答這些問題。一般常依投票與計票方式，將選制分為三大類：1. 政黨名單比例代表制，以政黨得票為準分配政黨席次；2.（相對）多數決選制（plurality/majority systems），依候選人得票高低決定當選者；3. 混合制（mixedmember systems），包含區域席次與比例代表席次，又可細分為「聯立式」和「並立式」兩類（Lijphart, 1994; Colomer, 2005; Lijphart, 1999b; 王業立，2011）。以本文的目的而言，這種分類方式不見得看得到政黨的利益：同樣屬於多數決選制，單一選區相對多數決選制和複數選區單記非讓渡投票制對政黨的席次分布就有很大的差異，遑論混合制中的並立式和聯立式，以及並立式混合制對於區域席次和比例席次的比重分配。

本文的目的既然在於探討政黨在選制變革中的角色，就不能完全依賴既有的分類方式，而應該根據政黨的席次率來進行區別。最明確的指標，就是當選門檻。[15] 對大黨而言，當選門檻越高（低），越（不）容易使其獲得過半席次，所以當選門檻會影響國會政黨的結盟方式以及選制變遷的方向。排除門檻（threshold of exclusion），是經常被提及的當選門檻。這個門檻，是指某個政黨在無法贏得任何席次時的最高得票率；換言之，政黨若能再多得一票，即可獲得席次。若假設應選名額為 m，每位選民可投票數為 v（$1 \leq v \leq m$），則排除門檻為 $v/(v + m)$（Rae, Hanby, and Loosemore, 1971）。依此公式，單一選區制的 m 為 1，所以排除門檻是 1/2；全額連記法下 $m = v$，所以排除門檻也是 1/2。這個公式也說明，排除門檻和 m 成反比，但會隨著 v 而上升。由於排除門檻是指可能敗選的最高得票率，必然高於實際上的當選門檻，因此學者常會估算其他的當選門檻。例如 Lijphart（1994: 27）就提出「有效當選門檻」：$[0.5/(m + 1)] + [(0.5/(2m)]$，其數值低於排除門檻。即便如此，排除門檻和其他當選門檻都用到應選名額，所以兩者高度相關。

當選門檻是量變項，但要能反映大小政黨的不同利益，所以也有質變項的性質。為兼顧兩者，可以用量的標準來區別質；至於要定義幾個質變項，取決於研究的課題和資料的範圍。本文的實證檢驗乃以全球選制變遷為對象，為產生跨國的共量性，應該採取最廣泛的二分法：多數決選制（majoritarian systems）和比例性選制（proportional systems）。[16] 依照前段的討論，多數決選制的排除門檻為 0.5，以單一選區制為主，比

---

[15] 另一種方式，是針對每次選舉各政黨所獲得的得票率和席次率，計算「比例性指標」（index of proportionality），其定義為 $0.5|V_i - S_i|$，其中 V_i 和 S_i 分別代表政黨 i 的得票率與席次率。這個指標的長處在於以每次選舉為分析單位，可以累積大量資料，但缺點在於難以辨識選制在性質上的轉換。請參閱 Loosemore 與 Hanby（1971）。

[16] 如果不進行這樣的二分法，可能會使小規模變動（例如複數選區下單記法和限制連記法間的轉

例性選制的排除門檻小於 0.5，涵蓋政黨名單比例代表制和應選名額大於 1 但選民投票數小於應選名額的複數選區制。

　　表 13.1 顯示各種選制所歸屬的類別，其中有兩個部分需要進一步說明。第一，這是一個依據當選門檻所劃分的雙層表，最左層是以多數決選制和比例性選制進行的二分法，其下再分爲第二層，也就是一般所熟知的選舉制度。根據此表，選制變遷可以小到只是比例性選制或多數決選制之內的位移，也可大到第一層的變化；依照表 13.1 的邏輯，小幅變動不見得代表大幅變動，但第一層的變化必然伴隨著第二層的變化。[17]第二，二分法雖然可以涵蓋大部分的選制，但難免有所疏漏，其中最複雜的是混合制。在混合制中，聯立式單一選區兩票制（mixed-member proportional system, MMP）乃以政黨得票來分配席次，應歸於比例性選制；並立式單一選區兩票制（mixed-member majoritarian system, MMM）的區域席次和比例代表席次分開計算，的確可能發生最大黨不能得到過半席次的可能。某些人將並立式單一選區兩票制視爲多數決選制，是因爲此制的區域選舉的確有利大黨。本文也將「單一選區席次至少占總席次一半」的並立式單一選區兩票制視爲多數決選制，但主要理由在於假設檢定。說明如下：

　　表 13.2 根據表 13.1 的定義，列出曾在 1978 到 2012 年經歷選制變遷的國家，其中並立式單一選區兩票制和多黨制並存的比例，高於和一黨過半並存的比例。這讓我們可以根據以下的方法來進行實證檢驗：本文希望將該選制歸爲對假設檢定較爲不利的類別時，仍能顯現假設的有效性。換言之，如果將此種選制歸爲對假設檢定較爲有利的類別，則假設的有效性可能來自歸類，而非假設本身。何以如此？從以下針對各種可能性的分析可知，將並立式單一選區兩票制歸爲比例性選制，有可能增加符合假設的案例。

1. 多數決選制變爲比例性選制，而並立式單一選區兩票制是變遷的結果。由於後者多屬多黨制，正好可以檢證本文的主要假設：「當多數決選制變爲比例性選制，無黨過半的變遷率高於一黨過半」（詳下節）。

2. 多數決選制變爲比例性選制，而現狀是並立式單一選區兩票制。由於後者被歸類爲比例性選制，故不屬於此類變遷。

　　變）等同於更高層性質轉變的狀態。其實 Lijphart（1994）和 Colomer（2005）也將選制二分爲「多數決選制」和「比例代表制」兩類，但涵蓋的選制有限，所以本文未採用他們的分類。再者，既有選制分類多以投票和記票方式爲基準，本文則以當選門檻進行劃分，兩者的性質不同。

[17] 「選制變動」的定義，涉及分析層次的選擇。我們可以依據研究議題，決定第二層的轉變是否可定義爲選制變動。蘇子喬、王業立（2010）即認爲，泰國在全額連記制和單一選區兩票制間的移動，屬於選制變遷。就該文作者所要探討的問題（亦即混合式選制的廢棄與否）來看，這樣的定義當然不會有問題。但這也表示，我們可以根據研究範圍或主題來調整變遷的定義。

表 13.1　由當選門檻所區別的選舉制度

第一層	第二層
多數決選制 （當選門檻有利於是大黨取得過半席次）	1. 單一選區制 　(1) 單一選區相對多數決（first past the post, FPTP）：應選名額一，得票最高者當選。 　(2) 多（兩）輪投票（two round system, TRS）：若無人得票過半則舉行下一輪投票，直至有人當選（通常前兩名參選，舉行兩輪投票）。 　(3) 絕對多數（absolute majority, AM）：需得多數才能當選：無兩輪投票。 　(4) 排序投票（alternative vote, AV）：選民依偏好將候選人排序，若無人過半，則排除最少人列爲第一順位之候選人並將其選票依排序加給其他候選人，直到有人得到過半選票。 2. 波達法（Borda count, BC）：選民將候選人排序，依次給予不同分數，總分最高者當選。 3. 全額連記複數選區制（block vote, BV）：選民投票數等於選區席次，以得票高低補滿應選名額。 4. 並立式單一選區兩票制（mixed-member majoritarian system, MMM）：席次分爲區域與比例代表兩部分，區域席次以單一選區相對多數決或多（兩）輪投票選出，和政黨名單比例代表席次分開計算：單一選區席次至少應占總席次之一半。
比例性選制 （當選門檻不利於大黨取得過半席次）	1. 聯立式單一選區票制（mixed-member proportional system, MMP）：席次分爲區域與政黨名單比例代表兩部分，區域席次以單一選區相對多數決或多（兩）輪投票選出，政黨總席次以政黨票爲計算基準，單一選區最高票必爲勝選者。 2. 部分並立式單一選區兩票制：區域選區席次不到總席次一半，或採取複數選區。 3. 複數選區制 　(1) 限制連記法（limited vote, LV）：選民投票數小於選區席次，以得票高低補滿應選名額。 　(2) 單記非讓渡投票制（single nontransferable vote, SNTV）：通常爲複數選區，每位選民投一票給候選人，候選人所得選票不得轉讓，以得票高低補滿應選名額。 　(3) 單記可讓渡投票制（single transferable vote, STV）：複數選區，選民依偏好將候選人排序後，計算到達當選門檻的候選人，將當選者超過當選門檻所需之選票依序分給其他候選人，直到補滿應選名額爲止。 4. 政黨名單比例代表制（proportional representation, PR）：以政黨的開放式或封閉式名單得票率爲準，依據最大平均數法或最大餘數法分配席次。

資料來源：由 IPU PARLINE 所定義的選舉制度整理。

表 13.2　選制變遷的國家（1978-2012）

變遷模式	國家	變遷前	變遷後	首次使用新選制年度
多數決選制之內	尼泊爾聯邦民主共和國（Nepal）	FPTP	MMM	2008
	吉爾吉斯共和國（Kyrgyzstan）	TRS	MMM	2000
	吉爾吉斯共和國（Kyrgyzstan）	MMM	TRS	2005
	亞塞拜然共和國（Azerbaijan）	MMM	FPTP	2005
	東加王國（Tonga）	BV	FPTP	2010
	阿爾巴尼亞共和國（Albania）	TRS	MMM	1997
	哈薩克共和國（Kazakhstan）	MMM	TRS	1995
	哈薩克共和國（Kazakhstan）	TRS	MMM	1999
	埃及阿拉伯共和國（Egypt）	BV	MMM	2011
	泰國（Thailand）	BV	MMM	2001
	泰國（Thailand）	MMM	BV + PR	2007
	烏克蘭（Ukraine）	FPTP	MMM	1998
	馬其頓共和國（Macedonia）	TRS	MMM	1998
	斐濟共和國（Fijo）	BV	AV	1999
	塔吉克共和國（Tajikistan）	TRS	MMM	2000
	蒙古國（Mongolia）	TRS	BV	1992
	蒙古國（Mongolia）	BV	TRS	1996
	蒙古國（Mongolia）	TRS	BV	2008

（接下頁）

變遷模式	國家	變遷前	變遷後	首次使用新選制年度
多數決選制之內	摩納哥侯國（Monaco）	TRS	MMM	2003
	緬甸聯邦共和國（Burma）	AM	TRS	2010
從多數決選制到比例性選制	巴基斯坦伊斯蘭共和國（Pakistan）	FPTP	PR	2002
	伊拉克共和國（Iraq）	BV	PR	2005
	吉爾吉斯共和國（Kyrgyzstan）	TRS	PR	2007
	多哥共和國（Togo）	TRS	PR	1999
	克羅埃西亞共和國（Croatia）	MMM	PR	2000
	法蘭西共和國（France）	TRS	PR	1986
	阿爾巴尼亞共和國（Albania）	MMM	PR	2009
	俄羅斯聯邦（Russia）	MMM	PR	2007
	保加利亞共和國（Bulgaria）	MMM	PR	1991
	哈薩克共和國（Kazambstan）	MMM	PR	2007
	約旦哈希米王國（Joradn）	BV	SNTV	1997
	烏克蘭（Ukraine）	MMM	PR	2006
	紐西蘭（New Zealand）	FPTP	MMP	1996
	馬其頓共和國（Macedonia）	MMM	PR	2002
	菲律賓共和國（Philippines）	BV	MMP	1998
	義大利共國和（Italy）	MMM	PR	2006
	摩洛哥王國（Morocco）	FPTP	PR	1997
	賴索托王國（Lesotho）	FPTP	MMP	2002

（接下頁）

變遷模式	國家	變遷前	變遷後	首次使用新選制年度
從比例性選制到多數決選制	中華民國（台灣）（Republic of China; Taiwan）	SNTV	MMM	2008
	日本（Japan）	SNTV	MMM	1996
	委內瑞拉共和國（Venezuela）	MMP	MMM	2010
	法蘭西共和國（France）	PR	TRS	1988
	馬達加斯加共和國（Madagascar）	PR	MMM	1998
	獅子山共和國（Siern Leone）	PR	FPTP	2007
	義大利共和國（Italy）	PR	MMM	1994
在比例性選制內	委內瑞拉共和國（Venezuela）	PR	MMP	1993
	玻利維亞（Bolivia）	PR	MMP	1997
	突尼西亞共和國（Tunisia）	MMP	PR	2011
	羅馬尼亞（Romania）	PR	MMP	2008

資料來源：根據 IPU PARLINE 資料計算。

說明：國家名稱依據中華民國外交部翻譯，在變遷模式下依筆畫順序排序。選制的中英文名稱，請參考表 13.1。

3. 比例性選制轉變為多數決選制，而現狀是並立式單一選區兩票制。如果假設是「此種變遷不會發生在一黨過半時」，則符合假設的資料將會增加。如果假設是「變遷起於外生因素」，則此一選制不應造成解釋力的大幅變動。

4. 比例性選制轉變為多數決選制，而並立式單一選區兩票制為變遷後果。此時，此一選制應屬未變遷組。

由此可知，將並立式單一選區兩票制歸類為比例性選制，對大部分的假設沒有影響，但在第三種狀況下有可能增加符合假設的案例。綜合以上分析，本文之所以將此選

制歸類為多數決選制，一方面是為了要符合直觀，另一方面則是要顯示在對假設檢證較為不利的狀況下，仍能檢證假設的有效性。至於不符合「單一選區席次至少占總席次之一半」的並立式混合制，就應該視為比例性選制。

次節將提出主要的假設，以連結本節所述的選制變遷分類表。

肆、選制變遷的假設

選制影響國會席次分配，國會議員又多屬政黨，顯示政黨體系和選制變遷有關。就政黨的偏好來看，因為選制和政黨的大小有關，所以變遷也應依選制是否對大黨有利，分兩個方向觀察。前節已經說明選制變遷和選制類型的關係，指出多數決選制的變遷和政黨體系有關，而比例性選制的變遷則受到外生因素的影響較大。作為自變項，外生因素難以窮盡，但選舉有可能導致政黨席次的重分配甚至政黨輪替，我們至少可以根據「政黨席次極大化」的假定，思考與其有關的自變項。以下提出本文採用的自變項，以及能否從選制變遷的理論推得特定變項的相關性和影響方向。

第一，是威權政體。本文採取 Freedom House 的「非自由」（not free）來判定政體是否為威權，所以在變項操作上稱威權政體為「非自由國家」。我們可以延伸 Boix （1999）的理論而得到以下的推論：如果挑戰者尚不足以與威權政黨抗爭，則多數決選制可以防杜新政黨獲取席次，所以較受執政者歡迎。[18] 就此變項的相關性而言，可以比較（半）自由與非自由國家。首先，假設現狀是多數決選制。以非自由國家而言，執政者除了偏好多數決選制，應該也不樂見選制變遷。[19] 但理論模型已顯示，就（半）自

---

[18] 威權政體舉行選舉，在近來受到學界的注意。對威權政體而言，選舉競爭存在一定的風險和機會。在風險方面，政治競爭如果導致國家財政的危機，容易造成威權政黨在選舉中失利，但欠缺自然資源的威權政體，比較可能透過選舉來轉型。也有研究發現，身處民主國家陣營的威權國家，比較可能透過選舉來轉型，被威權國家包圍的政權，則較難進行競爭性的選舉。無論如何，威權政體可以透過選舉來掌握更多的訊息，並在可控制的範圍內鞏固權力。請參閱 Carey 與 Reynolds（2011）、Greene（2010）、de Mesquita 與 Smith（2008）、Boix（2011）、Miller（2013）。

[19] 我們可以用國會選舉為分析單位，觀察多數決選制與比例性選制的比重是否因國家自由度而有異。結果發現，自由與半自由國家使用兩類選制的百分比分別為 38.70 與 61.30，非自由國家百分比分別為 73.48 與 26.52。之所以出現這樣的相關性，是因為選舉的角色因自由度而有別。非自由國家通常處於一黨專政，較多偏好多數決選制，也多反對將其改變為比例性選制。對自由國家中的先進民主國家而言，選制通常呈現一定的穩定性，主要是因為已經經歷過重要的選

由國家而言，一黨過半也是阻礙多數決選制轉變的重要原因。所以，多數決選制下的一黨過半，不論在（半）自由國家與非自由國家下都不利選制變遷，所以統計上的顯著性較弱。其次，如果現狀是比例性選制，非自由國家可能藉著轉變為多數決選制來鞏固權力，但其顯著性取決於其他變項是否出現類似的情況。

　　第二，是新興民主國家。本文以 Freedom House 的指標為判定標準。新興民主國家，多在第三波民主化潮流中建立民主體制，其中有許多是半自由和自由的國家，所以和非自由國家不同（Huntington, 1993; Diamond, 2008）。所謂「非新興民主國家」，包含非民主國家、先進民主國家以及曾遭遇民主倒退的國家。兩相比較，新興民主國家有以下的特性。首先，和非民主國家相比，新興民主國家的選舉對於政權重組扮演更重要的角色；和先進民主國家相比，新興民主國家的市民社會較弱，選舉往往成為決定政策方向的主要依據。此外，新興民主國家多以總統制或半總統制為主要的憲政體制。雖然有學者指出，這些國家的總統應該和能形成總統多數的多數決選制搭配，但現實上採行比例性選制的國家相當多（Jones, 1995）。就「新興民主國家」與選制變遷的相關性來看，此類國家大多欠缺能主導決策的力量，再加上經常出現的地域或族群分歧，使其較難形成選制改革的共識（Brady and Mo, 1992; Mozaffar, Scarrit, and Galaich, 2003; Barkan, Densham, and Rushton, 2006）。如果現狀是多數決選制，而新興民主國家又往比例性選制的方向變動，則動力應該在於多黨化，但這和非新興國家的動力一致，所以統計上的顯著性應該不強。如果現狀是比例性選制，則新興民主國家變為多數決選制的個案數應該很少；其顯著性取決於其他變項是否有同樣阻礙選制改變的原因，如果沒有，則其顯著性高。

　　第三，是區域特性。誠如 Reilly（2007b：1366）所言，亞洲國家的選制變遷反映「亞洲價值」，和其他區域有明顯差異。相較於歐美對於個人自由的重視，亞洲較強調集體價值和社會連結。亞洲國家的政黨可能有較強的人治色彩，甚至產生「反政黨」的傾向，但領導亞洲選制改革的，可能正是威權時代的政黨或領袖。亞洲的選制改革者很可能以減少政黨數目為訴求，以呼應希望提升政府效能的民意（Hicken and Kuhonta, 2011）。依此理，如果現狀是比例性選制，則亞洲和其他區域具有明顯的差異，應會顯現正向且顯著的影響力。但若現狀是多數決選制，我們尚難判定驅使亞洲國家走向比例

制轉變。反觀自由與半自由中的新興民主國家，正處於意見分化、欠缺領導中心的狀況，所以比較容易從多數決選制轉為比例性選制，但卻不利相反方向的轉變。此外，自由和非自由國家的選制變遷比例雖然都不高，但非自由國家卻有可能產生威權解體，逐漸變為新興民主國家；若然，其選制變遷的可能性會開始提高，類似其他的新興民主國家。相對而言，先進民主國家的選制已達均衡狀態，較難改變。

性選制的動因，而此一動因的顯著性，取決於是否和非亞洲區域相似。

　　最後，是憲政體制的類型。本文以政黨是否掌握國會半數以上席次爲主要自變項，隱含國會是主要的選制改革機構。然而，在某些憲政體制中，國會外的力量（例如總統）有可能扮演重要角色，甚至可以否決國會的決策。以此推論，憲政體制對於選制改革應該有所影響。簡言之，當選制變革從多數決選制走向比例性選制時，內閣制的國會直接反映多黨的選制偏好，而其他憲政體制的國家則可能出現持有相反意見的憲政機關，所以「內閣制」的影響力爲正而顯著。如果選制改革是從比例性選制變爲多數決選制，因爲政黨體系並非顯著的動因，所以很難判定內閣制的影響力。順帶一提，「總統選舉」是另一個重要變項，但必然發生在總統制和半總統制下，和「內閣制」幾乎是反義詞，所以就不另外設定這個變項。

　　以上推論，是以政黨體系對選制變遷的可能影響爲起點，延伸到其他面向。因爲本文要比較兩種選制變遷模式，所以兩個模型會考慮同樣的變項，不論其影響方向和顯著性是否明確。需要強調的是，全球資料庫並非抽樣所得，變項在統計上的顯著性，對照的是理論上的母體（亦即假定資料爲隨機抽樣所得），而非實存的母體。至於變項的影響方向，目的在於檢測是否和理論預期一致。以下的敘述以自變項 X 爲例，摘要說明相關性與顯著性的三種情況：

1. 從政黨角度出發，推得變項 X 的影響方向和非 X 不同，所以 X 具有明確的影響方向和統計上的顯著性。

2. 從政黨角度出發推得變項 X 的影響方向，但因和非 X 類似，所以統計上的顯著性不強。

3. 無法從理論推得明確的影響方向。

整理前述分析後，得出本文的主要假設如下：

假設一：當多數決選制變爲比例性選制時，「無黨過半」具有正向且顯著的影響力，「非自由國家」和「新興民主國家」的顯著性弱，「亞洲國家」的影響力無法從理論推得，「內閣制」的影響力爲正且顯著。

假設二：當比例性選制變爲多數決選制時，「無黨過半」的顯著性弱，「非自由國家」的顯著性無法從理論推得，「新興民主國家」的影響力爲負，若其他變項欠缺類似影響力時顯著性高，「亞洲國家」具有正向且顯著的影響力，「內閣制」的影響力無法從理論推得。

假設三：如果絕大多數的比例性選制產生多黨制，但多數決選制會造成一定比重的多黨制，則後者的變遷率高於前者。

假設四：當多數決選制轉變爲比例性選制，選制轉變前後皆爲多黨制，兩者差異
　　　　不大；當比例性選制轉變爲多數決選制，有效政黨數在選制轉變後應該變
　　　　少，產生較爲明顯的差異。

在這些假設中，假設三延伸自前兩個假設。既然多數決選制的變遷條件是多黨制，而比例性選制原本就以多黨制爲主，前者的變遷率應該比較高。再者，假設三、四涉及政黨數，我們將以「有效政黨數」（effective number of parties）當作主要變項。其中假設四的目的，在於重新檢視杜弗傑假說。如果有效政黨數在比例性選制變爲多數決選制後明顯減少，就反映出杜弗傑假說的核心論證。

在進入實證分析前，還需要說明兩個相關議題。第一，本文不以「有效政黨數」爲自變項，是因爲其定義與「無黨過半」不同。有效政黨數關切的是選制的後果而非影響選制變遷的直接因素，而且一黨過半的國家，有效政黨數不見得大於無黨過半的國家。[20] 第二，政黨看重的是下一次的選舉，所以應該用期待席次率作爲估算的標準。但是政黨對席次的期待，在現實上不易觀測，而不同政黨的期待有別，也欠缺統一指標。再者，某些國家的政黨體系會隨著選制改革而重組，不易進行前後比對。替代的方法，是假定政黨能「鑒往知來」，亦即根據以前的選舉紀錄，形成對未來的預期。次節會對相關議題提出進一步的說明。

伍、實證研究

在驗證上述假設之前，先說明資料庫的性質和研究設計。資料庫是由各國各次國會選舉所構成，包含所有從 1978 到 2012 年舉行過直接國會選舉的國家，如果爲兩院制，則以下議院（或眾議院）選舉爲準。[21] 選擇 1978 至 2012 年這個時間點有幾項意義。第一，1980 年代適逢第三波民主化浪潮，所以資料庫包含許多新興民主國家。「新興民主國家」是自變項之一，可以顯示民主化對選制變遷的影響。第二，這是最新的選制資料庫，而關於選制的相關研究大多未涵蓋新興民主國家，所以可以用新資料來驗證舊理論。第三，「非自由國家」也是自變項之一，可顯現選舉競爭是否因自由度而有別。

---

[20] 例如，假設 A 國有三黨，席次率分別爲 51%、45% 和 4%，B 國有四黨，席次率分別爲 49%、49%、1% 和 1%，則 B 國的有效政黨數低於 A 國，但 A 國有一黨過半，B 國無。

[21] 許多國家對於少數族群或區域設有特定的選制，應先扣除這些特殊席次，才能決定該國的選制類別。

第四，本資料庫的個案數超越其他研究，可減緩樣本過少的偏誤，並提升理論的可信度。本文建構的資料庫乃以 IPU PARLINE 爲本，並對照其他的資料庫、書籍與論文，以確認資料的正確性；若有不一致之處，則以 IPU PARLINE 爲準。[22] 資料庫中未被 IPU PARLINE 登錄的個案只有台灣，顯現此一資料庫的完整性。

在研究設計方面，關鍵問題在於分析層次的設定。選制是否變遷，是國家層次的問題，但本文的關切重點在國會選舉，亦即國家之下的現象。所謂政黨體系，是從每次的國會選舉累積起來的結果，所以兼具兩個層次的特色。一個直覺的分析方法，是以國家爲分析單位，並以該國在某種選制下政黨體系最常出現的類別爲主要變項。這是一種簡潔的研究設計，但個案數大量減少，而且不同國家的選舉次數有別，有可能造成統計推論的誤差。另一種方法，是以每次選舉爲分析單位，觀察政黨變項和選制變遷的關係。舉例而言，若某國採用多數決選制，則出現無黨過半的選舉次數越多，選制就越可能變爲比例性選制。這種分析法假定，政黨之所以需要一段時間來推動選制變革，可能因爲需要多次選舉的證明，也可能因爲結成多數聯盟要耗費時日。這種分析方法的分析單位仍是選舉，但選舉結果累積了變遷的動能，最終得以完成國家層級的選制改革。此種方法保持了最大的個案數，發生偏誤估計的機率也比較低。

本文強調的是選制的質性轉變，所以將「多數決選制和比例性選制」之間是否轉換視爲依變項。資料庫將國家區分爲「有變遷」和「無變遷」兩組。在資料庫中登錄爲「未變遷」的個案，是指未在 1978 到 2012 年發生第一層次的變遷，但不代表未在此期間發生其他層次的變化或在其他期間發生第一層次的變化。所以，本文所界定的是一種最廣義的「選制變遷」，範圍包含全球國家。其他針對小範圍國家的研究，可以包含第二層的選制變遷，但和本文的關切不同。

這組資料，包含國會選舉的縱橫面向，理論上可以同時考慮空間和時間，但實際上各國狀況不一。假設國會選舉每四年舉行一次，資料庫所能蒐集到的選舉最多只有四、五次；某些國家政局不穩，能放入資料庫的選舉更少。所以，我們並不假設時間是自變項，只能盡量擴大空間的範圍，讓個案總數超過既有研究。

在操作程序上，「變遷組」的資料，來自所有曾經在觀察期間內發生選制變遷的國家所舉行過的國會選舉，並扣除發生變遷的那次國會選舉，其他所有資料則歸於「無變遷組」。以下說明各變項及其定義。

1. 選制變遷：觀察 1978 至 2012 年間「多數決選制」和「比例性選制」之間是否發生變遷，1＝是，0＝否。

---

[22]　IPU PARLINE，http://www.ipu.org/parline。檢索日期：2015 年 7 月 2 日。

2. 無黨過半：每次選舉是否沒有政黨掌握國會過半議席，1 = 是，0 = 否。

3. 有效政黨數：$1/\sum S_i^2$，S_i 為國會黨派 i 的席次率，i 為政黨（包括無黨籍的議員）。[23]

4. 內閣制：國家元首為世襲或間接選舉產生，國會對政府有倒閣權；1 = 是，0 = 否。[24]

5. 非自由國家：以選舉年為基準，1 = 是，0 = 不是。[25]

6. 新興民主國家：1 = 是，0 = 不是。新興民主國家的定義，是指在 1970 年代之後進入民主化的國家。[26]

7. 國家是否在亞洲：1 = 是，0 = 不是。

作為本文的依變項，「選制變遷」的分析分為兩類模式來進行。其他變項，在前節已經討論其定義、理論意涵與預期發現。第一、二項假設，目的在於探詢影響選制變遷的因素。由於依變項是二元類別變項，本文採取「二元勝算對數模型」（binary logit model）為分析方法。[27] 在進行統計顯著性檢定時，假定標準差皆為「獨立且相同的分布」（independent and identically distributed, i.i.d.），Exp(B) 則表示「變遷對未變遷」的勝算比。

根據假設一，當多數決選制轉變為比例性選制時，「無黨過半」和「內閣制」具有正向且顯著的影響力，「非自由國家」和「新興民主國家」的顯著性弱，「亞洲國家」的影響力無法從理論推得。表 13.3 顯示，「無黨過半」係數的顯著性和預期一致，「內閣制」也出現預期的影響方向但顯著性稍弱，其餘變項大多符合預期。其中最重要的發

---

[23] 有效政黨數的算法有許多種，差別在於如何計算無黨派議員。當無黨派議員人數不多時，不同計算方法結果差異不大。但若無黨派議員數目很大，且將每位無黨派議員視為單一政黨，或在公式中考慮這個因素，都會使有效政黨數被放大，進而影響估計值的準確性。本文採取的是 Taagepera 提出的「最小成分法」（least component approach），亦即最大值與最小值的平均值。請參閱 Taagepera（1997: 147-148）。

[24] World Bank Database of Political Institutions，http://www.nsd.uib.no/macrodataguide/set. html?id=11&sub=1。檢索日期：2015 年 7 月 2 日。

[25] Freedom House，各年度報告：http://www.freedomhouse.org/reports。檢索日期：2015 年 7 月 2 日。

[26] 不同文獻對於哪些國家屬於新興民主國家，界定方式會有一些差異。本文以 Moestrup 和 Kapstein 與 Converse 的交集為準。請參閱 Moestrup（2007: 44-46）、Kapstein 與 Converse（2008: 163-166）。

[27] 國會選舉發生在同一國之內，而各國間的狀況有別，所以國會選舉可能帶有定群追蹤資料（panel data）的性質。但因本文並非針對同一選舉在不同時間點上進行調查，所以未將國家視為群集（cluster）進行標準差檢定。

現，就是「無黨過半」符合理論預期，其係數 0.831 的勝算對數比為 2.296，顯現此自變項是影響多數決選制變遷的關鍵要素。這表示，內生性理論在多數決選制的變遷上是成立的。

表 13.3　多數決選制變遷的二元勝算對數模型

	B	S.E.	Sig.	Exp(B)
無黨過半	0.831	0.361	0.021	2.296
內閣制	0.653	0.351	0.063	1.921
非自由國家	0.383	0.354	0.280	1.467
新興民主國家	0.280	0.324	0.388	1.323
亞洲國家	0.063	0.341	0.854	1.065
常數	-3.241	0.444	0.000	0.039

N = 429
Log likelihood = -140.95182
Pseudo R-square = 0.0356

資料來源：IPU PARLINE。

　　必須說明的是，「無黨過半」是必要條件而非充分條件，所以仍有些無黨過半的國家沒有發生變遷。解釋有無變遷的原因很多，其中之一在於多數決選制的投票方式。和其他的多數決選制相比，並立式單一選區兩票制包含了一定數量的比例代表席次，以政黨為劃分席次的基準，所以即使有利大黨掌握多數，小黨還是可能從比例區取得一定的政黨名單席次。如果此時產生多黨制，小黨即有機會組成選制改革聯盟，推動有利小黨參政的比例性選制。在其他的多數決選制中，多黨制有可能反映地域主義，雖然在全國為多黨制，但區域席次卻為大黨壟斷，所以欠缺改變選制的誘因。這個猜想，得到經驗資料的支持：在表 13.3 的 429 個案例中，有 91 個採行並立式單一選區兩票制，之後轉變為比例性選制的百分比為 19.78（占 46 個變遷案例的 18 個），在採行其他選制的 338 個個案中，轉變為比例性選制的百分比為 8.28，是前者的一半。

　　在其他的變項中，「內閣制」的影響力為正，可能原因在於政府決策較不受其他憲政機關的干擾，但其顯著性低於政黨體系。「新興民主國家」的影響力也是正的，反映出類似多黨化的趨勢，但效果不明顯。至於「非自由國家」的係數為何不顯著，可能因

爲這個變項和威權政黨高度相關,而後者又很少處於「無黨過半」的狀態,所以不太會發生選制變遷。

假設二探討比例性制變遷的動因。根據此一假設,當比例性選制變爲多數決選制時,「無黨過半」的顯著性弱,「內閣制」和「非自由國家」的顯著性無法從理論推得,「新興民主國家」的影響力爲負(顯著性要看和其他變項的相關性),「亞洲國家」則具有正向且顯著的影響力。表 13.4 印證了這些預期。其中值得注意的是「新興民主國家」和「亞洲國家」都具有顯著性,而兩者對於選制變遷的影響方向是相反的。一方面,前述 Reilly 的論證,已經說明爲何「亞洲國家」對比例性選制的變遷具有正向且顯著的影響。另一方面,許多「新興民主國家」呈現多元分歧的社會,一旦選擇比例性選制就欠缺改革動機,而其影響力在眾變項中具有獨特性,所以顯著性很強。

在 Reilly 理論的基礎上,可以進一步思考亞洲國家和其他區域(尤其是當中的新興民主國家)有何不同。[28]「亞洲國家」是區域的概念,也是顯現潛在變項的替代變項,正如「歐洲」相對於特定的價值一樣。相較於歐洲的多黨制和英美的兩黨制,亞洲國家較看重社會關係和集體價值。從這個角度看,日本和台灣長期採用的單記非讓渡投票制,具有一定的亞洲特性:一方面,此一選制有助一黨獨大,另一方面,個人選票(personal vote)對於勝選也相當重要。基於同樣的邏輯,當一黨獨大瓦解並走向多黨制時,即會出現以減少政黨數目來提升政府效能的呼求。除了台灣與日本,某些亞洲國家也出現降低選制比例性的變化(雖然本文未將其定義爲選制變遷)。亞洲國家的確和特定的選舉制度有關,但後者本身是被解釋的對象,所以本文仍以前者爲自變項。

假設三,是要藉著假設一、二的發現,探討不同選制發生變遷的機率。一般而言,比例性選制因多黨化而不利轉變,假設一又已確認多數決選制在無黨過半時比較容易發生變遷,使多數決選制可能產生一部分的多黨制,所以多數決選制的變動率應高於比例性選制。以實際的有效政黨數來觀察,多數決選制的平均值是 2.46,比例性選制是 3.59,以中位數而言,多數決選制是 2.09,比例性選制是 3.24。由此可知,少數的多數決選制選舉將有效政黨數的平均值拉高,所以多數決選制的變遷機率應該高於比例性選制。[29] 表 13.5 以「國家 / 選制」爲單位,顯示兩種選制變遷模式的「國家 / 選制」總數、

---

[28] 「亞洲國家數」和「亞洲個案數」不同。依照表 13.2,從比例性選制轉變爲多數決選制的國家共有七個,亞洲國家雖然只有日本和台灣,但以選舉次數來看,兩者所占的比重最高,而且都是從單記非讓渡投票制轉變爲並立式單一選區兩票制。在亞洲以外的國家中,法國和義大利都在轉爲比例性選制後很快改回原有的多數決選制,獅子山和馬達加斯加則因爲政局因素所以選舉的次數不多。有關日本的選制改革,請參閱王鼎銘、郭銘峰、黃紀(2008)。

[29] 比例性選制的平均數和中位數也有差距,但方向是往更高的比例性移動。

變遷的「國家／選制」數及比例，印證了這個假設。[30] Colomer 曾言，政黨名單比例代表制的穩定度相當高。本文使用的資料庫，時間橫跨 1978 到 2012 年，所謂比例性選制的範圍又大於政黨名單比例代表制，由此推知的「比例性選制比多數決選制穩定」，比 Colomer 的說法更具有普遍性。

表 13.4　比例性選制變遷的二元勝算對數模型

	B	S.E.	Sig.	Exp(B)
無黨過半	-0.748	0.627	0.233	0.473
內閣制	-0.419	0.449	0.351	0.658
非自由國家	-0.611	0.695	0.379	0.543
新興民主國家	-1.194	0.464	0.010	0.303
亞洲國家	1.844	0.448	0.000	6.322
常數	-1.823	0.667	0.006	0.162

N = 478
Log likelihood = -89.526294
Pseudo R-square = 0.1134

資料來源：IPU PARLINE。

表 13.5　兩種選制變遷模式之比較

	總數	變遷數	變遷比例（%）
多數決選制	98	17	17.35
比例性選制	97	9	9.28
總數	195	26	13.33

資料來源：IPU PARLINE。
說明：分析單位為「國家／選制」，某些國家因為選制變遷，所以出現的次數大於 1。

---

[30] 因為表 13.5 以「國家／選制」為單位，所以數量超過實際國家數。

　　假設四的目的，在於分析選制變革如何引發政黨數目的變化。我們以有效政黨數當作變項，比較兩種選制變遷模式的差別。如果假設四成立，有效政黨數在多數決選制變遷的前後不會有太大差別，只有在比例性選制變遷後才會明顯減少。如果以有選制變遷的國會選舉爲分析單位，並計算變遷前後各選舉的有效政黨數，則 One-Way ANOVA 是最簡明的比較方法。此一方法在考量各自標準差的情況下，觀察變遷前後的兩個有效政黨數平均值是否達到顯著的差距。因爲「非自由國家」不見得舉行公平的選舉，表 13.6 僅考慮自由和半自由國家。結果不但印證了假設四，也間接支持杜弗傑假說所蘊含的結果：有效政黨數在多數決選制變爲比例性選制後增加幅度有限，是因爲變遷前後都屬於多黨制；比例性選制變爲多數決選制後有效政黨數明顯減少，符合杜弗傑假說的意涵。換言之，多黨制雖非杜弗傑對多數決選制後果的預期，卻會內生性地轉向比例性選制，而比例性選制雖因外生因素而變遷，但變遷後有效政黨數下降，也符合杜弗傑假說。隨著兩種選制變遷路徑而來的政黨體系，正趨向杜弗傑假說所預期的均衡。

表 13.6　以 One-Way ANOVA 比較選制變遷前後有效政黨數的差異

	多數決選制變爲比例性選制	比例性選制變爲多數決選制
變遷前有效政黨數 平均值	4.011 (1.898)	3.607 (1.330)
變遷後有效政黨數 平均值	3.649 (1.786)	2.470 (0.609)
sig, <	0.444	0.001

資料來源：IPU PARLINE。
說明：以「選舉」爲單位；括弧內爲標準差；限於自由與半自由國家。

陸、結論

　　本文以選制和政黨體系的因果關係爲分析起點，探討選制變遷的兩派理論。杜弗傑假說，乃以選制的機械效應和心理效應來解釋政黨體系爲什麼是選制的後果。Colomer 認爲，縱使兩個變項相關，但選制多由政黨所選擇，所以政黨體系是選制變遷的變因。然而，也有學者指出，選制的變化，起於和政黨沒有關連的外生因素。爲了釐清這個辯論，本文以機率形式陳述杜弗傑假說，並以其預期之外的政黨體系作爲選制變化的源

頭。分析的焦點，在於釐清政黨體系在什麼情況下會成爲選制變遷的內生變因，什麼時候不會。結果發現，在多數決選制下，如果始終未出現一黨過半，小黨即有可能相互結盟，改採對其比較有利的比例性選制；在並立式單一選區兩票制下，小黨席次多來自政黨名單比例代表區，相互結盟的動機更強。反論之，如果比例性選制造成一黨獨大，則此政黨欠缺改變選制的誘因，如果此類選制帶來多黨制，則很難出現小黨爲了改革選制而結盟的可能。根據這樣的推論，多數決選制的變遷受到政黨體系的內生性影響，比例性選制的改革則取決於外生因素。爲了驗證這個假設，本文以全球選制資料庫爲檢測對象，得到以下的發現：1. 無黨過半，是影響多數決選制變遷的關鍵因素；2. 比例性選制的變革受到「亞洲國家」的正向影響，而其方向和「新興民主國家」相反；3. 絕大部分的比例代表制產生多黨制，而多數決選制下的政黨數則呈現偏斜分布，使後者的變遷機率高於前者；4. 比例性選制變爲多數決選制後，政黨數目的確下降，所以這種變化符合杜弗傑假說的意涵。

　　以上就是本文的理論和檢證。必須說明的是，理論採取的是簡化的假定，不可能涵蓋所有的變因。正如 Renwick（2010）所言，選制改革涉及複雜的變因，不但參與的行動者繁多，行動者對選制的認知也有程度不一的限制。量化研究以建構通則爲目的，其誤差項有可能正是某些選制改革的重點。對此，可以用個案研究來補充。其中一項個案研究的關鍵問題是，某些採取比例性選制的國家，爲何可以形成改革選制的政黨結盟？我們還是可以從政黨的席次變化來回答這個問題，而日本在 1994 年的選制改革，正好說明了這個情況。該國長期採用的單記非讓渡投票制，具有一定的亞洲特性：一方面，該選制鼓勵派系化，但爲了確保資源分配，需要獨大政黨壟斷政權；另一方面，該選制屬於比例性選制，讓小黨有獲得席次的空間；無論何者，個人選票都是勝選關鍵。但這種「一大多小」的政黨體系，使政黨席次率產生很大的差距，也爲選制改革埋下伏筆。這就解釋了爲什麼自民黨在 1993 年選舉失去了衆議院多數席次後，仍然是國會最大的政黨，並能透過政黨結盟主導選制改革，在 1994 年將衆議院選制改爲有利大黨的並立式單一選區兩票制。台灣的選制改革歷程和日本相當類似。國民大會在 2005 年修憲時，將立法院長期使用的單記非讓渡投票制改爲並立式單一選區兩票制，而中國國民黨和民主進步黨就是選制改革的推手；這兩個政黨之所以要改變選制，目的之一就在於壓縮小黨的參政空間。但台灣和日本仍有差異：日本是內閣制國家，單一選區兩票制企圖強化執政黨對同黨議員的控制；台灣屬於半總統制，單一選區兩票制使國會容易出現一黨過半，但代表行政權的總統和代表立法權的立法院立場不見得一致，總統又不能否決法案，所以新選制不見得能提升政府效能。總論之，政黨席次分配以及憲政體制，都是理論模型所未能涵蓋的變項，我們只能透過個案研究來加以補強。

　　即便如此，本文仍然提出了一些值得思考的理論問題。誠如本文一開始所言，杜弗傑假說是研究選舉制度和政黨體系的典範。本文透過理論推演和實證分析，帶動了對於杜弗傑假說的思考。該假說認爲選制決定國會的席次分配，而國會議員多屬於政黨，所以選制會影響政黨體系。這也表示，爲了擴大政黨獲取議席的能力，某些議員可能有誘因推動選制改革。本文發現，一部分的比例性選制雖然受到外生因素的影響而轉變爲多數決選制，但變遷後的有效政黨數確實降低，符合杜弗傑假說的意涵。換言之，比例性選制可被視爲多數決選制內生性變遷的產物，並在多黨制下達到新的均衡。本文將杜弗傑假說轉換爲機率的形式，舉出這個假說沒有預期到的後果，但也間接證實了機率式杜弗傑假說的有效性。

兩岸關係

主題導讀

林繼文的兩岸關係研究

吳文欽、冷則剛

壹、前言

綜觀林繼文教授多年來在兩岸關係研究上的耕耘，其特色在理論的充實與突破，同時也兼顧了現實的政策意涵。兩岸在 1987 年開始逐步開放以來，經貿互動日益密切，但安全問題未解，在政治認同上則逐漸分道揚鑣，形成多層次、多面向的兩難困境。環顧全球各種分立政權案例，兩岸問題可謂獨樹一幟，引起學者們持續的關注。與兩岸關係快速發展的同時，也是台灣民主化從萌芽、發展到鞏固的重要轉型期。有關國內利益、制度變遷、認同變化，以及政黨政治等諸多變局，每一項均與兩岸關係產生不同程度的互動影響。林繼文教授在兩岸關係開展的初期，就極具洞見地指出內政外交連鎖的重要性，並引用理性抉擇與雙重賽局等重要概念分析，試圖解釋為何經貿交往無法促使政治突破的學術謎團。林繼文教授在較後期的著作中，並以空間模型分析美中台雙層三角互動，展現了進一步拓展的學術企圖心。事實上，林教授多年來累積有關兩岸研究概念的延伸，更充實了政策界耳熟能詳的「雙贏」、「零合」等概念。而林教授應用「勝集」（winset）等概念分析兩岸關係，不但在學術界有不少追隨者，在政策界也引用此一概念闡述兩岸互動的困境與可行性。限於篇幅關係，本書僅收錄林繼文教授在此主題的四篇文章，但是在本文的討論中，我們也會帶到林繼文教授其他關於兩岸關係的研究，讓讀者能全面掌握他對於這塊文獻的慧見與貢獻。

貳、兩岸經貿交流的賽局意涵

首先是林繼文教授與羅致政教授合著、刊登於《人文及社會科學集刊》的「零和或雙贏？兩岸經貿交流新解」（林繼文、羅致政，1998）。這篇文章的著眼點在於海峽兩岸在 1990 年代之後不斷擴大的經貿交流，開始對台灣與中國雙方戰略所帶來的挑戰。在台灣方面，固然兩岸經貿合作會帶來經濟利益，但也擔憂中國可能進一步蠶食台

灣經濟，甚至藉此達到「以商圍政」、「以通促統」的目標；另一方面，北京也無法確保對台灣的不斷讓利，是否能夠達到其祖國統一的政治目的。這種各自的矛盾使得兩岸的經貿關係，發展成一種「雙贏」與「零和」並存的特殊現象。所謂「雙贏」，即是在貿易往來中各取所需、互謀其利後所創造的「貿易利得」；所謂「零合」，則是指兩岸在主權議題上無法妥協。於是，在這篇文章中，兩位作者引入了「相對獲利敏感度」這個概念，為兩岸經貿互動建構了一個賽局模型，以解釋兩岸經貿關係如何隨著政治情勢而改變。

根據本文的論點，「相對獲利敏感度」來自於國際關係文獻中對於國家間進行合作時，究竟是偏向「絕對獲益」（absolute gain）或「相對獲益」（relative gain）。「絕對獲益」指的是自己國家在國際交流與合作時所獲得利益多寡，而不考慮對手國的獲利。然而，對新現實主義者而言，由於國際社會屬於無政府狀態，國家為了生存，不只是要關心自己權力大小，也要注意它國權力的變化，這種思維使得新現實主義者偏向認為「相對獲益」是國家之間能否進行國際合作的主要考量，因為它國的獲益可能是己國的損失。

在這篇文章中，作者採用了 Powell（1991）的觀點，認為國家對於相對獲益或絕對獲益的重視，無本質之異，而只有程度之別。他們引入了一個介於 0 與 1 之間的變數 k，表示某國對於相對獲利的重視程度。當 k = 0 時，國家只重視絕對獲益，但是當 k = 1 時，則只重視相對獲益。在這樣的設定下，k 的大小決定了在雙方政府眼中，兩岸經貿交流究竟是雙贏（k = 0）還是零和（k = 1）。

本文的洞見便是在於討論 k 值對於兩岸關係發展的影響。首先，在沒有任何一方可以將「對抗」當成優勢策略時，k 值的升高反而讓合作更為可能，因為雙方皆有誘因避免彼此對抗。然而，當 k 值高過某個臨界點時，超過了善意的限度，讓雙方合作的機率陡降為 0，並採取互相對抗的策略。另一方面，這篇文章也指出，雙方的獲利差距越大，合作的基礎便更為脆弱。這樣論點解釋了為何兩岸經貿交流在國際貿易理論上該屬於「雙贏」的局面，往往會因為政治互信度的降低，而突然變成零和賽局，使得雙方進入對抗情勢。

這篇文章雖寫於 1997 年，但很大程度預示了之後兩岸經貿往來的演變。國民黨在 2008 年贏得總統大選之後，進一步擴大兩岸的經貿互動，先是簽署《海峽兩岸經濟合作架構協議》，並開放中國大陸民眾訪台觀光。然而，當 2014 年我國立法院通過《海峽兩岸服務貿易協議》（簡稱《服貿協定》）後，由於協定內容與審查程序都有爭議，引發學生佔領立法院的「太陽花學運」，《服貿協定》也隨後被擱置。這事件印證了林繼文教授的觀點：兩岸經貿的交流，會隨著彼此對於相對獲利的敏感度上升，由可能創造雙贏的局面，變為零合賽局。

參、雙層賽局下的美中台戰略三角關係

　　前述文章所關注的兩岸關係發展的主要行為者，僅包含台灣與中國政府，但是現實世界中，「外交是內政的延伸」，政府的對外政策會受制於國內政治的制度與發展脈絡。此外，兩岸關係也可從更大的國際關係架構去加以理解，特別是美國在兩岸關係中的角色。因此，學者發展「雙層賽局」（two-level game）的分析架構，探討國內因素如何影響國際談判與互動，亦有學者採用「戰略三角（strategic triangle）理論」，並發展出「美中台關係」的研究議程。本節先簡述雙層賽局與戰略三角理論的基本概念，並說明林繼文教授如何成功結合兩者，為美中台關係研究提出整合性的動態研究視角。

一、雙層賽局

　　學界很早就注意到一國的國內政治運作，會影響其對外關係，但是一直到 Putnam（1988）提出的「雙層賽局」的觀點，才讓這個研究議程得以進一步開展。所謂「雙層賽局」，即是政府在對外談判或交涉時所涉及的兩場賽局，第一場是它和對手國的交涉與談判，第二場則是政府與國內支持者的互動。在國際談判中，由於談判雙方都希望極大化本國利益，甚至是壓縮對手國的利益，因此當對手國讓步太多時，其談判代表會失去其國內支持基礎，使得談判失敗。所以，談判代表最大的挑戰，就是如何在國際與國內兩場連動的賽局中，取得最大的利益。

　　早在 2000 年，林繼文教授便於 *Issue & Studies* 發表 "Two-Level Games Between Rival Regimes: Domestic Politics and the Remaking of Cross-Strait Relations" 乙文（Lin, 2000），採用雙層賽局來分析兩岸關係。[1] 在 Putnam（1988）所提出的雙層賽局中，假定了賽局結構為「非零合賽局」（non-zero sum game），因此推導出當國內行為者對於現狀越不滿時，談判代表可以和對手國斡旋的空間越大，國際合作越可能發生（即談判越可能成功）。不過，林繼文教授在本文中，區分了零合賽局（zero-sum game）與非零合賽局（non-zero-sum game）對於雙層賽局的影響，並指出在零合賽局時，因為對手國之得利，即為己國之損失，因此國內改變現狀的呼聲，並無法取得對手國之讓步，反而可能導致國際衝突。例如，當非民主政權的當權者屬於溫和派，但權力基礎卻處於相對弱勢時，則可能迫於國內壓力而掀起國際衝突，反之，若是當權者為弱勢的激進派，倒比較可能維持和平。這篇文章區分了經濟利益和主權地位對於賽局的影響，也成為林繼

---

[1]　限於篇幅關係，本書並未收錄此文。

文教授後續採用雙層賽局分析兩岸關係的基礎。

在 "The PRC as a Player in Taiwan's Domestic Politics: A Two-Level Game Analysis" 一文中（Lin, 2016c），[2] 林教授另外建立了一個雙層賽局模型，分析中國如何能夠影響台灣的內部政治。該模型包含三個行爲者：北京當局、國民黨、以及民進黨，它們對於台灣的主權定位有各自的偏好。但是，對北京而言，在尋求統一台灣時，也必須顧及台灣民眾對於統一（或獨立）的支持，而國民黨與民進黨爲了勝選，必須滿足中間選民的偏好。由於中國政府的終極目標是兩岸統一，它一方面必須「促統」，另一方面也必須「防獨」。在資源有限的情況下，林繼文教授指出，中國政府的最佳策略是說服那些在藍綠陣營遊走、不具特定政黨傾向的選民（nonpartisan voter），不要投票給支持台獨的政黨。在此，中國政府用來說服台灣選民的工具，即是中國對台灣的經貿政策。也就是說，針對那些沒有固定政黨認同的選民，北京可以透過提升台灣經濟對於中國的依賴，例如採購台灣的產品、或者鼓勵赴中國投資，來增加台灣民眾的所得，也藉此降低這些人對於台灣獨立的支持。選民可以預期當某個政黨（即國民黨）勝選後，中國將會擴大和台灣的經貿交流，也讓自己可以從中獲利。

根據這個雙層賽局模型，林繼文教授提出了四項命題，解釋兩岸關係的發展。首先，當台灣對於中國的經濟依賴度低、且台灣的領導人反對獨立時，則兩岸可以和平共處；然而，當台灣領導人偏向獨立時，中國將會採取較爲強硬的立場。另一方面，當台灣經濟高度依賴中國時，若是台灣領導人反對獨立時，則兩岸則可能簽署自由貿易協定（例如馬英九政府時期），因爲中國希望透過經貿交流，提升中間選民的利益；若是台灣領導人偏獨時，中國同樣也會希望可以透過其他惠台方案，吸引中間選民的支持。換言之，台灣民眾即使可以選總統，但是對某些人來說，他們的投票選擇，將受北京提供給台灣的經濟誘因所影響。林繼文教授這篇文章發表於 2016 年，但證諸 2018 年中國發佈「關於促進兩岸經濟文化交流合作的若干措施」，包含了 31 條惠台政策，給予台灣企業和人民在租稅與就業上之便利，並藉此將其融入中國經濟發展，可再次看出林繼文教授的先見之明。

二、戰略三角理論

所謂「戰略三角理論」，旨在分析一組國家（通常是三個）彼此之間的戰略狀態所構成的環境，而其中任兩國的關係，也會影響第三國在三角關係中的戰略地位

2　限於篇幅關係，本書並未收錄此文。

（Dittmer, 1981, 1987; 吳玉山，2000a、2000b）。例如當三個國家彼此都處於友好狀態時，則屬於「三邊家族型」，若是它們都彼此處於敵對狀態時，則是「單邊否定型」，介於這兩種形式之間的狀況，則有「羅曼蒂克型」（兩個國家彼此處於敵對，而第三國和兩個國家保持友好）與「結婚型」（兩個國家彼此處於友好，並同時和第三國處於敵對）。

傳統的戰略三角理論屬於靜態的分析，亦即給定三個國家彼此屬於友好或敵對關係後，找出相對應的戰略型態，再進行分析，特別是藉此用來解釋第三國的戰略地位的變化。林繼文教授則對該理論進行以下三點延伸，從更為動態的角度來分析三角關係的變化：首先，基於理性選擇理論中「空間模型」的分析思維，研究者可用「理想點」（ideal point）來代表國家彼此之間的利益，而各國之間的關係，可用其理想點之間的差距來表示：差距越近則表示彼此利益衝突越小、關係越友好；其次，理想點和現狀（status quo）之間的距離，也可以用來解釋國家之間如何透過合作（或對抗）來改變（或捍衛）現狀的空間；第三，各國改變現狀的能力，則可以解釋現狀將如何改變，並影響三角關係的變化。

如此將戰略三角理論延伸之後，有兩個好處。首先，透過理想點的界定，以及理想點和現狀的距離，可以具體解釋國家之間合作或對抗的空間；其次，由於國家的理想點可能隨著政府或領導人更迭而改變，所以戰略三角關係也會因時而易，使得傳統偏向靜態分析的戰略三角模型，有了動態的個體基礎。基於這項動態觀點，林繼文教授另外引入前述雙層賽局的分析架構，與戰略三角理論結合，並建構了「雙層三角」（two-layered strategic triangle）的賽局模型。

三、雙層三角模型

林繼文教授在「雙層三角：以空間模型分析國內政治對美中台戰略三角的影響」這篇文章（林繼文，2009b），將雙層賽局與戰略三角理論與結合，建構了一個「雙層三角」的賽局模型。這個模型有三個特色：第一，模型的第一層是各方政府，第二層是國家，其中各國對它國的態度，由政府所代表的民意決定；第二，對三角關係的描繪，從原本「友好／敵對」的二分法，延伸為連續的空間，在該空間中，國與國之間理想點的距離，表現了其利益差距的程度；第三，國內政權（或領導權）的變動和各方改變現狀的能力，是影響戰略三角型態的主要變數。

這個雙層三角賽局模型，奠基於理性選擇中的空間模型，並借用林繼文教授博士論文指導教授 George Tsebelis 的「否決者理論」（veto player theory）推論相關命題，說

明國內政治如何影響戰略三角的總體後果。在林繼文教授提出的五個命題中，有兩個比較關鍵。首先是命題三：當一個國家內部的局卵越大、勝集寬度越長、勝集中點離對手國的理想點越近。在此，「局卵」（york）和「勝集」皆屬於合作賽局（cooperative games）的分析概念，表示給定決策制度下，所有可能改變現狀的集合，也就是雙層賽局裡面國內與國外行為者所同意的方案的加總，而這些方案的多寡—也就是勝集或局卵的大小—取決於決策的制度安排。換句話說，一個以多數決進行決策但是內部意見紛歧的國家，正因為內部意見的分裂，讓現狀可以改變的空間變大（即局卵較大），越容易和它國合作以改變現狀（即勝集越大），但也因此增強對手國談判時的議價空間，使本國代表在談判時居下風。因此，命題三揭示了台灣的民主體制對於兩岸談判的雙重效果：在一致政府時期，可以增加談判籌碼，但是分立政府卻可能弱化政府的談判能力。

　　此外，命題五則是探討現狀相對於其他三個行為者理想點之間的距離，將如何影響三者之間的結盟行為。這項命題為傳統戰略三角理論，引入動態變化的觀點。例如，當現狀位於三國的理想點所構成的三角形（又稱為帕雷圖集合），表示任何兩方結盟而改變現狀時，新的現狀將偏離第三方的理想點更遠，成為「結婚型」的三角關係。但是當現狀位於帕雷圖集合之外，或是三方的理想點其實處於同一直線上時，就會演變成「三邊家族型」或「羅曼蒂克型」的三角關係。也就是說，現狀相對於行為者理想點之間的距離，以及行為者是否可以單方面改變現狀，決定了現狀將如何改變，以及戰略三角關係將如何演變。林繼文教授也在本文的後半段，運用此雙層三角模型來解釋台灣在李登輝、陳水扁、以及馬英九等歷任總統任期間，美中台戰略互動的差異和演變。

肆、台灣民眾統獨立場與兩岸關係演變

　　台灣民眾的的統獨立場，一直是台灣政治學研究中的重要的主題。政治大學選舉研究中心從 1992 年起，便長期追蹤這項民意變化，由這筆追蹤資料所累積的相關研究汗牛充棟。然而，這項研究議程最大的挑戰在於，從歷年的民調資料來看，支持「急統」與「急獨」的民眾皆屬少數，而大部分民眾則支持某種形式的「維持現狀」。也就是說，如果把民眾的統獨立場視為一個在單維空間上的議題，而把「現狀」當成是統獨兩個端點之間的中間立場，那麼絕大部分民眾的立場皆位於中間地帶。然而，同樣由政治大學選舉研究中心長期追蹤的資料顯示，台灣民眾的政黨意識型態趨向兩極化，也就是泛藍與泛綠陣營支持者，在政黨立場上並無法相容。換句話說，既然「泛藍」與「泛綠」政黨對於兩岸關係未來的發展有不同立場，其各自的支持者為何又認為應該「維持現狀」？

　　對於有大量台灣民眾支持兩岸關係應該維持現狀的現象，學者發展不同的理論和方法進行分析，其中又以「條件式統獨」的研究最爲豐富（吳乃德，2005）。根據該研究議程的發現，部分台灣民眾對於統一或獨立，是屬於「有條件的支持」，例如支持維持現狀的民眾，可能會因爲中國大陸在各方面的發展台灣相當時，轉而支持統一；但這些人也可能在中國放棄武力攻打台灣後，進而支持獨立，對於某些支持維持現狀的民眾而言，之所以選擇維持現狀，不一定僅是受其意識型態所影響，也可能是經過務實的考量（物質利益或和平）所呈現的「交纏偏好」（non-separable preferences）（Lacy and Niou, 2013）。

　　林繼文教授在「論述如何框限選擇？條件式統獨偏好對 2012 年台灣總統選舉的影響」（林繼文，2015a）一文中，援引了交纏偏好的概念，來解釋這種「民眾統獨立場趨中、但政黨立場兩極化」的民意趨勢。首先，本文延續先前針對「條件式統獨」的研究，認爲有些民眾的統獨立場具有條件性，是屬於交纏偏好。基於對於這些條件的論述、以及政黨所傳遞的訊息，導致了民眾多數支持「維持現狀」，但卻又有不同政黨屬性的結果。簡言之，台灣的政黨—特別與中國關係較近的國民黨—可以透過對於兩岸關係的論述，來影響民眾在總統選舉時的投票選擇。

　　具體來說，對於兩岸關係的未來有許多不同的可能性，可以統稱爲「兩岸論述」。總統選舉連結了台灣不同政黨採取的兩岸論述和民眾的投票選擇。因爲論述策略隱含了對於現狀未來可能的發展，例如「維持現狀，以後走向統一」或是「維持現狀，以後走向獨立」，因此政黨的不同論述策略，可以讓民眾認知道自己所處的訊息結構爲何，並和自己的偏好進行比較而決定投票對象。此時，國民黨既然具有詮釋兩岸關係的優勢，又在 2008 年起執政八年，這段期間更容易操作兩岸關係的相關訊息，並影響投票抉擇。

　　基於上述理論，這篇文章的主要發現在於，支持條件式統一的獨派選民（林繼文教授稱爲「一中獨派」），也就是雖然支持「儘快獨立」或「維持現狀，以後走向獨立」、但同時又支持若「大陸在經濟、社會、政治方面發展跟台灣差不多，兩岸就應該統一」的人，在 2012 年「台灣社會變遷調查」中所訪問的偏獨民眾中，佔了 13.12%。這群「一中獨派」的選民，便會受到國民黨總統選舉時的論述策略所影響，特別是對於「九二共識」所帶來和平紅利，將吸引他們在總統選舉中投票給馬英九。但是另一方面，但對於偏獨且不支持條件式統一的選民，這些人的偏好並未交纏，此時若他們以台灣爲祖國、且對台灣民主政治具有光榮感，仍然不太會投票給馬英九。換句話說，透過不同的論述策略，台灣的政黨可以利用民眾對於統獨立場的條件式支持，進而吸引選票。

　　既然有大部分台灣民眾長期支持「維持現狀」，那麼這樣的民意態勢，對於兩岸關係的發展又會有什麼樣的影響？林繼文教授以台灣在 2004 年所通過的《公民投票法》（以下簡稱《公投法》）爲對象，分析民意在《公投法》實施後所產生的制度後果。在

"Taiwan's Referendum Act and the Stability of the Status Quo" 一文中（Lin, 2004），林繼文教授指出，《公投法》是對於兩岸關係各種可能的發展路線，引入一了位新的否決者，從而增加現狀的穩定性。就制度上來說，2004 年版的《公投法》有兩項特色，第一項是關於「防禦型公投」的條文：「當國家當國家遭受外力威脅，致國家主權有改變之虞，總統得經行政院院會之決議，就攸關國家安全事項，交付公民投票」。這樣的制度設計，讓任何改變台灣主權現狀的方案（無論是統一或獨立），都可能因為大部分民眾支持現狀，而被公民投票所否決。第二項則是「雙二一門檻」，即公投案中「投票權人總數二分之一以上，且有效投票數超過二分之一同意者，即為通過」，其中前項關於投票率的高門檻設計，使得公投不易通過，強化了現狀的穩定性。[3]

　　在本文中，林繼文教授也引進「否決者理論」中關於「議程設定」（agenda setting）的概念，並比較了各種不同的公投制度─特別是創制（initiative）與複決（reconsideration）─對於現狀產生的影響（他稱之為「現狀改變力」）。透過分析誰具有議程設定權（即發起公投）、以及公投結果對於現狀將產生何種影響，他發現同樣是公民投票，卻會因為制度細節的不同，使得民意對於改變現狀有不同的效果。例如，創制由於是人民直接發動，議程比較不會受到行政或立法機關所操控，因而較可能改變現狀；另一方面，複決雖然也讓民眾直接參與決策，但發動權在於行政或立法機關，而且一旦發動，行政或立法機關也可以針對議程內容進行操控，讓人民無法成功否決已通過之法案，進而達到維持現狀的效果。在這樣的區分下，「防禦性公投」是屬於後者，可以用來避免台灣主權現狀為單方面政治勢力所改變。讀者可以將此觀點帶入前述「雙層三角」一文中，將公投結果視為台灣政府的理想點，或者是約束台灣政府理想點位置的制度設計，並進而影響美中台的三角互動。

伍、總結

　　吾人在從事複雜萬端的兩岸關係研究時，最重要的是問對問題，掌握方向。從林繼文教授過去二十餘年來有關兩岸關係研究的成果來看，兩岸糾結的源頭已在他的縝密推演下牢牢掌握住。林繼文教授以紮實的學理論證，處理了單一研究途徑或調查研究無法全盤解析的兩岸難題。重要概念如「條件式統獨」的分類意涵，以及「兩岸維持現狀」

---

[3]　在此要特別說明的是，這項「雙二一門檻」已經於2017年《公投法》修正時放寬，並促使隔年的九合一地方選舉中，有七件公投案通過。

與台灣內政變化及諸如公投等重要議題的關連，都在理論分析的推演中得到進一步的釐清。林教授的學術論文從理論出發，但事實上提供了兩岸政策關鍵概念的開創性貢獻。由此可見，林繼文教授有關兩岸關係的經驗研究及案例分析，不是象牙塔式的虛幻論述。從林教授的兩岸著作中可以得知，每一項研究假設均有經驗資料佐證；每一套論證都有紮實的邏輯推演過程。從林教授豐富的理論演繹中，也可以看出解決當前兩岸困境的企圖心，以及正本清源，以中道結合理論與實務的強烈使命感。

第十四章

零和或雙贏？兩岸經貿交流新解*

林繼文、羅致政

壹、前言

　　回應李登輝總統的美國之旅，中共於 1995 年 6 月 16 日片面宣布推遲籌備當中的第二次「辜汪會談」，包括其他事務性會談也全部中止。而在一波波綿密的文攻武嚇折騰之下，兩岸多年以來好下容易建立的友好與穩定氣氛，頓時之間陰霾再現。中共這種不惜以惡化台海關係來抵制台灣務實外交的做法，讓我們重新認清兩岸之間的互信是如何的不足，而彼此關係又是如何的脆弱禁不起考驗。近期以來，對於台北政府要求恢復兩岸事務性會談的要求，中共在有計劃的安排下，刻意採取所謂的「冷處理」，要求台灣對「一個中國」的原則作出可以爲北京所接受的表態，並以此作爲恢復雙方會談的前提。此外，除了在軍事上持續威脅恫嚇，外交上加強圍堵封殺之外，更利用兩岸不斷深化的經貿交流，企圖推展其「以商圍政」、「以民逼官」、「以通促統」的策略。

　　面對北京方面的敵視態度與政治野心，同時考量台灣對大陸經濟依賴度的日益加深，如何維持台灣在經濟與政治上的自主性已成爲眾所關心的議題。李登輝總統於 1996 年在「全國經營者大會」以及「國統會第十一次委員會議」中所揭示的，「亞太營運中心計劃不以大陸爲唯一腹地」與「戒急用忍、行穩致遠」的兩項原則主張，可以視爲台灣方面對於兩岸經貿發展趨勢以及中共攻勢轉變的一種具體回應。[1]

　　然而，李總統的這兩項原則性說法，在國內卻激起了相當兩極的解讀與評價（鍾琴，1996；吳惠林，1996）。許多人認爲，台灣對大陸經貿依存度不斷攀升的結果，勢將損及台灣未來的談判籌碼以及安全利益，所以政府的謹慎做法絕對有其必要性。相對於此，也有論者以爲，以政治力來干預兩岸經貿往來，只會造成市場的「扭曲效果」，

---

* 本文曾刊登於《人文及社會科學集刊》，第 10 卷第 1 期（1998 年 3 月），頁 33-77。感謝中央研究院人文社會科學研究中心《人文及社會科學集刊》同意轉載。
　承蒙謝復生教授及兩位匿名審查人的寶貴意見，指正不少初稿的疏失，作者謹致上最高謝意。文責由作者自負。羅致政感謝國科會專題研究計畫（NSC-87-2414-H-031-002）補助。

[1] 有關李總統在國統會致詞全文，見余紀忠（1996）。

恐將危及兩岸經濟雙贏的出現。此外，更有人樂觀地主張，兩岸經濟整合的結果，將促進雙方在政治上的和解，創造彼此共存共榮的局面。很明顯的，對於兩岸經貿互動的政策主張，之所以出現百家爭鳴的局面，主要是因為眾人對於經濟利益與政治安全兩者之間的互動邏輯，有所不同的本質評估與理論推演所致。而台灣本身政治民主化發展的結果，更使得內部對於大陸政策主張更趨多元與複雜化（Nathan, 1992; Cheng, 1993; Jia, 1994）。但在 1996 年底所召開的國家發展會議中，朝野兩大黨對於兩岸經貿關係仍達成一致的原則共識：「由於中共對我仍存敵意，兩岸經貿發展應格外考量政治風險。因此，必須在維持我國家安全及兩岸和平的前提下，循序漸進地推動相關政策」（國家發展會議祕書處，1996）。由此可見，國家安全與經濟利益兩者之間如何相互影響，進而左右兩岸關係的變化，是研究台北與北京之間關係互動時，所不可忽視的重要切入點。

　　本文旨在探討台海雙方在安全與主權問題上的零和對峙，如何影響彼此在經濟合作上的雙贏追求；同時也試圖分析經濟整合的利益分配，是否可能轉化雙方在安全議題上的零和僵局。文章首先分析兩岸目前經貿交流的現況與發展趨勢，並評析因之所引發的各種問題與爭論。其次，我們將檢閱國際關係研究中，現實主義與自由主義二大學派對於國家之間衝突與合作現象的解釋與理論途徑，藉此尋找適以分析兩岸政經互動的理論基礎。接著，本研究以賽局理論作為主要的分析工具，透過國際關係研究中「相對獲利」（relative gains）的概念來界定國家對於安全議題的敏感度，並將此一變數融入兩岸經貿互動的賽局之中；並以此為基礎，推論多項基本命題，以供實證檢驗與分析之用。最後，文章將根據研究發現進行理論評估與政策建議。

貳、變動中的兩岸經貿交流

　　自 1970 年代末期中共推動經濟改革，採取對外開放政策後，兩岸之間政治對峙的局面逐漸出現解凍，而海峽間的經貿交流也開始走出過去近三十年來的停滯與隔絕狀態。兩岸之間經貿交流日益密切與繁榮，具體表現在兩方面：一是兩岸間轉口與間接貿易的激增；二是台商赴大陸投資的範圍與數量的不斷擴大。有鑑於兩岸間經濟整合的樂觀演變，海內外均有人提出類似成立華人經濟共同體的構想。然而，在兩岸經貿關係快速發展的背後，卻受到許多經濟與非經濟因素的制約，阻礙不斷隱憂重重。雙方一再指責對手，動輒以政治考量，隨處設限刻意阻撓。此外，各自內部也對兩岸經濟互賴的利弊評估看法分歧，政策主張出現極大的差異。因此，為了探尋影響兩岸經貿交流的變

數，吾人有必要檢視過去十餘年來台海經貿關係的變化，以及因之產生的問題與政策爭論。

1979 年元旦，中共「全國人大」常委會發表《告台灣同胞書》，要求展開「三通、四流」，而為表示善意，中共國防部也下令停止對大、小金門等島嶼的炮擊。雖然台灣方面並沒有立即的回應，但兩岸之間的經貿交流已出現較佳的政治格局。由於台灣目前仍堅持兩岸貿易採取間接的方式進行，因此，貿易額的估算有其困難，但僅以經由香港的兩岸轉口貿易來看，兩岸之間近十餘年的貿易發展，成果十分可觀。從表 14.1 中我們可以清楚地看出此一發展趨勢。

兩岸之間的貿易金額一直呈現著上升的趨勢，尤其是自 1986 年之後增加的幅度更快。這與 1984 年政府放寬自港澳轉口輸入大陸產品的限制，1985 年 7 月台灣宣布對轉口貿易不予干預，以及後來陸續擴大兩岸間接貿易項目有關。此外，台灣也加速對大陸貿易政策的法制化。1989 年 6 月經濟部公布實施《大陸地區物品管理辦法》，次年並通過《對大陸地區間接輸出貨品管理辦法》。隨著 1991 年《台灣地區與大陸地區人民關係條例》法律依據的建立，經濟部於 1993 年 4 月通過《台灣地區與大陸地區貿易許可辦法》以取代原有的《管理辦法》。根據此一《許可辦法》及其相關規定，業者與行政機關只要符合「不危害國家安全、對相關產業無不良影響、有助產品外銷競爭力的提升」三條件，均可向國貿局建議開放輸入大陸物品。簡言之，台灣的兩岸貿易政策一直採取審慎的態度在規劃，而基本上依循著「出寬進嚴」的原則在運作。

中共在處理兩岸經貿關係時，除了要配合其推動改革開放和完成「四化」建設的國家目標之外，更有為中國和平統一鋪設有利條件的特殊考量。1979 年 5 月，中共頒布《關於開展對台灣貿易的暫行規定》，給予台灣製品關稅免稅的待遇；次年 3 月中共商業部更頒發了《購買台灣產品的補充規定》內部文件一種，規定凡進口台灣貨品視同「國內貿易」免徵關稅，台灣商人購買大陸產品，不但優先供應，並有八折以下之優待；此一關稅與價格的優惠，在 1981 年 5 月取消。而為了應付日益頻繁的兩岸經貿交往，中共在 1988 年底在對外經貿部下增設「對台經貿關係司」。與台灣的謹慎態度相較，中共對兩岸間的貿易往來，抱持著開放與鼓勵的立場，強調所謂的「政經分離」，並不斷批評台灣方面「不對等雙向往來」的政策，要求儘早實行三通，以加強兩岸的經貿交流。

儘管存在著實施直接貿易的障礙，兩岸之間的貿易往來不僅在實際金額上不斷攀升，在兩岸貿易總依存度、出口依存度以及進口依存度上，也呈逐年上升的趨勢。表 14.2 顯示兩岸此一互賴情勢的發展狀況。可以看出來的是，台灣對大陸貿易的依賴度遠遠大於對岸依賴台灣的程度。

表 14.1　台海兩岸經香港轉口貿易金額統計

單位：百萬美元

年度	貿易總額		台灣向大陸出口		台灣從大陸進口		順（逆）差
	金額	成長率（%）	金額	成長率（%）	金額	成長率（%）	
1979	77.8		21.5		56.3		-34.8
1980	311.2	300.2	235.0	994.4	76.2	35.4	158.8
1981	459.3	47.6	384.2	63.5	75.2	-1.4	309.0
1982	278.5	-39.4	194.5	-49.4	84.0	11.8	110.4
1983	247.7	-11.1	157.9	-18.8	89.9	6.9	68.0
1984	553.2	123.3	425.5	169.6	127.8	42.2	297.7
1985	1,102.7	99.3	986.9	132.0	115.9	-9.3	870.9
1986	955.6	-13.4	811.3	-17.8	144.2	24.4	667.1
1987	1,515.5	58.6	1,226.5	51.2	288.9	100.4	937.6
1988	2,720.9	79.5	2,242.2	82.9	478.7	65.7	1,763.5
1989	3,483.4	28.0	2,896.5	29.2	586.9	22.6	2,309.6
1990	4,043.6	16.1	3,278.3	13.2	765.4	30.4	2,512.9
1991	5,793.1	43.3	4,667.2	42.4	1,126.0	47.1	3,514.2
1992	7,406.9	27.9	6,287.9	34.7	1,119.0	-0.6	5,169.0
1993	8,689.0	17.3	7,585.4	20.6	1,103.6	-1.4	6,481.8
1994	9,809.5	12.9	8,517.2	12.3	1,292.3	17.1	7,224.9
1995	11,457.0	16.8	9,882.8	16.0	1,574.2	21.8	8,306.8
1996	11,300.0	-1.4	9,718.0	-1.7	1,582.0	0.5	9,718

資料來源：《兩岸經濟統計月報》。

　　自 1980 年代末期開始，因為所謂「大陸投資熱」所形成的兩岸投資關係，已日漸取代貿易關係而成為兩岸經貿互動的重要主導力量。中國大陸自推動改革開放以來，吸引外商投資一直是其經濟現代化政策能否成功的重要關鍵，而台商便是其積極爭取的外

資對象之一。1983 年 4 月，中共國務院公布《台胞經濟特區投資三項優惠辦法》，更在 1988 年 7 月發布施行《關於鼓勵台灣同胞投資的規定》第二十二條，以各式優惠做法，鼓勵台灣的公司、企業和個人前往大陸投資，促進兩岸之間經濟技術的交流。在次年 9 月，中共國務院正式批覆設置「台商投資區」，隨後陸續公布各項給予台商優惠待遇的政策措施。很清楚地，不論從中央或地方的一系列做法，都可以看出大陸方面吸取台資的積極主動態度。

表 14.2　兩岸貿易互賴趨勢（1981-1995）

單位：百分比

年度	對大陸輸出占台灣對外輸出比	兩岸貿易占台灣對外貿易比	對台灣輸出占大陸對外輸出比	兩岸貿易占大陸對外貿易比
1981	7.19	3.54	0.34	0.77
1982	5.93	3	0.38	0.73
1983	5.51	2.85	0.4	0.69
1984	5.79	3.12	0.49	0.69
1985	7.27	4.17	0.42	0.56
1986	6.31	3.7	0.46	0.62
1987	6.66	3.71	0.73	0.89
1988	8.19	4.07	1.01	0.99
1989	9.61	4.88	1.12	1.18
1990	11.62	5.78	1.23	1.61
1991	15.15	7.49	1.57	1.99
1992	17.85	8.75	1.32	9.46
1993	20.78	10.21	1.2	9.58
1994	21.83	12.42	1.53	9.36
1995	21.49	12.27	n.a.	n.a.

資料來源：Leng（1996: 120）。

在台灣方面，自 1980 年代後期始，由於國內經濟投資環境的惡化，國際區域整合趨勢的發展，以及大陸提供的特殊優遇，加上台商投資大陸所具有語言、地緣、文化、以至於政治上的優勢地位，台資的流向大陸便形成了一股熱潮。自 1987 年台灣准許人民赴大陸探親以來，部分台商便已藉機從事對大陸的投資。爲了管制日益熱絡的兩岸投資，經濟部在 1990 年 7 月通過《對大陸地區投資及技術合作管理辦法》，正面表列包括 24 類的 2,500 項產品可赴大陸投資。同年 9 月公告《對大陸地區從事投資或技術合作管理辦法》，正面表列 67 類 3,353 項產品准赴大陸投資或技術合作。兩岸人民關係條例通過後，行政院於 1993 年 2 月公布施行《在大陸地區從事投資或技術合作許可辦法》。隨即在 4 月，經濟部發表官方報告，指出台灣上年對大陸投資已躍居我對外投資的第一位。綜觀台灣的大陸投資政策，主要是希望透過正面表列投資項目的許可方式，達到「管理」與「輔導」的目的，以避免對台灣經濟造成不良影響。

表 14.3 說明台資流入大陸的情形。很明顯地，大陸方面所公布的台商協議投資金額遠遠大於台灣官方的統計數字。但不論從那一方公布的資料來看，台商在大陸的投資的確顯現穩健的成長。更值得注意的是，台商在大陸投資除了數量的增加外，不論在投資形式、範圍、地域等方面都出現結構性的轉變，這包括投資期延長，獨資企業增加，投資範圍擴大，以及投資地域延伸等（劉映仙，1993：10-12）。中共《經濟日報》更報導分析台商投資大陸具有「廣、深、高、大、久、全」的六大發展趨勢（魏華，1992：39-40）。許多研究報告也指出，台商在大陸投資已不僅止於「量變」，更出現了「質變」的現象。

表 14.3　台商對大陸地區投資金額統計

單位：百萬美元

年度	件數	經濟部核准資料金額	平均每件金額	件數	大陸對外公布資料協議金額	平均每件金額	實際金額
1991	237	174.16	0.73	3,800	3,450	0.91	872
1992	264	246.99	0.94	6,430	5,540	0.86	1,053
1993	9,329	3,168.41	0.34	10,948	9,970	0.91	3,139
1994	934	962.21	1.03	6,247	5,397	0.86	3,391

資料來源：左原（1996），引自《經濟統計月報》。

　　目睹台、港和大陸地區各項經貿交流的逐步擴展，兩岸三地的部分人士紛紛提出成立一個類似「經濟圈」的構想，企圖透過經濟整合的方式，以達成「三贏」的目的。表 14.4 列出這類構想的名稱、提出者與所包含的範圍。雖然贊成建立「經濟圈」者提出各種理由來支持其構想的推動，但在現實層面上，台、港及大陸間的經濟整合面臨著許多困難，而這些困難同時也正是左右兩岸經貿關係變化的主要因素（陳德昇，1994：113-127）。

表 14.4　兩岸經濟整合的主張與構想

名稱	提出者（時間）	主要範圍
中國人共同體	黃枝連（1980）	福建、廣東、廣西、海南、港澳、台灣
中國圈	陳坤耀（1987）	大陸、台灣、香港
大中華共同市場	鄭竹園（1988）	台灣、大陸、港澳、新加坡
中國經濟圈	陳憶村（1988）	大陸、台灣、香港
亞洲華人共同市場	高希均（1988）	台灣、大陸、香港、新加坡
海峽兩岸經濟圈	金泓汎（1989）	福建、廣東、廣西、海南、港澳、台灣
華東南自由貿易區	周八駿（1989）	長江三角洲、珠江三角洲、港澳、閩南、台灣
華南經濟協作區	翁成受、許心鵬（1990）	福建、廣東、海南、港澳、台灣
中華港經濟圈	邱創煥（1991）	大陸、台灣、香港
中華文化經濟共同體	關中（1991）	大陸、台灣、香港
大中華經濟圈	劉泰英（1992）	大陸、台灣、香港、新加坡

資料來源：王鳳生（1992：167）。

　　關於兩岸不斷深化的經貿互賴關係，如何評估其利弊得失，海峽兩岸的看法並不一致，而各自內部也是意見分歧。在台灣方面，有人認為不斷放寬與加速的兩岸經貿交流，對台灣之政經發展已經造成一定的負面影響。這包括台灣對大陸之經濟依賴度逐年攀升、台灣產業的空洞化、大陸政策共識的瓦解以及對大陸戰略的籌碼與選項的限制。因此，有學者呼籲政府當局重視兩岸深化的經貿互賴所造成「脆弱性」與「敏感性」的

問題（吳安家，1996：62）。持此論者，也認爲應積極配合政府「戒急用忍」的主張，提防因爲對大陸經貿過度依賴所造成對台灣經濟安定與政治安定的不利影響。但也有部分人士認爲，兩岸經貿互賴對台灣而言並不必然是弊多於利，所以應該因勢利導、「大膽西進」，大幅開展兩岸經貿與民間交流，以創造「雙贏」的局面（許信良，1995：355-380）。大陸方面，基本上是肯定兩岸經貿交流所帶來的政經利益，但也不時指責台灣方面企圖透過經貿交流來實現其「政治登陸、和平演變」的目的。

　　基本上，任何人都無法否認，兩岸之間的經貿關係絕非單純的經濟問題，而是牽扯到極爲複雜的政治因素。之所以主觀地要求「政經分離」，正是因爲無法漠視「政經掛鉤」此一客觀事實的存在。因此，在探討兩岸政經互動的問題時，絕不能一廂情願，而是要認清此一政經糾葛的關係本質，並以此作爲分析的基礎，唯有這樣才能確實掌握兩岸互動的眞相，提出可行的政策建議。

　　從單純的經濟面考量，海峽兩岸雙方均肯定「合則兩利」的經貿關係的存在。但即使如此，兩岸貿易、投資互動發展的結果，很可能導致彼此的貿易摩擦加劇，而到時如果雙方採取反制措施，或進行經貿談判時，彼此所擁有的籌碼就直接建立在如今發展中的經貿方向。正基於這種考量，兩岸政府所關心的不僅是經貿關係發展爲各自所帶來的絕對利益，同時也留意兩者之間所建立的是何種的經貿關係，以及經濟利益分配的對比。換言之，雙方都關心經貿交流是否會使自己在互賴關係中處於下風。結果，單純的經貿利益追求（allocation）問題，變成了經貿雙方利益分配（distribution）的問題，進而使得兩岸經貿關係複雜化，增添了雙方合作的困難度。

　　阻礙兩岸關係正常順暢進展的更重要變數，是雙方政治立場與目標上的嚴重分歧。大陸的對台經貿政策除了有其經濟利益的考量之外，更重要的是要爲兩岸的統一創造有利的條件。中共於 1991 年初傳達的《中共中央關於進一步加強對台工作的通知》中發 3 號文件中，即明白的揭示，「要從祖國和平統一的戰略高度認識對台經貿工作的意義。發展雙方經貿往來，密切兩岸聯繫，是遏制台灣分離傾向、促進和平統一的有力措施。對台經貿工作既要按照經濟規律辦事，又要爲促進和平統一的政治任務服務」。經貿交流的推展策略則是從單向走向雙向、從間接走向直接、從民間走向官方，實現「以商圍政」、「以民促官」，經由事務性、功能性談判提升擴及政治性談判，以達成和平統一的最終目的。同時，台灣方面也不斷強調要推行「台灣經驗」，增強對大陸的影響力；最終促成大陸實現「政治民主化、經濟自由化、社會多元化、文化中國化」的目標。很明顯地，台灣的大陸政策實具有和平演變的積極意涵，而其主要目的可以歸納有二（Hickey, 1991: 523-525）。首先，透過民間交流，向大陸傳播「台灣經驗」，創造台海和平的契機。換言之，希望藉由兩岸密切的經濟、社會、文化交流，增加大陸方面

對台灣之瞭解，並透過自由民主思潮的傳播，營造彼此合作與平等對待的環境與心態。其次，台灣方面希望以經貿籌碼來交換中共的政治讓步。例如，台北方面要求中共必須在「不對台使用武力」、「承認台灣為對等政治實體」、「允許台灣在國際拓展生存空間」等三條件上作出善意回應，台灣才會在三通問題上作出讓步，進而邁入國統綱領的第二階段。

事實上，中共於各種場合不斷強調其必要時將以武力解決台灣問題的立場，基於此一現實考量，台灣實無法排除中共在未來以經濟脅迫台灣的可能。[2]因此，在敵意未消威脅未減之前，政治與經濟實為一體的兩面；經濟實力很可能成為未來政治對抗的籌碼，而政治的適度運作也可以爭取更多的經濟利益。同時，從「國家安全」的角度來看，減少對敵人一分的依賴便增加自己一分的力量（power）；而增加我方在經濟力量對比上的優勢，也相對提升武力上敵我對比的優勢，尤其是在當經濟力量形成國力的重要性日益增加之際。所以，也唯有在經濟利益上保有優勢，才能確保在安全與政治議題上占有較佳的地位。

總言之，在經濟議題上摻雜政治上的安全考量，絕非缺乏理性的作為；而在進行合作的過程當中，思考未來雙方可能對抗時的籌碼利用，也不是杞人憂天的做法。在台海政經互動的結構中，「對抗」與「合作」、「雙贏」與「零和」的思考是透過不同議題面向（issue-dimension）與時間面向（time-dimension）的串聯而同時存在的。任何分析兩岸政經互動的嘗試都不能忽略此一重要的關係本質。而台灣在尋求建構一套兼顧國家安全與經濟繁榮的大陸政策時，更不能脫離此一重要的思考方向。這樣的問題，其實已涉及國際關係的本質。以下，我們就先從國際關係理論的角度來思考這個問題。

參、安全與富裕，零和與雙贏

國家之間如何消弭衝突產生合作，一直是國際關係學者所共同關心的焦點。然而國際關係研究的兩大學派對於國際間合作的可能，卻有相當不同的看法與期待。現實主義者（realists）對於國家之間的合作一般都抱持著較為悲觀的看法，這其中古典現實主義者將國際衝突的不可避免歸因於人性中追求宰制（domination）或畏懼被宰制的本能（Morgenthau, 1978），而新現實主義者則強調國際體系本身無政府狀態（anarchy）的

2　根據新聞局的統計，在 1979 至 1994 年間，中共至少曾發表 104 次「不放棄對台使用武力」的談話（行政院新聞局，1995）。

特質對於國際合作所造成的阻礙（Waltz, 1979; Grieco, 1988a, 1988b）。正由於特別重視國家安全對於國家行為的指引作用，新現實主義者認為，在缺乏任何國際權威足以保障國家生存安全的情況下，國家不僅要關心自己權力的變化，更要隨時注意他國權力的消長。因此，「在無政府狀態下」，當國家在與他國交往時，「相對獲利」（relative gains）比「絕對獲利」（absolute gains）要來的重要（Waltz, 1979）。而由於經濟問題屬於「下層政治」（low politics）的範疇，因此勢將無法擺脫在「高層政治」國家安全上關注相對地位（relative position）的這種邏輯。如此尋求相對獲益的結果便是造成了零和的賽局，因而限制了國家之間合作的可能。事實上，有研究指出，相對獲利的追求不僅出現在安全議題之上，在其他政治經濟問題方面亦有可能產生，進而增加國際合作的困難（Gowa, 1986; Grieco, 1990; Gilpin, 1987）。

相對於現實主義者的悲觀看法，自由主義學派則認為，國際社會當中存在著利益的和諧以及合作的可能，不論是商業自由主義（commercial liberalism）、民主自由主義（democratic liberalism）或者是規範自由主義（regulatory liberalism）均抱持類似的樂觀主張（Keohane, 1989a）。隨著國際經濟互賴（economic interdependence）趨勢的不斷深化，以及眾多「國際建制」（international regimes）的形成與運作，新自由機制主義學派（neoliberal institutionalism）對於國際合作現象的分析與研究，已構成對現實主義理論的極大挑戰（Krasner, 1983; Keohane, 1989b）。不同於新現實主義對於國家追求相對獲益的基本假設，新自由主義者認為國家真正關心的焦點在於自身的絕對獲益，而對於別人的獲益不予關心（Keohane, 1984）。因此，國家間仍有可能積極地透過相互調整的方式，建立合作的安排，以共同提升彼此的絕對獲益。這種依據自我主義（egoism）所建構出來的國家行為模式，讓研究者提出各種化解國際合作困難度的可行途徑，這些包含在戰略上、報酬結構、議題串聯、互動次數、互動者數目等各方面的調整，以提高國家之間合作的可能性（Jervis, 1978; Axelrod, 1984; Oye, 1986）。

由此可知，國家之間對於相對獲益的敏感程度，與國家之間合作的可能性有極大的關聯。許多國際關係學者認為，國家重視相對獲益的程度愈高，一個國家的獲益便愈可能被視為另一國家的損失，也因此彼此之間的合作也愈不容易達成（Grieco, 1990）。但如果說現實主義與自由主義對於國際合作可能性的不同看法，只是基於彼此對於國家行為動機的不同假設（assumptions）所推論出來的結果，那麼兩大學派之間的爭辯將無法產生太大的交集。事實上，不論是現實主義者或自由主義者都傾向於認為國家對於相對獲益的敏感度不是一個常數（constant variable），而應該是一個可以根據情境所造成（induced）的變數（Powell, 1994: 335）。

本文的主張是，任何國家對於相對獲益與絕對獲益的重視，只有程度的差別，而無

性質的不同（Powell, 1991）。我們可以用一個變數 k 來表示某國對於相對獲利的重視程度。假設 $0 \leq k \leq 1$，且 k 值越大表示越重視相對獲利。再設該國在某情況下所得報酬（payoff）為 X，而對手國得 Y。(X, Y) 是雙方都只考慮絕對獲利時的利益分配。我們可以加進 k 這個變數，而將該國的獲利改寫為 $(1-k)X + k(X-Y) = X - kY$。當 $k = 1$ 時，兩方的獲利差距決定了該國的利益（即 $X-Y$）。如果對手國也採取同樣的態度，賽局即轉變為零和（$X-Y+Y-X=0$）。

　　那麼，什麼因素決定了 k 的大小？議題性質是第一個值得考慮的原因。任何人都不難發現，國家之間在安全議題上合作的困難度遠比在經濟議題上，要來的高。與目前在國際社會當中充滿的各式國際經濟建制（international economic regimes）相較，安全建制（security regimes）是非常侷限而且少有的（Jervis, 1982）。之所以如此，主要是因為這兩項議題之間不同的互動本質所致。雖然不論是經濟或安全議題，雙方都有可能因為共同合作而獲利，但兩者之間有一個很大的差別，即是在安全議題的賽局當中，萬一遭到背叛時，所付出的代價是十分昂貴的（Lipson, 1984）。在無政府的國際社會當中，這種沒有永久敵人與永久朋友的現象，迫使國家必須隨時擔心來自對手的可能威脅，所以也更須注意與對手互動時的相對獲益。

　　但在國際關係研究當中，安全與經濟議題卻是經常彼此掛鉤的。由於在無政府狀態之下，國家不時要面對可能的戰爭威脅，而經濟力量的強弱是國力展現不可或缺的要素，通常經濟力愈強的國家也愈有可能在戰場上占有優勢。因此，國家之間經濟的交往常無法擺脫國家追求安全的邏輯。但國家關心相對獲益的程度卻也不是一成不變的，很可能受到外在環境因素的影響。鮑威爾（Robert Powell）即認為，在一個國際體系當中，動用武力的成本高低會左右國家對於對手相對獲利的關心程度。簡言之，當動武的成本很低，亦即使用武力的可能性提高時，即使是經濟上的絕對獲益都很可能被詮釋為影響安全地位上的相對獲益，因此在經濟議題上合作的可能性也受到較大的限制。相反地，當一般動武的成本很高，亦即使用武力的機會降低時，經濟上追求絕對獲益的行為也較不會影響國家安全，而國家之間的合作也出現較佳的局面（Powell, 1991）。當然，將經濟資源轉化為軍事資源的能力，也影響到國家關心相對獲益的大小。此外，在軍事戰略上到底是攻勢優勢（offense-dominance）或守勢優勢（defense-dominance），也是左右國家對彼此之間相對獲益的敏感度之重要體系因素。[3]

　　根據葛瑞柯（Joseph Grieco）（1988b）的說法，國家對於相對獲利的敏感度至少

---

[3]　有關攻守優勢與戰爭可能性的研究，參閱 Quester（1988）、Hopf（1991）、Christensen 與 Snyder（1990）。

受到六項因素的運作。首先，敏感度會因為在某一合作安排下，報酬可以轉化成影響力的程度而有所不同。其次，敏感度也受到不同議題之間談判力量可移轉程度的影響。再者，互動時間的長短也可能影響敏感度。同時，國家之間過去互動的經驗，也會左右當前對於彼此相對獲益的關心程度。此外，如同前面提及的，國家的敏感度會因議題的不同而有不同的反應。最後，互動對象的不同，也可能產生國家對於相對獲益關心程度的差異。

　　在實證研究上，史奈多（Snidal, 1991）指出，當互動國家的數目增加時，相對獲益阻礙國際合作的影響力也愈小。因此，當雙邊合作因為彼此在乎相對獲益而造成合作上的困難時，可以透過引進第三者的方式，提高合作的機會。在新自由機制主義理論當中，國際建制或國際組織即是扮演這種促進多邊合作的功能。此外，日本學者鈴木（Motoshi Suzuki）（1994）的研究發現，即使在單純的雙邊互動當中，經濟互賴程度的提升將降低追求相對獲益所造成的負作用。總之，雖然國家對於對手獲益程度的關心會因為許多因素的影響而有所不同，但不可否認的是，國家追求相對獲益的敏感度左右著彼此之間合作的可能性。因此，任何分析國家之間合作衝突現象的理論架構，絕不可忽視此一重要變數的存在。

　　兩岸政府對於經貿交流如何影響彼此的政治或經濟籌碼，有不同程度的重視。而這種對未來力量對比的關心程度，即可用上述相對獲利敏感度來表示。如果當雙方都完全不用擔心未來可能的經濟或政治衝突時，k 值將是 0，而雙方也能專注於經濟雙贏的追求。相反地，當兩岸安全對立或政治僵持局面浮現時，k 值可能快速增大，而兩岸的經貿賽局也轉變成零和的困局。下文將針對 k 值的大小與兩岸合作衝突的關係，作進一步的分析與探討。

肆、兩岸經貿互動的賽局模型

　　如前所述，海峽兩岸間的經貿往來，自 1980 年代中期以來逐漸密切。對於這樣的趨勢，自然有正負兩面的評價。然而，細究各種意見，我們可以發現，對兩岸經貿來往持保留看法者，其主要的論點多為政治性的。簡言之，這派觀點認為過度依賴大陸市場將危害台灣的國家安全。[4] 然而，若單就經濟利害而言，即使是傾向獨立者也不能否認兩

4　參閱林向愷（1994）及王塗發（1994）。吳介民（1996）對這種看法提出了批判，認為中國不易對台灣進行經濟制裁。本文的看法則是，無論兩岸經貿有害論是否正確，這樣的可能性的確

岸在經濟分工上的互補性，及其對台灣之重要性。[5]樂觀者，甚且認爲經濟整合有助於化解政治衝突（王拓，1996）。

其實，經濟互動與政治（包含安全）間的關係，並非變動不居的，也不能全以主觀判斷。在不同的情境下，行動者會根據接收自對方的「訊號」（signal）來判斷經濟行爲的政治性，並予以適當的反應。經濟合作是否可能，即取決於雙方對於彼此政治意圖的判斷。我們可以這樣說：在完全沒有政治干預下的經濟交換，基本上應是互利的。然而，當某一行動者認定對方的行爲是有政治意圖時，就會在意對方從經濟合作中得到的好處。換言之，經濟互動的雙贏或零和，取決於彼此獲利的敏感程度。

這樣的觀點，事實上不斷出現在媒體或時事評論中。然而，對於兩岸經濟互動與政治互信間的具體關係，卻鮮少有作提出系統性的分析；某些問題，也未曾獲得清楚的回答。例如，對於相對獲利的重視，必然會減低合作的可能性嗎？如果真有這種傾向，其效果是漸進的還是突發的？如何才能打開相互對抗的僵局？這些問題當然是環環相扣的。以下，我們把影響兩岸經貿互動的主要因素放入一個賽局模型（game-theoretic model）中，藉此勾勒出一個整體的圖像。

我們依照一般的做法，分三個部分來建構一個賽局：行動者（players）、策略（strategies）及偏好（preference）（Osborne and Rubinstein, 1994: 11）。

【行動者】我們的模型所描繪的，是一個由兩岸政府所構成的雙人賽局（two-person game）。影響兩岸經貿互動的當然還有其他的角色，例如台商、政黨、其他利益團體等。然而，我們所關切的主要是政府部門的決策，因此可以暫不計入其他的行動者。當然，政府的決策必須考慮其他部門的反應。

【策略】兩岸的交流包含了許多細微的項目，其互動也是持續進行的。理想上，我們應該建構一個多回合賽局（repeated game）的模型，並考慮兩岸政府在各項事務上的態度。然而，這樣的模型不但難以操作與分析，由此所導出的理論也不具簡潔性（parsimony）。我們的做法，是將焦點放在兩岸政府的基本政策上。基本政策的特徵有二。第一，該政策具有指導其他政策的作用。第二，基本政策不會任意更動。在客觀環境不變的前提下，我方基本政策的變動完全取決於對方的基本政策。反之亦然。

國際關係研究者往往使用「合作」（cooperation）與「對抗」（defection）來描述行動者的策略選擇。兩岸政府的經貿政策，也存在著這兩種選項。不過，在具體的做法上，北京政府與台北政府稍有不同。就台灣而言，「合作」表示全面開放兩岸的資本、

5　存在於政治菁英的計算中，進而影響了其政策決定。
最具代表性者，應爲前民進黨主席許信良所提出的「大膽西進論」及「政經分離論」。

商品、人力交流；最具體之作爲，即是開放三通。相對地，「對抗」則表示閉鎖兩岸經貿交流。對北京而言，「合作」除表示開放市場、提供台商優惠外，更包含建立與台灣進行事務性協商的建制化管道，並充分利用此管道。「對抗」，則表示取消台商優惠、終止與台灣的協商，以及封閉兩岸交流，甚至對台進行貿易制裁。[6]

我們以 C_i 及 D_i 分別表示行動者 i 的合作策略與對抗策略，並以 $C_{\sim i}$ 及 $D_{\sim i}$ 表示對方政府 ~i 的策略。爲便於行文，以下先界定幾個賽局理論的基本概念。所謂的「策略」（strategy），是所有「訊息集」（information set）內行動方案的總和。[7]根據「純粹策略」（pure strategy），行動者在每一個訊息集中都可以找到獨一的行動指令。以方程式表示：

$$S_i : w_i \rightarrow a_i$$

這個式子表示，行動者 i 根據策略 S_i 決定在訊息集 w_i 採取行動 a_i。舉例而言，S_i 說得可能是：「如果對方合作我就合作」（C_i if $C_{\sim i}$），或是「對抗到底」（D_i always）。當然，完全的合作或對抗是極端的狀況，事實上的作爲可能介於兩者之間。在此情形下，策略指的是採取各種行動方案的機率分布：

$$S_i : w_i \rightarrow \pi(a_i), \pi \geq 0, \Sigma\pi(a_i) = 1$$

在這個式子中，S_i 代表行動者 i 的「混合策略」（mixed strategy），$\pi(a_i)$ 則是其在訊息集 w_i 中採取行動 a_i 的機率。舉例而言，i 政府可以採取傾向於合作，但又不完全合作的策略。若然，則 $1 > \pi(C_i) > \pi(D_i)$，而 $\pi(C_i) + \pi(D_i) = 1$。在本文中，我們分別以 p 與 q 表示兩岸政府採取合作策略（C）的機率，亦即前述式子中的 $\pi(C_i)$。

圖 14.1 所顯示的是這個賽局的展開式（extensive form）。如圖所示，這是一個資訊不充分的賽局（a game of imperfect information）。之所以如此，是因爲 i 政府在制定基本政策時，不能確定對方的基本政策是否會變動。然而，由於兩方的企圖都清楚而且公開，其互動也構成一個資訊完全的賽局（a game of complete information）。[8]由於賽局涉及基本政策的制定，雙方都只有一個訊息集。據此，表 14.5 顯示了這個賽局的正規式（normal form）。表中所示的獲利（payoff），將於以下討論。

---

6 兩岸政府的策略並不對稱（symmetrical），乃因其處境之不同。中共是資本的接受者，因此無所謂開放問題；但是否對台協商卻有強烈的政治意涵。同樣地，台灣固然會謹慎處理兩岸政治性協商，卻需要與中共進行事務性協商以確保交往過程中的權益。

7 我們可以約略將訊息集理解爲賽局中行動者必須採取行動的關卡。關於此概念的嚴格定義，可參考 Rasmusen（1989: 48）。

8 所謂資訊充分的賽局，是指每一個訊息集內都只有單一的行動選項。在資訊完全的賽局中，行動者的類型（type）是單一的。

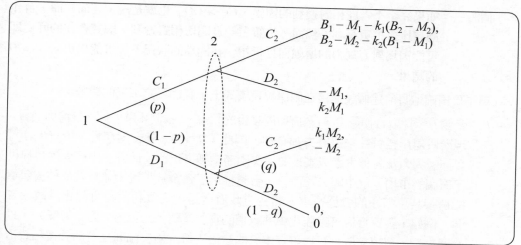

圖 14.1　兩岸經貿賽局的展開式

表 14.5　兩岸經貿賽局的正規式

行動者 1　行動者 2	C_2		D_2
C_1	$B_1 - M_1 - k_1(B_2 - M_2)$	$B_2 - M_2 - k_2(B_1 - M_1)$　$- M_1$	$k_2 M_1$
D_1	$k_1 M_2$	$- M_2$　0	0

【獲利】行動者的策略選擇，取決於其在各種局面中的獲利（payoff）大小。為了行文方便，我們把「i 政府採取合作策略，而對方也採合作策略」時，i 政府的獲利簡寫為 CC。同理可推 CD、DC、DD 的意義。我們認為，經貿來往的互利效果取決於雙方的合作機率。因此，兩岸經貿互動的賽局基本上須符合下列三項假設：

假設一：$DD \geq CD$。當對方採取對抗策略時，我方獲利不會因為改採合作策略而增加。

假設二：$DD \leq DC$。當兩方都堅持對抗策略時，如果對手改採合作策略，則我方獲利並不因此而減少。換言之，合作需要雙方共同努力，對抗卻可以單方誘發之。

假設三：如果完全不考慮相對獲利的因素，$CC > CD$。也就是說，在商言商，合作應該比對抗更有利。然而，決策者一旦關切相對獲利，經貿合作的好處即可能因為對方實力的增強而打折扣。在極端的狀況下，可能出現 $CC < CD$ 的結果。

為了更精確地將前述假設運用在兩岸經貿賽局上，我們界定下列的變數：

B_i：當雙方皆採取合作態度，i 政府所能獲得的利益。[9]我們認為，純就經濟面而言，現階段兩岸經貿往來對雙方都有利。因此，$B_i > 0$。就台灣而言，投資大陸可以節省人力及各種生產成本，並使夕陽產業獲得出路。此外，中國大陸也提供了廣闊的市場。就中國大陸而言，台灣提供了資金及技術，並較其他經濟體更能銜接其現階段的發展需求。對雙方政府而言，經貿利益也可轉化為政治資源。例如，經貿合作可以強化中共政權的物質基礎，乃至擴大對台影響力。以台灣來看，經貿交流可以換得資本家的政治支持，兩岸協商且有助於緩和政治對立，增進執政當局在國內外的聲望。

M_i：為維持合作所需付出的成本。任何的經濟活動都涉及資源的投入。台灣在大陸的投資，即受制於工資、土地、資本乃至於政治環境等各項生產因素的限制。中國大陸則必須以低價提供人力物力資源，以吸引台資。此外，外資的進入則對其國內的資本形成有一定的排擠作用，經濟的成長也可能帶來通貨膨脹等問題。除此之外，經貿活動也蘊含了政治的風險和成本。就中共而言，吸引台資可能導致外來勢力進入中國大陸，乃至造成和平演變。應台灣之要求進行協商，更有提高後者聲勢之虞。在台灣方面，開放資本流入大陸則有可能導致本身的產業空洞化、過度依賴大陸市場，或促成跨海利益集團的形成。儘管有這些成本的存在，我們認為（純就經濟面而言）現階段兩岸的經貿交流應可產生淨利益，因此 $B_i > M_i > 0$。

k_i：行動者 i 對於對方所獲利益之敏感度。假設 $0 \leq k_i \leq 1$，而 k_i 越高表示越在意對方所得。最能提高中共對於台灣獲利敏感度的因素在於：台灣當局是否將兩岸合作所獲得的政治經濟資源，用在開拓國際空間上，亦即挑戰中共的主權堅持。相對而言，台灣則可能由於兩種因素而增加對於中共獲利的敏感度：中共因為經濟成長而增強實力，及中共利用台商對台灣當局施加壓力，進而危及台

9　政府的利益當然不等同於整個社會的利益。我們從政府的角度來界定經貿利益，是因為賽局的結果取決於兩岸政府的互動。然而，非政府部門並非毫無影響力。政府和社會的利益越分歧，決策的成本就越高。

灣本身的安全（Lo and Lin, 1995）。[10]

如果 $k = 0$（完全不在乎相對獲利），則經貿合作的獲利應是 $CC = B_i - M_i$。這個結果應該好於 CD（我方合作，對方抵制；見假設三）。當然，即使只有單方採取合作策略，獲利也不一定是 0。但爲方便分析起見，可以假定 $CD = -M_i$。[11]當 $k > 0$，行動者必須顧及對方的獲利。在此情況下，我們可將 CC 的獲利寫爲 $B_i - M_i - k_i(B_{-i} - M_{-i})$。同理，$DC = k_iM_{-i}$。最後，我們可以假設 $DD = 0$，以符合假設一與假設二。[12]圖 14.1 與表 14.5 中的獲利（payoff），就是根據這些設定所寫出的。

【均衡解】本文運用「納許均衡」（Nash equilibrium）的概念來預測兩岸經貿互動的結果。其定義如下：

$$S^* 爲納許均衡 \Leftrightarrow \forall i, \beta_i(S_i^*, S_{-i}^*) \geq \beta_i(S_i', S_{-i}^*), \forall S_i'$$

在式子中，$\beta_i(S_i, S_{-i})$ 是指雙方分別採取 (S_i, S_{-i}) 策略時 i 的獲利。S 可能是我們早先所界定的「純粹策略」，也可以是「混合策略」。納許均衡可以在三種狀態下存在：

1. 當雙方都有優勢策略時，納許均衡必爲「純策均衡」（pure strategy equilibrium）。其原因是行動者在每個訊息集的行動都是單一的。

2. 當純策均衡不存在時，納許均衡必爲「混策均衡」（mixed strategy equilibrium），因爲行動者找不到最好的單一策略。[13]

3. 純策均衡和混策均衡同時存在。這種情形的發生，必是因爲有許多個純策均衡並存，而行動者無法判斷何種純粹策略的期待效用值（expected utility）較大。[14]

根據以上的概念界定，我們可以得到以下的結果：

結果 1：對任何一方的行動者 i 而言，若 $k_i > \dfrac{B_i - M_i}{B_{-i}}$，則 $k_iM_{-i} > B_i - M_i - k_i(B_{-i} - M_{-i})$，$D_i$ 成爲優勢策略。若此情形爲對手得知，必不會以合作的態度應之，相互對抗（DD）因而成爲唯一的納許均衡。這個結果可以理解爲，當行動者

---

[10] 本文將 k 值當作外生變數，從模型本身並不能解釋 k 爲何變動。但我們可以把 k 當作一個「經驗前提」（empirical precondition）：只要我們有經驗資料可以判斷 k 的大小，就可以輸入模型而作出預測。

[11] 即使假定 $CD = B' - M < B - M$，我們主要的結論還是不變。

[12] 當然，這不是滿足假設的唯一情況。但只要假設一與假設二得到滿足，分析的結果是一樣的。

[13] Lo 與 Lin（1995）與羅致政（1996）都曾運用這樣的概念分析兩岸關係。

[14] 換言之，純策均衡的存在並不表示混策均衡不存在。這是賽局論中一個常引起誤解的觀念。Rasmusen（1989: 73-74）就曾以 Chicken 賽局爲例，說明兩種均衡如何並存。Lohmann（1995: 134-138）也曾以集體行動爲例，顯示兩者的並存。

對於對方獲利的在意程度超越了某個門檻，相互對抗將成為唯一的結果。

結果 2：若對雙方而言，$k_i \leq \dfrac{B_i - M_i}{B_{\sim i}}$，則 $B_i - M_i - k_i(B_{\sim i} - M_{\sim i}) \geq k_i M_{\sim i}$。又因 $-M_i$ < 0，*CC* 與 *DD* 成為兩個納許均衡。但只有 *CC* 滿足帕雷圖最適（Pareto optimal）條件。[15]

第二種情形（*CC* 與 *DD* 同為均衡）的出現，顯示雙方都不是非常在意對方的獲利；對抗的可能性雖然存在，但非唯一的選擇。我們可以根據混策均衡的概念，來計算合作或對抗發生的機率。

就行動者 1 來看，策略 C_1 與 D_1 的期待效用值分別為：

$$EU_{C1} = q[(B_1 - M_1) - k_1(B_2 - M_2)] - (1 - q)M_1 \tag{1}$$

及

$$EU_{D1} = qk_1 M_2 \tag{2}$$

基於混策均衡的前提，（1）＝（2）。由此可推出行動者 2 追求 *C* 戰略的機率

$$q = \frac{M_1}{B_1 - k_1 B_2} \tag{3}$$

我們可以用同樣的方法，求得行動者 1 追求 *C* 戰略的機率

$$p = \frac{M_2}{B_2 - k_2 B_1} \tag{4}$$

式（3）及式（4）所顯示的是，在雙方對彼此均有一定的信任時（*k* 值低），採取合作策略的機率。我們可將之視為本研究的主要發現。以下，我們根據式（4），以比較靜態分析法（comparative static analysis），探討影響合作機率的因素。式（3）可用同法分析之，故不再重複。

我們首先確立各變數在數學上的關係。其實證意涵，將於次節討論之。

---

[15] 國際關係學者習慣將這種情形名為 Assurance Game。在此賽局中，行動者的合作與否，取決於對方的態度。

【結果 2-1】p 與 k_2 的關係：

$$\frac{\partial p}{\partial k_2} = \frac{M_2 B_1}{(B_2 - k_2 B_1)^2} \geq 0 \tag{5}$$

$$\frac{\partial^2 p}{\partial k_2^2} = \frac{2M_2 B_1^2 (B_2 - k_2 B_1)}{(B_2 - k_2 B_1)^4} \tag{6}$$

並可推知

$$(6) \leq 0 \leftrightarrow k_2 \geq \frac{B_2}{B_1}; \ (6) \geq 0 \leftrightarrow k_2 \leq \frac{B_2}{B_1}$$

然因 $k_2 > \frac{B_2}{B_1} \geq 1$ 違反假設，故（6）≥ 0。

【結果 2-2】p 與 B_1、B_2 關係：

$$\frac{\partial p}{\partial B_1} = \frac{M_2 k_2}{(B_2 - k_2 B_1)^2} \geq 0 \tag{7}$$

$$\frac{\partial p}{\partial B_2} = \frac{-M_2}{(B_2 - k_2 B_1)^2} < 0 \tag{8}$$

以上乃針對個別行動者的策略進行分析。然而，我們更有興趣瞭解的是，個體的選擇如何影響「相互合作」（CC）作爲一種集體後果（collective outcome）的發生機率。如前所述，只有在 $k_1 \leq \frac{B_1 - M_1}{B_2}$ 與 $k_2 \leq \frac{B_2 - M_2}{B_1}$ 同時成立時，才有合作的可能。若然，我們可將 CC 發生的機率寫爲

【結果 2-3】

$$r = pq = \frac{M_1 M_2}{(B_1 - k_1 B_2)(B_2 - k_2 B_1)} \tag{9}$$

根據此式，可以推出下列兩項結果。首先：

$$\frac{\partial r}{\partial M_i} > 0 \tag{10}$$

其次，若合作機率爲正，則 $k_i < \frac{B_i}{B_{-i}}$ 或 $k_i > \frac{B_i}{B_{-i}}$。若爲後者，則 $k_i > 1$ 或 $k_{-i} > 1$，違反了我們的假設。由此可知，

$$r > 0 \Rightarrow k_i < \frac{B_i}{B_{\sim i}} \tag{11}$$

我們可將式（11）稱為合作的必要條件。

以上的分析顯示了什麼？很明顯地，政治因素對於經貿交往有著重大的影響。然而，其間關係之複雜，卻超乎我們所想像。我們的模型固然印證了許多常識性的看法，卻也挑戰了不少既存的觀念。其中關鍵所在，即是行動者對於對手所獲利益的敏感度（k 值）。我們姑且將其簡稱為 SRG（sensitivity coefficient to relative gains，相對獲利敏感度），以便於行文。我們可將前述結果歸納為下列四大命題。

命題 1：當「對抗」對於雙方而言皆非優勢策略時，則某方採取合作策略的機率將隨著對方 SRG 接近臨界點而加速度上升。

我們是從式（5）及式（6）推出這項命題的。這項命題挑戰了「追求相對獲利有害合作」的傳統說法。事實上，出現這樣的結果是有理可循的。我們已經知道，當雙方皆不以對抗為上策時，CC 與 DD 是兩個可能發生的結果，而且前者優於（Pareto dominates）後者。為了追求雙贏，行動者自然希望以善意的作為引起對方的回應。對方對我方的行動越敏感（SRG 越高），我方的善意作為就越重要，而且越有效果。同時，越接近臨界點，即表示越有可能陷入相互對抗的泥淖中；我方乃更須以積極的合作以挽救情勢於未然。我們可以用一個具體的案例來說明這個命題。假設政府 1 與政府 2 從合作中分別可獲得 50 與 40 的利益，而兩方採行合作策略所須付出的成本分別為 20 與 30，則雙方從可能合作到放棄合作的臨界點分別是 0.75 與 0.2。在到達臨界點前，雙方都會放出善意訊息來避免對抗爆發。有趣的是，對方的 SRG 越高，這種善意訊號的效果就越好（r 較高）。圖 14.2 描繪了這種情況。

命題 2：當任一方的 SRG 超越臨界點，則相互對抗立即產生。

然而，善意的試探是有限度的。根據結果 1 得知，一旦當 SRG 超越了某一臨界點，「對抗」成為唯一的選擇。若然，則合作的機率立即降為零，並不會再上升。[16] 圖 14.2 也顯示了策略轉變之突然性。在到達臨界點前後，合作的機率突然由 1 滑落為 0。這種情形的發生，意味著「純策均衡」DD 的存在。

---

[16] 只要任一行動者的 SRG 超過臨界點，相互合作的機率即為零。

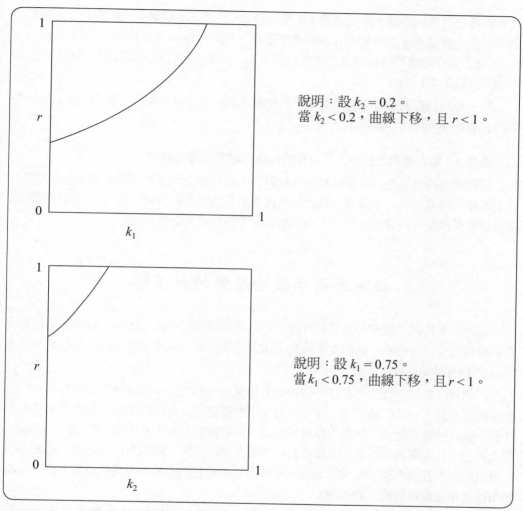

說明：設 $k_2 = 0.2$。
當 $k_2 < 0.2$，曲線下移，且 $r < 1$。

說明：設 $k_1 = 0.75$。
當 $k_1 < 0.75$，曲線下移，且 $r < 1$。

圖 14.2　合作機率（r）與獲利敏感度（SRG）

　　當然，SRG 不是影響合作的唯一變數。根據式（7）與式（8），我們可以推出下列命題：

命題 3：當對方之 SRG 低於臨界點時，我方採取合作策略的機率與己方獲利成正比，並與對方獲利成反比。

正因爲經貿往來可以創造本身的利益，所以可能帶來雙贏的局面。因此，利益的擴

大自然增強合作的動機。此由結果 2-2 可以得知。然而，在經貿交往的同時，也須顧及對方是否會將經濟上的獲利轉化為對抗的籌碼。因此，除非全無政治因素的干預（$k = 0$），我方合作的機率將會隨著對方獲利的增加而減低，但影響的程度則取決於 SRG 的大小（由結果 2-1 可知）。[17]

以上分析乃以個別行動者為對象。就整體而言，式（11）指出了雙方皆採取合作態度的必要條件。該式之含意如下：

命題 4：雙方獲利差距越大，合作的局面就越容易遭受破壞。

這個命題的意思是，某方獲利越低於對方，即越可能因為些微的因素而完全放棄合作的希望。同理可推：當雙方透過合作所獲得的利益完全均等時，式（11）所指出的必要條件恆得滿足（$k < 1$）。至此，合作與否全然取決於互信的程度。

伍、對兩岸政經互動的新理解

透過以上的模型推演，我們是否能重新詮釋兩岸經貿交流的變動？前述命題是否能得到事實的支持？為此，我們重新檢視了過去三年多來（1994-1997）的兩岸經貿關係，並以表 14.6 描繪其變化。

我們以「對抗—合作」這樣一個面向來描繪兩岸的作為。就台灣方面而言，「中止兩岸經貿交流」與「開放三通」分別代表完全對抗與完全合作的策略。對中共而言，合作的行動包括優遇台資、放寬兩岸貿易限制、並維持與台灣事務性協商的制度化管道。反之，若中共關閉協商管道，或採取對台經貿緊縮的政策，即是對抗的表現。從表 14.6 所呈現的兩岸互動形態中，我們發現一些值得特別注意的現象。而這些現象，正可由前節所述諸項命題得到充分的解釋。

第一，兩岸都曾突然由合作轉變為對抗。這種毫無預警的關係惡化，曾出現在 1994 年 4 月的千島湖事件、10 月的廣島亞運等。中共方面，更在李登輝總統訪美後，於 1995 年 6 月 16 日宣布推遲第二次「辜汪會談」及其預備性磋商的時間。另一方面，李登輝總統則在 1996 年 8 月 14 日，宣稱「以大陸腹地來建設亞太營運中心的論調，必須加以檢討」。9 月 14 日，李更提出「戒急、用忍」說，提醒台灣企業界北京「以民逼官」、「以商圍政」的意圖，並要求其自制。雙方的政策轉折，都是出人意表的。

---

[17] 我們可以把成本（M）也當作一個變數，而推出相同的結論。

表 14.6　兩岸經貿互動表

日期	台北 衝突	台北 合作	北京 合作	北京 衝突
940112		TC	BC	
940118		TC	BC	
940120		TC		
940122		TC		
940130		TC		
940201		TC	BC	
940203		TC		
940206		TC		
940215		TC		
940304	■			
940305			BC	
940315		TC		
940325		TC	BC	
940402		TC		
940405		TC		
940407	■			
940408	■			
940410				■
940411			BC	
940412				
940413				
940415			BC	
940426		TC		
940519		TC		
940616	■			
940709		TC		
940719		TC		
940730		TC	BC	
940730		TC2		
940804		TC		
941005				■
941020				■
941103	■			
941107		TC		
941111		TC	BC	
941121		TC		
941122		TC	BC	
941208		TC		
941221		TC		
941223		TC		
950103		TC		
950113		TC		

日期	台北 衝突	台北 合作	北京 合作	北京 衝突
950122		TC	BC	
950210		TC		
950220		TC		
950301		TC		
950321		TC		■
950327		TC		
950411	■			
950414		TC		
950415		TC		
950419			BC	
950420		TC		
950421		TC		
950422		TC		
950507		TC		
950512		TC		
950515		TC	BC	
950526		TC	BC	
950601			BC	
950616				■
950616				■
950630				■
950721		TC		■
950727		TC1		
950727		TC2		
950728		TC		
950803			BC	■
950810				■
950815				■
950818		TC		
951002		TC		
951003		TC		
951004			BC	
951005		TC		
951107		TC	BC	
951117			BC	
951121		TC		
951125	■			■
951128		TC		
951204			BC	
951208		TC	BC	
951209		TC		
960202		TC	BC	

日期	台北 衝突	台北 合作	北京 合作	北京 衝突
960215		TC		
960303		TC		
960307			BC	
960308				■
960309			BC	
960312		TC		■
960317		TC		
960401		TC		
960403		TC		
960415		TC		
960416		TC		
960418		TC		
960520		TC		
960527		TC		
960608		TC		
960624		TC		
960626			BC	
960703		TC		
960705				■
960711		TC		
960812		TC		
960820			BC1	
960820			BC2	
960821	■		BC	
960827		TC		
960903			BC	
960914	■			
961007	■			
961018		TC		
961020		TC		
961021		TC		
961104		TC		
961201			BC	
970204		TC	BC	
970205			BC	
970210		TC		
970318	■			■
970331			BC	
970402			BC	
970416		TC	BC	
970417			BC1	
970417			BC2	

說明：TC 表示台灣的合作策略，TD 表示台灣的對抗策略；BC 表示北京的合作策略，BD 表示北京的對抗策略。具體事件內容，請參見本章附錄──兩岸經貿交流大事記。

一般多將中共推遲第二次「辜汪會談」，視為是對李登輝總統訪美的報復。然而，中止兩岸事務性會談明顯違反中共「政經分離」的宣示；事前，也無人預測到中共的反應。[18]對於李登輝的「戒急、用忍」說，媒體更以「急轉彎」來形容其突然性。

　　若根據前節的賽局模型（命題2），則很容易解釋這種政策轉變：對抗行為的突然出現，乃因行動者對對手獲利的敏感度跨越了臨界點。李登輝的訪美，使中共警覺到，兩岸合作可能使台灣有更大的籌碼可以爭取國際生存空間。一旦涉及此一因素，兩岸交流就帶有零和賽局的性質。跨海利益集團的成長，使中共的籌碼（B）變多，台灣的成本（M）增加。台灣的決策者一旦認定中共吸引台資是有政治意圖的，就會突然轉換兩岸經貿政策。[19]對台灣而言，經貿也成了政治工具。1996年8月19日，李總統曾明言「中共最怕哪一套，我們就用哪一套作我們的策略」，應該就是最好的說明。

　　第二，兩岸在關係突然惡化之前，皆處於善意的交往氣氛中。1995年1月22日至27日，海基會與海協會進行了第三次焦唐會談。同月30日，中國國家主席江澤民發表了著名的「江八點」，提出「不要讓兩岸政治分歧妨礙經貿發展」及「中國人不打中國人」等被視為有善意的談話。即使在美國國會已經通過歡迎李登輝訪美的決議後，雙方仍在台北舉行了第二次「辜汪會談」的預備磋商會議，並商定會談日期與地點。

　　台灣方面的善意作為則更為明顯。即使是在中共頻頻發動軍事演習之刻，台灣仍然採取了一系列的善意措施。1995年12月29日，外交部長錢復明確宣示「大陸政策位階高於外交政策」的原則。1996年2月2日，陸委會代主委高孔廉表示，《國統綱領》中程階段的兩岸通航，可以彈性移至近程階段處理。3月12日，經濟部長江丙坤表示，即使中共密集對台演習，兩岸經貿仍將持續開放。3月24日李登輝當選總統後，開放措施更加明顯。副總統當選人連戰清楚地揭示了新政府的政策目標：兩岸恢復溝通管道，尋求雙贏。次日，交通部長劉兆玄宣布，月底前將明確宣布兩岸三通方案。4月1日，台北政府全面解除汽車零組件赴大陸投資禁令。同月3日，經濟部決定大幅開放大陸農工產品進口。15日，陸委會通過相關辦法，放寬兩岸證券與期貨往來；翌日，

---

[18] 事實上，美國眾議院在5月初就已通過歡迎李登輝訪美案，但中共卻等到6月中才做出反應。在此之前，兩岸仍持續進行會談的準備。這顯示中共的做法，不全然是情緒性的報復，而帶有政策調整的性質。

[19] 台灣的大陸經貿政策出現急轉彎後，首當其衝的就是大企業。李登輝批評「大陸腹地論」後，台塑立即撤回漳州電廠的投資申請書。統一集團則表示不急於進行武漢電廠的投資計畫。有媒體報導，李登輝發表「戒急用忍」說，乃因統一集團的高清愿未先向政府報備即面見江澤民。「戒急用忍」政策的政治背景由此可見一斑。此外，命題3、4也指出，中共獲利增加及台灣成本擴大（因資本外移）也會降低台灣的合作意願。

經濟部決定大幅放寬大陸工商人士赴台的資本與層級限制。5 月 25 日，陸委會通過大幅放寬大陸物品進口範圍，以及大陸專業人士來台。6 月 1 日，陸委會表示將研擬開放大陸傳播媒體長期駐台。同月 8 日，經濟部作出放寬限制證券商赴大陸投資的決議。24 日，陸委會決定大幅放寬大陸經貿人士來台。7 月 4 日，經濟部通過十三件重大赴大陸投資案。7 月份台灣赴大陸投資金額，創下了歷年來的最高記錄。

　　以上的過程，相當程度印證了命題 1：當政治顧慮尚未到達臨界點時，行動者可能用善意的作爲，來防範對抗的發生。同時，對方的不信任度越高，我方就必須付出更大的努力，才能避免兩敗俱傷。舉例而言，台灣在千島湖事件中展現對中共的不信任態度，但中共並不因此立刻採取對抗措施，反而採一系列低調的做法，希望挽回台灣人民的信心。此外，即使美國宣布同意李登輝訪美，海協會常務副會長唐樹備仍然按計畫抵台，參加第二次辜汪會談第一次預備性磋商。然而，我們在前面也談到，這種善意的行爲不會一直持續下去。只要某方失去耐心，相互對抗很快就會爆發，造成不能挽回的傷害。當李登輝返台，而連戰又接著出訪歐洲時，中共才宣布推遲兩岸協商。

　　表 14.6 還透露了一個值得玩味的現象。李登輝總統提出「戒急用忍」說，距離中共片面中止二次辜汪會談已超過一年的時間。這點和我們的預測有所差距。根據前述模型，當一方採取對抗策略時，另一方應以同樣的策略應之。我們如何解釋兩岸政策轉變的時間差距？台灣方面爲何不在中共推遲辜汪會談，並宣布軍事演習後就立刻降低兩岸經貿往來？

　　其中的原由可能相當複雜。我們認爲以下兩點因素值得進一步的探討。首先，政策轉換是要付出代價的。台灣在 1996 年 3 月進行總統直選，迫使當局必須愼重考慮降低兩岸經貿往來所須付出的政治代價。當然，我們可以進一步的提出這樣的假設：李登輝總統所最在意的，其實是工商界的政治支持。據此，我們即不難瞭解中共的「以商圍政」爲何引發了李總統的「戒急用忍」說。其次，「訊息成本」（information cost）在政策轉換過程中扮演重要的角色。由於相互對抗是比相互合作更壞的結果，決策者必須經過不斷的測試，方能確定對方的眞正態度。在中共中止協商後，台灣方面曾不斷重提「江八點」、「李六條」；中共方面則一再強調要對台灣當局「聽其言」、「觀其行」。這些訊息其實都具有試探作用：當對方有任何政策改變的可能時，必會對其有所反應。互相放話，其實是爲了避免因爲溝通不良（miscommunication）而造成兩敗俱傷。台灣當局在大陸經貿政策上踩煞車，應該是確認了中共態度的不可改變。

陸、結論

「雙贏」與「零和」可能是台灣媒體或學界評論兩岸關係時最常使用的字眼。近來，「以商圍政」、「戒急用忍」等名詞更已深入人民的日常生活中。然而，大多數人僅把這些概念當作政治修辭來使用，而忽略了其原本的意涵。事實上，這些概念不只具有分析上的意義，彼此更有密切的關係。本文即從賽局論的角度，將這些概念整合在同一個分析架構之下，並將之用來分析兩岸關係。我們發現，「雙贏」的賽局，可能隨著政治互信的降低而「零和」化。但這種轉化往往是突發其然的，而且一旦陷入僵局就不易化解。

我們的發現也挑戰了一些國際關係理論的定見。追求「相對獲利」固然有害於國際合作，但其衝擊只有在到達某個臨界點時才會顯現。在此之前，國家反而可以利用對方的政治敏感度，以善意的行動來誘發對方的合作。我們認為，這樣的模型具有一定的普遍性。在完全沒有政治因素的干預下，國家間的經貿往來非常類似於我們所描繪的「互信賽局」（assurance game）：對抗固然引發對抗，合作卻也能引發合作，進而帶來雙贏。自由主義者眼中由「貿易國家」（trading states）所構成的世界，應該就是如此。然而，從我們的研究也可推知：只有當這樣的國家占了絕大多數時，相互合作才能成為國際規範。原因很簡單：合作需要雙邊共同的努力，但對抗卻可以由任何一方單獨引發。「貿易國家」如果碰上了「領土擴張國家」（territorial states），也不得不謹慎應對，並以政治的手段來保障經貿利益。[20]

台海兩岸目前就處於這樣的局面中。由於中共堅決主張擁有對台灣的領土主權，使得兩岸關係必然帶有強烈的政治色彩。即使像經貿往來這種應能互蒙其利的事務，也不能免於政治因素的干預。兩岸政府當然也看到了這個問題，亦不約而同地提出「政經分離」論。不幸的是，事實的發展並未依照這個原則進行。

不過，本文的結論並非是全然悲觀的。我們認為，政治對立的產生固然有其結構性背景，其對於非政治事務的影響卻不是絕對的。同理，以政治邏輯來思考經貿議題，也不一定能解決政治問題。如果追求雙贏不是政治口號，兩項步驟是必要的。首先，兩岸政府必須確定不信任感的來源。在某些情況下，對立是現實使然（例如主權即具有不可妥協性），溝通協調的效果必然有限。然而，就經貿議題而言，政治因素的介入卻不是必然的。例如，中共可以這樣認知和台灣的關係：台灣爭取國際空間，是任何執政者為

---

[20] 關於貿易國家與領土國家的討論，詳見 Rosecrance（1986）。

求生存皆會採行的政策；中共即使反對這種政策，開放或關閉對台協商管道並無助於改變這項事實。就台灣而言，亦須體認到中共對台灣國際空間的擠壓並不會隨著兩岸經貿的冷熱而有明顯的改變。簡言之，避免不必要的政治猜測是合作的前提。[21] 其次，即使雙方都有善意，還是必須透過「同時行動」（simultaneous actions）來完成合作。本文所描繪的兩岸關係，也是一種「協調賽局」（coordination game）。在此賽局中，可能發生的結果不只一種，而某些結果比他者更符合共同利益。然而，若是雙方已處在相互的對抗狀態中，卻無任何一方願意先表示善意，僵局將持續下去。這可以說是一種「兩敗」的狀態：雙方皆可以更好，卻因為協調不良而無法突破現狀。由此，我們認為制度化的協商管道是非常重要的。這種協商管道的設立並無害於兩岸各自追求的政治目標，卻能在必要的時候防止雙方皆不願見到的結果發生。

我們的分析也顯示，雙方獲利的差距越大，合作的基礎就越脆弱。據此，我們可以推論，互賴（interdependence）比依賴（dependence）更有利於合作。舉例而言，台灣對於大陸市場依賴越深，就越可能擔憂對方以此為籌碼進行政治脅迫，進而阻斷兩岸交流。必須強調的是，這種憂慮起因於經濟計算，而非單純只是政治考量。只要經貿依賴關係不改善，僵局的出現是難免的。從這個觀點來看，台灣採取適當的分散市場策略，反而有利於兩岸交流的穩定化；「南向」與「西進」，其實是互補的。

---

[21] 必須說明的是，我們並不主張兩岸政府不會或不應將政經掛鉤。我們只是要強調，以經貿交流作為政治工具，無助於改變政治目標。

附錄　兩岸經貿交流大事記

日期／策略	內　　容
940112BC	海協會第一屆理事會第三次會議於 12 至 13 日在北京舉行，唐表示1994 年工作重點有三：一為推動兩會人士互訪，以推動二次辜汪會談；二為協助兩岸交流，以推動和平統一；三為促成兩會就「台商在大陸權益及相關議題」、「兩岸工商界人士互訪」等議題進行對話。
940112TC	經濟部向陸委會建議開放三項大陸產品或商業行在台刊登以利促銷。
940118BC	中共「對外貿易經濟合作部」、「海關總署」頒布《對台灣地區小額貿易管理辦法》。
940118TC	由陸委會主導的「中華發展基金」已獲行政院同意，近日正式運作。
940120TC	陸委會近日原則同意我民航局提出的《兩岸航空聯運許可辦法》，未來將可在國內航空公司購買大陸段機票，行李也可直接轉機。經濟部召開「赴大陸地區投資及技術合作專案審查小組」會議，決定開放營造業、租賃業以工程顧問業赴大陸間接投資。
940122TC	經濟部國貿局最近完成修訂《台灣地區與大陸地區貿易地區許可辦法》，將由目前國貿局核發輸入許可證的做法，第一階段改為事前銀行簽證；第二階段改為免輸入許可證，為進口大陸物品實施負面表列預作準備。
940130TC	經濟部公布實施《在大陸地區從事商業行為許可辦法》，於下月 1 日正式接受申請。
940201TC BC	一日至五日在北京舉行「焦唐會談」。
940203TC	經濟部決定擴大放寬大陸經貿人士來台許可辦法，放寬赴台條件。
940206TC	經濟部今召開「赴大陸地區投資專案小組」會議，決定准許營造業、租賃業以工程顧問業赴大陸間接投資。
940304TD BD	「海峽兩岸產業科技交流合作研討」因故延後。大陸成員全由中共國台辦圈選，具幾乎都有中共官方身分，但因大陸代表團不願更動人選，因而決定放棄組團。
940215TC	外貿協會研訂《大陸市場策略聯盟拓展工作規劃綱要》，積極撮合外商和台商拓展大陸市場。
940305BC	八屆人大常委六次會議通過《台胞投資保護法》，據規定，對台商投資不實行國有化和徵收；其投資收益、合法收入和清算後的資金，可以匯回台灣或匯往境外等。

（接下頁）

日期／策略	內　　　容
950315TC	陸委會公布《現階段兩岸文化交流實施原則》。
940325TC BC	海協會與海基會開始舉行第四次工作會談，主要有關人員遣返問題。
940402TC	經濟部決定大幅放寬國內汽車工業前往大陸投資，同時也開放大陸汽機車零組件進口。
940405TC	經濟部工業局初步開放紡織業赴大陸投資項目 325 項，成衣服飾產品也將全部開放間接進口。
940407TC	經濟部長江丙坤：千島湖事件未明朗前，台商對大陸投資或增資計畫應全面暫停。
940408TD	黃昆輝表示，若中共未對千島湖事件有妥善明確交待，政府將調整兩岸交流。
940410BD	大陸游泳教練孫紅標來台任教，超過大陸期限，大陸方面電催未果，日前電中華奧會表示，若孫今日之前未返大陸，「將嚴重影響兩岸體育關係」。
940411BC	中共國務院召開為期五天的「對台經濟工作會議」今日在北京開幕，繼續推動兩岸經濟全面交流。
940412TD	陸委會文教會報決定因千島湖事件暫停七項交流。
940413TD	行政院支持國內旅行業者決定，在中共未公布真相與追究責任之前，自 5 月 1 日起暫停組團赴大陸。
940415BC	中共國務院召開為期五天的「對台經濟工作會議」今日在北京閉幕，繼續推動兩岸經濟全面交流。
940426TC	經濟部工業局決定再大幅放寬廠商赴大陸投資項目，同時擴大開放大陸物品進口。
940519TC	行政院討論通過《台灣地區與大陸地區貿易許可辦法》部分條文修正案，決定大幅簡化自大陸進口物品的簽審程序，以適應兩岸經貿情勢的需要。
940616TD	陸委會通過教育部所提，將自 7 月 1 日起停止受理大陸地區「非文教類」人士申請來台從事兩岸學術交流活動。
940709TC	經濟部認為，中油公司在政策許可前提下，在平等互惠基礎上可以間接參與大陸探油計畫。
940719TC	經濟部表示自千島湖後暫停審查赴大陸投資項目，迄今已累積近一百件，自今日起將恢復審查。

（接下頁）

日期／策略	內　　　容
940730TC BC	海基會副秘書長許惠祐與海協會孫亞夫，在台北舉行兩會第五次後續性會談。
940730TC2	陸委會通過財政部所提《台灣地區與大陸地區保險業務往來許可辦法》，並限定祇能從事再保業務。陸委會同時決定以「負面表列方式」，再擴大開放兩岸金融業務往來。
940804TC BC	第二次「焦唐會談」於 4 至 7 日在台北舉行。
941005BD	中共在舟山群島附頻海域舉近二十年來最大規模之「神聖九四」演習。
941020BD	海協會來函再一次拒絕海基會的經貿團赴大陸武漢等地訪問。
941103TD	行政院大陸工作策劃小組開會決定《台灣地區境外漁船雇用大陸船員暫行要點》暫緩公布實施。
941107TC	立院經濟司法聯席會通過經濟部提交的《台灣地區與大陸地區貿易許可辦法》、《大陸地區產業技術引進許可辦法》、《在大陸地區從事投資或技術合作許可辦法》以及《廢除現對大陸地區從事間接投資或技術合作管理辦法》等案。
941111TC BC	中共海峽兩岸經貿協調會和台灣海峽兩岸商務協調會在北京簽定新的合作協議書。
941121TC	陸委會同意中油公司以間接方式向大陸採購原油。
941122TC BC	海基會與海協會於 22 至 27 日在南京舉行兩岸第六次事務性協商。
941208TC	中央銀行宣布開放國內指定外匯銀行可以承作「大陸進口，台灣結匯」。
941221TC	經濟部公告再開放 132 項產品赴大陸投資，總計使得台灣至大陸投資項目達 4,644 項。
941223TC	陸委會決定放寬大陸記者來台採訪申請手續。
950103TC	中央銀行決定近日開放國內指定外匯銀行直接辦理台商大陸出口、台灣押匯業務，取消原規定的兩岸轉口貿易必須透過第三地開信用狀、融資的限制。
950113TC	陸委會通過「現階段兩岸經貿發展規劃案」，該案以擴大經貿為主軸，推動兩岸互利互惠的經貿關係，以及建設台灣為亞太營運中心為主要方向。
950122TC	兩會第三次焦唐會談和第七次事務性協商會談於 22 至 27 日在北京舉行。

（接下頁）

日期／策略	內　　　容
950210TC	財政部公布，同意由國內保險業同業公會赴大陸設立聯絡辦事處。
950220TC	陸委會核准保險同業公會赴大陸設辦事處。
950301TC	交通部宣布，行政院已核准開放外輪和權宜輪行駛兩岸之間，待作業要點研擬完成後即可實施，屆時並將成立境外營運中心。
950321TC	政府已正式授權台灣工商協進會理事長辜濂松，代表台灣民間工商界與大陸「中華全國工商聯合會」建立對口單位。
950321BD	根據《星島日報》報導，中共「國務院台灣事務辦公室」為統一對台工作口徑，明令各地政府部門不得與海基會直接聯繫，遇有海基會的詢問、交涉、交流等，都必須報告海協會統一處理。
950327TC	陸委會通過《大陸地區人民進入台灣地區許可辦法》部分條文修正案，大幅放寬大陸人民許可來台規定。
950411TD	台灣證管會宣布，台商在大陸設立的公司，將視為中資企業，不能回台上市、或從事投資。
950414TC	法務部今天決議，今後台灣漁船在公海雇用中國大陸漁工，不須經台灣主管機關同意。
950415TC	連戰正式核定《大陸地區人民赴台從事經貿活動許可辦法修正草案》，該修正案放寬中共經貿官員來台規定。此辦法將於19日公布實施。
950419BC	海協會唐副會長在山東台商座談會上，就台商所提「如果台灣政權生變，台獨勢力執政，台商利益是否還會得到保護」問題表示，不論在何情況下，中共都將保護台商在大陸利益。
950420TC	行政院農委會決定自5月1日起，開放大陸專業農業人士來台，除參觀外並可接受培訓。
950421TC	交通部表示，政院已核定公布《大陸地區交通專業人士來台從事交通相關活動許可辦法》，自本月26日起施行。
950422TC	交通部正式宣布，該部籌劃的「境外航運中心」將於5月1日起正式展開運作，並以高雄港先單獨作業。
950507TC	陸委會通過《境外航運中心設置作業辦法》，並於次日起由高雄港務局接受申請，採取設置「境外航運中心」模式，先開放外籍貨輪在兩岸間直航，船上貨物必須以大陸或第三地為目的地，貨物不可以進入台灣。

（接下頁）

日期／策略	內　　　容
950512TC	境管局向陸委會建議，將大陸配偶來台配額由每年 600 人調增至 1,080 人。
950515TC BC	海基會石齊平副秘書長和海協會副秘書長劉剛奇通電確定，二次辜汪會談訂 7 月中、下旬在北京舉行，同時為了建立辜汪會談在兩地輪流舉行的制度，雙方也同意第三次在台北召開。
950526TC BC	大陸海協會常務副會長唐樹備等八人抵台，參加第二次辜汪會談第一次預備性磋商。
950601BC	中共對外經貿合作部港澳台司副司長王暉表示，李總統訪美一事不會影響中共鼓勵台商投資、加強兩岸經貿交流的一貫政策。
950616BD1	大陸海協會致函海基會，宣布推遲兩岸協商。
950616BD2	海基會文教參訪團由李慶平率領抵上海，海協會長汪道涵以身體不適不克出席歡迎晚宴。同時取消汪與訪問團會見之行程。
950630BD	海協會正式推遲第四次焦唐會談。
950721BD	中共舉行試射飛彈演習，台北股市重挫。
950721TC	連戰在國建會閉幕會上強調，兩岸交流仍將秉持「經貿為主軸的原則」，兼顧經濟發展安全，並透過國際多邊活動，追求雙方互重共處，以促進兩岸互補互利，最終邁向和平統一。
950727TC1	行政院通過《台灣地區人民進入大陸地區許可辦法修正案》，根據此法，擔任行政職務的政務官可以申請參加在大陸國際組織舉辦的國際會議或活動。
950727TC2	中央社報導，陸委會通過大陸地區產業技術引進許可辦法。
950728TC	經濟部決定近期內再開放 84 項來自大陸的半成品進口，這使得累計核准進口的對岸半成品總數達 2,447 項。
950803BC	中共國台辦主任王兆國，會見陸潤康等金融大老時，明確表示將繼續加強兩岸經貿往來，不受其他事件影響。
950810BD	中共宣布在東海海域進行導彈、火炮射擊。
950815BD	中共再度舉行「東海演習」。
950818TC	李總統接見日本產經新聞總編輯住田良能時表示，兩岸關係陷入谷底令人遺憾，確保海峽和平安定應為最基本原則，台灣會繼續尋求對話協商的窗口。

（接下頁）

8

日期／策略	內　　容
951002TC	陸委會邀集交通部和經濟部等相關單位討論決定，同意澳門航空以原班機、改班號續飛大陸，使台澳航權解決，台澳航線可望成為兩岸第一條一機底，仍解釋為「間接通航」的航線。
951003TC	行政院國科會主任委員郭南宏前往北京，出席亞洲暨太平洋經濟合作會議科技部長級會議，這是六年來繼財政部長郭婉容後，第二位部長級前往大陸。
951004BC	江澤民在接受《美國新聞與世界報導》訪問時表示，「我歡迎李登輝到北京來，而若受邀請也隨時可以出發。」，《新華社》隨後發表修正版報導，江表示：我們歡迎台灣當局領導人以適當身分前來訪問，我們也願意接受台灣方面的邀請，前往台灣。中國人的事我們自己辦，不需要借助任何外力。
951005TC	行政院通過經濟部所提《大陸地區產業技術引進許可辦法修正草案》，同意擴大引進技術者範圍。
951107TC BC	大陸偷渡客遣返重新展開。
951117BC	中共副總理在亞太經合會閉幕會上稱，台灣海峽兩岸進行經貿有利雙方。
951121TC	交長劉兆玄宣布，嘉縣布袋港升為台灣境內第四座商港，已報政院核定，其升格將為兩岸直航預作準備。
951125TD	為避免資本及技術密集的大型製造業前往大陸投資，造成台灣產業空洞化，經濟部工業局宣布製造業赴大陸投資的審查門檻。
951125BD	中共舉行「東山島演習」。
951128TC	政府為進一步協助大陸台商解決融資問題，決定政策性開放台灣租賃間接赴大陸投資。
951204BC	江澤民已正式批示，通過《台灣海峽兩岸間水路航行運輸管理辦法》。
960202TC	陸委會高代主委表示，國統綱領三階段沒有時間表，在不違反我大陸政策的安全、對等、尊嚴三原則前提下，中程階段的兩岸通航，可以彈性提前移至近程階段處理。
960202BC	中共對外經貿部長吳儀發表談話強調：一、在一個中國原則下，採取務實、靈活的措施，推進兩岸直接通商；二、貫徹《中華人民共和國台灣同胞投資保護法》，積極吸引台商到大陸投資；三、改善投資環境，促進兩岸貿易發展，擴大對台出口，減少對台貿易逆差。
960215TC	經濟部通過 45 項間接赴大陸投資案，並決定今後在對岸投資金額在二百萬美元以下的逐由投審會進行核准，不必再開會討論。

（接下頁）

日期／策略	內　　容
960303TC	連戰表示，兩岸關係不是低聲下氣，委曲求全就能解決，問題癥結在於中共的霸權心態。今後兩岸關係，要以經貿爲主軸，按部就班，循序漸進來促進交流合作。
960307BC	中共農業部長劉江表示，大陸希望能進一步與台灣進行農業貿易往來。
960308BD	中共人民解放軍將於3月8至15日進行地對地彈導發射訓練。
960309BC	對外經貿部長吳儀在人大記者會表示，中共將依江八點的「不以政治分歧影響和干擾兩岸經濟合作」方針繼續致力兩岸經貿關係的發展。
960312BD	人民解放軍於3月12至20日在台灣海域和空域，進行海空實彈演習。
960312TC	經濟部長江丙坤表示，雖然兩岸關係受中共對台密集軍事演習的影響，但兩岸經貿政策持續開放的方向不變，以利靈活運用比較利益，垂直分工，提升國際競爭力。
960317TC	國貿局再開放進口原油等61項大陸物品。
960401TC	台灣決定將汽車零組件業赴大陸投資的禁令全面解除。
960403TC	經濟部國貿局，將自7月1日起大幅開放對岸農工產品進口，並由現行的正面表列改爲負面表列。
960415TC	陸委會通過有關辦法，放寬台灣業者與大陸證券及期貨業務往來。
960416TC	經濟部及有關單位開會，決定大幅放寬申請大陸人士來台的台灣廠商資本額。另根據修訂辦法，台灣邀請對岸工商團體層級則放寬爲省、市級，對岸主管級與高級技術人員也可來台接受訓練。
960418TC	交通部宣布開放大陸貨櫃可直接進出台灣地區。
960520TC	李登輝在第九任總統就職演說再次呼籲：海峽兩岸都應正視處理結束敵對狀態這項重大問題，並表示願意前往大陸從事和平之旅。
960527TC	陸委會通過放寬大陸物品進口範圍，開放公營事業無須經專案許可，即可申請大陸物品進口。
960608TC	經濟部投審會召開跨部會議，決定放寬限制證券商到大陸投資營業的決議。
960624TC	陸委會討論經濟部所提《大陸人民來台從事經貿相關活動許可辦法修正草案》，決定大幅放寬大陸經貿人士來台。

（接下頁）

日期／策略	內　　　容
960626BC	在西班牙訪問的江澤民對西班牙《國家報》發表訪談，指稱：舉行兩岸和平統一談判是中共的一貫主張，雙方可先就「在一個中國的原則下正式結束兩岸敵對狀態」，進行談判。中共歡迎台灣當局領導人以適當身分來大陸訪問，也願意接受台灣方面的邀請前往台灣；兩岸領導人可在「一個中國」前提下就雙方關注的問題交換意見。
960703TC	海基會經陸委會授權，將 6 月 25 日通過「兩會組團互訪」案，正式去函海協會，提議兩會理（董、監）事進行互訪，並期海協對此作出正面積極回應。
960705BD	海協回覆海基稱，台灣應就中共中央台辦、國台辦發言人 6 月 22 日所提「就結束兩岸敵對狀態與其他政治議題進行商談」作出回應，才是當務之急；對互訪案，未見回應。
960711TC	政院通過內政部所提《大陸土地及營建人士赴台從事相關活動許可辦法》。
960812TC	陸委會張主委指出，國統綱領本身就有相當大的彈性和解釋空間。兩岸互動是延續性的，從近程階段過渡到中程階段，很難有明確的切割點來區分，也很難由某一個人或單位作宣示。
960820BC1	中共交通部根據「一個中國、雙向直航、互惠互利」原則，發布「台灣海峽兩岸間航運管理辦法」，並決定即日起實施。
960820BC2	中共交通部長黃鎮東宣布，開放廈門、福州兩個港區，作為兩岸間船舶直航的試點口岸。
960821TD	經濟部最近對台商赴大陸投資作出進一步限制規定，要求對 12 個重點產業的「兩岸分工模式」進行檢討修正。
960821BC	中共對外經貿部發布《關於台灣海峽兩岸間貨物運輸代理業管理辦法》全文 14 條，即日實施。
960827BC	自中共宣布開放廈門、福州為直航試點港口後，台中港將於本月底接受島內航商申請。
960903BC	中共國家主席江澤民接受法國《費加羅報》採訪時稱，中共將堅持貫徹江八點主張；呼籲舉行兩岸和平統一談判，在一個中國前提下，歡迎台灣領導人以適當身分來大陸訪問，也願意接受台灣方面的邀請，前往台灣。
960914TD	李總統在「全國經營者大會」致詞，提出面對中共以民逼官、以商圍政等冷處理做法，採「戒急用忍」的大原則。

（接下頁）

日期／策略	內　　　容
961007TD	經濟部長王志剛 7 日在向立法院經濟委員會提出的施政報告中表示，陸委會、經濟部日前對大陸經貿政策看法已經一致，在經貿特區方面，都認為應放眼全球，不將大陸排除在外，至於台商赴大陸投資，在兩岸關係未改善前將取審慎態度，專案審查的標準將趨嚴。
961018TC	副總統兼行政院長連戰會見美國西東大學亞洲系主任楊力宇時表示，在「一個中國」問題上，由於兩岸對其涵意的解釋各有不同，因此，雙方應建立在「台灣與大陸均是中國領土」的共識基礎上，才能打開兩岸目前的僵局。並提出具體如下看法：一、兩岸應以「協商代替對抗」；二、雙方應強化互惠、互利的經貿關係；三、兩岸應在平等、相互尊重的基礎上，推動和平協定的談判和簽署，早日結束敵對狀態。
961020TC	教育部政務次長楊朝祥 20 日下午率團經香港前往大陸考察兩岸文教交流業務，這是第一位因公前往大陸，但不是參加國際會議或活動的政務官。
961021TD	李總統在國家統一委員會第十一次委員會議發表談話重申，我們的大陸政策，必須以根留台灣、加強建設、充實國力為出發點，戒急用忍，行穩致遠，逐步實現國家和平統一的終極目標；李總統還重申了去年回應「江八點」的六點主張，再次鄭重呼籲「兩岸應正視處理結束敵對狀態這項重大課題」，並表達從事「和平之旅」的意願，以及「與中共領導當局見面直接交換意見」的主張。
961104TC	陸委會通過《大陸記者來台常駐規定》，新聞局兩周內即可對外發布並接受申請。
961201BC	中共國務院台灣事務辦公室發布《關於台灣記者來祖國大陸採訪的規定》，共 12 條。
970204TC BC	海峽兩岸航運界日前在香港就兩岸試點直航會談達成協議。
970205BC	中共人大常委會辦公廳、政協辦公廳宣布，歡迎台灣記者前往北京採訪中共八屆人大第五次會議和政協八屆第五次會議。
970210TC	交通部航政司長謝明輝表示，該部已接獲行政院公文，原則同意開放外輪定期航線船舶間接航行兩岸，至於貨的部分，依經濟部門的貿易許可辦法，只要允許進口的大陸貨物以間接運輸方式運送即可。
970318TD	陸委會、經濟部等單位開會研究台商赴大陸投資處理原則，對違規赴對岸投資的台商作出罰款新台幣三百萬至一千五百萬不等處罰的決定。
970331TD	中央銀行總裁許遠東指出，依目前政府法令，政府將全面清查國內大企業赴大陸投資的資金往來情形，並從台塑開始。

（接下頁）

日期／策略	內　　　容
970331BC	海協會就台灣發生豬隻口蹄疫事致函海基會稱，大陸在口蹄疫防治方面具備充分技術能力，並可提供高效能 O 型疫苗。
970402BC	大陸海峽兩岸航運交流協會以傳真，告知我台灣海峽兩岸航運協會，大陸五家航商已獲得中共交通部核准經營兩岸定點通航業務。
970416TC BC	在中華民國紅十字會及廈門紅十字會派員見證下，兩岸根據金門協議在台海中線附近的吳嶼，交換偷渡犯。
970417BC1	海協會致函海基會稱，中共對 3 月 10 日劫機犯劉善忠已完成必要審查，即依金門協議予以遣返；具體事宜將由兩岸紅十字會聯繫。
970417BC2	中共交通部 16 日晚完成相關行政程序，並於 17 日照會我方，正式批准六家航商的申請開航。（核准後一週）

第十五章

雙層三角：以空間模型分析國內政治對美中台戰略三角的影響[*]

壹、兩岸關係與內部政治

在現實主義者（realist）的眼中，國際關係由追求最大利益的國家所構成。[1] 所謂「國家」（state），不但在分析上經常被視為單一個體的行動者（unitary actor），在許多人的心中也是真實存在的本體。這樣的視野，可能帶來一項分析上的困難：不同的執政者，是否追求同樣的國家利益？政治體制，會不會影響國家的對外行為？這並不是新問題（Evans, Jacobson, and Putnam, 1993; Rosenau, 1969），而在諸派理論中，又以 Robert Putnam（1988）的雙層賽局（two-level game）模型受到最多的注意和引用。[2] 到今天，很少人能忽略國內政治為國際關係帶來的影響。

兩岸關係亦不例外。過去十年，台灣和大陸的經濟互動日漸加深，政治上卻趨向對立；在同一時間，台灣完成了兩次政黨輪替，中國大陸的政治結構則進一步的體制化。要理解這些現象，我們必須解釋台灣的內部政治變遷如何和國際環境的變化產生互動：過去十年，李登輝和陳水扁兩位前總統，在建構本土政權的同時，也試圖替加溫中的兩岸經貿互動踩煞車，但主權獨立的呼求和台灣意識的上升畢竟難以抵擋全球化的趨力和中國經濟的壯大。隨著中國在國際舞台影響力的擴大和美國對中國大陸依賴度的增加，台灣逐漸在新的國際秩序中被邊緣化。在此情勢下，主張「不統、不獨、不武」的馬英九在 2008 年 3 月贏得總統選舉，是否能突破台灣的困境？還是會加深台灣對中國經濟的依賴、進一步弱化台灣的國際地位？[3]

---

[*] 本文曾刊登於包宗和、吳玉山（編），《重新檢視爭辯中的兩岸關係理論》（2009 年 9 月），頁 277-304，台北：五南。感謝中央研究院政治學研究所、五南圖書同意轉載。

[1] 關於現實主義的流派以及對現實主義的批評，請參閱 Donnelly（2000）。

[2] 知名的國際關係期刊 *The Journal of Conflict Resolution* 曾在 1997 年 2 月號（第 41 卷第 1 期）出版專號，探討賽局理論在連結政治上的運用。

[3] 馬英九在 2007 年 11 月 20 日公布他的外交政策白皮書，強調他主張兩岸關係「不統、不獨、不武」，以「活路外交」為中華民國在國際找出路（陳志平，2007）。

　　欲回答上述問題，我們不但要解析短期的政策變化，更要能著眼長期，提出普遍性的理論架構。這個架構，要能以同一個理論整合國內政治、兩岸關係和美中台三角互動。在兩岸關係的研究上，一些學者探討過台灣的選舉、民主化和認同政治對兩岸關係的影響（吳玉山，2000a；Chan, 2005; Garver, 1997; Hsieh, 2004; Li, 2005; Wu, 1999, 2006），基本上是把台灣的內部因素視爲影響兩岸關係的變數。也有不少研究採取戰略三角（strategic triangle）的途徑（吳玉山，2000a、2000b；Dittmer, 1981, 1987），從三角關係的形態來分析美中台的國際處境（例如吳玉山，2000a、2000b；包宗和，1999；Wu, 1996, 2005b, 2006）。本章希望在這些研究的基礎上，建構一個採取以下假定的「雙層三角」（two-layered strategic triangle）模型：第一，模型的第一層是各方政府，第二層是國家，各國對其他國家的態度，由政府所代表的民意決定；[4] 第二，對三角關係的描繪，從「友好／敵對」的二分延伸爲連續空間，國與國的距離，表現其利益差距的程度；第三，國內政權（或領導權）的變動和各方改變現狀的能力，是影響戰略三角形態的主要變數。立基於這些假定，「雙層三角」模型賦予傳統戰略三角理論動態的個體基礎。此一模型以各方的政府爲分析單位，各方互動產生總體效應，並回過頭來影響各方的利益。因爲各國政府的利益又受制於選民結構和內部競爭，國內政治就和國際關係產生了動態的聯繫。

　　「雙層三角」模型既然以構成戰略三角的政府爲行動主體，國家之間的關係又取決於各政府的利益，最適合的分析框架就是理性選擇中的空間模型（spatial model）。由於國內相關的理論著作有限，所以本文將以一定的篇幅介紹相關概念，並借用 George Tsebelis 的「否決者理論」（veto player theory）推論相關命題，說明國內政治如何影響戰略三角的總體後果。之後，將以台灣過去十年三位總統的兩岸政策爲案例，說明如何運用「雙層三角」模型來解釋國內政治對戰略三角的影響。

貳、理性選擇、賽局理論與空間模型

　　本節介紹重要的分析概念。當我們以台、美、中三方政府爲行動者，並根據各方利益來探討他們的互動結果時，已經隱含了「理性選擇」（rational choice）的分析途徑。理性選擇研究的是「意向性」（intentional）的行爲，假定行爲者有特定的目標，並會

4　這個假定，並不預設國家一定採取民主體制。對於非民主國家，可以將「民意」定義爲「參與決策的菁英」所呈現的集體偏好。

儘可能地實現其目標。更詳細言之，理性選擇途徑採取以下的假定（林繼文，2005：76-77）：

1. 方法論上的個體主義（methodological individualism）：發生於某個層次的現象，乃由構成這個層次的個體之行爲所產生。

2. 具有完全性（completeness）與遞移性（transitivity）的偏好（preference）：所謂完全性的偏好，是指行爲者對於所有的選項都能進行偏好排序；遞移性的偏好，是指偏好排序（preference order）可以在不同選項間遞移，例如 a 比 b 好，b 比 c 好，則 a 比 c 好。

3. 利益的極大化。

這三個假定彼此相關：如果偏好沒有完全性或遞移性，行爲者就不知道最大利益是什麼，當然也就無所謂利益極大化，也不能藉此推論集體選擇。理性選擇途徑最大的挑戰，不在偏好的假定，而在如何由個體的偏好推論其行爲，並加總爲集體的後果。理性選擇途徑之下的各種理論，就是在處理「個體偏好如何轉爲集體選擇」的「加總機制」（aggregation mechanism）問題，其中又以賽局理論（game theory，或譯博弈理論）是最爲人所熟知。

賽局理論，又可依加總機制的不同區分爲非合作賽局理論（non-cooperative game theory）和合作賽局理論（cooperative game theory）。合作賽局假設行爲者可以根據共同利益而持守某些約定（例如形成聯盟），非合作賽局則無此假定。非合作賽局的均衡是指「所有行爲者都無法獨自求得更大利益」的狀態，可以用來處理細緻的情境（例如具體的談判過程），但較難處理多行動者的問題。合作賽局的均衡，是指無法被任何聯盟改變的狀態，可以用在人數眾多、議題複雜的情境。非合作賽局理論和合作賽局理論並不矛盾，兩者所描繪的均衡可能是同樣的狀態，而透過合作賽局建構的一般理論正可和非合作賽局的細緻分析相輔相成。本文所要建構的雙層三角模型，處理的問題是美、中、台三方的互動如何受到內部政治的影響，因爲牽涉的因素眾多，比較適合運用合作賽局的概念，一些細節的部分則可透過非合作賽局來處理。[5] 爲便於分析，以下使用形式

---

[5] 以賽局理論探討兩岸關係的研究，絕大部分採用非合作賽局，主題則是以安全、遏阻戰略（deterrence strategy）最多，例如 Franck 與 Melese（2003）；Huang、Kim 與 Wu（1992）；王玉玲（1996）；包宗和（1993、2000）；吳秀光（1995、1999）；李英明、賴皆興（2005）；沈有忠（2006）；胡均立（1996）；黃秋龍、王正光（2000）；鄧志松、唐代彪（2006）等。也有少數的賽局論文從經濟互賴探討兩岸的政治關係，如林繼文、羅致政（1998）；Benson 與 Niou（2007）。純粹處理兩岸經貿關係的賽局分析，則有葉國俊（2005）；葉國俊、侯乃榕（2007）。以合作賽局探討兩岸關係的則有 Lin（2000）。

理論（formal theory）的語言來界定本文所用到的基本概念。

第一個概念是「勝集」（winset）。令 O 爲所有選項（alternatives）所構成的集合，則選項 $x \in O$ 的勝集爲 $W(x) = \{y \mid y \neq x，y$ 可替代 $x\}$。y 之所以可以替代 x，和制度或遊戲規則有關。在多數決制下，只要支持 y 的人多於支持 x 的人，y 就可以替代 x；在共識決制下，只有所有的人都覺得 y 比 x 好，y 才能替代 x。在國際關係中，改變某種狀態的能力和國家實力以及議題性質有關。一般而言，各國政府都有某些可獨自改變的狀態，而這種能力隨國家實力而改變。但若議題涉及雙邊乃至多邊協議，參與協議的各方必須要有共識才能通過協議；此時，參與協議的國家成爲「否決者」（veto player）。第二個概念是「局心」（core），和勝集有關。對任何的合作賽局而言，局心的定義是 $\{x \mid W(x) = \varnothing\}$。換言之，局心就是所有無法被替代的選項所構成的集合，也就是合作賽局的均衡。當 x 爲現狀（status quo，以下稱爲 SQ）時，$W(x)$ 就是可以替代現狀的選項所構成的集合，$W(x)$ 的元素越少，表示現狀越難改變；局心，就是無法被改變的現狀。以「勝集」和「局心」的概念來分析國際關係，可以協助我們解決一項合作賽局的弱點：行動者之間的結盟是否具有可行性（enforceability）。國際政治中的結盟關係原本就欠缺穩定性，敵我關係也時常產生變化，所以「局心不存在」（亦即沒有不可被聯盟改變的現狀，請參考 Plott（1967））原本就是常態，以「勝集」作爲主要的分析概念，剛好可以反映國際政治的特性，也可描繪出國家間的結盟空間。

運用以上的概念來分析戰略三角，要先處理三個問題：誰是行動者？在三角互動中，「選項」是指什麼？對於這些選項，如何描繪行動者的偏好？第一個問題比較簡單，我們可以假定行動者是各方政府，其利益由所代表的民意決定。至於選項和偏好，是一體的兩面，傳統的戰略三角理論提供了一些啓示。在戰略三角的理論中，每兩國之間具有「友善」或「敵對」兩種關係，所以三國構成一個三角形。本文以理性選擇爲出發點，對戰略三角理論做了一些修正：首先，從分析層次而言，「友善」或「敵對」是各國政府互動之後產生的集體後果，所以應將政府視爲行爲者，將其關係視爲被解釋項；第二，將「友善」或「敵對」的二分延展爲連續的空間。做了這樣的修正，最適合表達選項和偏好的就是前面提到的「空間模型」（spatial model）。

空間模型的基本概念，是以距離表達偏好。所謂空間，指的是「歐氏空間」（Euclidean space），其維度（dimensionality）可以從 0 到無限多。在空間模型中，每個行動者都有一個最喜歡的結果，稱之爲理想點（ideal point）；在 k 維的空間中，理想點就是一個 k 維的向量（vector）。所謂選項，即可用空間中的向量來表達。[6] 對任意

6　爲便於分析，我們假設選項所構成的是一個緊緻的凸集合（compact and convex set）。這表示議題不會無限延伸，而選項之間的空間也可列爲選項。

選項 x 而言，i 行動者的效用函數為：

$$U_i(x) = -[\sum \alpha_{ij}(x_j - t_{ij})^2]^{1/2}$$

其中 t_i 是 i 的理想點，x_j 和 t_{ij} 分別是 x 和 t_i 在第 j 維的位置，α_{ij} 則 i 是對第 j 維向度的加權值。這個效用函數，其實就是一般化的歐式距離（Euclidean distance），在 $x = t_i$ 的時候達到極大值。因為我們以歐氏空間來表達效用，所以必然符合理性選擇關於完全性與遞移性的假定。

　　以空間模型來分析戰略三角，關鍵的問題在於「空間」如何構成，以及如何界定政府在空間中的位置。對於這個問題，有兩種殊途同歸的思考方式。第一，我們可以將各方政府關切的議題視為空間的軸線，並透過各政府在各議題上的立場歸納出其理想點。由於戰略三角的行動者有三個，不論議題有多複雜、空間的維度有多大，都可以把三者的理想點投射在一個二維的空間上，構成一個三角形、直線或點。第二種方式，是將三方的理想點視為空間中的三個點，點和點的距離表達國與國之間的利益差距，所以三方政府構成三組關係，也可用二維空間表達。這兩種方式，不論是以具體議題為基礎，或以理想點為基準，都可以用三角形表達三者的關係，三角形的三個邊長越相等，表示三者之間的關係越等距，三個邊長差距越大，越表示其中兩者的關係好於第三者。圖 15.1 描繪一個假想的狀況。假設美、中、台三方的理想點分別是 (0.6, 0.6)、(0, 0) 與 (0, 1)，這三個點，剛好就是戰略三角的三個頂點，這三個頂點間的距離，反映各方的利益差距。以圖 15.1 為例，台美的距離為 0.72，美中的距離為 0.85，中台的距離則是 1。

　　根據各國的理想點和效用函數，我們可以描繪三方政府對於現狀的勝集。如果我們假設行動者對議題的加權值相等，一國政府對現狀的無異線（indifference contour），就是以其理想點為圓心，以其理想點到現狀為半徑的圓。[7] 假設改變現狀需要兩國合作，則雙方的利益交集區域就是勝集。如果現狀果真被勝集中的選項取代，將導致兩國關係往友善方向前進，但兩國與第三方的關係則往敵對的方向發展。以圖 15.1 為例，如果我們假設現狀為 (0.3, 0.3)，則三個圓交集的區域就是能夠改變現狀的區域。當然，國際政治沒有什麼固定的結盟規則，有共同利益的國家，可能因為諸多障礙而不能立即改變現狀，但能被單一國家改變的現狀也不少。圖 15.1 所顯示的勝集，是由兩方所構成的潛在合作空間。

---

[7]　不同面向的加權值不見得相等。若然，要證明相關命題的技術層次較高，超出本文的範圍，不過，無論是否假設面向的加權值相等，現狀點移動的方向仍不會改變，所以本文所提出的命題仍然成立。

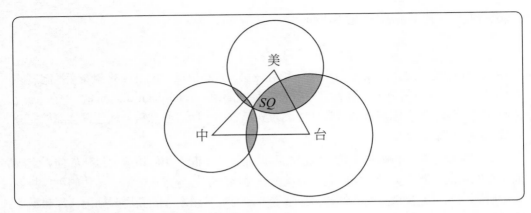

圖 15.1 空間模型中的美中台戰略三角

空間模型的另一個用處，是能清楚地顯示國內政治對三角關係的影響。再以圖 15.1 為例，假設台灣因為政黨輪替，理想點由 (0, 1) 變為 (0, 0.5)，所以新的理想點距離美、中的理想點都更近。此時，美中距離不變，但中台距離變為 0.5，台美距離變為 0.61，表示台灣對美中兩方都是朝友善的方向前進。我們可以用同樣的方法，顯示其他各方內部權力的變化對三角關係的影響，甚至可以在各國之內放入不同的行動者，觀察國內競爭如何影響三角關係。

上面的例子說明如何運用空間模型來建構雙層三角理論。這個例子中所用到的分析概念，可以當成模型的變數，用來解釋三角關係的轉變。主要的自變數包括國家之間的利益差距、國內政權的變化、決策體制的性質、現狀的位置以及各方對現狀的改變力等。對於這些變數間的關係，George Tsebelis（2002）的「否決者理論」（veto player theory）提供了相當有用的分析工具。所謂否決者，如其名所示，是能夠否決某一集體選擇（如議案、條約）的行動者。某些否決者是個別行動者，某些則是所謂的集體否決者（collective veto player）。否決者理論的核心概念，正是勝集。次節先說明雙層三角理論的內涵，再根據否決者理論的概念建構相關命題。

參、雙層三角模型的空間化

傳統的戰略三角模型，分析的焦點在於國家在不同形態戰略關係中的處境。本文也以國家之間的敵對或友好為關切對象，但採取較為動態的觀察角度。主要步驟有二：首

先，以理想點的差距來描繪國家之間的利益差距；其次，探討理想點和現狀的位置如何影響國家之間的合作空間；第三，以各國對現狀的改變力來預估現狀的改變方向，以及對三角關係的影響。以空間模型的概念來說，雙層三角模型要尋找的是國家間的勝集，勝集越大（小），代表合作的空間越大（小）。不過，勝集包含的範圍還是相當大，其中的選項仍有好壞之別。一個合理的假定是，結盟國應該在勝集中尋找最符合雙方共同利益的選項，而這些選項應該位於結盟國的「帕雷圖集合」（Pareto set）上。帕雷圖集合的定義為：如果選項 x 屬於兩國的帕雷圖集合，即表示對任意 $y \neq x$ 而言，y 必然比 x 距離其中一個結盟國的理想點更遠；反論之，如果 x 不屬於帕雷圖集合，即表示必然存在比 x 更靠近兩方理想點的選項。依此理，任意兩方在空間模型中的帕雷圖集合，就是連結兩方理想點的線段。所以，結盟國勝集和其帕雷圖集合的交集，應該就是他們最可能用來替代現狀的選項，而兩國之間的談判也應該集中在此交集的選項上。為便於說明，以下將勝集和其帕雷圖集合的交集稱為 V 集合。我們若假設聯盟由兩國構成，V 集合就是一個線段。根據這些概念，以下是雙層三角模型依變數的形式化定義（見圖 15.2）：

1. 勝集的寬度：如果結盟國有兩國，V 集合是一個線段；線段越長表示兩國合作空間越大。

2. 勝集的中點：V 集合既然是線段，就會有中點，而此一中點距離某國的理想點越近，表示合作對此國越有利。

3. 現狀的改變方向：新現狀應該位於 V 集合之內，但具體位移受制於現狀改變力。

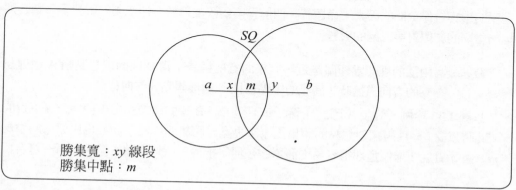

圖 15.2 勝集的寬度與中點

主要的自變數包括：

1. 理想點和現狀的位置：理想點由國內政權的特性決定，現狀的位置可能受到外生因素（例如國際情勢的變化、重大危機等）的影響，也可能是內生於三角關係的，亦即對既有現狀的改變。

2. 改變現狀的能力：改變的現狀方式，包括國家間的聯盟（例如簽署協議）或單一國家的行為（例如增加武力、宣告獨立）。某些國家在某些議題上沒有改變現狀的能力，例如美國不能替台灣宣告獨立，台灣不能替美國增加軍備。若然，即使某些國家間的合作空間很大，現狀也不見得能立即改變。我們只能說這些國家具有強大的結盟動機，但現狀究竟如何變動，要看國家的可行選項（feasible alternatives）為何。

3. 國內政治制度：國內有幾個多數聯盟？除了政府，一國之內是否有其他的否決者？關於前者，我們將以「局卵」（yolk）的大小測量國內的分歧度。所謂「局卵」，是指和所有「中位線」（median line，在二維以上的空間稱為中位面）相交的圓中最小的圓，而「中位線」的定義則是線上的理想點加上任意一邊的理想點皆構成多數的線。對集體否決者而言，「局卵」是衡量決策穩定性的重要指標，局卵越小，表示決策越不容易被推翻；如果局卵的半徑等於 0，局卵即等於局心，也就是合作賽局的均衡（Feld, Grofman, and Miller, 1988; Miller, Grofman, and Feld, 1989）。

為便於分析，以下假定兩國理想點之間的距離大於兩國理想點和現狀之間的距離。[8] 在此假定下，我們可以根據否決者理論的概念，推論出以下的命題，其中前兩個命題說明影響合作空間的因素，命題三、四解釋國內政治對於合作空間的影響，命題五則描繪兩國的結盟對第三國的影響。

命題一：兩國的理想點距離越近，勝集的寬度越長；當 B 國的理想點朝 A 國理想點的方向靠攏時，勝集的中點也往 A 國理想點的方向移動。

以圖 15.3 為例，假設 A 國的理想點 a 不變，而 B 國的理想點由 b 變為離 a 更近的 b'。此時以 a、b' 為兩國理想點的勝集比原來更寬，勝集的中點（m'）也比原來的中點（m）離 a 更近。這個道理很容易從簡單的幾何學推得，所以命題一適用於所有符合假

---

8 如果兩國理想點間的距離小於現狀距離兩國理想點的距離，則兩國的帕雷圖集合將被包含在勝集之內，所以勝集和帕雷圖集合的交集就是連接兩個理想點的線段，勝集的中點就是此一線段的中點。這表示，當結盟雙方都非常希望改善現狀時，雙方的談判地位是平等的。

定的案例。[9]命題一的現實意涵是，結盟國之間的利益差距越小，合作的空間越大；如果利益差距的縮小來自某國理想點的改變（例如政權替換），反而會減少對手國的讓步空間。

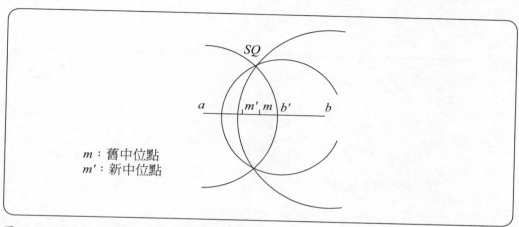

圖 15.3　理想點的變動對勝集寬度與中點的影響

命題二：現狀距離結盟國越遠，勝集寬度越長。

勝集的寬度由 SQ 和理想點的距離決定，而 V 集合又是由兩國的理想點和 SQ 的距離所決定，所以 SQ 離理想點越遠，V 集合的寬度也越長。這個命題的現實意涵是，結盟國越需要改變現狀，其利益交集越大。

命題三：一個國家內部的局卵越大，勝集寬度越長，勝集中點離對手國的理想點越近。

作爲集體否決者，國家內部可能存在著一個「小三角」。我們可以將局卵想像成這個小三角形成的內部妥協空間。令 c 爲集體否決者局卵的圓心，r 爲其半徑，d 爲 c 與 SQ 的距離，則該國對於 SQ 的勝集被包含在以 c 爲圓心，以 $d + 2r$ 爲半徑的圓內（Miller, Grofman, and Feld, 1989; Tsebelis, 2002: 45-51）。所以，局卵的半徑越長，勝集的寬度

---

[9]　以圖 15.3 爲例，假設以 b 爲圓心、以 SQb 線段爲半徑的圓與 ab 線段相交於 y，以 b' 爲圓心、以 SQb' 線段爲半徑的圓與 ab 線段相交於 y'，則只要計算各點之間的距離，即可得知 by 線段必定短於 by' 線段。

就越長，勝集中點也離對手國的理想點越近。由於局卵建立在多數決制之上，此一命題同時顯現政治制度以及意見分歧對戰略三角的影響：一個以多數決制進行決策但內部意見分歧的國家，和他國的合作空間最大，但在談判上處於較不利的地位。這表示，多數決制的民主國家之間的合作空間最大，而威權國家較易在和民主國家的結盟過程中占有上風。

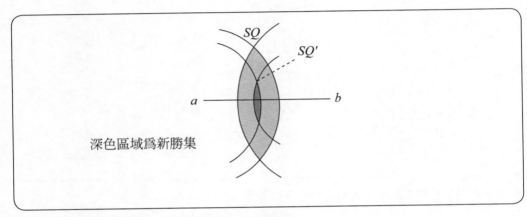

圖 15.4　現狀點的變動對勝集寬度與中點的影響

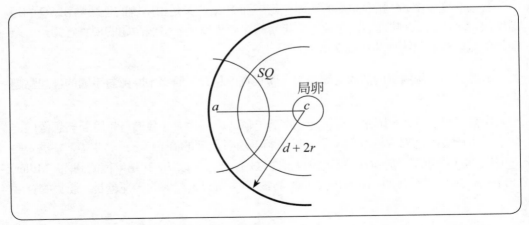

圖 15.5　國內分歧對勝集寬度與中點的影響

命題四：極端位置的否決者將減少合作空間。

　　圖 15.6 顯示，當 B 國出現極端否決者 b' 時，勝集的寬度比 b' 不存在時窄很多。這個命題也具有兩個重要意涵。多數決並非唯一的決策體制，某些民主國家採共識決，而極端的黨派若具有否決能力，就會降低與對手國合作的空間。事實上，即使是威權國家也可能存在著不利結盟的鷹派或激進派。從談判的觀點來看，極端否決者的出現，一方面會降低談判空間，另一方面卻可以讓處於不利談判地位的國家向對手表示讓步空間有限，藉以提高談判籌碼。

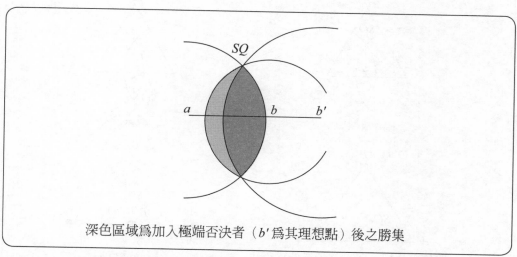

深色區域為加入極端否決者（b' 為其理想點）後之勝集

圖 15.6　內部否決者對勝集寬度的影響

命題五：當現狀位於三方的帕雷圖集合時，任何兩方結盟所產生的新現狀，必然比舊現狀距離第三方的理想點更遠。

　　如果三個國家的理想點構成一個三角形而現狀位於三角形（即三方的帕雷圖集合）內，則現狀的改變至少會使一方的理想點距離新現狀更遠。我們可以延伸這個命題，根據現狀的位置來探討戰略三角的性質（見圖 15.7）。首先，若現狀位於三方的帕雷圖集合內，表示三方不可能形成改變現狀的共識，所以任何兩方合力改變現狀，就會使第三方成為孤雛，亦即產生「結婚型」（marriage）的三角關係。其次，如果現狀不在三方的帕雷圖集合內，兩方的結盟可能使第三方獲利，造成「三邊家族型」（ménage à trois）的三角關係。第三，關於「羅曼蒂克型」（romantic）的三角關係，只可能在一

種狀況下產生：三方的理想點構成一條直線，居中的國家是其他兩方的好友，也是現狀的維持者，但兩端的國家彼此敵對。此時，「現狀即局心」，任何對現狀的變動都會被中間行動者和其中一者反對。最後，如果每個國家都可以獨自否決現狀的變動，而現狀剛好又位於任何三方的帕雷圖集合中，則國家間沒有結盟的誘因，因而形成「單位否決型」（unit-veto）的三角關係。這也表示，對於「結婚型」的孤雛而言，突破困境的方法之一就是讓自己具有否決現狀改變的能力，使三角關係轉為「單位否決型」。[10]

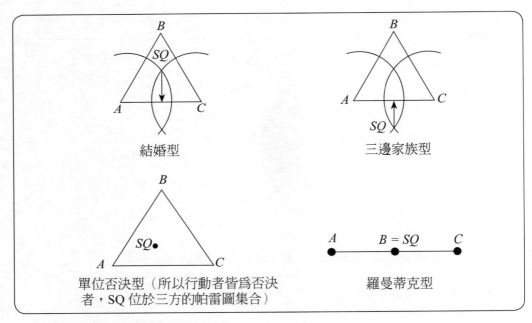

圖 15.7　四種戰略三角形態的空間化

　　現狀如何改變，是一個外生性的問題。以上推論假設現狀要靠國際合作改變。如果現狀可以被單一國家改變，戰略三角的形態取決於該國如何改變現狀。如果某國政府使現狀更加偏離其他兩國的理想點，將給予其他兩國更大的合作空間，並使自己陷入孤雛的困境；如果該國使現狀更接近自己和另一個國家的理想點，等於是在創造合作空間，並使第三國變為孤雛。如果現狀位於三國的帕雷圖集合之外，能獨自改變現狀的國家可

---

[10] 舉例而言，台灣可以設置「改變現狀需要公民投票」的機制，預防國家定位被大國決定。

以同時使三方獲利，創造三邊家族的形態。以下，將以台灣的實際情況說明現狀如何改變。

肆、以雙層三角模型分析美中台的戰略互動

前節探討國家利益、政治制度和現狀位置如何影響國家間的結盟空間，但仍未觸及現狀改變的軌跡。原因在於各國改變現狀的能力不一，而且因個案而有差別。本節將前述命題運用在美中台三角關係上，指出各方政府在個別議題上的現狀改變力，並分析台灣的政權替換如何影響三角關係的改變。過去十多年，美國雖然歷經不同黨籍的總統，但兩岸政策並沒有太大的變動，中國大陸也並未大幅調整對台的官方立場。反觀台灣，歷經李登輝、陳水扁和馬英九三位總統，採取的兩岸政策具有相當的差異性，正可讓我們觀察國內政治的變化如何影響戰略三角關係。

在進入分析之前，先說明美中台戰略三角所處之空間。和美中台相關的議題相當多，例如台灣的主權歸屬、兩岸經貿關係、中國和美國在東亞的競逐等。不過，某些議題可能具有高度相關性，所以議題的數目不見得等於空間的維度。即使空間維度很高，我們仍可將三個行動者的理想點投射到一個二維的空間上，而此空間的向度，將由最具爭議性的議題主導。以美中台的現況觀之，應該有兩個最重要的面向：兩岸關係與中美關係。以兩岸關係而言，最重要的議題是台灣的統獨。在此面向上，台灣的統獨立場因執政者而有不同，中國大陸當然希望達成統一，美國在形式上接受一個中國，但認為兩岸應該進行協商，所以位置介於中、台之間。在中美關係上，對重要的課題是美國如何面對崛起的中國。在此面向上，美國政府可以採取平衡者的角色，也可以讓中國扮演區域霸權（亦即從中國勢力所及之處「撤離」）；影響其策略的因素除了執政者的意識形態，還有美國的全球戰略以及美中的國力變化等。台灣的政府大致希望美國能平衡中國大陸的擴張，北京則希望美國隨著中國崛起而從其勢力範圍撤離。

至於現狀改變力，我們可以做出以下的假定。第一，台灣可以決定走向獨立或統一，但最終結果受制於美國和中國大陸是否支持；台灣對美中關係所能產生的影響，則是相當有限的。第二，美國和中國大陸可以決定彼此的關係，對於台灣的統獨走向，則只能間接促成或直接反對。第三，雙邊關係若需透過協議來改變，則雙方都是否決者。根據這些假定，以下分為不同時期說明台灣政府的政策如何影響美中台關係。[11]

---

[11] 有關於歷任總統的兩岸關係談話或是相關事件，請參考行政院大陸事務委員會網站，http://www.mac.gov.tw/。

　　第一，在 1996 年台灣總統選舉前，李登輝政府的兩岸政策比蔣經國時代更偏離中共政府的立場（理想點），但並未大幅偏離美國政府的立場，再加上推動民主化和總統直選符合美國的意識形態，因此創造台美的合作空間。命題一指出，兩國的理想點差距越大，勝集的寬度就越窄；反過來說，兩國理想點越接近，其合作空間也越大。命題二則顯示，現狀距離兩國越遠（近），兩國合作的空間就越大（小）。我們可以根據這兩個命題得出這項推論：李登輝比蔣經國更強調台灣的主體性，又透過修憲推動台澎金馬人民直選總統，使台灣更具有實質獨立的樣貌，兩岸在國家認同上的差異隨之擴大。不過，李登輝在 1996 年之前的政策並未大幅偏離美國的立場，反而因為推動民主化而符合美國的意識形態，等於為美國創造一個民主盟邦，因此擴大了和美國合作的空間。

　　更詳細言之，李登輝政府關於台灣的國家定位，先在 1992 年 8 月由國家統一委員會提出「海峽兩岸均堅持一個中國之原則，但雙方所賦予之涵義有所不同」的決議（亦即所謂的「一個中國，各自表述」），和對岸的「一國兩制」具有一定的交集。兩岸自 1993 年舉行辜汪會談，並展開相關會議，李登輝則在 1995 年發表兩岸關係正常化的談話。然而，李登輝在 1994 年與日本作家司馬遼太郎的會談提到「身為台灣人的悲哀」，被看成是他台灣主體意識的表徵。1994 年修憲確立中華民國總統由台澎金馬地區人民直選產生，在實質上將這些地區視為一個獨立國家；1995 年訪問美國，發表有關台灣民主化的演講，一般多以「台灣總統」視之。面對此情勢，中共推遲二次辜汪會談，並在台海進行飛彈演習。此一危機，在美國柯林頓總統派遣兩艘航空母艦穿越台灣海峽後停止。很明顯地，飛彈危機顯現中共政府企圖遏止現狀滑向台灣獨立，美國則在其中扮演了平衡者的角色。

　　圖 15.8 顯示了上述變化：在蔣經國總統時期，台灣在統獨上的立場和對岸差異並不大。李登輝推動總統直選和本土化政策，使現狀往獨立的方向移動，但並未大幅偏離美國和台灣的合作空間。

　　第二，1996 年李登輝當選總統後，立場繼續偏離中共政府，導致台灣與中國大陸談判空間的進一步減縮；美國政府的態度則取決於台海現狀被武力破壞的可能。這個推論同樣來自命題一和命題二。李登輝在 1996 年勝選後，推動民主化和總統直選的效應降低，柯林頓則在 1996 年 11 月贏得美國總統選舉，希望能與北京修補關係，同時倡議各種版本的「中程協議」，希望台灣不要走向獨立，中國不要對台動武。1998 年 6 月，柯林頓訪問中國大陸，發表「不支持台灣獨立、不支持一中一台與兩個中國、不支持台灣參加以國家為主體的國際組織」的「三不政策」，等於是在平衡台灣在總統選後的情勢。

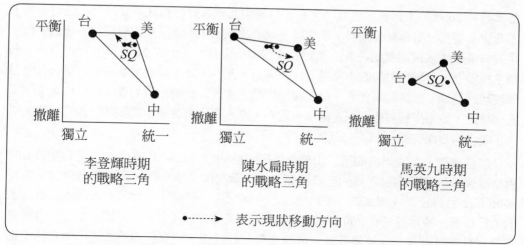

圖 15.8　台灣不同政權下之戰略三角變化

　　相對於美中關係的改善，李登輝在 1999 年接受德國媒體訪問時提到「台灣與中國大陸是特殊的國與國關係」（一般稱為「兩國論」），等於是把台灣的位置往偏離中、美立場的方向移動。根據圖 15.8，此時台灣對現狀的改變已經超越了美國所能接受的範圍，美國和中國反而因此產生合作空間。從實際面觀之，面對李登輝的兩國論，中共政府在 2000 年 2 月發表白皮書，措辭強硬地批評李登輝和「分裂勢力」，抨擊台灣的憲政改革是在將台灣製造為獨立的政治實體，並表示「中國政府只能被迫採取一切可能的斷然措施、包括使用武力，來維護中國的主權和領土完整，完成中國的統一大業」。中共政府的強硬態度顯示台海現狀有可能受到武裝衝突的破壞，柯林頓政府因此很快對北京發出警告，表示中國大陸若使用武力將帶來嚴重的後果。這表示，兩岸政府企圖改變現狀的企圖，增加了美國平衡台海現狀的壓力。

　　上述變化，同樣呈現在圖 15.8 中：李登輝在第二任總統期間持續推動本土化政策，使台灣更加偏離北京的理想點：如果北京以武力反制台灣的走向，美國雖然可能扮演平衡者的角色，卻也讓新現狀位於台美的帕雷圖集合上，大幅減縮兩方的合作空間。反觀美中的合作空間，卻因新現狀偏離兩者立場而擴大。

　　第三，陳水扁擔任總統後，立場更加偏離中共政府的立場，並逐漸擴大與美國的差距，導致中美合作空間進一步擴大；九一一事件後美國在國際舞台上對中國的需求增加，進一步使台灣邊緣化。陳水扁於 2000 和 2004 年當選總統，相較於李登輝時期的中國國民黨，陳水扁所代表的民主進步黨更明確地主張「台灣不是中國的一部分」。陳水

扁雖然在 2000 年 5 月宣示就職時主張「只要中共無意對台動武，其保證在任期之內，不會宣布獨立，不會更改國號，不會推展兩國論入憲，不會推展改變現狀的統獨公投，也沒有廢除國統綱領與國統會的問題」（四不一沒有），但在 2002 年 8 月又表示「台灣主權獨立，台灣和對岸的中國是一邊一國」。此外，陳水扁並推動一系列嘗試改變台灣現狀的措施，包括制憲正名、公民投票捍衛主權等。台灣政府的立場再度往北京的反方向移動，使兩岸談判空間快速縮小。此外，陳水扁推動改變台灣現狀的作為，再次擴大了美中的合作空間。

　　這個趨勢，在陳水扁的第二個總統任期更為明顯（Lin, 2008）。「正名運動」的對象從國家到擴展到海內外的政府機關，《中華民國憲法》則被視為不合時宜；他在 2006 年 2 月終止了「國家統一委員會」和《國家統一綱領》，並推動台灣進入聯合國的公民投票。陳水扁又在 2007 年 3 月 4 日提出「四要一沒有」：台灣要獨立，台灣要正名，台灣要新憲，台灣要發展；台灣沒有左右路線，只有統獨的問題。面對陳水扁的台獨路線和改變現狀的企圖，中共政府在 2005 年 3 月由全國人大通過《反分裂國家法》，特別提及「得採取非和平方式及其他必要措施，捍衛國家主權和領土完整」。更重要的變化在於美國的態度：如命題二所示，當陳水扁嘗試推動多項突破現狀的行動時，美、中的合作空間反而因此擴大。美國不但公開反對台灣推動進入聯合國的公民投票，布希總統更在 2007 年 8 月 31 日表示「台灣或中華民國都不是一個國家」。另一個促成美國態度轉變的因素在於國際情勢的變化。2001 年 9 月 11 日美國遭受恐怖份子的攻擊，之後相繼發動對阿富汗和伊拉克的戰爭，不但需要其他大國在國際事務上的支持，也難以全力處理其他區域的危機。作為崛起中的大國，中國對國際事務的影響力日漸增加，自然成為美國尋求支持的對象。台灣政府在此時採取傾向獨立的行動，即使是透過憲政改革或公民投票等民主程序來進行，仍然難以獲得美國的支持。

　　圖 15.8 描繪了這些變化。陳水扁的總統任內，現狀有兩個移動軌跡。首先，他的策略比李登輝更趨向台灣獨立，也就是使現狀往獨的方向移動。然而，此種移動反而擴大了美中合作的空間，使美中形成「共管台灣」的默契，共同遏止台灣走向獨立，所以使現狀又往統的方向移動。此外，中國逐漸崛起，美國在國際事務上對中國的需求增加，使兩方的利益差距縮小。兩項變化相加，使台灣趨向獨立的困難度增加，美國逐漸失去作為「平衡者」的力量，台灣進一步被邊緣化。

　　第四，馬英九於 2008 年當選總統後，採取對美、中的等距交往，立場較陳水扁政府大幅往北京政府立場接近，使兩岸談判空間大幅擴大，但兩岸距離的拉近起因於台灣立場的調整，所以談判空間的中點也往北京方向移動，最後的談判結果則與國內政治結構有關。圖 15.8 顯現了這個變化。在統獨立場上，馬英九政府反對台灣獨立，在美中

關係上，馬政府採行等距交往，使馬英九政府的新立場離美中雙方都更接近。再加上現狀位於三者之間，使馬政府同時擴大了和雙方交往的空間，其中又以兩岸關係的變化最受到注目。

我們可以從馬英九當選總統後的變化來印證上述推論。相較於陳水扁和李登輝，馬英九更強調維持台海現狀，主張「不統、不獨、不武」的「三不政策」。2008 年 9 月，馬英九在回答「兩個中國」的問題時，認為兩岸不是國與國的關係，和李登輝的「特殊國與國」以及陳水扁的「一邊一國」有很大的區別。馬英九的主張當然不等於統一，但仍是往北京方向移動。根據命題一，馬政府的新兩岸政策雖然擴大了兩岸的合作空間，但也使勝集的中點往北京方向移動。這表示，如果談判不成，損傷較大的可能是馬政府，所以北京似乎居於較有利的談判地位。再加上台灣經濟情勢不佳，馬英九又背負著總統改選壓力，亟需提振台灣經濟，所以將兩岸協商視為優先議題。此種情況，顯現在馬英九政府對於兩岸經濟協議的態度上。[12]

馬英九當選總統後，台灣的六大工商團體為因應「東協加三」的態勢，要求馬政府盡速與中國大陸簽署《綜合性經濟合作協議》（Comprehensive Economic Cooperation Agreement, CECA），以圖解決兩岸經貿整合的關鍵問題，例如關稅減讓、投資保障、雙重課稅等，馬政府也將簽訂此項協議視為既定政策。CECA 後來被更名為《兩岸經濟合作架構協議》（Economic Cooperation Framework Agreement, ECFA），彰顯其為「架構性的協議」。對於 ECFA，台灣社會出現一些不同的意見，包括是否圖利特定企業、台灣失業率是否增加、協商過程是否透明化、台灣主權是否弱化等。面對這些質疑，馬英九並未承諾將協議送交立法院事前審查，而表示「今天不做，明天就會後悔」（林修全、陳志平，2009）。

這種急迫性，使馬政府希望能盡速簽訂 ECFA，北京因此居於優勢談判位置。縱使如此，最後結果仍然受到內部政治結構的影響，對何方有利仍有待觀察。首先，談判中點雖然往北京方向移動，但究竟距離台灣的「中位選民」（median voter）更遠還是更近，取決於馬英九政府的理想點，無法從模型本身得知。其次，台灣在野力量對於馬英九政府的批評，不見得對談判不利。根據命題四，民進黨若能在兩岸談判的議題上扮演否決者的角色（例如質疑未經民主程序同意的談判結果），將會縮減談判空間。此時，

---

[12] 另一個相關事件是中國海協會會長陳雲林的來台訪問。陳於 2008 年 11 月 3 日訪台，和海基會董事長江丙坤簽署兩岸空、海運直航、郵政合作、食品安全等四項協議。行政院陸委會表示，如果立法院 30 日內未針對海空協議作出決議，法律上視為同意。此一安排顯示馬政府對於兩岸協商的急迫性。

如果談判對兩岸政府都有利，台灣內部的極端意見等於是把台灣的位置拉往與北京相反的方向，進而增加馬英九政府的籌碼。至於馬政府是否會採取此一策略，取決於其真實理想點究竟是較為靠近北京還是台灣的中位選民。如果是後者，馬政府可以利用內部否決者使談判結果趨近自己的理想點，以避免喪失多數選民的支持。

　　第五，台灣如果出現分裂的多數，將使其居於較為不利的談判位置。命題三指出，國內利益差距越大、決策越依賴多數決，勝集的中點就越接近對手國。以兩岸政府的形態來看，中共政府為威權體制，台灣則為民主體制，因此較可能出現分裂多數，使其處於較不利的談判地位。更詳細言之，台灣採行的是半總統制，雖然大多數人以總統為最高的實質領袖，但總統不見得能完全掌控行政機關，更可能和立法院的多數不同黨。陳水扁擔任總統的八年，就處於「分立政府」（divided government）的狀況，此時兩岸雖然沒有展開正式的協商，但北京卻與中國國民黨建構了「國共論壇」的協商管道，給予民進黨政府相當大的壓力。

　　「國共論壇」起於國民黨黨主席連戰在 2005 年 4 月在中國大陸的訪問。此次訪問由中國國家主席胡錦濤邀約，連胡會後提出四點主張，強調「九二共識」、「一個中國」原則，中國絕不能分裂、中華民族絕不能分裂，並應加強兩岸經濟上的交流合作，展開平等協商等；之後，國共兩黨又共同舉辦了「兩岸經貿文化論壇」。很顯然地，國共論壇不論在主張或形式上，都是針對陳水扁政府而來的。陳水扁政府之所以面臨相當的壓力，正是因為國民黨代表的是占有國會多數的泛藍陣營，而這個多數是有可能根據國共論壇通過相關法令的。

　　綜合馬英九和陳水扁的經驗，我們發現台灣的民主體制對於兩岸談判具有雙面作用：在一致政府時期，內部的否決者可以增加談判籌碼，但分立政府卻可能弱化政府的談判能力。反觀北京，始終處於威權政府狀態，所以不會出現分裂多數的問題，反而可以利用內部極端派的否決聲音來增加其談判籌碼。

伍、結論

　　本文透過空間模型將戰略三角理論動態化，並探討國內政治對國際結盟的影響。戰略三角理論原本就有空間的意涵，本文更明確地以「空間距離」來描繪國家間的敵友關係，以理想點和現狀的空間位置與現狀改變力為自變項，解釋三角關係的變化。從理論的角度來看，本文所建構的「雙層三角」模型，對相關理論提出幾個補充。首先，對戰略三角理論而言，雙層三角模型是建立在個體論的基礎（micro foundation）上，以

各國政府爲行動者，以其所代表的民意定位其理想點，並以空間模型分析其互動結果，使得我們能從個體的角度解釋集體的後果。第二，雙層三角模型運用「否決者理論」的分析概念，指出不利國際合作的因素，例如極端的國家利益、使國際競爭趨於零和的現狀等。這些因素的變化不但影響兩國間的合作空間，也牽涉到與第三國的關係，所以可以解釋戰略三角關係的轉變。從這個觀點，可以看出國內政治如何影響戰略三角關係。例如，某國政府如果因爲內部競爭而逐漸採取極端的立場，將強化其他國家間的合作空間，並使自己陷入孤雛困境。某國的新政權如果採取向他國靠攏的策略，將可擴大國際合作的空間，但不見得能取得有利的談判位置。

從經驗研究的角度觀察，雙層三角模型，提供我們解釋兩岸關係過去十年重要變化的線索。兩次的政黨輪替，不但爲台灣的民主化立下重要的里程碑，也深刻影響兩岸關係的發展。李登輝從「九二共識」變爲「特殊國與國關係」，陳水扁從「四不一沒有」轉爲「四要一沒有」，無論是基於理念或政治考量，都使中國大陸找到和美國「共管台灣」的理由。馬英九當選總統後亟欲解凍兩岸關係，但究竟能否取得有利的談判位置，或是更進一步成爲北京與美抗衡的工具，仍有待時間考驗。從長遠的角度來看，美國與中國的競合關係固非台灣所能左右，但台灣卻很難不成爲兩國棋盤上的重要棋子，而台灣內部的政治變化，勢必也影響到北京和華盛頓的關係。

本文的主要目的是介紹研究兩岸關係的空間模型途徑，在理論和實證上必然有所不足，不過正可和其他各章搭配運用。例如，雙層三角模型以「勝集」描繪國家之間的合作空間，但在特定的勝集中如何協商，涉及動態的談判過程，可以採用非合作賽局進行分析。再者，國家實力的消長涉及複雜的因素，對理性選擇而言屬於外生因素，所以應該參照政治經濟學、政治社會學的分析途徑。最後，政治領袖的立場固然受制於選民，但我們不能忽略個人理念以及政策的正當性，而政治心理學和規範研究正好可以彌補這個空缺。

第十六章

論述如何框限選擇？條件式統獨偏好 對 2012 年台灣總統選舉的影響[*]

壹、常態分布的統獨選擇，爲何會產生兩極化的政黨競爭？

　　台灣存在國家認同（national identity）的爭議，隨之而來的統獨選擇則深刻影響選民的投票行爲。[1] 以民主進步黨（民進黨）爲主的政黨組成泛綠陣營，認爲台灣主權獨立，「中華人民共和國」是另一個國家。以中國國民黨（國民黨）爲首的政黨組成泛藍陣營，反對台灣獨立，並視台灣爲「一個中國」的一部分。兩大陣營相互對抗，將許多議題視爲統獨的延伸，使台灣政治趨向兩極化。介於統獨之間的民衆，似乎逐漸邊緣化。[2]

　　這個表象之下，隱含了一個困惑：儘管台灣出現政黨兩極化的現象，但國家認同和統獨選擇卻是同質性高於異質性。根據政治大學選舉研究中心的研究，認同自己是台灣人的民衆，在過去 22 年持續升高，從 1992 年的 17.6% 攀升到 2014 年的 60.4%；相對而言，認同自己是中國人的民衆則持續降低，從 1992 年的 25.2% 滑落到 2014 年的 3.4%（國立政治大學選舉研究中心，2015）。這個趨勢顯示，認同自己爲台灣人，已經是當前的社會主流。在統獨選擇方面，民衆的態度更是違反兩極化。以「台灣選舉與民主化調查」（Taiwan's Election and Democratization Study, TEDS）針對 2012 年總統選舉所進行的民意調查爲例，在 1,826 位受訪者中，回答「維持現狀（看情形再決定獨立或統一）」的人數有 1,076 人，占 58.93%。再看「台灣社會變遷調查」（Taiwan Social

[*]　本文曾刊登於《政治科學論叢》，第 63 期（2015 年 3 月），頁 55-90。感謝台灣大學政治學系《政治科學論叢》同意轉載。
　　非常謝謝兩位匿名審查人及編輯委員所提供的寶貴意見。本人感謝中央研究院社會學研究所張茂桂教授所主持的「台灣社會變遷基本調查國家認同組」計畫，以及參與計畫同仁所提供的意見。本文曾發表在中央研究院社會學研究所在 2014 年 12 月 5 日主辦的「國家認同」研討會，非常謝謝吳乃德教授的評論。本文若有任何問題，由本人負擔全責。

[1]　統獨選擇受到國家認同（或譯國族認同）的影響，但兩者是不一樣的概念。詳見吳乃德（1993：46-56）。
[2]　兩極化不見得有負面的意涵。在某些情況下，改革要透過不同立場的辯論才會發生。這裡所說的兩極化，是指「維持現狀」的邊緣化，使統獨兩派欠缺對話的空間。

Change Survey）針對 2012 年總統選舉的面訪，選擇「永遠維持現狀」的人數，在 1,952 位受訪者中占有 763 人，比例爲 39.09%，是諸選項中最高的。[3] 不管用哪份問卷，主張維持現狀的民眾都最多。這和藍綠陣營的兩極化，有明顯的差距。

　　本文的目的，就是要解答這個困惑。在被解釋項的部分，本文以「統獨選擇」爲對象，理由如下。首先，台灣的國家認同逐漸同質化，即便反對台灣獨立的政治菁英，也經常以台灣人自居。[4] 這表示，台灣越來越以統獨爲主要分歧，國家認同的角色逐漸淡出。[5] 其次，國家認同逐漸同質化，統獨爭議卻涉及憲政層次的問題，不易消除。《中華民國憲法》規定「中華民國領土，依其固有之疆域，非經國民大會之決議，不得變更之」，但所謂「固有領土」，大部分卻爲「中華人民共和國」（以下簡稱中共）所統治。兩岸關係究竟是統是獨，牽涉台灣基本的國家定位，也必然出現在總統選舉中。政黨究竟主張台灣獨立還是堅持一個中國，都涉及領土主權範圍，難以閃躲。

　　台灣的統獨選擇，也有其理論意涵。按照 Maurice Duverger 的理論（Duverger, 1963: 217），台灣總統選舉既然採取單一選區相對多數決選舉制度，如果只有兩組候選人競選，理應趨向中位選民才有勝選可能。[6] 以勝選爲目的的政黨，爲何以兩極對立爲競選主軸，忽略「維持現狀派」的選民？回答這個問題，有兩個線索。第一，是有關訊息的操作。菁英和民眾都有兩極化的可能，但兩者的訊息不對稱。以台灣的案例來看，應該是政黨菁英主導，民眾接受政黨設定的議程。所以，兩極化是由上到下的動員過程，目的在於吸引偏向政黨的選民。問題是，主張維持現狀的選票，對於競爭激烈的選舉仍然非常重要。政黨，爲什麼要放棄這些選票？第二，是進一步拆解「維持現狀」的內涵。例如，說明「現狀」其實包含了各種非統非獨的選項，並無一致性；或承認「維持現狀」的確是選項之一，但具有條件性。

　　本文認爲，以上兩種解釋有其共通之處：政黨菁英的確掌握訊息優勢，方能給予「維持現狀」新的詮釋；但「維持現狀」可能包含了「在某些條件之下，主張台灣獨立或中國統一，甚或真正主張維持現狀」的選民，而這些條件與政黨所提供的訊息有關，

---

[3] 這兩項面訪對「維持現狀」的問法有些許差異，其他選項也非完全一致，或可解釋贊成此選項的百分比爲何有所差異。

[4] 例如，2014 年國民黨十九全第二次會議，馬英九主席的演講主題就是「我是台灣人，我支持中國國民黨」。

[5] 還有一個原因，就是「台灣人」既可指涉國家，也有族群意涵，兩者可能糾纏不清。相對而言，統獨涉及主權歸屬，比較不會混淆。

[6] 2012 年台灣的總統／副總統選舉候選人，還包括親民黨的宋楚瑜和林瑞雄。他們對總統選舉影響有限，所以仍可將此一選舉視爲兩大黨的競爭。

這些訊息若構成論述，則投票行為就會受到政黨論述的制約。所謂「條件式的立場」，是指立場隨著條件而改變，由此形成的議題態度，可稱為「不可分離的偏好」（non-separable preferences），亦即無法以單一議題來排序的偏好。本文認為，此種不可分離的偏好不但能解釋支持維持現狀的比例為何如此之高，也能說明其變動性，以及在何種情況下能被政黨論述所影響。如果本文的假設能得到證實，不但可以回答「常態分布下的兩極化」這個難題，也能連結兩岸論述和統獨選擇。

　　國家認同、統獨立場和投票行為都涉及情感與理性的互動。在常見的資料庫中，TEDS 詢問了不少與國家認同和統獨選擇有關的問題，但該資料庫較少處理影響這些立場或態度的因素。舉例而言，如果我們想瞭解某位支持台灣獨立的民眾，究竟是在情感上將台灣視為祖國，還是因為疑懼兩岸經貿互動將造成台灣財富分配的惡化，就只有把統獨選擇當成依變數，並找尋適當的解釋變數。相對於 TEDS，「社會變遷調查」的國家認同題組問了不少相關問題，因此較適合當作本文的資料庫，一方面呈現條件式統獨偏好與總統選舉的關係，另一方面解析影響統獨選擇的因素。

　　下節文獻檢討先說明如何將兩極化研究用在台灣的統獨選擇上，再指出既有研究很少討論這些影響統獨立場的條件從何而來。本文主張，政黨在論述中釋出的訊息，是重要的條件之一。第參節提出本文的理論模型，顯示同樣的偏好結構，會因為訊息的不同而產生不一樣的結果。依此模型，國民黨的兩岸政策，在 2012 年選舉時較有利其進行議題設定。[7]本節也根據這個推論，提出基本假設：主張條件式統一的獨派選民，較易受到國民黨兩岸論述的影響，使這群選民投票給國民黨總統候選人的比例高於國民黨籍區域立委候選人的比例，並以其差距解釋國民黨兩岸論述的影響力。

　　我們進一步探討偏獨選民的身分，指出他們越是重視中國大陸的經濟影響力或越不將台灣視為祖國，就越可能投票給馬英九。但這些推論建立在特定條件上，不能輕易推論到其他情境。結論討論本文的理論與實證意涵。

---

[7] 2008 年總統大選時國民黨尚未執政，選後馬英九提出的「不統、不獨、不武」政策，目的在於緩和兩岸情勢。2012 年國民黨已經執政四年，必須界定台灣的主權歸屬，但不管論述內容為何，都比 2008 年更容易陷入兩極對立。

貳、兩極化下的統獨選擇

常態分布的統獨立場，為何和兩極化的競爭模式並存？要回答這個問題，得先從兩極化的文獻著手。有關兩極化的研究，以美國經驗最豐富。美國和當前台灣有幾個類似性：總統都享有很大的權力，皆以兩大政黨為主，但政黨立場未如 Downs（1957）預測的那樣趨近中位選民。[8] 這表示，我們若要解釋台灣的兩極競爭，可以先從美國經驗談起。對於美國政黨為何沒有趨中競爭，Aldrich（1983）很早就修正了 Downsian 模型，指出政治上的活躍份子通常具有特定的政治立場，他們若決定參與選舉，將有可能造成「非中間化」的均衡。這個論點，受到有關美國國會投票行為研究的支持。其中最早，也最有名的是 Poole 與 Rosenthal（2001）的研究。他們透過對美國國會記名表決紀錄的長期觀察，證實美國政治出現兩極化的趨勢。[9] McCarty、Poole 與 Rosenthal（2006: 163-188）進一步指出，美國政治兩極化反映出少數保守菁英的結盟，其結果是財富分配更為惡化。Fukuyama（2013）甚至宣稱，美國的分權體系使菁英互信低落，不但造成政治上的極化，也和國力衰微有關。這些研究都挑戰了以 Downs 為代表的趨近模型（proximity model）。有學者提出方向模型（directional model），認為某些選民可能會選擇偏離中位點的政黨，以防止現狀往另一個極端滑動。[10] 不過，方向模型受到現狀所在位置的影響，能否產生更好的解釋力，仍有待檢驗。

美國的經驗顯示，分權制、兩黨制和菁英結盟，都是構成兩極化的要因。[11] 從全球的視角觀之，同時具有這幾種條件的國家的確不多，而台灣正是其中之一。關於台灣經驗，Dalton 與 Tanaka（2007）透過 Comparative Study of Electoral Systems 的資料，發現台灣民眾雖能辨認自己在「左右光譜」上的位置，但對於左、右的定義缺乏共識。

---

[8]　Levendusky（2009）曾以理論模型和經驗檢證來說明兩極化的形成。Curini 與 Hino（2012）發現不同體制下的職位分配模式也是兩極化政治的重要變數。

[9]　接續其後，Bartels（2000）、Fleisher 與 Bond（2004）等學者也進行了類似的研究。

[10]　關於趨近模型和方向模型的整合，請參考 Merrill III 與 Grofman（1999）。

[11]　某些學者認為，美國選民的態度並未出現明確的兩極化（DiMaggio, Evans, and Bryson, 1996），立場也比較曖昧（Fiorina and Levendusky, 2006）。Han 與 Brady（2007）則指出，1950 到 1960 年代美國之所以沒有出現明顯的兩極化，和早先的歷史經驗有關，但這表示美國政治並無趨中的內在動力。就菁英的角度來看，兩極化較易滿足其意識形態（Layman, Carsey, and Horowitz, 2006; Hetherington, 2001），也可在黨內排除溫和派的力量（Hirano, Snyder, and Ting, 2009; Thomsen, 2014），或遏阻中間選民投票（Callander and Wilson, 2007）。也有研究指出，媒體對於美國民眾的兩極化扮演重要角色（Ahler, 2014），而美國政黨和民眾的意識形態也的確日趨一致（Abramowitz and Saunders, 2008）。

相對而言，「國家認同」和「統獨選擇」卻是選民區別政黨的主要依據，Hsieh 與 Niou（1996）、Chu 與 Lin（2001）、Niou（2004）、蕭怡靖、鄭夙芬（2014）都提出類似的看法。從時間的變化，更可看出趨勢。二十多年前，台灣尚處在民主化前期，為了擴大選票基礎，即便主張台灣獨立的民進黨，也不見得會在選舉時標舉明確的台獨立場；到了 2000 年民進黨贏得總統選舉，出現分立政府（divided government），情況有所轉變。正如美國經驗所示，行政部門與立法部門若由不同政黨主導，很容易出現兩極化的傾向。Fell（2005: 119-122）透過菁英訪談，指出國家認同的確是台灣政黨的主要分歧，但自 2001 年才出現明顯的兩極化趨勢。一個具體的實例，就是 2004 年的「防禦性公投」。蔡佳泓、徐永明、黃琇庭（2007）認為，在 2004 年的總統選舉中，民進黨藉由議題操作，使選民必須在二選一的公民投票中選擇特定的立場，進而弱化中間選項，導致兩極化的後果。這個例子說明，總統選舉、菁英操作和兩黨競爭，的確都是台灣政治兩極化的要因。

以上的敘述，說明台灣的統獨選擇為何有兩極化的可能。但這種可能性，卻潛藏一個更根本的問題：有這麼多人支持的「維持現狀」，為什麼在兩極競爭中被邊緣化？對方向模型而言，這尤其是一個難題：如果馬英九的當選會使現狀更偏向統一，支持現狀的選民就應該投票給蔡英文，但這似乎與實情不符。關鍵因素，可能在於「統獨選擇」的多變性。所謂的「統獨選擇」，通常是問「你贊成台灣與中國大陸統一、台灣獨立、維持現狀後獨立、維持現狀後統一、維持現狀再決定統一或獨立還是永遠維持現狀？」對這些問題，即使答案一樣，實際意涵也可能隨著時空環境而有差別。在缺乏政治競爭的威權時期，受訪者的答案受到歷史經驗的影響，所以「台灣人」和「中國人」可能有省籍意涵，「獨立」或「統一」也是以國民黨所宣稱的「中華民國」為對象；進入民主化之後，威權時代的省籍差異逐漸透過選舉動員而轉變為認同差異，所謂「中國」也從「中華民國」轉化為「中華人民共和國」（吳乃德，2002）。

此外，問題怎麼問，也和受訪者怎麼答有關。我們可將相關文獻分為以下兩種。第一類研究採取固定的分類法（陳義彥、陳陸輝，2003），但有可能調整問法。例如，蕭怡靖、游清鑫（2012：75）在傳統的六分法之後，加上「最無法接受的選項」，就是想更完整地呈現受訪者的態度。其他相關的研究則在類似的分類基礎上，將受訪者的態度連結到某些重要的變數上，例如政黨競爭（張傳賢、黃紀，2011）、兩岸政策（Chu, 2004; 周陽山，2008；蔡宏明，2008；陳明通，2009；袁鶴齡、沈燦宏，2012；黃清賢，2012）、九二共識對 2012 年總統選舉的影響（蒙志成，2014）乃至性別政治（楊婉瑩、劉嘉薇，2009）等。後者通常是以統獨選擇連結特定現象，很少探討影響統獨立場的條件從何而來。

第二類研究，是將統獨立場視為條件題，並彰顯「維持現狀」的多變性。對於贊成維持現狀的比例為什麼這麼高，吳乃德（1993、2005）很早就提出疑問。他認為，國家認同和統獨選擇涉及理性與感性的糾結，所以「維持現狀」其實蘊含了一種兩難。Niou（2005）進一步指出，統獨選擇若會受其他條件影響，應視為「偏好不可分離」。他在2005年進行了「台灣國家安全調查」（Taiwan National Security Survey）（Niou, 2005: 95-96），發現有相當多台灣選民的統獨偏好受到其他條件的影響。[12] 例如，在同一時間內，同一位選民可以在確保兩岸和平時支持獨立，或在兩岸發展程度接近時接受統一。之後，有相當數量的研究，都探詢條件式的統獨立場（耿曙、陳陸輝，2003；耿曙、劉嘉薇、陳陸輝，2009；陳陸輝等，2009；劉嘉薇、耿曙、陳陸輝，2009；俞振華、林啟耀，2013；張茂桂、陳俐靜，2013）。正如這類研究所發現，很多受訪者因為條件式的統獨立場，很容易在各選項中選擇「維持現狀」，而這也暗示「現狀」的複雜多變。既然如此，選擇維持現狀的比例會隨著條件而變動，並不令人意外。

然而，上述文獻多未探討統獨立場的面向性問題，或隱含單一面向的假定（張茂桂、陳俐靜，2013：206-207），留下一些分析上的問題。在單一面向的假定下，維持現狀處於統獨的中間地帶，政黨理應爭取這些選票才能勝選，但這個意涵有悖於兩極化的現實。換言之，如果要解釋台灣的兩極化，不應將條件式的統獨偏好視為單一面向的議題，其變化不一定具有單一方向性，甚至不屬於實數（real number）系統。再者，即使是第二類的研究，也很少討論「條件」從何而來，在什麼情況下可以影響統獨立場，以及對哪些黨派有利。關鍵問題，在於不同條件是否可在同一時間內誘發同一位條件式偏好者出現偏獨或偏統的抉擇。如果答案是肯定的，就可解釋政黨對於條件式統獨偏好者的影響，而政黨若藉著「二選一」的方式來操作議題，可能就與兩極化有關。

為彰顯統獨立場在空間模型中的意涵，以下稱之為「條件式統獨偏好」。本文認為，統獨議題涉及國家定位，最容易和總統選舉產生關連。下節提出的模型，目標即為闡述論述中的訊息如何約制總統選舉的投票行為。透過模型，還可推導出幾項經驗假設，回過頭來驗證模型。

參、理論模型

大多數的統獨主張隱含法理論述，所以應先闡述後者，才能瞭解前者的差距從何而

---

[12] Niou 亦曾委託國立政治大學的選舉研究中心，執行了「兩岸關係和國家安全民意調查」。

來。從憲法的層次來看，目前實施於台灣、澎湖、金門與馬祖的《中華民國憲法》，在第四條規定「中華民國領土，依其固有之疆域，非經國民大會之決議，不得變更之」。所謂「固有領土」，根據大法官會議釋字第 328 號解釋（1993 年 11 月 26 日），「不應由行使司法權之釋憲機關予以解釋」，其理由在於憲法「不採列舉方式而爲概括規定，並設領土變更之程序，以爲限制，有其政治上及歷史上之理由」（司法院大法官，1993）。若以 1947 年 1 月 1 日《中華民國憲法》公布日來界定主權，領土範圍和當前中華人民共和國憲法施行的地區大致重疊，但並不一致，造成「一個中國」原則的不確定性。在此意義下，所謂「一個中國」包含以下幾種意涵：

（一）世界上只有一個中國，中華人民共和國政府是中國唯一的合法政府。

（二）世界上只有一個中國，依《中華民國憲法》主權範圍及於固有領上，目前大陸地區爲中共政權所管轄。

（三）一個中國，各自表述。世界上只有一個中國，台灣方面認爲是「中華民國」，大陸方面認爲是「中華人民共和國」，兩者認知的範圍不一致。

（四）九二共識：由中華民國行政院前陸委會主委蘇起在 2000 年 4 月 28 日提出，指中華民國政府以「一個中國，各自表述」來總結 1993 年的辜汪會談，但避免使用（三），以免中共不談「各自表述」。

中共政府一開始並不承認九二共識，直到 2005 年連戰開始密集走訪中國大陸，中共才在官方文件上使用此一名詞。馬英九在 2008 年當選總統，遂以「九二共識」來總括兩岸政策。很明顯地，上述立場雖然都符合「一個中國」的意涵，但是（一）是中共的立場，（四）則是國民黨在 2005 年之後的立場。

依照同樣的邏輯，「台灣獨立」至少包括以下選項：

（五）台灣、澎湖、金門、馬祖不屬於中國（無論以何種方式界定），目前國家名稱爲中華民國。[13]

（六）台灣不屬於中國（無論以何種方式界定），且應建立台灣共和國。[14]

雖然「一個中國」有其曖昧性，金門馬祖是否歸屬台灣也有爭議，但以上主張仍然有清楚的主權界線：從（一）到（四），台灣屬於中國，所以台灣沒有獨立的主權；在（五）和（六）下，台灣不屬於中華人民共和國，並擁有獨立的主權。在此前提下，政

---

[13] 民進黨在 1999 年 5 月 8 日通過的「台灣前途決議文」，即彰顯類似的主張。

[14] 1991 年 10 月 13 日民進黨修訂黨綱，指出應該「建立台灣共和國」（即一般所謂的「台獨黨綱」），和此一主張相當接近。

黨的兩岸論述難以迴避主權問題：國民黨反對台獨，所以中華民國的主權涵蓋全中國；民進黨主張台獨，所以國家主權不及於中華人民共和國。

我們可將以上立場統稱為「兩岸論述」。總統選舉，使兩岸論述和選民的投票抉擇產生關連。2012 年，國民黨和民進黨的實力接近，持有條件式統獨立場的選民成為決勝的關鍵。如果他們的投票抉擇受到兩岸論述的影響，問題就在於論述提供了什麼訊息。先看「支持條件式統一的偏獨選民」（以下簡稱「一中獨派」）。以 2012 年的脈絡觀察，「條件式統一」主要是指同意「如果大陸在經濟、社會、政治方面的發展跟台灣差不多，兩岸就應該統一」的人，而「獨派」則是指主張「盡快宣布獨立，或維持現狀後獨立」的選民。條件當然還有他種可能，例如「條件式的統派選民」，指的就是「如果台灣獨立不會引起戰爭，就應該宣布獨立」的偏統選民。「兩岸發展接近」和「兩岸不會戰爭」都是尚未發生的狀態，但前者已可看到中國大陸經濟的快速成長，後者卻仍有中共不放棄對台用武的可能性（如「反分裂國家法」所示）。再加上 2012 年的議程由國民黨設定，不會強調獨立，所以前者的可能性遠高於後者。以人數比例來看，「一中獨派」在 740 位偏獨選民中占 13.12%，具有統獨兩面性，對兩岸的政經互動特別敏感。相對於其他類別的選民，獨派投票給馬英九的比例最低，所以若能顯現「一中獨派」支持馬英九，他類選民的投票傾向自不待言。[15]

如前所述，法理上的統一或獨立涉及清楚的主權範圍，是難以迴避的問題。總統候選人，是否會提出「一個中國」或「台灣獨立」來界定他們的主權論述？面對立場互異的選民，哪種論述能增加選票？我們不難猜想，在前列各種統獨論述中，越接近選項（一），台灣選民反對的比例就越高。對國民黨而言，若以「一中各表」為兩岸共識，中共可能會忽略「各表」，進而緩進到方案（一）。和「一中各表」相比，「九二共識」的主權意涵較為曖昧，並且隱含兩岸的和平互利，而「一中各表」則蘊含主權和政體選擇，欠缺想像空間。基於這個道理，國民黨和中共的默契相當重要：在台灣的總統選舉期間，中共是否會默認國民黨所提出的「九二共識」，以讓馬英九能增加他的選票？「一個中國」的定義，是否等馬英九當選後再議？

賽局模型，可以更細緻地描繪上述推論，並透過策略互動推導命題。本章附錄一以賽局模型呈現三種訊息結構，用在同樣的策略互動和報酬分配模式上，希望顯示訊息的差異可以導致不同的後果。為幫助大家瞭解訊息結構與選票流動的關係，在此以直觀方式敘述推論過程。模型的關鍵問題是：台灣要不屬於一個中國，要不享有獨立主權，那

---

[15] 在主張「永遠維持現狀」的 763 人中，有 23% 的人同意這個條件式的統一立場；在偏統的 281 人中，有 73.56% 的人同意此一條件式的統一立場。

麼國民黨是否要倡議「一中各表」，民進黨要不要主張「台灣獨立」？「一中獨派」希望爭取台灣的國際生存空間，但又疑懼中共的壓制。所以，他們是否接受某種兩岸論述，要看中共的態度。中共雖然堅持一個中國，但可以默認或否認「一中各表」的「各表」，而這種態度會影響「一中獨派」的投票抉擇。在這兩種狀態下，兩黨的訊息結構有三種可能。

　　第一種訊息結構，是假設兩黨都瞭解中共的意圖。在總統選舉時，如果中共默認「各表」，民進黨也沒有提出台獨來反制，則國民黨即使提出「一中各表」，「一中獨派」也不太會支持國民黨，理由在於各方的對策沒有太多衝突，所以「一中獨派」欠缺支持國民黨的理由。如果中共強調「一中」但明白反對「各表」，民進黨就會以強調台灣主權獨立來回應；此時國民黨若倡議「一中各表」即落入親中陷阱，「一中獨派」的選票也不太會流向國民黨。所以，在雙方都有充分訊息的假設下，國民黨應該不會強調「一中各表」，以免喪失「一中獨派」的支持。第二種訊息結構，是假設兩黨都不瞭解中共的態度。此時國民黨和民進黨都必須猜測中共的真實意圖。如果民進黨猜測中共否認「各表」的機會不高，就應採取善意的兩岸論述，少提台獨；如果民進黨認為中共很有可能否認「各表」，則會採取抗衡的準備。無論是哪種情況都對民進黨有利，所以國民黨都會避免讓「一中各表」成為焦點議題，以防止「一中獨派」的選票流向民進黨。所以，如果兩黨都不清楚中共的真實意圖，國民黨仍會採取保守策略，避免讓統獨問題主導選舉。[16] 在這兩種情況下，國民黨的兩岸論述都不會觸及主權問題，以免民進黨藉此增加選票。

　　第三種訊息結構，是假設只有國民黨瞭解中共的態度。這裡所說的「瞭解」，是指在總統選舉期間，馬英九能預判中共的態度，而中共也預先瞭解馬英九的兩岸論述。民進黨只能決定是否倡議台灣獨立，但無論其選擇為何，都不能維持均衡：如果民進黨強調台獨而中共也準備否認「各表」，則瞭解狀況的國民黨應會避免提出「一中各表」，以防杜民進黨藉著統獨議題而獲利；如果民進黨避談台獨而中共也默認「各表」，則國民黨也不會倡議「一中各表」，以防止民進黨藉機增加選票。既然台獨與否都會使國民黨避談「一中各表」，民進黨應該會採取混合策略；同理，國民黨也會將風險分散到「強調一中各表」和「避談一中各表」之間。此時兩黨會處於混合策略的均衡狀態：因為無法確知另一政黨的策略，所以會採取兩種純粹策略之間的選項。國民黨既然瞭解中共的態度，所以能在滿足混策均衡的報酬組合中，選擇對其最有利的選項。簡言之，國

16　還有一種狀況，就是中共對「各表」的態度曖昧。此時，民進黨和國民黨都會分散風險。在討論訊息結構三時，會提出進一步說明。

民黨得以利用訊息優勢選擇對其最有利的結果，最後的均衡就是接近「一中各表」的「九二共識」。國民黨既然避談「一中各表」，處於被動的民進黨很難找到反制點。

　　總結以上三種訊息結構，國民黨最可能在掌握訊息優勢時操作兩岸論述，以「九二共識」替代「一中各表」；「九二共識」的確和主權問題有關，但卻不讓「一中」出現在論述中。這個模型有其理論上的道理，但如何證明其實證效力？理論模型雖然簡化現實，但可幫助我們掌握選舉策略的基本樣態。從實證研究的角度來看，也只有透過理論模型，才能推想常識所不能及的命題，並加以檢證。所謂的檢證（verification），比「尋找變數間的相關性」要複雜一些。第一，檢證要有理論基礎，才能透過檢證的結果來修正理論。對本文而言，核心課題就是兩岸論述與選票流動的關係。第二，某些重要因素很難找到直接證據，我們只能檢測其「蘊含」（implications）。所謂的蘊含，是指「若 A 則 B」的 B。此時，觀察到 B 並不能證明「若 A 則 B」，但若能找到「非 A」且顯示「非 A 則 B」的機率低，我們對「若 A 則 B」的信念就會增強。第三，所有的策略選擇都涉及篩選，被放棄的策略固然扮演重要的角色，但無法觀察。對這些看不見的變數，我們只能驗證其蘊含，其方法也與第二點一致。

　　在進入實證分析之前，先提示幾個能證成推論的短期因素。第一，從 2012 年年初開始，有部分台灣重量級的企業家表態，認為要支持「九二共識」，台灣經濟才能繼續發展。第二，某些民調曾經顯示國民黨、民進黨的支持度接近，甚至預測民進黨的蔡英文勝選。例如，TVBS 曾在 2012 大選前針對總統候選人進行密集的民意調查，發現馬英九和蔡英文的支持度一度相持不下，但在選前一個月開始拉大。[17] 這些轉變，是否反映某些選民的統獨偏好受到兩岸論述的影響？如果是，馬英九的得票率應該高於其支持度，TVBS 的民意調查，已經透露一些端倪：該台預測馬英九的得票率是 49%，但支持度只有 43%。由此推論，這種變化可能起因於部分選民在選前改變支持對象，而企業家的表態可能是一個訊號。第三，行政院大陸事務委員會所公布的資料，顯露中共在總統競選期間的言談：2011 年 5 月 11 日，中共國台辦說，台灣以「中華台北」的名義參加世界衛生組織（World Health Organization）的觀察員，是「大陸方面釋放的善意」；同年 12 月 16 日，全國政協主席賈慶林宣稱，「九二共識」是一個客觀事實，否定「九二共識」，兩岸協商就難以為繼。從整個競選期間來觀察，很難找到中共倡議「一個中

---

[17] 候選人的支持度和得票率是不一樣的概念，但多數媒體只能追蹤支持度。TVBS 的民調雖以電話訪問進行，但是是少數每週進行的民調，可以針對候選人支持度進行短期但密集的觀察。關於 TVBS 的民意調查，請參考 TVBS（2012）。此外，遠見雜誌民調一直預測蔡英文勝選，但選前幾個月卻停止民調，該民調中心主任也辭職。

國」並否決「各自表述」的證據。[18]

　　由此可知，國民黨在競選期間向選民傳達一定的訊息，只要中共默認，這些訊息就可以增強其一致性和說服力，使某些偏獨選民期望能從兩岸經貿往來中得利，進而增加馬英九的選票。我們因此可以提出本文的關鍵假設：如果「九二共識」是造成馬英九勝選的重要原因，增加的選票最可能來自「一中獨派」。[19] 我們不難想像，如果國民黨在選舉時主張「一中各表」但遭中共否認「各表」，這些「一中獨派」投票給馬英九的比例就不會這麼高。這個假設延伸出以下的三個命題，說明兩岸論述與投票行為的關係。

命題一：2012 年的總統大選，來自「一中獨派」的選票，是解釋馬英九得票的重要因素。

　　此一命題的依變數是投票行為。如果「一中獨派」的確受到「九二共識」的影響，就表示這個變數是解釋選舉結果的重要因素。我們觀察的方式是，比較是否放入「一中獨派」變數對其他變數係數及顯著性的影響。

命題二：在 2012 年選舉，「一中獨派」投票給馬英九的機率明顯高於投票給國民黨籍區域立委候選人的機率。

　　這是本文的關鍵命題：我們希望檢測「非條件」的後果。這裡的「非條件」，是指區域立法委員選舉。2012 年的總統選舉和立法委員選舉在同一天舉行，區域立委也是採取對大黨有利的單一選區相對多數決制，等於控制了所有的干擾因素。命題二的目的，就在觀察「九二共識」對同屬國民黨籍的馬英九與區域立委候選人，是否產生不同的投票選擇。如果答案是肯定的，就會增強我們對理論模型的信心。

命題三：在偏獨選民中，投票給馬英九的機率隨著與對岸經濟往來的密切程度而上升，隨著台灣認同的強度而下降。

　　按照中共的設想，偏獨選民越能在兩岸經貿互動中得利，就越可能因為物質利益而轉變情感認同。我們也可從反面來驗證此一命題：越具有台灣認同的選民，就越不易受

---

[18] 2012 年總統選舉，馬英九是在 2011 年 4 月 23 日獲得國民黨的提名。行政院陸委會的資料，是以有關國家主權的論述為對象，請參考中華民國行政院大陸委員會（2011）。

[19] 陳陸輝、耿曙、王德育（2009：12）發現「宣布獨立是否引起武力相向」對 2008 年總統選舉並未產生顯著的影響。2008 年總統選舉的現任者是民進黨的陳水扁，本文則以是否投票給2012 年的現任總統馬英九為依變數，並以相反方向的「一中獨派」為自變數。如前所述，「兩岸發展接近」比「宣布台獨而未引發戰爭」更具體，也更容易改變條件式偏好者的行為。這也表示，就兩岸論述而言，2008 與 2012 年的總統選舉是不同的。

到物質利益的左右而投票給馬英九。這個命題，也能檢證中共經濟戰略的效果。

　　以上的命題，是從不同角度來驗證兩岸論述對於 2012 年總統選舉的影響。這些命題，也是要挑戰將國家認同和統獨選擇的變數值視為不變的假設。前述模型，已經指出論述中的訊息能影響某些選民的投票行為。在 2012 年的總統選舉中，接受中共所默許的「九二共識」，可以維持兩岸的和平關係和擴大經貿往來；某些選民也認識到，當國民黨掌握訊息優勢時，才會鼓吹此種共識。這種認知，使具有獨立傾向，但又依賴中國大陸經濟而存活的選民，有可能轉變其總統選舉的投票對象。以下，將說明如何將理論命題運作化為經驗假設。

肆、兩岸論述如何影響投票行為

　　本文以第六期第四次的「台灣社會變遷調查」，以下簡稱「社變」）資料來驗證上述命題。在社變資料中，國家認同組的有效樣本共有 1,952 份，執行期間為 2013 年整年。在本文所運用的社變資料中，主要的變數包括個人背景、投票選擇、國族認同、統獨選擇以及經濟行為或評價等。詳細的變數，在說明分析結果時會加以解釋。為顧及行文的一致性，本文將某些變數重新編碼（詳附錄三）。以下將以「一中獨派」來描繪 1. 在統獨選擇上選擇「支持台灣獨立」或「維持現狀，以後走向獨立」且；2. 同意「兩岸在經濟、文化、政治上發展一致則支持統一」的受訪者。遺漏值，包括「無法決定」、「無意見」、「不瞭解題意」、「不知道」、「拒答」等。在扣除遺漏值後，本文的樣本大約有 1,800 人左右（因變數不同而稍有差異）。這些受訪者包含未投票者，而回答有投票給馬英九的人占 36.0%，此實際數字 38.4% 稍低，但仍可信賴。因為本文的目的在於瞭解為什麼有些獨派會投票給國民黨籍的總統候選人，所以並未再細分有無投票，以免降低樣本數以及分類後各類別的人數。

　　命題從模型而來，具有理論意涵；在考慮變數的性質和編碼方式後，可以將命題運作化為以下的假設。

假設一：「一中獨派」的選票，是解釋馬英九在 2012 年大選得票的顯著變數。

　　透過「一中獨派」這個變數，我們可以檢測「九二共識」論述對投票行為的影響。檢測顯著性的方法，是比較是否加入「一中獨派」這個變數，對兩個模型各變數係數與

顯著性的影響。[20]

假設二：「一中獨派」投票給馬英九的機率與投票給國民黨籍區域立委候選人的機率，在統計上有顯著的差異。

這個假設是要檢測「非條件」的影響。區域立委選舉是在選區的層次進行，比較不受兩岸論述的影響。我們以「單因子變異數分析」（One-Way ANOVA）來檢測這兩個變數在分布上的差異。如果差異顯著，即表示同樣的選民在不同層級的選舉，對同屬國民黨籍的候選人有不同的偏好。如果得到驗證，即可間接觀察不同程度的「九二共識」是否對「一中獨派」產生不同的作用。

假設三：在「一中獨派」的選民中，越覺得中國大陸經濟重要或越欠缺對台灣的情感認同，越可能投票給馬英九。

這個假設是要檢測經濟利益和情感認同的交互作用。如果經濟利益真能改變人的政治態度，應該最容易從「一中獨派」選民的投票行為看出。需要說明的是，社變資料中有好幾個變數都與經濟利益與情感認同有關。為了避免共線性，假設三只挑選了某些變數。在檢證此一假設時，會對挑選步驟提出詳盡說明。

簡言之，假設一比較是否加入「一中獨派」的差別，假設二觀察「一中獨派」是否對馬英九和國民黨籍區域立委候選人有不同的支持度，假設三探討「一中獨派」和「扣除一中獨派後的偏獨選民」投票給馬英九的原因。

先說明假設一的檢證方式。一個可能的方法，是透過比較 2012 和 2008 年的民調，觀察「一中獨派」和他類選民的差別，以確認「一中獨派」對馬英九勝選的影響。但國民黨在 2012 年是執政黨，2008 年不是，難以比較該黨如何在不同的選舉中藉著兩岸論述影響「一中獨派」的投票行為。所以，我們仍以馬英九在 2012 年的得票為依變數，找出相關的因素。由於「是否投票給馬英九」是類別變數（投 = 1，未投 = 0），本文以「二元勝算對數模型」（binary logit model）為分析方法。[21]

---

[20] 其他的自變數，主要包括政黨認同、國家認同及統獨選擇等。既有文獻大多發現具有泛藍（泛綠）認同且反對（主張）台灣獨立的受訪者，有很高的機率支持泛藍（泛綠）的候選人。

[21] 在勝算對數模型中，自變數需要彼此獨立才能滿足 Independence of Irrelevant Alternatives（IIA）的假定。以假設一來看，「一中獨派」和「國家認同」的相關係數不高，只有 -0.07。「國家認同」和「統獨選擇」可能有相關性，但若分別將「國家認同」或「統獨選擇」移除，其他變數的係數縱使稍升，但大致與表 16.1 相同，顯示仍可同時考慮這兩個因素。再者，如果排除「國家認同」和「統獨選擇」，則「一中獨派」的顯著程度變低，所以前兩者仍是重要變數。在檢證假設三時，也採取同樣的方法。

　　在此需要進行兩項說明。第一，「一中獨派」共有 97 人，若以 95% 的信賴區間爲準，其上下誤差幅度稍大。[22] 我們可將「永遠支持現狀」加入偏獨選民，稱這個類別爲「非統派」，並定義「一中非統」爲「非統派，且贊成兩岸發展一致則接受統一」的選民。表 16.1 的模型都放入「國家認同」和「統獨選擇」這兩個和投票行爲最相關的連續變數，但模型二和模型三則分別放入「一中獨派」和「一中非統」這兩個類別變數以觀察其影響。結果如表 16.1 所示，「一中獨派」的顯著性達到 0.038，雖比多數變數低，但已可說明兩岸論述的影響。[23] 再就「一中非統」來看，模型三的顯著程度達到 0.000，不但方向與「一中獨派」一致，係數也相當接近。所以，「一中非統」雖不似「一中獨派」那樣偏向獨立，但可視爲是對後者穩定度的檢測。第二，表 16.1 的「國家認同」和「統獨選擇」是連續變數，其假定爲變數值具有同一方向性。本文因爲以下的理論目的而暫時採取這樣的假定：兩極化表示兩極對立，所以應該有方向性，與此相關的統獨問題和國家認同，可能也有方向性，而本文想要顯示，即使假設「國家認同」和「統獨選擇」是連續變數，仍不能改變「一中獨派」或「一中非統」這些類別變數的影響力。簡言之，本文希望以條件式的統獨偏好來修正統獨方向性的假定，所以應將後者視爲具有方向性的連續變數，結果的確顯示前者不受方向性的影響。就變數性質而言，當然不一定要將「國家認同」和「統獨選擇」視爲連續變數。附錄二說明，如果將這兩個變數視爲沒有方向性的類別變數，「一中獨派」和「一中非統」的相關性並沒有因變數性質的改變而下降，也間接顯示這些變數的穩定性。由此可知，不論如何替統獨選擇歸類，或如何認定相關變數的性質，結果都相當類似，也說明條件式統獨偏好有其獨特性。

　　表 16.1 的其他發現則符合一般的認知：投票給馬英九的機率，會隨著外省人身分、泛藍政黨認同而上升；在個人背景方面，男性比女性更容易支持馬英九，教育年數的影響也是正向的。[24] 比較三個模型，可以發現大部分變數的係數和顯著性並無明顯變化，顯現「一中獨派」和「一中非統」都具有獨立於其他自變數的影響力。

---

[22] 這個樣本數雖然不大，但應該高於 King 與 Zeng（2001: 138）所說的「稀少事件資料」（rare events data）。

[23] 如前所述，2012 和 2008 年，國民黨的兩岸論述對「一中獨派」產生不一樣的影響。同一群選民，在 2008 年投票給馬英九的比例只有 31%，比 2012 年的 34.02% 低。由此可知國民黨兩岸論述在 2012 年選舉的作用。

[24] 國家認同和統獨選擇之所以對投票給馬英九的機率有正向影響，是因爲前者是以「台灣人、兩者都是、中國人」的順序爲變數值，後者則是由「儘快宣布獨立」到「儘快與中國大陸統一」劃分五個等級的獨統指標。

表 16.1　是否投票給馬英九的二元勝算對數模型

自變數	模型一				模型二				模型三			
	B	S.E.	Sig.	Exp(B)	B	S.E.	Sig.	Exp(B)	B	S.E.	Sig.	Exp(B)
常數	-2.399	.342	.000	.091	-2.539	.351	.000	.079	-2.559	.348	.000	.077
性別	.240	.109	.028	1.271	.250	.109	.022	1.283	.246	.109	.025	1.278
出生年	-.027	.004	.000	.973	-.028	.004	.000	.973	-.028	.004	.000	.973
教育年數	.054	.017	.001	1.055	.056	.017	.001	1.057	.057	.017	.001	1.058
省籍	.947	.189	.000	2.578	.953	.190	.000	2.594	.951	.190	.000	2.587
偏向泛藍政黨	1.069	.177	.000	2.912	1.059	.177	.000	2.884	1.054	.177	.000	2.869
國家認同	.944	.123	.000	2.570	.940	.123	.000	2.559	.931	.123	.000	2.538
統獨選擇	.343	.063	.000	1.409	.377	.065	.000	1.457	.366	.063	.000	1.442
一中獨派					.519	.251	.038	1.680				
一中非統									.521	.149	.000	1.684
-2 Log likelihood	2022.470				2018.363				2010.419			
Cox and Snell R-square	0.166				0.168				0.172			
觀察值	1,787				1,787				1,787			

資料來源：第六期第四次的「台灣社會變遷調查」。

說明：這三個模型的差別，在於是否考慮「一中獨派」或「一中非統」。

　　那麼，「一中獨派」的投票選擇和其他選民有什麼差別？表 16.2 顯示，「一中獨派」的選民，投給馬英九的比例比其他選民稍低，但仍達到 34.02%。必須說明的是，所謂的「非一中獨派」包含「非一中獨派的獨派」以及「非獨派」兩類選民，前者投票給馬英九的比例為 22.04%，後者投票給馬英九的比例為 45.15%。「兩岸發展接近則接受統一」這個條件使獨派投票給馬英九的比例上升了 11.98%，可見其影響力。

表 16.2　馬英九的得票分布

是否為一中獨派	是否投票給馬英九		
	未投	投	總計
否	1,086 (63.21%)	632 (36.79%)	1,718 (100.00%)
是	64 (65.98%)	33 (34.02%)	97 (100.00%)
人數	1,150	665	1,815

資料來源：第六期第四次的「台灣社會變遷調查」。
說明：括弧為列百分比；「非一中獨派」包含「非一中獨派的獨派」以及「非獨派」兩類選民；
　　　前者投給馬英九的比例為 22.04%，後者投給馬英九的比例為 45.15%。

　　為確認兩岸論述的影響，我們比較「一中獨派」在總統與立委選舉上的投票行為，是否達到統計上的顯著差異。在 2012 年的選舉中，每位選民都可投下一張總統選票和兩張立委選票，而總統和區域立委選舉都是採取單一選區相對多數決制，對大黨有利。如果「一中獨派」選民對於總統選舉和區域立委選舉投下的選票分屬不同政黨，而前者的選票多於後者，即可間接顯現兩岸論述對總統選舉的影響。表 16.3 以「單因子變異數分析」進行兩類選舉的比較，結果符合預期。「一中獨派」投給馬英九的比例，的確高於投給國民黨籍立委候選人的比例，而且差異達到顯著水準。若以「一中非統」為對象，則其 F 值為 177.093，顯著性也達到 0.000。所以，無論怎麼定義統獨選擇，都可發現「獨派」或「非統派」對兩種選舉所採取的不同態度，而其源由之一很可能就是兩岸論述。

　　下一個問題是，「九二共識」影響「一中獨派」的原因何在？以經濟理性的邏輯來看，物質利益能轉變政黨認同，尤其是當後者欠缺動員基礎時。依此理，「一中獨派」之所以會投票給馬英九，很可能是為了從兩岸的經濟關係中得利，尤其是中共默認

表 16.3　對於「一中獨派」投票行爲的差異分析

	Sum of squares	df	Mean square	F	Sig.
組間	7.763	1	7.763	52.638	0.000
組內	14.01	95	0.147		
總計	21.773	96			

資料來源：第六期第四次的「台灣社會變遷調查」。
說明：以「單因子變異數分析」計算；「一中獨派」總數爲 97 人；兩組分別代表 1. 一中獨派投票給馬英九及；2. 一中獨派投票給國民黨籍區域候選人。

「九二共識」，使某些獨派欠缺支持台獨的理由時。反論之，某些獨派選民之所以沒有投票給馬英九，可能是因爲台灣意識強烈或覺得台灣過度依賴中國大陸，而這些因素的作用力強於短期的經濟利益。是否如此，我們可以檢視假設三。

　　假設三的依變數仍是「是否投票給馬英九」這個類別變數，所以我們仍要處理自變數的相關性問題，以免造成估計值的偏誤。處理方法包括以下步驟。首先，找出和國家認同與統獨選擇有關的變數，若有某些變數具有相關性，則從其中篩選普遍性最大的爲自變數。第二，以因素分析法找出主成分，並根據成分矩陣（component matrix）挑選係數較高的變數。第三，找出第二和第三的交集。結果共挑出六個自變數，涵蓋認同的情感面、對台灣民主的光榮感以及與兩岸經濟有關的幾項因素。最後，用這些變數和一些個人背景變數，解釋「一中獨派」的投票行爲。

　　假設三以「一中獨派」爲模型一的樣本，「扣除一中獨派後的偏獨選民」爲模型二的樣本，並比較兩者的異同。在進入假設檢證前，先概述這兩群選民的基本樣態。如前所述，如果扣除「一中獨派」，偏獨選民投票給馬英九的比例是 22.04%，比「一中獨派」低很多。[25] 扣除「一中獨派」後，偏獨選民投給國民黨籍區域候選人的百分比是 18.51，比投給馬英九的百分比只少了 3.53；相對而言，「一中獨派」投票給國民黨籍區域候選人的比例，比他們投票給馬英九的比例少 7%，顯現兩岸論述對「一中獨派」的影響力。因此，對照這兩個模型，可以看出「條件式統一」對偏獨選民的作用。根據理論模型，「九二共識」對「一中獨派」最大的影響在於經濟因素。反論之，扣除「條件式統一」後的獨派之所以較少人投票給馬英九，可能是因爲情感因素重於經濟因素。是否如此，我們以「不顯著性小於 0.05」來判斷變數的顯著性。

---

[25] 「兩岸發展接近則接受統一」是影響「一中獨派」的重要條件，但不是唯一的條件。所以，非屬「條件一中」的偏獨人士仍有可能因爲其他因素而投票給馬英九，只是比例沒有「一中獨派」那麼高。

表 16.4　影響「一中獨派」和「偏獨選民」投票行為的因素

自變數	模型一 （一中獨派）				模型二 （偏獨選民且非一中獨派）			
	B	S.E.	Sig.	Exp(B)	B	S.E.	Sig.	Exp(B)
常數	2.088	1.729	.227	8.070	2.109	.956	.027	8.239
性別	1.297	.588	.027	3.658	.051	.214	.812	1.052
出生年	-.054	.026	.039	.947	-.015	.009	.074	.985
教育年數	.107	.100	.284	1.113	.056	.035	.104	1.058
祖國是台灣	-1.637	.711	.021	.194	-1.319	.287	.000	.267
同胞要有感情	.970	.542	0.73	2.638	.387	.184	.035	1.472
民主政治光榮感	-.417	.341	.220	.659	-.418	.132	.002	.658
中國大陸市場是重要的	.934	.626	.136	2.546	.190	.246	.441	1.209
若為經濟發展則支持統一	-.729	.301	.015	.482	-.425	.109	.000	.653
去中國大陸次數	-.048	.137	.728	.953	-.003	.049	.950	.997
-2 Log likelihood	81.913				558.151			
Cox and Snell R-square	0.266				0.090			
觀察值	97				643			

資料來源：第六期第四次的「台灣社會變遷調查」。
說明：觀察值的差別來自樣本不同。

　　模型一以「一中獨派」為對象，有四個變數達到前述標準：「性別」、「出生年」、「祖國是台灣」和「若為經濟發展則支持統一」。我們可分幾方面來解讀這個結果。首先，「若為經濟發展則支持統一」的高顯著性並不令人意外，因為「一中獨派」原本就預設兩岸如果在社會、經濟與文化各方面發展接近則支持統一，並由此推知「九二共識」的影響力。[26] 其次，「祖國是台灣」的係數是負而顯著的，表示這種情感因素會阻礙投票給馬英九。第三，性別之所以是顯著變數，很可能和產業分工模式有關：在中國大陸經商的人士，男性應該遠多於女性，也使前者投票給馬英九的比例高於後者。第四，以出生年來看，人的生日決定其世代歸屬，而逐漸民主化的台灣，在不同世代的確面對不同的政治社會化機制，應該會對台灣的國家定位帶來不同想像。出生年

[26] 此一連續變數的影響方向為負，因為值越大越不同意「若為經濟發展則支持統一」這個說法。

係數的負值，反映出威權時代出生的民眾較有可能支持馬英九，年輕世代成長於民主化時期，支持馬英九的比例就比較低。其他變數雖未達到前述標準，但係數方向皆與預期一致。值得關注的是，「中國大陸市場是重要的」為什麼不顯著。一個合理的推論是，中國大陸經濟的重要性可能反映了台灣的依賴度，而過度依賴可能有負面效果，降低了投票給馬英九的可能性。為了確認「一中獨派」估計值的可信度，本文也以「一中統派」為檢測對象，結果發現兩者的顯著程度和方向性皆為一致。由此可知，兩個統獨選擇的分類法都能透露類似的訊息。

最後的問題，在於哪些因素影響排除「一中獨派」後的偏獨人士。從影響方向來看，表 16.4 的兩個模型完全一致，但顯著性有差別。首先，性別變數不再顯著，很可能是因為這群選民與中國大陸經濟的互動程度較低，所以較不受性別分工的影響。其次，和模型一相比，「若為經濟發展則支持統一」的係數較低但顯著性更強。一個可能的解釋是，這個變數的影響力很大，但仍有其他解釋投票行為的重要變數。第三，只有在模型二才看得到情感因素的作用，包括「祖國是台灣」、「同胞要有感情」和「民主政治光榮感」。這是三組相關但是不盡相同的概念，分別涉及國家、族群及體制。這三組概念的顯著性，表示扣除「一中獨派」後的偏獨人士，是因為非經濟利益的因素而沒有投票給馬英九。換言之，雖然利益與情感都影響這兩群選民的投票行為，但「一中獨派」較看重經濟利益，扣除「一中獨派」後的偏獨選民更受到情感認同的影響。中共如果只給後者經濟利益而不能體會其情感依附，不見得能改變他們的認同。

總論之，以上的經驗假設是運作化理論命題所得，而命題的基礎是賽局模型。賽局模型假定候選人以贏得總統選舉為目的，當馬英九掌握訊息優勢，最有可能利用中共的默認，以「九二共識」替代「一中各表」並影響偏獨選民的投票抉擇。因此，本文的推論是否合理，和模型假定的合理性有關，也要受到實證檢驗。若以實證究來看，本文以受訪者對問卷問題的回答為分析對象，必然有所疏漏與不足，也無法窮盡所有相關的問題，但透過賽局模型建構了一套因果機制，解釋反對台獨的總統候選人在什麼情況下可以得到偏獨選民的支持。透過理論模型和經驗分析，我們在既有研究的基礎上增加了對條件式選民的理解，也解釋了為何台灣會出現兩極化的競爭：如果現任總統的訊息優勢能夠影響條件式統獨偏好者的投票選擇，當然也會減縮其他選民的選擇空間，而正因為現任者擁有訊息優勢，這種「二選一」的兩極競爭是很難逆轉的。

伍、結論

　　台灣究竟應該追求獨立還是與大陸統一，是兩岸關係的核心議題，也是選民區別政黨的主要依據。這樣重要的課題，吸引了相當多的關注，也累積了豐富的研究成果。關於統獨問題，既有文獻發現多數民眾選擇「維持現狀」；許多政治人物，不論其黨派立場，也都認知這個現實。然而，政黨競爭卻仍然出現兩極化的趨勢，中道選擇似乎逐漸邊緣化。或許，這是因為兩極化的競爭弱化了無黨派選民的投票意願。但選舉競爭如此激烈，即便無黨派選民投票意願低，仍然是不可忽視的關鍵少數。維持現狀和兩極化，似乎是相悖的趨勢。為了解答這個困惑，本文重新詮釋「維持現狀」的意涵，指出論述中的訊息，可能改變投票的對象。同一個人，可能會因為台灣獨立不至於引起戰爭而贊同台獨，但也可能在兩岸發展接近時支持統一。這群「偏好不可分離」的選民正是各方候選人所爭取的對象。

　　以 2012 年總統選舉的時空觀之，馬英九擔任總統職務已有四年，兩岸也已簽署了《兩岸經濟合作架構協議》（Cross-Straits Economic Cooperation Framework Agreement），並展開密切的經貿往來。馬政府之所以鮮少提及「一中各表」而以十分相近的「九二共識」替代之，很可能是希望避免中共不提「各表」而使台灣進入「一中」的框架。對某些聽者而言，「九二共識」是和平紅利，對遊走兩岸的經商者特別有吸引力。因為馬英九已經執政四年，此一共識很可能已經得到中共政府的默許。至少，某些「一中獨派」存在這樣的想像，並因此決定支持馬英九連任總統。但很多「一中獨派」並未因此而轉變政黨認同，所以在同一天舉行的區域立委選舉中，並未投票給國民黨籍的候選人。對「一中獨派」而言，支持馬英九是基於經濟考量，所以越是覺得可以從中國大陸經濟獲利，越有可能投票給馬英九。但也正因為「一中獨派」是以「九二共識」所蘊含的物質利益來決定投票對象，所以他們很可能在其他條件的導引下，轉而支持其他政黨的候選人。

　　政黨的實力越接近，條件式統獨偏好者的角色就越重要。這些選民對統獨的看法，比「維持現狀」更為積極，但不容易被既有問卷所掌握。隨著兩岸經貿互動日趨密切，條件式統獨偏好者的人數也在上升。但這不代表兩岸經濟互賴必然對國民黨有利。單以經濟因素來看，所謂「中國因素」就有很多面向，除了競爭結構和企業利潤，還包括市場所在、投資方式、就業結構以及所得分配等，其中以政治機會最為關鍵。某些選民可能覺得中國大陸市場相當重要，但必須以掌握特定政治關係為前提。如果喪失政治依靠乃至投資管道，可能會有人對進一步的經濟開放採取保留態度。本文也發現，對台灣的情感依附，會降低投票給馬英九的機率。台灣認同是一種情感，但經濟利益不是。在財

富分配日漸惡化的狀況下，前者是否會逐漸替換後者，可以進一步研究。

　　本文還產生兩個值得深究的理論議題。第一個問題，在於問卷調查的理論意義。「國家認同」和「統獨選擇」的選項，是由問卷設計而來，回答同一個選項的受訪者，可能各有不同的理由。如果能在答案與理由間找到連繫，將可拓展理論深度。相較於其他資料庫，社變調查的長處在於提供許多相關問題，讓我們可以檢視它們與依變數的關係。例如，受訪者表達不同層次的族群情感或對兩岸經濟利益的看法，都可以幫助我們瞭解同一個問卷答案之下的不同動機。如果要對國家認同進行更深層分析，這些問題扮演重要角色。第二個議題，在於模型與理論的關係。很多學者爲求模型的簡潔，都將重要的社會分歧想像成單維的歐式空間（one-dimensional Euclidean space），並得出重要的推論，例如「中位選民定理」。[27] 但我們發現，即使把趨近模型修正爲方向模型，仍然不能完全解釋台灣的案例。更根本的問題是，單維的空間模型是否簡化了重要的現實，甚至誤導經驗假設的提出？以台灣而言，的確可以將統獨想像成單維的空間，而既有研究也時常這樣假定。但這種設定，在某些情況下並不能充分解釋選舉結果。本文發現，要處理條件式的偏好，的確要修改單維空間的假定。但這也表示，我們只要瞭解條件從何而來，就可以分析條件如何驅動偏好的改變。政治的能動性，正在於創造條件，改變趨勢，而掌握這種能動性的理論意義，將能幫助我們拓展理論的廣度。

---

[27] 中位選民定理只能用在單維空間，其他假定包括候選人數爲 2，其目標在於極大化選票，且所有選民皆投票等。

附錄一　訊息結構與統獨選擇的賽局模型

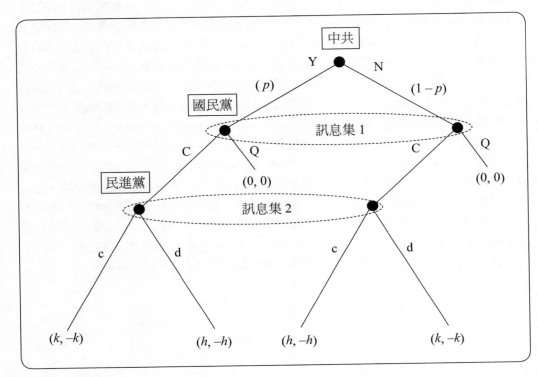

圖 16.1　賽局展開式

行動者爲國民黨與民進黨。

中共爲行動者所不能掌握的狀態（Nature），有兩種可能的態度：

Y：中共默認「一個中國，各自表述」的「各自表述」，其機率爲 p。

N：中共否認「一個中國，各自表述」的「各自表述」，其機率爲 $1-p$。

行動者策略：

C：國民黨主張「一中各表」。

Q：國民黨避談「一中各表」。

c：國民黨若採 C，民進黨以避談台獨來回應。

d：國民黨若採 C，民進黨以主張台獨來回應。

報酬分配方式：

1. 國民黨若採取 Q 行動則賽局結束，兩黨報酬皆爲 0。

2. 總統選舉爲零和競爭，故國民黨與民進黨之報酬總和爲 0。

3. $h > 0$，中共爲 Y，國民黨採 C，民進黨在中共爲 Y 時採 d（或中共爲 N 時採 c）之後，「一中獨派」轉向國民黨的淨比例。[28]

4. $k < 0$，中共爲 N，國民黨採 C，民進黨在中共爲 N 時採 d（或中共爲 Y 時採 c）之後，「一中獨派」轉向國民黨的淨比例。

以上用 h 和 k 來描繪「一中獨派」在各種策略組合下轉向國民黨的淨比例。如果要分析詳細的互動細節，需要加入其他變數，但只要這些變數與 h 和 k 有關，以下推論仍能成立。

訊息結構一：國民黨和民進黨都瞭解中共的眞實意圖

這個結構表示訊息是完善（perfect）的，兩黨都知道 $p = 1$ 或 $p = 0$，所以圖 1 中的訊息集 1 和訊息集 2 都不存在。由於 $h > 0 > k$，以逆向歸納法（backward induction）可知以下兩種均衡的存在：

若 $p = 1$，則（Q●, c●）爲子賽局均衡，其中 ● 表示其他訊息集之行動。

若 $p = 0$，則（Q●, d●）爲子賽局均衡，其中 ● 表示其他訊息集之行動。

訊息結構二：國民黨和民進黨都不瞭解中共的眞實意圖

此時兩黨都無法得知中共的眞實意圖，所以訊息集 1 和訊息集 2 都存在。以下是此賽局的正規式（normal form）：

表 16.5　賽局正規式

	c	d
C	$kp + h(1-p), -kp - h(1-p)$	$hp + k(1-p), -hp - k(1-p)$
Q	0, 0	0, 0

純粹策略（pure strategy，簡稱純策）的均衡如下：

1. 當 $p > 0.5$，$-kp - h(1-p) > -hp - k(1-p)$，對民進黨而言 $EU_c > EU_d$，對國民黨而言

---

[28] 此處使用「淨比例」，是因爲訊息的改變可能造成多方的選票流動，所以 h 代表的是扣除各方變動之後的結果。

$kp + h(1 - p) < 0$。

2. 當 $p < 0.5$，$-kp - h(1 - p) < -hp - k(1 - p)$，對民進黨而言 $EU_c < EU_d$，對國民黨而言 $hp + k(1 - p) < 0$。

在兩種情況下皆為 $EU_Q > EU_C$，所以國民黨都會採取 Q 策略，最後的純策均衡就是（Q, c）或（Q, d）。[29]

訊息結構三：國民黨瞭解中共的真實意圖，但民進黨不瞭解

依此假設，只有訊息集 2 存在，訊息集 1 是不存在的。國民黨有 CC、CQ、QC 和 QQ 等四個策略，民進黨有 c 和 d 兩個策略。因民進黨可以觀察到國民黨的行動，所以能透過貝氏法則（Bayes rule）來更新其對於中共態度的信念。令 Pr(Y) 時國民黨採取 C 行動的機率為 q，Pr(N) 時國民黨採取 C 行動的機率為 q'。

因為民進黨在國民黨之後行動，故可計算其期待效用：

1. 若 $EU_c > EU_d$，則 $\dfrac{-kqp - hq'(1 - p)}{qp + q'(1 - p)} > \dfrac{-hqp - kq'(1 - p)}{qp + q'(1 - p)} \rightarrow q/q' > (1 - p)/p$。此時國民黨的策略是 QC，但民進黨可以透過國民黨的行動，充分推知其節點屬於 Y 或 N。在 N 的情況下，民進黨不可能採取 c 策略。所以 $EU_c > EU_d$ 不可能是均衡。

2. 若 $EU_d > EU_c \rightarrow q/q' < (1 - p)/p$。基於同樣的理由，民進黨不可能在 Y 的情況下採取 d 策略。所以 $EU_d > EU_c$ 不可能是均衡。

3. 此外，(CQ, c) 和 (QC, d) 也不可能是純策均衡。所以，兩黨必對剩下的四種情況採取混策均衡。令 Pr(CC) = x，Pr(c) = y。在混策均衡下，$EU_{CC} = EU_{QQ}$ 在 $y^* = 0.5$ 時成立；$EU_c = EU_d$ 在 x^* 在 $h = -k$ 時成立。根據此一混策均衡，$EU_c = EU_d$，符合前述分析，$h = -k$ 則有無限多組解。對操作議程的國民黨而言，可以選擇對其最有利的 h，達到此一混策均衡。

比較以上分析可知，國民黨在三種訊息結構下都不會採行「一中各表」的純策，以免民進黨將統獨問題帶入選舉。在訊息結構一、二之下，國民黨的純策均衡是避談「一中各表」。在訊息結構三下，雙方都未採行純策，在混策均衡中，國民黨會主張「九二共識」並取得高報酬；民進黨很難在 c 和 d 中取捨，且其報酬與國民黨報酬有零和關係。換言之，國民黨可以選擇對其最有利的策略組合，使其所論述的「九二共識」很接近「一中各表」，但又無須擔心中共將「一中各表」詮釋為「一個中國」。此一賽局驗證了本文的關鍵假設：具有訊息優勢的政黨，能夠吸引條件式統獨偏好者的選票，並創造對其有利的選舉結果。

---

[29] 若 $p = 0.5$，還存在混策（mixed strategy）的均衡。

附錄二　將「國家認同」與「統獨選擇」視為類別變數

表 16.6　對「是否在 2012 年總統選舉投票給馬英九」的分析

自變數	模型一				模型二			
	B	S.E.	Sig.	Exp(B)	B	S.E.	Sig.	Exp(B)
常數	.998	.665	.133	2.712	1.034	.666	.120	2.813
性別	.245	.110	.025	1.278	.252	.110	.022	1.286
出生年	-.027	.004	.000	.974	-.027	.004	.000	.974
教育年數	.057	.017	.001	1.059	.056	.017	.001	1.058
省籍	.968	.190	.000	2.633	.963	.190	.000	2.619
偏向泛藍政黨	1.070	.178	.000	2.914	1.064	.178	.000	2.898
是台灣人	-1.181	.620	.057	.307	-1.191	.621	.055	.304
是台灣人也是中國人	-.199	.621	.749	.820	-.222	.622	.722	.801
偏獨	-.895	.159	.000	.409	-.893	.156	.000	.410
永遠維持現狀	-.313	.145	.030	.731	-.448	.150	.003	.639
一中獨派	.571	.254	.025	1.771				
一中非統					.528	.153	.001	1.696
-2 Log likelihood	2015.927				2009.096			
Cox and Snell R-square	.169				.17			
觀察值	1,787				1,787			

資料來源：第六期第四次的「台灣社會變遷調查」。

說明：1. 對虛擬變數的說明如下。在「國家認同」部分，設定「是台灣人」與「是台灣人也是中國人」兩類，並以「是中國人」為參照組；在「統獨選擇」部分，分為「偏獨」（包括「儘快宣布獨立」與「維持現狀，以後走向獨立」）與「永遠維持現狀」兩類，並以「偏統」（包括「儘快與中國大陸統一」與「維持現狀，以後走向統一」）為參照組。

　　　2.「是台灣人也是中國人」的比例很低，可能是此一變數不顯著的原因之一。若以「是純粹之台灣人」為虛擬變數，並將「是台灣人也是中國人」與「是中國人」合併為參照組，則「是純粹之台灣人」的相關性會比較高。但在不同的模型中，「一中獨派」和「一中非統」的顯著性並沒有明顯變化。

附錄三　變數及其編碼方式

變數	題目	編碼方式
性別	性別	1 = 男性 0 = 女性
出生年	請問您是什麼時候出生的（以身分證上的為主）？民國__年（民國前以負數表示，填答範圍 -8 至 -1，1 至 83）	依所填年度
教育年數	從國小一年級算起，請問您總共受幾年的學校教育？__年（填答範圍 1 至 30。31 年或以上請填 31）	依所填年數
省籍	父親省籍	1 = 外省人（含金門、馬祖、大陸） 0 = 非外省人
祖國是台灣	如果有人問您的祖國是哪裡，請問您會怎麼回答？	1 = 台灣 0 = 不是台灣（包括中華民國、中國、中華人民共和國）
同胞要有感情	有人認為下列條件重要，也有人認為不重要。請問您覺得它們重不重要？ 在感情上認同我們的國家	1 = 非常重要 2 = 有點重要 3 = 不怎麼重要 4 = 一點也不重要
民主政治光榮感	我國民主政治運作的情形，請問您感到光榮或是不光榮？	1 = 非常光榮 2 = 有些光榮 3 = 不太光榮 4 = 一點也不光榮
國家認同	目前社會上有人會說自己是台灣人，有人會說自己是中國人，也有人會說兩者都是。請問您認為自己是台灣人、中國人還是兩者都是？	1 = 台灣人 2 = 兩者都是 3 = 中國人
是台灣人	目前社會上有人會說自己是台灣人，有人會說自己是中國人，也有人會說兩者都是。請問您認為自己是台灣人、中國人還是兩者都是？	1 = 是台灣人 0 = 是中國人；是台灣人也是中國人
是台灣人也是中國人	目前社會上有人會說自己是台灣人，有人會說自己是中國人，也有人會說兩者都是。請問您認為自己是台灣人、中國人還是兩者都是？	1 = 是台灣人也是中國人 0 = 是台灣人，是中國人

（接下頁）

變數	題目	編碼方式
統獨選擇	對於未來台灣與中國大陸的關係，有人主張台灣獨立，也有人主張與大陸統一。請問您比較贊成哪一種主張？	1 = 儘快宣布獨立 2 = 維持現狀，以後走向獨立 3 = 永遠維持現狀 4 = 維持現狀，以後走向統一 5 = 儘快與中國大陸統一
偏獨	對於未來台灣與中國大陸的關係，有人主張台灣獨立，也有人主張與大陸統一。請問您比較贊成哪一種主張？	1 = 儘快宣布獨立；維持現狀，以後走向獨立 0 = 永遠維持現狀；維持現狀，以後走向統一；儘快與中國大陸統一
永遠維持現狀	對於未來台灣與中國大陸的關係，有人主張台灣獨立，也有人主張與大陸統一，請問您比較贊成哪一種主張？	1 = 永遠維持現狀 0 = 儘快宣布獨立；維持現狀，以後走向獨立；維持現狀，以後走向統一；儘快與中國大陸統一
條件式統一	是否同意如果大陸在經濟、社會、政治方面的發展跟台灣差不多，兩岸就應該統一？	1 = 非常同意；同意 0 = 不同意；非常不同意
一中獨派	偏獨選民 × 條件式統一	1 = 兩者都是 0 = 非兩者都是
一中非統	非統選民 × 條件式統一	1 = 兩者都是 0 = 非兩者都是
中國大陸市場是重要的	請問大陸的市場對您或您的家人所服務的公司，有沒有很重要？	1 = 有 0 = 沒有
若為經濟發展則支持統一	有人說，為了台灣的經濟發展，必要時可以和中國大陸統一，請問您同不同意這種說法？	1 = 非常同意 2 = 同意 3 = 既不同意也不反對 4 = 不同意 5 = 非常不同意
去中國大陸次數	請問您去過中國大陸（不含港澳）嗎？一共去了幾次？	1 = 0-3 次 2 = 4-6 次 3 = 7-9 次 4 = 10-19 次 5 = 20 次或以上
偏向泛藍政黨	請問您是否偏向泛藍政黨？	1 = 國民黨，親民黨，新黨，其他泛藍政黨 0 = 其他

（接下頁）

變數	題目	編碼方式
投票給馬英九	2012 年的總統選舉，請問您有沒有投票給馬英九？	1 = 有 0 = 沒有
區域立委投票	去年 1 月的區域立委選舉是否投票給國民黨籍候選人？	1 = 是 0 = 否

資料來源：第六期第四次的「台灣社會變遷調查」。

說明：編碼為 1 或 0 者為虛擬變數，0 為參照組，其餘變數為連續變數。

第十七章

Taiwan's Referendum Act and the Stability of the Status Quo[*]

On March 20, 2004, the citizens of Taiwan cast their ballots in the island's first-ever national referendum.[1] Although the ballots were predominantly in favor of the posed questions, the referendum was annulled because the number of voters who cast a referendum ballot failed to reach the required 50% mark.[2] The international community has watched this referendum with great concern for fear that it would destabilize the status quo across the Taiwan Strait. This referendum originated in the "defensive clause"(防禦性條款) of Taiwan's Referendum Act (公投法), which authorizes the President to initiate a referendum when the nation's sovereignty is confronted by external forces. This clause, however, is just one of the sixty-four articles of the law. An interesting question is thus whether the defensive referendum reflects the general nature of the Referendum Act or is an exceptional design. The answer to this question would lead to different expectations of Taiwan's referendum system.

The purpose of this article is to give a detailed account of Taiwan's Referendum Act in order to answer some important questions: How can a referendum be initiated in Taiwan?

[*] Reproduced from [Lin, Jih-wen. "Taiwan's Referendum Act and the Stability of the Status Quo." *Issues & Studies* 40(2): 119-153, 2004], with kind permission of the Institute of International Relations, National Chengchi University.

The earliest draft of this article was presented at the Institute of Political Science, Academia Sinica. The author expresses his appreciation for the helpful comments of the seminar's participants as well as those provided by two anonymous reviewers.

[1] For a comprehensive description of the process of this referendum and its relationship with the presidential poll, see Kaufmann and Goldmann (2004).

[2] About 45% of the eligible electors participated in this referendum. The first question was: "If the PRC refuses both to withdraw the missiles it has targeted at Taiwan and to openly renounce the use of force against us, would you agree that the government should acquire more advanced anti-missile weapons to strengthen Taiwan's self-defense capabilities?" The second question was: "Would you agree that our government should engage in negotiations with the PRC about the establishment of a 'peace and stability' framework for cross-Strait interactions in order to build consensus and for the welfare of the peoples on both sides?" About 88 percent and 85% of the eligible voters answered "yes" for the first and second questions, respectively. See *Taipei Times*, January 17 and March 21, 2004.

Who actually makes the decision? Will the referendum become a constant component of Taiwan's political process? If so, will the system undermine the status quo of the referendum issue? This article tackles these problems from a theoretical perspective, and begins by introducing the rise of Taiwan's referendum movement and then clarifying the definition of the referendum system. The next section then discusses how various types of referendum designs can produce opposite outcomes and allow room for strategic manipulation. The analysis will then apply these findings to reassess the Referendum Act passed by Taiwan's Legislative Yuan (立法院), and measure the possibility for the status quo to be changed by the referendum under different circumstances. The approach of this article is institutional. Unlike many countries where the constitution (or convention) is the only legal foundation of referendum, Taiwan defines the system's details by a law. The Taiwan case will show how the constitutional legitimacy of referenda can sometimes be affected by an article in a law.

I. Referendum and Decision-Making

As an essential institution of direct democracy,[3] the referendum has been used to scotch the abuse of legislative powers (Cronin, 1989). The legitimacy of this institution grows, therefore, when the distrust of representative democracy broadens. The referendum calls on the citizens to vote on issues, and is thought to be more reasonable than electoral democracy.[4] Although having been used most frequently in the advanced democracies—Switzerland in particular, the popularity of the referendum has spread quickly in nascent political entities.[5] This mechanism has been widely employed by both the post-communist states to legitimize new constitutions (Auer and Bützer, 2001) and by European states in deciding whether or not to seek European Union (EU) membership (Butler and Ranney, 1997).[6] Despite the growing

---

[3]　Direct democracy requires other conditions, however. See Lijphart (1984: 30-32).

[4]　A cross-regional econometric analysis shows that direct democracy via initiative and referendum systematically and sizably raises self-reported individual well-being. See Frey (2000: 918-939).

[5]　Since 1793, nearly one thousand referenda have taken place, and only four advanced democracies have not held a nationwide referendum—interestingly, the United States is one of them. See Anderson (1999).

[6]　An empirical study verifies that, in the case of European integration, referendum use has led to more supportive voters than when this system was excluded. See Christin and Hug (2002).

popularity of referendum use, however, some critics are questioning whether this system, by presenting only one issue at a time, can really reflect the voice of the people (Clark, 1998: 434). There are also studies showing the complicated roles of the use of referenda in policymaking, particularly the ability to change the status quo.[7]

Taiwan has been experiencing a similar debate on the merits of the referendum. In the past two decades, the island has witnessed a quick advancement of democratization.[8] The process has been accompanied by intensive constitutional reforms in which instituting a referendum system was placed on the agenda right from the beginning. This goal was never fulfilled, however.[9] The Democratic Progressive Party (DPP, 民主進步黨)—Taiwan's major opposition party before May 2000—has taken the establishment of this system as its major platform. Supposedly able to give the power back to the people, the referendum system is also popular among social activists. Having gained control over the presidency in May 2000, the DPP was still a minority legislative party and thus failed to halt the building of a fourth nuclear power plant; the referendum thus became an appealing alternative. In the Legislative Yuan (Taiwan's parliament), DPP legislators attempted to present their proposals for a Referendum Act, but could not overcome the roadblocks set up by the Kuomintang (KMT, 國民黨) and the People First Party (PFP, 親民黨). When President Chen Shui-bian (陳水扁), who is also the DPP's Chairman, emphasized again in mid-2003 his intention to set the referendum movement into action, the attitude of opposition parties on the referendum issue suddenly made a U-turn. The major cause was the presidential election of 2004. The race was such a close one that each camp sough to woo voters from the other side.[10] The opposition's engagement of the referendum issue was certainly a counter-strike to Chen's campaign strategy.

To compete with the DPP's Referendum Act proposal, the opposition parties—or the pan-Blue (泛藍) camp—on July 3, 2003 announced their principles on the issue. Later on, the

---

[7] See, for example, Clarke, Kornberg, and Stewart (2004). The issue of the status quo will be addressed later.

[8] For the history of Taiwan's democratization, see Tien (1997).

[9] For details, see Lin (2002).

[10] Most opinion polls released by Taiwan's mass media indicated that the gap between the KMT's presidential candidate Lien Chan (連戰) and the DPP's Chen Shui-bian was within about 5%, a difference which might have been due to sampling error.

pan-Blue camp even conceded that they would not exclude the use of the referendum on such topics as constitutional revision and the changing of national symbols.[11] The contest soon put the issue on the legislative agenda, prompting the Legislative Yuan to pass the Referendum Act on November 27, 2003. According to this new law, Taiwan's citizens can now initiate new laws or vote on both existing laws and constitutional amendments.[12] This outcome is not a surprise, however, because the pan-Blue parties have long claimed themselves to be the followers of Sun Yat-sen (孫逸仙). The Constitution of the Republic of China─the official national name professed by the government of Taiwan─stipulates that the people shall have the right of election, recall, initiative, and referendum (Article 17). The referendum had never been used in Taiwan because the Constitution also stipulates that the exercise of the rights of initiative and referendum shall be prescribed by law (Article 136). This stipulation also explains why, unlike the cases of many other democracies, Taiwan's referendum process must be regulated by law.

The Referendum Act specifies in detail the process through which initiative and referendum can be initiated and put to vote. As will be discussed later, the law opens only one channel for the executive branch to initiate a referendum.[13] In Article 17, the law stipulates that the President is entitled to launch a referendum when the nation's sovereignty is being threatened. Since Chen Shui-bian has long been promoting referendum use and that his first term was to end in a few months, this article became his only instrument to realize that goal. For several reasons, Chen's announcement that he would put Article 17─or what is usually called the "defensive referendum"─into practice, soon put the international community on alert. First, President Chen comes from an independence-leaning party. In addition to social movements, nation-building is another source of Taiwan's referendum movement. The DPP party platform clearly states the relationship between Taiwan independence and the use of referendum. Most notably, the platform states that "the proposal to establish the Republic of

---

[11] There have been other proposals of the Referendum Act, the most noticeable being the version recommended by DPP legislator Trong Chai (蔡同榮), a major advocator of the referendum movement. I will address the difference among the competing versions of the law in a later section of this paper.

[12] *Taipei Times*, November 28, 2003.

[13] According to Taiwan's current constitutional system, the executive branch is composed of the Presidential Office (總統府) and the Executive Yuan (行政院). I will use these names to designate the initiators of Taiwan's referendum.

Taiwan and a new constitution should be decided by the people in Taiwan via referendum" and that "any change of Taiwan's independent status quo should be decided by the people of Taiwan via referendum."[14] Second, President Chen himself has reiterated in his campaign speeches that he hopes to establish a new constitution via the referendum mechanism in 2006. To those who already suspect Chen's intentions, the abolishment of the Constitution of the Republic of China will substantiate Taiwan's independence furthermore; to them, the defensive referendum use marks the first step toward reaching this end. For the same reason, the referendum becomes an indispensable component of Taiwan's national identity politics, which gives the DPP a powerful leverage to mobilize its supporters in the presidential election.

In this context, the defensive referendum was regarded by the government of the People's Republic of China (PRC) as preparation for independence.[15] Even U.S. President George W. Bush sternly rebuked Chen's attempt to initiate the defensive referendum when meeting with Wen Jiabao (溫家寶), the PRC Premier, on December 9, 2003.[16] Some analysts hold that the United States is justified in discouraging Chen's referendum attempt "as part of [Washington's] broader effort to establish the conditions underlying its political and military support to the island" (Swaine, 2004: 39). The leaders of Japan, France, and the European Union followed the lead of the United States, criticizing President Chen's decision with unprecedented harshness. The reason that these democracies sought to repudiate Taiwan's right to hold a referendum can be explained by their reluctance to anger the PRC, a country that is playing an ever important role in international political economy. Many countries fear that Taiwan's referendum will provoke the PRC to take preemptive action, thereby forcing the United States and her allies to recast their global strategies.

More specifically, the international community is concerned that Taiwan's referendum will destabilize the status quo across the Taiwan Strait. The DPP's platform has already made

---

[14] See http://www.dpp.org.tw.

[15] According to Kong Quan (孔泉), the spokesman of the PRC's Foreign Ministry, "some people on Taiwan are using the false pretext of democracy to hold what is in reality a Taiwan independence referendum damaging the stable situation in the Taiwan Strait." See *New York Times*, March 19, 2004.

[16] Bush's remark was more than lip service to the PRC delegate. Chen Chien-jen (程建人), head of the Taipei Economic and Cultural Representative Office in Washington, returned to Taipei to issue a warning to the government about the deteriorating relationship between Taiwan and the United States after President Chen announced the referendum proposal. See *Taipei Times,* December 30, 2003.

clear that any change of Taiwan's sovereignty status would involve the use of a referendum. Initiating the referendum, therefore, becomes a necessary step in the pursuit of Taiwan's independence. If the result or the practice of the referendum violates the "one-China" principle, the PRC would be forced to respond. Thus the international community has felt the need to discourage Taiwan's referendum effort in order to maintain a tight relationship with the PRC.

This apprehension is based on the assumption that the use of the referendum would provoke a change in the status quo. Here a distinction must be made regarding the meaning of the term "status quo." While many believe that the holding of a referendum is enough to modulate the existing process of decision-making—which can itself be regarded as a status quo, this article focuses on whether the result of a referendum can change the content of a policy or decision. For example, Taiwan's defensive referendum, a threat to Beijing no matter what the outcome may be, could very well likely change the *political* status quo across the Strait. By contrast, this article is concerned with the *policy* status quo: if the success or failure of the defensive referendum would influence either the procurement of Taiwan's anti-missile devices or the government's stance in cross-Strait negotiations. In fact, if referendum use fails to influence policymaking or legislation on a regular basis, its function as a political institution will be diminished. The purpose of this article is to show that, as an instrument of decision-making, the impact of the referendum mechanism is determined by its institutional designs. Thus, the subsequent sections will challenge the intuition that referendum is prone to upset the status quo.

This argument is made by first introducing the various types of referendum systems and then demonstrating their different status quo-changing capabilities. The focus of the analysis will be on how the referendum interacts with other parts of the decision-making process and whether referenda can be manipulated. This discussion will then facilitate our understanding of Taiwan's referendum system and its likely future impacts. The analysis will help us answer some important questions: How unique is the "defensive referendum"? Will other referendum designs undermine the status quo for other issues as well? Who will benefit from referendum use? Can referendum achieve what representative democracy cannot? Most important, will referendum transform the nature of Taiwan's democracy?

II. Referendum: Definition and Types

Defined most loosely, referendum refers to the people's decision on public affairs. This definition is far from sufficient, however, being unable to capture the nature of the system. In fact, the term "referendum" is conceptually confusing. A plebiscite, for example, indicates almost the same process, except that it is usually applied to public decisions regarding sovereignty change or constitution-making. Since the plebiscite is utilized to legitimatize the political system itself, the decision process involves only the citizens. Nonetheless, the plebiscite (defined in this way) is rarely used in this day and age. The referendum, in contrast, involves the participation of both the legislature and executive, through which many subtypes of the system are created.

In a narrower sense, the referendum designates the institution where the people reject or approve laws passed by the legislature.[17] In Switzerland, where the term was first coined, referendum means "to report to"; in the United States, it describes the process where delegates make laws *ad referendum* to the voters. In sum, a referendum is a public vote on resolutions, laws, or constitutional amendments adopted by the legislature.[18] Sometimes the policies of the executive organizations can also become the object of a referendum. The initiator of a referendum is most frequently the legislature or the executive, and less so the people. A referendum initiated by the people is called the popular referendum (or petition referendum). In some cases, the referendum is advisory and imposes no legal constraints. The referendum can be mandatory or optional, depending on whether such a procedure is required by law.

In contrast, an initiative is a public motion on legislative measures, constitutional amendments, or government policies. The initiative is most frequently brought into being by the people, yet the decision can be carried out in various ways. An initiative is indirect if the motion is sent either to the legislature or the executive in order to be realized, and is returned to the people only if the legislature or the executive fails to realize the object. A direct initiative is submitted straight to the people for a decision, and is procedurally similar

---

[17] A referendum is rejective if the target is a recently passed law, and is abrogative if the target is an existing law. In both cases, the people enjoy only veto power and cannot amend the proposal.

[18] In the United States, citizens cannot cast votes on national issues, although constitutional amendments must be approved by referendum in all states except Delaware. See Cronin (1989: 2-3).

to direct legislation. Under some situations, the people's initiative can call for a referendum on the motion—a process which is called the referendum initiative.

The above are all standard definitions. They are, however, too general to specify the difference among various referendum systems, let alone the impacts on decision-making.[19] Scholars tend to classify referendum by whether they are mandatory, decisive, constitutionally pre-regulated, or whether the people's role is active.[20] Keeping these categories in mind, we still need to highlight the interplay among the citizens, the parliament, and the executive—for this is the key dynamic that shapes the outcomes of the referendum.

To facilitate analysis, I first define some key terms. To begin with, the "agenda-setter" is the one—be it the people, the executive, or the legislature—who writes the motion to be put to vote. When a referendum on a passed law is launched, the agenda-setter is naturally the legislature (the agenda-setter varies in other cases). Second, an "initiator" is one who calls the referendum or initiative into action. While an initiative is usually begun by the people, a referendum could—depending on law—be initiated by the people, the executive, or the legislature. Third, an "approver" is the body that makes the final decision on an initiative or referendum. The decision will have legal effect if the initiative or referendum is decisive. For all systems of initiative and referendum, the final approver must be the people, although in an indirect initiative the legislature or the executive can preempt the decision by passing a similar resolution. Meanwhile, we should consider the legal outcomes of these systems by specifying the decision-making process. Table 17.1 summarizes the players in various referendum institutions. Finally, to be consistent with the popular understanding of the term "referendum," the following analysis will apply in its broader sense—i.e., it includes all kinds of referenda on public affairs. I will use "reconsideration" to indicate the people's decision on an existing law or policy. A successful initiative suggests that the people are able to create a new law or a new policy by their motion. If a reconsideration is passed, the legal effect of the object—a law or a policy—is temporarily annulled.[21]

---

[19] For a referendum typology and the concrete experiences of its implementation, see Gallagher and Uleri (1996).

[20] For example, see Suksi (1993: 1-14).

[21] In Chinese, initiative, reconsideration, and referendum are respectively translated as *chuangzhi* (創制), *fujue* (複決), and *gongmin toupiao* (公民投票).

Table 17.1 The Players in the Initiative and Reconsideration Institutions

Institution	Agenda-setter	Initiator	Approver	Result (if passed)
Direct initiative	The people**	The people	The people	New law or policy
Indirect initiative	The people	The people	Legislature or executive (if they accept the motion)	New law or policy
Legislature-initiated initiative	Legislature	Legislature	The people	New law or policy
Executive-initiated initiative	Executive	Executive	The people	New law or policy
Popular reconsideration* (referendum)	The people	The people	The people	Annulment of law or policy
Legislature-initiated reconsideration	Legislature	Legislature	The people	Annulment of law or policy
Executive-initiated reconsideration	Executive	Executive	The people	Annulment of law or policy

Notes:

* In reconsideration, the agenda is confined by the content of its object (i.e., a law or a policy previously made by the legislature or the executive).

** Political parties and interest groups may play important roles in mobilizing the people to participate in referenda.

III. Referendum and the Status Quo: Theories of Veto-Playing and Agenda Manipulation

To proponents, the greatest merit of the referendum system is the direct involvement of the people in the decision-making process; to opponents, greater participation does not ensure better quality. This section will address this debate by focusing on two issues. The first is how the various types of referendum affect the stability of the status quo. The second is whether the referendum is less manipulable than a parliamentary vote. The commonsense view would suggest that citizen participation should make the reform of the status quo easier, with the decision-making process thus being done in a more transparent manner. In the following, I will utilize two social science theories to cast doubt on this intuition. The derived findings will also enable us to decipher the political implications of Taiwan's Referendum Act.

First, according to the veto player theory, the increase of veto players (those whose agreement is required to alter the status quo) or the broadening of their policy distance will enhance the stability of the status quo (Tsebelis, 2002). A veto player can be a collective one if a quorum is required for this body to pass a resolution. For example, the legislature usually applies certain majority rules to initiate a referendum. In some countries, a referendum is invalid if either the number of endorsers or the turnout rate fails to reach the thresholds required by law. In this article, *the status quo is defined as the situation before a decision is being made*. Each constitutional system will depict its own decision-making process. The status quo can be modified by a legislative act or a government policy. If the decision-making process includes a referendum, several outcomes can follow (see Figure 17.1). The initiators of an initiative can create a law or set up a new policy if this process is successful and decisive. If an initiative is claimed invalid, the situation will return to the status quo. A reconsideration must be based on the existence of a law or a policy. Suppose a law or a policy has been adopted to change the status quo. If a reconsideration is passed under this situation, the law or the policy is temporarily annulled and the status quo is restored. If this referendum fails, the status quo will be changed by the law or the policy.[22]

Second, agenda-setting plays a very important role in the strategic manipulation of decision-making.[23] In some sense, a referendum is always vulnerable to manipulation, no matter what the procedure is. Even direct initiative or direct legislation can be the result of elite manipulation. Here, however, we must distinguish between two kinds of manipulation tactics. The first is generally related to issues that are divisive; the alternatives are by nature

---

[22] In some cases, the status quo is set to change by itself, and a law or a policy is made to prevent this change. In this case, we should define the status quo as the situation that exists right before the law or the policy is to be adopted.

[23] For how the initiative and referendum have been manipulated to serve political ends, see Walker (2003).

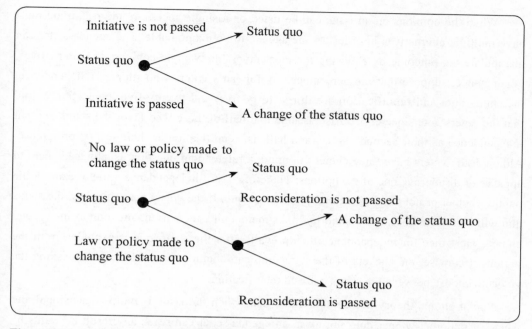

Figure 17.1 Initiative, Reconsideration, and the Fate of the Status Quo

binary, and the voters are "mobilized" to support or reject one of them.[24] The second type involves issues that are complicated and have multiple options. Since a referendum presents one issue at a time and asks the voters to approve or disapprove a statement, the room for manipulation is great in this circumstance. This is the "manipulation" defined by social choice theory: it occurs if an individual or a minority group can change the outcome of collective choice through agenda-setting or strategic voting (Ordeshook, 1986: 86). Agenda-setting refers to the decisions on which issue to present and what binary choices to select. To distinguish this concept from what is intuitively understood as "manipulation," we will use the term "agenda manipulation" to depict this situation. Social choice theory has shown that agenda manipulation can lead to contradictory outcomes. To see how this is so, consider the following cases.

---

[24] For how conservatives in the United States have used direct legislation to propagate their political ideas, see Cronin (1989: 3).

When the opinions on an issue can be listed on a single spectrum, the resolution must have multiple alternatives in order for the agenda to be manipulable. The agenda-setter can manipulate the outcome by choosing the most favorable ways to compare the alternatives. For instance, suppose that the percentages of Taiwan's voters who support independence, the status quo, and reunification are thirty, forty-five, and twenty-five, respectively (and that the voters vote sincerely).[25] Also assume that half of those who favor the status quo put independence as their second choice, and half list reunification as their second preference. Although the voters have three choices in mind, a referendum question usually asks them to approve or disapprove one of the options. Therefore, a pro-independence initiator can ask the public whether or not they want to keep the status quo. If the voters vote sincerely, the status quo will be rejected because a majority ranks maintaining the current situation as the second choice. The voice for independence then prevails after the status quo is excluded from the options. Likewise, the backers of the status quo can obtain a favorable result by asking the voters to choose between the status quo and reunification.

Social choice theory has demonstrated that, when the issue is multi-dimensional and when a Condorcet winner does not exist, an agenda-setter can reach any result he wants by asking the voters to decide on issues where he enjoys majority support.[26] When the voters' preferences are nonseparable (i.e., the total utility of an individual is not a summation of his utilities on each issue dimension), even a Condorcet winner is not guaranteed to win.[27] In the legislature, this problem could be solved by either issue-by-issue voting or vote-trading, but such mechanisms cannot be used in a referendum, making the system more manipulable than a legislative decision (Lacy and Niou, 2000b).

It is beyond the scope of any model to predict the type of a referendum issue. One thing, however, is certain: an initiator who belongs to a minority party or group can benefit from a referendum only if the issue belongs to the second type. Meanwhile, he must be able to

---

[25] This distribution in fact quite closely resembles Taiwan's actual situation.

[26] An alternative is a Condorcet winner if it beats all other options in pairwise comparisons using majority rule. See McKelvey (1976: 472-480).

[27] A good example of nonseparable preference is the sovereignty dilemma that many people in Taiwan face. To this group, Taiwan independence is an acceptable choice only if it incurs no military threat. Thus we cannot determine their attitudes on the independence issue without considering the security condition.

estimate carefully the latent outcomes of a complicated issue. To accomplish this, the initiator must have sufficient political knowledge and be capable of strategic thinking. Assuming that most people do not have these talents, it follows that the likelihood of agenda manipulation goes up as the threshold to initiate a referendum goes down. In the most extreme case, the agenda-setter and the initiator can be just one person (the president, for instance), who thus basically has a free hand when designing the agenda, and can single-handedly launch a referendum. In the other extreme, agenda manipulation is difficult, if not impossible, when the initiation of a referendum has to be endorsed by the general public.[28] The writer of the motion can of course be a strategic calculator, but the probability for a manipulated referendum question to be put on the agenda is reduced when the required number of endorsers increases.

These two theories can then be used to classify the referendum systems by their potential to change the status quo and their agenda manipulability. The findings are summarized in Table 17.2. According to Table 17.1, the people, the legislature, and the executive are all collective veto players in particular settings. A referendum is ineffective if the designated actors refuse to initiate or approve the petition, whereby the status quo is made unchangeable. It follows from Figure 17.1 that the institution most conducive to status quo change is the direct initiative; this is because the people constitute the only veto player in this institution.[29] The agenda-setter, the initiator, and the approver can be composed of different subsets of the people, but no other organization is involved. If we assume that the agenda-setter and the initiator are subsets of the approver, viewing people as a single veto player is still reasonable; this is because the agenda-setter, the initiator, and the approver in a direct initiative must take the same stance. With an indirect initiative, the legislature or the executive could redefine the objective of the initiative and adjust the shift of the status quo. An initiative put forward by the legislature or the executive is also prone to change the status quo, but the motion is more likely to be rejected because two collective veto players are involved.

---

[28] Concerning Taiwan's legislative reform, electoral system and legislative size are the most critical issues. When the reformists attempted to collect public signatures to protest the Legislative Yuan's inaction, the issue of electoral system had to be dropped because it was too complicated for the ordinary citizen. Even the question of legislative size has been simplified into: "Do you agree that the Legislative Yuan should be halved?"

[29] In this case, the lower the petition threshold, the easier it is for the status quo to be modified. Similarly, the status quo is more likely to be kept if the law requires a higher turnout rate for the referendum to be valid.

Table 17.2　Referendum Institutions Classified by Status Quo-Changing Potential and Agenda Manipulability

Institution	Status quo-preserving?	Agenda manipulation?
Direct initiative	No. Initiative involves the change of the status quo.	Difficult. The cost for the public to reach a consensus on a manipulated agenda is high.
Indirect initiative	No. Initiative involves the change of the status quo (yet the legislature or the executive could modify the substance of the initiative).	Difficult. The cost for the public to reach a consensus on a manipulated agenda is high.
Legislature-initiated initiative	No. Initiative involves the change of the status quo (yet there are two veto players, so the chance for the initiative to fail becomes higher).	Relatively easy. The legislature can modify its resolution so that the public finds it hard to reject.
Executive-initiated initiative	No. Initiative involves the change of the status quo (yet there are two veto players, so the chance for the initiative to fail becomes higher).	Easy. The cost for the executive to launch a manipulated initiative is small.
Popular reconsideration (referendum)	Yes. Reconsideration involves the annulment of law or policy.	Difficult. The cost for the public to reach a consensus on a manipulated agenda is high.
Legislature-initiated reconsideration	Yes. Reconsideration involves the annulment of law or policy (yet the increase of veto player reduces the chance for the motion to pass).	Relatively easy. The legislature can modify its resolution so that the public find it hard to reject.
Executive-initiated reconsideration	Yes. Reconsideration involves the annulment of law or policy (yet the increase of veto player reduces the chance for the motion to pass).	Easy. The cost for the executive to launch a manipulated reconsideration is small.

As illustrated in Figure 17.1, the effect of the reconsideration is the opposite of that of the initiative. If successful, a reconsideration can restore the situation before a law or a policy is made. The chance for a reconsideration to be adopted is again affected by the number of veto players. In a popular referendum, only one collective veto player is involved in reconsidering the object. The likelihood for the status quo to be reinstated under this institution is thus high. The reconsideration initiated by the legislature or the executive displays a similar status quo-preserving force, but the increase in the number of veto players reduces the probability for the motion to pass, in which case the status quo cannot be brought back.

In terms of the likelihood of agenda manipulation, several factors must be considered. Manipulation is difficult if a referendum is mandatory and no agenda selection is allowed. Otherwise, two variables are most crucial: the nature of the issue and the composition of the veto players. At the theoretical level, only the latter condition can be discussed. We have already seen how the likelihood for manipulation to occur is increased by the elitist inclination of the agenda-setting group. Ranking the groups according to the costs they face to manipulate the agenda from lowest to highest, we have: the executive, the legislature, and the people. For the legislature and the people, the cost goes up as the threshold to pass a resolution rises. When initiating a referendum, the executive could reframe the questions in order to generate maximum support. Similarly, a legislature asking the people to reconsider a policy will select the wording that maximizes the distrust toward the executive.

To summarize the foregoing analysis, we can identify four major types of referendum systems. Referendum systems in the first type are built to remove the status quo and are hard to manipulate. Examples are the direct and indirect initiative systems. Both systems are designed to create new laws or policies through the people's own volition. These features make the initiative the ideal type of referendum. Institutions in the second type also challenge the status quo, but are easier to manipulate. Examples are the initiatives put forward by the legislature or the executive. Most likely, this type is employed when the legislative and executive branches are controlled by different parties. The legislature can initiate a policy that the executive branch refuses to implement, and the executive branch can ask the people to reconsider the law passed by the legislature. The third type includes referendum systems that are status quo-preserving and difficult to manipulate. The popular referendum is the only example we have studied. This system provides a channel for popular desire to halt the abuse of executive or legislative powers. The last type contains status quo-preserving systems that are manipulable. The reconsideration systems promoted by the executive and the legislature are the typical cases; again, they give the executive and the legislature more instruments with which to discipline each other.

Some referendum systems require that both the number of initiators and the turnout rate exceed particular thresholds. Since all referendum systems at some stage ask the people to cast their ballots, these requirements affect not only the ability of the citizens to enjoy veto power, but also the likelihood for the agenda to be manipulable. A referendum is more likely to be valid if the requirement on minimum turnout rate is low. Several scenarios are possible. First, suppose the supporters of the referendum questions have a higher chance to participate. A low threshold would then facilitate the passing of a manipulated agenda in this referendum. The effect on the status quo may vary by institution, however. A low threshold may reduce the cost to modify the status quo in an initiative, but the status quo also becomes more stable if the system is a reconsideration. Second, the reverse may occur if more people intend to reject the referendum question. By the same token, a referendum is more likely to be invalid if the minimum turnout rate is set high. In this case, attempts to change the status quo through an initiative have a higher probability to fail, regardless of the distribution of opinions. For the same reason, the people will find it harder to preserve the status quo by reconsidering the related law or policy. We can thus derive an interesting observation: for a referendum to become an effective political instrument, the system must relax its requirement on the minimum threshold of participation.

The foregoing framework not only provides a guideline to examine Taiwan's referendum system, but also brings to the fore the theoretical contribution of this study. In particular, it shows that referendum includes various institutions that exert diverse outcomes, so that the normative judgment of referendum should also specify the details of the institution. The referendum adds a new veto player only if it asks the people to reconsider a passed law or policy. With a popular initiative, the people can bypass the executive or legislative body and single-handedly establish a law—that is, the institution makes the people the only collective veto player.[30] As for the role of referendum in agenda-setting, the above analysis suggests that the petition threshold matters. The next section will use the Taiwanese case to demonstrate how the institutional particulars affect the outcomes of a referendum system. This analysis will demonstrate how a phrase in a law can determine the fate of a referendum.

---

[30] For how referendum use adds to the number of veto players, see Tsebelis (2002: ch5).

IV. Reassessing Taiwan's Referendum Act

On the basis of the above analysis, how do we evaluate Taiwan's Referendum Act? What kind of referendum system does Taiwan have? What political outcomes could result from this law? The following will first elucidate the vital parts of this Act and compare the major differences between the proposals submitted by the Executive Yuan and the opposition camp. The discussion will then fit the Act into the theoretical framework.

The first fact to be emphasized is that, when the Referendum Act was passed by Taiwan's Legislative Yuan, the anti-government seats out-numbered the pro-government ones, but neither camp controlled a clear majority. The pan-Blue alliance, composed of sixty-six KMT and forty-four PFP legislators, was three seats away from a majority.[31] Gaining support from independent legislators has thus been crucial to the pan-Blue camp. Meanwhile, the upcoming presidential election forced the opposition parties to be wary about the attitudes of the undecided voters. On the whole, the Legislative Yuan was leaning toward the opposition, although room for bargaining still existed.

The Referendum Act specifies early on (Article 2) the matters for which a referendum may be held. At the national level, a referendum can be held to reconfirm a law, to create a legislative principle, to initiate or confirm a major policy, or to confirm the constitutional amendments.[32] Except for constitutional amendments, the referendum can be held at the local level on parallel matters. Budgets, taxation, investments, wages, and personnel matters cannot be proposed as referendum issues. This article not only details the allowable issues for the referendum, but also considers the institution's legal results. The initiative can only be applied to legislative principles or major policies, whereas reconsideration is permitted on laws, major policies, or constitutional amendments.

According to Article 31, a passed initiative on legislative principles should be adopted by related executive organizations into bills and sent to the legislature for review. For established referenda on important policies, the related authorities should take the necessary measures

---

[31] The New Party (新黨) also participates in the pan-Blue alliance, but the party has only one legislator in the Legislative Yuan.

[32] The Chinese version of the Referendum Act can be found on the website of the Legislative Yuan, http://www.ly.gov.tw.

to realize the content. Most importantly, for a law that is approved to be reconsidered, the original law should be annulled three days after the public announcement of the passage of the ballot. Article 20 stipulates that, if the legislative branch realizes the purpose of an initiative or reconsideration on a law before it is publicly announced, the referendum should be halted. Taken together, these articles suggest that Taiwan's voters are not given the right to launch a direct initiative, but must rely on the executive or legislative organization to realize the goals of the initiative.

The Referendum Act specifically excludes the executive branch from using any means to initiate the referendum (Article13), yet gives this right to the Legislative Yuan (Article16). The Act leaves only two options to the people: the indirect initiative and the popular referendum. Nevertheless, the likelihood for the public to improve the status quo through these means is affected by the legal requirements on turnout rate and petition threshold. The Act sets up three thresholds for a referendum to be valid. First, the number of initiators of a referendum proposal must reach 0.5% of the total number of electors in the most recent presidential election (Article 10). Second, the number of endorsers of a referendum must reach 5% of the total number of electors in the most recent presidential election (Article 12).[33] Lastly, a referendum is passed only if more than half of the qualified voters in the related constituency cast a ballot and more than half of the valid ballots are in support of the proposed measure (Article 30).[34]

Compared with some democracies that have long used the referendum as a decision-making tool, Taiwan's 50% turnout requirement may seem stringent.[35] However, there are

---

[33] Using the 2000 presidential election as a base, the 5% threshold would be 773,130 electors.

[34] An interesting question is why the Act sets up such a high passage threshold. Since the versions proposed by the Executive Yuan and the pan-Blue alliance both installed a 50% threshold, the most possible answer is the concern of legitimacy. Both camps might be concerned that a referendum that fails to attract half of the voters to participate would be criticized as illegitimate. Another possibility is that, when less than half of the people turnout to vote, the number of people who approve the question might be outnumbered by those who vote against it.

[35] These countries usually set the threshold on the number of initiators rather than the minimum turnout rate that makes a referendum valid. The Swiss Constitution stipulates that popular initiative for total or partial revision of the Federal Constitution must be proposed by at least 100,000 people, and that the referendum on Federal Statutes requires the proposal of 50,000 people. Given the size of the Swiss population, these thresholds amount to less than 2% of the eligible voters. Some states in the United States require that the signatures to start a referendum exceed certain thresholds, which could be higher

also other countries that adopt strict regulations for referendum passage.[36] In any case, the turnout requirement creates a dilemma for Taiwan's referendum initiators. Many people will have no incentive to cast a ballot if the answer is obvious, which undermines the likelihood that the referendum will become valid. If the referendum involves sensitive or divisive issues (e.g., Taiwan's sovereignty), many people will be discouraged to vote in order to prevent political turmoil. Again, the result could be the nullification of the referendum. Concerning the initiation of a referendum, the 5% endorsement threshold could be hard to reach if no political party or interest group is organizing the petitioners. To exceed the 50% turnout rate, the issue has to be simplified, if not politicized.

Additionally, the Referendum Act has set other obstacles for the initiators to surpass. According to the Act, the Executive Yuan shall establish a Review Commission (公民投票審議委員會) both to verify whether a matter is qualified for national referendum and to determine the similarity between referendum proposals (Article 34). This Commission is beyond the control of the executive branch, however. According to Article 31, the Review Commission is composed of twenty-one commissioners, each appointed for a three-year term, and the composition of the Commission must reflect the proportion of seats held by political parties in the Legislative Yuan. To deliberate a referendum proposal, more than half of the commissioners must be present. A proposal on the agenda will be passed when more than half of the commissioners present vote in favor of the proposal (Article 36). As such, the political parties can veto a referendum by either not showing up or by voting negatively for the proposal. This article has made the Review Commission another veto power, one composed of party elite.

In terms of the role of the executive branch in the referendum, the Referendum Act has provided the President with a peculiar power. According to Article 17, the President may, via

---

[36] than that in Taiwan, but do not specify the minimum turnout rate to validate a referendum. The French Constitution defines the procedure to initiate a referendum but imposes no legal threshold requirement. Italy is another European country where the referendum is frequently used. However, the system has been weakened by the 50% turnout quorum. See http://www.iri-europe.org. The United Kingdom uses simple majority rule to determine if a referendum question is accepted, but under some circumstances stipulates a more restrictive requirement. For example, the Scotland Act of 1978 stated that, for the Act to be repealed, more than 40% of the electorates must vote "yes" in the referendum. That explains why the Scotland referendum of 1979, which saw a turnout rate of 64% and an approval rate of 52%, was invalidated. See Balsom (1996).

a resolution of the Executive Yuan general meeting, propose as a referendum to the citizens a matter crucial to national security; the one stipulation is that this can only be done when the nation is being confronted by an external force that could be regarded as a threat to national sovereignty. This is the so-called "defensive referendum,"[37] and it is the only channel through which the executive branch can initiate a referendum. Given that the Referendum Act was passed only four months before the presidential election, and that its application requires no legislative approval, the President was provided with a strong motivation to put the defensive referendum into practice. Indeed, President Chen announced on January 16, 2004 that he intended to initiate a defensive referendum to be held jointly with the March 20 presidential election.

Nonetheless, there were objections to the President's proposal of this defensive referendum. First, some questioned the legality of holding the referendum and the presidential election on the same day. Article 17 stipulates that Article 24—which itself requires that the referendum and the national election may be held on the same day—shall not apply to the referendum described in Article 17. The vagueness of this stipulation caused a controversy concerning the true negation of Article 24. Second, some constitutional scholars argued that Article 17 is equivalent to the President's emergency power, so that legislative approval should still be needed.[38] Similarly, some cited Article 2 to contend that the Review Commission should determine whether an issue is a qualified referendum issue. Finally, some doubted the existence of the precondition of Article 17. The PRC's military threat does exist, they believe, but the emergency is neither present nor immediate. To Chen's opponents, the referendum was simply a ploy by the President to boost his popularity. The strategy of the pan-Blue camp was thus to deny the legality of this referendum.

Overshadowed by both these technical difficulties and the pan-Blue camp's boycott, the defensive referendum was nevertheless carried out on March 20, 2004. From a theoretical point of view, this verifies the previous conjectures about the executive-initiated referendum. The fact that no public deliberation was held regarding the forming of the referendum questions suggests that the issue was highly manipulable. Most likely, the President

---

[37] This is the term used by the media to characterize Article 17. Since this article says nothing about reconfirming a law, the term could cause some misunderstanding. Another peculiar feature is that this "referendum" does not necessarily aim at resolving a dispute.

[38] *Lianhe bao* (*United Daily News*), February 12, 2004.

meticulously endeavored to refine the questions so that they would not likely be found objectionable by either the international community (the United States in particular) or the electors in Taiwan. In any case, the questions would have been designed to garner the support of undecided voters.[39]

As for whether the holding of this referendum foretells a change in the status quo, there are many different interpretations. First, one should note that, as an institution, the defensive referendum is equivalent to an executive-initiated reconsideration on government policies. The executive branch can, of course, decide whether to procure the anti-missile devices or to engage in cross-Strait negotiation, but the legitimacy of implementing these contentious policies will be strengthened if they are accepted by the people in a referendum. When speaking to his supporters on the evening of March 20, 2004, Chen Shui-bian remarked that "the referendum has shown the majority will of the Taiwanese people" and the government will follow this opinion to implement policies related to national defense and cross-Strait negotiation.[40] This statement signifies that, although the referendum failed to reach the required turnout rate, the predominance of the approval votes still shows strong support for the questions posed by President Chen. Second, the referendum itself is something new. To the PRC, the establishment of the referendum system presents another outlet for the use of pro-independence elements. Third, given that the defensive referendum was annulled, we are unable to evaluate the substantial impact of the referendum on cross-Strait relations. President Chen's intention was, however, to claim that the defensive referendum—even if it had passed—was meant to maintain the status quo across the Taiwan Strait and had nothing to do with independence.[41] The reaction of the international community toward the defensive referendum implies, however, that worry about its impact still exists.

What about other articles in the Referendum Act? For instance, can The Legislative Yuan initiate a referendum that challenges the status quo in other issue areas? Table 17.3 describes the referendum institutions articulated in Taiwan's Referendum Act. The Act gives the legislature and the people extensive rights to propose both initiatives and reconsiderations on law and policy, but excludes the executive organizations from launching any referenda.

---

[39] According to the DPP's calculation, voting in favor of these referendum questions would likely increase the likelihood that one would also vote for Chen Shui-bian.

[40] *Lianhe bao* (*United Daily News*), March 21, 2004.

[41] *Taipei Times*, December 5, 2003.

Table 17.3 Taiwan's Referendum Institutions as Stipulated in the Referendum Act

Institution	Agenda-setter	Initiator	Approver	Result (if passed)
Reconsideration on legislative principle (2, 31)	The people	The people	The people	Annulment of law
Initiative on legislative principle (2, 31)	The people	The people	The people (legislature)	New law
Initiative on important policy (2, 31)	The people	The people	The people (executive)	New policy
Reconsideration on important policy (2, 31)	The people	The people	The people	Annulment of policy
Initiative on important policy (2, 16, 31)	Legislature	Legislature	The people	New policy
Reconsideration on important policy (2, 16, 31)	Legislature	Legislature	The people	Annulment of policy
Reconsideration on constitutional amendment (2, 31)	The people	The people	The people	Annulment of the constitutional amendment
Defensive referendum (17)	President	President	The people	Change of policy

Note: The numbers in parentheses designate the articles that result in the institution.

Still, the initiator of a referendum faces several obstacles. One such problem relates to the matter that a referendum is allowed to raise. We have already specified above the items that are explicitly included or excluded as a referendum matter. Although issues related to national identity and symbols are neither included nor excluded, putting them as referendum questions would be highly controversial.[42] If constitutional revisions related to sovereignty issues or national symbols are passed by the legislature, there would also be strong demands to reconsider the amendments. One can thus conclude that, except for the "defensive clause," the current Referendum Act opens little room for national identity issues to be raised.

Next, consider the status quo-changing capability and agenda manipulability of other referendum designs. The likelihood that an indirect initiative can be manipulated is low, given the high endorsement threshold. Among the institutions stipulated in the Act, the indirect initiative has the best chance to modify the status quo. In contrast, a popular referendum can at best disapprove a passed law or policy, and is therefore status quo-preserving. Agenda manipulation is difficult under the popular referendum, because the Act sets a high threshold of initiation. Although the legislature-initiated reconsideration is manipulable, the consequence is status quo-protecting. Since the Referendum Act does not make the legislature-initiated reconsideration on law mandatory, the most likely initiator is the minority party dissatisfied with the adopted resolution. The majority will have to accept the referendum proposal if the issue could weaken the legitimacy of the legislature. Even so, there is still the opportunity for the legislative majority to reframe the issue so that it can be passed more easily. The Referendum Act also allows the legislature to activate an initiative or a reconsideration on important policies. This could be used as a legislative tool to force the executive to modify its policy output.

For all cases, the 50% turnout rate requirement and the supervision of the Review Commission both reduce the likelihood for a valid referendum and this in turn reduces the likelihood that the status quo will be changed. Although the Act adds more veto powers into Taiwan's political system, the high passage threshold mitigates their forces. Similarly, for the designs that facilitate the change of the status quo, the same threshold impedes their ability to do so. This last outcome is what occurred during Taiwan's first referendum.

---

[42] Compared with the drafts proposed by the pan-Blue alliance and the Executive Yuan, the vagueness of Article 2 reflects a compromise that provides both sides with some benefit. Although small, the possibility for matters related to national identity or sovereignty to be raised is still maintained. For the pan-Blue alliance, the absence of these matters from the Act could be interpreted as if they were excluded.

V. The Contending Versions of the Referendum Act

Taiwan's Referendum Act was doubtlessly the product of power struggle. The passage of the law was prompted by a closely contested presidential election, but the stringent regulations also reflected the conservative atmosphere in the Legislative Yuan. This fact can be brought to the fore by a comparison of the various versions of the Referendum Act. From this comparison, we can also foresee the possible ways that the Referendum Act might be amended should the seats of the Legislative Yuan be reallocated in the year-end legislative election of 2004.

When the Legislative Yuan proceeded to the last reading of the Referendum Act, only the versions proposed by the Executive Yuan and the pan-Blue alliance were left on the table.[43] These two versions differ in regard to the petition and endorsement thresholds, the initiation procedure, the Review Commission, the defensive clause, the schedule of voting, and the subject matter coverable by referenda. Piecing these items together, these two drafts would have led to quite different laws that would have exerted diverse impacts on the stability of the status quo.

To begin with, the two political camps held disparate views on the permissible matters of referendum. While the pan-Blue version attempted to exclude issues concerning constitution-making and the change of national symbols (such as the official name, the anthem, the flag, and the territorial boundaries)—all issues mentioned by the Executive Yuan, the pan-Blue camp sought to prohibit the referendum from applying to national security, diplomacy, military, budget, taxation, wages, and personnel matters. The Executive Yuan's draft excluded only budget, taxation, wages, and personnel affairs. Moreover, the pan-Blue alliance sought to assign the initiative and reconsideration procedures to different matters, while the Executive Yuan made no such distinction. The passed version maintains the pan-Blue's specification of the applicable procedures, but keeps the national identity issues in an undefined position. Most interestingly, the Executive Yuan's proposal of the "defensive referendum," a measure that could enhance the President's power, was accepted by the pan-Blue alliance.[44]

---

[43] For the various versions of the Referendum Act and the general deliberation process, see *Lifayuan gongbao* [立法院公報] (2003: 118-296).

[44] Why did the pan-Blue camp give up their original insistence on the exclusion of national identity

The second dispute concerned the decision-making process of the referendum. While the Executive Yuan's version allowed the President to initiate a referendum via resolution by the Executive Yuan general meeting, the pan-Blue camp attempted to exclude both the executive branch and the Legislative Yuan as the initiator, even though the adopted Referendum Act keeps the initiative power of the Legislative Yuan (Article 16). Furthermore, the Legislative Yuan is allowed to launch a referendum concerning the principle of important policies, a stipulation regarded by the Executive Yuan as a violation of the separation of powers. A related controversy regards the reviewing of referenda. While the pan-Blue camp intended to institute a Referendum Review Commission, the Executive Yuan saw this design as a disenfranchisement of the people's rights. The pan-Blue camp prevailed again on this item.

The threshold of petition was another point of disagreement. For referenda at the national level, the Executive Yuan proposed that the number of initiators must reach or exceed 0.5% of the total number of electors in the most recent presidential election. The pan-Blue alliance raised the number to 1% of the number of electors. As for the number of endorsers, the Executive Yuan suggested 2% for the referendum on matters related to legislative principle and important policy, and 5% for those on constitutional amendment. The pan-Blue alliance proposed 5% for all national-level referenda. The adopted article is a compromise between the two versions: 0.5% for the initiators and 5% for the endorsers.

Finally, regarding the issue of time period, the Executive Yuan proposed that the Central Election Commission (中央選舉委員會) should carry out the referendum within twenty-eight days to six months after its announcement, and that the referendum could be held concurrently with national elections. The pan-Blue camp was more specific. According to their proposal, the referendum should be carried out within three months after its announcement, and could be held simultaneously with the Legislative Yuan or county council elections. Their version prohibited, however, the referendum to be carried out together with the elections for the President or county councilors. The adopted Referendum Act stipulates that the referendum may be held on the same day as a national election (Article 24), but excludes the defensive referendum from this article's coverage.

---

matters? Most observers agreed that the presidential election was the crucial factor. The pan-Blue camp has simply been hesitant to take a strong stance on national identity issues in order not to hurt their chances for election. For a similar reason, the "defensive referendum" was included in the passed Act.

With the current Referendum Act, no initiative on constitutional amendment (let alone constitution-making) is allowed.[45] Any referendum that attempts to make adjustments to the national symbols would encounter the objection of the Review Commission. Had the Executive Yuan's version been approved, Taiwan would have had quite a different referendum system.[46] For instance, in line with the Executive Yuan's proposal, the citizens or the executive branch would have had a chance to initiate a constitutional amendment and hold the referendum jointly with the presidential election. A similar process could even have been used to adjust the symbols of national identity. In such a case, the status quo—particularly that concerning cross-Strait relations—would become more unpredictable. For this above situation to occur, seat distribution in the Legislative Yuan would have to be changed so that the pan-Green (泛綠) camp could garner the legislative majority to amend the Referendum Act according to the DPP government's proposal.[47]

VI. Conclusion

From the starting point of Taiwan's recently held "defensive referendum," this paper has studied the impact that various initiative and reconsideration institutions have on decision-making. The resulting findings could shed light on the debate concerning the value and necessity of the referendum mechanism.[48] To the advocates of this system, its greatest merit is the involvement of the people in the decision-making process. Giving power back to the citizens can also help break legislative deadlock or prevent special interests from usurping

---

[45] If the current Referendum Act remains unchanged, the only way for President Chen to establish a new constitution by 2006 is to launch a plebiscite that puts the legitimacy of the whole state at stake.

[46] The Executive Yuan attempted an item veto on the Referendum Act, contending that the law deprives the people of their basic rights and allows the legislature to dominate the decision-making process. Since the override from the Legislative Yuan requires only a majority vote, the veto was unsuccessful. See *Lianhe bao* (*United Daily News*), November 28, 2003.

[47] On April 21, 2004, the Ministry of the Interior (內政部) drafted a revision of the Referendum Act. This proposal covers the adjustment of thresholds, the initiative of constitutional revision, the removal of the Legislative Yuan's right to launch a referendum, and the abolishment of the Referendum Review Commission. This revised Act will unlikely be passed by the current Legislative Yuan, which is still dominated by the pan-Blue alliance. For details, see *Lianhe bao* (*United Daily News*), April 22, 2004.

[48] For a review of the pros and cons of referendum, see Cronin (1989: 182-184).

the privileges of the public. Most important, this "participationist" view sees referendum as a necessary mechanism to deepen democratization. To the critics of referendum, however, this institution is costly and does not necessarily produce the optimal social outcome.[49] Worse, referenda actually downgrade the quality of policymaking by fostering populist tendencies.

The picture illustrated in this paper is more complicated than either view would expect. I began by defining the existence of the status quo and investigated how it could be affected by the different systems of initiative and reconsideration. A simple analysis of the decision-making process suggests that the major institutions of referendum are all different. Generally speaking, the initiative institutions are more favorable to changing the status quo, and are less likely to be manipulated by the agenda-setter. The initiative, which involves the people's direct participation, could be difficult to initiate, however. The executive and the legislature can sometimes initiate a referendum that affects the stability of the status quo, but the process is highly manipulable and the purpose is usually a political one. In sum, no general assessment can be given in regard to the various institutions of referendum.

As for whether the referendum can improve the quality of democracy, the key variables are the nature of the status quo and the design of the institution. A status quo that results from legislative gridlock can be broken by an executive-initiated referendum or a direct initiative.[50] Nonetheless, a status quo that is already socially optimal can be shifted by an executive-initiated referendum or a direct initiative to favor special interests. Likewise, special interests could be protected by a status quo-preserving referendum system. The participationist argument holds only if a referendum is able to create a socially optimal outcome, whereas the representative government cannot. Presumably, this institution is the direct initiative. Even this outcome is contingent, however, upon many intervening factors, such as the distribution of the citizens' preferences.

We can use this framework to address the political consequences of Taiwan's Referendum Act. There exist four possible scenarios constituted by two variables: whether the status quo is socially optimal or not, and whether the referendum will destabilize the status

---

[49] In welfare economics, the social optimum denotes the state where no changes can improve the collective benefit of the decision-makers. Thus defined, the social optimum is different from the maximization of individual preference.

[50] A good example is how New Zealand fulfilled her electoral reform through referendum. See Vowles (1995).

quo. The most desirable situations are for the referendum to reduce the cost of replacing an unwanted status quo, or to increase the cost of removing a desirable status quo. The less fortunate situations are for the referendum to increase the cost of abandoning an undesirable status quo, or to decrease the cost of upsetting an optimal status quo. Whether the status quo is viewed as advantageous, of course, often varies by actor. Competing political interests may thus have different preferences toward referendum design. That explains why the pan-Blue alliance would set up a restrictive Referendum Act, and why Chen Shui-bian would hasten to activate the defensive referendum.[51] Most likely, the power struggle to amend Taiwan's Referendum Act will be carried on, and cross-Strait relations will continue to face an unpredictable future.

---

[51] Interestingly, the pan-Blue alliance changed their attitude after Chen Shui-bian won the 2004 presidential election. After the election, the pan-Blue alliance suggested the initiation of referenda on whether to establish a committee that would investigate the assassination attempt on Chen Shui-bian and whether to review documents related to the implementation of the national security mechanism on voting day eve. In response, Chen Shui-bian proposed that two referenda could be held regarding whether or not to halve the number of seats in the Legislative Yuan and whether to establish a committee to review the KMT's party assets. These referenda are apparently indirect initiatives. See *Taipei Times*, April 12, 2004.

第十八章

學者之路[*]

壹、何謂「學者」？

　　許多人常將「學者」和「專家」這兩個詞連用，甚至混用。這兩個稱謂，雖然相關卻不盡相同。我們每個人，對某些事務的瞭解一定超越他人，例如自己每天的生活路徑。但這樣的人不會被當成專家，因為這些事務太狹隘，而且沒有任何專業性。專家所專精的事務，得有一定的專業性和技術性，從所謂「生態保育專家」、「網路安全專家」這些稱謂，可以一窺端倪。但是，對於鑽研某些知識領域的人，例如物理學、經濟學或人類學，我們常稱為學者而非專家。原因似乎是因為這些知識的廣博性，超越了特定的專門技術。

　　區別學者和專家，是要界定學者的特性，進而探索學者的養成。如果說專家在於精，學者在於廣，能夠又精又廣不是很好？但這並不是容易的事。知識的產生有一定的步驟，通常得將資料（例如數據或文字）再製為可被解讀的資訊，再將資訊彙整為具有系統性的知識。這個過程環環相扣，沒有前面的功夫就沒有後面的結果。所以，學者應該都是某方面的專家，但專家卻不一定是學者。舉個例子，某人喜歡觀察選舉，蒐集了歷來所有候選人的個人資料和得票記錄，但可能並不被當成研究選舉的學者，因為此人可能一直是業餘的選舉資料蒐集專家。反之，研究選舉的學者，要能夠將這些資訊轉化成知識。這樣看來，學者既可滿足「精深」的要件，又能符合「廣博」的期待。本文關切的對象，應該就是這群人。

　　要如何才能又專又廣？我們的社會，存在一些明星級的學者，他們可能是某些專業領域的專家，但知名度遠超過專業領域；對社會大眾而言，他們是教育者（所以尊稱其為老師），是解決各項疑難雜症的專家，是關懷公共事務的知識份子。不過，明星級的學者畢竟是少數，他們的意見是否正確，一般人也欠缺判斷的能力。大多數的學術從業人員，正辛苦地參與一場沒有止境的馬拉松競賽。對參賽者而言，「學術裁判」的哨聲，比觀眾的掌聲重要多了，與其成為明星學者，存活更重要。所以，這篇短文的第一

---

[*]　本文曾刊登於《人文與社會科學簡訊》，第 11 卷第 4 期（2010 年 9 月），頁 21-26。感謝科技部人文及社會科學研究發展司《人文與社會科學簡訊》同意轉載。

個目的，是要想像這個問題的答案：不論路途多坎坷，哪些人可以跑得比較穩、比較久、比較遠？找到答案後，我們再回來看台灣的學術體制，到底是在培育學者，還是在訓練專家？而年輕學者要如何自處？這是本文的第二個目的。

貳、學術這一行

　　學者一定得受過專業訓練，但這只是必要條件。重點在於是否能讓其他學者分享研究成果。台灣的學術界有個潛藏的規則，不但影響研究經費的分配，更和聘用、升等乃至學術地位密切相關。這個規則很簡單：越能在聲譽卓著的期刊（或出版社）發表研究成果，「排序」就越前面，也越能獲得各項獎勵。這個道理大家都知道，問題是如何做到。關鍵既然在出版，我們就先想像一下，什麼樣的論文最容易通過審查？我們先以期刊爲模擬範本，再將結論延伸到其他的學術活動。盡責的論文審查人，大多會問以下的問題：

　　第一，論文是否問了好問題。好問題，除了要能引起好奇心，大多具有理論意涵。舉例來說，若有學者根據美國的實證資料，指出政黨認同會影響投票抉擇，問題重點就不是美國，而是政黨認同和投票行爲的關係。而問題的好壞，是由論文對話的對象來判別的。如果大多數的讀者都相信理論 A 是對的，而某論文卻認爲 A 是錯的或 B 才是對的，這個提問就很重要。因此要表達這樣的立場，論文作者就必須瞭解讀者是誰，以及讀者對此一主題的看法，文獻檢討則是達到這個目的的必要手段。每檢討一篇文獻，都是與讀者的一段對話；文獻檢討的聽眾，不但是這些論文的讀者，更可能是這些論文的作者。透過文獻檢討，不但可以綜觀潛在讀者群的想法，更可探知相關研究的現況及可改進之處。

　　在台灣，「文獻檢討」幾乎已是學位論文乃至學術論文的必要元素，但是問題也不少。許多碩、博士論文大量引用其他碩、博士論文，某些學術論文也列出洋洋灑灑的參考文獻，卻不見得能達到文獻檢討的主要目的：找出既有研究的不足。而與其參考大量的學位論文或未經仔細閱讀的學術論文，不如將焦點放在最重要、最有代表性的論文，並直接與作者對話。越是重要的論文，就越能表達學界主流的看法（也越容易被其他人引用）；能夠超越這些論文，就等於直接與最大的讀者群對話。其實，只要瀏覽一下重要期刊論文的參考文獻，就可發現文獻的多寡不是重點，與重要文獻的對話才是。

　　第二，論文課題越吸引人，審查人越會仔細檢視論文的論證。所謂論證，依學科性質而有不同。社會科學的論證，應該立基於可被檢證的理論上。好的社會科學理論，除

了要清晰一致，還要有邏輯上的延展性，一方面能連結理論命題與經驗假設，另一方面得以推演出其他可被檢證的命題，以擴張理論的涵蓋面。這裡要特別強調，「檢證」並不必然指量化分析。某些個案研究，足以彰顯理論的現實意涵，或挑戰既存理論。舉例而言，政黨認同影響投票抉擇，已經是投票行為的基本理論。那麼如果政黨在同一選區提名好幾個候選人，選民又只能投一票，則依據是什麼？台灣的縣市議員選舉制度，正有這樣的特性。如果能透過訪談瞭解選民是如何投票的，就能與重要的理論對話。其他常見的驗證法，包括量化研究、比較研究等，而分析單位（或個案）數目雖有多有少，邏輯卻得一致。另外，好的理論既然具有延伸性，當然也可以推論出很多待證假設；不論這些假設所陳述的是變數的相關性還是單一事件，都可以透過經驗資料來驗證。理論越能產生可通過檢驗的命題，可信度也越高。

　　第三，論文是否能被接受，和資料的品質密切相關。前面提到，所有的研究都建立在資料的蒐集上，資料的品質因而影響研究的品質。資料的性質當然因學科、研究途徑而有別，但仍有一些共通的基本原則。首先是效度：資料是否能表達研究者想表達的概念？效度不但是科學研究的基本原則，也適用於人文學科。例如，針對某位法國思想家的研究，如果全都是靠翻譯（甚至二手資料），效度就會引起質疑。第二個原則是信度：別人是否可以蒐集到同樣的資料？不同的蒐集方式，是否導致資料的差異？某些重要的科學發現，其實是從複製別人的資料展開的。某些資料當然不易蒐集，但研究者至少要交代資料來源和資料蒐集的過程。第三，對社會科學而言，資料的蒐集應該具有理論依據。許多資料庫是獨立於理論存在的，但若根據理論來使用這些資料，將產生不少分析優勢。然而沒有理論就沒有假設，對資料的蒐集就欠缺方向感；反之，理論不但讓資料的蒐集具有方向感，還可擴展資料蒐集的範圍，進而增進理論的可信度。從研究的成本來看，耗費很大的功夫蒐集資料，卻無法回答任何理論問題，不是很可惜嗎？第四，對社會科學而言，資料是否有代表性、是否偏誤、是否有足夠的變異性，都是基本問題。其中最容易被忽視的，是資料的變異性。舉個例子，某研究如果要證明黨紀在立法過程的重要性，就不能只以記名投票為樣本，因為記名投票的記錄公開，違反黨紀付出的代價高，只用這筆記錄可能看不到違反黨紀的情況；同理可推，如果黨紀在非記名投票所發揮的效用低，對立法過程的影響小，不看（或看不到）非記名投票的記錄，就等於忽視了可能否證假設的資料。

　　以上的原則不僅適用於論文寫作，也可應用在研究計畫的撰寫上。撰寫研究計畫時，通常已進行了問題的釐清和文獻檢討，但尚未進行全面的資料蒐集，自然也還不能檢證理論，所以需要提出研究設計，並據此估算研究經費。如果研究計畫問了好問題，對相關研究進行了確實的檢討，並提出清楚而合理的研究設計，就比較能說服審查者。這樣的研究計畫，完成後也較容易轉換成論文。

參、審查體制下的學者

　　上面所談的是一般原則，也是理想狀況。如果能持守這些原則，論文被接受（或計畫通過）的可能性比較高，但是絕對不代表「世界是公平的」。許多知名學者都有一些慘痛的記憶，例如論文連審都沒審就被拒絕，而這篇論文可能就是日後讓他成名的著作。審查人的人數有限、所知有限，即使在最健全的論文（或計畫）審查制度下，都還是有機運的成分。我們不難想像，某些年輕學者花了很大功夫完成的論文卻一直被退稿，從此挫折感侵蝕研究動力，就算未造成惡性循環，也喪失對學術的熱情。沒有人喜歡收到退稿信，不少人甚至看了前兩句話就丟進垃圾桶。這樣太可惜了。

　　某些退稿信充滿偏見、誤解、甚至羞辱，但這還是機率問題，而且無法被改變。論文作者要如何降低被莫名退稿的機率？除了參考前述原則，一個簡單的方法是「大數法則」：越多人參與一篇論文的「前置作業」，論文最後被刊登的機會應該越大。所謂前置作業，是指一篇論文在被接受刊登之前的所有過程。越多相關學者曾對一篇論文提出意見，作者就越不會犯下明顯的錯誤；如果不同審稿人所給的意見大致相同，就表示學界對論文的評價差不多也是這樣。此時就算論文被拒絕，還是可以根據審查意見仔細的進行修改，並改投其他期刊。從機率上而言，給予論文意見的人（包括會議評論人、不同期刊的審查人）越多，論文就越不容易被挑出重大缺失，也就越有被刊登的機會。這也表示，如果論文作者不想按照審查意見來修改論文，只想改投其他期刊試試，那就真的要碰碰運氣了。

　　這個方法好不好用，要看「相關學者」的質量。學術論文，要對相關領域有所貢獻才能被接受。這也表示，論文對話的對象最好能集中於特定的專業讀者群。挑戰最基礎、最廣為人知的理論，雖然可能得到國際性的認可，但付出的代價也相當龐大。在「出版至上」的時代，很多人之所以選擇較為技術性或應用性的研究問題，原因就在於此。這樣一來，學者變成專家，又增加了學術審查的困難度。以台灣而言，學術分工和主要國家差不多，但學術人才的規模卻比大國小很多，即使某些領域已經高度國際化，仍然會面臨「專家」數目不足的情況。專業人才不足，論文卻又走向高度專業，常使期刊找不到足夠的論文審查人；縱使有人願意審，也不見得能提出有用的意見，如果論文被退稿，更容易引起審查不公的抱怨。此外，專業規模過小，也可能使匿名審查名存實亡，甚至產生小圈圈。

　　上述情況，可能隨著整體學術品質的提升或審查倫理的建立而逐漸改善。對學者而言，審查評鑑制度的合理化、公平化自然是值得高興的事。不過，審查評鑑體制一旦健全，學者就會更進一步地受制於此一體制，以「體制不公」來反抗體制將越來越困難。

關鍵問題仍是如何積極正面地面對審查體制。論文能被重要期刊或出版社接受固然可喜可賀，被拒絕也不用氣餒。只要論文眞的有貢獻，總會找到出路；如果論文被所有的期刊拒絕，大概就是有問題了。這也不打緊，許多知名學者，抽屜裡都有很多的半成品。重點是如何在錯誤中學習，從退稿信中累積經驗。

肆、結語

很多人以學術爲志業，是因爲這一行的自由度很高。的確，學者沒有老闆，沒有員工，沒有上下班時間；即使擔任學術行政工作或聘用助理，也是暫時的。思想和行動的自由，的確是學問的基礎。但是，學者也充分承擔了自由的代價。很多學者的生活，像是無聲的戰役：剛出道時必須躲過許多「退稿彈」才能存活，幾年以後還是要躲這些風險，但是也開始向別人扔退稿彈。有人開玩笑說，什麼是學者？就是自己不斷質疑人家，而人家也不斷質疑自己的一群人。在台灣和美國，都有系所將重要研究成果的出版高舉在入口處，像是彰顯戰功的勳章，也像是中學時代模擬考的排行榜。這樣的生活，使「傑出學者」走路有風，但也讓更多人備感壓力。學術工作是沒有什麼回頭路的，大多數人拿到博士學位都已經三十好幾，好不容易找到工作，幾年下來也已屆中年，如果還無法升等甚至續聘，眞會產生無路可退的危機。

學術工作是馬拉松賽跑，需要耐力和信心，而且大部分時間是一個人在跑。但我們很難向年輕學者說：「跑慢一點，以後路還很長。」我們的體制並沒給年輕學者太多時間。越來越多的機構立下一定的升等期限，但並不把和博士論文有關的研究列入考慮；以社會科學而言，像樣的期刊論文至少都有兩、三年的製成期。前扣後扣，難怪許多人選擇輕薄短小的量產路線。在這種時代氛圍下，很多人不再覺得自己是社會大眾所認定的學者，而比較像是專家——生產論文的專家。這篇短文有點像「教戰守則」。喜歡戰爭的人不多，但既然上了戰場，就得想辦法活下來。這份守則的要義，可以歸納成這句話：學者要先聽懂別人的話，然後根據別人的話說出別人沒說過，但很想聽下去的話。學術的路是孤獨的，但卻絕對不是獨角戲。

參考文獻

中文文獻

《立法院公報》，2003，〈公民投票法草案〉，92（54）：118-296。

《自由時報》，2014，〈綠委提修憲案，擴充憲法人權清單〉，12 月 17 日：http://news.ltn.com.tw/news/politics/breakingnews/1183641。檢索日期：2016 年 6 月 25 日。

TVBS，2012，〈TVBS 民意調查〉：http://www1.tvbs.com.tw/FILE_DB/PCH/201201/flece50d2gpdf。檢索日期：2015 年 3 月 24 日。

TVBS 聯合調查中心，2001，〈聯合政府民意調查〉：http://www.tvbs.com.tw/code/tvbsnews/poll/20010831/010831.asp。檢索日期：2009 年 3 月 10 日。

中央選舉委員會，2008，〈選舉資料庫〉，中央選舉委員會網站：http://www.cec.gov.tw。檢索日期：2008 年 2 月 9 日。

中央選舉委員會，2009，〈歷屆公職選舉資料——立法委員選舉〉：http://210.69.23.140/cec/cechead.asp。檢索日期：2009 年 2 月 26 日。

中共中央，1995，《中共中央關於進一步加強對台工作的通知》（中共中央文件），中發（1991）3 號。

中華民國行政院大陸委員會，2011，〈兩岸大事紀〉：http://www.mac.gov.tw/ct.asp?xItem=93745&ctNode=6501&mp=1。檢索日期：2015 年 4 月 18 日。

中華民國總統府，2005，〈中華民國憲法修條文〉：http://www.president.gov.tw/1_roc_intro/law_add_94.html。檢索日期：2009 年 3 月 10 日。

王玉玲，1996，《由兩岸關係探討台灣的統獨問題——以博奕理論析之》，台北：桂冠。

王貝林，2008，〈謝：考慮馬組閣兩黨共治〉，《自由時報》，1 月 18 日：http://www.libertytimes.com.tw/2008/new/jan/18/today-fo4.htm。檢索日期：2009 年 3 月 12 日。

王拓，1996，〈從經濟整合解決兩岸政治問題〉，《中國時報》，11 月 3 日，11 版。

王泰升，1997，《台灣法律史的建立》，台北：三民。

王健壯，2010，〈國會失控：馬英九的最大夢魘〉，《中國時報》，1 月 7 日，A18 版。

王塗發，1994，《獨立建國確保台灣經濟永續發展》，台北：民進黨中央黨部。

王業立，1995，〈單記非讓渡投票制的政治影響：我國民意代表選舉制度的探討〉，《選舉研究》2（1）：147-167。

王業立，2001a，〈總統直選與憲政運作〉，《理論與政策》15（3）：1-17。

王業立，2001b，《比較選舉制度》，第三版，台北：五南。

王業立，2011，《比較選舉制度》，第六版，台北：五南。

王鼎銘、郭銘峰、黃紀，2008，〈選制轉變過程下杜弗傑心理效應之檢視：從日本眾議院選制變革的經驗來觀察〉，《問題與研究》47（3）：1-28。

王鼎銘、蘇俊斌、黃紀、郭銘峰，2004，〈日本自民黨之選票穩定度研究：1993、1996及2000年眾議院選舉之定群追蹤〉，《選舉研究》11（2）：81-109。

王鳳生，1992，〈兩岸經貿互動關係與共同體之形成〉，《大陸情勢與兩岸關係學術研討會論文集》，高雄市：中山大學中山學術研究所。

包宗和，1993，《台海兩岸互動的理論與政策面向1950-1989》，第三版，台北：三民。

包宗和，1999，〈戰略三角角色轉變與類型變化分析——以美國和台海兩岸三角互動為例〉，包宗和、吳玉山（編），《爭辯中的兩岸關係理論》，台北：五南，頁337-364。

包宗和，2000，〈台海兩岸互動之和平機制〉，《遠景季刊》1（1）：1-15。

台灣省行政長官公署（編），1946，《台灣省五十一年來統計提要》，台北：台灣省行政長官公署統計室。

台灣總督府，1945，《台灣統治概要》，台北：台灣總督府。

司法院大法官，1993，〈大法官解釋〉：http://www.judicia1.gov.tw/constitutionalcourt/p03_01.asp?expno=328。檢索日期：2015年4月18日。

左原，1996，〈兩岸投資與貿易關聯性之分析〉，《中國大陸研究》39（5）：10-11。

民主進步黨，2015，〈民進黨提出現階段憲主張，蔡英文：修憲要看國家長遠利益〉，3月30日：http://www.dpp.org.tw/m/index_content.php?sn=7790。檢索日期：2016年7月3日。

田習如，2010，〈A攔發？政客「早收清單」大公開〉，《財訊》（343）：106-107。

行政院，2009，〈歷任院長〉：http://www.ey.gov.tw/lp.asp?ctNode=988&CtUnit=77&BaseDSD=14&mp=1。檢索日期：2009年3月2日。

行政院新聞局，1995，《對中共所謂「不排除使用武力犯台」之研析》，台北：行政院新聞局。

余克禮、朱顯龍（編），2001，《中國國民黨全書》，西安：陝西人民出版社。

余紀忠，1996，〈以「戒急用忍」與「慎謀致遠」作平行思考——在國家統一委員會第十一次全體委員會議上發言全文〉，《中國時報》，10月22日，2版。

吳乃德，1993，〈國家認同與政黨支持〉，《中央研究院民族學研究所集刊》74：33-61。

吳乃德，2002，〈認同衝突和政治信任：現階段台灣族群政治的核心難題〉，《台灣社會學》4：75-118。

吳乃德，2005，〈麵包與愛情：初探台灣民眾民族認同的變動〉，《台灣政治學刊》9（2）：5-39。

吳介民，1996，〈經濟躍進，政治僵持？後冷戰時兩岸關係的基調與變奏〉，《台灣政治學刊》（1）：211-253。

吳玉山，2000a，〈台灣總統大選對於兩岸關係產生的影響：選票極大化模式與戰略三角途徑〉，

《遠景季刊》1（3）：1-33。

吳玉山，2000b，〈非自願的樞紐：美國在華盛頓一台北一北京之間的地位〉，《政治科學論叢》12（7）：189-222。

吳安家，1996，《台海兩岸關係的回顧與前瞻》，台北：永業。

吳秀光，1995，〈理性決策途徑適用於兩岸關係的一些思辯〉，《中國大陸研究》38（3）：58-65。

吳秀光，1999，〈兩岸談判之結構分析：由博弈理論出發〉，包宗和、吳玉山（編），《爭辯中的兩岸關係理論》，台北：五南，頁119-152。

吳東野，1996a，〈「半總統制」之探討〉，《美歐月刊》11（1）：72-85。

吳東野，1996b，〈「半總統制」政府體系的理論與實際〉，《問題與研究》35（8）：37-49。

吳重禮，2000，〈美國「分立性政府」研究文獻之評析：兼論台灣地區政治發展型〉，《問題與研究》39（3）：75-101。

吳重禮，2001，〈分立政府：肇因、影響、改革〉，《中國行政評論》10（4）：1-22。

吳重禮、王宏忠，2003，〈我國選民「分立政府」心理認知與投票穩定度：以2000年總統選舉與2001年立法委員選舉爲例〉，《選舉研究》10（1）：81-114。

吳重禮、徐英豪、李世宏，2004，〈選民分立政府心理認知與投票行爲：以2002年北高市長暨議員選舉爲例〉，《政治科學論叢》21：75-116。

吳重禮、黃紀、張壹智，2003，〈台灣地區「分立政府」與「一致政府」之研究：以1986年至2001年地方政府府會關係爲例〉，《人文及社會科學集刊》15（1）：147-186。

吳重禮、楊樹源，2001，〈台灣地區縣市層級「分立政府」與「一致政府」之比較：以新竹縣市與嘉義縣市爲例〉，《人文及社會科學集刊》13（3）：251-305。

吳惠林，1996，〈大陸投資不應設限〉，《經濟前瞻》，11月5日：34-38。

李英明、賴皆興，2005，〈從理性博弈向結構博弈轉：兼論兩岸結構博弈〉，《遠景基金會季刊》6（4）：1-29。

沈有忠，2005，〈制度制約下的行政與立法關係：以我國九七憲後的憲政運作爲例〉，《政治科學論叢》23：27-60。

沈有忠，2006，〈從台灣的政治競爭推論《反分裂國家法》下的美中台賽局〉，《遠景基金會季刊》7（3）：105-137。

周育仁，2002，〈少數政府對行政立法互動之影響〉，《政治學報》34：17-30。

周添城，1993，《意見領袖的大陸經貿主張》，台北：業強。

周陽山，1995，〈「半總統制」概念及其實施經驗的反思：芬蘭模式的探討〉，《美歐月刊》10（5）：67-78。

周陽山，1996，〈總統制、議會制、半總統制與政治穩定〉，《問題與研究》35（8）：50-61。

周陽山，2008，〈「不統不獨不武」與統合前景〉，《臺灣民主季刊》5（2）：141-148。

林向愷，1994，《台灣、中國經貿關係的潛在危險及化解之道》，台北：民進黨中央黨部。

林修全、陳志平，2009，〈上任十月，再上火線說政策〉，《聯合晚報》，3月20日，A2版。

林濁水，2002，〈「半總統制」憲政運作展望〉，《行政暨政策學報》34：1-28。

林繼文，1997，〈制度選擇如何可能：論日本之選舉制度革〉，《台灣政治學刊》，（2）：63-106。

林繼文，2000，〈半總統制下的三角政治均衡〉，林繼文（編），《政治制度》，台北：中央研究院中山人文社會科學研究所，頁135-175。

林繼文，2005，〈虛假霸權：台灣政治學研究中的理性選擇〉，《政治科學論叢》，25：67-104。

林繼文，2006，〈政府體制、選舉制度與政黨體系：一個配套論的分析〉，《選舉研究》，13（2）：1-42。

林繼文，2008，〈以輸為贏：小黨在日本單一選區兩票制下的參選策略〉，《選舉研究》15（2）：37-66。

林繼文，2009a，〈共治可能成為半總統制的憲政慣例嗎？法國與台灣的比較〉，《東吳政治學報》，27（1）：1-51。

林繼文，2009b，〈雙層三角：以空間模型分析國內政治對美中台戰略三角的影響〉，包宗和、吳玉山（編），《重新檢視爭辯中的兩岸關係理論》，台北：五南，頁283-310。

林繼文，2015a，〈論述如何框限選擇？條件式統獨偏好對2012年台灣總統選舉的影響〉，《政治科學論叢》（63）：55-90。

林繼文，2015b，〈選舉制度為何變遷？理論與檢證〉，《問題與研究》54（3）：1-29。

林繼文、羅致政，1998，〈零和或雙贏？兩岸經貿交流新解〉，《人文及社會科學集刊》10（1）：33-77。

邱珮文，2015，〈朱立倫：18歲、不在籍投票都是世界趨勢〉，新頭殼newtalk，3月27日：http:// newtalk.tw/news/view/2015-03-27/58307。檢索日期：2016年6月30日。

俞振華、林啟耀，2013，〈解析台灣民眾統獨偏好：一個兩難又不確定的選擇〉，《台灣政治學刊》17（2）：165-230。

洪永泰，1995，〈分裂投票：八十三年台北市選舉的實證分析〉，《選舉研究》2（1）：119-145。

胡均立，1996，〈兩岸以合作代替對抗能實現嗎？一個賽局論的觀點〉，《台灣經濟研究月刊》19（2）：86-88。

徐正戎，2001，〈「左右共治」憲政體制之初探──兼論法、我兩國之比較〉，《台大法學論叢》30（1）：1-43。

徐正戎，2002，《法國總統權限之研究》，台北：元照。

耿曙、陳陸輝，2003，〈兩岸經貿互動與台灣政治版圖：南北區塊差異的推手？〉，《問題與研究》42（6）：1-27。

耿曙、劉嘉薇、陳陸輝，2009，〈打破維持現狀的迷思：台灣民眾統獨抉擇中理念與務實的兩難〉，《台灣政治學刊》13（2）：3-56。

袁鶴齡、沈燦宏，2012，〈從美中台戰略三角的演變看兩岸信心建構措施的建立〉，《東吳政治學報》30（3）：51-107。

高朗，2001，〈評析我國少數政府與聯合政府出現的時機與條件〉，《理論與政策》15（1）：1-11。

國史館，1994，《中華民國行憲政府職名錄（三）》，台北：國史館。

國史館，1998，《中華民國行憲政府職名錄（四）》，台北：國史館。

國史館，2001，《中華民國行憲政府職名錄（五）》，台北：國史館。

國立政治大學選舉研究中心，2015，〈台灣民眾台灣人／中國人認同趨勢分布（1992 年 6 月至 2014 年 12 月）〉：http://esc.nccu.edu.tw/course/news.php?Sn=166。檢索日期：2015 年 4 月 18 日。

國家發展會議秘書處，1996，《國家發展會議：兩岸關係議題總結報告》，台北：國家發展會議秘書處。

張世賢，1995，〈日本眾議院議員選舉區制革之研究〉，《中國行政評論》4（3）：1-42。

張台麟，1995，《法國總統的權力》，台北：志一。

張佑宗，2006，〈選舉事件與選民的投票抉擇：以台灣 2004 年總統選舉為分析對象〉，《東吳政治學報》22：21-159。

張壯熙，1996，〈法國「左右共治」經驗的啓示〉，《問題與研究》35（1）：73-86。

張茂桂、陳俐靜，2013，〈民眾政治「兩極化」現象初探：「中間」的變動與啓示〉，張茂桂、羅文輝、徐火炎（編），《台灣的社會變遷 1985-2005：傳播與政治行為》，台北：中央研究院，頁 175-240。

張菁雅、彭顯鈞，2008，〈馬：府院同一黨才會和諧〉，《自由時報》，1 月 18 日：http://www.libertytimes.com.tw/2008/new/jan/18/today-fo5.htm。檢索日期：2009 年 3 月 12 日。

張傳賢、黃紀，2011，〈政黨競爭與台灣族群認同與國家認同間的聯結〉，《台灣政治學刊》15（1）：3-71。

張榮豐，1989，《台海兩岸經貿關係》，台北：國家政策中心。

盛杏湲，2003，〈立法機關與行政機關在立法過程中的影響力：一致政府與分立政府的比較〉，《台灣政治學刊》7（2）：51-105。

盛治仁，2006，〈單一選區兩票制對未來臺灣政黨政治發展之可能影響探討〉，《臺灣民主季

刊》3（2）：63-86。

符芳碩，2015，〈修憲若不納入人權清單，學者：立院愧對人民〉，新頭殼 Newtalk，5 月 7 日：
　　http://newtalk.tw/news/view/2015-05- 07/59857。檢索日期：2016 年 6 月 25 日。

許介鱗，1991，《日本現代史》，台北：三民。

許志雄，1997，〈從比較憲法觀點論「雙首長制」〉，《月旦法學雜誌》26：30-37。

許信良，1995，《新興民族》，台北：遠流。

郭正亮，1996，〈尋求總統和國會的平衡：雙首長制對台灣憲的時代意義〉，《問題與研究》35
　　（7）：56-72。

陳宏銘，2007，〈台灣半總統制下「少數政府」的存續：2000-2004〉，《東吳政治學報》25
　　（4）：1-64。

陳宏銘，2012，〈半總統制下總統的法案推動與立法影響力：馬英九總統執政時期的研究〉，
　　《東吳政治學報》30（2）：1-71。

陳宏銘、蔡榮祥，2008，〈選舉時程對政府組成形態的牽引力：半總統制經驗之探討〉，《東吳
　　政治學報》26（2）：117-180。

陳志平，2007，〈公布外交政策白皮書：馬倡活路外交〉，《聯合晚報》，11 月 20 日，5 版。

陳志華，2002，〈「雙首長制」的迷思──突破總統制的侷限與革趨向〉，《行政暨政策學報》
　　34：1-28。

陳明通，2009，〈當前北京對台策略剖析〉，《東吳政治學報》27（2）：127-202。

陳明通、林繼文，1998，〈台灣地方選舉的起源與國家社會關係轉變〉，陳明通、鄭永年
　　（編），《兩岸基層選舉與政治社會變遷》，台北：月旦，頁 23-69。

陳彥廷、陳慧萍，2014，〈跨黨派 37 立委提案要求成立修憲委員會〉，《自由時報》，12 月 12
　　日：http://news.ltn.com.tw/news /politics/paper/838395。檢索日期：2016 年 6 月 25 日。

陳陸輝、耿曙、王德育，2009，〈兩岸關係與 2008 年台灣總統大選：認同、利益、威脅與選民
　　投票取向〉，《選舉研究》16（2）：1-22。

陳陸輝、耿曙、涂萍蘭、黃冠博，2009，〈理性自利或感性認同？影響台灣民眾兩岸經貿立場因
　　素的分析〉，《東吳政治學報》27（2）：87-125。

陳慈陽，2004，《憲法學》，台北：元照。

陳義彥、陳陸輝，2003，〈模稜兩可的態度還是不確定的未來：台灣民眾統獨觀的解析〉，《中
　　國大陸研究》46（5）：1-20。

陳德昇，1994，《兩岸政經互動──政策解讀與運作分析》，台北：永業。

彭威晶，2000，〈扁：不可能讓國民黨「整碗捧去」〉，《聯合報》，4 月 1 日：http://issue.udn.
　　com/FOCUSNEWS/TAN/a3.htm。檢索日期：2009 年 3 月 2 日。

曾盈瑜，2015，〈國民黨修憲小組，聚焦閣揆同意權〉，《中央社》，1 月 15 日：http://www.

ly.gov.tw/03_leg/0301_main/leg_news/newsView.action?id=119457&lgno=00104&stage=8&atc id=119457。檢索日期：2016 年 6 月 25 日。

游清鑫，2012，〈初體驗與粗體驗：台灣民眾對立委新選制的認知、參與及評價〉，《選舉研究》19（1）：1-32。

湯德宗，1998，〈論九七憲後的權力分立——憲工程的另類選擇〉，《台大法學論叢》27（2）：135-178。

童振源、林馨怡、林繼文、黃光雄、周子全、劉嘉凱、趙文志，2009，〈台灣選舉預測：預測市場的運用與實證分析〉，《選舉研究》16（2）：131-166。

黃秀端，2003，〈少數政府在國會的困境〉，《台灣政治學刊》7（2）：1-46。

黃昭元，1998，〈九七修憲後我國中央政府體制的評估〉，《台大法學論叢》27（2）：183-215。

黃秋龍、王正光，2000，〈兩岸統獨對峙之賽局分析：以連鎖體系（Chain-Store）賽局為例證〉，《問題與研究》39（10）：59-78。

黃紀，2001，〈一致與分裂投票：方法論之探討〉，《人文及社會科學集刊》13（5）：541-574。

黃紀、王鼎銘、郭銘峰，2005，〈日本眾議院 1993 及 1996 年選舉——自民黨之選票流動分析〉，《人文及社會科學集刊》17（4）：853-883。

黃紀、吳重禮，2000，〈台灣地區縣市層級「分立政府」影響之初探〉，《台灣政治學刊》4：105-147。

黃紀、張益超，2001，〈一致與分裂投票：嘉義市一九九七年市長與立委選舉之分析〉，徐永明、黃紀主（編），《政治分析的層次》，台北：韋伯文化，頁 183-218。

黃清賢，2012，〈兩岸關係的辯證性建構〉，《遠景基金會季刊》13（3）：49-94。

黃德福，2000，〈少數政府與責任政治〉，《問題與研究》39（12）：1-24。

楊婉瑩、劉嘉薇，2009，〈探討統獨態度的性別差異：和平戰爭與發展利益的觀點〉，《選舉研究》16（1）：37-66。

葉國俊，2005，〈建立兩岸經濟合作機制是台灣免於經濟邊緣化的唯一選擇？一項總體經濟賽局模擬初評〉，《經濟論文叢刊》33（4）：229-261。

葉國俊、侯乃榕，2007，〈探索台灣經濟邊緣化問題：國際總體經濟政策協作思維〉，《社會科學論叢》1（2）：71-104。

廖達琪、洪澄琳，2004，〈反對黨獨大下的分立政府——高雄縣府會關係的個案研究（1985-2003）〉，《台灣政治學刊》8（2）：5-50。

蒙志成，2014，〈「92 共識」對 2012 年台灣總統大選的議題效果：「傾向分數配對法」的應用與實證估算〉，《選舉研究》21（1）：1-45。

劉映仙，1993，〈兩岸經貿問題的現狀、問題和趨勢〉，劉映仙（編），《海峽兩岸經貿關係探討》，北京：友誼出版社，頁 8-26。

劉國銘（編），2005，《中國國民黨百年人物全書》，北京：團結出版社。

劉康彥，2015，〈民進黨憲會議，黨中央擬提「改良的總統議會民主制」〉，ETtoday 新聞雲，1 月 29 日：http://www.ettoday.net/news/20150129/460601. htm?feature=fashion&tab_id=110。檢索日期：2016 年 6 月 25 日。

劉嘉薇、耿曙、陳陸輝，2009，〈務實也是一種選擇─台灣民眾統獨立場的測量與商榷〉，《臺灣民主季刊》6（4）：141-168。

劉維開（編），1994，《中國國民黨職名錄》，台北市：中國國民黨黨史委員會。

蔡宏明，2008，〈兩岸關係的新情勢與新政府的新作為〉，《遠景基金會季刊》9（3）：199-243。

蔡佳泓、徐永明、黃琇庭，2007，〈兩極化政治：解釋台灣 2004 總統大選〉，《選舉研究》14（1）：1-31。

蔡宗珍，1999，〈威瑪憲法與政黨政治〉，《當代》140：72-79。

鄧志松、唐代彪，2006，〈兩岸賽局：一個新情勢的開始〉，《國家發展研究》5（2）：21-50。

鄭夙芬、陳陸輝、劉嘉薇，2005，〈2004 年總統選舉中的候選人因素〉，《台灣民主季刊》2（2）：31-70。

鄭夙芬、陳陸輝、劉嘉薇，2008，〈選舉事件與政治信任：以 2004 年總統選舉為例〉，《問題與研究》4（3）：29-50。

盧瑞鍾，1995，〈總統制與內閣制優缺點之比較〉，《政治科學論叢》6：1-32。

蕭怡靖、游清鑫，2012，〈檢測台灣民眾六分類統獨立場：一個測量進的提出〉，《台灣政治學刊》16（2）：65-116。

蕭怡靖、鄭夙芬，2014，〈台灣民眾對左右意識形態的認知：以統獨議題取代左右意識形態檢測台灣的政黨極化〉，《台灣政治學刊》18（2）：79-138。

戴雅真，2014，〈鄭麗君提案人權入憲降修憲門檻〉，《中央社》，12 月 17 日：http://www.cna.com.tw/search/hydetailws。檢索日期：2016 年 6 月 25 日。

薛化元，1997，〈中華民國憲政藍圖的歷史演變：行政權為中心的考察〉，《月旦法學雜誌》26：10-22。

謝相慶，1999，〈日本眾議院議員新選舉制度及其政治效應──以 1996 年選舉為例〉，《選舉研究》6（2）：45-87。

謝復生，1986，〈選舉制度與政黨多寡：兼論科學法則的建立〉，《國立政治大學學報》54：151-163。

謝復生，2011，《實證政治理論》，北京：中國人民大學出版社。

謝復生，2013，《實證政治理論》，台北：五南。

謝復生、林繼文，2013，〈理性抉擇與台灣的政治學研究〉，吳玉山、林繼文、冷則剛（編），

《政治學的回顧與前瞻》，台北：五南，頁 65-87。

鍾琴，1996，〈爲何大陸投資應該設限？〉，《經濟前瞻》，11 月 5 日：24-32。

魏華，1992，〈對當前兩岸經貿情勢之探討〉，《中共研究》26（8）：38-46。

羅致政，1996，〈美國戰略性模糊政策對兩岸互動的影響〉，《東吳政治學報》6：175-202。

蘇子喬，2006，〈我國「雙首長制」爲什麼不會換軌？——制度因素之分析〉，《政治學報》40：41-84。

蘇子喬、王業立，2010，〈爲何廢棄混合式選制？——義大利、俄羅斯與泰國選制革之研究〉，《東吳政治學報》28（3）：1-81。

蘇方禾，2015，〈修憲又破局，綠：國民黨想總統立委脫鉤選〉，《自由時報》，6 月 12 日：http://news.ltn.com.tw/news/politics/breakingnews/1350365。檢索日期：2016 年 7 月 3 日。

英文文獻

Abramowitz, Alan I. and Kyle L. Saunders. 2008. "Is Polarization a Myth?" *The Journal of Politics* 70(2): 542-555.

Ahler, Douglas J. 2014. "Self-Fulfilling Misperceptions of Public Polarization." *The Journal of Politics* 76(3): 607-620.

Aldrich, John H. 1983. "A Downsian Spatial Model with Party Activism." *American Political Science Review* 77(4): 974-990.

Alesina, Alberto and Howard Rosenthal. 1995. *Partisan Politics, Divided Government, and the Economy.* Cambridge, UK: Cambridge University Press.

Amorim Neto, Octavio and David J. Samuels. 2010. "Democratic Regimes and Cabinet Politics: A Global Perspective." *Revista Iberoamericana de Estudos Legislativos* 1(1): 10-23.

Amorim Neto, Octavio and Gary W. Cox. 1997. "Electoral Institutions, Cleavage Structures, and the Number of Parties." *American Journal of Political Science* 41(1): 149-174.

Anderson, Benedict. 1991. *Imagined Communities: Reflections on the Origin and Spread of Nationalism*, revised ed. London, UK and New York, NY: Verso.

Anderson, Gary M. 1999. "Electoral Limits." In *Limiting Leviathan*, eds. Donald P. Racheter and Richard Wagner. Cheltenham, England: Edward Elgar, pp. 176-202.

Andrews, Josephine T. and Gabriella R. Montinola. 2004. "Veto Players and the Rule of Law in Emerging Democracies." *Comparative Political Studies* 37(1): 55-87.

Ardant, Philippe and Olivier Duhamel. 1999. "La Dyarchie." *Pouvoirs* 91: 5-24.

Arter, David. 1987. *Politics and Policy-making in Finland.* New York, NY: St. Martin's Press.

Arrow, Kenneth J. 1953. *Social Choice and Individual Values*, 2nd ed., New York, NY: Wiley.

Auer, Andreas and Michael Bützer, eds. 2001. *Direct Democracy: The Eastern and Central European Experience*. Aldershot, Hants, England and Burlington, VT: Ashgate.

Axelrod, Robert. 1984. *The Evolution of Cooperation*. New York, NY: Basic Books.

Axelrod, Robert and Robert O. Keohane. 1985. "Achieving Cooperation under Anarchy: Strategies and Institutions." *World Politics* 38: 226-54.

Bagehot, Walter. 1867. *The English Constitution*. Ithaca, NY: Cornell University Press.

Bahro, Horst. 1999. "Virtues and Vices of Semi-Presidential Government." *Journal of Social Sciences and Philosophy* 11(1): 1-35.

Bahro, Horst, Bernhard H. Bayerlein, and Ernst Veser. 1998. "Duverger's Concept: Semi-presidential Government Revisited." *European Journal of Political Science* 34: 201-224.

Balsom, Denis. 1996. "The United Kingdom: Constitutional Pragmatism and the Adoption of the Referendum." In *The Referendum Experience in Europe*, eds. Michael Gallagher and Piervincenzo Uleri. New York, NY: Macmillan, pp. 209-225.

Banks, Arthur S., Alan J. Day, and Thomas C. Muller, eds. 1997. *Political Handbook of the World: 1997*. Binghamton, NY: CSA Publications.

Barkan, Joel D., Paul J. Densham, and Gerard Rushton. 2006. "Space Matters: Designing Better Electoral Systems for Emerging Democracies." *American Journal of Political Science* 50(4): 926-939.

Bartels, Larry M. 2000. "Partisanship and Voting Behavior, 1952-1996." *American Journal of Political Science* 44(1): 35-50.

Batto, Nathan F., Henry A. Kim, and Natalia Matukhno. 2016. "Presidents and Blank Votes in the Bolivian and Russian Mixed-Member Systems." In *Mixed-Member Majoritarian Electoral Systems in Constitutional Context: Taiwan, Japan, and Beyond*, eds. Nathan F. Batto, Chi Huang, Alexander C. Tan, and Gary W. Cox. Ann Arbor, MI: University of Michigan Press, pp. 278-299.

Baylis, Thomas A. 1996. "Presidents Versus Prime Ministers." *World Politics* 48(3): 297-323.

Beliaev, Mikhail V. 2006. "Presidential Powers and Consolidation of New Postcommunist Democracies." *Comparative Political Studies* 39(3): 375-398.

Benoit, Kenneth. 2001. "District Magnitude, Electoral Formula, and the Number of Parties." *European Journal of Political Research* 39: 203-224.

Benoit, Kenneth. 2002. "The Endogeneity Problem in Electoral Studies: A Critical Re-examination of Duverger's Mechanical Effect." *Electoral Studies* 21(1): 35-46.

Benoit, Kenneth. 2004. "Models of Electoral System Change." *Electoral Studies* 23: 363-389.

Benoit, Kenneth and Jacqueline Hayden. 2004. "Institutional Change and Persistence: The Evolution of Poland's Electoral System, 1989-2001." *The Journal of Politics* 66(2): 396-427.

Benson, Brett V. and Emerson M. S. Niou. 2007. "Economic Interdependence and Peace: A Game-theoretic Analysis." *Journal of East Asian Studies* 7(1): 35-59.

Blais, André. 2008. *To Keep or To Change First Past The Post? The Politics of Electoral Reform.* Oxford, UK: Oxford University Press.

Bogdanor, Vernon and David Butler. 1983. *Democracy and Electoral Systems and Their Political Consequences.* Cambridge, UK: Cambridge University Press.

Boix, Carles. 1999. "Setting the Rules of the Game: The Choice of Electoral Systems in Advanced Democracies." *American Political Science Review* 93(3): 609-624.

Boix, Carles. 2011. "Democracy, Development, and the International System." *American Political Science Review* 105(4): 809-828.

Bosco, Joseph. 1994. "Taiwan Factions: Guanxi, Patronage, and the State in Local Politics." In *The Other Taiwan, 1945 to the Present*, ed. M. A. Rubinstein. Armonk, NY: M.E. Sharpe, pp. 114-144.

Bowler, Shaun and Bernard Grofman. 2000. *Elections in Australia, Ireland, and Malta Under the Single Transferable Vote: Reflections on an Embedded Institution.* Ann Arbor, MI: University of Michigan Press.

Brady, David and Jongryn Mo. 1992. "Electoral Systems and Institutional Choice: A Case Study of the 1988 Korean Elections." *Comparative Political Studies* 24(4): 405-429.

Brady, David W. and Craig Volden. 1998. *Revolving Gridlock: Politics and Policy from Carter to Clinton.* Boulder, CO: Westview Press.

Brazier, Rodney. 1988. *Constitutional Practice.* Oxford, UK: Clarendon Press.

Brennan, Geoffrey and Alan Hamlin. 1992. "Bicameralism and Majoritarian Equilibrium." *Public Choice* 74(2): 169-180.

Broschek, Jörg. 2010. "Federalism and Political Change: Canada and Germany in Historical—Institutionalist Perspective." *Canadian Journal of Political Science* 43(1): 1-24.

Broschek, Jörg. 2011. "Historical Institutionalism and the Varieties of Federalism in Germany and Canada." *Publius: The Journal of Federalism* 42(4): 662-687.

Bryce, James. 1905. *Constitutions.* Oxford, UK: Oxford University Press.

Buchanan, James M. and Gordon Tullock. 1962. *The Calculus of Consent: Logical Foundations of Constitutional Democracy.* Ann Arbor, MI: University of Michigan Press.

Budge, Ian and Michael Laver. 1986. "Office Seeking and Policy Pursuit in Coalition Theory." *Legislative Studies Quarterly* 11(4): 485-506.

Butler, David and Austin Ranney, eds. 1997. *Referendums Around the World: The Growing Use of Direct Democracy*. New York, NY: Palgrave/Macmillan.

Cabestan, Jean-Pierre. 1997. "Is Taiwan Moving Towards a French-Style Semi-presidential System?" *China Perspectives* 14: 40-44.

Callander, Steven and Catherine H. Wilson. 2007. "Turnout, Polarization, and Duverger's Law." *The Journal of Politics* 69(4): 1047-1056.

Carey, John M. and Andrew Reynolds. 2011. "The Impact of Election Systems." *Journal of Democracy* 22(4): 36-47.

Carey, John M. and Matthew Soberg Shugart. 1995. "Incentives to Cultivate a Personal Vote: A Rank Ordering of Electoral Formulas." *Electoral Studies* 14(4): 417-439.

Carter, John R. and David Schap. 1987. "Executive Veto, Legislative Override, and Structure Induced Equilibria." *Public Choice* 52: 227-244.

Central Election Commission. 2015. http://db.cec.gov.tw/histMain.jsp?voteSel=19960301A9.

Chan, Steve. 2005. "Taiwan in 2005: Strategic Interaction in Two-Level Games." *Asian Survey* 46(1): 63-68.

Chao, Linda, Raymon H. Myers, and James A. Robinson. 1997. "Promoting Effective Democracy, Chinese Style: Taiwan's National Development Conference." *Asian Survey* 37(7): 669-682.

Cheibub, Jose Antonio. 2002. "Minority Governments, Deadlock Situations, and the Survival of Presidential Democracies." *Compatative Political Studies* 35(2): 284-312.

Chen, Ching-chih. 1984. "Police and Community Control Systems in the Empire." In *Japanese Colonial Empire, 1895-1945*, eds. Ramon H. Myers and Mark R. Peattie. Princeton, NJ: Princeton University Press, pp. 213-239.

Chen, Ming-tong. 1995. "Local Factions and Elections in Taiwan's Democratization." In *Taiwan's Electoral Politics and Democratic Transition: Riding the Third Wave*, ed. Hung-mao Tien. Armonk, NY: M.E. Sharpe, pp. 174-193.

Cheng, Tun-jen. 1993. "Democracy and Taiwan-Mainland China Ties: A Critique of Three Dominant Views." *Journal of Northeast Asian Studies* 12(1): 72-89.

Chou, Wan-yao.1996. "The Kōminka Movement in Taiwan and Korea: Comparisons and Interpretations." In *The Japanese Wartime Empire, 1931-1945*, eds. Peter Duus, Mark Peattie, and Ramon Myers. Princeton, NY: Princeton University Press, pp. 40-68.

Christensen, Raymond. 1994. "Electoral Reform in Japan." *Asian Survey* 34: 589-605.

Christensen, Thomas J. and Jack Snyder. 1990. "Chain Gangs and Passed Bucks: Predicting Alliance Patterns in Multipolarity." *International Organization* 44: 137-168.

Christin, Thomas and Simon Hug. 2002. "Referendums and Citizen Support for European Integration." *Comparative Political Studies* 35(5): 586-617.

Chu, Yun-han. 1992. *Crafting Democratic Institutions in Taiwan*. Taipei: Institute for National Policy Research.

Chu, Yun-han. 1994."Social Protest and Political Democratization in Taiwan." In *Other Voices/Other Visions: Responses to Directed Political and Socio-economic Change in Taiwan, 1945-1991*, ed. Murray Rubinstein. Armonk, NY: M.E. Sharpe.

Chu, Yun-han. 1999. "A Born-Again Dominant Party? The Transformation of the Kuomintang and Taiwan's Regime Transition." In *The Awkward Embrace: One Party Domination and Democracy*, eds. Hermann Giliomee and Charles Simkins. London, UK: Harwood Academic Publishers.

Chu, Yun-han. 2004. "Taiwan's National Identity Politics and the Prospect of Cross-Strait Relations." Asian Survey 44(4): 484-512.

Chu, Yun-han and Chia-lung Lin. 1999. "Democratization and Growth of Taiwanism: Competing Nationalisms and National (In) Security." Paper delivered at the Second Annual Conference of the EU-China Academic Network (ECAN), January 21-22, Spain: Centro de Estudios de Asia Oriental, Universidad Autonoma de Madrid.

Chu, Yun-han and Jih-wen Lin. 2001. "Political Development in the 20th Century Taiwan: State-Building, Regime Transformation and the Construction of National Identity." The China Quarterly 165: 102-109.

Clark, Sherman J. 1998. "A Populist Critique of Direct Democracy." *Harvard Law Review* 112(2): 434-482.

Clarke, Harold D., Allan Kornberg, and Marianne C. Stewart. 2004. "Referendum Voting as Political Choice: The Case of Quebec." *British Journal of Political Science* 34(2): 345-356.

Cole, Alistair. 1994. *François Mitterrand: A Study in Political Leadership*. London, UK: Routledge.

Colomer, Joseph M., ed. 2004. *Handbook of Electoral System Choice*. Houndmills, Basingstoke, Hampshire and New York, NY: Palgrave/Macmillan.

Colomer, Joseph M. 2005. "It's Parties That Choose Electoral Systems (or Duverger's Laws Upside Down)." *Political Studies* 53(1): 1-21.

Conley, Richard S. 2006. "From Elysian Fields to the Guillotine? The Dynamics of Presidential and Prime Ministerial Approval in Fifth Republic France." *Comparative Political Studies* 39(5): 570-598.

Constitution Finder. 2009. "The Constitution of the Republic of Mali." *WIPO*: http://confinder.richmond. edu/admin/docs/Mali.pdf (accessed March 12, 2009).

Cox, Gary W. 1990. "Centripetal and Centrifugal Incentives in Electoral Systems." *American Journal of Political Science* 34(4): 903-935.

Cox, Gary W. 1991. "SNTV and d'Hondt are 'Quivalent'." *Electoral Studies* 10: 118-132.

Cox, Gary W. 1994. "Strategic Voting Equilibria under the Single Nontransferable Vote." *American Political Science Review* 88: 608-621.

Cox, Gary W. 1997. *Making Votes Count: Strategic Coordination in the World's Electoral Systems.* Cambridge, UK and New York, NY: Cambridge University Press.

Cox, Gary W. and Emerson M. S. Niou. 1994. "Seat Bonuses under the Single Non-Transferable Vote for Large Parties: Evidence from Japan and Taiwan." *Comparative Politics* 26: 221-236.

Cox, Gary W. and F. M. Rosenbluth, 1994. "Reducing Nomination Errors: Factional Competition and Party Strategy in Japan." *Electoral Studies* 13: 4-16.

Cox, Karen and Leonard J. Schoppa. 2002. "Interaction Effects in Mixed-Member Electoral Systems: Theory and Evidence from Germany, Japan, and Italy." *Comparative Political Studies* 35(9): 1027-1053.

Croissant, Aurel. 2003. "Legislative Powers, Veto Players, and the Emergence of Delegative Democracy: A Comparison of Presidentialism in the Philippines and South Korea." *Democratization* 10(3): 68-98.

Cronin, Thomas. 1989. *Direct Democracy: The Politics of Initiative, Referendum, and Recall.* Cambridge, MA: Harvard University Press.

Cubitt, Robin P. and Robert Sugden. 2003. "Common Knowledge, Salience and Covention: A Reconstruction of David Lewis' Game Theory." *Economic and Philosophy* 19: 175-210.

Cunningham, David E. 2006. "Veto Players and Civil War Duration." *American Journal of Political Science* 50(4): 875-892.

Curini, Luigi and Airo Hino. 2012. "Missing Links in Party-System Polarization: How Institutions and Voters Matter." *The Journal of Politics* 74(2): 460-473.

Dalton, Russell J. and Aiji Tanaka. 2007. "The Patterns of Party Polarization in East Asia." *Journal of East Asian Studies* 7(2): 203-223.

Davis, Otto A., Morris H. DeGroot, and Melvin J. Hinich. 1972. "Social Preference Orderings and Majority Rule." *Econometrica* 40: 147-157.

de Mesquita, Bruce Bueno and Alastair Smith. 2008. "Political Survival and Endogenous Institutional Change." *Comparative Political Studies* 42(2): 167-197.

Dearden, James A. and Thomas A. Husted. 1990. "Executive Budget Proposal, Executive Veto, Legislative Override, and Uncertainty: A Comparative Analysis of the Budgetary Process." *Public*

Choice 65: l-19.

Delury, E., ed. 1987. *World Encyclopedia of Political Systems & Parties.* New York, NY: Facts on File Inc.

Diamond, Larry. 2008. *The Spirit of Democracy: The Struggle to Build Free Societies Throughout the World.* New York, NY: Times Book.

DiMaggio, Paul, John Evans, and Bethany Bryson. 1996. "Have Americans' Social Attitudes Become More Polarized?" *American Journal of Sociology* 102(3): 690-755.

Dittmer, Lowell. 1981. "The Strategic Triangle: The Elementary Game-Theoretical Analysis." *World Politics* 33(4): 485-515.

Dittmer, Lowell. 1987. "The Strategic Triangle: A Critical Review." In *The Strategic Triangle: China, the United States and the Soviet Union*, ed. Ilpyong J. Kim. New York, NY: Paragon House Publisher, pp. 29-47.

Diwakar, Rekba. 2007. "Duverger's Law and the Size of the Indian Party System." *Party Politics* 13(5): 539-562.

Donnelly, Jack. 2000. *Realism and International Relations.* Cambridge, UK: Cambridge University Press.

Dow, Jay K. 1999. "Voter Choice in the 1995 French Presidential Election." *Political Behavior* 21(4): 305-324.

Downs, Anthony. 1957. *An Economic Theory of Democracy.* New York, NY: Harper.

Druckman, James N. and Michael F. Thies. 2002. "The Importance of Concurrence: The Impact of Bicameralism on Government Formation and Duration." *American Journal of Political Science* 46(4): 760-771.

Dunleavy, Patrick and Helen Margetts. 1995. "Understanding the Dynamics of Electoral Reform." *International Political Science Review* 16(1): 9-29.

Duverger, Maurice. 1963. *Political Parties: Their Organization and Activity in the Modern State.* New York, NY: Wiley.

Duverger, Maurice. 1964a. *An Introduction to the Social Sciences: With Special Reference to Their Methods.* Trans. Malcolm Anderson. New York, NY : Frederick A. Praeger.

Duverger, Maurice. 1964b. *Political Parties: Their Organization and Activity in the Modern State*, 3rd ed. Trans. Barbara and Robert. London, UK: Methuen.

Duverger, Maurice. 1969. *Political Parties: Their Organization and Activity in the Modern State*, 3rd ed. Trans. Barbara and Robert. London, UK: Methuen.

Duverger, Maurice. 1972. *Party Politics and Pressure Groups: A Comparative Introduction.* New York,

NY: Thomas Y. Crowell.

Duverger, Maurice. 1974. *La Monarchie Republicaine ou Comme Les Democraties se Donnent des Rois*. Paris, France: R. Laffont.

Duverger, Maurice. 1978. *Echec au Roi*. Paris, France: Albin Michel.

Duverger, Maurice. 1980. "A New Political System Model: Semi-presidential Government." *European Journal of Political Research* 8(2): 165-187.

Elgie, Robert. 1997. "Models of Executive Politics: A Framework for the Study of Executive Power Relations in Parliamentary and Semi-presidential Regimes." *Political Studies* 45(2): 217-231.

Elgie, Robert. 1999. *Semi-presidentialism in Europe*. Oxford, UK: Oxford University Press.

Elgie, Robert, ed. 2001a. *Divided Government in Comparative Perspective*. Oxford, UK: Oxford University Press.

Elgie, Robert. 2001b. "'Cohabitation': Divided Government French-Style." In *Divided Government in Comparative Perspective*, ed. Robert Elgie. Oxford, UK: Oxford University Press, pp. 106-127.

Elgie, Robert. 2004. "Semi-presidentialsm: Concepts, Consequences, and Contesting Explanations." *Political Studies Review* 2: 314-330.

Elgie, Robert. 2005. "Variations on a Theme." *Journal of Democracy* 16(3): 98-112.

Elgie, Robert. 2007. "What is Semi-Presidentialism and Where is it Found?" In *Semi- presidentialism Outside Europe: A Comparatice Study*, eds. Robert Elgie and Sophia Moestrup. London, UK: Routledge, pp. 1-13.

Elgie, Robert and Steven Griggs. 2000. *French Politics: Debates and Controversies*. London, UK: Routledge.

Elgie, Robert and Howard Machin. 1991. "France: The Limits to Primeministerial Government in a Semi-presidential System." *West European Politics* 14: 62-78.

Elgie, Robert and Sophia Moestrup, eds. 2007. *Semi-presidentialism Outside Europe*. New York, NY: Routledge.

Elkins, Zachary, Tom Ginsburg, and James Melton. 2014. "Characteristics of National Constitutions, Version 2.0." *Comparative Constitutions Project*: http://www.comparativeconstitution-sproject.org.

Evans, Peter B., Dietrich Rueschemeyer, and Theda Skocpol, eds. 1985. *Bring the State Back In*. Cambridge, UK: Cambridge University Press.

Evans, Peter B., Harold K. Jacobson, and Robert D. Putnam, eds. 1993. *Double Edged Diplomacy: International Bargaining and Domestic Politics*. Berkeley, CA: University of California Press.

Feld, Scott L., Bernard Grofman, and Nicholas Miller. 1988. "Centripetal Forces in Spatial Voting: On the Size of the Yolk." *Public Choice* 59(1): 37-50.

Fell, Dafydd. 2005. *Party Politics in Taiwan: Party Change and the Democratic Evolution of Taiwan, 1991-2004.* London, UK: Routledge.

Ferrara, Federico. 2004. "Electoral Coordination and the Strategic Desertion of Strong Parties in Compensatory Mixed Systems with Negative Vote Transfers." *Electoral Studies* 23(3): 391-413.

Ferrara, Federico and Erik S. Herron. 2005. "Going It Alone? Strategic Entry under Mixed Electoral Rules." *American Journal of Political Science* 49(1): 391-413.

Filippov, Mikhail and Olga Shvetsova. 1999. "Asymmetric Bilateral Bargaining in the New Russian Federation: A Path-Dependence Explanation." *Communist and Post-Communist Studies* 32(1): 61-76.

Finer, S. E., Vernon Bogdanor, and Bernard Rudden. 1996. *Comparing Constitutions.* Oxford, UK: Oxford University Press.

Finke, Daniel. 2009. "Estimating the Effect of Nonseparable Preferences in EU Treaty Negotiations." *Journal of Theoretical Politics* 21(4): 543-569.

Fiorina, Morris P. 1996a. *Divided Government.* Needham Heights, MA: Simon and Schuster.

Fiorina, Morris P. 1996b. *Divided Government*, 2nd ed. Boston, MA: Allyn and Bacon.

Fiorina, Morris P. and Matthew S. Levendusky. 2006. "Disconnected: The Political Class versus the People." In *Red and Blue Nation? Characteristics and Causes of America's Polarized Politics*, eds. Pietro S. Nivola and David W. Brady. Washington, DC: Brookings Institution Press, pp. 49-71.

Fleisher, Richard and John R. Bond. 2004. "The Shrinking Middle in the U.S. Congress." *British Journal of Political Science* 34: 429-451.

Franck, Raymond E. and Francois Melese. 2003. "A Game Theory View of Military Conflict in the Taiwan Strait." *Defense and Security Analysis* 19(4): 327-348.

Frey, Bruno S. 2000. "Happiness, Economy, and Institutions." *The Economic Journal* 110(466): 918-939.

Friend, Julius W. 1998. *The Long Presidency: France in the Mitterrand Years, 1981-1995.* Boulder, CO and Oxford, UK: Westview Press.

Frye, Timothy. 1997. "A Politics of Institutional Choice: Post-Communist Presidencies." *Comparative Political Studies* 30(5): 523-552.

Fukuoka, Masayuki. 2001. *Nihon no senkyo* [Japan's Elections]. Tokyo, Japan: Waseda Daigku Shuppankai.

Fukuyama, Francis. 2013. "The Decay of American Political Institutions." *The American Interest*: http://www.the-american-interest.com/2013/12/08/the-decay-of-american-political-institutions/ (accessed April 18, 2015).

Fukuyama, Frances, Bjorn Dressel, and Boo-Seung Chang. 2005. "Facing the Perils of Presldentialism?" *Journal of Democracy* 16(2): 102-116.

Gallagher, Michael. 1998. "The Political Impact of Electoral System Change in Japan and New Zealand, 1996." *Party Politics* 4(2): 203-228.

Gallagher, Michael and Piervincenzo Uleri, eds. 1996. *The Referendum Experience in Europe*. New York, NY: Macmillan.

Garver, John W. 1997. *Face Off: China, the United States, and Taiwan's Democratization*. Seattle, WA: University of Washington Press.

Gellner, Ernest. 1983. *Nations and Nationalism*. Ithaca, NY: Cornell University Press.

Gerhardt, Michael J. 2000. *The Federal Appointments Process: A Constitutional and Historical Analysis*. Durham, NC: Duke University Press.

Gerring, John. 2004. "What Is a Case Study and What Is It Good For?" *American Political Science Review* 98(2): 342-354.

Gillespie, Richard. 1990. "The Consolidation of New Democracies." In *Politics in Western Europe Today*, eds. D. W. Urwin and W. E. Paterson. London, UK: Longman, pp. 227-250.

Gilpin, Robert. 1987. *The Political Economy of International Relations*. Princeton, NJ: Princeton University Press.

Goodin, Robert E., ed. 1996. *The Theory of Institutional Design*. New York, NY: Cambridge University Press.

Goodin, Robert E. and Hans-Dieter Klingemann, eds. 1996. *A New Handbook of Political Science*. Oxford, UK: Oxford University Press.

Gowa, Joanne. 1986. "Anarchy, Egoism, and Third Image." *International Organization* 40: 67-86.

Greene, Kenneth F. 2010. "The Political Economy of Authoritarian Single-Party Dominance." *Comparative Political Studies* 43(7): 807-834.

Greif, Avner and David D. Laitin. 2004. "A Theory of Endogenous Institutional Change." *American Political Science Review* 98: 633-652.

Grieco, Joseph M. 1988a. "Anarchy and the Limits of Cooperation: A Realist Critique of the Newest Liberal Institutionalism." *International Organization* 42: 485-507.

Grieco, Joseph M. 1988b. "Realist Theory and the Problem of International Cooperation: Analysis with an Amended Prisoner's Dilemma Model." *Journal of Politics* 50: 600-624.

Grieco, Joseph M. 1990. *Cooperation among Nations: Europe, American, and Non. Tariff Barriers to Trade*. Ithaca, NY: Cornell University Press.

Grofman, Bernard. 1975. "A Review of Macro-election Systems." In *Sozialwissensch-aftliches Jahrbuch fur Politik*, ed. R. Wildenmann, Munich, German: Gunter Olzog Verlag, pp. 303-352.

Grofman, Bernard. 1999. "SNTV, STV, and Single-Member-District Systems: Theoretical Comparisons and Contrasts." In *Elections in Japan, Korea, and Taiwan under the Single Non-Transferable Vote: The Comparative Study of an Embedded Institution*, eds. B. Grofman, S. C. Lee, E. A. Winckler, and B. Woodall. Ann Arbor, MI: University of Michigan Press.

Grofman, Bernard. 2005. "Comparisons Among Electoral Systems." *Electoral Studies* 24: 735-740.

Grofman, Bernard and Arend Lijphart, eds. 1986. *Electoral Laws and Their Political Consequences*. New York, NY: Agathon Press.

Grofman, Bernard, André Blais, and Shaun Bowler. 2009. *Duverger's Law of Plurality Voting*. New York: Springer.

Grofman, Bernard, Sung-Chull Lee, Edwin A. Winckler, and Brian Woodall, eds. 1999. *Elections in Japan, Korea, and Taiwan Under the Single Non-Transferable Vote*. Ann Arbor, MI: University of Michigan Press.

Gross, Oren and Fionnuala Ní Aoláin. 2006. *Law in Times of Crisis: Emergency Powers in Theory and Practice*. Cambridge, UK: Cambridge University Press.

Grumm, John G. 1958. "Theories of Electoral Systems." *Midwest Journal of Political Science* 2: 357-376.

Grunberg, Gérard. 1999. "Du Cohabitationnisme de l'Opinion." *Pouvoirs* 91: 83-95.

Gschwend, Thomas. 2007. "Ticket-splitting and Strategic Voting under Mixed Electoral Rules: Evidence from Germany." *European Journal of Political Research* 46(1): 1-23.

Guomin dahui [National Assembly]. 1998. *Disan jie guomin dahui dier ci huiyi shilu* [Records of the Second Session of the Third National Assembly]: http://lis.ly.gov.tw/nacgi/ttsweb?@0:0:1:dbini/ly meetingdb@@0.6962012632289616. Taipei, Taiwan: National Assembly.

Hall, Peter A. and Rosemary C. R. Taylor. 1996. "Political Science and Three New Institutionalisms." *Political Studies* 44: 936-957.

Hammond, Thomas H. and Gary J. Miller. 1987. "The Core of the Constitution." *American Political Science Review* 81(4): 1155-1174.

Han, Hahrie and David W. Brady. 2007. "A Delayed Return to Historical Norms: Congressional Party Polarization After the Second World War." *British Journal of Political Science* 37(3): 505-531.

Hardin, Russell. 1989. "Why a Constitution?" In *The Federalist Papers and the New Institutionalism*, eds. Bernard Grofman and Donald Wittman. New York, NY: Agathon Press, pp. 100-120.

Hardin, Russell. 1999. *Liberalism, Constitutionalism, and Democracy*. New York, NY: Cambridge University Press.

Harding, Harry. 1992. *A Fragile Relationship*. Washington, DC: Brookings.

Harrison, Michael M. 1986. "France in Suspense." *SAIS Review* 6(1): 91-115.

Heller, William B. 2001. "Political Denials: The Policy Effects of Intercameral Partisan Differences in Bicameral Parliamentary Systems." *Journal of Law, Economics, and Organization* 17(1): 34-61.

Herron, Erik S. 2002. "Mixed Electoral Rules and Party Strategies: Responses to Incentives by Ukraine's Rukh and Russia's Yabloko." *Party Politics* 8(6): 719-733.

Herron, Erik S. and Misa Nishikawa. 2001. "Contamination Effects and the Number of Parties in Mixed-Superposition Electoral Systems." *Electoral Studies* 21(1): 63-86.

Hetherington, Marc J. 2001. "Resurgent Mass Partisanship: the Role of Elite Polarization." *American Political Science Review* 95(3): 619-631.

Hicken, Allen. 2009. *Building Party Systems in Developing Democracies*. New York, NY: Cambridge University Press.

Hicken, Allen and Erik Martinez Kuhonta. 2011. "Shadows from the Past: Party System Institutionalization in Asia." *Comparative Political Studies* 44(5): 572-597.

Hicken, Allen and Yuko Kasuya. 2003. "A Guide to the Constitutional Structures and Electoral Systems of East, South and Southeast Asia." *Electoral Studies* 22(1): 121-151.

Hickey, Dennis Van Vranken. 1991. "Will Inter-China Trade Change Taiwan or the Mainland?" *Orbis* 35(4): 517-531.

Higley, John, Tong-yi Huang, and Tse-min Lin. 1998. "Elite Settlements in Taiwan." *Journal of Democracy* 9(2): 148-163.

Hirano, Shigeo, James M. Snyder, and Michael M. Ting. 2009. "Distributive Politics with Primaries." *Journal of Politics* 71(4): 1467-1480.

Hopf, Ted. 1991. "Polarity, the Offense-Defense Balance, and War." *American Political Science Review* 85: 475-493.

Horowitz, Donald L. 1990. "Comparing Democratic Systems." *Journal of Democracy* 1(4): 73-79.

Horowitz, Donald L. 2004. "The Alternative Vote and Interethnic Moderation: A Reply to Fraenkel and Grofman." *Public Choice* 121(3/4): 507-516.

Hsieh, John Fuh-sheng. 2004. "National Identity and Taiwan's Mainland China Policy." *Journal of Contemporary China* 13(40): 479-490.

Hsieh, John Fuh-sheng. 2011. "The Logic of Semi-Presidentialism: Loopholes, History, and Political Conflict." *Issues & Studies* 47(1): 57-78.

Hsieh, John Fuh-sheng. 2013. "Continuity and Change in Party Politics in Japan, Taiwan and South Korea." *East Asian Policy* 5(3): 76-85.

Hsieh, John Fuh-sheng and Emerson M.S. Niou. 1996. "Issue Voting in the Republic of Chinaon Taiwan's 1992 Legislative Yuan Election." *International Political Science Review* 17(1): 13-27.

Hsieh, John Fuh-sheng and Jih-wen Lin. 2016. "East Asia: Variable Support for Democracy in a Diverse Region." In *Citizens and Democracy: Does Growing Up Democratic Make a Difference?* eds. David Denemark, Robert Mattes, and Richard G. Niemi. Boulder, CO: Lynne Rienner, pp. 83-104.

Hu, Fu. 1987. "The Mutation and Reconstruction of the Constitutional Structure." *National Taiwan University Law Review* 16(2): 1-32.

Huang, Chi, Ming-Feng Kuo, and Hans Stockton. 2016. "The Consequences of MMM on Party Systems." In *Mixed-Member Majoritarian Electoral Systems in Constitutional Context: Taiwan, Japan, and Beyond*, eds. Nathan F. Batto, Chi Huang, Alexander C. Tan, and Gary W. Cox. Ann Arbor, MI: University of Michigan Press, pp. 25-51.

Huang, Chi, Woosang Kim, and Samuel Wu. 1992. "Conflicts across the Taiwan Strait, 1951-1978." *Issues & Studies* 28(6): 35-58.

Huang, Mab. 1976. *Intellectual Ferment for Political Reforms in Taiwan*. Ann Arbor, MI: Center of Chinese Studies, University of Michigan.

Huber, John D. 1996. *Rationalizing Parliament: Legislative Institutions and Party Politics in France*. New York, NY: Cambridge University Press.

Huntington, Samuel P. 1993. *The Third Wave: Democratization in the Late 20th Century*. Norman, OK: University of Oklahoma Press.

Immergut, Ellen M. 2005. "Historical-Institutionalism in Political Science and the Problem of Change." In *Understanding Change: Models, Methodologies, and Metaphors*, eds. Andreas Wimmer and Reinhart Kössler. Basingstoke, UK: Palgrave Macmillan, pp. 237-259.

Inter-Parliamentary Union. 2008. "Assemblée nationale (National Assembly)." http://www.ipu.org/ parline-e/reports/ 2113_B.htm (accessed November 24, 2008).

Ishikawa, Masumi. 1995. *Sengo seiji shi* [Postwar Political History]. Tokyo, Japan: Iwanami shoten.

Jacob, Bruce. 1990. "Taiwanese and the Chinese Nationalist, 1937-1945." *Modem China* 16(1): 84-118.

Jacob, Neil. 1996. *U.S. Aid to Taiwan*. New York, NY: Praeger.

Jaconelli, Joseph. 1999. "The Nature of Constitutional Convention." *Legal Studies* 19(1): 24-46.

Jaconelli, Joseph. 2005. "Do Constitutional Conventions Bind?" *Cambridge Law Journal* 64(1): 149-176.

Jennings, Ivor. 1959. *The Law and the Constitution*. London, UK: University of London Press.

Jervis, Robert. 1978. "Cooperation under the Security Dilemma." *World Politics* 30: 167-214.

Jervis, Robert. 1982. "Security Regimes." *International Organization* 36: 357-378.

Jia, Qingguo. 1994. "Toward the Center: Implications of Integration and Democratization for Taiwan's Mainland Policy." *Journal of Northeast Asian Studies* 13: 49-63.

Jones, Mark P. 1995. *Electoral Laws and the Survival of Presidential Democracies*. Notre Dame, Indiana: University of Notre Dame Press.

Jou, Willy. 2009. "Electoral Reform and Party System Development in Japan and Taiwan: A Comparative Study." *Asian Survey* 49(5): 759-785.

Jung, Jai Kwan and Christopher J. Deering. 2015. "Constitutional Choices: Uncertainty and Institutional Design in Democratising Nations." *International Political Science Review* 36(1): 60-77.

Kapstein, Ethan B. and Nathan Converse. 2008. *The Fate of Young Democracies*. Cambridge, UK: Cambridge University Press.

Katz, Richard. 1980. *A Theory of Parties and Electoral Systems*. Baltimore, MD: Johns Hopkins University Press.

Katz, Richard. 2005. "Why Are There So Many (or So Few) Electoral Reforms?" In *The Politics of Electoral Systems*, eds. Michael Gallagher and Paul Mitchell. Oxford, UK: Oxford University Press, pp. 57-76.

Kau, James B. and Paul H. Rubin. 1979. "Self-interest, Ideology, and Logrolling in Congressional Voting." *Journal of Law and Economics* 22(2): 365-384.

Kaufmann, Bruno and Mattias Goldmann. 2004. *Taiwan 2004 Referendum Assessment Report*. Initiative and Referendum Institute Europe.

Keohane, Robert O. 1984. *After Hegemony: Cooperation and Discord in the World Political Economy*. Princeton, NJ: Princeton University Press.

Keohane, Robert O. 1989a. "International Liberalism Reconsidered." In *Economic Limits to Modern Politics*, ed. J. Dunn. Cambridge, UK: Cambridge University Press.

Keohane, Robert O. 1989b. *International Institutions and State Power*. Boulder, CO: Westview Press.

Kernell, Samuel. 1997. *Going Public: New Strategies of Presidential Leadership*. Washington, DC: CQ-Roll Call Group Books.

King, Gary and Langche Zeng. 2001. "Logistic Regression in Rare Events Data." *Political Analysis* 9: 137-163.

King, Gary, Robert O. Keohane, and Sidney Verba. 1994. *Designing Social Inquiry: Scientific Inference in Qualitative Research*. Princeton, NJ: Princeton University Press.

Kirschke, Linda. 2007. "Semipresidentialism and the Perils of Power-sharing in Neopatrimonial States." *Comparative Political Studies* 40(11): 1372-1394.

Krasner, Stephen D. 1983. *International Regimes*. Ithaca, NY: Cornell University Press.

Krehbiel, Keith. 1998. *Pivotal Politics: A Theory of U.S. Lawmaking*. Chicago, IL: University of Chicago Press.

Kyofu, Utsu. 1996. S*aishin rekidai naikaku soran* [A Compendium of the Updated Chronicle of Cabinets]. Tokyo, Japan: Kabushiki kaisha jepi tsushinsha.

Lacy, Dean and Emerson M. S. Niou. 2000a. "Nonseparable Preference and the Elections in Double-Member Districts." *Journal of Theoretical Politics* 10(1): 89-110.

Lacy, Dean and Emerson M. S. Niou. 2000b. "A Problem with Referendums." *Journal of Theoretical Politics* 12(1): 5-31.

Lacy, Dean, and Emerson M. S. Niou. 2013. "Nonseparable Preferences and Issue Packaging in Elections." In *Advances in Political Economy: Institutions, Modeling, and Empirical Analysis*, eds. Norman Schofield, Gonzalo Caballero, and Daniel Kselman. Berlin, Germany: Springer-Verlag, pp. 203-215.

Lai, Tse-han, Raymond Myers, and Wou Wei. 1991. *A Tragic Beginning: The Taiwan Uprising of February 28, 1947*. Stanford, CA: Stanford University Press.

Laing, J. D., S. Nakabayashi, and B. Slotznick. 1983. "Winners, Blockers and the Status Quo: Simple Collective Decision Games and the Core." *Public Choice* 40: 263-279.

Lakeman, Enid. 1984. "The Case for Proportional Representation." In *Choosing an Electoral System: Issues and Alternatives*, eds. Arend Lijphart and Bernard Grofman. New York, NY: Praeger, pp. 41-52.

Lakeman, Enid and James D. Lambert. 1955. *Voting in Democracies: A Study of Majority and Proportional Electoral Systems*. London, UK: Faber and Faber.

Lane, Jan-Erik and Svante Ersson, eds. 1999. *Politics and Society in Western Europe*. London, UK: Sage Publication Inc.

Laver, Michael and Kenneth A. Shepsle. 1996. *Making and Breaking Governments: Cabinets and Legislatures in Parliamentary Democracies*. Cambridge, UK: Cambridge University Press.

Laver, Michael and Norman Schofield. 1991. *Multiparty Government: The Politics of Coalition in Europe*. Oxford, UK: Oxford University Press.

Layman, Geoffrey C., Thomas M. Carsey, and Juliana Menasce Horowitz. 2006. "Party Polarization in American Politics: Characteristics, Causes, and Consequences." *Annual Review of Political Science* 9(1): 83-110.

Leng, Tse-Kang. 1996. *The Taiwan-China Connection: Democracy and Development Across the Taiwan Straits*. Westview, FL: Boulder.

Lepsius, M. Ranier. 1978. "From Fragmented Party Democracy to Government by Emergency Decree and National Socialist Takeover: Germany." In *The Breakdown of Democratic Regimes: Europe*, eds. Juan J. Lina and Alfred Stepan. Baltimore, MD: Johns Hopkins University Press, pp. 34-79.

Levendusky, Matthew S. 2009. "The Microfoundations of Mass Polarization." *Political Analysis* 17: 162-176.

Lewis, David. 1969. *Convention: A Philosophical Study*. Cambridge, MA: Harvard University Press.

Leyenaar, Monique and Reuven Y. Hazan. 2011. "Reconceptualising Electoral Reform." *West European Politics* 34(3): 437-455.

Li, Chenghong. 2005. "Two-Level Games, Issue Politicization, and the Disarray of Taiwan's Cross-Strait Policy after the 2000 Presidential Election." *East Asia: An International Quarterly* 22(3): 41-62.

Liao, Da-Chi and Herlin Chien. 2005. "Why no Cohabitation in Taiwan?" *China Perspectives* 58: 55-59.

Lijphart, Arend. 1984. *Democracies: Patterns of Majoritarian and Consensus Government in Twenty-One Countries*. New Haven, CT and London, UK: Yale University Press.

Lijphart, Arend. 1990. "The Political Consequences of Electoral Laws, 1945-85. "*American Political Science Review* 84(2): 481-496.

Lijphart, Arend. 1994. *Electoral Systems and Party Systems: A Study of Twenty-Seven Democracies, 1945-1990*. Oxford, UK: Oxford University Press.

Lijphart, Arend. 1997. "The Difficult Science of Electoral Systems: Acommentary on the Critique by Alber to Penades." *Electoral* Studies 16: 73-77.

Lijphart, Arend. 1999a. *Democracies: Patterns of Majoritarian and Consensus Government in Thirty-Six Countries*. New Haven, CT: Yale University Press.

Lijphart, Arend. 1999b. *Patterns of Democracy: Government Forms and Performance in Thirty-Six Countries*. New Haven, CT: Yale University Press.

Lijphart, Arend. 2012. *Patterns of Democracy: Government Forms and Performance in Thirty-Six Countries*, 2nd ed. New Haven, CT: Yale University Press.

Lijphart, Arend and Bernard Grofman, eds. 1984. *Choosing an Electoral System: Issues & Alternatives*. New York, NY: Praeger.

Lijphart, Arend, Rafael Lopez Pintor, and Yasunori Sone. 1986. "The Limited Vote and the Single Non-transferable Vote: Lessons from the Japanese and Spanish Examples. "In *Electoral Laws and Their Political Consequences*, eds. Bernard Grofman and Arend Lijphart. New York, NY: Agathon Press Inc., pp.154-169.

Lin, Chia-Lung. 1998. *Paths to Democracy: Taiwan in Comparative Perspective*. Doctoral dissertation,

Department of Political Science, Yale University, New Haven, CT.

Lin, Jih-wen. 1999. "Democratization under One-party Dominance: Explaining Taiwan's Paradoxical Transition." *Issues & Studies* 35(6): 1-28.

Lin, Jih-wen. 2000. "Two-Level Games Between Rival Regimes: Domestic Politics and the Remaking of Cross-Strait Relations." *Issues & Studies* 36(6): 1-26.

Lin, Jih-wen. 2003. "Looking for the Magic Number: The Optimal District Magnitude for Political Parties in d'Hondt PR and SNTV." *Electoral Studies* 22(1): 49-63.

Lin, Jih-wen. 2002. "Transition through Transaction: Taiwan's Constitutional Re-forms in the Lee Teng-hui Era." *American Asian Review* 20(2): 123-155.

Lin, Jih-wen. 2004. "Taiwan's Referendum Act and the Stability of the Status Quo." *Issues & Studies* 40(2): 119-153.

Lin, Jih-wen. 2008. "The Institutional Context of President Chen Shui-bian's Cross-Strait Messages." *Issues & Studies* 44(1): 1-31.

Lin, Jih-wen. 2011a. "The Endogenous Change in Electoral Systems: The Case of SNTV." *Party Politics* 17(3): 365-384.

Lin, Jih-wen. 2011b. "A Veto Player Theory of Policy Making in Semi-Presidential Regimes: The Case of Taiwan's Ma Ying-jeou Presidency." *Journal of East Asian Studies* 11(3): 407-435.

Lin, Jih-wen. 2011c. "The Rules of Electoral Competition and the Accountability of Semi-Presidential Governments." In *Semi-Presidentialism and Democracy*, eds. Robert Elgie, Sophia Moestrup, and Yu-Shan Wu. London, UK: Palgrave Macmillan, pp. 61-80.

Lin, Jih-wen. 2016a. "The Consequences of Constitutional Systems on Party Systems." In *Mixed-Member Majoritarian Electoral Systems in Constitutional Context: Taiwan, Japan, and Beyond*, eds. Nathan F. Batto, Chi Huang, Alexander C. Tan, and Gary W. Cox. Ann Arbor, MI: University of Michigan Press, pp. 52-72.

Lin, Jih-wen. 2016b. "Taiwan's Semi-Presidential System Was Easy to Establish but Is Difficult to Fix: A Comparison between the Constitutional Reform Efforts of 1997 and 2015." *Taiwan Journal of Democracy* 12(2): 39-57.

Lin, Jih-wen. 2016c. "The PRC as a Player in Taiwan's Domestic Politics: A Two-Level Game Analysis." In *Taiwan and the 'China Impact': Challenges and Opportunities*, ed. Gunter Schubert. London, UK and New York, NY: Routledge, pp. 15-35.

Lin, Jih-wen. 2017. "How Are the Powers of the President Decided? Vote Trading in the Making of Taiwan's Semi-Presidential Constitution." *International Political Science Review* 38(5): 659-672.

Linz, Juan J. 1990. "The Perils of Presidentialism." *Journal of Democracy* 1(4): 51-69.

Linz, Juan J. 1994. "Presidential or Parliamentary Democracy: Does It Make a Difference?" In *The Failure of Presidential Democracy: Comparative Perspectives*, eds. Juan J. Linz and Arturo Valenzuela. Baltimore, MD: Johns Hopkins University Press, pp. 3-87.

Linz, Juan J. 1997. *Presidentialism and Democracy in Latin America.* Cambridge, UK: Cambridge University Press.

Linz, Juan J. and Alfred Stepan. 1996. *Problems of Democratic Transition and Consolidation: Southern Europe, South America, and Post-Communist Europe.* Baltimore, MD: Johns Hopkins University Press.

Linz, Juan J. and Arturo Valenzuela, eds. 1994. *The Failure of Presidential Democracy: The Case of Latin America.* Baltimore, MD: Johns Hopkins University Press.

Lipset, Seymour Martin. 1963. *Political Man: The Social Bases of Politics.* New York, NY: Anchor Books.

Lipson, Charle. 1984. "International Cooperation in Economic and Security Affairs." *World Politics* 37: 1-23.

Lo, Chih-cheng and Jih-wen Lin. 1995. "Between Sovereignty and Security: A Mixed Strategy Analysis of Current Cross-Strait Interaction." *Issues & Studies* 31(3): 64-91.

Lohmann, Susanne. 1995. "The Poverty of Green and Shapiro." In *The Rational Choice Controversy*, ed. Jeffrey Friedman. New Haven, CT: Yale University Press, pp. 127-154.

Loosemore, John and Victor J. Hanby. 1971. "The Theoretical Limits of Maximum Distortion: Some Analytic Expressions for Electoral Systems." *British Journal of Political Science* 1(4): 467-477.

Mainwaring, Scott. 1993. "Presidentialism, Multipartism, and Democracy: The Difficult Combination." *Comparative Political Studies* 26(2): 198-228.

Mainwaring, Scott and Matthew Soberg Shugart, eds. 1997. *Presidentialism and Democracy in Latin America.* Cambridge, UK: Cambridge University Press.

Mann, Michael. 1993. *The Sources of Social Power: Volume II. The Rise of Classes and Nation-State, 1760-1914.* Cambridge, UK: Cambridge University Press.

Marshall, Geoffrey. 1984. *Constitutional Conventions: The Rules and Forms of Political Accountability.* Oxford, UK: Clarendon Press.

Martin, Pierre. 2000. *Comprendre les Évolutions Électorales: La Théorie des Réalignements Revisitée.* Paris, France: Presses de Science Po.

Massicotte, L. and A. Blais. 1999. "Mixed Electoral Systems: A Conceptual and Empirical Survey." *Electoral Studies* 18(3): 341-366.

Mayhew, David R. 1991. *Divided We Govern: Party Control, Lawmaking, and Investigation, 1946-*

1990. New Haven, CT: Yale University Press.

Maynard, John and George R. Prince. 1973. "The Logic of Animal Conflict." *Nature* 246: 15-18.

McCarty, Nolan, Keith T. Poole, and Howard Rosenthal. 2006. *Polarized America: The Dance of Ideology and Unequal Riches.* Cambridge, MA: MIT Press.

McCubbins, Mathew D. and Frances M. Rosenbluth. 1995. "Party Provision for Personal Politics: Dividing the Vote in Japan." In *Structure and Policy in Japan and the United States,* eds. Peter F. Cowhey and Mathew D. McCubbins. Cambridge, UK: Cambridge University Press, pp. 35-55.

McFaul, Michael. 1999. "Institutional Design, Uncertainty, and Path Dependency During Transitions: Cases from Russia." *Constitutional Political Economy* 10(1): 27-52.

McKelvey, Richard D. 1976. "Intransitivities in Multidimensional Voting Models and Some Implications for Agenda Control." *Journal of Economic Theory* 12: 472-482.

Meitetsu, Haruyama. 1980. "Kindai nihon no shokuminchi toji to hara takashi." (Modern Japanese Colonial Rule and Hara Takashi) In *Nihon shokuminchi shugi no seijiteki tenkai (1895-1934)* (The Political Development of Japan's Colonialism, 1895-1934), eds. Haruyama Meitetsu and Wakabayashi Masahiro. Tokyo, Japan: Ajia seikei gakkai, pp. 1-75.

Merrill III, Samuel and Bernard Grofman. 1999. *A Unified Theory of Voting.* New York, NY: Cambridge University Press.

Metcalf, Lee Kendall. 2000. "Measuring Presidential Power." *Comparative Political Studies* 33(5): 660-685.

Michelat, Guy. 1993. "In Search of Left and Right." In *The French Voter Decides,* eds. Daniel Boy and Nonna Mayer. Trans. Cynihia Schoch. Ann Arbor, MI: University of Michigan Press, pp. 65-90.

Miller, Michael K. 2013. "Electoral Authoritarianism and Democracy: A Formal Model of Regime Transitions." *Journal of Theoretical Politics* 25(2): 153-181.

Miller, Nicholas R., Bernard Grofman, and Scott L. Feld. 1989. "The Geometry of Majority Rule." *Journal of Theoretical Politics* 1(4): 379-406.

Ministère de l'Intérieur. 2009. "Résultats électoraux en France." http://www.interieur.gouv.fr/sections/a_votre_service/elections/resultats/ (accessed March 2, 2009).

Mao, Tien-hung and Yun-han Chu. 1996. "Building Democratic Institutions in Taiwan." *The China Quarterly* 148: 1103-1132.

Mo, Jongryn and David Brady. 1999. "The SNTV and the Politics of Electoral Systems in Korea." In *Elections and Campaigning in Japan, Korea, and Taiwan: Toward the Study of Embedded Institutions,* eds. Bernard Grofman, Sung-Chull Lee, Edwin A. Winckler, and Brian Woodall. Ann Arbor, MI: University of Michigan Press.

Moestrup, Sophia. 2007. "Semi-presidentialism in Young Democracies: Help or Hindrance?" In *Semi-Presidentialism Outside Europe: A Comparative Study*, eds. Robert Elgie and Sophia Moestrup. Oxon, UK: Routledge, pp. 30-55.

Moon, Eric P. 1997. "Single Non-Transferable Vote Methods in Taiwan in 1996: Effects of an Electoral System." *Asian Survey* 37: 652-668.

Morgenthau, Hans J. 1978. *Politics Among Nation.* New York, NY: Knopf.

Moser, Robert G. 1999. "Electoral Systems and the Number of Parties in Postcommunist States." *World Politics* 51: 359-384.

Moser, Robert G. and Ethan Scheiner. 2004. "Mixed Electoral Systems and Electoral System Effects: Controlled Comparison and Cross-National Analysis." *Electoral Studies* 23(4): 575-599.

Moser, Robert G. and Frank C. Thames, Jr. 2001. "Compromise Amidst Political Conflict: The Origins of Russia's Mixed Member System." In *Mixed-Member Electoral Systems: The Best of Both Worlds?* eds. Matthew Soberg Shugart and Martin P. Wattenberg. Oxford, UK: Oxford University Press, pp. 255-278.

Mozaffar, Shaheen, James R. Scarritt, and Glen Galaich. 2003. "Electoral Institutions, Ethnopolitical Cleavages, and Party Systems in Africa's Emerging Democracies." *American Political Science Review* 97(3): 379-390.

Mueller, Dennis C., ed. 1997. *Perspectives on Public Choice.* New York, NY: Cambridge University Press.

Mueller, Dennis C. 2003. *Public Choice III.* Cambridge, UK and New York, NY: Cambridge University Press.

Muller, Wolfgang C. and Kaare Strom, eds. 2000. *Coalition Governments in Western Europe.* Oxford, UK: Oxford University Press.

Muller, Wolfgang C., W. Philipp, and B. Steininger. 1996. "Austria." In *Party and Government: An Inquiry into the Relationship between Government and Supporting Parties in Liberal Democracies*, eds. Jean Blondel and Maurizio Cotta. Houndmills, UK: Macmillan Press, pp. 91-109.

Naikaku seido hyakujunen kinen shi henshu iinkai. 1996. *Naikaku seido hyakunen shi, II tsuiroku* [The Cabinet System in One Hundred Years, Appendix II]. Tokyo, Japan: Okura sho insatsu kyoku.

Nakamura, Yutaka. 2009. "SSB Preferences: Nonseparable Utility or Nonseparable Beliefs." In *The Mathematics of Preference, Choice and Order: Essays in Honor of Peter C. Fishburn*, eds. Steven Brams, William V. Gehrlein, and Fred S. Roberts. Berlin, German: Springer, pp. 39-55.

Nathan, Andrew. 1992. "The Effects of Taiwan's Political Reforms on Taiwan-Mainland Relations." In *Political Change in Taiwan*, eds. Tun-jen Cheng and Stephan Haggard. Boulder, CO: Lynne

Rienner, pp. 207-219.

Neustadt, Richard E. 1990. *Presidential Power and the Modern Presidents: The Politics of Leadership from Roosevelt to Reagan.* New York, NY: Free Press.

Niou, Emerson M. S. 2004. "Understanding Taiwan Independence and Its Policy Implications." *Asian Survey* 44: 555-567.

Niou, Emerson M. S. 2005. "A New Measure of Preferences on the Independence-Unification Issue in Taiwan." *Journal of Asian and African Studies* 40(1/2): 91-104.

Nishikawa, Misa and Erik S. Herron. 2004. "Mixed Electoral Rules' Impact on Party Systems." *Electoral Studies* 23(4): 753-768.

Noble, Gregory W. 1999. "Opportunity Lost: Partisan Incentives and the 1997 Constitutional Revisions in Taiwan." *The China Journal* 41: 89-114.

Nohlen, Dieter. 1984a. "Changes and Choices in Electoral Systems." In *Choosing an Electoral System: Issues and Alternatives*, eds. Arend Lijphart and Bernard Grofman. New York, NY: Praeger, pp. 217-224.

Nohlen, Dieter. 1984b. "Two Incompatible Principles of Representation." In *Choosing an Electoral System: Issues and Alternatives*, eds. Arend Lijphart and Bernard Grofman. New York, NY: Praeger, pp. 83-89.

Norris, Pippa. 1997. "Choosing Electoral Systems: Proportional, Majoritarian and Mixed Systems." *International Political Science Review* 18(3): 297-312.

Nousiainen, Jaakko. 1988. "Bureaucratic Tradition, Semi-Presidential Rule and Parliamentary Government: The Case of Finland." *European Journal of Political Research* 16(2): 229-249.

O'Malley, Eoin. 2006. "Investigating the Effects of Directly Electing the Prime Minister." *Government and Opposition* 41(2): 137-162.

Ordeshook, Peter C. 1986. *Game Theory and Political Theory: An Introduction.* Cambridge, UK: Cambridge University Press.

Ordeshook, Peter C. 1990. "The Emerging Discipline of Political Economy." In *Perspectives on Positive Political Economy*, eds. James E. Alt and Kenneth A. Shepsle. Cambridge, UK: Cambridge University Press, pp. 9-30.

Ordeshook, Peter C. and Olga V. Shvetsova. 1994. "Ethnic Heterogeneity, District Magnitude, and the Number of Parties." *American Journal of Political Science* 38(1): 100-123.

Osborne, Martin J. and Ariel Rubinstein. 1994. *A Course in Game Theory.* Cambridge, UK: MIT Press.

Oye, Kenneth A. 1986. *Cooperation Under Anarchy.* Princeton: Princeton University Press.

Pasquino, Gianfranco. 1997. "Semi-presidentialism: A Political Model at Work." *European Journal of*

Political Research 31(1/2): 128-137.

Peattie, Mark R. 1984. "Japanese Attitudes toward Colonialism, 1895-1945." In *Japanese Colonial Empire, 1895-1945*, eds. Ramon H. Myers and Mark R. Peattie. Princeton, NJ: Princeton University Press, pp. 80-127.

Pempel, T. J. 1990. *Uncommon Democracies: The One-Party Dominant Regimes*. Ithaca, NY: Cornell University Press.

Pierce, Roy. 1991. "The Executive Divided Against Itself: Cohabitation in France, 1986-1988." *Governance* 4(3): 270-294.

Pierson, Paul. 1996. "The Path to European Integration: A Historical Institutionalist Analysis." *Comparative Political Studies* 29(2): 123-163.

Plott, Charles. 1967. "A Notion of Equilibrium and Its Possibility under Majority Rule." *American Economic Review* 57(4): 787-806.

Poast, Paul. 2012. "Does Issue Linkage Work? Evidence from European Alliance Negotiations, 1860 to 1945." *International Organization* 66(2): 277-310.

Poast, Paul. 2013a. "Can Issue Linkage Improve Treaty Credibility? Buffer State Alliances as a 'Hard Case'." *Journal of Conflict Resolution* 57(5): 739-764.

Poast, Paul. 2013b. "Issue Linkage and International Cooperation: An Empirical Investigation." *Conflict Management and Peace Science* 30(3): 286-303.

Poole, Keith T. and Howard Rosenthal. 2001. "D-Nominate after 10 Years: A Comparative Update to Congress: A Political-Economic History of Roll-Call Voting." *Legislative Studies Quarterly* 26: 5-29.

Portelli, Hugues. 1999. "Arbitre ou Chef de l'Opposition?" *Pouvoirs* 91: 59-70.

Poulard, Jean V. 1990. "The French Double Executive and the Experience of Cohabitation." *Political Science Quarterly* 105(2): 243-267.

Powell, Robert. 1991. "Absolute and Relative Gains in International Relations Theory." *American Political Science Review* 85: 1303-1320.

Powell, Robert. 1994. "Anarchy in International Relations Theory: The Neorealist-neoliberal Debate." *International Organization* 48: 313-344.

Putnam, Robert D. 1988. "Diplomacy and Domestic Politics: The Logic of Two-Level Games." *International Organization* 42(3): 427-460.

Quester, George. 1988. *Offense and Defense in the International System*. New York, NY: Wiley.

Rae, Douglas W. 1967. *The Political Consequences of Electoral Laws*. New Haven, CT: Yale University Press.

Rae, Douglas W. 1971. *The Consequences of Electoral Laws*, 2nd ed. New Haven, CT: Yale University Press.

Rae, Douglas W., Victor Hanby, and John Loosemore. 1971. "Thresholds of Representation and Thresholds of Exclusion: An Analytic Note on Electoral Systems." *Comparative Politics* 3(4): 479-488.

Rahat, Gideon. 2004. "The Study of the Politics of Electoral Reform in the 1990s: Theoretical and Methodological Lessons." *Comparative Politics* 36(4): 461-479.

Ramseyer, J. Mark and Frances M. Rosenbluth. 1993. *Japan's Political Marketplace*. Cambridge, MA: Harvard University Press.

Ramseyer, J. Mark and Frances M. Rosenbluth. 1997. *Japan's Political Marketplace: With a New Preface*. Cambridge, MA: Harvard University Press.

Rasmusen, Eric. 1989. *Games and Information: An Introduction to Game Theory*. Cambridge, UK: Blackwell.

Reed, Steven R. 1990. "Structure and Behaviour: Extending Duverger's Law to the Japanese Case." *British Journal of Political Science* 20: 335-356.

Reed, Steven R. 1996. "Seats and Votes: Testing Taagepera in Japan." *Electoral Studies* 15: 71-81.

Reed, Steven R. 1999. "Strategic Voting in the 1996 Japanese General Election." *Comparative Political Studies* 32(2): 257-270.

Reed, Steven R., ed. 2003. *Japanese Electoral Politics: Creating a New Party System*. London, UK: Routledge Curzon.

Reed, Steven R. and Michael F. Thies. 2001. "The Causesquences of Electoral Reform in Japan." In *Mixed-Member Electoral Systems: The Best of Both Worlds?* eds. Matthew Soberg Shugart and Martin P. Wattenberg. Oxford, UK: Oxford University Press, pp. 152-172.

Reilly, Benjamin. 2007a. "Electoral Systems and Party Systems in East Asia." *Journal of East Asian Studies* 7(2): 185-202.

Reilly, Benjamin. 2007b. "Democratization and Electoral Reform in the Asia-Pacific Region: Is There an 'Asian Model' of Democracy?" *Comparative Political Studies* 40(11): 1350-1371.

Renwick, Alan. 2010. *The Politics of Electoral Reform: Changing the Rules of Democracy*. Cambridge, UK: Cambridge University Press.

Rhodes, R. A. W., Sarah A. Binder, and Bert A. Rockman, eds. 2006. *The Oxford Handbook of Political Institutions*. New York, NY: Oxford University Press.

Riker, William H. 1962. *The Theory of Political Coalitions*. New Haven, CT: Yale University Press.

Riker, William H. 1982. "The Two-Party System and Duverger's Law: An Essay on the History of

Political Science." *American Political Science Review* 76(4): 753-766.

Riker, William H. 1992. "The Justification of Bicameralism." *International Political Science Review* 13(1): 101-116.

Riker, William H. and Peter C. Ordeshook. 1968. "A Theory of the Calculus of Voting." *American Political Science Review* 62(1): 25-42.

Riker, William H. and Steven J. Brams. 1973. "The Paradox of Vote Trading." *American Political Science Review* 67(4): 1235-1247.

Rogers, James R. 2005. "The Impact of Divided Government on Legislative Production." *Public Choice* 123: 217-233.

Rokkan, Stein. 1968. "Elections: Electoral Systems." In *International Encyclopedia of the Social Sciences*. New York, NY: Crowell-Collier-Macmillan, pp. 256-281.

Rokkan, Stein. 1970. *Citizens, Elections, Parties: Approaches to the Comparative Study of the Process of Development*. Oslo, Norway: Universiteitsforiaget.

Roper, Steven D. 2002. "Are All Semipresidential Regimes the Same? A Comparison of Premier—Presidential Regimes." *Comparative Politics* 34(3): 253-272.

Rosecrance, Richard. 1986. *The Rise of the Trading State*. New York, NY: Basic Books.

Rosenau, James N. 1969. *Linkage Politics: Essays on the Convergence of National and International Systems*. New York, NY: Free Press.

Rosenbluth, Frances McCall. 1996. Internationalization and Electoral Politics in Japan. In *Internationalization and Eomestic Politics*, eds. Robert O. Keohane and Helen V. Milner. New York, NY: Cambridge University Press, pp.137-158.

Rothstein, Bo. 1996. "Political Institutions: An Overview." In *A New Handbook of Political Science*, eds. Robert E. Goodin and Hans-Dieter Klingermann. Oxford, UK: Oxford University Press, pp. 133-166.

Sakamoto, Takayuki. 1999. "Explaining Electoral Reform: Japan Versus Italy and New Zealand." *Party Politics* 5(4): 419-438.

Samuels, David J. 2004. "Presidentialism and Accountability for the Economy in Comparative Perspective." *American Political Science Review* 98(3): 425-436.

Samuels, David J. and Matthew S. Shugart. 2010a. *Presidents, Parties, Premiers: How the Separation of Powers Affects Party Organization and Behavior*. New York, NY: Cambridge University Press.

Samuels, David J. and Matthew S. Shugart. 2010b. *Presidents, Parties, Prime Ministers: A Framework for Analysis*. Cambridge, UK: Cambridge University Press.

Sankoff, D. and K. Mellos. 1972. "The Swing Ratio and Game Theory." *American Political Science*

Review 66: 551-554.

Sartori, Giovanni. 1968. *Representational Systems, International Encyclopedia of the Social Sciences.* New York, NY: Crowell-Collier-Macmillan.

Sartori, Giovanni. 1994. "Neither Presidentialism nor Parliamentarism." In *The Failure of Presidential Democracy, Vol. 1: Comparative Perspectives*, eds. Juan J. Linz and Arturo Valenzuela. Baltimore, MD: Johns Hopkins University Press.

Sartori, Giovanni. 1997. *Comparative Constitutional Engineering: An Inquiry into Structures, Incentives and Outcomes*, 2nd ed. Washington Square, New York, NY: New York University Press.

Schelling, Thomas. 1960. *The Strategy of Conflict*. Cambridge, MA: Harvard University Press.

Schwartz, Thomas. 1977. "Collective Choice, Separation of Issues and Vote Trading." *American Political Science Review* 71(3): 999-1010.

Schmitter, Philippe C. and Terry Lynn Karl. 1991. "What Democracy Is…and Is Not." *Journal of Democracy* 2(3): 75-87.

Shepsle, Kenneth A. and Barry R. Weingast. 1981. "Structure-induced Equilibrium and Legislative Choice." *Public Choice* 37: 503-519.

Shields, Todd G. and Chi Huang. 1995. "Presidential Vetoes: An Event Count Model." *Political Research Quarterly* 48(3): 559-572.

Shiratori, Rei. 1986. *Shinpan: Nihonno naikaku III* [A New Edition: The Cabinets of Japan III].Tokyo, Japan: Kabushikikaisha shinhyoron.

Shiratori, Rei. 1987. *Shinpan: Nihonno naikaku II* [A New Edition: The Cabinets of Japan II]. Tokyo, Japan: Kabushikikaisha shinhyoron.

Shiratori, Rei. 1995. "The Politics of Electoral Reform in Japan." *International Political Science Review* 16: 79-94.

Shugart, Matthew Soberg. 1995. "The Electoral Cycle and Institutional Sources of Divided Presidential Government." *American Political Science Review* 89(2): 327-343.

Shugart, Matthew Soberg. 2001. "'Extreme' Electoral Systems and the Appeal of the Mixed-Member Alternative." In *Mixed-Member Electoral Systems: The Best of Both Worlds?* eds. Matthew Soberg Shugart and Martin P. Wattenberg. Oxford, UK: Oxford University Press, pp. 24-51.

Shugart, Matthew Soberg. 2005. "Semi-presidential Systems: Dual Executive and Mixed Authority Patterns." *French Politics* 3(3): 323-351.

Shugart, Matthew Soberg and John M. Carey. 1992. *Presidents and Assemblies: Constitutional Design and Electoral Dynamics*. Cambridge, UK and New York, NY: Cambridge University Press.

Shugart, Matthew Soberg and Martin P. Wattenberg, eds. 2001. *Mixed-Member Electoral Systems: The*

Best of Both Worlds? Oxford, UK: Oxford University Press.

Siaroff, Alan. 2003. "Comparative Presidencies: The Inadequacy of the Presidential, Semi-presidential and Parliamentary Distinction." *European Journal of Political Research* 42(3): 287-312.

Site de Premier Ministre. 2009. "Histoire des Chefs de Gouvernement." http://www.premier-ministre. gouv.fr/acteurs/premier_ministre/histoire_chefs_gouvernement_28/ (accessed March 2, 2009).

Skach, Cindy. 2005. *Borrowing Constitutional Designs: Constitutional Law in Weimar Germany and the French Fifth Republic.* Princeton, NJ: Princeton University Press.

Slinko, Arkadii and Shaun White. 2010. "Proportional Representation and Strategic Voters." *Journal of Theoretical Politics* 22(3): 301-332.

Snidal, Duncan. 1991. "Relative Gains and the Pattern of International Cooperation." *American Political Science Review* 85: 701-726.

Solum, Lawrence B. 2008. "Constitutional Possibilities." *Indiana Law Journal* 83(1): 307-337.

Soma, Masao. 1986. *Nihon senkyo seido shi: futsu senkyoho kara koshoku senkyoho made* [History of Japan's Electoral Systems: From the Law of General Election to the Law of Public Office Election]. Fukuoka, Japan: Kyushu Daigaku Shuppankai.

Stein, Arthur. 1980. "The Politics of Linkage." *World Politics* 33: 62-81.

Stein, Arthur. 1982. "Coordination and Collaboration: Regimes in an Anarchic World." *International Organization* 36: 299-324.

Steunenberg, Bernard. 2004. "Coordinating Sectoral Policy-making: Searching for Countervailing Mechanisms in the EU Legislative Process." In *A Constitution for the European Union*, eds. C. B. Blankart and D. C. Mueller. Cambridge, MA: MIT Press, pp. 139-167.

Stratmann, Thomas. 1992. "The Effects of Logrolling on Congressional Voting." *American Economic Review* 82(5): 1162-1176.

Stratmann, Thomas. 1995. "Logrolling in the U.S. Congress." *Economic Inquiry* 33(3): 441-456.

Stratmann, Thomas. 2008. "Logrolling." In *The Encyclopedia of Public Choice, Vol. II*, eds. Charles Rowley and Friedrich Schneider. Berlin, Germany: Springer Science & Business Media, pp. 372-374.

Suksi, Markku. 1993. *Bringing in the People: A Comparison of Constitutional Forms and Practices of the Referendum. The Netherlands.* Dordrecht, Notherlands: Martinus Nijhoff.

Suzuki, Motoshi. 1994. "Economic Interdependence, Relative Gains, and International Cooperation: The Case of Monetary Policy Coordination." *International Studies Quarterly* 28: 475-498.

Swaine, Michael D. 2004. "Trouble in Taiwan." *Foreign Affairs* 83(2): 39-49.

Taagepera, Rein. 1986. "Reformulating the Cube Law for Proportional Representation Elections."

American Political Science Review 80: 489-504.

Taagepera, Rein. 1997. "Effective Number of Parties for Incomplete Data." *Electoral Studies* 16(2): 145-151.

Taagepera, Rein. 1998. "Nationwide Inclusion and Exclusion Thresholds of Representation." *Electoral Studies* 17: 405-417.

Taagepera, Rein. 2007. *Predicting Party Sizes: The Logic of Simple Electoral Systems.* Oxford, UK: Oxford University Press.

Taagepera, Rein and John Ensch. 2006. "Institutional Determinants of the Largest Seat Share." *Electoral Studies* 25(4): 760-775.

Taagepera, Rein and Matthew Soberg Shugart. 1989. *Seats & Votes: The Effects & Determinants of Electoral Systems.* New Haven, CT and London, UK: Yale University Press.

Tanaka, Zenichiro. 2005. *Nihon no sosenkyo* [Japan's General Elections]. Tokyo, Japan: Tokyo Daigaku Shuppankai.

Tavits, Margit. 2008. *Presidents with Prime Ministers: Do Direct Elections Matter?* Oxford, UK: Oxford University Press.

Thayer, Nathaniel B. 1996. "The Japanese Prime Minister and His Cabinet." *SAIS Review* 16(2): 71-86.

Thelen, Kathleen. 1999. "Historical Institutionalism in Comparative Politics." *Annual Review of Political Science* 2: 369-404.

Thiébault, Jean-Louis. 2000. "France: Forming and Maintaining Government Coalitions in the Fifth Republic." In *Coalition Governments in Western Europe*, eds. Wolfgang C. Muller and Kaare Strom. Oxford, UK: Oxford University Press, pp. 498-528.

Thody, Malcolm Waller Philip. 1998. *The Fifth French Republic: Presidents, Politics, and Personalities.* London, UK: Routledge.

Thomsen, Danielle M. 2014. "Ideological Moderates Won't Run: How Party Fit Matters for Partisan Polarization in Congress." *The Journal of Politics* 76(3): 786-797.

Tien, Hung-mao. 1997. "Taiwan's Transformation." In *Consolidating the Third Wave Democracies*, eds. Larry Diamond, Marc F. Plattner, Yun-han Chu, and Hung-mao Tien. Baltimore, MD and London, UK: Johns Hopkins University Press, pp. 123-162.

Tien, Hung-mao and Yun-han Chu. 1994. "Taiwan's Domestic Political Reforms, Institutional Change and Power Realignment." In *Taiwan in the Asia-Pacific in the 1990s*, ed. Gary Klintworth. Sydney, Australia: Alien & Unwin, pp. 1-20.

Toshio, Otaka. 1990. *Seijika jinmei jiten* [A Dictionary of Politician Names]. Tokyo, Japan: Nichigai asoshietsu kabushiki kaisha.

Tsebelis, George. 1990. *Nested Games: Rational Choice in Comparative Politics*. Berkeley, CA: University of California Press.

Tsebelis, George. 1994. "The Power of the European Parliament as a Conditional Agenda Setter." *American Political Science Review* 88(1): 128-142.

Tsebelis, George. 1995. "Decision Making in Political Systems: Veto Players in Presidentialism, Parliamentarism, Multicameralism and Multipartyism." *British Journal of Political Science* 25(3): 289-325.

Tsebelis, George. 1999. "Veto Players and Law Production in Parliamentary Democracies: An Empirical Analysis." *American Political Science Review* 93(3): 591-608.

Tsebelis, George. 2002. *Veto Players: How Political Institutions Work*. Princeton, NJ: Princeton University Press.

Tsebelis, George and Eduardo Aleman. 2006. "Presidential Conditional Agenda Setting in Latin America." *World Politics* 57(3): 396-420.

Tsebelis, George and Jeannette Money. 1997. *Bicameralism*. New York, NY: Cambridge University Press.

Tsurumi, E. Patricia. 1977. *Japanese Colonial Education in Taiwan, 1895-1945*. Cambridge, MA: Harvard University Press.

Tullock, Gordon. 1959. "Problems of Majority Voting." *Journal of Political Economy* 67(6): 571-579.

Veser, Ernst. 1999. "Semipresidentialism—Duverger's Concept—A New Political System Model." *Journal of Social Sciences and Philosophy* 11(1): 39-60.

Vowles, Jack. 1995. "The Politics of Electoral Reform in New Zealand." *International Political Science Review* 16(1): 95-115.

Walker, Mark Clarence. 2003. *The Strategic Use of Referendums: Power, Legitimacy, and Democracy*. New York, NY: Palgrave/Macmillan.

Waltz, Kenneth N. 1979. *Theory of International Politics*. Reading, MA: Addison-Wesley Publishing Co.

Wang, T. Y., Chang-chih Lin, and Yi-ching Hsiao. 2016. "Split-Ticket Voting under MMM." In *Mixed-Member Majoritarian Electoral Systems in Constitutional Context: Taiwan, Japan, and Beyond*, eds. Nathan F. Batto, Chi Huang, Alexander C. Tan, and Gary W. Cox. Ann Arbor, MI: University of Michigan Press, pp. 194-226.

Wiatr, Jerzy J. 1996. "Executive-Legislative Relations in Crisis: Poland's Experience, 1989-1993." In *Institutional Design in New Democracies*, eds. Arend Lijphart and Carlos H. Waisman. Boulder, CO: Westview Press, pp. 103-116.

Winckler, Edwin A. 1983. "Mass Political Incorporation, 1500-2000." In *Contending Approaches to the Political Economy of Taiwan*, eds. Edwin A. Winckler and Susan Greenhalgh. New York, NY: M.E. Sharpe, pp. 41-66.

Wu, J. R. and Michael Gold. 2015. "Taiwan's New Political Voices Want More Openness on China Ties," *Reuters*, May 13: http://www.reuters.com/ article/2015/03/13/us-taiwanpolitics-idUSKBN0M90JB20150313 (accessed July 1, 2016).

Wu, Yu-Shan. 1996. "Exploring Dual Triangles: The Development of Taipei-Washington-Beijing Relations." *Issues & Studies* 32(10): 26-52.

Wu, Yu-Shan. 1999. "Taiwanese Elections and Cross-Strait Relations: Mainland Policy in Flux." *Asian Survey* 39(4): 565-587.

Wu, Yu-Shan. 2000a. "Theorizing on Relations across the Taiwan Strait: Nine Contending Approaches." *Journal of Contemporary China* 9(25): 407-428.

Wu, Yu-Shan. 2000b. "The ROC's Semipresidentialism at Work: Unstable Compromise, Not Cohabitation." *Issues & Studies* 36(5): 1-40.

Wu, Yu-Shan. 2005a. "Appointing the Prime Minister under Incongruence." *Taiwan Journal Democracy* 1(1): 103-132.

Wu, Yu-Shan. 2005b. "From Romantic Triangle to Marriage? Washington-Beijing-Taipei Relations in Historical Comparison." *Issues & Studies* 41(1): 113-159.

Wu, Yu-Shan. 2006. "Domestic Political Competition and Triangular Interactions among Washington, Beijing and Taipei: The U.S. China Policy." *Issues & Studies* 42(1): 1-46.

Zafrullah, H. M. 1981. *Sri Lanka's Hybrid Presidential and Parliamentary System and the Separation of Powers Doctrine*. Kaula Lumpur, Malaysia: University of Malaya Press.

Ziegfeld, Adam. 2012. "Coalition Government and Party System Change: Explaining the Rise of Regional Political Parties in India." *Comparative Politics* 45(1): 69-87.

日文文獻

リード，スティーブン・R. [Reed, Steven R.]，2003，〈並立制における小選挙区候補者の比例代表得票率への影響〉，《選挙研究》18：5-11。

上田修一，2006，〈世襲議員（126名）五十音順〉，2005年総選挙選出衆議院議員一覧／世襲：http://www.geocities.co.jp/WallStreet/1251/ses.html。檢索日期：2008年6月30日。

大嶽秀夫，1995，〈自民党改革派と小澤グループ：政治改革を目指した二つの政治勢力〉，《ルゥアイアサン》17：7-29。

小林良彰，1985，《計量政治學》，東京：成文堂。

川人貞史，1987，〈中選區制における得票率の分布〉，《北大法學論集》，38（2）：143-206。

不入斗智，1990，《選舉改革をあぐる暗斗》，《世界》11 月：40-50。

日本共產党中央委員会，2007，〈選舉方針見直し、なぜ？〉，しんぶん赤旗：http://www.jcp.or.jp/akahata/aik07/2007-10-03/ftp20071003faq12_01_0.html。檢索日期：2008 年 6 月 30 日。

日本衆議院，1990，《議會制度百年史：議會制度篇》，東京：衆議院。

日本總務省自治行政局選舉部，2007，〈衆議院議員總選舉〉，總務省（選舉関連資料）：http://www.soumu.go.jp/senkyo/senkyo_s/data/index.html#chapter2。檢索日期：2008 年 6 月 30 日。

水崎節文、森裕城，1995，〈中選舉區制における候補者の選舉行動と得票率の地域的分布〉，《選舉研究》10：16-31。

水崎節文、森裕城，1998，〈得票データからみた並立制のメカニズム〉，《選舉研究》13：50-59。

台灣總督府，1945，《台灣統治概要》，台北：台灣總督府。

平野貞夫，1994，〈証言：政治改革への長い道程〉，《中央公論》9：84-94。

田中善一郎，2005，《日本の總選舉：1946-2003》，東京：東京大学出版会。

石川眞澄，1993，《小選舉區制と政治改革》，東京：岩波書店。

林崎理，1994，〈公職選舉法の改正について〉，《地方自治》559：10-35。

河野勝，1995，〈九三年政府變動─もう一つの解釋〉，《ルゥァイアサン》17：30-51。

政界往來社，各年，《政界往來》。

降矢敬義，1994，〈中選舉區制に關する覺書〉，《自治研究》60：6-8。

宮川隆義（編），各年，《政治ハンドブック》，東京：政治廣報センター。

宮川隆義（編），2000，《政治ハンドブック No. 37》，東京：政治廣報センター。

堀江湛，1989，〈改革案の利害得失〉，杉林昇（編），《日本の選舉、世界の選舉》，東京：読売新聞社。

富森叡兒，1993，〈過大な勝利─選舉制度の行方〉，《日本型民主主義の構圖》，東京：朝日新聞社。

森田朗，1994，〈公職選舉法の改正について〉，《地方自治》559：10-35。

菅原琢，2004，〈2003 年衆議院選舉区別都市度〉，菅原研究室 / 日本政治データ：http://freett.com/sugawara_taku/data/2003did.html。檢索日期：2008 年 6 月 30 日。

福岡政行，2001，《日本の選舉》，東京：早稻田大学出版部。

読売新聞社（編），1996，《大變革への序章：檢証，新制度下の 96 衆院選》，東京：読売新聞社。

読売新聞社（編），1999，《大変革の序章：証検・新制度下の衆院選》，東京：読売新聞社。

附錄：林繼文學術著作

一、博士論文

1. Lin, Jih-wen. 1996. *Consequences of the Single Non-Transferable Voting Rule: Comparing the Japan and Taiwan Experiences*. The Department of Political Science, University of California, Los Angeles, 229 pages.

二、期刊論文與專書論文

1. Lin, Jih-wen. Nov. 2017. "How Are the Powers of the President Decided? Vote Trading in the Making of Taiwan's Semi-Presidential Constitution." *International Political Science Review* 38(5): 659-672. (SSCI)
2. Lin, Jih-wen. Sept. 2017. "How Electoral Systems Shape the Life of a Democracy: The East Asian Model." In *Routledge Handbook of Democratization in East Asia*, eds. Tun-jen Cheng and Yun-han Chu. London, UK: Routledge Press, pp. 161-174.
3. Lin, Jih-wen. Dec. 2016. "Taiwan's Semi-Presidential System Was Easy to Establish but Is Difficult to Fix: A Comparison between the Constitutional Reform Efforts of 1997 and 2015." *Taiwan Journal of Democracy* 12 (2): 39-57.
4. Hsieh, John Fuh-sheng and Jih-wen Lin. Jul. 2016. "East Asia: Variable Support for Democracy in a Diverse Society." In *Growing Up Democratic: Does It Make a Difference?* eds. David Denemark, Robert Mattes, and Richard G. Niemi. Boulder, CO: Lynne Rienner, pp. 83-104.
5. Lin, Jih-wen. Jun. 2016. 〈選舉制度的改革，究竟改革了什麼？〉(What Has Taiwan's Electoral Reform Reformed?). In 〈臺灣民主之反思與前瞻〉(*Reflections and Prospects for Taiwan's Democratization*), ed. Yeh-li Wang. Taipei, Taiwan: Taiwan Foundation of Democracy, pp. 69-93.
6. Lin, Jih-wen. Jun. 2016. "The Democratic Progressive Party in Majoritarian Elections". In *Taiwan's Democracy Challenged: The Chen Shui-bian Years*, eds. Yun-han Chu, Larry Diamond, and Kharis Templeman. Boulder, CO: Lynne Rienner Publishers, pp. 51-72.
7. Lin, Jih-wen. Apr. 2016. "The Consequences of Constitutional Systems on Party Systems." In *Mixed-Member Electoral Systems in Constitutional Context: Taiwan, Japan, and Beyond*, eds. Nathan F. Batto, Chi Huang, Alexander C. Tan, and Gary W. Cox. Ann Arbor, MI: University of Michigan Press, pp. 52-72.
8. Lin, Jih-wen. Nov. 2015. "The PRC as a Player in Taiwan's Domestic Politics: A Two-Level Game

Analysis." In *Taiwan and the 'China Impact': Challenges and Opportunities*, ed. Gunter Schubert. London, UK and New York, NY: Routledge, pp. 15-35.

9.　Jensen, Michael J. and Jih-wen Lin. Nov. 2015. "Conclusion: Voting Advice Applications, Information, and Democracy." In *Political Behavior and Technology: Voting Advice Applications in East Asia*, eds. Da-Chi Liao, Bo Yu Chen, and Michael J. Jensen. Basingstoke, UK: Palgrave Macmillan, pp. 157-165.

10.　Lin, Jih-wen. Sept. 2015.〈選舉制度為何變遷？理論與檢證〉(Why did Electoral Systems Change? Theories and Verification)《問題與研究》(*Wenti Yu Yanjiu*) 54(3): 1-29. (TSSCI)

11.　Tung, Chen-yuan, Tzu-chuan Chou, and Jih-wen Lin. Aug. 2015. "Using Prediction Markets of Market Scoring Rule to Forecast Infectious Diseases: A Case Study in Taiwan." *BMC Public Health* 15: 766. (SCI)

12.　Lin, Hsin-yi, Chen-yuan Tung, Jih-wen Lin, and Tzu-chuan Chou (林馨怡、童振源、林繼文、周子全). Jun. 2015.〈影響選舉預測市場準確度的因素：以2008-2010年未來事件交易所的選舉資料為例〉(Factors Best Predict Election Results: A Case Study of 2008-2010 Election Data from the Exchange of Future Events)《臺灣民主季刊》(*Taiwan Democracy Quarterly*) 12(2): 87-122. (TSSCI)

13.　Lin, Jih-wen. Mar. 2015.〈論述如何框限選擇？條件式統獨偏好對 2012 年台灣總統選舉的影響〉(How Is Choice Constrained by Discourses? The Impact of Conditional Unification-Independence Preferences on Taiwan's 2012 Presidential Election)《政治科學論叢》(*Political Science Review*) (63): 55-90. (TSSCI)

14.　Lin, Jih-wen. Jun. 2014. "Resource Allocation and the Performance of Taiwan's Democratic Progressive Party in Mixed-Member Majoritarian Elections." *Issues & Studies* 50(2): 1-38.

15.　Wu, Yu-Shan, Jih-wen Lin, and Tse-Kang Leng (吳玉山、林繼文、冷則剛). Nov. 2013.〈台灣政治學的回顧與前瞻〉(Introduction to Political Science: The State of the Discipline). In《政治學的回顧與前瞻》(*Political Science: The State of the Discipline*), eds. Yu-Shan Wu, Jih-wen Lin, and Tse-Kang Leng. Taipei, Taiwan: Wunan, pp. 1-18.

16.　Hsieh, John Fuh-sheng and Lin Jih-wen (謝復生、林繼文). Nov. 2013.〈理性抉擇與台灣的政治學研究〉(Rational Choice and the Research of Taiwan's Political Science). In《政治學的回顧與前瞻》(*Political Science: The State of the Discipline*), eds. Yu-Shan Wu, Jih-wen Lin, and Tse-Kang Leng. Taipei, Taiwan: Wunan, pp. 65-87.

17.　Wu, Yu-Shan, Jih-wen Lin, and Tse-Kang Leng (吳玉山、林繼文、冷則剛). Nov. 2013.〈台灣政治學的發展：議題、方法與評鑑〉(Issues, Methodologies, and Evaluations In Taiwan's Political Science). In《政治學的回顧與前瞻》(*Political Science: The State of the Discipline*), eds. Yu-

Shan Wu, Jih-wen Lin, and Tse-Kang Leng. Taipei, Taiwan: Wunan, pp. 493-500.

18. Liao, Da-chi, Jih-wen Lin, and Bo Yu Chen (廖達琪、林繼文、陳柏宇). Jul. 2013.〈iVoter星座與政治參與〉(The Constellation and Political Participation of iVoters). In《網路民主：台灣iVoter投票諮詢網站建置紀實》(*The Net of Democracy: The Establishment of the iVoter Web for Their Vote Choice*), eds. Da-chi Liao, Yung-Tai Hung, and Jih-wen Lin et al. Taipei, Taiwan: Wunan, pp. 73-100.

19. Tung, Chen-yuan, Tzu-Chuan Chou, Jih-wen Lin, and Hsin-yi Lin. Dec. 2011. "Comparing the Forecasting Accuracy of Prediction Markets and Polls for Taiwan's Presidential and Mayoral Elections." *The Journal of Prediction Markets* 5(3): 1-26.

20. Lin, Jih-wen and Jung-hsiang Tsai (林繼文、蔡榮祥). Apr. 2012.〈半總統制下的分類研究與國際連結〉(The Typology of Semi-presidentialism and its International Linkage). In《權力在哪裡？從多個角度看半總統制》(*Where is Power? Semi-presidentialism in Multiple Perspectives*), eds. Yu-chung Shen and Yu-Shan Wu. Taipei, Taiwan: Wunan, pp. 459-477.

21. Lin, Jih-wen. Dec. 2011. "A Veto Player Theory of Policy Making in Semi-Presidential Regimes: The Case of Taiwan's Ma Ying-jeou Presidency." *Journal of East Asian Studies* 11(3): 407-435. (SSCI)

22. Tung, Chen-yuan, Tze-chuan Chou, Jih-wen Lin, and Hsin-yi Lin (童振源、周子全、林繼文、林馨怡). Sept. 2011.〈選舉結果機率之分析：以 2006 年與 2008 年台灣選舉為例〉(Analysis on Probability of Election Results: Case Studies of 2006 and 2008 Elections in Taiwan)《臺灣民主季刊》(*Taiwan Democracy Quarterly*) 8(3): 135-159. (TSSCI)

23. Tung, Chen-yuan, Tze-chuan Chou, Jih-wen Lin, and Hsin-yi Lin (童振源、周子全、林繼文、林馨怡). May 2011.〈2009年台灣縣市長選舉預測分析〉(Analysis on the Prediction Results of the 2009 Magistrate and Mayoral Election in Taiwan)《選舉研究》(*Journal of Electoral Studies*) 18(1): 63-94. (TSSCI)

24. Lin, Jih-wen. May 2011. "The Endogenous Change in Electoral Systems: The Case of SNTV." *Party Politics* 17(3): 365-384. (SSCI)

25. Lin, Jih-wen. Mar. 2011. "The Rules of Electoral Competition and the Accountability of Semi-Presidential Governments." In *Semi-Presidentialism and Democracy*, eds. Robert Elgie, Sophia Moestrup, and Yu-Shan Wu. London, UK: Palgrave Macmillan, pp. 61-80.

26. Lin, Jih-wen. Dec. 2009.〈時事評論：解析台灣2009年縣市長選舉〉(Analyzing Taiwan's 2009 County Magistrate and City Mayor Elections)《臺灣民主季刊》(*Taiwan Democracy Quarterly*) 6(2): 207-216. (TSSCI)

27. Tung, Chen-yuan, Hsin-yi Lin, Jih-wen Lin, G. George Hwang, Tzu-chuan Chou, Chia-kai Liu, and

Wen-chih Chao (童振源、林馨怡、林繼文、黃光雄、周子全、劉嘉凱、趙文志). Nov. 2009. 〈台灣選舉預測：預測市場的運用與實證分析〉 (*Prediction on Taiwan's Elections: Application and Empirical Studies of Prediction Markets*) 《選舉研究》 (*Journal of Electoral Studies*) 16(2): 131-166. (TSSCI)

28. Lin, Jih-wen. Sept. 2009. 〈雙層三角：以空間模型分析國內政治對美中台戰略三角的影響〉 (Two-layered Strategic Triangle: A Spatial Analysis for the Effects of Domestic Politics on U.S.-China-Taiwan Triangular Relations). In 《重新檢視爭辯中的兩岸關係理論》 (*Revisiting Theories on Cross-Strait Relations*), eds. Tzong-Ho Bau and Yu-Shen Wu. Taipei, Taiwan: Wunan, pp. 277-304.

29. Lin, Jih-wen. Jul. 2009. "The Evolvement of Taiwan's Constitutional System." In *The Political System of Taiwan*, eds. Markus Porsche-Ludwig and Chin-peng Chu. Baden-Baden, German: Nomos Verlagsgesellschaft, pp. 31-54.

30. Lin, Jih-wen. Mar. 2009. 〈共治可能成為半總統制的憲政慣例嗎？法國與台灣的比較〉 (Can Cohabitation Become a Constitutional Convention under Semi-presidentialism? A Comparison between France and Taiwan) 《東吳政治學報》 (*Soochow Journal of Political Science*) 27(1): 1-51. (TSSCI)

31. Lin, Jih-wen. Nov. 2008. 〈以輸為贏：小黨在日本單一選區兩票制下的參選策略〉 (To Lose is to Win: The Candidate-Placement Strategy of Minor Parties Under Japan's Mixed-Member Majoritarian System) 《選舉研究》 (*Journal of Electoral Studies*) 15(2): 37-66. (TSSCI)

32. Lin, Jih-wen. Mar. 2008. "The Institutional Context of President Chen Shui-bian's Cross-Strait Messages." *Issues & Studies* 44(1): 1-31. (SSCI)

33. Lin, Jih-wen. Nov. 2006. 〈政府體制、選舉制度與政黨體系：一個配套論的分析〉 (Power Division, Voting Rule, and Party System: What do We See When They are Considered Together?) 《選舉研究》 (*Journal of Electoral Studies*) 13(2): 1-42. (TSSCI)

34. Lin, Jih-wen. Arp. 2006. "The Politics of Reform in Japan and Taiwan." *Journal of Democracy* 17(2): 118-131. (SSCI)

35. Lin, Jih-wen. Sept. 2005. 〈虛假霸權：台灣政治學研究中的理性選擇〉 (Hegemony in Mirage: Rational Choice in Taiwan's Political Studies) 《政治科學論叢》 (*Political Science Review*) (25): 67-104. (TSSCI)

36. Lin, Jih-wen. Dec. 2004. "Can Social Solidarity be Institutionally Engineered? The Case of Presidential Election." *Issues & Studies* 40(4): 183-224. (SSCI)

37. Lin, Jih-wen. Jun. 2004. "Taiwan's Referendum Act and the Stability of the Status Quo." *Issues & Studies* 40(2): 119-153. (SSCI)

38. Lin, Jih-wen. Sept. 2003. "Institutionalized Uncertaintyand Governance Crisis in Posthegemonic Taiwan." *Journal of East Asian Studies* 3(3): 433-460. (SSCI)

39. Lin, Jih-wen. Jun. 2003. "A Blue Tango: Electoral Competition and the Formation of Taiwan's Opposition Coalition." *Issues & Studies* 39(2): 41-72. (SSCI)

40. Lin, Jih-wen. Jun. 2003.〈憲法作爲一種制度〉(Constitution as an institution)《政治與社會哲學評論》(*A Journal for Philosophical Study of Public Affairs*) (5): 35-74.

41. Lin, Jih-wen. Mar. 2003. "Looking for the Magic Number: The Optimal District Magnitude for Political Parties in d'Hondt PR and SNTV." *Electoral Studies* 22(1): 49-63. (SSCI)

42. Lin, Jih-wen. Jun. 2002. "Transition through Transaction: Taiwan's Constitutional Reforms in the Lee Teng-hui Era." *American Asian Review* 20(2): 123-155.

43. Lin, Jih-wen. May 2002.〈選舉制度、選民偏好與政黨體系的分化：東亞三國的比較〉(Electoral Systems, Voter Preference, and Effective Number of Parties: The East Asian Cases)《選舉研究》(*Journal of Electoral Studies*) 9(1): 137-171. (TSSCI)

44. Lin, Jih-wen. Mar. 2002. "Democratic Stability under Taiwan's Semi-Presidentialist Constitution." *Issues & Studies* 38(1): 47-79. (SSCI)

45. Lin, Jih-wen. Jan. 2002. "Taiwan's 2001 Elections and their Political Impact." *China Perspectives* (39): 53-61.

46. Lin, Jih-wen. Dec. 2001.〈創設、選擇與演化：制度形成的三個理論模式〉(Design, Choice, and Evolution: Three Models of Institution Formation)《政治學報》(*Chinese Political Science Review*) (32): 61-94. (TSSCI)

47. Chu, Yun-han and Jih-wen Lin. 2001. "Political Development in the 20th Century Taiwan: State-Building, Regime Transformation and the Construction of National Identity." *The China Quarterly* (165): 102-129 (SSCI).

48. Lin, Jih-wen. Nov. 2000. "Two-Level Games between Rival Regimes: Domestic Politics and the Remaking of Cross-Strait Relations." *Issues & Studies* 36(6): 1-26. (SSCI)

49. Lin, Jih-wen. Apr. 2000.〈半總統制下的三角政治均衡〉(Triangular Equilibrium under Semi-presidential Systems). In《政治制度》(*Political Institutions*), ed. Jih-wen Lin. Taipei, Taiwan: Sun Yat-sen Graduate Institute of Humanities and Social Sciences, Academia Sinica, pp. 135-175.

50. Lin, Jih-wen. Nov. 1999. "Democratization under One-party Dominance: Explaining Taiwan's Paradoxical Transition." *Issues & Studies* 35(6): 1-28. (SSCI)

51. Lin, Jih-wen. Dec. 1998. "Vote Buying vs. Noise Making: Two Models of Electoral Competition under the Single Non-transferable Vote-Multimember District System."《政治學報》(*Chinese Political Science Review*) (30): 93-122.

52. Lin, Jih-wen. Nov. 1998.〈地盤劃分與選舉競爭：對應分析法在多席次選舉研究上之應用〉(Territorial Division and Electoral Competition: The Application of Correspondence Analysis on the Study of Multi-seat Elections)《選舉研究》(*Journal of Electoral Studies*) 5(2): 103-128. (TSSCI)

53. Lin, Jih-wen and Chih-cheng Lo (林繼文、羅致政). Mar. 1998.〈零和或雙贏？兩岸經貿交流新解〉(Zero-Sum or Win-Win? A Reinterpretation of Cross-Strait Economic Exchanges)《人文及社會科學集刊》(*Journal of Social Sciences and Philosophy*) 10(1): 33-77. (TSSCI)

54. Chen, Ming-tong and Jih-wen Lin (陳明通、林繼文). Feb. 1998.〈台灣地方選舉的起源與國家社會關係轉變〉(The Origin of Taiwan's Local Election and the Transformation of State-Society Relations). In《兩岸基層選舉與政治社會變遷》(*Local Elections and Political-Social Changes across the Strait*), eds. Ming-tong Chen and Yong-nian Zheng. Taipei, Taiwan: Yuedan, pp. 23-69.

55. Lin, Jih-wen. Dec. 1997.〈制度選擇如何可能：論日本之選舉制度改革〉(How can an Institution End Itself: The Case of Japan's Electoral Reform)《台灣政治學刊》(*Taiwan Political Science Review*) (2): 63-106. (TSSCI)

56. Lin, Jih-wen. Dec. 1997〈日本占領期下台灣之戰爭動員體制〉(日本占領期における台灣の戰争動員体制/Taiwan's War Mobilization System under Japanese Rule)《中国21》(*China 21*) 2: 111-134.

57. Lin, Jih-wen. Jun. 1997. "Multi-candidate Equilibria with Rank-improving Objective."《政治學報》(*Chinese Political Science Review*) (28): 141-157.

58. Lo, Chih-cheng and Jih-wen Lin. Mar. 1995. "Between Sovereignty and Security: A Mixed Strategy Analysis of Current Cross-Strait Interactions." *Issues & Studies* 31(3): 64-91. (SSCI)

59. Lin, Jin-wen. Jun. 1994. "Two Models of Legislative Coalition Formation."《政治學報》(*Chinese Political Science Review*) (22): 103-119.

三、他類論文（含書評）

1. Lin, Jih-wen. Jan. 2012.〈台灣的民主轉型與"憲 政"選 〉(Taiwan's Democratic Transition and Its Constitutional Choice). In《台灣民主轉型的經驗與啓示》(*The Experience and Implications of Taiwan's Democratic Transition*). Beijing, China: Social Sciences Academic Press, pp. 125-158.

2. Lin, Jih-wen. Jul. 2010.〈憲改為何休市？〉(Who Shut down the Market of Constitutional Reform?) In《秩序繽紛的年代：1990-2010》(*A Decade of Chaotic Order: 1990-2010*), eds. Jieh-min Wu, Erde Gu, and Yun Fan. Taipei, Taiwan: Zuoan, pp. 213-228.

3. Lin, Jih-wen. Sept. 2010.〈學者之路〉(Becoming a Scholar)《人文與社會科學簡訊》

(*Newsletter of Humanities and Social Sciences*) 11(4): 21-26.

4. Lin, Jih-wen. Sept. 2005.〈政治學計量方法研習營的緣起、進展與未來〉(The Origin, Progress, and Prospect of the Summer Camp of Political Methodology)《人文與社會科學簡訊》(*Newsletter of Humanities and Social Sciences*) 6(4): 43-51.

5. Lin, Jih-wen. 2002. "Book Review: Politics in Taiwan: Voting for Democracy. By Shelley Rigger, New York and London: Routledge, October 1999." *Issues & Studies* 28(3): 220-224.

6. Lin, Jih-wen. Nov. 2001.〈選舉制度：國會改革的基礎〉(Electoral System: The Foundation of Legislative Reform)《當代》(*Contemporary Monthly*) (171): 58-77.

7. Lin, Jih-wen. Aug. 2001.〈從憲政工程學的角度論行政權之改革〉(Administrative Reform Viewed from the Perspective of Constitutional Engineering)《國家政策論壇》(*National Policy Forum*) (18): 8-10.

8. Lin, Jih-wen. Jun. 2001.〈政黨輪替改變了什麼〉(What has been Changed by Regime Transition?)《二十一世紀》(*Twenty-First Century*) (65): 20-24.

9. Lin, Jih-wen. Jul. 1999. "Comparative Politics in East Asia: A Discipline for the Nation, or of the Nations?" *Comparative Politics Newsletter of the American Political Science Association*.

10. Lin, Jih-wen. Jun. 1999.〈單一選區兩票制與選舉制度改革〉(Mixed-member Majoritarian Systems and Electoral Reform)《新世紀智庫論壇》(*Forum of New Century Institute*) (6): 69-79.

四、專書

1. Lin, Jih-wen. Mar. 1996.《日本據台末期戰爭動員體系之研究：1930-1945》(*Japan's War Mobilization System at the End of Its Colonization of Taiwan: 1930-1945*). Taipei, Taiwan: Daw-Shiang Publishing.

五、主編之專書

1. Wu, Yu-Shan, Jih-wen Lin, and Tse-Kang Leng (吳玉山、林繼文、冷則剛) (eds.). Nov. 2013.《政治學的回顧與前瞻》(*Political Science: The State of the Discipline*). Taipei, Taiwan: Wunan.

2. Liao, Da-chi, Yung-Tai Hung, and Jih-wen Lin et al.(廖達琪、洪永泰、林繼文等人) (eds.). Jul. 2013.《網路民主：台灣iVoter投票諮詢網站建置紀實》(*The Net of Democracy: The Establishment of the iVoter Web for Their Vote Choice*). Taipei, Taiwan: Wunan.

3. Lin Jih-wen (ed.). Apr. 2000.《政治制度》(*Political Institutions*). Taipei, Taiwan: Sun Yat-sen Graduate Institute of Humanities and Social Sciences, Academia Sinica.

國家圖書館出版品預行編目資料

政治學的理性與感性——林繼文精選集／林繼
文等著. －－初版.－－臺北市：中央研究院
政治學研究所, 2019.07
　面；　公分
ISBN 978-986-05-9290-0（平裝）

1.政治學　2.文集

570.7　　　　　　　　　　　　108008322

中研政治系列叢書　第五輯

政治學的理性與感性——林繼文精選集

主　　　編／冷則剛、吳文欽、吳玉山、吳親恩

作　　　者／林繼文、朱雲漢、羅致政

導 讀 者／謝復生、吳玉山、吳親恩、吳文欽、冷則剛

責任編輯／賴芊卉、林佳瑩

校　　　對／林文正、楊君婕、呂英鈒、謝孟君

出 版 者／中央研究院政治學研究所

發 行 人／冷則剛
　　　　　　地　　址：115台北市南港區研究院路二段128號
　　　　　　電　　話：(02)26525300（代表號）
　　　　　　傳　　真：(02)26546011
　　　　　　網　　址：http://www.ipsas.sinica.edu.tw/
　　　　　　電子郵件：ipsas@gate.sinica.edu.tw

總 經 銷／五南圖書出版股份有限公司
　　　　　　地　　址：106台北市大安區和平東路二段339號4樓

版　　　刷／2019年 7 月初版一刷

定　　　價／新臺幣300元

劃撥帳號／01068953，請逕洽五南圖書出版股份有限公司